MARSHAL WILLIAM CARR BERESFORD

Marcus de la Poer Beresford read history at Trinity College Dublin, before qualifying as a lawyer. Marcus retired from legal practice in 2010 after three decades as a partner in the Dublin firm of A & L Goodbody in order to return to his first love, history. His earlier research and postgraduate thesis focused on Ireland in the eighteenth century and the Irish diaspora following the Treaty of Limerick in 1691. He is a distant relative of William Carr Beresford. www.marcusdelapoerberesford.ie

MARSHAL WILLIAM CARR BERESFORD

'The ablest man I have yet seen with the army'

MARCUS DE LA POER BERESFORD

Irish Academic Press

First published in 2019 by
Irish Academic Press
10 George's Street
Newbridge
Co. Kildare
Ireland
www.iap.ie

© Marcus de la Poer Beresford, 2019

9781788550321 (Cloth)
9781788550338 (Kindle)
9781788550345 (Epub)
9781788550352 (PDF)

British Library Cataloguing in Publication Data
An entry can be found on request

Library of Congress Cataloging in Publication Data
An entry can be found on request

Interior design by www.jminfotechindia.com
Typeset in Garamond Premier Pro 11/14 pt

Jacket design by edit+ www.stuartcoughlan.com
Jacket front: Marshal Beresford by Thomas Lawrence. By kind permission of Historic England.
Jacket back: Marshal Beresford unhorsing a Polish lancer at the Battle of Albuera, 16 May 1811,
by Franz Joseph Manskirch, engraved by M. Dubourg. Author's own collection.

CONTENTS

DE LA POER BERESFORD FAMILY TREE

Abbreviated Family Tree of de la Poer Beresford Family in the Eighteenth and Nineteenth Centuries

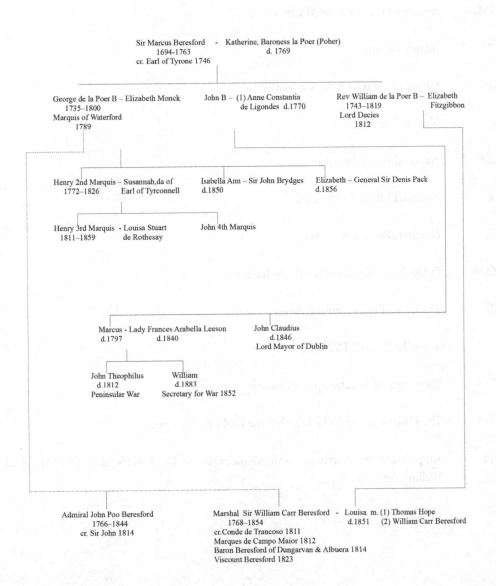

Sir Marcus Beresford - Katherine, Baroness la Poer (Poher)
1694-1763   d. 1769
cr. Earl of Tyrone 1746

George de la Poer B – Elizabeth Monck   John B – (1) Anne Constantia   Rev William de la Poer B – Elizabeth
1735–1800   de Ligondes d.1770   1743–1819   Fitzgibbon
Marquis of Waterford   Lord Decies
1789   1812

Henry 2nd Marquis – Susannah,da of   Isabella Ann – Sir John Brydges   Elizabeth – General Sir Denis Pack
1772–1826   Earl of Tyrconnell   d.1850   d.1856

Henry 3rd Marquis - Louisa Stuart   John 4th Marquis
1811–1859   de Rothesay

Marcus - Lady Frances Arabella Leeson   John Claudius
d.1797   d.1840   d.1846
                                 Lord Mayor of Dublin

John Theophilus   William
d.1812   d.1883
Peninsular War   Secretary for War 1852

Admiral John Poo Beresford   Marshal Sir William Carr Beresford - Louisa m. (1) Thomas Hope
1766–1844   1768–1854   d.1851   (2) William Carr Beresford
cr. Sir John 1814   cr.Conde de Trancoso 1811
                           Marques de Campo Maior 1812
                           Baron Beresford of Dungarvan & Albuera 1814
                           Viscount Beresford 1823

ABBREVIATIONS

AHM	Arquivo Historico Militar
AMM	Arquivo Municipal de Mafra
BL	British Library
HMC	Historical Manuscripts Commission
NA	National Archives, Kew
NAM	National Army Museum
NLI	National Library of Ireland
NYA	North Yorkshire Archives
PRONI	Public Record Office Northern Ireland
TCD	Trinity College Dublin Library
TT	Torre do Tombo, Lisbon
USL	University of Southampton Library
WD	The Dispatches of Field Marshal the Duke of Wellington
WSD	Supplementary Despatches and Memoranda of Field Marshal Arthur, Duke of Wellington K.G.

INTRODUCTION

Marshal William Carr Beresford
'The ablest man I have yet seen with the army'
Wellington's strong right arm

Ireland in the mid-eighteenth century was an island of many different components. The governing body represented some, but not all, of those who had fought in Ireland on the victorious side in the war of the two kings, a war which had pitted not just Catholic James II against Protestant William and Mary in the British Isles (sometimes with cavalier disregard for Mary's position as a daughter of James), but which was part of a wider conflict which had brought together other powers wishing to resist the domination of Louis XIV's France on the European continent (the War of the League of Augsburg).

The defeat of James II and his supporters at the battles of the Boyne (1690) and Aughrim (1691) followed by the Treaty of Limerick led to the establishment of the Ascendancy in Ireland, made up of those who belonged to the Church of Ireland or its sister Church, the Church of England. Not only did this exclude the majority Roman Catholic population but also Presbyterians, Quakers and other non-conformists. While the process had commenced earlier, the victory of William and Mary over James completed the means whereby the Ascendancy secured political, economic and social control of the island of Ireland through a transfer of landownership and the introduction of restrictions on their opponents brought about primarily by the penal laws. Outwardly, Ireland remained at peace in the hundred years prior to the French revolution, with no substantial unrest taking place in support of the Jacobite risings in Scotland of 1708, 1715 or 1745, but underneath the surface those displaced not unnaturally resented the situation. This manifested itself in agrarian discontent and ultimately the explosion that was the rebellion of 1798.

One family that benefitted substantially from the conclusion of the war of the two kings was that of the Beresfords. Tristram Beresford had arrived in Ireland at the time of James I. His great grandson, Sir Tristram Beresford (1669–1701), supported William and Mary and as such was attainted in May 1689 by the Jacobite parliament in Dublin and forfeited his lands. Recovering these on the Williamite victory, he did not live long to enjoy them, dying in 1701 at the age of just thirty-two. His son, Sir Marcus, was just seven years old but it was this man that was to bring the family to the fore in Irish and for a time in British politics. Sir Marcus was one of a number of members of the family who made astute marriages by which they acquired not just wealth but political power. In his case, in 1717 he married Catherine, Baroness La Poer, the only daughter and heiress of James, 3rd Earl of Tyrone, a supporter of James II who after the collapse of the Jacobite cause in Ireland had submitted to William and Mary and who finished his days as Governor of Waterford.[1]

Following this marriage, Sir Marcus and his successors held substantial lands in Counties Derry and Waterford (where they settled and subsequently extended the family home of Curraghmore) and soon acquired further lands in the city of Dublin, and counties Dublin and Wicklow.[2] Their parliamentary power was based on the control of boroughs in these counties, combined with family alliances elsewhere. Sir Marcus was created Viscount Tyrone in 1722 and the Earl of Tyrone in 1746. His three surviving sons and six daughters made advantageous marriages and advanced the family politically. Marcus's eldest son, George, the 2nd Earl, married Elizabeth Monck, a granddaughter of the 1st Duke of Portland.[3] Marcus's second son, John, married first Anne de Ligondes and subsequently Barbara Montgomery. From his power base of Revenue Commissioner in Ireland, John became a major parliamentary figure and firm friend of William Pitt the Younger; and is reputed to have been referred to as 'virtually King of Ireland' by Earl Fitzwilliam.[4] The third son, William, took holy orders in the Church of Ireland, ultimately becoming Archbishop of Tuam and Lord Decies. He married Elizabeth FitzGibbon, sister of John, Earl of Clare and Lord Chancellor of Ireland. It was into this family that William Carr Beresford ('Beresford') was born on 2 October 1768, the younger of two sons (the other being John Poo) fathered by the second Earl prior to his marriage and acknowledged by him as his own.[5] Apart from his own siblings, the children and grandchildren of John (the Commissioner) and William (the Archbishop) were to be involved closely with the life of William Carr Beresford.[6]

While he would not inherit titles or wealth, William Carr was more fortunate than many. A lack of certainty exists as to the identity of his mother, but notwithstanding Thomas Creevey's suggestion late in William's life (1827) that it was rumoured to be Elizabeth Monck prior to her marriage to William's father, there is a strong family tradition that it was a local lady by the name of Carr; a tradition which is supported by both the fact that there was no family background to the name Carr, William being addressed as such by family members, and the existence then and today of families with the name Carr in the area adjacent to Curraghmore.[7] Creevey's suggestion was that it was rumoured both John Poo and William Carr were the children of Elizabeth. He referred to the affection in which they were held by her, and there certainly was a considerable bond, with John Poo and William Carr continuing to visit Elizabeth who lived much of her life in England after her husband's death in 1800.

Great Britain and France had fought four major wars in the eighteenth century prior to the French Revolution in 1789. Those wars had seen Britain emerge as the pre-eminent world naval power, but had left France as the dominant land power in western Europe. Between 1793 and 1814 the two nations were engaged in continuous conflict, with the exception of one short period of peace brought about by the Treaty of Amiens in 1802–3.

The distrust engendered by James II's attempt to build a royalist standing army meant that historically in the eighteenth century the British army had rarely exceeded an establishment of 40,000, falling on occasions to less than half that size. By 1814 there were some 250,000 men in the army. This required the securing of huge additional manpower, some of which was found in central Europe in German speaking lands, but the vast majority of which was sourced in England, Wales, Scotland and Ireland. In addition, substantial militia and fencible regiments were raised to perform duties at home and to guard against potential invasion. Unlike the continental powers, Britain did not introduce conscription to meet its military requirements relying instead on volunteers.

The simultaneous industrialisation of England in particular, with the rural population moving to urban centres, meant a lack of manpower was available for the army. Further, quite apart from the dangers of serving abroad, where disease killed many more than enemy forces, industrial wages reduced the attraction of a soldier's life. Britain found a substantial part of the resources it needed in the agrarian societies of Ireland and Scotland, often in circumstances where landholdings were of an insufficient size to support large families. To these soldiers of the British army were added the rejuvenated army of Portugal, aided by the various Spanish armies and the irregulars of both Iberian nations, without which it is doubtful Britain could have driven the French out of the Peninsula and successfully invaded the south of France, thus contributing substantially to Napoleon's downfall.

At the commencement of the wars with France in 1793, the British army was disorganised and suffering from the loss of morale caused by defeat in 1783 in America. Two men in particular were responsible for its resuscitation and emergence as a major fighting force over the next twenty years. The Duke of York, whatever his limitations as a battlefield general, proved to be an able administrator, while Arthur Wellesley, the future Duke of Wellington emerged as one of the most successful and effective campaign generals Britain has ever produced.

Britain's participation in the revolutionary and Napoleonic wars has been the subject of many excellent works. Wellington's campaigns and battles have been written about exhaustively. The generals who fought alongside and indeed against Wellington have in most cases been the subject of one or more biographies, yet Marshal William Carr Beresford is noticeable for the absence of any biography of his life, which is curious given that he was Wellington's right-hand man in the Peninsula, moreover, the man who was responsible for the rebuilding and reform of the Portuguese army. For some time it was thought that his papers might even have been destroyed, meaning that it was necessary to look for his letters in the collections of recipients, and often hope to find drafts of the replies there as well. The lack of any central repository of Beresford's papers makes the task of getting to grips with his life something of an endurance test, with papers to be found in different countries.

Gradually, however, a substantial correspondence has come to light. Beresford later remarked that due to the manner in which he had left Portugal in 1820, he apprehended many of his papers had been lost, though the greater part remained there. It appears that some papers were sold at auction or donated to archives by his step-grandson, Philip Beresford Hope, in the 1890s.[8] These have been augmented by documents now lodged in the archives of a number of countries and by papers still held by the family. Beresford's career was not without controversy, but that should not have discouraged the biographer given the nature and extent of his achievements. He suffered at the hand of William Napier, who had little good to say about Beresford in his monumental *History of the War in the Peninsula and the South of France*, but the Beresfords were strong supporters of the Tories, whom Napier passionately disliked. It is difficult to conclude that Napier's criticism of Beresford and other Tory leaders was not motivated, at least in part, by his own political affiliations. It was not just Beresford who engaged in a pamphlet war with Napier, and others resorted even to the courts. Sir Charles Oman, in what remains the definitive history of the Peninsular War, did much to redress the balance. His magisterial *History of the Peninsular War* rebutted Napier's assertions in a number of respects. However, neither of these works deal in any length with Beresford's early career, his rebuilding and reform of the Portuguese army, his active participation in the battles in the Peninsula and France, or his subsequent life in Portugal and the United Kingdom of Great Britain and Ireland as it had become by virtue of the Act of Union of 1800. In more recent times, the battle of Albuera (Albuhera) has attracted the attention of skilful and eminent historians whose contributions I have sought to acknowledge, even where I have been led to different conclusions.

The current work dealing with Beresford's métier and relationships is based on an aspiration to fill out the many parts of Beresford's life that I feel would merit from the telling of an interesting and exciting career. While this is the story of a man who chose the army as a way of life, I have tried to portray a flavour of his relationships with his family and colleagues. This undertaking is not intended to be a move by move account of the major battles and sieges of the Napoleonic wars. There exists now a wonderful array of such books. However, I have sought to address in some detail the events of three battles, because of Beresford's particular involvement. They are Albuera, where he commanded an Allied army in difficult circumstances, as well as Orthez and Toulouse, where he led the attacks, though under the watchful eye of Wellington. In all three battles the French were commanded by Maréchal Jean-de-Dieu Soult, one of Napoleon's most able generals.

Beresford did not serve with Arthur Wellesley until 1808, but clearly they knew each other previously. Coming from a similar Anglo-Irish background, it is perhaps not surprising that they allegedly shared some characteristics, though they differed in many ways. A certain reserve, hauteur and even arrogance was attributed by contemporaries, but both were tough, resolute and if necessary pragmatic. The case is not made that Beresford was a military commander comparable to Wellesley, but that great commander recognised his abilities and chose to prefer Beresford rather than doggedly follow the custom and practice of seniority. Beresford clearly respected Wellesley's great abilities and was happy to be the instrument of their implementation on most occasions. Instances of disagreement are few and far between.

In approaching the task of producing a biography on William Carr Beresford, I have sought to rely on as many primary and contemporary sources as possible. I quote extensively and deliberately from these sources as this helps the reader absorb and understand what the chief protagonists and ordinary men were saying about the issues of the day. Sources relied upon include the correspondence of Beresford, now located in a number of countries in both Europe and the Americas, as well as his Ordens do Dia (Orders of the Day), which are an invaluable source when dealing with the rebuilding of the Portuguese army and its operations. Beresford's pamphlet war with William Napier in the 1830s is also a useful reference point, though it was written twenty years after many of the events on which it comments and should be treated accordingly. Wellington's correspondence both published (*The Dispatches of Field Marshal the Duke of Wellington*, revised edition 1844) and unpublished is essential to an understanding of the issues and the conduct of the war. These sources are augmented by many other primary sources, including the correspondence of Generals Denis Pack, Rowland Hill, Thomas Picton, Nicholas Trant and other military men.

Beresford was a regular correspondent with a number of family members and this correspondence shows a more humane side of the man than might be commonly supposed, dealing with the life and death of family members as well as his own health and finances. Considerable correspondence exists in particular with his siblings John Poo Beresford, Lady Anne and Lady Elizabeth Beresford. In Portugal, the extensive correspondence between Beresford and Dom Miguel Forjaz, the Secretary for War and Foreign Affairs in the Regency Council established in Lisbon, is a mine of information that I have in no way exhausted. Added to these are numerous diaries and recollections which I have sought to reference throughout the text.

The use of primary documents in no way diminishes the debt I owe to those who have gone before me in writing about these wars and the remarkable men who fought in them or who directed the efforts of the various contestants. Several years into the research for this book I came across two excellent and informative writings on Beresford. The first of these was an unpublished script by the late Professor Harold Livermore, an authority on the history of Portugal and Spain as well as their former American colonies.[9] The second was a doctoral thesis by Samuel Vichness presented at the Florida State University.[10] These works both prompted me to consider in greater depth certain points and indeed challenged views I had formed on various issues. Had I known of their existence at the outset I might have been deterred from the journey I have followed to produce the current account of Beresford's life, though I have been fortunate enough to find materials I believe were not available to either Livermore or Vichness.

The thesis of Vichness was part of the extraordinary output from the Florida State University attributable to Dr Donald D. Horward, Director of the Institute on Napoleon and the French Revolution at that University. Horward's own works, including his translation of Jean Jacques Pelet's campaign account of Masséna's invasion of Portugal in 1810–11, led me not just to Vichness but to another doctoral thesis which has proved helpful; Francisco de la Fuente's work on Dom Miguel Pereira Forjaz.[11] Other accounts providing useful insights on Beresford and his relationships with others include those by Bernardo Almazán, J.D. Grainger, Ian Fletcher, Mark Thompson and a series of essays edited by Professor Malyn Newitt and Dr Martin Robson.[12]

My love of history was nurtured by my father and later by Dr Norman Atkinson at St Columba's College and Professor J.G. Simms at Trinity College Dublin. On this current project many people and organisations have given me help and encouragement. To the staff in the National Library of Ireland, the library of Dublin University (TCD), the Royal Irish Academy, the British Library, the National Archives, the National Army Museum, the Hartley Library at

Southampton University, the Arquivo Histórico Militar and the Arquivo Nacional da Torre de Tombo in particular I give my heartfelt thanks. Likewise, I owe a huge debt to Raquel Rocha, who while in Ireland taught me sufficient Portuguese to enable me to read documents in that language.

To those with whom I have discussed the project and who have made suggestions I am grateful. In Portugal they include Pedro d'Avillez, Major General Rui Moura, Clive Gilbert MBE, José Ermitão and Professor Paulo Miguel Rodrigues (Madeira). In Argentina, Rogelio Maciel and his daughter, Maria Laura, spent time showing me the sites of the *Reconquista* in Buenos Aires. In France I received kindness and assistance from the Mayors and others of towns in the Pyrenees, the Pays Basque and the Bearn; sometimes descendants of those who fought for Napoleon. In England my efforts were encouraged and helped by many, including Karen Robson at the Hartley Library Archives, Major Nick Hallidie and Dr Mark Thompson. I remain in awe of the works of Dr Rory Muir, who has also extended me a helping hand and sound advice. I have learnt much from scholarly presentations at conferences run under the auspices of the University of Southampton (The Wellington Congress), The Waterloo Association and The Friends of the British Cemetery, Elvas.

To the creators and organisers of 'The Napoleon Series' I take off my hat. I have had regard to these online discussions on numerous occasions when trying to resolve particular points. In Ireland I would like to record my thanks to the Marquis and Marchioness of Waterford for their generosity, as well as to Suzie Pack-Beresford.[13] I should also like to commend Julian Walton who has undertaken the assembly and indexation of the family archive at Curraghmore. In Scotland, Mindy Maclean has been most helpful (Susie and Mindy are both descendants of Major General Sir Denis Pack, who was not only a great friend of William Carr Beresford, but who married Elizabeth, the half-sister of Beresford). My family have responded with enthusiasm to my endless 'discoveries' about 'WCB', as he quickly became known. Edel has been a pillar of support on this project, and my children have assisted in so many ways, ranging from proofreading, the drawing of maps and the resolution of IT issues.

It was understandable that with the emergence of liberalism in Portugal, Beresford, as the representative of an authoritarian government as well as that of a not entirely disinterested ally, should have been regarded with distaste. Largely ignored by Portuguese historians of the nineteenth and twentieth century because of whom he had represented, a new interest in the Marshal has been awakened, linked rightly with the role played by the Portuguese army and people in defeating a hitherto invincible enemy who invaded and laid waste to their country on three separate occasions in five years; an army moreover which then played an important role for a further three years in the liberation of Spain and the defeat of Napoleon in south west France in 1814.

The reader will note that I have referred to Arthur Wellesley as Wellesley until 4 September 1809. Thereafter he is Wellington. This is possible because there is a natural break in events after the retreat following the tactical victory at Talavera. William Carr Beresford is referred to as 'William' or 'Beresford' save where the use of the name 'Carr' is used to make a particular point. I have sought to provide substantial details in the footnotes to each chapter to facilitate those who wish to research the topics further. I have also used these as an opportunity to bring forward information about events and personalities which, if not centre stage, deserved in my opinion their footnote in history.

I have been fortunate to have found in Irish Academic Press a publisher which has high standards, and whose staff have shown great interest in and been most attentive to this project. In particular I would like to thank my publisher Conor Graham, editor Fiona Dunne and Myles McCionnaith.

Finally I would like to acknowledge the support and assistance of Professor Malyn Newitt. The professor's encylopaedic knowledge of Portuguese and Brazilian history made it a pleasure as well as a privilege to discuss with him Beresford's part in these wars. He was kind enough to read my script and I am certain it is much improved as a result of his comments and suggestions. At the end of the day, the views expressed are my own as are any mistakes. I have tried to be objective and to avoid any sense of an apologia; dealing with both Beresford's achievements and the occasions on which success eluded him or was only partial. The reader will judge the degree of success or otherwise attaching to my endeavour.

1 THE EARLY YEARS

'A before marriage boy of the old Lords'[1]

William Carr, born in 1768, was the younger of the two boys fathered by George de la Poer Beresford, Earl of Tyrone, prior to his marriage to Elizabeth Monck. John Poo had been born two years earlier than William Carr. Little is known about their early lives but given that Elizabeth was reportedly fond of them, they presumably spent those days at the family home, Curraghmore, County Waterford. There they clearly formed close bonds with their siblings, as is borne out by their later correspondence. The Marchioness gave birth to six children and all bar the first, Lord la Poer, were to have a continuing and lifelong relationship with William Carr.[2] In the family, the boys were addressed in correspondence as 'Poo' and 'Carr' respectively, rather than John and William. They probably carried these as surnames in early years, for later in life both boys obtained licences to use the name 'Beresford'.[3] Obtaining these licences seems only to have regularised a pre-existing condition, for the naval and military records of the two boys refer to them as Beresford from the commencement of their service, and they signed documents as such from that time.[4]

Childhood at Curraghmore would have been comfortable by the standards of the day. Lying in a broad and beautiful valley in County Waterford, through which runs the river

Clodagh, the architecture of the house incorporates the mediaeval tower along with additions including those of the seventeenth and eighteenth centuries. William was not to enjoy those surroundings for long. At the age of eight he was sent (along with John) to a school in Catterick Bridge in Yorkshire to be educated.[5] Later, the two boys moved to a school in York, where they were looked after by two ladies whom they remembered with kindness later in life.[6] As might be expected, his elder brother, John, very much led the way at this time.[7] In his seventeenth year (1784), William entered the military academy in Strasbourg to train for the army.[8] His stay there was relatively short, for in 1785 he was appointed an ensign in the 6th Regiment of Foot (1st Warwickshire Regiment). It is likely this position was purchased, perhaps by his father with whom he remained in close contact, albeit mostly by correspondence given William's long absences abroad, for the rest of the Marquis's life.[9]

The 6th regiment was posted to Nova Scotia in 1786. One of William's fellow ensigns in the 6th regiment was Thomas Molyneux, who joined it in 1786 and also hailed from Ireland.[10] William and Thomas were part of a hunting party one day when a covey of partridges rose up. As Thomas shot at the birds, a pellet from his gun struck William in the left eye, entirely depriving him of sight in that eye.[11] While the loss is evident in some of the paintings of William in later life, in others it is as if airbrushed to produce a more sympathetic picture.

Promotion came rapidly, albeit by changing regiments. In 1789 he joined the 16th Regiment of Foot as a Lieutenant, a regiment of which in later life he became Colonel.[12] In the following year he became a Captain in the 69th Regiment of Foot, and in that capacity he served with the marines under Admiral Lord Hood.[13] He was present at the opening to a British force of the gates of Toulon by French royalists in August 1793. For some time prior to this event, Hood's fleet had been blockading that French naval base, but royalist success was to be shortlived. On 2 December of the same year, the town fell to French revolutionary forces (the French artillery was commanded by a certain Napoleon Bonaparte). However, Hood was able to ensure that much of the French fleet was burnt rather than to let it fall into revolutionary hands.

Admiral Hood then moved to take Corsica, having been invited to do so by the de facto ruler and Corsican patriot, Pasquale Paoli. William distinguished himself at the capture of the Martello at San Fiorenzo, as a result of which he achieved his majority in March 1794. Additionally, serving under Sir John Moore, he was present at the capture of Bastia and Calvi. The island briefly became a British protectorate, but was lost to the French again in 1796. By that time Beresford had returned to England (1794) where he was appointed Lieutenant Colonel of the Waterford Regiment (124th), a regiment raised by his father on his estates in Ireland.

In early 1795 the regiment was transferred to England, where it was based first at Romsey and then Netley barracks in Hampshire.[14] The regiment was almost full and recruiting was continued in Ireland throughout the first half of the year. Even at this early date, Beresford's ability to organise and train was recognised with the regiment's Major, Richard Lee, reporting that it was wonderful what Carr had made of it. Initially the 124th was designated to serve under Lord Moira, who had recently returned from an unsuccessful expedition to the Netherlands led by the Duke of York.

This decision delighted the Marquis of Waterford who, no doubt aware of the short life expectancy of soldiers in the West Indies, expressed the view that he was happy 'Carr' would not be going there.[15] His joy was to be short lived, for even though the Duke of York inspected the regiment at Southampton that summer and was most complimentary, a decision, which Waterford had apprehended, was made in the autumn to disband the 124th, transferring officers and men to the 88th regiment (the Connaught Rangers).[16] There was a silver lining to this particular cloud, as Beresford was appointed Lieutenant Colonel of the Connaught Rangers in September 1795. This appointment came at a time when the regiment was ravaged by sickness, both typhus and typhoid having broken out in the retreat from Bergen op Zoom to Ems during the previous winter. As a result, on its return to England the 88th was seriously deficient in numbers, the regimental return for June 1795 showing a mere 222 men fit for duty with 543 declared sick, which may explain the reversing of the Waterford regiment into that of the Connaught Rangers.

Beresford set his hand to the task of rebuilding a regiment, and his methods excited the admiration of the regimental surgeon, James McGrigor; himself later to achieve fame in the Peninsula.[17] This early dedication to and demonstration of a professional approach to the welfare and training of the regiment was to be repeated frequently in his later life resulting in the appreciation and high regard held for his organisational skills by other officers.

William's father's fears of a carribean sojourn were nearly realised in the autumn of 1795. The 88th was part of a force destined for service in the West Indies later that year under Sir Ralph Abercromby, but the fleet, and indeed the regiment, became widely dispersed as a result of severe storms and as a consequence most of it returned home. Beresford was granted three months leave of absence in 1796.[18] Between 1797 and 1798, the 88th and Beresford were stationed in Jersey for the defence of that island.[19] It was a not unimportant posting as the French were once again rumoured to be threatening the Channel Isles, which they had invaded as recently as 1779 and 1781. In later life Beresford was Governor of the island, from 1821 to 1854, a thirty-year period that is still commemorated by a street named after him in the capital, St Helier.

In 1797, Richard Wellesley (then Earl of Mornington) was appointed Governor-General of the Presidency of Fort William in India, an appointment which he was to hold until 1805.[20] His younger brother, Arthur Wellesley, later to become the Duke of Wellington, took a leading military role in the ensuing Indian wars which effectively extinguished resurgent French ambitions in the subcontinent and laid the ground for the development of British power there.[21] Beresford was sent to India with the 88th regiment to join a force under Sir David Baird, but he arrived at Bombay in June 1800 after the fall of Seringapatam (May 1799) had ended the resistance of Tipu Sultan, who was killed at that time.

Beresford's career was to be linked with that of Baird rather than Arthur Wellesley for the next seven years, notwithstanding his request to the Governor-General of India to serve under Arthur following his arrival in India, a wish that Richard Wellesley was happy to accede to in circumstances which imply a good relationship between the two families.[22] In late 1800, a British expedition from India under Arthur Wellesley was planned with two potentially rather different objectives; Batavia and/or Mauritius. However, following instructions received from England the destination was changed, and Marquess Wellesley, as Richard had now become, appointed Baird to command an expeditionary force to go to Egypt, much to his brother Arthur's chagrin.

It was intended this expedition should assist and join with the army under Sir Ralph Abercromby, at that time engaged in an attempt to dislodge Napoleon's army from Egypt. The Governor-General of India appointed his brother Arthur as second in command under Baird, but Arthur was taken ill with fever in Bombay and never joined Baird's expeditionary force.[23] Thus Beresford was denied the opportunity at this date to serve under Arthur Wellesley. In December 1800, Beresford, who had been appointed to command the first brigade, was ordered to prepare to sail with secret orders from Bombay. He arrived in Bombay ahead of Baird and by the time the latter reached Bombay, Beresford had himself sailed (before 3 April 1801) for Egypt with six transports containing troops and provisions. Wellesley, whose illness seems to have involved a recurrence of a previously debilitating fever, arrived in Bombay on 23 March and seems to have been actively involved in the preparations for the expedition.

Beresford's force put in to Mocha (the Yemen) on 21 April and sailed again the following day, without disclosing his destination to the Resident, Mr Pringle. Clearly he was not going to breach his secret orders. Colonel John Murray, who was Quartermaster General on Baird's staff, had also gone ahead of Baird with a separate detachment. Baird became concerned that Beresford and Murray would join up and attack Kosseir (Al Qusair) on the Red Sea coast of Egypt before they had adequate numbers to ensure success. A messenger was sent after Beresford to tell him to meet Baird at Jeddah on the Arabian coast, but the messenger did not find either Beresford or Murray. Baird's concern rose because in May 1799 the French under Belliard had captured and subsequently garrisoned Kosseir, and in the following year driven off a British force which had inflicted considerable damage on the fort. In fact the French subsequently abandoned the fort, but not before attempting to poison the wells.

Richard Wellesley's instructions to Baird were to conciliate the Arab chiefs (including the Sheriff of Mecca, the Imam of Sana and the Sultan of Aden) to ensure, if possible, their support for the British, or at the least to obtain their neutrality. This was no foregone conclusion, given the desire of at least some to see weakened Britain's ally, the Ottoman Empire. Baird eventually reached Jeddah, having himself called at Mocha, on 18 May where he learnt that the British force under Sir Ralph Abercromby had won a signal victory against the French in Lower Egypt on 21 March, though Abercromby himself had lost his life in the engagement. He was told also that Murray and Beresford had headed up the Gulf of Suez. In fact they had already landed at Kosseir on 16 May and were making preparations to cross the desert with a view to reaching Cairo. While Baird was engaged in diplomacy with Arab leaders, Sir Home Popham arrived in Kosseir from the Cape of Good Hope with further reinforcements. Baird, Popham and Beresford were to be involved again in interesting circumstances some five years later.

Baird caught up with Beresford and Murray at Kosseir on 8 June. At that stage Murray and Romney had apparently already made one abortive attempt to cross the desert from

Kosseir to Ghennah (also Ghenné, Kenné, or Qena) on the Nile. Kosseir and its immediate environs were pretty inhospitable, as described by the Count de Noé, an officer serving with the 10th Regiment of Foot: 'I shall never forget the deep impression of melancholy made upon my mind by the first sight of this desolate coast. Such barrenness, such solitude, such a total and wretched absence of every thing like verdure or foliage, except indeed in the shape of a few blighted date trees. The heart shuddered at the idea of even a temporary residence upon its arid shores.'

The challenge of how to transport an army of in excess of 6,000 across 120 miles of desert in blistering heat was a considerable one.[24] It involved the purchase of camels, horses and bullocks, but most importantly the securing of supplies of water.[25] Baird sent out advance parties to dig new wells along the route and provided for each detachment to carry with it a large quantity of water sacks (mussacks), though these ultimately proved problematic as a number leaked.

The first corps ordered to begin the 'perilous march', being the 88th Regiment and the Bombay sepoys, was that commanded by Beresford, which set off to Moilah where there was water and provisions. However, the wells built at various points proved insufficient and Baird was forced to delay sending the second body of men while the camels carried further water supplies to Beresford and his men.[26] Ultimately the entire force, less three who had died on the way, reached Ghennah (via Legeta), which Baird reported on 24 June was to be the intermediate destination of the 88th Regiment (Connaught Rangers), but not before Baird had been forced by the conditions to send his cannon back to Kosseir.[27] The troops suffered from dysentery, and Baird was perhaps fortunate to lose only three men on a journey which had been described some twenty-five years earlier, by the explorer James Bruce, in the following terms:

> Our road was all the way on an open plain, bounded by hillocks of sand and fine gravel, perfectly hard, and not perceptible above the level of the plain country of Egypt. About twelve miles distant there is a ridge of mountains, of no considerable height, perhaps the most barren in the world – between them our road lay, through plains near three miles broad, but without trees, shrubs, or herbs; there are not even the traces of any living creatures, neither serpent nor lizard, antelope nor ostrich, the usual inhabitants of the most dreary deserts; there is no sort of water on the surface, brackish or sweet; even the birds seem to avoid the place as pestilential, not having seen one of any kind so much as flying over. The sun was burning hot, and upon rubbing two sticks together, in half a minute they flamed.[28]

Once at Ghennah, Baird prepared to move his force by boat down the Nile with Cairo as his objective. Unbeknownst to Baird, Cairo had surrendered to the British on 27 June, as Baird's army was crossing the desert. Baird's army embarked on 31 July, leaving Colonel Murray and a detachment to garrison Ghennah. Baird travelled via Gizeh (which he left Colonel Ramsey to garrison). He reached the island of Rhouda just outside Cairo on 27 August and by 30 August had arrived at Rosetta. Baird's force arrived at Alexandria just as a truce had been arranged and this was followed by the surrender of the French on 2 September 1801, which meant

Beresford played no part in the siege of that city. He was, however, subsequently appointed Commandant of Alexandria and he remained in Egypt until the British forces were withdrawn in 1803.[29]

The march by Baird's force from Kosseir on the Red Sea across 130 miles of desert in nine days and then down the Nile to Cairo caught the public imagination at home. Beresford shared in the fame generated by these events. Perhaps even more importantly he had witnessed the vital necessity of good organisation and planning for military operations, as demonstrated by Baird's thorough preparations prior to crossing the desert.

On his return home from Alexandria in 1803, Beresford spent time in Ireland, one of the few occasions during the French wars that he was able to do so. Ireland had just witnessed the suppression of a further rebellion following that of 1798; for in 1803 Robert Emmet had sought to raise the flag of republicanism again; with the difference that now the Act of Union joining Ireland with England had been adopted (1801), the target was no longer the Irish parliament in Dublin but the British administration ruling in the name of the United Kingdom of Great Britain and Ireland.

The rebellion commenced in Dublin and County Wicklow on 23 July but was short lived. A number of those involved managed to avoid the government forces for some time. While back in Ireland in late 1803, Beresford was engaged in the search for some of Emmet's supporters hiding out in the Wicklow mountains. Beresford's appearance in Wicklow at this time probably resulted from the burning of the Beresford family property at Hollywood in County Wicklow in the 1798 rebellion. Michael Dwyer and Martin Burke were two prominent participants of the 1803 rising being sought by the militia. When Martin Burke was captured on 13 December, Beresford expressed the view that he merited mercy, as he had never been a murderer, and indeed he said he did not think Burke had been responsible for any particular crime since 23 July. However, he was prepared to use Burke to capture Dwyer. Dwyer in fact surrendered the next day, followed afterwards by a number of others who had been supporters of Emmet.[30] These leaders of the Wicklow-based insurrection were detained in Kilmainham Jail in Dublin before being sent to New South Wales in late 1805 as free men.

This short interlude in Wicklow also demonstrated a side of Beresford's character with which all were to become familiar in the Peninsula. A yeoman was caught plundering property during a search, whereupon Beresford sought instructions as to whether he could court martial him using the form of trial used for soldiers or whether he was required to use some other form? While the response from his superiors has not been located, the request is evidence of Beresford, the strict disciplinarian.[31]

The year 1804 remains a blank sheet in the life of William Carr Beresford. There is a family tradition that at some stage he sought the hand of his cousin Louisa, daughter of the Archbishop of Tuam; but that this union was prevented by the family.[32] No documentary evidence has been located to support this story, but the two were supposedly close. In 1806, Louisa, who was a renowned beauty and friend of the Irish authoress Maria Edgeworth, married Thomas Hope, the interior designer, author and collector. With him she had a family, but following his death in 1831 she was to marry William in 1832 and they then spent the next twenty years together.[33]

They were both mature persons at that time, with William having secured fame, titles and financial security. Nobody would then have been in a position to prevent their marriage at that stage in their lives. If there is substance to family tradition, then the period of 1804 and early 1805 is the only time when Beresford would have had the opportunity to get to know Louisa as an adult prior to her marriage.[34]

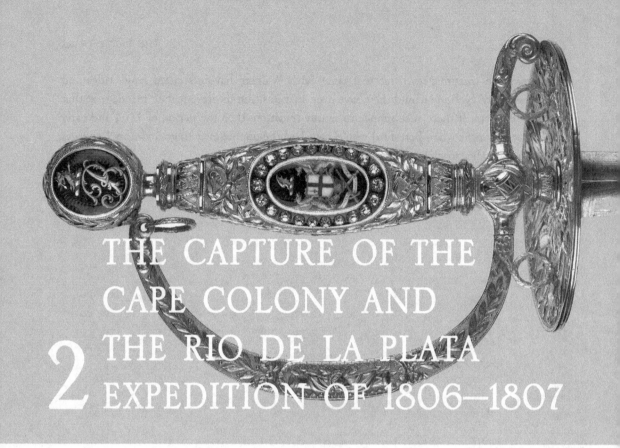

THE CAPTURE OF THE CAPE COLONY AND THE RIO DE LA PLATA EXPEDITION OF 1806—1807

2

'It grieved me to see my country subjugated in this manner, but I shall always admire the gallantry of the brave and honourable Beresford in so daring an enterprise.'[1]

Until the armistice of October 1801, which led to the Peace of Amiens in March 1802, Britain had been at war with not just France, but also with Spain and other French allies. War with France broke out again in 1803, and in 1804 Spain entered the war on the side of France following an attack on its treasure fleet by a squadron of the Royal Navy off Cape Santa Maria on 5 October without any declaration of war.[2] Britain's links with its colonies and trading partners were once again threatened, and the government developed a number of strategies to safeguard its position.

Possession of the Cape Colony, or at least the presence there of a friendly power, was a substantial asset to those interested in securing the sea route to India and the East Indies in the days of sail at a time prior to the construction of the Suez Canal. Lord Castlereagh, Secretary of State for War and the Colonies, expressed it thus:

' the true value of the Cape to Great Britain is its being considered and treated at all times as an outpost subservient to the protection and security of our Indian possessions.'[3] The British had conquered the Cape in 1795 but returned it to the Dutch (then the Batavian Republic) in 1803 pursuant to the Treaty of Amiens.[4]

French sea power, particularly when combined with that of Spain, remained a real threat to Britain in 1805 prior to the battle of Trafalgar in October of that year. Only two years previously, Napoleon had threatened an invasion of England by a massive force based around Boulogne and Calais.[5] Against this background the British government determined to seek to recapture the Cape Colony. An expedition under the command of Sir David Baird was dispatched, comprising some 6,000 soldiers divided into two brigades. The first brigade, led by Beresford, was made up of the 24th, 38th and 83rd regiments. The second brigade, the Highland Brigade, was made up of the 71st, 72nd and 93rd regiments and was commanded by Ronald Craufurd Ferguson, like Beresford a Brigadier General. The land forces were escorted by a fleet commanded by Sir Home Popham on HMS *Diadem*. This fleet fitted out and sailed from Falmouth on 5 August, and having assembled and taken on troops and further provisions departed on 31 August from Cork.[6]

The fleet called first at Madeira in the last week of September 1805. There the destination of the expedition was confirmed, ending weeks of speculation, as instructions had been declared secret to all but the commanders. The ships prepared to sail from Madeira on 1 October. A few days later, those ships destined for the West Indies separated from the remainder of Popham's fleet. After leaving Madeira, Popham raised his pennant as Commodore and appointed Captain Hugh Downman of the *Diomede* to command the *Diadem*, in a move that was to cause many disputes later when it came to claiming prize money. The fleet traversed the Atlantic, crossing the Equator on 3 November and arriving at São Salvador (now Bahia) on the Brazilian coast on 9 November after suffering some damage in a heavy storm. Two large vessels, the *King George* and the *Britannia*, were lost on Las Rochas with fatalities including Brigadier General Yorke, who had command of the artillery. Repairs and the sourcing of provisions and horses for the cavalry meant that the fleet did not depart São Salvador until late December.[7] It was not until 4 January 1806 that the fleet reached Table Bay, where it was sighted by the Dutch colonists.

Notwithstanding the rough seas, Beresford and a small landing party were sent ashore that day to ascertain a suitable disembarkation venue.[8] The next day, 5 January, there was an unsuccessful attempt to land Beresford's brigade at Leopard's Bay in high surf. Baird then detached Beresford with the 38th Regiment and some cavalry with orders to land at Saldanha Bay. This wonderful harbour is some 60 miles north of Capetown.[9] Orders were to secure the area (including seizing the postmaster) with a view to obtaining provisions for the army, and to prepare the site for a landing by the entire force if that should prove necessary. Beresford's force was carried by the *Diomede* (50-guns) and some smaller vessels, and disembarked without opposition on 6 January. As it turned out, landing at Saldanha Bay meant that Beresford missed the ensuing battle that determined the fate of southern Africa.

A change of wind direction abated the surf enough to allow Baird to land his main force at Leopard's Bay (now Melkbosstrand), some 16 miles north of Capetown, with only minor opposition on 6 January.[10] Two days later Baird comprehensively defeated the Dutch under Lieutenant General Jan Willem Janssens at the battle of Blaauwberg, and on 9 January the

9

commander of Capetown surrendered on terms which were ratified later that month.[11] In Capetown, the British learnt the welcome news of the victory of Nelson at Trafalgar over the combined Franco-Spanish fleets on 21 October of the previous year.

Beresford caught up with Baird in Capetown. Baird then sent him after Janssens, who had withdrawn into the interior in the Hottentots Holland Kloof area with his defeated force. He caught up and made contact with the Dutchman, having assumed a position in Stellenbosch on 14 January, and secured the environs. When Baird arrived the following day, Janssens surrendered after further discussions. In his dispatch home, Baird praised Beresford's 'spirit of conciliation and perseverance'.[12]

Up to this point the British expedition had followed its instructions and achieved its objectives with little loss. Baird's and Popham's orders provided (in the absence of a negotiated surrender) for the capture of the Cape with the granting to the inhabitants the continued enjoyment of their private property, usages and religion as nearly as might be possible consistent with the terms granted in the previous war when it had been occupied by Britain. Baird was then to send on to India the troops designated for that service. In the event of it being decided that an attempt to capture the Cape was not viable (there was concern the French might have fortified it by means of troops and provisions on vessels that had escaped from Rochfort), the instructions were for that part of the force not designated for India to return to St Helena to await further instructions, and in the event these were not forthcoming within fifteen days, to return to Cork, calling at Faial in the Azores in case instructions had reached that island.[13] There was no element of discretion that would allow for the expedition that Baird and Popham subsequently determined upon.

The renewal of the conflict with Spain offered the opportunity to weaken Spain as a military power and to open up trading opportunities, particularly in South America. The latter objective was particularly important in mercantile circles threatened by the loss of British and Irish trade with continental Europe.

One of the most vociferous advocates of British intervention in South America was Sir Home Popham. He had been trying to interest the British government in South America for some years. However, the attack on the Rio de la Plata in 1806 which now took place was pure opportunism and had not been sanctioned in advance by the British cabinet.[14] While in Capetown, Popham apparently heard from a number of sources that the Peruvian treasure (in fact primarily silver from the mines around Potosi in modern-day Bolivia, then part of the Viceroyalty of Peru) was on its way to Buenos Aires for transhipment to Spain.[15] With communications to London taking perhaps three months in each direction, there was no time to seek instructions. Popham approached Baird, and after some initial resistance persuaded the military commander to authorise Popham to take part of his fleet and some 1,400 troops from Capetown to support the enterprise. The voyage provided for a stopover at St Helena, where it was hoped that the expedition might pick up additional troops and artillery.[16]

Baird determined to appoint Beresford to command the expeditionary force, stating to Lord Castlereagh that he had: 'confided the command to an officer of rank and recognized ability, wise and zealous.' He further authorised the appointment of Beresford as Lieutenant-Governor if he should get possession of 'the Spanish establishment on the River Plate'.[17]

The core of Beresford's force (some 864 men) was made up of the 1st Battalion of the 71st Regiment of Foot, commanded by another Irishman, Lieutenant Colonel Denis Pack. Beresford and Pack were firm friends, though it is not known whether this factor played any part in the selection of the 71st Regiment to accompany Beresford.[18] Popham had wanted to take a different regiment, whose commanding officer was a close friend of his own.[19] Additional firepower was to be supplied by Royal Marines, Royal Artillery members and a picket of the 20th Light Dragoons, as well as sailors from the fleet accompanying Beresford's force.

Following the capture of Capetown, the 71st had been quartered at Wynnberg, about 7 miles outside the town. Once again secrecy was the order of the day and the speculation in Capetown concerned Macao or Manila as the destination of the expedition, given that the Ile de France was considered too strong a target. Popham's predeliction for South America was such that it was not long before opinion fixed on a marauding expedition along the coast of Peru. When later they heard of Beresford's success in capturing Buenos Aires, the reaction was one of incredulity that a city of this size could be taken by one regiment.[20] On 12 April 1806, the 71st Regiment and the other members of the expedition embarked, and Popham's fleet, which sailed on 20 April, arrived in Saint Helena nine days later. On the way there contact had been lost with *The Ocean*, one of the transports carrying some 200 men, but fortuitously this was waiting for the fleet when it arrived at the entrance to the Rio de la Plata. In Saint Helena, Beresford acquired some 250 additional soldiers including artillerymen and two 5½-inch howitzers. In all this little army numbered little more than 1,600 men.[21]

Arriving in the Rio de la Plata in early June, Popham and Beresford disagreed on their first objective. Beresford sought to strike against Montevideo rather than Buenos Aires, on the basis that Montevideo was reportedly well fortified and that it would be preferable to strike the stronger position first while the British force had the element of surprise and the men were fresh. He was overruled by Popham, allegedly on the basis that provisions, which were apparently in short supply, would be easier to obtain in Buenos Aires.[22] However, it seems not unreasonable to suppose that the suspected presence of 'Peruvian' silver in Buenos Aires in transit to Spain may have contributed to Popham's preference for an attack on Buenos Aires rather than Montevideo.[23] The troops then transferred from the men-of-war to frigates and transports as the former were too big to proceed up-river. The scene was set for a landing, though Beresford's disclosure that Baird had commissioned him as Major General on the eve of his departure from the Cape (12 April) upset Popham, who later lodged a complaint with the government in this respect.[24]

On 24 June, the force was off Buenos Aires and the Spanish Viceroy, Rafael Marquis de Sobremonte, was advised of its arrival while attending the theatre that evening. He had been warned in general terms of the presence of the British squadron in the Rio de la Plata some weeks earlier, in response to which Sobremonte had taken certain defensive measures. Buenos Aires at that time was a town of between 40,000 and 50,000 inhabitants.[25] There was a fort near the river with thirty-five 24lb guns and assorted other ordnance. However, the city was short of regular troops, for some of those designated to go there were still in northern Spain. A number of local regiments were augmented by a militia. When he was first warned of the British presence, Sobremonte called out the militia and stationed troops in Quilmes, Olivos and along the line of the Rio Riachuelo; the former to cover anticipated landing points, and the latter to create a defensive screen outside the city. However, the Viceroy's reaction to the landing of the British was to abandon Buenos Aires and to proceed inland towards Córdoba with some 600 troops and sixteen wagons loaded with the state treasure and the valuables of wealthy citizens. He left his aide-de-camp (ADC), Hilarión de la Quintana, to resist the British, and if necessary to negotiate terms.[26]

The following day (25 June) Beresford disembarked his forces, amounting to probably less than 1,450 men, at Quilmes, approximately 12 miles from Buenos Aires.[27] Having seized the beachhead, the small force spent the night near Reducción de Quilmes before proceeding towards Buenos Aires. The next day the British encountered a Spanish force estimated variously to be 2,000–3,000 strong with cavalry and cannon drawn up in a line. Beresford sent the 71st Regiment under Pack forward with bagpipes playing, while keeping the Saint Helena infantry in reserve. The British troops brushed aside resistance following a short but sharp fight. The Spanish retreated to a small village called Barracas, burning the bridge over the river Riachuello, but early on the morning of 27 June, following a brisk exchange of fire, Beresford's troops crossed the Riachuello on a pontoon bridge made up of small boats and planks, and quickly gained possession of Barracas.

Beresford sent one of his ADCs, Alexander Gordon, to summons the city of Buenos Aires. Quintana sought terms for surrender, but Beresford refused conditions save such as he was pleased to offer. On the afternoon of 27 June the British entered Buenos Aires and took possession of the fortress. From disembarkation to the surrender of the fortress the British force lost only one man killed and a further twelve wounded. In victory Beresford allowed generous conditions, which may have stood him in good stead later; he allowed the garrison to surrender with the honours of war. Captain A. Gillespie of the marines was appointed Commissary for Prisoners and the Spanish officers signed their parole papers at his lodgings, in the 'Inn of the Three Kings'. Beresford guaranteed security of property and freedom of commerce, together with the full exercise of religion. While this was entirely in line with British thinking on freedom of trade, it is likely that Beresford was motivated by a desire to cement the acquisition of Buenos Aires in a situation where he had landed with some 1,400 troops and needed to control a population of over 40,000 with many other potential enemies within striking distance in Montevideo and other towns.

Beresford's correspondence with both London and the Cape reveals his anxiety regarding his position. Indeed, even while in Saint Helena he had written home to the government stating that in the event of success he would require reinforcements and additional instructions.[28] He clearly felt that the best he could try and do was to hold Buenos Aires, and he indicated that he would not be undertaking further operations until reinforcements were received. In early July he requested an additional 2,000 infantry and 600 cavalry. Beresford must have received some degree of intelligence from the local community because he knew that Viceroy Sobremonte was trying to collect a large force from the towns of Córdoba in order to attempt the recovery of Buenos Aires.[29]

It was immediately evident that to have any prospect of retaining the city and its surrounding area would require additional troops. Popham's first letters after the capture of Buenos Aires were to Baird in Capetown advising him of the success and seeking reinforcements. Similar reports and requests were sent to London.[30] By way of response, Baird advised on 13 August that he was sending 2,000 men as soon as possible, a force that would include 350 cavalry. Understandably, given the length of time it took to communicate with England, a response from the government was somewhat slower.[31]

Beresford set up his headquarters in the fortress of Buenos Aires. He moved quickly in an effort to consolidate the tenuous hold he had on the city and with a view to garner support for British rule. While he secured the city, he sought to conciliate those accustomed to exercise power, the merchants and indeed other groups. In essence, he left in place the existing legal, administrative and ecclesiastical structures making just one major change in that he proclaimed the sovereignty of George III and assumed the position of Lieutenant-Governor in place of Viceroy Sobremonte.[32] He made a series of proclamations designed to reassure the population, which reduced many commercial tariffs. As late as 4 August 1806 he issued a proclamation containing sixteen commercial regulations designed to break the system of 'monopolies, restriction and oppression'.[33] Free trade was established subject to the payment of certain taxes to the British Crown and to the Consulate. The amount of these taxes depended on the origin of the goods, with lesser rates appertaining to trade with Great Britain, Ireland and the colonies of the British crown. There were specific taxes in respect of tobacco, Chilean wine, whiskey, Paraguayan herbs, horse hides and other skins as well as for gold and silver.

Beresford moved also to establish his supply lines, appointing an Irish merchant resident in Buenos Aires, Thomas O'Gorman, as purveyor of provisions to the army. Some funds were available for this purpose, as over 600,000 pesos was sequestered from government coffers in the fort and on the quayside.[34] In parallel with securing the city and encouraging commerce, he sought to recover the 'treasure' which it will be recalled had been sent inland with the Viceroy and an escort. To this end Beresford sent a party under Captain Robert Arbuthnot to attempt to retrieve the treasure, which had been sent to Luján, some fifty kilometres in the interior.[35]

Arbuthnot took with him seven dragoons, twenty infantry and two other officers from the 71st Regiment. They set out by horse on 3 July and remarkably returned with an immense sum one week later.[36] The total sum recovered from Luján was $1,291,323. Of this $1,086,208 (perhaps $70–77,000,000 in current value) was sent back to England on 17 July on a frigate, HMS *Narcissus*, while Beresford kept back $205,115 for the Buenos Aires treasury and the needs of the expeditionary force.[37] At the same time, over $100,000 worth of valuables was reportedly returned to Portenos (as the inhabitants of Buenos Aires were and are still known) in keeping with Beresford's promise of security of property.

The *Narcissus*, commanded by Captain Ross Donnelly, arrived at Portsmouth, England, on 12 September after a 57-day voyage, and the news was forwarded to London. Letters had been despatched by Popham to the City of London, the chambers of commerce of other towns and even Lloyds Coffee House extolling the potential of trade with South America. In what appears to have been a well-engineered propaganda occasion, the treasure was transported on wagons from Portsmouth to London escorted by a picket of cavalry. The convoy arrived in London on 21 September to a rapturous reception, as reported in *The Times* and other publications. Each wagon bore a large sign stating 'Treasure' and when the convoy reached St James's Square silk banners stating 'Buenos Aires, Popham, Beresford, Victory' were presented to the convoy as it made its way to the Bank of England.[38]

The lion's share of the proceeds seized in what is now Argentina went to the state, but each officer, soldier and sailor received a share. Baird, who had authorised but not participated in the expedition, was awarded £23,990-5-8d, the largest sum; but even the lowly soldier or sailor received £18-6-0d. Beresford's share at £11,995-2-10½d was deemed to be double that of Popham (£5,997-11-5d), notwithstanding the latter's angry representations.[39]

A grateful City of London, with an eye on future trade at least as much as the benefit accruing from the capture of the treasure, voted Beresford and Popham the Freedom of the City; the Court of Common Council resolving unanimously:

> that the thanks of this Court be given to Major-General Beresford and Commodore Sir Home Popham, and the officers and men under their respective commands, for their very gallant conduct and the very important services rendered by them to their country in the capture of Buenos Ayres, at once opening a new source of commerce to the manufacturers of Great Britain, and depriving her enemy of one of the richest and most extensive colonies in her possession.[40]

In addition to the Freedom of the City, Beresford and Popham were awarded jewelled freedom boxes and beautiful dress swords to the value of 200 guineas each, though they were not to collect these until after the abdication of Napoleon in 1814.[41]

Back in Buenos Aires, the situation – unbeknownst to the government in London – had changed dramatically. While Lord Grenville's administration prepared to send out a relieving force under Brigadier General Samuel Auchmuty, and indeed even before the *Narcissus* had arrived at Portsmouth with its cargo of precious metal, the British forces in Buenos Aires had suffered defeat and capture.[42] Though some Portenos took the oath of allegiance, by mid July 1806 Beresford was conscious of growing opposition to British rule. He observed that while people were desirous of change they were (quite wisely as it turned out) concerned that Spain would recover the conquered land and that factor inhibited people from coming forward to declare their support. Notwithstanding this difficulty, he seems personally to have developed a good relationship with some of the important families and individuals in Buenos Aires.[43] Later, after his return to England, Beresford was to send presents to a number of these. Furthermore, in light of later events, it is possible that Beresford sympathised with the ambitions of some Portenos to achieve independence, though he trod a very careful line in the absence of instructions from London. There were also rumours of masonic connections between erstwhile opponents, and the 'Southern Cross' masonic lodge may have been established at this time.

The population of the Spanish colony (the Virreinato) was made up of four components; the Spanish, the creoles, the native Indians and slaves. Those of political consequence were the Spanish and the creoles. While Beresford reportedly met a number of proponents of independence, including Juan Martin de Pueyrredón and J.J. Castelli, both of whom later pursued independence from Spain, neither the Spanish settlers nor the creoles were interested (with possibly a few exceptions) in exchanging one colonial power for another. The resistance and number of deaths arising from subsequent assaults by other British forces on Montevideo and Buenos Aires make this clear. Whether they were long-term residents, recent arrivals, Spanish or Creole, they realised quickly that the British force under Beresford was too weak to guarantee their independence.[44]

With the growth of opposition to the British presence, Beresford now faced two further problems. The first of these concerned Spanish officers released on parole who disappeared, thus breaking that parole. There was little that could be done once they had absconded.[45] The second problem, the desertion of some of his own troops, was met head on by Beresford. The force brought from the Cape and St Helena included a number of German and Spanish mercenaries, some of whom deserted. Beresford had already demonstrated his capacity to ensure discipline in Egypt and he was later to be recognised for his great organisational and administrative abilities. Here in Buenos Aires he showed those same qualities. Four Spanish deserters from the St Helena regiment were ordered to be given 500 lashes and one of those died in the process. However, when a Spanish cadet was sentenced to death on 17 July, Beresford reprieved him at the request of the Bishop of Buenos Aires, even though the latter was not well disposed towards the British. Two days later Beresford decreed that those assisting men to desert would be liable to the death penalty, a move that may have been inspired by the efforts of some of the clergy to persuade soldiers who were their fellow Roman Catholics to desert. Many of those targeted were Irish, and some reportedly deserted in late July and early August having been offered land and in some cases employment. Following the battle of Perdriel, a German deserter who was recaptured was given the death penalty, a not infrequent punishment at the time.[46]

At the end of July, Beresford was faced with an insurrection led by Juan Martin de Pueyrredón at the head of a force of perhaps 1,000–2,000 mostly mounted horsemen.[47] Pueyrredon had initially appeared well disposed to the British on their arrival, but he subsequently left the city to gather troops to resist the invaders. This force was put to flight in twenty minutes by Beresford at Perdriel on 1 August, with Colonel Pack and a force of 500 men from the 71st regiment assisted by six pieces of artillery.[48] A lack of cavalry prevented any pursuit and Pueyrredón escaped, fleeing to Colonia de Sacramento in modern-day Uruguay, where he joined another force being raised by Santiago de Liniers, a Frenchman who served for most of his life as a military officer in the service of Spain. In 1788 he had been promoted to Captain and put in command of the flotilla guarding the Rio de la Plata, and at the time of the British invasion he obtained sanctuary in the convent of San Domingo in Buenos Aires before escaping to Montevideo, where the governor authorised him to raise an army to resist the invasion.[49]

Popham had naval patrols in the Rio de la Plata to both report on and attempt to prevent the transfer of any force from the north to the south bank of the river. Some of the marines used in the initial capture of Buenos Aires were taken from the garrison to give teeth to these patrols. However, on the night of 4/5 August under cover of a storm, de Liniers managed to cross the river with a force of in excess of 2,000, augmented by further adherents as he advanced on the city. Arriving before Buenos Aires on 10 August, which itself was now in a state of unrest, he called on Beresford to surrender, reminding him that he was vastly outnumbered. Rather than surrender, Beresford determined to try and extract his forces, now reduced to about 1,300 men, but only succeeded in getting the sick and the wounded onto Popham's fleet before hostilities began in earnest on 11 August.[50] A running battle ensued over two days during which the British force suffered 45 deaths with 100 injured and a further 9 missing; while the enemy reportedly sustained some 700 losses.[51]

Beresford had insufficient forces to hold the city and initially sought to maintain himself in the fort, the Retiro barracks and a few other outposts including the Recova.[52] Indeed he could spare just fifteen men for the defence of the Retiro which only fell to the Spanish force when all but two of the fifteen defenders had been killed. The British drew back to the Plaza Mayor on 12 August, having been forced to abandon the Recova, where Beresford's secretary, Captain Kennett, was killed at his side. Beresford had placed riflemen in the steeple of the cathedral, but this position was also abandoned when the decision was made to retreat to the Plaza Mayor.

Beresford at one stage may have planned to retire to the docks at Ensenada and embark there but ultimately he fell back on the fortress, reportedly himself being the last man across the drawbridge.[53] Later that day (12 August), under a flag of truce, terms for surrender were negotiated. These included the security of person and property of all British subjects; the troops to march out with the honours of war, and a provision for their speedy embarkation for the Cape or England at the expense of Spain. Further, the British troops were not to serve against Spain directly or indirectly until exchanged for Spanish prisoners. Some of the troops at least appear to have been exchanged for Spanish prisoners previously taken by Beresford in June 1806, and on 17 August a number of Popham's transports arrived off Buenos Aires for the purpose of taking men on board.[54]

There seems to have been no doubt at this stage that the terms of the agreement between Beresford and de Liniers provided for the repatriation of the British force, for the appearance of Popham's transports followed de Liniers ADC visiting Popham on board the *Diadem* on 16 August under a flag of truce for the specific purpose of embarking the troops and effecting an exchange of prisoners.[55] De Liniers however, under pressure from his political masters, ultimately signed the terms on 20 August with the caveat 'so far as I am able' ('en cuánto puedo'). Terms clearly agreed were now rendered uncertain and Beresford immediately protested when there was a failure to release the prisoners with a view to repatriation. To this end he sent back the amended terms to de Liniers via his ADC, Robert Arbuthnot, on 21 August, reminding him that the Spanish version of the treaty had been written by Don Felix Casamayor, the Superintendant of Finances in Buenos Aires. Initially, de Liniers acknowledged the unfairness of this unilateral variation of the terms, which he condemned, and stated he would adhere to the original agreement. Subsequently, he indicated to Beresford that the people of the town were in a state of insurrection as a result of which he wished the British to embark at night from a place out of sight of the crowds. Even that plan was abandoned and clearly under pressure de Liniers denied any knowledge of an agreement in the terms originally reduced to writing.[56]

Popham supported Beresford's protests. He engaged in a vigorous correspondence with the Governor of Montevideo, Ruiz Huidobro, and subsequently Viceroy Sobremente, protesting strenuously at the non-fulfilment of the terms of the capitulation agreed between Beresford and de Liniers. These protests were to no avail as the Spanish authorities determined that de Liniers had no authority to agree the terms, and that in reality the terms had not been signed until after the surrender of the British forces in Buenos Aires.[57] Popham castigated the Governor of Montevideo for arguing that the agreement had been intended merely as a private document and not a public treaty, pointing out that it had been agreed in the presence of Casamayor antecedent to the surrender, and if this had not been the case Beresford would not have surrendered the castle. In a burst of righteous indignation, Popham claimed the Spanish conduct was disgraceful and contrary to the law of nations and he contrasted this behaviour with that of Beresford on the capture of Buenos Aires earlier.[58]

The treatment of the defeated force was a mixed one. A number of men were abused and even murdered, but alongside such incidents acts of considerable kindness took place.[59] In particular, the Bethlemite fathers administered medical treatment to the injured, and this was recognised by the 71st Regiment when it was later repatriated.[60] Colonel Pack kept up a correspondence with Don Luis, one of the Bethlemite Friars, for some years afterwards. He expressed his gratitude for the attention paid to the wounded and sent him the gift of a coffee service in English china in 1809.[61] Initial developments were far from satisfactory, for instead of release and repatriation the British soldiers were committed to various jails and other strongholds in and around Buenos Aires. Beresford (and other officers) were released on parole and he lodged with the family of Felix Casamayor in the city.[62] Casamayor was the official who had transcribed and witnessed the original terms of the treaty whereby Beresford surrendered.

Following the arrival of further British forces in the estuary of the Rio de la Plata from the Cape at the end of September, as part of the response designed to reinforce Beresford, there was a change of policy and the senior officers were rounded up in mid October and sent under guard to the Cabildo of Luján, the very town from which Beresford's force had seized the 'treasure'. Other officers were sent to San Antonio de Areco, Capilla del Señor and various estancias. Parallel with the decision to send the officers to Luján and other locations, the Cabildo dispersed the British troops to a number of inland towns, including Santiago del Estero, Tucumán, San Luis and Córdoba.[63] The decision to place them at a distance from Buenos Aires was taken in anticipation that Britain would either attempt their rescue, or, as in fact happened, seek to use reinforcements to restore and extend British rule. Moving officers to the interior and the failure to repatriate the force was seen by the British officers as a breach of the terms of surrender by the colonial government and this was made clear. Later the British officers were able to use this breach as a justification for their own conduct.

In Luján, Beresford and the officers with him were initially at liberty to exercise. They hunted, fished and played cricket; and at first were allowed to correspond.[64] Beresford was attended from time to time by Captain Saturnino Rodriguez de Peña, military secretary to de Liniers. De Peña was an opponent of Spanish dominion and he seems to have formed the opinion that Beresford supported the objectives of those who sought independence.[65]

The promised relief force of some 2,000 under Colonel Backhouse arrived in the Rio de la Plata from the Cape of Good Hope towards the end of September. Meeting up with Popham's fleet, Backhouse learnt of Beresford's defeat and capture. After an abortive attempt to capture Montevideo, a small force was landed and captured Maldonado, a then modest town on the left bank of the Rio de la Plata, together with a number of surrounding gun batteries. Maldonado then became the British shore base. Meanwhile British strategy, unaware until 25 January 1807 of Beresford's surrender, was being directed not just to the maintenance of the conquest of Buenos Aires, but with a view to taking control of Chile. Further reinforcements arrived from England in December with Rear Admiral Sir Charles Stirling, who relieved Popham of his command. Popham returned to England to face trial for his unauthorised campaign.

The main British relief force under Brigadier General Sir Samuel Auchmuty arrived off Montevideo in early January 1807. On 3 February, Auchmuty captured Montevideo. The reaction of the chief magistrate of Buenos Aires was to order the seizure of Beresford's papers. Judge Juan Bazo y Berry and another procurator fiscal, Dr Pedro Andrés García, with a military escort were sent to Luján for this purpose and despite Beresford's protests his papers were taken from his ADC, Robert Arbuthnot.[66] It was also decided to move Beresford and the other officers further away from the coast to Catamarca in the interior.[67] Colonel Pack was clear in his report that García was reminded that the British officers did not regard themselves as on parole due to the Spanish breach of the terms of surrender.[68]

These developments galvanised de Peña, who was in charge of bringing supplies and money to the detained officers. In possession of a free pass from de Liniers for that purpose, he and a colleague rode to Luján, arriving on 16 February to find that Beresford and the other officers had left under armed escort that very day for Catamarca.[69] De Peña and his colleague, in an act of daring, pursued and caught up with the escort party near the Estancia Grande of the Bethlemite Fathers at Arrecifes claiming to have orders to bring Beresford to Buenos Aires. De Peña apparently informed Beresford that he would be taken to Montevideo and that de Peña and his colleagues were undertaking this rescue for the good of the country. However, a difficulty arose in that Beresford refused to leave without Pack, so both were taken back to Buenos Aires by de Peña. There they were hidden by de Peña and his two colleagues, messrs Padilla and Francisco Gonzalez, for three days in the home of Gonzalez before being smuggled offshore in a small boat on 21 February.[70] On 22 February 1807 they were transferred to HMS *Charwell* in the estuary of the Rio de la Plata and they made good their escape to Montevideo.[71]

Auchmuty's forces had captured Montevideo three weeks prior to Beresford's arrival there. When Beresford arrived, Auchmuty was preparing to attempt the recapture of Buenos Aires. He proposed that Beresford should take command of the forces designated for the attempt, in accordance with his own orders to place his force under Beresford's command. Beresford refused this offer on the grounds that he wished to go to England to acquaint the government fully concerning the situation in the country (i.e. the Rio de la Plata). In this respect he may have wished to express views regarding the potential for Argentinian independence and possible British support for such a move, given the suggestion he had expressed sympathy for such a move to de Peña.[72] He also suggested that given the disgrace which had occurred he doubted whether he could really assume command; though it is not clear whether this remark was a reference to military defeat or the rows about the terms of surrender.

A Court of Inquiry held in Montevideo determined that neither Beresford nor Pack had broken their parole, but perhaps Beresford still felt honour-bound not to resume the fight personally.[73] Pack corroborated Beresford's evidence regarding the conditions under which they had surrendered and stated that he was present on 13 August when de Liniers dispatched a Spanish officer to Popham to request transports be furnished to execute the terms of the treaty. Insofar as they were able to controvert the evidence of the surrender document, the Spanish advanced an argument that Beresford had raised the Spanish flag over the fort at Buenos Aires prior to the signing the document and had thrown down his sword, both considered as evidence of unconditional surrender. However, it was pointed out that the Spanish flag had been raised at the specific request of de Liniers' ADC in order to stop the exchanges of fire which were continuing, and in fact Captain Patrick rather than Beresford had thrown down his sword in disgust.[74] Beresford conceded he had given his parole not to escape but maintained he was not bound by his word given the failure of the Spanish to return him and his troops to England and the subsequent placing of an armed guard on him and his fellow officers. Having been cleared of any improper conduct, Beresford sailed from the Rio de la Plata on the *Diomede* on 26 March, reaching Ireland on 22 May 1807. Pack remained with the army in Montevideo and only returned home following its defeat in the summer of 1807.[75]

Interestingly, Beresford wrote from Montevideo to Martín de Álzaga (then Mayor of Buenos Aires) to try and secure the release of the British prisoners in compliance with the terms of the capitulation in August 1806, declaring in that correspondence that he intended to take no further part in the campaign: 'but in spite of all that has happened to me I feel interested for the people of Buenos Aires' and if they heard from him again he wrote 'it will be from my striving to do what I consider will make them prosperous and happy'.[76]

Beresford's departure meant General Whitelocke ultimately came to be placed in charge of the army that attempted but failed to recapture Buenos Aires in the summer of 1807. His abject capitulation at the head of a force of over 9,000 – including 350 horse – led to a complete surrender of the British forces in the region, including the abandonment of Montevideo. This was one of Britian's most humiliating defeats in the Napoleonic wars and on returning home Whitelocke was court martialled and subsequently cashiered. Lieutenant Colonel Pack was amongst the British troops who were repatriated to Britain under the terms of the 1807 surrender. Those who came back included the remaining officers and many of the men who had served as part of Beresford's force.

Not all chose to return, however, and in particular a number of soldiers who appear to have been of predominantly Irish and Scots origin decided to stay on in South America. It is noticeable that many of those who determined to remain were members of Pack's 71st Highland

Regiment which had a large Irish cohort, probably recruited when that regiment was based in Ireland. They forfeited their share of the prize money, not just from the 'treasure' of Buenos Aires but from vessels taken off the coast during the time of the British occupation.[77]

The officers and men who sailed back with the British regiments, or in the case of those who had died in service their dependents, were paid dividends from this prize money, in some cases many years later; allocation of funds depending on rank. Popham became involved in litigation with some of his own captains over his share of prize money and the court (Mansfield J) found he was not entitled to a commanding officer's share as he was not a commodore with a captain serving under him.[78] Similarly, he engaged with Baird and Beresford in litigation in which he was ultimately unsuccessful.

Rather touchingly, on his return to England Beresford obtained from the British government pensions for de Peña, Padilla and Gonzalez, as well as for the boatman who had helped him escape, Antonio Luiz de Lima. De Peña and Padilla resided in Rio de Janeiro following their having rendered assistance to the British officers, de Lima eventually settled in London on his pension of £300 per annum.

Baird and Popham seem to have envisaged military conquest of the Rio de la Plata Viceroyalty, or a portion of it, rather than just a type of privateering venture. On that basis the size of the force sent there showed a distinct lack of realism. The knowledge of the crushing naval defeat suffered by the French and Spanish at Trafalgar would presumably have encouraged both Popham and Beresford to believe they had a secure exit strategy if events went against them in the Rio de la Plata; in that they were unlikely to be challenged at sea. On his own return to England, Popham had suggested his expedition had been supported in concept by a now-deceased Pitt. *The Times* rejected this argument and summed up the position adroitly:

> Who will believe that Mr Pitt, or any other person who might be the Prime Minister of England, would, if he had actually determined to occupy La Plata, consider 1046 soldiers and 480 seamen and marines, to be a force adequate to such an object? The first temporary success of this small expedition 'twas all that was contrary to probability; the ultimate failure, and the capture of all the troops that comprised it, was what might have been expected.[79]

In truth the British government had merely tried to capitalise on the initial success of the expedition under Popham and Beresford. Ultimately, the venture ended in the collapse of the military objective after Beresford had left South America. There had for some time been a faction within government advocating the development of commercial ties rather than physical conquest with South America, and this group now gained the upper hand.

In Great Britain, the legacy of this foreign expedition is perhaps best remembered in terms of the 'treasure' sent to England. As such the events of 1806 have been seen as a 'derring-do' voyage of virtual piracy along the lines of Drake, Raleigh and others. In the words of one soldier present, 'the object of our enterprise is to cripple the pecuniary resources of Spain'.[80] However, it seems highly likely that its consequences were far greater. The ease with which Beresford's small force had dismissed the Spanish colonial forces demonstrated to others that this was an empire in serious decline; and so it proved when the colonials moved against the Spanish monarchy less than four years later. Beresford clearly understood that it was going to be very difficult for Spain to recover control of the Rio de la Plata for he expressed that view in correspondence with the British government.

While the war of independence in what is now Argentina did not conclude until 1818, full independence was declared in 1816. One commentator has summed up Beresford's campaign by stating it 'cracked the monumental edifice of the Spanish Empire and began the process by which it collapsed into rubble'.[81] As such, while modern-day Argentines celebrate the Reconquista, Beresford is remembered today in Buenos Aires more with admiration than hatred.

While there are suggestions that Beresford was not inimical to the desire of a number of the inhabitants of the Rio de la Plata for greater freedom, and even independence, he prudently followed a cautious line. Supporting independence in a rival empire's colonies created potential danger in Britain's own dependencies. Napoleon's forcing of the Portuguese royal family into exile in 1807 and his seizure of the Spanish throne in 1808 made it important for Britain that the colonies of those nations did not succumb to French influence, an objective that was achieved by British naval power. The quid pro quo for British support for Portugal and Spain was the loosening of trade restrictions enabling British commerce with South America to grow considerably. Those in Britain who sympathised with aspirations for independence in the various colonies of South America appreciated that so long as Spain was fighting the Napoleonic threat, it was against the British interest to weaken Spain by encouraging insurrection by the colonials of South America. Whereas in early 1808, Britain was still planning a substantial expedition to South and even Central America in response to Napoleon's takeover of Spain, the subsequent Spanish revolt and the request for British assistance transformed policy, providing Britain with the opportunity to open up a new European front.[82]

What of the fate of the three principals in the expedition to the Rio de la Plata? The expedition had been unauthorised and both Baird and Popham faced criticism and risked serious censure. Baird was roundly criticised by the Secretary of State for War for authorising the expedition to South America without sanction or authority, and it was made clear to him that if the government had wished to attack the Spanish settlements at the Rio de la Plata, a more appropriate sized force would have been employed than that which Baird had dispatched under Beresford.[83] He was recalled from his position as Lieutenant-Governor of the Cape and he left there on 19 January 1807, arriving in England in March. He was soon employed again, taking part in the Copenhagen expedition of 1807 before going on to serve in the Peninsula under Sir John Moore. Later in life he was to be appointed Commander in Chief of the forces in Ireland between March 1820 and June 1822.

Popham was not so fortunate. On his return to England he was arrested and tried by Court Martial for both leaving the Cape in a defenceless state and for undertaking an expedition for which he had 'no direction or authority whatsoever'. Following a robust defence, in which Popham pleaded his various papers presented to and conversations with Pitt, Melville and Miranda, he was found guilty of both charges, but was only severely reprimanded 'in consideration of the circumstances'.[84] The finding does not seem to have inhibited his career even in the short term, for not only did he take part in the Copenhagen expedition of 1807, but he did so as First Captain in the fleet commanded by Lord Gambier.

For his part, Beresford was clearly not felt to be culpable. He had neither devised nor authorised the expedition, and the letter of recall to Baird makes it clear that a larger force would have been utilised had the British wished to attack the Spanish in the Rio de la Plata; the implication being that he had done well with the force at his disposal. His conduct of his small force was admired by those present and recognised by the government.[85] Beresford's own feelings that he had perhaps let the side down by surrendering rather than fighting to the end were not shared by others. Pack neither blamed him for the subsequent disputes surrounding the terms of surrender, nor for the act of surrender observing:

> A more gallant and honourable officer than General Beresford there cannot be, and I am fully persuaded he has acted from the purest motives of humanity, and I cannot help thinking it was to us a dreadful sacrifice. If the place ought to have been defended, I am afraid it will be thought we lost too few in the attempt; if not, too many.[86]

Beresford's experience in the Rio de la Plata colony was to stand him in good stead in the years to come in the Iberian Peninsula. He had demonstrated administrative abilities, an adherence to discipline and personal courage in leading his troops. Within six months of his return to England he was appointed to command an expedition to take control of the Portuguese island of Madeira. It was only following the abdication of Napoleon in 1814 that he was able to attend the Guildhall in the City of London on 11 June in that year and receive in person the Freedom of the City together with the freedom box and sword voted to him in 1806. In accepting this honour, Beresford described it as the proudest moment of his life.

While it was undoubtedly a high point of an already distinguished career, it was to prove one step in a life which subsequently saw him rise to become Marshal-General of Portugal and a cabinet minister in Wellington's government of 1828. His reputation was enhanced rather than tarnished by his South American experiences, though arguably had he thought through Popham's proposal he would not have agreed with it, as conquest of the Rio de la Plata had little chance of success with such a small force. Did he let an opportunity for glory cloud proper judgment? If he had not wished to support the decision of Baird to endorse Popham's proposal for the invasion of the Rio de la Plata, he would have had to resign from the expeditionary force at the Cape and return to England and might have been criticised in some quarters for such conduct; though this is what Sir Robert Wilson did when chastised by Home Popham for expressing doubts regarding the project.[87]

Even in Argentina Beresford was not without his admirers. The capture and 47-day occupation of Buenos Aires is frequently acknowledged by Argentine historians as part of the process which enabled Argentina to secure its own independence, beginning four years later.

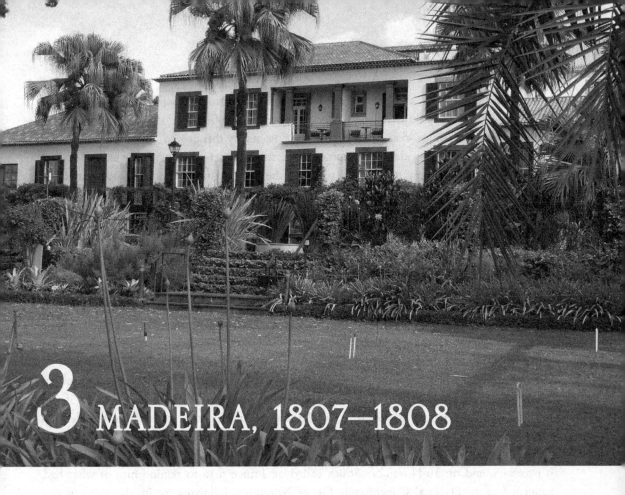

3 MADEIRA, 1807–1808

Portugal had long held a strategic importance for Great Britain and others. To this had been added a commercial relationship of considerable importance. The Portuguese had developed an empire based on maritime trade and Portugal proved to be invaluable to Britain in the latter's politico-economic struggle with first Spain and later France. In 1807, Portugal was governed by a Regent, Prince João, due to the fact that his mother Queen Maria had been deemed of unsound mind.[1] Britain and France, as well as other participants, had been at war again since 1803 with Portugal desperately seeking to maintain its neutrality.

The importance of Portugal to France lay in its continued resistance to the implementation of the imposed continental system, whereby Napoleon sought to block Great Britain from access to continental markets.[2] Furthermore, France had not given up its ambition to invade Great Britain. After Trafalgar, the French engaged in a naval rebuilding programme but at the same time perceived the potential benefit of securing the only two remaining navies other than the Royal Navy in western Europe, both representing neutral powers.[3] The French failed to secure the Danish fleet when the British pre-empted Marshal Bernadotte's invasion by itself acquiring twenty-nine ships of the line and frigates following the bombardment of Copenhagen in late August and early September 1807. Napoleon was also prepared to invade Portugal, should that country fail to comply with French demands.

In the summer of 1807, France gave Portugal an ultimatum to seize British property, to close its ports to British shipping and to declare war on Great Britain. Portugal tried to appease Napoleon while keeping Great Britain onside but ultimately this proved impossible.[4] Deeming the Portuguese response inadequate, Napoleon determined to send a French army under Marshal Junot to invade the country. Prior to this invasion, the British envoy to Lisbon, Lord Strangford, had negotiated in August an arrangement whereby the Governor of Madeira would surrender when British forces appeared off the island; subject to the Portuguese government being informed first of the intention to send an expedition to Madeira. Separately, in October 1807 the British Foreign Secretary George Canning, and the Portuguese envoy to London, Domingos António de Sousa Coutinho, drew up a secret agreement providing for the occupation of Portuguese possessions only on notice and for a British fleet to escort the Portuguese court to Brazil should that prove necessary.[5] In Britain, however, there remained both unease and uncertainty as to Portuguese intentions both prior to and subsequent to these agreements. This was not just because of the apparent desire of the Portuguese to appease Napoleon, but also because of the existence of a pro-French faction in the Portuguese government.

When Portugal succumbed entirely to France's demands on 20 November, expelling Britons, seizing property and closing Portuguese ports to British vessels, it seemed as if the British fleet off the Tagus under Rear Admiral Sidney Smith might be called upon to undertake offensive operations against Portugal rather than come to the defence of that kingdom.[6] His orders provided for the destruction of the Portuguese fleet and the bombardment of Lisbon if necessary, and on 16 November Smith called on Prince João to remind him of what had happened to the Danes at Copenhagen. On 24 November, following receipt the previous day of the news that Junot and the French army had crossed the Portuguese frontier and was at Abrantes, the decision was taken by João and his advisers to move to Brazil; an outcome that determined the Portuguese Empire would remain an ally of Great Britain.

The Portuguese royal family, the court and much of the administrative apparatus left Lisbon for Rio de Janeiro in a massive fleet of some fifty ships carrying reputedly 15,000 people a couple of days prior to Junot's arrival in the Portuguese capital.[7] In addition to ships of the Portuguese navy, it was protected by a Royal Navy convoy under Admiral Sidney Smith with nine ships of the line.[8] In concept this was no last-minute flight but the adoption of a well-thought-out strategy followed by the Portuguese court when all attempts to remain neutral failed to secure that status.[9] Repair work on the Portuguese fleet had commenced in August. When the moment came for embarkation on 27 November, notwithstanding a system of permits and allowances, many could not obtain passage and on Junot's arrival on 29 November much of value was simply sitting abandoned on the Lisbon docks.[10] The French General watched helplessly as the fleet sailed down the Tagus estuary and out of sight on its long seven-week voyage to São Salvador (Bahia) and Rio de Janeiro.

By virtue of the secret Treaty of Fontainebleau, Napoleon initially agreed to carve up Portugal with Spanish assistance. The treaty envisioned three separate states: In the north a new kingdom centred on Porto and to be known as the Kingdom of Northern Lusitania was proposed to compensate the Spanish Bourbon King of Etruria for the loss of his kingdom to

France. In the centre, a French dependency to include Trás-os-Montes, Beira and Portuguese Estremadura would be centred on Lisbon, and in the South a promised principality for the Prime Minister of Spain, Manuel Godoy, the 'Prince of the Peace', was to be made up of the Alentejo and the Algarve.

The treaty enabled Junot's army to march through Spain with Spanish approval. Even so, because of the duress placed on Junot to move with speed to capture both the Portuguese royal family and its navy, the French force straggled piecemeal into Lisbon on 29 November with three Spanish armies under Taranco (Porto), Carafa (Lisbon) and Solano (Algarve), respectively, following it into Portugal some days later.[11] The presence of these Spanish forces in Portugal helped maintain Junot's rule there until the late spring of 1808.

Prior to the departure of the Portuguese court to Brazil, the Regent had provided for Portugal to be ruled by a Regency Council. Initially this was made up of the Marquês de Abrantes (Pedro de Lancastre da Silveira Castelo Branco Sá Meneses); the Marquês de Olhão (Francisco de Melo da Cunha de Mendonça e Meneses); 'The Principal' Sousa Coutinho; Pedro de Mello Breyner; Tenente-General Francisco Xavier de Noronha; and the Conde de Sampãio, but its composition changed from time to time and in particular Dom Miguel Forjaz, who had started as Secretary to the Council, came to wield considerable influence. The Regent's instructions to the Council and the army were not to resist the French forces, but within a short time Junot was to replace the Regency Council with one of his own on which served a number of members of the previous council.

The archipelago of Madeira is located approximately 32° North and 16° West. Discovered and colonised by the Portuguese in the fifteenth century, it lies just over 500-kilometres from the African coast and in the early nineteenth century remained an important point of replenishment for those sailing to India, the East Indies, Southern Africa, South America and the West Indies. It was strategically important in time of war. The capital and main port, then, as now, was Funchal. In 1801 British troops under Lieutenant General Clinton had occupied the two forts guarding the harbour of Funchal. The garrisoning of these forts had been undertaken jointly with the local Portuguese forces. No attempt was made on that occasion to interfere with the civil administration of the island and it was made clear to the Portuguese government that the occupation would end once peace was achieved with France. Nevertheless the Portuguese were still intensely irritated by this episode. The occupation lasted only six months and the troops were withdrawn on 19 January 1802 during the negotiations leading to the Peace of Amiens, effective on 27 March 1802.

Months before Junot's invading army had crossed into Portugal, orders had been given for 3,000 men to be detached from Sir John Moore's army returning from Sicily for the purpose of securing Madeira, but lack of knowledge of the whereabouts of this army led to William Carr Beresford being appointed in mid November to command a force of approximately 3,600 men for that purpose, though instructions were given to keep the destination of this small army secret. He was given a briefing document outlining the characteristics of the Governor of the island and other influential persons in Madeira, together with an assessment as to whether they were likely to serve a British administration. Beresford sought clarification as to the civil rank he was to hold along with the salary he should draw in respect of that position.[12] In response he was informed he should assume the position of Lieutenant-Governor at a salary of £3,000 per annum.[13] His small staff included a number of those who had served with him in the 88th regiment and who were to serve again with him later in the war.[14]

Escorted by a fleet under Admiral Hood (comprised of four ships of the line, four frigates, one brigantine and fifteen transports), the force made up of the 3rd and 11th regiments left Plymouth on 29 November (ironically the day Junot entered Lisbon).[15] It arrived off the island of Porto Santo, part of the Madeiran archipelago, shortly before Christmas 1807. The frigate *Comus* had been sent ahead to the island of Madeira to collect intelligence and its crew ascertained that the island had received news of the flight of the Portuguese court to Brazil and that no attack on the island was anticipated.[16] On 24 December in mid afternoon, Beresford sent ashore Captains Nurse and Murphy of the 88th regiment demanding that the Governor, Pedro Fagundes Bacelar d'Antas e Menezes, surrender within thirty minutes.[17] This was agreed and by nightfall the two regiments had been landed without resistance.

Overwhelming force, or at least the perception of it, must presumably have determined the Governor's quick acquiescence to Beresford's demand for it would seem that he was unclear regarding the arrangement made by his own government. He assumed perhaps that the occupation was to be of a similar nature to that of General Clinton in 1801, involving merely the taking over of military installations. It is not clear exactly when he realised that on this occasion the intent was to annex the island as a crown colony, but at the latest it would seem to have been following the landing of the troops. There was some delay in accepting the new situation, but within forty-eight hours the Governor had ceded both civil and military power by signing terms of capitulation on 26 December.

While the declared intention was to create a Crown Colony, with the British King enjoying 'all the right and privileges and jurisdictions which heretofore belonged to the Crown of Portugal', the Terms of Capitulation made it clear that the island 'shall be evacuated and delivered' to the Portuguese Crown 'when the free ingress and egress to the Ports of Portugal and its colonies shall be re-established as heretofore; and when the sovereignty of Portugal shall be emancipated from the control or influence of France'. Thus there existed, at least on paper, an unequivocal statement that there was no intention to permanently annex Madeira. Instead the creation of a British colony may have been part of an elaborate charade designed not to imperil Portuguese neutrality by emphasising the forceful nature of British occupation. In the event, strategic considerations meant that the terms of capitulation were to be altered in a relatively short time, long before the liberation of Portugal.[18]

Beresford was now the Lieutenant-Governor of a crown colony and he installed himself in the palace of São Lourenço, at the same time procuring a private residence in the surrounding hills known as the Quinta da Achada, now the Quinta Jardins do Lago.[19] The sovereignty of George III was proclaimed on 31 December. Beresford confirmed officials in the positions they had held previously subject to their taking the oath of allegiance.[20] Beresford proceeded to act much as he had done in Buenos Aires with a view to securing local support. He guaranteed the safety of private property and the freedom to practice religion. Civil administration of the island under Beresford was vigorous as well as enlightened. He undertook a review of the island's finances (it was a net contributor to the Portuguese State) and his report sent to Castlereagh at the end of January 1808 envisaged long-term occupation. He terminated the State monopolies on soap and tobacco trading; provided for the licensing of beggars and introduced a close season for the shooting of birds. He established a Court of Appeal on the island, since cases were no longer to be appealed to Portugal. In doing so he removed the existing Corregidor, Dom J.C. Pereira, from office, a move which was approved by the British government.[21]

French and Spanish citizens were sent to the Canary Islands. Beresford's instructions provided for the sending of the Governor and the garrison of Funchal to Lisbon or Brazil and for the disarming of the militia (surrender with the honours of war, usually provided for those surrendering to march out with arms and to return home or at least leave the location of surrender). This was effectively part of the charade of military conquest. However, he deemed his orders to repatriate soldiers to Lisbon undesirable given that city was now occupied by the French; and given that the Portuguese court had made good its escape from French influence he determined to keep the regiment of Portuguese artillery on the island, pending further instructions, on the basis that it would assist with its defence and its maintenance would avoid creating disquiet.[22]

On finding that even the regular Portuguese regiments on the island were largely made up of islanders, and observing that the disarming of the local militia would cause discontent and be at odds with the policy of friendly cooperation that he was striving to implement, he sought to incorporate part of these forces in the defence of the island of Madeira. He took the precaution of storing the arms of the militia in Funchal in the fort of St Jago but military expediency presumably led to his decision to permit the militia in the outlying districts to keep their arms.[23] In disregarding his instructions to repatriate trained soldiers, Beresford showed an understanding and feel for the situation on the ground as well as a degree of confidence in his own judgment. Beresford's policy of working with the Portuguese in Madeira may have made him all the more acceptable as the appointee to reform the Portuguese army in 1809. He reported to Castlereagh that when the people of Madeira had discovered the British came as sole rulers of the island there was 'a little sensation and fermentation' but that it had soon subsided.[24]

The British troops were billeted for the most part in two monasteries, the Incarnation and the Jesuit College. This was in accordance with Portuguese custom and caused no difficulties. Indeed, not only did Beresford first obtain the permission of the Bishop of Funchal but he ensured the religious orders were financially compensated for this arrangement, a move which was unusual at the time. Further, he ensured that the payment of the troops was a burden on the British treasury and provisions for his force were purchased rather than plundered. Food was in short supply in January because the victuallers to the fleet had not appeared, but Hood ordered the landing of such supplies as the transports with the fleet could spare.[25] Meat was brought in from the Azores and other provisions from Africa.[26] However, medicines had to be sought from England as due to the speed of departure a considerable amount had been left at Portsmouth. Here, as throughout the Peninsula, British policy directing payment for provisions was in marked contrast to that of the French, which required its armies to live off the land.

The defences of the island, while they had been improved by the Governor prior to Beresford's arrival, he found to be inadequate. This was particularly the case with the artillery (a common problem for the British in Portugal) which Beresford described as 'unserviceable and much more dangerous to those that fire them than those they may be fired at'. Beresford told Castlereagh that if the island was to be properly defended guns must be sent from England.[27]

British policy, however, was undergoing change within weeks of Beresford's arrival in Madeira. Britain was highly desirous of obtaining the right to trade directly with Brazil, a privilege previously reserved to Portugal, and the Portuguese made their agreement to granting such a right conditional on the ending of British sovereignty over Madeira. In mid February, Beresford was informed by Castlereagh that the emigration of the Portuguese court had materially changed the circumstances under which orders had been given to occupy the island and accordingly it had been resolved to adopt a system which would 'remove suspicion from the Portuguese government that we occupy the island with any other view than to preserve the sovereignty of the Crown'.[28] Accordingly the civil government would be returned to Portugal while the military command would remain with Britain which would be responsible for the defence of the island.

On 1 March 1808, Castlereagh wrote to Beresford formally informing him of the plan to return Madeira to the Regent, and this was announced on 26 March.[29] The island's former Governor was reinstated on 24 April just four moths after Beresford had landed at Funchal. Writing that day to Castlereagh, Beresford was able to inform him that he and the Portuguese governor enjoyed the 'best of friendly relations'.[30] However, the restoration of Portuguese authority led to the rescission of many of Beresford's civil reforms.

Beresford, promoted to the rank of Major General in March 1808, was clearly hungry for action and very concerned that he would miss out in the enduring conflict with France.[31] Shorn of his civil powers in Madeira he repeatedly sought a transfer from the island and was delighted when notified by letter of 16 July that he should transfer to Portugal. He was directed to take with him the 3rd regiment together with one company of artillery. If the British army was not employed there or in Spain, his orders were to proceed to Gibraltar.[32] Beresford left the island on HMS *Undaunted* on 23 August for Portugal. His successor in Madeira was General Meade, and henceforth the British role in Madeira was confined to a military one. While the military occupation of Madeira did not end until 1814, it is noteworthy that the quality and number of the troops sent there was reduced. Not only was the 3rd Regiment sent to Portugal with Beresford in the summer of 1808, but the 11th Regiment was subsequently replaced by a regiment of veterans. This attitude probably reflected an assessment by the British government that French intervention was extremely unlikely due to maritime weakness.

The British citizens on the island obviously appreciated his time in the archipelago, for in 1810 the Factory authorised the presentation to Beresford of a sword and a piece of plate valued at £310.[33] An entry in the books of Cossart Gordon and Company, the wine merchants in

Funchal for 6 September 1808, refers to the arrival of General Meade and goes on to state: 'His predecessor General Beresford rendered himself extremely popular with all ranks in the island and it was with extreme regret we parted with him.'[34] One of Beresford's achievements while on the island was to acquire the land which became the new burial ground for the Anglican church in Funchal, at the time as a military cemetery.[35] In 1811 he was to repeat that success by persuading the Portuguese government and religious authorities to establish a military graveyard at Elvas following the battle of Albuera.

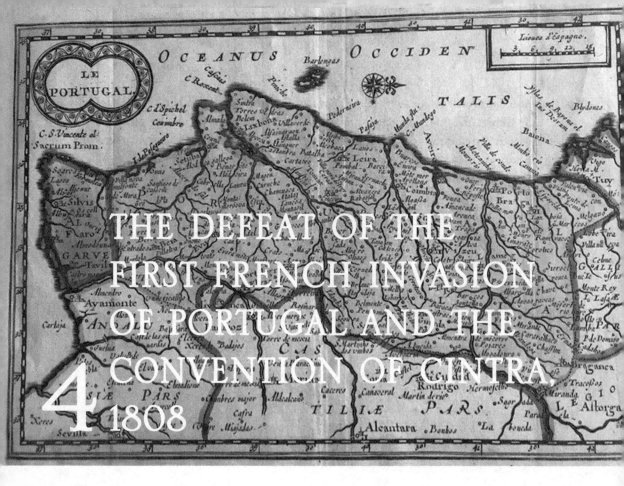

THE DEFEAT OF THE FIRST FRENCH INVASION OF PORTUGAL AND THE CONVENTION OF CINTRA, 1808

4

The increasingly harsh rule of Junot during the winter of 1807 and spring of 1808 gave rise to an incremental unwillingness by the Portuguese to obey Prince João's instruction to cooperate and not oppose the Franco-Spanish invader. Junot's despotic behaviour resulted in the withdrawal of local officials' cooperation and active popular resistance. It is sometimes not fully appreciated that such resistance emerged very quickly, notwithstanding the royal directive to cooperate with the French invader. The replacement of the Portuguese flag with that of France on the Castelo de São Jorge on 13 December 1807 led to unrest in Lisbon that was quickly put down by French arms.[1] Junot's intentions became even clearer when nine days later, on 22 December, he reduced the numbers of regiments in the Portuguese army, ultimately virtually extinguishing it with the formation of the Portuguese Legion, which was dispatched to northern Europe where they fought for Napoleon under pro-French officers with considerable distinction until the end of the war.[2] In early 1808 Junot dissolved both the militia and the ordenança.[3] The situation was further aggravated by acts of aggrandisement along with the plundering of Portuguese churches and households.[4]

On 1 February, Junot disclosed that Napoleon had declared that the house of Braganza had ceased to rule in Portugal and imposed a substantial imposition of 40 million cruzados on the country.[5] Napoleon's real intentions were now made clear with the announcement that the entire kingdom of Portugal would become a French dependency with Junot as Governor. On the same day he dissolved the Regency Council and replaced it with a council of his own appointees, made up of French and Portuguese.[6] Resentment was rising. In February, nine Portuguese were brutally executed in Caldas da Rainha on the orders of General Loison, who was to make a name for himself as a merciless soldier in the Peninsula.[7] In March, the French army occupied the fort of Elvas.

The spark that ignited serious opposition to Napoleonic ambitions in the Iberian peninsula proved to be the enforced abdication of Carlos IV of Spain and the waiving under duress of a claim to his throne by his son Ferdinand VII.[8] The French managed to crush the resistance of the 'Dos de Mayo' in Madrid, but opposition to French rule in the shape of Joseph Bonaparte as King of Spain soon spread throughout much of the country. The divisions of the Spanish army in northern and southern Portugal managed to extricate themselves to Galicia and Badajoz, respectively, though Junot disarmed and imprisoned the division under Carafa based in Lisbon on 11 June.[9]

While Junot retained his grip on Lisbon and a number of important strongholds including the fortresses of Almeida, Elvas and Peniche, the vacuum left by the departing Spanish soon resulted in the emergence of increased opposition to French rule. In Alentejo that opposition was firmly put down by General Loison, but Porto witnessed an uprising on 6 June and the emergence of the self-styled Supreme Junta under the Bishop of Porto, which could dispose of a not inconsiderable armed force under Lieutenant General Bernardim Freire de Andrade (Bernardim Freire).[10] On 1 May, the Prince Regent declared war on France from the safety of Rio de Janeiro, having been informed that the Regency Council he had left in Lisbon had been dismissed by Junot.

In London, the risings against French domination in Spain and Portugal were seized upon with alacrity. In early July the government was informed of the rising in Porto and on 7 July a delegation was sent to London to request help with arms and soldiers.[11] The government had been assembling a force at Cork for embarkation for South America, where it was designated to assist Francisco de Miranda in his quest for Venezuelan independence from Spain. The emergence of Spain as Britain's ally changed the political dynamic. In late June, Sir Arthur Wellesley received orders to proceed to Cork and to sail with the force for the Peninsula, without any particular destination being named. There was talk of a landing in the Asturias or Galicia, but also Cádiz as well as Portugal.[12] Wellesley was directed to proceed to La Coruña to ascertain the situation there, as it was understood that while the Spanish wished for arms they were not keen on British forces landing on Spanish territory. Wellesley was told that another force of 10,000 would follow about three weeks behind his own, and that the objective was 'the entire and absolute evacuation of the Peninsula by the troops of France'.[13]

Wellesley sailed from Cork (Cobh) with his force of just under 10,000 men on 12 July.[14] Stopping briefly at La Coruña, he ascertained the local junta did not wish for British troops to be landed to assist in Galicia. Wellesley therefore proceeded to Porto, arriving there on 24 July, and on the following day met the Bishop who headed the Supreme Junta. Bernardim Freire informed Wellesley that he had about 5,000 men under his command available, though some of them were in Coimbra; additionally about 12,000 peasants were armed 'in different modes'.[15]

A small portion of the Portuguese forces, with some Spanish assistance, was blockading French occupied Almeida while others were trying to guard Trás-os-Montes against a background of the Spanish having suffered defeat at Rio Seco on 14 July.[16] The Bishop promised to supply the British commander with 150 horses for his dragoons together with 500 mules for transport purposes to be delivered at Coimbra.

Wellesley himself then sailed to the British squadron off the Tagus, where he met with Admiral Sir Charles Cotton undertaking a blockade of Lisbon, which included the confinement and isolation of a Russian fleet anchored in the Tagus.[17] Cotton advised disembarkation at Mondego or Peniche, both north of Lisbon; Peniche being a somewhat curious choice as it contained a strong French garrison. From General Brent Spencer in Andalucia, Wellesley received intelligence which suggested there were perhaps 20,000 French troops in Portugal rather than the local estimate of 16,000–18,000. The latter figure is not necessarily incompatible as it may reflect the number of troops available to Junot given that there were 600–800 in each of Elvas, Almeida, São Julião and Peniche fortresses. Wellesley ordered Spencer and his force to join him in Portugal and returned to the estuary of the river Mondego, where a landing – though physically challenging through the Atlantic surf – was made eminently feasible tactically due to the seizure of Figueira da Foz, the port at the river mouth, by the students from Coimbra University on 26 June.

Arriving off Mondego, he heard of the Spanish victory at Bailén on 20 July.[18] He began disembarkation of the British army at Mondego on 1 August, but not before he apparently received some important news on the previous day. On 15 July, Castlereagh had written to him telling him the troops from the Baltic under Sir John Moore would follow as soon as they were re-victualled, together with another 5,000 under Generals Anstruther and Ackland as more French than were previously thought were stationed in Portugal. A total force of 30,000 was promised for the Peninsula. These included the 3rd Regiment ('The Buffs') which were being dispatched from Madeira under Major General William Carr Beresford to join Wellesley. A second letter, dated 15 July, was also received on the 31 July. It may not have been so welcome for it notified him of the appointment of Lieutenant General Sir Hew Dalrymple to command with Lieutenant General Harry Burrard as second in command. Wellesley was slipping down the command chain.[19]

Wellesley lost little time in moving south from Mondego towards Lisbon. He met Lieutenant General Bernardim Freire de Andrade and General Manuel Pinto Bacelar with their Portuguese forces at Montemor-o-Velho on 7 August and by 12 August the combined forces were at Leiria.[20] A disagreement on tactics followed, with Wellesley wishing to take a coastal route to Lisbon (with a view to staying in touch with his provisioning fleet) and Bernardim Freire anxious to secure central and eastern Portugal by following a route through Santarém.[21] Wellesley also claimed that the Portuguese General had demanded the British feed the Portuguese force, which they were unable to do. As a result, only some 1,600 Portuguese troops under Colonel Nicholas Trant, out of a total of some 6,000, joined Wellesley.[22] Bernardim Freire's decision is sometimes criticised, but he marched the balance of his force to Santarém where he managed to delay Loison's corps for three days, preventing it from uniting with that under General Henri

Delaborde at Roliça at a time when the reinforcements under Ackland and Anstruther had yet to join with Wellesley. On 17 August, Wellesley fought an initial engagement against a French force under Delaborde at Roliça before meeting the main French army under Junot at Vimeiro on 21 August and inflicting a comprehensive defeat on the French General.[23] However, there was to be no pursuit of the defeated French.

General Burrard had arrived in Maceira roads aboard HMS *Brazen* on 20 August.[24] Wellesley went on board this sloop that evening to report and hand over command. The British army was then before Vimeiro and Wellington proposed to advance the next day. Burrard, perhaps feeling he needed further information, suggested delaying any advance. Matters were taken out of Wellesley's hands on the morning of 21 August when the French chose to attack the British force. After the battle, the victorious Wellesley wished to pursue the defeated French but Burrard, who had by then joined the army, prohibited such a move even though the French were in considerable disorder.[25] Burrard clearly felt the French still had their reserve intact and a substantial superiority in cavalry and accordingly caution was required in his mind. He wished to wait for Sir John Moore with reinforcements.[26] As a result the French were able to retire on Torres Vedras.

Dalrymple, stationed at Gibraltar, had received his instructions from Castlereagh on 7 August.[27] He was directed to seek to expel the French from Lisbon and cut off their retreat to Spain if possible. Sailing from Gibraltar on 13 August, he reached the mouth of the Tagus on 19 August and there conferred with Admiral Cotton. He left the 42nd Regiment, which had travelled with him from Gibraltar, with Cotton in case the opportunity arose to land at Lisbon; while Dalrymple proceeded to Maceira where he landed on 22 August, establishing there his initial headquarters. Assuming command, he met Wellesley who once again urged an advance. Dalrymple made it clear he was not in a position to form an opinion on the merits of such a proposal, having just landed, but he did authorise Wellesley to prepare to march the army.[28]

Within hours of Dalrymple landing at Maceira, General François Étienne Kellerman (who had commanded the reserve at Vimeiro) arrived under a flag of truce to propose an armistice.[29] This suspension of arms was stated to be for the specific purpose of negotiating a convention for the evacuation of the French army from Portugal. Furthermore the armistice provided:

> it is agreed provisionally that the French army shall not, in any case, be considered as prisoners of war; that all the individuals who compose it shall be transported to France with their arms and baggage, and the whole of their private property, from which nothing shall be exempted.[30]

The balance of the armistice provided for the neutrality of the port of Lisbon so that the Russian fleet trapped there could sail at will, guarantees of security for those who had supported France in Portugal, the transport of French artillery and the horses of the cavalry to France, and a forty-eight hour notice of termination of the suspension of arms.[31]

While the clause quoted above was to become central to the disagreements that followed, each of the provisions referred to gave rise to debate, both during the formation of the terms for the suspension of arms and the subsequent convention.[32] Importantly, Kellerman assured the British that the words used regarding baggage and private property meant their strict grammatical meaning and did not cover merchandise of any sort. Wellesley for his part advocated unavailingly that the suspension of arms should be for only forty-eight hours rather than determinable on forty-eight hours notice.

The days following the signing of the suspension of arms were spent negotiating the terms of the convention, on the one hand, and the preparation for the renewal of conflict, on the other. However the ink was barely dry on the suspension of arms terms before Bernardim Freire expressed his dissatisfaction. The Portuguese commander visited Dalrymple at his new headquarters at Ramalhal on 23 August. He was given a copy of the terms of armistice and immediately objected on a number of grounds including the failure to consult the Junta of Porto, as the Portuguese leadership, and the provisions designed to protect those who had cooperated with the French during the occupation of Portugal. Dalrymple was clearly sensitive to the potential for friction with Britain's ally for he requested the objections in writing, but apparently these were not forthcoming. Bernardim Freire agreed to establish Major Ayres Pinto de Souza as a liaison officer to attend on the British commander.[33]

Meanwhile, Lieutenant Colonel Murray had taken a copy of the terms to Admiral Cotton who insisted that the Russian fleet should not be allowed to sail free, and in effect should be excluded from the terms of any convention and subject to a separate agreement.[34] Ultimately this was to involve the surrender of the Russian fleet to Admiral Cotton, on the basis it would be returned at the conclusion of hostilities, and the repatriation to Russia of its crews.[35] However, when Murray returned to headquarters on 25 August with the news that Cotton objected to the proposed inclusion of the Russian fleet in the convention, Dalrymple, having called a conference with both Burrard and Wellesley in attendance, determined to tell the French that the cessation of hostilities would end at twelve noon on 28 August, given the terms were not acceptable. Murray was dispatched to Junot with this instruction, but with authorisation to extend the cessation for a further twenty-four hours if he was making progress with negotiations.

Murray did make progress in further discussions with Kellerman and on the morning of 29 August, Captain Adolphus John Dalrymple, a son of the British commander, arrived back at Ramalhal with an amended treaty agreed between Murray and Kellerman. Once again Dalrymple convened a meeting of his Lieutenant Generals.[36] Objections were raised to the proposals, and a further draft containing alterations was sent back to Murray.[37] Meanwhile, the cessation of hostilities ended and Dalrymple moved his headquarters into Torres Vedras. Junot accepted the convention as altered and signed the terms, together with some additional articles of an administrative nature, at his headquarters in Lisbon on 30 August.[38] In ratifying the terms, he signed as Duke of Abrantes. No one may have noticed at the time, but the acknowledgment of this title was itself to cause resentment in Portugal when it became known.[39]

On 31 August at 7.30 am, Captain Dalrymple arrived back at Torres Vedras with the definitive treaty. Sir Hew Dalrymple convened a further meeting of his Lieutenant Generals in Burrard's headquarters; a meeting which on this occasion did not include either Wellesley or Paget who were with their troops. Dalrymple ratified the 'Convention of Cintra' with no disapproval being made by those present. It was noted that Junot had failed to sign one part of the treaty, and Lieutenant Colonel Lord Proby was sent to Lisbon with both copies in order that this might be rectified.[40] One copy was later returned to the British commander but meanwhile in its absence Murray was detailed to explain its substance to Pinto da Souza.

The Convention contained twenty-two articles and three supplementary articles.[41] In essence, the French army was to evacuate Portugal and be transported to any French port between Rochefort and Lorient, the means for doing so to be supplied by the British government. The Convention provided for the hand over of the strong places in Portugal to the British army and for the gradual embarkation of the French army in three divisions. The execution of the Convention and its terms was to give rise to discussion and disagreement when it became known in the United Kingdom, but more immediately a number of articles became the subject of anger and dispute in Portugal, rendering its implementation fraught with difficulty. While several articles were to prove contentious between the British and their Portuguese allies, the interpretation of Article V by the French leadership and the manner in which the British command reacted gave rise to complaint and recrimination in Portugal and criticism at home. Article V provided:

> The French army shall carry with it all its equipments, and all that is comprehended under the name of property of the army; that is to say, its military chest, and carriages attached to the Field Commissariat and Field Hospitals; or shall be allowed to dispose of such part of the same, on its account, as the Commander-in-Chief may judge it unnecessary to embark. In like manner, all individuals in the army shall be at liberty to dispose of their private property of every description; with full security hereafter for the purchasers.

The possibility of disagreement as between the contracting parties relating to the Articles had been recognised in the Convention, which provided for commissioners to be named by both sides to regulate and accelerate the arrangements (Article XIII), and the Convention further provided that when doubts arose on the meaning of any article, it was to be interpreted in favour of the French army (Article XIV). The latter provision was a standard one in favour of the defeated side. Dalrymple appointed Lieutenant Colonel Lord Proby as the British commissioner to work with his opposite number, General Kellerman, on 2 September.

The French command chose to interpret 'military chest' as set out in Article V to include public and private property seized during its occupation of Portugal, even that taken after the execution of the Suspension of Arms of 22 August. A strong protest was not long in coming. The Bishop of Porto sent Dalrymple a letter of protest on 1 September to which Dalrymple responded the following day pointing out that he had sent Bernardim Freire a copy of the terms of agreement, the basis of the Convention, and sought his views but had heard nothing in return.[42] On 2 September Bernardim Freire lodged a written protest with Dalrymple asserting that the French 'are practicing in Lisbon a species of plunder on the Publick Treasury, Museums, Arsenals, Churches, Library, as also the houses and stores of private persons, which it is my duty to communicate to your Excellency information of, that you may take such measures as you may think proper'.[43]

The first division of the French army was reportedly ready to embark as early as 3 September. In a taste of things to come, General Junot had sought the use of five neutral Danish vessels then in the river to carry his own 'personal effects' but this was declined by Proby on Darymple's instructions.[44] The disturbing reports reaching Dalrymple regarding the behaviour of the French prompted him to appoint a second commissioner to oversee the implementation of the Convention. He chose Major General William Carr Beresford, who had arrived from Madeira with the 3rd Regiment (The Buffs) after the Battle of Vimeiro.[45] Dalrymple indicated to Proby that Beresford's appointment was 'to ease you of at least part of your vexation and labour'.[46]

Dalrymple's motives in choosing Beresford over any other staff officer for the position are not clear, though his familiarity with the Portuguese and French languages combined with recognition of his administrative abilities already demonstrated in Egypt, South America and Madeira may have played their part. On arriving at the estuary of the Tagus, Beresford's initial assignment had been to occupy the forts on the river under the terms of the Convention. This he had undertaken with the 3rd and 42nd regiments on 2 September.[47] Whatever the motives, the choice of Beresford as a commissioner proved inspired. Beresford, upon taking up the post of commissioner, made an early call on Junot at his Lisbon headquarters. While they apparently breakfasted together, the meeting was perhaps not unsurprisingly a far from happy one. Writing to Wellesley, Beresford stated: 'Junot did not appear to have taken any great liking to me, at which you will believe I am not breaking my heart.'[48] One of Junot's officers, General Thiébault, probably identified why Junot was not taken with Beresford when he wrote: 'Beresford était un home tres poli, mais tres ferme de caractère.'[49]

It is interesting and perhaps indicative of his relationship with Wellesley that Beresford was writing not only to the Commander of the British army in Portugal, Dalrymple, but also to his fellow Irishman about the implementation of the Convention. An extensive correspondence took place between Proby and Beresford, on the one part, and Dalrymple, on the other, relating to the work of the commissioners, who clearly faced a very substantial challenge in their efforts to ensure that the French left only with their 'military chest'. Most letters were signed by Beresford and Proby but a number bear the signature of just one of the commissioners.[50]

In their first letter to Dalrymple on the topic of their work on 4 September, Beresford and Proby outlined the issues and expressed concern that the 'articles of the treaty' appeared to favour the French as allowing them to keep whatever was in their possession on 30 August (the date the French signed the Convention). The French, they wrote, seemed to be intent on taking everything other than military and naval arsenals and ships.[51] The commissioners went on to list some of the categories of moveable property that the French were seeking to take. These included:

  i) valuables belonging to HRH the Prince Regent;
  ii) valuables taken from churches. In many cases church plate appears to have been melted down into bars of bullion;

iii) valuables taken from individuals;

iv) the contents of the royal libraries;

v) a sum of approximately £22,000 from the Depósito Público, which was made up of monies belonging to individuals.[52]

A day later the commissioners added a further complaint, namely that the French were still appropriating the revenues of the country.[53] Wellesley was obviously consulted. He opined that the property to be carried off by the French was 'limited to military baggage and equipments and that the French must restore what had been taken from churches and individuals'.[54]

An unnamed diarist visited Beresford's house in Lisbon on 6 September and reported:

> On our arrival at Lisbon, we visited General Beresford, at whose house we met Lord Paget, his aides de camp, and Colonel Graham. We here found that nothing could surpass the audacity of the attempts which had been made by the French to carry off all the articles of value which could be found in Lisbon, whether public or private property. They had actually packed up two state carriages, the property of His Royal Highness the Duke of Sussex; but at the remonstrance of General Beresford, they were compelled to relinquish their booty.[55]

Beresford and Proby were able to make some progress in negotiations with General Kellerman. On 6 September they reported that the French had conceded that they were not entitled to keep anything other than military baggage and private property, and that public property appropriated since the first day of the truce must be restored. The monies taken from the Depósito Público were to be replaced. The artefacts taken from the royal and public libraries and museums would be restored 'if insisted upon' but Kellerman suggested many of the items from the museums were in fact duplicates and were items they did not have in Paris and that it was in the interest of all that scientific examination take place. The commissioners sought instructions from Dalrymple who responded that 'the French have no right to carry off plunder of any sort, at least not in its original form'. Dalrymple complimented Beresford and Proby on the firm manner in which they were executing their mission, at the same time confirming that the articles which were allegedly duplicates must not be removed.[56]

Indeed, 6 September may have been a critical day in the sequence of events. On that day Dalrymple received a deputation from the merchants of Lisbon and noted that their ire was directed almost as much against the English as against the French. They also wrote to him in strong terms expressing their outrage.[57] The anger of the Portuguese was summed up by José de Abreu Campos:

> Our churches plundered of their ornaments, the royal palaces damaged, the royal treasury plundered, and in general, the people reduced to such poverty and misery, as to render the streets and squares of the capital impossible; nothing of this is taken into consideration. Yet these objections are of extreme importance, as an example not to be passed with impunity

... The safeties of monarchies depends on not letting their rights be invaded without punishing the offender, and the consequence of permitting such crimes with impunity will occasion incalculable misfortune.[58]

Bernardim Freire had lodged a protest as soon as he had heard of the terms of the Convention, even before he had received a written copy of the document. In doing so he listed particular criticisms and concerns. He made the point that the Portuguese should have been, but were not included, as a party. Furthermore, since he had not been consulted he declined to take any responsibility for its terms.[59] A formal protest was not long in forthcoming. In a lengthy Memorial of 3 September, Bernardim Freire pointed out that the British army was in Portugal as an auxiliary force at the invitation of the Portuguese government and that accordingly discussions with the French should have been in conjunction with the Portuguese.[60] Further, he complained that certain stipulations in the Convention, such as the surrender of forts to British rather than Portuguese troops, were such as could only have been made if Portugal was a conquered country. Dalrymple was urged to explain that this happened only to avoid friction between French and Portuguese troops. Objection was also made to the proposals to allow those who had cooperated with the French to remain in Portugal, in circumstances where they would not have to answer for their actions. To these complaints was added a general one regarding the plundering by the French continuing to take place in Lisbon.[61] This Memorial was followed a day later by an article-by-article complaint.[62]

Further protests were received at British headquarters. Lieutenant General Dom Francisco da Cunha Menezes, Count of Castro Marim and Monteiro-mor, Governor of Algarve, who commanded the army of the south, wrote in the first instance on 9 September to Admiral Cotton seeking his intervention to prevent the French leaving the port of Lisbon.[63] Cotton passed on the correspondence to Dalrymple. In an arguably cavalier approach, Dalrymple took the view that he was only required to discuss matters with the government of the country; and the Supreme Junta of Porto was not so appointed. Of course, Junot had dissolved the Council of Regency so Dalrymple had a point, but that was to ignore the fact that the Monteiro-mor had been a member of that Council, and therefore a member of the government. Nevertheless, Dalrymple was sensitive to the issue of plunder and its potential for friction. When Kellerman called to his headquarters at Oeiras on 6 September to complain of the demands made by commissioners Beresford and Proby, Dalrymple told him in their presence that if any person from the General-in-chief to the lowest person in the French army should prove guilty of plunder, that person would forfeit the benefit of the treaty and be considered a prisoner of war.[64]

Pressure was mounting on Kellerman, and following further representations from Beresford and Proby, Junot issued an *Ordre du Jour* dated 6 September. This directed every person having private property, whether in pictures or other moveables, to restore them immediately to the owners. For some time the French had maintained they were entitled to keep melted down church plate in their possession prior to the signing of the truce, but ultimately Junot conceded it should not be taken out of the country but should be used to pay the debts of the French army. Dalrymple felt that providing this offer was implemented it was fair.[65] Beresford and Proby were clearly making some progress, as was testified by Charles Stewart writing to his brother, Castlereagh, then Secretary of State for War and the Colonies, on 8 September having arrived in Lisbon the previous day:

> I found Proby and Beresford hard at work endeavouring to make these robbers disgorge their plunder and I hope they have in part succeeded although much remains to be done & it is impossible things can have been worse managed on our side than they have been. When Proby was first sent in to see the articles of the Treaty executed, he was not even furnished with a copy of it and owned to Sir Hew his complete incompetence to manage so intricate an affair especially as there were parts of the convention he did not understand – many points unsettled. Sir Hew however persevered in sending him in with plein pouvoirs, & no treaty. The French endeavoured to impose a spurious one and this he detected. Beresford at last came in and since his arrival things have gone on better. He has got back the museum and £25,000 taken from the Deposito Publico [*sic*], during the time the treaty was going on. They are now at issue on the Church Plate ... The Duc D'Abrantes is the greatest robber of the whole and set the example by seizing everything in every shop and house without payment.[66]

Junot may well have been 'the greatest robber of the whole' but he was also extremely astute, reportedly using two mints to convert melted down church plate into Napoleon D'Ors, thus enabling him to claim they were part of his military baggage.[67]

The British, pushed by the Portuguese, set about investigating the persistent allegations of plunder and to this end established a three-man Committee for Receiving Reclamations. Its composition reflected the three nations involved: Lieutenant Colonel Nicholas Trant, St António Rodrigues de Oliveira and a Monsieur Duplier, *commissaire de guerres*.[68] On 10 September, the Committee published a proclamation under the names of the three commissioners informing the inhabitants of Lisbon of their right to claim restoration. On 11 September, Beresford and Proby reported that this committee had given general satisfaction at its initial sittings.[69]

However the French, including Junot, were continuing to play for time hoping that they would get away from Lisbon without having to make further concessions with which they might have to comply. The first division of the French army, it will be recalled, was reportedly ready to sail on 3 September, but ultimately did not do so until over a week later. The rows went on, delaying the departure of the French. Junot had allegedly appropriated ten chestnut horses from the royal stables, but he was able to convince the commissioners they were his own which he had stabled there.[70] Fifty-three boxes of indigo reportedly worth about £5,000 were found on board a vessel destined to receive the baggage of the French Commander in Chief. He disclaimed all knowledge of the boxes, which were seized on behalf of the commissioners. Beresford and Proby felt they had done their best. Nevertheless, in their report to Dalrymple of 18 September they made their disquiet known:

> We will conclude this report by stating that the conduct of the French had been marked by the most shameful disregard to honor [*sic*] and probity, publicly evincing their intentions

of carrying off their plundered booty and leaving acknowledged debts unpaid; and finally they have only paid what they were obliged to disgorge, and were not permitted to carry off, though the British Commissioners represented to General Kellerman, that whatever their words, it could never be the spirit of any convention that an army would, as a military chest, or otherwise, carry off public money, leaving public debts unpaid; and called upon him, for the honour of the French army and nation, to act justly; and yet, unmindful of any tie of honour or of justice, the French army has taken a considerable sum in the military chest, leaving its debts unpaid to a very large amount.[71]

On 15 September most of the French were embarked at Cais do Sodré (Lisbon). In the first two weeks of September they had led an uncomfortable existence in Lisbon, running the gauntlet of Portuguese intent on revenge.[72] On 18 September Junot went on board the vessel intended to carry him to France without repaying the monies taken from the Depósito Público, as a result of which Beresford and Proby applied successfully to Admiral Cotton to detain the second division of the French army as well as Junot. Only when £40,000 had been transferred by the French *Payeur General* to cover these monies and other items extracted from the public magazines (stores) were the French allowed to leave the Tagus. In addition, chests of natural history exhibits from the royal museum were restored along with a quantity of books.[73]

By 21 September the French force, together with a number of followers, was largely embarked and it sailed a week later.[74] The exceptions were the garrisons of Almeida and Elvas, which were transported afterwards to France.[75] Beresford and Proby's job as commissioners was complete and Dalrymple praised their conduct to Castlereagh saying they had 'performed their duty in a most firm and honourable manner'.[76] Dalrymple was to state at a later stage that the French had got away with a very small amount of plunder due to the work of the commissioners. While he had a vested interest in pursuing this line, it is of note that Kellerman also gets a measure of approbation from another source for having acted in a gentlemanly manner in interpreting the convention.[77]

Beresford's role in dealing with the fallout from the Convention of Cintra was not yet at an end. It will be recalled that on the occurrence of the risings in Spain, Junot had disarmed and imprisoned the Spanish division of General Carafa in Lisbon. The Convention provided for the repatriation of those troops amounting to some 5,000 men. With a view to sending them home, Beresford liaised with the Portuguese to ensure the troops were reissued with arms and their officers given back the horses taken by the French.[78] Before they were sent home Beresford reviewed them at the Campo d'Ourique, presenting their general with a ceremonial sword. He took the opportunity to address the troops in an emotional address designed no doubt to fire their ardour and encourage them to maintain the struggle against the French forces of occupation:

In an animated speech [Beresford] requested that the latter [the Spanish troops] would again accept their arms from the King of England, never to lay them down till the cause of Ferdinand VII, of Europe, and of humanity had triumphed. This address which was forcibly and well delivered, had not yet come to a close, when it was drowned in the reiterated vivas of soldiers and inhabitants, whilst the roar of cannon, and the braying of trumpets, echoed from one end of Lisbon to the other.[79]

One wonders what the Spanish made of the representative of their historical foe urging them to accept their arms from the King of England.

Dalrymple also gave Beresford a liaison role with the reconstituted Portuguese Regency Council, with a view to restoring order in Lisbon and improving relations with the Portuguese.[80] Order had partially broken down in the run up to the departure of the French and a number of Portuguese had demonstrated hostility not only towards the French but also to their liberators. Lieutenant General John Hope had been Dalrymple's original appointee to the post of Commandant of Lisbon, but Beresford was given this command when Hope was sent into the Alentejo to enforce the terms of the Convention.[81] The appointment of Beresford to this role is probably significant as it required liaison with the Portuguese authorities. It may reflect not only his grasp of and interest in Portuguese affairs, but also a recognition of his growing reputation as an able administrator. He had clearly achieved a degree of approval for his role as a commissioner under the Convention. To the post of Commandant of Alexandria, Governor of Buenos Aires, Governor of Madeira was now added, albeit for a short period, responsibility for Lisbon. By 22 September he was able to tell Dom Miguel Pereira Forjaz, the Portuguese Secretary for War and Foreign Affairs of the Regency Council, that he was returning responsibility for Lisbon to the Portuguese government.[82]

The news of the British victory over the French at Vimeiro reached England on 1 September and resulted in much celebration, as it was presented as a complete victory.[83] The content of the definitive Convention arrived in England with Dalrymple's letter of 3 September 1808 headed 'Cintra' on 15 September.[84] Church bells were again rung and cannon fired but jubilation soon turned to anger and recrimination. Dalrymple gave his reasons for entering into the Convention rather than continuing hostilities. These were: first, the time of year and the ability of the enemy to consume much time in the defence of strong places in the absence of a convention, and secondly, when terms had been agreed for the armistice Sir John Moore had not arrived with his army, and he had doubts about the ability to land such a large army on an open and dangerous beach. While of course Dalrymple did not at the time of negotiating the Convention possess either Lisbon or the Tagus Estuary, Wellesley had already landed an army at least as big as that of Moore on the beaches about the Mondego estuary.

A storm of protest was launched by the Whig opposition in parliament, and in the media, where Whig publications were perhaps surprisingly joined by their Tory counterparts. Within days of the news becoming widespread, condemnatory editorials were joined by satirical poems and commentary of a highly critical nature. Byron's *Childe Harold's Pilgrimage* and Wordsworth's tract *Concerning the Convention of Cintra* will forever live in the minds of English-speaking peoples interested in the topic because of who they were and the quality of their writing, but the daily and weekly press contained a plethora of amusing and sometimes vicious poetry, prose and caricatures, of which it is noticeable featured Wellesley as much as Burrard and Dalrymple.[85]

This may well have been because Wellesley's brother, Richard, was part of the government and thus an objective to attack by opposition supporters.[86]

Part of the responsibility for the build up of public anger may have been that not only of Arthur Wellesley but also politicians at home 'over egging' the nature of the victory at Vimeiro. Newspaper reports were full of statements to the effect that this was the end of Napoleonic tyranny in Portugal and Spain and that the battle was more significant than that of Trafalgar, in that it had shown French troops were not invincible.[87] Some eleven days before the arrival of Dalrymple's dispatch containing the definitive terms of the Convention, the cabinet was aware of the terms of the armistice because the Bishop of Porto had furnished these to the Portuguese Minister in London, who in turn had drawn them to the attention of George Canning to whom he made a formal protest.[88] Canning and others found it difficult to believe the veracity of these statements and the government did not publicise the true nature of the agreement until the terms were printed in the Gazette on 16 September. As one British soldier put it, the news occasioned a 'political electric shock'.[89]

The Whig opposition had been lukewarm in its support of the war with France. There was, however, a very keenly held view that the terms of the Convention were not only foolish but inimical to the interests of Portugal and Spain. Wordsworth, who had previously exhibited republican sympathies, tried along with others to hold a meeting in Cumbria with a view to submitting an address to the King on the subject, and it was probably only when this stratagem failed that he turned to writing his tract.[90]

For the Whigs, 'Cintra' was a heaven-sent opportunity to attack the Tories and the government found themselves in some difficulty. As unpalateable as it seemed, the convention could not in reality be abandoned, though Canning wrote to Bathurst, Percival and others, including the King, railing against it. In that correspondence he argued that Britain should repudiate those parts of the convention repugnant to the Portuguese and not within the competence of a military commander.[91] There were comparisons drawn with the loss of Minorca in 1756, following which Admiral John Byng had been court martialled and shot, and the debacle at Buenos Aires leading to Whitelocke's court martial in 1808.[92]

The government moved quickly, Castlereagh recalling Dalrymple on 17 September to England to explain his conduct. In his letter Castlereagh made the point that His Majesty was disappointed with certain Articles of the Convention which were deeply upsetting to England's allies and stating that no ally should be exposed to an injury so offensive under the countenance of a British army.[93] The uproar was such that Richard Wellesley advised his brother to return home, which Arthur did, taking leave of the army on the basis that his duties in Ireland required him there.[94] Wellesley's own trumpeting of his success at Vimeiro, which he called a 'complete victory' with only half his army over 'the whole of the French force in Portugal', was now coming home to roost.[95] The government realised that it was in danger of being blamed for the terms of the Convention and that if it did not investigate the matter further, the public would hold it responsible. While recognising the *fait accompli*, it was decided to establish a Board of Inquiry. On 1 November, the King ordered the establishment of an Inquiry into the conditions of the Armistice and Convention, the causes and circumstances which led to them, and into 'the conduct, behaviour, and proceedings of the said Lieut. General Sir Hew Dalrymple, and any other officer or officers who may have held the command of our troops in Portugal'.[96] General Sir David Dundas was appointed President and six other experienced soldiers and statesmen nominated to the Board.[97]

The Inquiry sat from 14 November to 27 December 1808 at the Royal Hospital, Chelsea. It took evidence from Dalrymple, Burrard and Wellesley, the three principal officers present in Portugal at the time the Armistice and Convention were negotiated and signed; as well as from a number of more junior staff officers. A voluminous amount of documentation was submitted to the Inquiry and this was listed in its Report placed before the House of Commons in January 1809.[98]

In essence, Dalrymple gave as his evidence that his instructions and objective had been to get the French out of Portugal and cut off their retreat to Spain, so as to enable the British army to assist Spain. Bearing in mind that Junot still had an intact army and held strong positions, combined with the difficulties of holding his provisioning fleet on station, he felt this was best achieved by the Convention. He not unreasonably pointed out that he had consulted his Lieutenant Generals, including Burrard and Wellesley, and that none of them had objected to the terms as eventually settled (there had been considerable negotiation).[99] Where he differed from Wellesley was in his assertion that Wellesley had been involved in the negotiation of the Armistice. Dalrymple also felt that Burrard had played no great part in the negotiation of the Armistice.

Burrard gave evidence to the effect that he felt the army was exhausted after the battle of Vimeiro. It suffered from a lack of provisions and its cavalry was heavily outnumbered by the French and any advance as it approached Lisbon would be entering countryside more favourable to cavalry. He had therefore ordered a halt, anticipating in due course the arrival of Sir John Moore with a substantial force.

Wellesley had moved to distance himself from the terms of the Convention while still in Portugal. On his arrival in London he made it very clear that he had not approved the terms of the Armistice.[100] He maintained that while he had favoured an advance following the victory at Vimeiro, Burrard's decision to halt was not unreasonable. Further, while Wellesley had favoured such an advance with a view to cutting off the French from Lisbon, he pointed out that was in no way incompatible with his support for an armistice and convention when the circumstances had changed on 22 August, for by then the French were no longer in confusion. Wellesley made it clear he had not negotiated the armistice, but had merely signed it at Dalrymple's request, given that he held a rank of equivalence with the French signatory, General Kellerman. Furthermore, Wellesley stated that he had objected to various terms of the armistice including that pertaining to the Russian fleet in the Tagus (which Cotton rejected in any event) and the agreement to give forty-eight-hours' notice to end the suspension of hostilities. Wellesley confirmed he had in fact suggested the suspension of hostilities should be only for forty-eight-hours.

All three of these Generals expressed the opinion that if the Convention had not been entered into, the French might have passed the Tagus and gone to either Almeida or Elvas and therefore frustrated the British desire to help Spain. Furthermore, they might have held up the

British by defending Lisbon and other strongholds which would have required protracted siege warfare with the same result. Indeed it was widely reported that Junot had threatened to destroy Lisbon rather than let it fall into British hands intact.[101]

The attention of the Board was drawn to earlier Conventions, including those whereby the French had been allowed to evacuate Genoa (1800), Malta (1800), Egypt (1801) and indeed the arrangement whereby terms for the repatriation of Dupont's army had been agreed following the French defeat at the hands of the Spaniards at the Battle of Bailén (1808); though these were not subsequently honoured.[102] Dalrymple solicited the assistance of two generals in his own defence, with Anstruther and Lord William Bentinck furnishing supportive letters.[103] Though neither Beresford nor Proby were called as witnesses (they remained in the Peninsula), the correspondence with the Commissioners employed to carry the provisions of the Convention into effect was listed with a view to bolstering the cases of the generals as the subject of scrutiny, as they were able to demonstrate their determination to prevent the French taking home items of value not encompassed by the articles.[104]

The Board of Inquiry Report accepted that Burrard's conduct in not advancing after the battle of Vimeiro had been justified, particularly when two commanders succeeded each other within the space of twenty-four-hours. Further, the Convention had immediately liberated Portugal and relieved a large section of the Spanish frontier from the danger of attack, enabling the Spanish to make a more effective defence of Spain without an enemy at its back. It noted much firmness had been taken in restricting the French interpretation of the Convention, with the French being forced to disgorge their plunder. The Convention was similar to those entered into in Egypt, where the garrisons of Alexandria and Cairo could not have held out for long and had no prospect of succour. The Convention had not been objected to by five experienced Lieutenant Generals and in the opinion of the Board 'no further military proceeding is necessary'. The Report concluded with the statement that while the Board might have differences respecting the fitness of the Convention it was unanimous in recognising the unquestionable zeal and firmness of Dalrymple, Burrard and Wellesley.

The Commander in Chief, the Duke of York, was not impressed with one aspect of the Report. Three days later, on Christmas Day, he ordered the Board to express their opinion on whether the conditions of the Armistice and Convention were advisable and should have been agreed upon. As a result, the Board agreed that each member should indicate whether he approved of the Armistice, and separately whether he approved of the Convention. The results of those deliberations on 27 December showed a 6:1 majority in favour of the Armistice but only a 4:3 majority in favour of the Convention. The minority felt that the appearance of John Moore with reinforcements, together with the arrival of the 3rd and 42nd regiments following the Armistice, meant that Dalrymple could have taken a stronger position in the discussions leading to the Convention and would in all probability have obtained a more advantageous result had he done so. Only Moira felt there should have been no armistice as it effectively established the terms of the Convention.[105]

It is well known that Dalrymple and Burrard were never again given active commands. The King went further. While he adopted the unanimous opinion of the Board that no further military proceeding was necessary, he made a formal declaration of his disapprobation of the Armistice and Convention which was communicated to Dalrymple. It is most interesting that in doing so he highlighted his disapproval of the Articles in which stipulations were made directly affecting the interests or feelings of the Spanish and Portuguese nations. It was declared improper and dangerous to include in military conventions articles of such description. While the King's disapprobation does not list the articles complained of, it is easy to see that these must be those that had caused so much grief in Portugal. The inclusion of Spain may relate to the promise to secure the restoration of French subjects, whether military or civilian, detained in Spain. Dalrymple was being criticised for his acceptance of political articles in a military convention.[106]

Napoleon initially reserved his opinion on Junot and the Convention, writing to General Clarke on 2 October saying that on landing Junot should be told Napoleon did not know if he should approve the Convention but that there had been no harm to French honour in that the troops did not lay down their arms and no standards had been lost.[107] He seems to have felt that Junot should have entrenched himself and waited for reinforcements and is reported to have been considering a court martial, but the establishment of an Inquiry by the English avoided the need for him to punish an old friend.[108] Indeed, on his return to France Junot was given command of the 3rd Corps to prosecute the siege of Zaragoza.[109]

The holding of the Inquiry bears the hallmarks of political expediency. No inquiry had been called for under circumstances where deals had been done in recent years to allow the French home on surrender, and indeed such arrangements were the norm for other countries as well.[110] Indeed, Whitelocke's army had been allowed home from Buenos Aires[111] so why was the case of Portugal so different? The Report exculpated all three Generals in respect of their military conduct but clearly Portugal was felt to be a valuable ally whose feelings needed to be assuaged.[112] Furthermore, the fact that some of the French returnees were back in Spain by the beginning of December and the more immediate realisation they would be available to fight again caused considerable upset. Criticism of Dalrymple and Burrard as military commanders may be justified and it may be that a better result could have been obtained by making use of Moore's army, but is it sustainable to argue that all the parties to the conflict benefitted considerably by the Convention?[113]

While it was hard to get the message accepted, Britain had removed the French from Portugal without suffering serious losses and on a short time scale. The early capture of Lisbon enabled the provisioning of an army to go into Spain under Sir John Moore, and the deliverance of Portugal made the march on Spain feasible. All the other strongholds in Portugal were secured without fighting and Portugal became the British base for future operations. Furthermore, the British now had a safe harbour for their navy. On the negative side there was a perception that Britain could have struck a tougher bargain with Junot, perhaps ensuring the troops did not return to the Peninsula. There was also the more cosmetic criticism of the recognition of Napoleon's Imperial title for the first time, as well as the recognition of Junot as the Duke of Abrantes. The British Generals in overall command had failed to take the Portuguese into account, a situation which was recognised within government. Moreover, the psychological effect of winning victories in the Peninsula at a time when British forces were faring dismally elsewhere must have been a great morale booster for the British army and the government. Condemnation of the convention was not universal, and often depended on political allegiance. On balance it is argued Britain emerged a winner.

The English government was perhaps fortunate that the hullabaloo concerning Cintra died down remarkably quickly because of a fresh scandal which erupted in late January 1809, shortly after the publication of the report of the Board of Inquiry.[114] The new scandal concerned alleged corruption in the army arising from the sale of commissions under the influence of the Commander in Chief's mistress, Mary Ann Clarke. While the Duke of York was acquitted of the charges against him, he had to stand down for a considerable time as Commander in Chief.

Portugal had rid itself of the French army of occupation. While plundered to a degree, the Convention had saved Lisbon.[115] Henceforth, it obtained protection from a British army which paid its way. The fact that Moore was able to take an army into Spain and draw the French towards northern Spain and La Coruña probably prevented a fresh and more substantial invasion of Portugal by the French at this time. Of course, the involvement with Britain drew it into a lengthy war and huge suffering in terms of property and people, but in return it received a well trained army and financial assistance in its defence through British subsidies. It was not the Convention of Cintra, but the removal of the Court to Brazil in 1807 and the ensuing six years of warfare, combined with the opening up of direct trade by other nations with Brazil, that caused seismic changes to the politics and economics of Portugal. While Britain's failure to consult with the Portuguese over the proposals leading to the Convention of Cintra proved a real irritant, it is arguable Portugal emerged a winner.

Spain is not often thought of in terms of the Convention. However, it resulted in the repatriation of the imprisoned division of its army under Carafa. The march of the British army under Sir John Moore into central Spain and its subsequent withdrawal to La Coruña may have contributed to the saving of Andalucia in that Napoleon turned troops northwards which might otherwise have been used to crush resistance in the south. Finally, Spain no longer had an enemy behind it in Portugal, which enabled Spanish forces to concentrate elsewhere. A win also for Spain.

France lost Portugal, but in doing so recovered almost intact an army which was soon redeployed.[116] With some justification, the Convention was portrayed as a diplomatic triumph, as while the British feared a long engagement in Portugal the reality was that with the additional forces at the disposal of Dalrymple, a French withdrawal would have been a strategically demanding affair and might have resulted in unconditional surrender. If not a win, then a measured loss. France was still in the driving seat on mainland Europe, including the Peninsula.

The removal of the French army from Portugal enabled British propaganda to present the Convention of Cintra in a favourable light, but there were losers under its terms. A number of Portuguese lost possessions, and national treasures were looted from museums, libraries, churches and palaces. The full extent of those losses is difficult to quantify, not least because as Junot observed to Napoleon 50 million Francs worth of goods had been removed from Portugal to Great Britain when Portugal had initially come under French threat.[117] In addition, the Portuguese had already suffered a brutal taxation imposed by Junot. This situation should be set against the gain of a liberated country and the recovery of a considerable amount of goods and valuables. Without defending the theft of items, it is difficult to estimate the extent of plunder when it is recalled that substantial royal and independent valuables had been shipped to Brazil in 1807.[118] Further, it was a surprising oversight that Dalrymple did not seek to incorporate in the Convention provision for the return to Portugal of Portuguese prisoners detained in France.

Dalrymple and Burrard certainly emerged as losers, not being given further commands. Poor Burrard lost three sons fighting in the Peninsula and is said to have died of grief in 1813. However, fortune did not entirely desert Dalrymple. Though his son's military career suffered in that while he purchased promotion he was not given any future command, the General, with the support of Castlereagh, was created a baronet in 1815, perhaps in recognition that judgment on him had been somewhat harsh.[119]

The findings of the Board of Inquiry proved to be of great consequence. In supporting the actions of the military on the ground, those findings made it possible for Wellesley to be placed in command of Britain's next foreign expedition. In the autumn and early winter of 1808, Beresford was to participate in the attempt of Sir John Moore to assist Spain deliver itself of the French invader. Beresford's star was in the ascendant as a result of his efforts to limit the French interpretation of the Convention, his role in policing Lisbon, and in improving relations between the British military in Portugal and the Portuguese political elite remaining in that country. One British officer arriving in Lisbon at the close of September reckoned that the vigilance of Beresford had saved the populace of in excess of £200,000 in recovered private and public wealth. He credited Beresford with proving to the inhabitants that 'we were not the sanctioners of robbery, the protectors of plunderers, and the carriers of violated property'.[120] Given the reported strength of the ill feeling towards the British following the execution of the Convention of Cintra, it is not difficult to see why Beresford's conduct in the implementation of the Convention would ensure he would be welcomed back to Portugal in 1809.[121]

5 PORTUGAL AND SPAIN: FROM LISBON TO LA CORUÑA, 1808–1809

*'I well remember what a fine looking soldier he was.
He was equal to his business too'[1]*

Beresford was certainly very active while stationed in Lisbon. We have already seen his involvement with the implementation of the Convention of Cintra and his role in securing calm in Lisbon. Apart from his relationship with a number of Portuguese military personnel, it is clear that Beresford at this time began to forge contacts with the various members of the Regency Council. Dalrymple was using Beresford as a go-between with Forjaz and others during September and this continued under Burrard in October.[2]

In a move which may have had some bearing on subsequent events, Beresford studied the current state of the Portuguese army and sent a report on it to General Bernardim Freire de Andrade, commander of the Portuguese forces in the northern part of the country, as well as to the reconstituted Regency.[3] Beresford had displayed an interest in the organisation of the Portuguese military while in Madeira, deliberately ignoring government instructions in order to do so. Now we see him exhibiting a keen interest in the means of defending Portugal. In the report, Beresford advocated that troops should be transferred away from their home towns in order to be trained, so that they could develop into a fighting unit.[4] He also stressed the need for regular pay, proper equipment and ready supplies. Finally, he recognised the need to reform the officer corps. All of these recommendations were to play a part in the reform of the Portuguese army in the period after 1809, though Burrard, in sending a copy of Beresford's 'plan' home in October 1808, expressed no great hopes for its implementation:

> Major General Beresford gave in a plan to the Regency for the reorganization of the Portuguese army of which I send a copy, as I do not believe it has been transmitted home. I am afraid little has been done on it, but consultation and debate, and I must repeat that without a Minister here equal to the task of instructing, urging and conciliating the government and people I think nothing beneficial will ensue either to Portugal, Great Britain or the general cause of Europe.[5]

Beresford expressed his frustration at this time about both the inactivity of the British army and uncertainty as to who would command it, a frustration born perhaps of having missed the battles in August 1808. On 30 September he wrote to his old friend Edward Cooke referring to Dalrymple's recall and expressing a desire shared by many: 'who is finally to have command of this army is what we are all anxious to know, and we trust a speedy decision as we do not understand rotting here doing nothing, while our friends the Spaniards are, with such earnestness, demanding our assistance'.[6]

Beresford was soon given another task. No sooner had he handed responsibility for Lisbon back to the Portuguese when riots broke out in Porto, instigated it was widely believed by the Bishop, António de São José de Castro, who initially expressed the view that the Regency Council had no authority given their cooperation with the French.[7] When appointed one of the Regency Council to replace those removed on the grounds of collaboration with the French, he feared that his influence might be threatened by that body.[8] There is little room for doubt that this concern led the Bishop to avoid coming to Lisbon at this time. Beresford was directed to Porto with some 2,500 troops to put an end to the disturbances.[9] Subsequently, some of the troops were intended to occupy Almeida, surrendered by the French on 2 October under the terms of the Convention of Cintra. The decision to send Beresford reflects his high standing at the time with Burrard writing to Castlereagh: 'I trust Major General Beresford will be successful in putting a fortunate termination to insurrection, as he has been happy in conducting some very intricate and difficult affairs in this town.'[10]

Burrard directed Sir Robert Wilson, in command of the recently constituted Loyal Lusitanian Legion, to meet Beresford at Coimbra.[11] When Beresford arrived there on 22 October he learnt that peace had been restored in Porto. Sending on the troops to garrison at Almeida, Beresford visited the Bishop personally in Porto on 31 October. He secured the agreement of the Bishop that the latter would go to Lisbon in about a month to join the other members of the Council. In the event it was April 1809 before he did so. Beresford clearly realised the Bishop was seeking to advance his own position, but he managed to avoid taking sides while remaining on good terms with the cleric. Because Beresford could combine a cold demeanour with a considerable temper when roused, his diplomatic skills have perhaps not been adequately acknowledged. These skills had already been evidenced at Buenos Aires and during his time as Governor of Madeira. Now they were being honed further, with his involvement in the implementation of the Convention of Cintra and his mission to Porto. While there were many disagreements with the Regency Council before the end of the war in 1814, it will become clear that Beresford, in conjunction with Forjaz and Wellington (and with the financial support of Great Britain), managed to motivate the Portuguese army in such a manner as to enable Portugal to play a vital part in what was to become an Allied success.

With the recall of Wellesley along with Burrard and Dalrymple, the British army came under the command of Sir John Moore. His instructions envisaged the British force providing auxiliary help to the armies of Spain. Spanish success at Bailén resulted in Napoleon going to the Peninsula to conduct the war, and by the end of 1808 in excess of 200,000 French troops were in Spain to quell the insurrection there. Moore felt that an invasion of Spain was justified in order to help the Spanish, but he soon found himself on the back foot when his army of over 30,000 was faced by superior French forces. Initially he was delayed by lack of resources, the subject of correspondence with Castlereagh.[12] Logistics led Moore to direct the army from Portugal to Salamanca in three divisions marching by different routes. Moore's forces entered Spain from Portugal in early November, with Moore reaching Ciudad Rodrigo on the eleventh of that month. A portion of his forces reached Salamanca two days later. Beresford's brigade initially formed part of the 3rd Division under Lieutenant General Mackenzie Fraser, who took his troops from Coimbra via Viseu to Salamanca. Beresford's Brigade was used as a flanking brigade on the march there and by 6 November was stated by Moore to be at Pinhel and Celorico and their environs.[13] Two weeks later, Beresford confirmed to his half-brother, the 2nd Marquis of Waterford, that they had reached Salamanca where he was quartered in the Bishop's house, mentioning that he had a very good cook with him but surprisingly there was a shortage of wine. He observed that Salamanca was somewhat like Oxford with its colleges and churches, though the difference being that the Spanish city had monasteries for men and women. The buildings he found beautiful and the cathedral decidedly so.[14] The news from Spain was all bad, with the successive defeats of armies under Blake and Castaños at Espinosa de los Monteros and Tudela, causing Beresford to opine that there was no prospect of his meeting his half-brother before the passing of another winter. Following the French capture of Madrid, Beresford was to observe that the defence had been trifling 'not from want of inclination of the people but there is little spirit in the upper classes, less energy, and if possible less knowledge, at least such as is suitable for the present times'.[15]

Moore received additional support with the arrival at Mayorga on 20 December of a further British force under Lieutenant General Sir David Baird from La Coruña. This force of approximately 16,000 men arrived off La Coruña on 13 October.[16] However, because of Spanish concerns it was not allowed to disembark initially and only commenced doing so on 26 October, following receipt of approval from the government in Madrid, with the last units only getting ashore on 4 November. Baird's initial puzzlement as to why he was in northern Spain was intensified when having advanced with his force as far as Astorga he was ordered back to La Coruña, with Moore having decided that he would retire with his own army to Portugal after receiving news of the defeat of the Spanish army under General Castaños at Tudela.[17]

In a further volte-face, Moore then determined to stay in Spain following news of what appeared to be determined Spanish resistance and to this end he ordered Baird forward again. Moore then learnt on 11 December of the fall of Madrid to the French on the 4th of the month. Captured communications led him to believe he might be able to attack a French army in León in northern Spain under Marshal Soult before Napoleon could come from Madrid to its support. On 20 December Moore and Baird linked up and began an advance on Soult's position at Carrión. Following this junction of the two British forces, Moore reorganised his army but Beresford's brigade continued to form part of the 3rd Division under Mackenzie-Fraser. Initially the British enjoyed some success with Henry, Lord Paget, commanding the 10th and 15th Hussars getting the better of General Debelle at Sahagún in a cavalry action on 21 December.[18] However, before Moore could come up with Soult he learnt on 23 December that the main French army, with Napoleon in command, was moving north from Madrid at speed in pursuit of his own far smaller force. He therefore abandoned the envisaged attack on Soult and ordered the retreat which was to end at La Coruña.

The story of the difficult mid-winter retreat of the British army from Salamanca to La Coruña is well known, with substantial losses being suffered to both the advancing French and the weather. James Ormsby, a chaplain to the army, described the intense suffering of marching 'over a stupendous high chain of mountains, which were deeply covered with snow, and as many of the troops had not received either bread or wine for the two preceding days, their sufferings were extreme'.[19] Two days later, on 6 January 1809, he referred to men lying down in the snow never to rise again and an awful silence pervaded the ranks, only interrupted by the faint groans and fruitless exclamations of the dying. In a graphic description of what it was like for camp followers he wrote: 'Here lies an infant upon a lifeless mother's breast; it fondly labours to imbibe the wonted nourishment.'[20]

Discipline broke down in a number of regiments and there are many stories involving destruction of Spanish property and the appropriation of goods, particularly alcohol.[21] It was not just the Spaniards who suffered. Even British officers were not safe from the depradations of their men. Lieutenant William Henry Sewell, recently arrived from England to serve as ADC to Beresford, had a gold watch, gold toothpick case and a silver essence box stolen from him at Lugo for which Private Charles Rankin of the 22nd Regiment was found guilty and sentenced to death by hanging.[22]

Lieutenant Colonel George MacGregor had his rum bottle stolen by a corporal to whom he had given it to fill, and his saddle bags stolen by, he suspected, men of another British regiment. He recorded a scene of complete desolation on the retreat from Villafranca to Lugo noting: 'there was not a hundred yards of the road free from the carcasses of horses and other beasts of burden; which had given up and were shot by their owners.' He went on to contrast the condition of the British soldiers with their French counterparts: 'Nor was it all pleasant to observe the French, every one of them, provided with one of the blankets which had been thrown away upon the road in cart loads, together with the arms, the dollars and the shoes!

– The enemy had no occasion for them. They were remarkably well clothed.'[23] Many British soldiers under the influence of drink lost their lives to the inclement weather or the pursuing French when they were unable or unwilling to march.

Moore decided to split his force, sending some 3,500 under Generals Craufurd and Alten to Vigo to embark there while he took the main army to La Coruña. He reached La Coruña on 11 January 1809 to find that the British fleet had not yet arrived, and had no choice but to defend the town.[24] In the ensuing battle, Moore was killed, and his second, Baird lost an arm.[25] However, the French were repulsed and the bulk of the British forces successfully withdrawn.[26] La Coruña was claimed by Soult a French victory, but Great Britain was also able to claim success.[27] The British army had stopped the French with a successful strategic defensive action which brought it sufficient time to salvage its one standing army, albeit with substantial losses in terms of men and equipment.

Some reports suggest that Beresford's brigade was part of the British rearguard in the retreat to La Coruña, but it would appear that it was just ahead of the rearguard, though called upon repeatedly to assist that rearguard under Paget. Beresford leaves us in no doubt that the retreat was difficult. Writing from Sobrado to his half-sister Anne on 5 January 1809, he stated:

> I arrived here this day between Lugo and St Jago on my way to Vigo to re-embark, and to which all the army was making, but a counter-order has just arrived and tomorrow we measure back our steps to Lugo. We have had for the last twenty days the most extraordinary marching and the most intolerable weather. Most have lost their baggage from the latter cause and the roads, and I fear no good will arise from the counter-order. Our men are completely fatigued.[28]

The British Fleet under Rear Admiral Hood arrived with transports about 2 pm on 14 January and embarkation of the army began almost immediately. During that night and on the following day, the cavalry was dismounted and the sick and fifty-two pieces of artillery were loaded onto the fleet. Only twelve light guns were retained on shore. Fighting took place on 15 January and more intensively on 16 January, with Moore killed on the second day. By the latter date much of the baggage, the remaining horses and artillery and the reserve division had been embarked.[29] The following day (17 January) the embarkation continued in worsening weather and under heavy fire from Soult's artillery, which had begun shelling the harbour the previous day from the heights of St Lucía.[30] The guns of the ships of war responded in kind and succeeded in silencing those of the French.

The embarkation was covered by Major General Hill's brigade which was stationed on the promontory at the rear of the town and by Beresford's brigade on the inland front of La Coruña directly facing the enemy.[31] During the day (17 January) Hill's brigade was embarked and all but Beresford's brigade were on board.[32] Spanish troops under the command of the Marquis de la Romana occupied the citadel. Beresford's brigade, now reduced to about 2,000 men, covered the ongoing embarkation and that night his troops lit huge fires and kept them fully supplied with a view to deceiving the enemy.[33]

Early on the morning of 18 January, Beresford's force embarked from behind the citadel, though he reported that his friends had despaired of his getting off and he thought himself fortunate to have escaped 'my friends the French'. [34] As soon as this small force was embarked the fleet set sail.[35] The Spanish, commanded by General Alcedo, the military and political governor of the town, only surrendered La Coruña to Soult on 20 January, when the British were safely out at sea. Lieutenant General Sir John Hope (who commanded the 2nd Division) had taken over the command on Moore's death and he subsequently wrote most favourably of Beresford's conduct:

Major General Beresford, with that zeal and ability that is so well known to yourself and the whole army, having fully explained, to the satisfaction of the Spanish governor, the nature of our movement, and having made every previous arrangement, withdrew his corps from the landfront of the town soon after dark, and was, with all the wounded that had not been previously moved, embarked before one this morning.[36]

Beresford wrote to his half-sister, Anne, back in Ireland to tell her he was safe after a great deal of fatigue and some anxiety. Like so many in the army he was relieved that there had been a trial of strength with the enemy:

who attacked us in our position near Corunna and got a most complete beating for his pains. We have however lost our Commander Sir John Moore who was killed and Sir David Baird lost his arm but is as yet doing as well as could be expected. The troops with the exception of my brigade embarked the night after the action, and the ensuing day I was left as the rear guard to cover and protect the embarkation of the army, and the enemy having driven among our transports during the day, I was given up at least as to be a prisoner, however, I completed the service and embarked my own Brigade and the wounded, and got on board at two o'clock this morning, and the enemy will be astonished. I can say no more than that I hope shortly to see my dearest Anne and I now long for your being in London ...[37]

Beresford could, and clearly did, feel positive about his own contribution to the circumstances allowing for that evacuation.

Beresford and Moore had served together prior to the campaign in Spain ending with the retreat to La Coruña. At Toulon and in Corsica they had soldiered side by side and there is no evidence of other than cordial relations between the two men. That did not stop Beresford criticising Moore's decision to retreat to La Coruña, calling it a most inglorious and unnecessary flight which had cost five times the numbers than would have been the case if they had stopped to oppose the enemy. He was not alone in his criticism of the retreat, with the now-deceased Moore being castigated both in England and Spain.[38] Certainly, huge numbers were lost on the retreat but Moore's achievement in enabling a large part of Britain's Peninsular army to be brought home was considerable.[39]

FIRST STEPS IN THE REBUILDING AND REFORM OF AN ARMY: THE CAMPAIGN IN NORTHERN PORTUGAL, 1809

6

Sometimes military reform becomes an engine for change for an entire society, intended or otherwise. Given the global reach of British and French military practices and the compulsive energy and hypermilitarization of Imperial Germany, it is not surprising that the great reformers are Europeans: William Carr Beresford in Portugal, Charles George Gordon in China, Ivor Herbert in Canada, H.H. Kitchener in Egypt, Orde Wingate in Jewish Palestine, John Bagot Glubb in Jordan, Joseph-Simon Gallieni in Indochina, Hubert Louis Lyautey in Morocco, Colmar von der Goltz and Liman von Sanders in Turkey, Emil Korner in Chile, Hans Kundt in Bolivia and Max Bauer and Hans von Seeckt in China.[1]

After the evacuation of the British army at La Coruña, Beresford's stay in England on his return from Spain was to prove a short one. He did not even have the opportunity to return to Ireland to visit his relatives, and indeed it was to be a further five years before he was reunited with his family. Soon after returning from Spain he was offered the command of the British forces in Jamaica, with the expectation of Governorship of that island. He declined on the basis that he wished to see active service.[2] Within days of turning down this opportunity, on 9 February 1809 he was ordered to Portugal in response to a request from the Regency Council for a British officer to reform and rebuild that country's army. While he noted that he would not have refused this opportunity to be involved in active service, he also made clear that he had been told that his appointment to command the Portuguese army was not open to refusal.[3]

Notwithstanding the victories at Roliça and Vimeiro, the position of Portugal was fraught with danger by the close of 1808. The optimism which surrounded the British advance into Spain that autumn had perished in the retreat to La Coruña and Vigo. Once again, in early 1809 Portugal was faced with a French invasion.

In the aftermath of the Convention of Cintra and the deportation of the French army, on 18 September 1808 General Dalrymple had re-established the Regency Council subject to the removal of its French supporters. It faced huge difficulties, not least because of the need to obtain instructions from the Prince Regent in Rio de Janeiro before making major decisions. This restriction was born of a determination by the royal family and its advisers in Brazil not to allow the growth of an alternative power base, a policy which was to make difficult Portuguese participation in the war, and which on occasion was to provide a convenient stratagem for those opposed to British suggestions. It is important to realise that on arrival in Brazil in January 1808, Prince João effectively set up a full royal government and state apparatus there.[4] It included a Council of State, four ministries, a Supreme Court of Justice, Royal Treasury, Royal Mint, Royal libraries, a military academy, a law school and more. This government-in-exile not only established the conditions for the development of Brazilian independence, but for thirteen years led to a role reversal whereby Portugal was in many respects ruled from Brazil.

This situation created difficulties which were manifested in different ways, such as when Prince João, in confirming the reinstatement of the Regency by order of 2 January 1809, made it clear that all matters other than those requiring immediate decision should be referred to the appropriate ministry in Rio de Janeiro. This requirement included all reforms as well as promotions in the army and even the universities. In effect, the Regency Council were governors rather than a body standing in lieu of the Queen (or in reality the Prince Regent) with all the difficulties in making decisions required to govern on behalf of a ruler some 5,000 kilometres away in an age when communication was by sail and subject to the vagaries of the prevailing weather system.[5]

Furthermore, the Regency experienced considerable difficulty in establishing its own authority in Portugal. It was split by rival factions and undermined by, amongst others, the Bishop of Porto whose reluctance to recognise its authority reflected a desire to promote himself and the Junta of Porto as a leadership uncontaminated by collaboration with the French. The serious riots which had occurred in Porto in early October, riots in which many of the soldiers stationed there were involved, were brought under control but there remained an inflamed mood with the threat of further outbreaks. Anarchy was matched by apathy, with many thinking the war with France was now at an end and that the French would soon be driven from the Iberian Peninsula. French success in the winter of 1808–9 meant that apathy amongst some was quickly replaced by terror, and the febrile atmosphere in Lisbon was not helped by persistent rumours of an intention by Britain to withdraw its remaining troops from Portugal, rumours which were not without foundation for that possibility was recognised by Sir John Cradock, the new commander of the British forces in Portugal, on his arrival in Lisbon in mid December. British government policy was itself uncertain.

Remarkably, at the end of January – the very moment the government was considering further involvement in Portugal – it simultaneously recognised the possibility of withdrawal. Following La Coruña and the bringing home of Moore's army in what must have been a particular low point for British ministers, Castlereagh wrote to Cradock on 28 January 1809 urging him to maintain himself as long as possible in Portugal in order to give the Spanish an opportunity to regroup and to force the enemy to engage in long marches. If Cradock had to withdraw he was to go to Cádiz, if the Spanish wanted the British army there, but if the response was negative he should proceed to Gibraltar.[6] Cradock for his part was clearly worried about his ability to maintain a presence in Portugal, and following receipt of the news of the departure of the British army from La Coruña he closed a number of provisioning depots in northern Portugal – at Almeida and Lamego – and sought to concentrate his army of about 10,000 men in and around Lisbon; though the 40th Regiment was garrisoned strategically at Elvas and Brigadier General Charles Stewart, with a force of 2,700, occupied Santarém. British popularity in Portugal was less than universal, with its troops in Lisbon not immune from attack by Portuguese.[7]

In addition, the departure of a number of the pro-French party in Portugal, whether through going to France with the Portuguese Legion under d'Alorna or from taking sail with Junot, did not mean there was not a pro-French faction still in Portugal. A British observer, the Reverend James Wilmot Ormsby, detected in October 1808 that there was still a strong French party in Lisbon, though in most of the country people detested the French. He noted the joy of the Portuguese at the extermination of the French but added, 'it does not follow that because they hate them they should love us. Had they behaved with moderation the French might have been hailed as deliverers.'[8] The result of this state of affairs was that little rebuilding of either administrative or military structures was achieved in Portugal in the autumn of 1808 and early spring of 1809. Ultimately the Regency would be reformed in the summer of 1809, but before the end of the previous year it had at least recognised that it was incapable of reforming the Portuguese army and sought the assistance of Great Britain to do so.

If Portugal was in a state of chaos in 1808, it is equally clear that its army was not fit for purpose. No discussion of the rebuilding and reform of the Portuguese army would be complete without looking at its historical evolution prior to the Peninsular War and the career of the man who more than any other provided the Portuguese impetus for change, Dom Miguel Pereira Forjaz.[9] Beresford was to prove to be the instrument of reform and the creation of an efficient fighting force was made possible by the provision of financial and material support from Great Britain; but the undertaking and progression of this task owed much to the foresight and determination of Forjaz, one of the Secretaries to the Regency Council. The much maligned General Burrard had identified that nothing would be done in Portugal without a minister 'equal to the task of instructing, urging and conciliating the government and people' and Forjaz proved to be that man of vision and determination.[10]

Forjaz joined the re-established Regency Council as Secretary for Foreign Affairs, War and Marine and remained one of those most influential and supportive of the Anglo-Portuguese war effort throughout the Peninsular War.[11] A lack of military organisation and modernisation in the Portuguese army had been identified as far back as the 1790s, and the need for reform had been advocated by Forjaz and some of his compatriots since that time. Following the conclusion of the 'War of the Oranges' in June 1801, the appointment of Karl Alexander von der Goltz as Commander in Chief of the Portuguese army led to recommendations for reform aimed at producing a trained and disciplined force, but internal resistance led to Goltz's departure a year later.[12] His short period in Portugal was not without result, for it led to the appointment of a military Commission to examine how the army could be improved, and Forjaz served as Secretary to the Commission. The Commission did not agree a final report and its resolutions were not acted on by the government. Forjaz, however, worked closely with successive Ministers for War and made suggestions for appointments to be made on merit and the reform of logistical support, which had they been acted upon might have reduced the serious problems encountered by the Portuguese army in the Peninsular War. It is likely that the policy of appeasement adopted towards Napoleon by António de Araújo, the Francophile Minister for War from 1804, was an important factor in the failure to address the issues required for the proper defence of the realm.[13]

Forjaz had been dismissed from the army by Junot, and having withdrawn from public life rather than support the French regime he had been one of the first to become involved in the re-establishment of a Portuguese army under the Supreme Junta of Porto in the summer of 1808. Serving under General Bernardim Freire de Andrade (his cousin), Forjaz sought to introduce many of the reforms he had long advocated for the Portuguese army.[14] Relatively little had been achieved in the run up to the defeat of the French in August 1808, and indeed thereafter progress was very slow prior to Beresford's arrival and appointment as Commander in Chief in the spring of 1809. The combination of Forjaz's vision and application and Beresford's commitment to the creation of a well disciplined fighting force, where promotion was based on merit rather than merely birth, meant that over the next few years these two men effectively combined to produce one of the finest armies in Europe.

In the autumn of 1808, the prospect of Portugal possessing an army to be reckoned with in the Napoleonic wars must have seemed remote. In despair the Regency Council reported to Rio in mid October that the country was effectively a demilitarised zone; a rather startling and pessimistic assertion given there were then over 30,000 British soldiers in the country in addition to the Portuguese forces.[15] Junot had denuded Portugal of some of its best soldiers by creating the Portuguese Legion under the Marquis d'Alorna.[16] The regiments raised by the Supreme Junta of Porto and others in 1808–9 were for the most part badly armed, poorly trained and in some cases lacking in leadership. There was a shortage of money to pay the troops, discipline was weak and there was a chronic lack of supplies. In addition to the troops raised in Portugal in 1808, the Loyal Lusitanian Legion had been formed in England, and this force commanded by Sir Robert Wilson had landed in Porto in the autumn of that year. Made up principally of Portuguese who had escaped from Portugal it consisted of two battalions of infantry and an artillery unit, and the Loyal Lusitanian Legion was to perform useful service until ultimately subsumed into the Portuguese army in 1811.[17]

The steps taken by the Regency involved a declaration of 30 September recalling all officers retired by Junot to the colours. This step could only have been moderately successful given that many officers had either gone to Brazil with the Court, joined the Loyal Lusitanian Legion or the Portuguese Legion. At the same time a radical move was made in creating six battalions of caçadores (light troops). This decision was not entirely innovative; one such regiment had been created previously under the Marquis d'Alorna as part of the reforms suggested by the members of the military commission, but this had been part of the force dispatched to France designated to become the Portuguese Legion in the service of Napoleon. In October and November, further decrees were issued designed to reorganise the army on previously existing lines, recalling men to their regiments and including a pardon for deserters.[18] Forjaz instigated the formation of volunteer regiments in Lisbon in late 1808.

The restored format for the army thus envisaged twenty-four infantry regiments of the line (37,200), six battalions of caçadores (3,768) twelve cavalry regiments (7,128) and four artillery regiments (4,800), giving a regular army of some 52,000 men. In addition, there was theoretically a militia force of comparable size and a *levée en masse*, known as the ordenança, which could be called out in time of crisis. However, the reality was very different. Early in September a report prepared by Baron Frederick von Decken for the British Government suggested there were in fact 13,272 infantry, 3,384 caçadores, 1,812 cavalry and 19,000 militia.[19] Portuguese returns for 26 November 1808 suggested that this figure had risen to 22,361 infantry, 3,422 cavalry, 4,031 artillery and 20,800 militia by that date, but Portuguese historians query the veracity of these and later figures when set against the much more strictly tabulated figures for 1810 and 1811.[20]

Portuguese forces raised in 1808 were lacking in equipment, provisions and discipline.[21] A return for 5 January 1809 lists 21,094 infantry but some without arms or uniforms. A theoretical cavalry force of 3,691 could not be put in the field due to a lack of horses, while there was an artillery force of 2,419. The remaining British force under Sir John Cradock amounted to just over 10,000 men, with a rather alarming number of a mere 5,221 effectives. These were centred on Lisbon from whence it was anticipated initially they would sail for England in the event of a major French advance, though later a retreat to Cádiz or Gibraltar was contemplated.[22]

Furthermore, it is clear from the correspondence of Sir John Cradock with the British Envoy to Lisbon, Sir John Villiers, that the former had been told by Forjaz that the quality of those recalled to the Portuguese army did not greatly impress him and further there were less than 10,000 serviceable arms for the Portuguese forces in mid December.[23] At the beginning of the month, Major General MacKenzie, who had just arrived in Lisbon, observed to Castlereagh: 'I am sorry to say that very little assistance can be relied on from the government of this country. The reestablishment of their military force goes on, but very slowly and without energy.' Forjaz had told him that there was an extreme lack of arms for both the regular forces and the militia.[24] A month later, in early January 1809, Villiers wrote to Canning stating, 'this part of the Peninsula will fall whenever it is attacked, unless measures for its defence are immediately taken', going on to add that at present it may be considered as defenceless.[25]

By February 1809 there were two Portuguese armed forces of any size operational in Portugal together with garrisons in fortresses such as Almeida and Elvas. The larger of the two forces, under the command of Lieutenant General António José de Miranda Henriques, was headquartered at Tomar with the objective of protecting Lisbon. This corps nominally amounted to just under 15,000 regulars and 2,000 cavalry with artillery support. The second force was operative north of the Douro in the provinces of Minho and Trás-os-Montes. This corps was split into two forces, with that under Lieutenant General Bernardim Freire de Andrade covering Porto and another group under Brigadier General Francisco da Silveira operating in Trás-os-Montes with headquarters in Chaves. The combined total of these two forces was calculated at only 6,444 with some cavalry. It was supplemented by a large force of militia.[26]

In London, notwithstanding the successful expulsion of the French from Portugal following the battle of Vimeiro, there was recognition by government ministers that the rebuilding of the Portuguese army would require financial assistance. Indeed, even prior to Vimeiro Arthur Wellesley had suggested it would require substantial British help to rebuild the Portuguese army.[27] The Government proceeded with caution, given its own requirement for troops to meet disorder at home and the possibility of French invasion. However, Portugal clearly fell into the category of an ally who could and would fight if given the materials to do so. Additionally, both Portugal and Brazil offered important military, naval and economic advantages to Great Britain, just as they would have done to France. The initial decision to give financial aid was communicated to Villiers in November 1808, when it was agreed that cloth for uniforms, leather and materials for 10,000 men would be sent to Portugal. It was to be March 1809 before arms and clothing for this number was in fact delivered to the country.[28]

Credit should be given to the Regency for recognising the need to bring in outside help in order to reorganise and rebuild the army. By letter of 26 December 1808, Cipriano Ribeiro Freire on behalf of the Portuguese government requested a British officer to reform and rebuild the Portuguese army, and in what proved to be an inspired choice, Beresford was nominated for that position in February 1809.[29] The request baldly stated: 'Present circumstances rendering it extremely desirable that there should be at the head of the Portuguese army a general officer, whose experience and other qualifications may fit him to command the Military Force of this kingdom, whether for its own immediate defense [sic], or for the general cause and liberty of the Peninsula ...'.[30] That the decision to send a British general to help build the Portuguese army was taken at all, let alone within weeks following the retreat to and evacuation from La Coruña, is perhaps remarkable but shows a determination not to allow the hard-earned fruits of the victory at Vimeiro to slip away. Indeed, the decision when first announced was ridiculed by some who expressed the view that Lisbon would be in French hands before the appointee could reach the Tagus.[31]

How and why was Beresford chosen by the Duke of Portland's administration to reform and rebuild the Portuguese army? The decision was made within a month of the request being received by the government in London, surely indicating an understanding at cabinet level of the imminent dangers facing Portugal and a wish to capitalise on the military success of the 1808 campaign in that country. Beresford's appointment was no racing certainty. While no specific general was requested by the Portuguese, Villiers was told privately that Wellesley would be most welcome.[32] It is unclear whether Wellesley indicated that he was not interested, but in any event Castlereagh felt he was too valuable to be put forward for the job and opposed his appointment.[33] Lieutenant General Sir John Doyle's name was mentioned, probably at the behest of the Duke of York. He was senior to Wellesley, so it was perhaps as well that this suggestion was not implemented, as it would have made it difficult, if not impossible, to appoint Wellesley commander of all Allied forces a month later. There were certainly more senior candidates than Beresford, a relatively junior Major General. Canning favoured Sir John Moore, but by the last week of January news of his demise had reached London. Canning then appears to have decisively supported Beresford's nomination, explaining that his appointment was due not only on account of his military ability but because of his knowledge of Portugal and the Portuguese people and language.[34] Further factors leading to his selection may have included the interest Beresford had shown in training Portuguese infantry while in Madeira, and his own recommendations for the creation of a modern Portuguese army shortly after arriving in Portugal in 1808, before leaving for Spain with Sir John Moore's army.[35]

The decision to appoint Beresford seems to have been the result of strong support from Robert Stewart, Viscount Castlereagh, at this time Minister for War and the Colonies and an ally of the Wellesleys. Castlereagh had also been born in Ireland in the same year as Arthur Wellesley (1769), just one year after Beresford. In his seminal work on the Peninsular War, Sir Charles Oman hypothesised as to whether Wellesley had had any influence on the appointment.[36] Certainly Wellesley and Beresford were on good terms and remained so throughout the war, as is ascertainable not just by their mode of familiar address but by Wellington's frequent exchanges with Beresford, whether in person or through correspondence.[37] Furthermore, the rebuilding of the Portuguese army with British assistance was the subject of a proposal which Wellesley had put forward in the summer of 1808, as part of a plan to secure Portugal from the French and give support to the various Spanish armies. Wellesley foresaw that the combined numbers of a rebuilt Portuguese army with a British army in Portugal would give this alliance a very strong say in the conduct of the war.[38] While there seems to be no irrefutable evidence that Wellesley played a hand in Beresford's nomination, Sir Charles Oman's speculation that the appointment was part of a plan by Castlereagh and Wellesley to involve another of the Anglo-Irish Tory coterie is an attractive theory.[39] A further factor which may have assisted Beresford's appointment was the relationship by marriage of his father with the Prime Minister, the Duke of Portland.[40]

Beresford was nominated less than two weeks after his return from La Coruña.[41] Napier suggested that parliamentary interest was the deciding factor in Beresford's appointment and that this caused great discontent amongst those officers of superior rank.[42] If there is justification in Napier's assertion that the appointment arose through parliamentary influence, then it would not be the first or last occasion such appointments were due to political influence. Beresford's *Strictures*, written in the 1830s in response to Napier's suggestion, make some relevant points regarding the appointment. Those fall into two categories: The first concern his previous experience in Portugal and Spain, which involved his tenure as Governor of Madeira, his nomination as a commissioner to implement the Convention of Cintra by Dalrymple, whom Beresford did not know, and his selection by Sir John Moore to cover the retreat and embarkation at La Coruña.[43] The second point Beresford makes is that in 1809, after his return from La Coruña, he had hoped to visit his family in Ireland, a family which he had not seen much of since 1793; but that when summoned by Castlereagh he was told he could not decline the appointment to command the Portuguese army.[44] That is born out by the contemporary correspondence. It is clear that even if parliamentary influence was at work in securing the appointment, it was not solicited by Beresford.

Beresford's reputation as an able administrator and a strict disciplinarian appear likely to have been factors in his appointment, combined with qualities already referred to here. While Canning was now committed to the defence of Portugal, he was under no illusions as to the challenge faced by Beresford, referring to it as an 'arduous and difficult undertaking'. It involved placing a British army officer in a position of power in a country with different laws, a fractured government, a divided society, a different religion, and different customs and climate. The appointment was to give him command of the Portuguese army, but on the basis that Beresford was to be subject to the overall command of the commander in chief of the British forces in Portugal. As such he was thrown into a complex series of relationships where political, economic and military factors fell to be decided by a number of parties who were sometimes geographically distant, personally jealous and whose policies were not perfectly aligned. The lack of any meaningful central authority with the ability to make things happen in Portugal had to be altered, and it is a tribute to Forjaz, Wellington and Beresford that an efficient war machine was created over relatively few years. That this could be achieved in the face of French military might was doubted by many at the outset and Beresford himself expressed the view that it was not impossible, indeed not improbable that he would go to and return from Portugal given the state of affairs there.[45]

The Portuguese had requested an officer of the rank of Lieutenant General to command their army. Beresford, whom we have seen had only been promoted to Major General in 1808, was made up to Lieutenant General 'during the time in which he shall be employed the [sic] command of the Portuguese forces'.[46]

Beresford arrived in Lisbon on 2 March 1809 after an eight-day voyage, during which his vessel 'missed the French fleet by little'.[47] While it was rumoured that the French were on their way back to Portugal he found the Portuguese in high spirits and full of enthusiasm.[48] Five days later he was appointed Marshal and Commander in Chief of the Portuguese army. He wrote to Charles Stewart, brother of Castlereagh and soon to be Wellington's adjutant general in the Peninsula, explaining that he had not wished to be made a Marshal, but that the Portuguese had insisted that this was necessary for the command of the army. Beresford's suggestion that he be appointed a Lieutenant General in the Portuguese army would not give him command of that army because it contained a considerable number of Lieutenant Generals already, all of whom would have been senior to Beresford and thus would have had command over him.[49] Probably wisely, Beresford determined that the terms of his appointment and the extent of his authority required clarification before he took up his duties. In particular, he was understandably anxious to establish that he would have authority over all military appointments and promotions and it was only when agreement on this point and his ability to discipline those who would not obey commands was secured that he moved to finalise his appointment.[50] Indeed, he had stressed the necessity of such powers in a paper sent to Castlereagh in early February prior to taking up his appointment.[51] As a result it was a further week before he formally took command of the Portuguese forces on 15 March.[52]

The Portuguese may have been full of enthusiasm but Beresford found the army, both officers and men, in a state of insubordination, to such an extent that officers no longer gave orders and if they did so, there was no certainty they would be obeyed.[53] Hence his initial task was to get control of the army. It is not therefore surprising that in his first Order of the Day (Ordem do Dia) Beresford made it clear that discipline and subordination would be key elements of his command and in a carrot and stick approach he stated that he had confidence in the Portuguese people and their ability to build an army as good as any in Europe. Sensing perhaps potential distrust of a foreigner he specifically asserted that he was a 'Portuguese Officer, and to the Portuguese he confers his honour and his reputation.' [54] Serving the Portuguese crown while bearing in mind Britain's interests was to be a challenging task for Beresford over the next eleven years.[55]

The means of instilling discipline and authority, combined with ensuring the ability to fight as a unit through understanding and training in military regulations, was the introduction of British officers into the Portuguese regiments. This had been agreed with Castlereagh before Beresford's departure from England, though at the time neither had perhaps envisaged the number of officers which would be required or the consequences of the inducement to be offered to those officers. Beresford had travelled with a small personal staff to Portugal. These included William Warre of the Anglo-Portuguese wine family, and Robert Arbuthnot, who had served with him previously in South America, Madeira and in the campaign of 1808–9 ending at La Coruña. Arbuthnot was now to serve Beresford as ADC and military secretary until the close of the war. Soon after taking up his appointment in Lisbon, Beresford was to make a number of appointments which not only established the way he intended to work, through a combination of British and Portuguese working together, but which were to endure throughout the war and beyond in many cases.[56] His four adjutants were the aforementioned Major William Warre, who had been born in Porto and was able to speak and write Portuguese fluently, Captain William H. Sewell, Captain Conde de Lumiares and Captain Dom José Luiz de Sousa.[57] In addition he appointed Manuel de Brito Mosinho as Adjutant General of the army and António de Lemos Pereira de Lacerda his Portuguese military secretary. Both of these men were to play a vital part in keeping the show on the road over the ensuing years.[58]

On arrival in Portugal in March 1809, Beresford was faced with a theoretically unified command but in practice a series of small forces operating of necessity independently. In addition to being poorly armed, clothed and fed, many regiments fell far short of a full complement. A report of 10 March 1809 sent to the Prince Regent contained an appendix purporting to set out the real state of the Portuguese army. In effect it identified an army based north of Lisbon to guard the city of some 16,000 with 7,500 militia under Lieutenant General António José de Miranda Henriques, and a second army of some 6,000 with 12,000 militia designed to protect Porto and the north under Bernardim Freire.[59] There were in addition garrisons in various forts and forces of a lesser size in the southern provinces. That report made no reference to the Loyal

Lusitanian Legion but in any event in view of the steps subsequently taken to raise regiments and fill existing regiments, the figures are suspect.[60] Later, following the efforts of Forjaz and Beresford combined, with the financial assistance of the British government, the annual size of the army including artillery and policemen has been calculated at between 48,000 and 53,500 during the period 1809–11.[61]

The moulding of a well-disciplined fighting force required experienced officers with the ability to drill and train recruits. Beresford secured these by obtaining their secondment from the British army, while simultaneously enforcing the retirement of those Portuguese officers not up to the task and promoting promising younger officers within the Portuguese service.[62] Obtaining men of fighting age necessitated an efficient recruiting system combined with a commissary to feed, clothe, arm and pay the soldiers. These requirements meant Beresford had to persuade the Portuguese political (both in Portugal and Brazil) and military establishment of the potential benefits if he was to make substantial progress. Self-evidently, the task could not be achieved in the short term, not least because the country was in the course of being invaded for the second time in three years, and steps needed to be taken to meet that threat. Nevertheless, immediate actions were taken which ensured the incremental improvement of the army over a surprisingly short period of time.

History did give Beresford one advantage. There had been a practice of foreigners being brought in to advise and indeed to command the Portuguese army in times of crisis. The British had sent the Marquis de Ruvigny, Earl of Galway, to assist the Portuguese during the war of the Spanish Succession. In the mid-eighteenth century, during the Seven Years War (1756–63), the Portuguese had engaged the Prussian General the Count of Schaumburg-Lippe to command their army. He effected considerable reforms with the help of British and Prussian officers, but on his dismissal many of these changes were reversed, as inimical to the ruling elite. A further attempt to reform the Portuguese army took place after reverses in the war of 1801, 'The War of the Oranges', led to Portugal giving up possession of Olivença and its surrounding territory to Spain.[63] Reference has already been made to a military commission established in the autumn of 1801 to advise on reforms with Dom Miguel Forjaz as its Secretary. Because of disagreements it did not present a formal report. Nevertheless, Forjaz produced a summary of its deliberations for the Minister for War, Dom João de Almeida. Political infighting, partly the product of the existence of both pro-British and pro-French factions at court, severely limited the reforms introduced by Almeida and his successors. A particular success was the introduction of light troops of the line, the caçadores, who were to earn their laurels in the Peninsular War.[64]

The Regent João and his ministers had sought to walk a tightrope with a view to alienating neither Britain nor France after war between those two countries resumed in 1803. Pressure from French emissaries combined with that of the Francophile party in Portugal led to the reduction in size of the Portuguese army following Dom António de Araújo's appointment as Minister for War in 1804. By 1806 there was widespread recognition of the need for further reform and an internal reorganisation was commenced in order to streamline the command and logistical supply of an army that contained perhaps 10,000–15,000 effectives; though in theory it was made up of 24 regiments of infantry, 12 regiments of cavalry, 4 regiments of artillery and 43 regiments of militia.[65] However, little had been achieved when Junot led his forces into Lisbon in November 1807; and the small gains were swept away in his subsequent dismemberment of the Portuguese army. Nevertheless, the seeds had been sown and when the time came for Beresford to institute reform and rebuild the army he was to find in Forjaz an enthusiastic and able architect for change.

The nature and size of the challenge facing Beresford as well as the Portuguese and British armies in Portugal in early March was immense. Soult was on Portugal's northern border, while Victor was on the Guadiana with the French 1st Corps and Sebastiani with the 4th Corps in the region of Salamanca, with the Spanish armies in disarray. Immediately Beresford had been appointed to command the army he had to face the invasion of Soult. Intelligence of Soult's movements was obviously fairly good, for he was able to tell Brigadier General Charles Stewart on 17 March that the French had tried unsuccessfully to cross the Minho near its embouchure but had now crossed the river higher up and were attacking through Trás-os-Montes, where Silveira was retreating in what Beresford felt was a bad start. However, he sent two officers north to see what might be done, rather plaintively hoping the French might be pressed for provisions.[66] He was obviously very concerned about the extent to which he might be able to organise the Portuguese regiments at short notice.[67]

Soult's troops arrived at Porto and captured the city on 29 March, following a difficult march through northern Portugal during which they had been continuously harassed by Portuguese regular and irregular forces.[68] Beresford declined a request to send Portuguese troops to defend that city on the basis that in their present state it would merely result in the loss of men and arms. He was aware that the city was in a state of 'the greatest anarchy and insubordination and by the latest accounts the population entirely govern the civil and military'.[69] His decision was almost certainly justified by the chaotic and vicious defence of Porto which followed the massacre of a number of Portuguese leaders, including their commander Lieutenant General Bernardim Freire and Brigadier Luis de Oliveira by fellow Portuguese.[70] Beresford discussed the question of aid to Porto with General Cradock, passing on a request for help from the Regency. While recognising it was a decision for Cradock, he urged the latter to advance a British force as far north as Leiria in an effort to dissuade Soult from attempting to march on Lisbon. In response, Cradock did advance troops from his growing army to Óbidos and Rio Maior, moving his headquarters to Leiria.[71]

Both Beresford and Cradock realised that Lisbon was the key to Portugal and that it would be important not to allow Soult join with Marshal Victor's corps, which was in Spain threatening the Portuguese frontier to the east of Lisbon. To that end Beresford directed the dispatch of 2,500 troops with Sir Robert Wilson to support the Spanish under General Cuesta on the Guadiana.[72] Victor, however, advanced towards Badajoz and Cuesta suffered a bad defeat at Medellín on 28 March and was attempting to regroup. At the end of the month of March 1809 the Allied position appeared perilous. Cuesta's defeat had opened up Andalucía to the French and the capture of Porto by Soult threatened to suffocate the rebirth of the Portuguese army, with the possibility that Soult would move on Lisbon in accordance with Napoleon's orders. While some Portuguese regular troops and a considerable force of largely untrained militia had escaped across the Douro at the time of the fall of Porto, there was disagreement as to whether the Allies should try and hold the country between the Douro and the Mondego or merely concentrate on the defence of Lisbon.

With its wonderful natural harbour, Lisbon was recognised as the key to the country, but there was considerable unease amongst the Portuguese at the prospect of the abandonment of rich and fertile countryside and its population, and concern as to the intentions of the Portuguese Regency, as well as the British political and military establishment. General Silveira expressed his reluctance to leave the people and country north of the Douro, notwithstanding Beresford's instructions that it was more important to maintain his force in retreat.[73] The issue of whether to attempt to defend Portugal on its frontiers or to withdraw to a defensible position with the objective of making the defence of Lisbon the priority was one which was to raise its head repeatedly during the next few years.

The difficulties faced by Beresford at this time are exemplified by the experiences of the Irishman, Colonel Nicholas Trant, a British officer in the Portuguese service since 1808. Trant was at Coimbra when the news of the fall of Porto came through. He advised Beresford he had barely 1,100 militia and 200 students from Coimbra at his disposal, the first in the worst possible state, never having fired a blank cartridge, the latter in no way as enthusiastic as he had anticipated. His first action on arriving in Coimbra on 28 March had been to imprison the police guard corporal who had accompanied him from Lisbon, because he had shot a courier from General Miranda on the road from Pombal. Trant had hoped to march north but this would not be possible due to a lack of preparations and he opined the *levée en masse* would be of no assistance, and there was much despondency amongst all classes of the population.[74] Trant determined to try to hold the line of the river Vouga and his little force was augmented by those who had escaped from Porto. He ordered the destruction of the bridge over the Vouga but was doubtful of his ability to check the French at the river if the enemy moved forward other than with reconnoitring parties. There were almost daily skirmishes along the rivers Vouga and the Ovar. Trant put the situation succinctly to Beresford. He explained that even after retreating southwards from Porto a forward movement with a force inferior to the enemy was required to assuage the fears of the people of the country and to inspire confidence in his own troops, who were by no means at his disposal following recent events, and a move forward was needed to calm their suspicion of 'every movement of mine'. Clearly Trant was concerned that his own troops could turn on him and his officers if he retreated further, a not unsurprising fear given recent events prior to and during the siege of Porto.[75] A mutiny by artillery sergeants required them to be treated as prisoners. Trant was clearly in a difficult position.

The position regarding the assembling of the ordenança was even more dire than the problems Beresford and his commanders faced with the army and the militia. Once again we have Trant's opinion, this time that the *levée en masse* was of no assistance. The ordenança would assemble to defend their own village but were not inclined to form a disposable force. The Inspector General of Ordenança north of the Mondego had fled at the first approach of the French, and when Lieuteneant General de Mello ordered Major Albuquerque to join Trant with 8,000 ordenança, only 2,000 arrived. Desertion meant that only 200 remained a day after their arrival and this number had been reduced to 50 on the following day. Trant, however, found Albuquerque a most zealous fellow and made him an Inspector General. He also found time to praise other Portuguese officers.[76]

Trant may have been proposing to take on the French under a disadvantage, but he clearly did not lack initiative and even confidence in these early days for he sought Portuguese cavalry from Beresford in the beginning of May with a view to delivering a left hook around the back of the French as Soult advanced south from Porto.[77] He even envisaged trying to take Porto by a *coup de main*.[78] A year later, when Trant was threatened with removal from the Royal Staff Corps unless he returned to Britain, Wellington intervened telling Liverpool that 'there is no officer the loss of whose services in this country would be more sensibly felt by the government and the people, and Marshal Beresford and myself, than those of Col. Trant'.[79] Wellington won the argument for the time being, though in 1813 Trant did have to return to England.

By early April Beresford was proceeding with his staff to army headquarters at Tomar (some 140 kilometres north of Lisbon) with a view to ascertaining the strength and quality of the troops there and organising new levies in that city. The reorganisation of the Portuguese army was about to begin with the assistance of British officers. In this task he was greatly aided by the arrival of Benjamin D'Urban, whom he made his Quartermaster General and who was to remain an integral part of Beresford's command structure throughout the war and for some years thereafter.[80]

Beresford's approach to the rebuilding of the army was multi-faceted and indeed comprehensive. He directed that each regiment should prepare accurate records of men and equipment.[81] He engaged William Warre to translate the British army regulations into Portuguese and these were subsequently published. Immediate implementation of those regulations was begun and Warre reported on 27 April that under the instruction of the British officers the Portuguese troops were 'coming on very well'.[82] The importance of this move was clearly shown when the time came for the British and Portuguese forces to work together. As early as 24 March Beresford had begun to introduce an informal brigading of regiments under British as well as Portuguese officers.[83]

The use of and performance of the British officers will be dealt with in a later chapter, but Beresford had been authorised initially to engage up to twenty-four such officers (perhaps one for each infantry regiment). That number was to prove woefully inadequate and was considerably augmented in due course, though when Beresford first sought additional officers from the British army the then Commander in Chief, Sir David Dundas, told Wellesley that the King's instructions were not to exceed the twenty-four initially approved.[84] These original appointees were given one step up in the British service and a further step in the Portuguese service; thus a captain became a major in the British service and a Lieutenant Colonel in that of Portugal; at the same time retaining their seniority in the British army. Later appointees only received a step in the Portuguese army. Not all twenty-four original officers came out from England and Cradock was asked to facilitate the move to the Portuguese army of those he could spare who were requested by Beresford. From 9 March onwards these British officers were being appointed in the Portuguese army.[85] While Cradock clearly facilitated Beresford in respect of the request for officers, eighteen of the twenty-one who availed of the opportunity to transfer at this time were Lieutenants or Ensigns, whereas what Beresford desperately needed was officers with substantial experience.[86] Beresford and Cradock would seem to have got on reasonably well, even if Cradock proved reluctant to move the troops under his command too far from Lisbon, for later Cradock's only son, John Hobart Cradock, was to serve in Lisbon as Beresford's aide-de-camp.[87]

While witness accounts suggest considerable progress with training was made in the first five or six weeks following Beresford's appointment as Marshal, work was cut short by the need to move the forces north as part of the Anglo-Portuguese campaign against General Soult, which began in May.[88]

Allied to the introduction of a strenuous training regime, Beresford moved quickly to impose his authority on the army. Nowhere was the lack of discipline and the disregard for authority more forcefully demonstrated within weeks of Beresford's arrival than in the defence of northern Portugal. Silveira had abandoned Chaves following a disagreement on whether to stand or withdraw from that town in early March, which split his force in two; and he himself proved reluctant to implement Beresford's order to withdraw south of the Douro with a view to protecting Lisbon, on the basis that his force would be of greater use maintaining itself in and protecting the northern provinces. Further, he argued a number of his officers would desert if he retired south, for nine-tenths of his officer corps were from the two northern provinces (Minho and Trás-os-Montes) and would be unwilling to leave their houses and families to the mercy of the enemy.[89]

General discipline was imposed forcefully, with even small infractions leading to serious consequences. Court martials became a regular feature, not just for desertion, which was a serious problem, but for other substantial misdemeanours. The Portuguese court martial process was extremely cumbersome and Beresford moved to replace it with a more streamlined version. Once again Beresford approached this subject with a carrot and stick. Exhortation was matched with consequences for failure to obey. This was vital because the lack of discipline was not just a problem in the ranks but had to be tackled at officer level as well; for Beresford was faced with a situation where officers frequently took leave without the permission of their superiors. In the case of desertion the consequences were usually, but not always, dire. He made it clear that a soldier's duty was to fight for the nation, and a failure would be punished.[90] Beresford left no doubt that the practice of soldiers selling equipment was prohibited, and would be punished severely. Likewise, he made it clear to officers that the practice of brutality towards the ranks would not be tolerated and he outlawed it and provided that infractions would be severely punished.

In order to impose a system of immediate justice Beresford demanded the replacement of the Portuguese court martial processes, telling Forjaz that if they were not changed it would be impossible to introduce discipline to the army, declaring that the trial of a deserter which 'should have taken five minutes took five days'.[91] The core of the problem for Beresford was extensive pre-trial and trial processes reduced to writing and the fact that a decision then had to be referred to the Council of War before any sentence was carried out. On his own authority Beresford short-circuited the trial and post-sentence procedures, and it was only some time later that authorisation for his own procedures was received from Prince João, and even then it was limited to when the army was on campaign, though Beresford seems to have continued to apply it in other circumstances.[92] In order to get the process under way, Beresford appointed a well established lawyer Judge Advocate for the army, José António de Oliveira Leite de Barros.[93]

Initial sentences were severe. An early case, which was determined on 20 April 1809, resulted in ten years' hard labour being imposed on a soldier who refused to march on the basis that it was illegal to move a soldier more than three leagues from his encampment.[94] Insubordination could involve a prison sentence, such as the one-year imprisonment in the Torre de Belém imposed on Major Manoel Xavier Botelho in January 1810.[95] Desertion usually, but not always, resulted in execution by shooting, as Beresford insisted that the alternative of garrotting be terminated.

Beresford needed to tackle other aspects of army organisation involving both personnel and logistics. Recruitment went on remorselessly under the hand of Forjaz, but with Beresford very often hounding him.[96] Where Beresford played a major role involved the removal of non-performing officers and their replacement by either experienced officers from the British service or young, active and interested Portuguese. Many of the latter filled the junior officer ranks initially, but appointments made in the first few years of the war were later to rise to high positions. Beresford showed a determination to promote on merit, which was both feared and admired. On initial enquiry Beresford found that many of the junior officers (captains and lieutenants) had been *in situ* for upwards of thirty years, or in some cases much longer. Others had risen to command regiments, but they were now too old and in some cases too infirm to face the rigours of a campaign. Some of their appointments had been purely political, with no real intention of pursuing a military career, but in any event many were too old to march with their regiments and deemed incapable of performing the training or leading in battle. The process of weeding out those deemed incapable or unwilling to perform their functions was commenced immediately.

To counter a practice of leave taken on the grounds of illness, Beresford persuaded Forjaz to support the introduction of a system whereby those officers who reported sick had to go before a special board of physicians who in turn reported to a panel of officers empowered to make the decision on whether or not to grant leave.[97] Officers who went absent without leave were liable to be demoted to the ranks.[98] In March and April 1809, Beresford began the process of remodelling the officer corps of the Portuguese army ultimately reaching a situation where each infantry regiment had a balance of British and Portuguese officers. Nowhere was this more noticeable than at the top of the regimental command structure, where frequently first and second in command would come from different nationalities. The Ordens do Dia (Orders of the Day) reveal the promotions made. Not unnaturally, the promotion of British officers caused some resentment, which Beresford met by assuring the Portuguese that the appointments were only temporary as the officers involved would retain their British rank.[99]

While Beresford did not hesitate to remove or suspend officers he also moved quickly to praise those who had performed valiantly, even in defeat. Brigadier António Teixeira Rebelo, the Inspector of Artillery, was suspended on 8 April in order to establish better discipline. A few days later Ordens do Dia were published commending Brigadier António Marcelino da Vitória for his part in the defence of Porto and a pension directed for the only daughter of Captain António Pereira Vahia who had died for his country at Chaves.[100]

The struggle to equip the army was compounded by the difficulties faced in transporting supplies, whether of provisions or equipment. Captain Alexander Dickson, who was to play a significant role in the utilisation and direction of artillery in the war, arrived in Portugal on 2 April 1809, joining the Portuguese service as a lieutenant colonel. It became immediately apparent that the Portuguese army needed to tackle the problem of transporting guns and ammunition. His diary contains many entries reflecting these requirements from the moment of his arrival. Musket ammunition could only be carried in quantity on the backs of mules or in ox wains, both of which were hard to procure. Parties were sent out to secure these but there were still shortages and the decision was taken to transport as much as possible by water. The guns required horses, or in some cases mules, to draw them. Once again there was a shortage. Captain Cleves of the King's German Legion artillery was sent to Tangiers to acquire horses, but the mission was not a success as the animals there were found not to be suitable. A better source for horses was Ireland and on 7 April 300 'excellent horses' were landed and distributed to the brigades of guns, having been shod and fitted for harness on arrival. Provisions had to be brought to the army then and later in the war from Lisbon, a continual logistics challenge. Likewise, the army was frequently dependent on forage being brought to the front.[101] This problem was by no means unique to the Portuguese army, with Cradock advising Beresford in mid April that the forward movement of his force had been held back by a lack of supplies, forage and straw.[102]

Within days of Beresford landing at Lisbon to take up his post as Commander in Chief of the Portuguese army, the British government had determined to send a further British army to Portugal. Towards the end of March, Wellesley was told privately that he was to command this army and it was announced officially on 2 April.[103] A further 20,000 troops were to be sent to augment the force already there under Cradock, making a total of about 30,000 British soldiers. Wellesley had left the army in Portugal in late August 1808, citing an obligation to take up again his position as Chief Secretary for Ireland, his substitute having passed away while Wellesley was on active service. While factually this was the situation, there is little doubt that he wished to remove himself from an environment where he had been superseded in command and where he was concerned at the strategy being followed by Dalrymple.

However, absence from the Peninsula did not mean that Wellesley's views were not sought and given on what should be undertaken there in the period between September 1808 and the spring of the following year. Prior to Vimeiro he had advocated that the British raise, organise and pay an army in Portugal to be made up of 30,000 Portuguese and 20,000 British troops, including 4,000–5,000 cavalry.[104] A month later, in the wake of the Convention of Cintra, Wellesley, in the knowledge that the government intended to send a force of at least 10,000 to help the Spanish under Castaños, was suggesting a British force of 5,000 be kept in Lisbon and Elvas, while the remainder of the army then in Portugal (about 10,000) would be reinforced with a further 10,000 men from England. He was not sanguine about Spanish success and he envisaged that it might well be necessary for the British to evacuate the Peninsula 'and that retreat must be the sea'. While the use of the Asturias was seen as a possibility which would secure any line of retreat, clearly Lisbon offered this option too.[105]

In a memorandum of 7 March 1809, Wellesley returned to the theme of British military involvement in Portugal, arguing now for a British force of 30,000 rather than the 20,000 advocated previously. At the same time he suggested the development of the Portuguese militia.[106] Strategically, Wellesley saw the army in Portugal as linking with the Spanish armies in Galicia and Andalucía to create a barrier to French domination of the Peninsula and to provide a springboard for future advance. The decision to send Wellesley back to Portugal was taken at cabinet on 26 March and on the same day a decision was made to offer Cradock the command at Gibraltar.[107] As soon as the formal announcement of his appointment to head the expedition to Portugal was made, Wellesley resigned as Chief Secretary for Ireland on 4 April and having embarked for Portugal on 16 April arrived in Lisbon on 22 April. Part of his army had arrived before him but regiments designated for his army at this time were continuing to disembark at Lisbon over the next few weeks.

Wellesley did not let the grass grow under his feet on arrival in Portugal. He assumed command of the British forces from Cradock (who soon sailed for Gibraltar), and made two significant staff appointments; placing Charles Stewart as Adjutant General and Colonel George Murray as Quartermaster General. He requested Beresford to come to Lisbon for what was in effect a council of war, in order to determine how best to move against Soult while simultaneously safeguarding Lisbon should Victor move against it with the 1st Corps then on the Spanish border.[108]

On 27 April they met in Lisbon (with Cradock still in attendance) and decided the strategy which was subsequently followed almost without deviation, namely to strike at Soult before he and Victor could effect any merger of their respective forces. This was a strategy which Beresford had suggested to Cradock on 28 March but which Cradock had rejected on the basis that it would put Lisbon at risk.[109] Beresford was requested to move the Portuguese army from Tomar to Coimbra and simultaneously Wellesley ordered the English force to march there from Leiria where it was in the course of assembling.[110] A containing force was left at Lisbon and an outer screen under Major General John Randoll MacKenzie pushed towards Abrantes to watch for any sign of Victor moving forward from the Spanish frontier, and if necessary to defend the line of the Zêzere. On 27 April, Wellesley was presented to the regency at the Palace of Inquisition in the Rossio and two days later, on 29 April, he was appointed Marshal-General of Portugal, assuming overall command of both armies. He made it clear to Beresford that he wished the latter to take the lead in all matters dealing with the Portuguese government. Their relationship over the remainder of the war was one of mutual support and was evidenced by a lack of friction.[111]

On 2 May, Wellesley and Beresford were at Coimbra and a review of the two armies was held there a few days later. Beresford felt he had made progress with the Portuguese regiments and Warre, while wishing they had had more time, felt they were coming along well under the instruction of the British officers.[112] Wellesley and other British officers were not as impressed, the British commander observing to Beresford that his troops made a bad 'ligne' this morning at Review, the battalions very weak, none of them with more than 300 men, the body of them, particularly the 10th, very bad 'and the officers worse than anything I have seen.'[113] Beresford noted with regret that some battalions had paraded so weakly, observing that the English officers should have 'brought them into some method'. He felt the march from Tomar might have been partly responsible but still felt they were a stout body of men capable of being made into soldiers. He used the occasion to plead for Wellesley to lend him more British officers as 'in their own I have not the slightest dependence'.[114]

In a slightly more nuanced vein, Major the Hon. Charles Edward Cocks, later to become one of Wellesley's favourite and most effective intelligence officers, observed: 'The bridge over the Vouga in our front is occupied by the Portuguese. Their troops are superior to what I expected, at least in appearance, but I fear their officers are bad.'[115] Nonetheless, Wellesley must have been sufficiently confident to brigade two Portuguese regiments (10th and 16th together with a detachment of 1st Portuguese Grenadiers) with English regiments, and the 16th was to show considerable promise at a brisk encounter with the French at Grijó during the advance on Porto.[116] Wellesley was sufficiently impressed to tell Villiers, 'they tell me that the Portuguese riflemen, the students I believe behaved remarkably well' and referring separately to the 16th Portuguese regiment under Colonel Doyle 'this last regiment behaved remarkably well'.[117]

Leaving a mixed Anglo-Portuguese force under Major General J.R. Mackenzie to cover Lisbon against any sudden move from Spain by Marshal Victor, Wellesley determined on a three-pronged attack on Marshal Soult's force, centred in Porto.[118] While the main army (of some 20,000 infantry and 1,400 horse) would take the central or main road northwards, a force under General Hill was dispatched along the coastal route. Beresford's force was designated to head north east via Viseu and Lamego with a view to crossing the Douro if possible, joining up with Silveira's Portuguese and cutting off Soult from a retreat east into the province of León in north west Spain. Before leaving Coimbra, news had reached Wellesley and Beresford of the capture of Amarante by a French force under General Loison with Silveira being driven back to Lamego.[119]

It is not clear whether the commanders of the Anglo-Portuguese army thought Loison's brigade was the advance guard and was an indication that Soult was planning to head east to Spain, but rumours abounded, and Soult later claimed in his *Mémoires* that he had formed the intention to retreat from Porto into Spain rather than to try to defend the city.[120] Wellesley was very conscious that the strategy devised might expose Beresford's relatively small contingent of between 6,000 and 7,000 (the latter figure probably included his small cavalry detachment) to the full force of Soult's army, and if a crossing of the Douro did not prove practical, then at least he was to prevent the French coming south over the Douro.[121]

Beresford was aware that if Soult's entire force moved east against him, he would not be able to prevent him passing, but with considerable foresight suggested that if Wellesley attacked Porto, and then detached to his right such force as he could spare, the French could be stopped in their retreat and forced to abandon their guns and baggage; in the process probably losing a great number of men.[122] Wellesley was adamant that if Soult moved east from Porto with his entire army, Beresford should not attempt to obstruct him for he did not wish 'to see a single British brigade supported by 6,000–8,000 Portuguese exposed to be attacked by the French army in any but a very good post'.[123] Accordingly, Wellesley's instructions to Beresford were specific. He was not to endanger his force unless he felt strongly he would defeat the enemy:

If the French should weaken their corps about Amaranthe [*sic*] and Villa Real so as to give you any reason to hope that you can do anything against them, then I wish you to attack them and take any opportunity of getting possession of either of these points. But remember that you are a Commander in Chief of an army & must not be beat & therefore do not undertake anything with your troops if you have not some strong hopes of success.[124]

Beresford's force was designated to include the 3rd Brigade under Major General Tilson, but this force of some 1,500 men of the 60th, 87th, 88th and Portuguese grenadiers was delayed amid suggestions that Tilson did not take gladly to being under Beresford's command.[125] Beresford expressed his disappointment to Wellesley at Tilson's failure to respond to the order to join him with alacrity, more particularly as he failed also to communicate with Beresford on receiving the order.[126] Tilson had made it clear he did not wish to serve under Beresford, and in making his report to Wellesley, Beresford castigated Tilson's performance and made repeated pleas to Wellesley to accede to Tilson's request.[127] Tilson's wish not to serve under Beresford was clearly not personal but based on the principle of not having to serve under an officer who had been promoted Major General at the same time as himself.[128]

Following the expedition to clear northern Portugal of the French, Tilson asked to be allowed to resign the command of his brigade and go to England, making the further request that in future he would be employed in the Portuguese army, and therefore under Beresford, but presumably with the step up in rank to Lieutenant General. Wellesley was not prepared to agree to this proposition and Tilson was urged to reconsider his position, being reminded that he must obey the orders of his superior and commanding officer. He gave Tilson leave to resign his command, which Tilson opted to do, though he subsequently sought and obtained leave to withdraw his resignation acknowledging that he had been mistaken regarding his responsibilities.[129] Tilson served under Hill at the battle of Talavera later in 1809, but he was to leave the Peninsula the following year, though returning again later in the war.

Wellesley's successful march on Porto and the surprise crossing of the Douro, causing Soult to flee eastwards on 12 May, is well known. Before setting off from Coimbra with the main army on 7 May, Wellesley started Beresford on his flanking march a day earlier, given the greater distance he had to cover. Beresford reached Viseu on 7 May where he was joined by Wilson and two battalions drawn from Almeida. Beresford proceeded to Lamego on 8 May and the Portuguese regiments of infantry and part of the artillery designated to join the Marshal's column assembled at Lamego by 9 May, while Tilson's brigade had reached Viseu.[130] Urgent instructions were despatched to Tilson to join Beresford at Lamego by 11 May.[131] On 8 May Loison had reached Vila Real and on 10 May he closed up on Mesão Frio. On 10 May, Beresford sent Silveira and a force including the 6th Caçadores over the Douro at Peso da Régua. Loison was engaged and thrown back on Amarante. Beresford followed with his main force, crossing the Douro on 11 May and on approaching Amarante the next day Loison retreated to the far side of the River Tamega to a position of considerable strength.

On 12 May, Wellesley not only captured Porto but put a considerable force under Major General Sir John Murray across the Douro upstream to get behind Soult, who now marched east to join with Loison in the hope of marching to Spain to link up with the French forces there.[132] Murray did not seek to stop Soult, perhaps fearing his own force was too small. Soult had expected Loison to stand his ground at Amarante, but instead he retired north west to Guimarães on 13 May, thus leaving Soult's army in a potential trap between Wellesley and Beresford.[133] In difficult conditions Beresford's army, including Tilson's brigade which had joined it early that day, crossed the Tamega with the river rising fast because of the rain.[134] The crossing took four hours and was led by the 60th, 87th and 88th regiments from Tilson's brigade, but two companies were unable to cross and a number of men were lost.[135]

Much of Amarante had been burnt by the retreating French. Soult, realising his danger, destroyed his artillery and abandoning heavy baggage marched to join Loison in Guimarães. Meanwhile, Wellesley was still bringing equipment, including guns and supplies, across the Douro and combined with the exertions of the army this meant he needed a day in Porto before setting off in pursuit of Soult. The latter, with his full force, headed for Braga and Beresford, whose advance guard had come across Soult's abandoned baggage and destroyed guns on 14 May, when he learnt of the recapture of Porto anticipated that Wellesley would head to Braga. Beresford left a screening force in Amarante and proceeded himself to Chaves by forced march, reaching it late on the evening of 16 May with only part of an exhausted force after three days marching in the rain.[136]

On the same day, 14 May, he ordered Silveira to Montalegre. The objective was to deny Soult the Montalegre and Chaves exit routes to Spain. While the latter was achieved, the delay in Silveira's troops reaching Montalegre left open a door for Soult to escape. The French Marshal, now aware that Wellesley was coming up behind him to Braga, ordered Loison in turn to destroy his artillery and the men to abandon anything other than essential food and a reserve of ammunition. With the help of local guides the French army led a desperate but ultimately successful escape to Orense in Spain over the mountains, via Montalegre; Silveira's force only arriving as the French were leaving on the afternoon of 17 May.[137] Though the Portuguese were themselves much wearied, they picked up some French stragglers.

Those of Beresford's troops who had reached Chaves were exhausted and needed to rest on 17 April while he waited for Tilson's brigade and that of Bacelar to catch up.[138] On 18 May, Beresford did march from Chaves to Monterey, catching up with some of the French near Ginzo, but Soult's main force by now was far to the east and pursuit was abandoned the following day on Wellesley's orders, perhaps because of a lack of supplies but also alarming news had reached the latter from MacKenzie that Victor's corps was on the move into the Tagus valley, having expelled the Loyal Lusitanian Legion from the bridge at Alcantara.[139] While Victor had indeed captured the bridgehead at Alcantara, the news that he was advancing into Portugal turned out to be false. Beresford's exhausted force then returned south to Castelo Branco via Lamego picking up those abandoned on the route north. Beresford himself then proceeded to meet Wellesley at Lamego on 27 May to take stock of the position and coordinate plans for the future.

There was a suggestion in some quarters that Beresford might have driven his forces with greater intensity so as to shut the door on Soult's escape, but such comment fails to recognise the nature of the extended marches undertaken in appalling weather conditions. Beresford had ordered Silveira with a body of troops to Montalegre to try to deny Soult's force that road into Spain, but Silveira had reached the town only as the French departed. Ironically it was Silveira, who was jealous of Beresford's command, that later sought to blame Beresford for the escape of part of the French army.[140] Wellesley was not critical of Beresford, indeed he had had to stop to rest his own troops and obtain supplies after the capture of Porto, but Beresford seems to have been sensitive to the criticism, for writing to his half-sister Anne on 26 May he referred to the escape of some of the French 'for which I need not be much criticised, as it is really wonderful how they escaped, tho in so miserable a condition having abandoned everything and trusting simply to their getting off by their lightness'.[141] If anything, Beresford perhaps drove his men too hard, as is witnessed by the large number of losses suffered through exhaustion on the march from Amarante to Chaves adverted by then Major (later Field Marshal) Hugh Gough.[142] Wellesley realised the reality of the situation echoing Beresford's remarks to Anne, when he wrote to Castlereagh:

> It is obvious, however, that if an army throws away all its cannon, equipments and baggage, and everything which can strengthen it, and can enable it to act together as a body; and abandons all those who are entitled to its protection, but add to its weight and impede its progress; it must be able to march by roads through which it cannot be followed, with any prospect of being overtaken, by an army which has not made the same sacrifices.[143]

The campaign had been a huge success. Wellesley had achieved his objective, even if the elusive Soult had escaped with part of his corps. Within two weeks of leaving Coimbra the Anglo-Portuguese army had driven a French army out of Portugal in a precipitous flight causing it to abandon artillery, carriages, horses and large numbers of men, not to mention seized property. A number of regiments of the Portuguese army had performed well in the first campaign of 1809. Further, while Wellesley and Beresford had been chasing Soult out of northern Portugal, the Loyal Lusitanian Legion and the militia of Idanha-a-Nova had proved brave and tenacious when holding off Marshal Victor's much larger French corps at Alcantara for nine hours, before retiring in good order on 14 May. Beresford, in his order of the day, praised the conduct of Colonel Mayne and the Legion observing that: 'The army will see, that although troops are sometimes obliged to retreat, at the same time they may cover themselves with glory, and merit the greatest praise.'[144]

Soult's force was degraded and no longer an immediate threat. Wellesley and Beresford were now able to turn their attentions elsewhere. Wellesley needed to meet the threat posed by Victor and King Joseph, whereas Beresford badly needed time to train an army that had begun to show its metal, so much so that when Mackenzie had expressed the view the Portuguese would not fight Wellesley retorted: 'You are in error in supposing the Portuguese troops will not fight. One battalion has behaved remarkably well with me, and I know of no troops that could behave better than the Lusitanian legion.'[145]

CONTINUING REFORM OF THE PORTUGUESE ARMY: THE SUMMER CAMPAIGN OF 1809 AND PREPARATIONS FOR THE DEFENCE OF PORTUGAL

7

> *When I arrived here the army was in a terrible state...One found it without*
> *discipline and without subordination. The soldiers were lacking in confidence in*
> *their officers who were negligent in their duties and had an attitude and behaviour*
> *which encouraged insubordination among the soldiers. There was completely lacking*
> *in the officers any strength or application of military laws, and the army I saw was*
> *an ungovernable machine.*[1]

Following the successful campaign on the Douro, Beresford continued the serious business of reforming and rebuilding the Portuguese army. In this he was helped by both Forjaz and Wellesley in enforcing structural and command change; and over the years by several hundred British officers in drilling and training the infantry, cavalry and artillery. Portuguese officers, trained in accordance with the British regulations, increasingly played a part in training their own men.

Castlereagh's letter to Beresford of 15 February confirming his appointment to command and organise the Portuguese army had merely specified 'a due proportion of British Officers will be appointed to assist you, and a supply of arms to the extent of 10,000 stand has been for some time embarked ...'[2] The number of officers allocated at the outset was twenty-four,

75

but Beresford soon realised this number would not be nearly enough. The original twenty-four officers came both from Britain and from the British army in Portugal.[3] Those already with the British army in Portugal who chose to join Beresford included Lieutenant Colonels Blunt and Campbell.[4] Many of those who applied from the British army in Portugal were relatively junior and Beresford needed more senior officers, not just for training and disciplinary purposes but to lead the regiments and brigades in battle.[5] The strongest attraction for those in the British army to join the Portuguese army may well have been double or later single step promotion, but an additional incentive was that serving officers in the British army also received pay both for their rank at home and in respect of their Portuguese appointment. Many of them elected to have their British salary paid at home while living in Portugal on their Portuguese salary.[6]

By early April 1809, if not earlier, Beresford had realised he would need many more than twenty-four British officers if he was to train the Portuguese army to a sufficient level of competence. His request for a total of 150 such officers caused some concern at government level, even though it had been suggested originally by Castlereagh.[7] On Wellesley's advice, Beresford was offered a further twelve to fourteen officers, though Wellesley was quick to realise once he arrived in Portugal that this number would be insufficient.[8] Furthermore, those now accepted to join the Portuguese army were only given a step up in rank in that army, a far less attractive proposition than hitherto. As late as 23 April Beresford was telling his sister, Lady Anne Beresford, that 'officers in abundance are volunteering to serve under me in the Portuguese service, nay even from the Guards, two colonels of which have offered their services'.[9] However, he realised that notwithstanding the British commitment to Portugal and to rebuilding the Portuguese army, it was not going to be easy to obtain a sufficient number of officers with the requisite experience to train the Portuguese army, irrespective of whether they were to come from the British Isles or from the British forces in Portugal, for he went on:

> As usual however at home after agreeing to everything before I left them, and directing Cradock to give me in officers every assistance he could, they now throw some doubt on the propriety of my having officers from regiments on service, and propose to send them to me from England, alas they propose making it a business of patronage and they have thereby put a very great delay in my advancing the discipline of the Portuguese troops.

He had received notice of this objection from Brigadier General Stewart some days previously and had immediately remonstrated to Castlereagh.[10] Apart from the question of delay, it is clear from his letter to his sister that Beresford was concerned that appointments would not be made on merit, a principle of which he was a steady advocate.

Towards the end of 1809, Beresford was to revise the figure of British officers he required slightly, seeking a total of 179 officers, being five for each infantry regiment, three for each regiment of caçadores and three for each of the twelve regiments of cavalry.[11] Now, however, he had a far more pressing problem, for although the government had approved the appointment of thirty more British officers to the Portuguese army in May, it was on the basis of only one step up in the Portuguese service, but even that move was threatened by a suggestion by Wellesley that all promotion should be done away with as it was liable to cause command difficulties when the armies were operating together.[12] Beresford was seriously concerned that this suggestion would mean that not only would he not be able to persuade a sufficient number of British army officers to join the Portuguese service but that those, other than the original twenty-four appointees who had joined in expectation of promotion in the British army, would now resign.

Beresford raised this concern with Wellesley in mid May and his apprehension was soon proved to have a valid foundation. While the British government refused to modify its new stance on the matter, a compromise of sorts was eventually achieved, though not before the number of resignations had threatened to destroy the work Beresford and his fellow officers were seeking to undertake. The compromise involved an assurance that the quality of service in the Portuguese army would be taken into account when promotions were being considered in the British army.[13] In coming to its decision the government appears to have had regard for a change of heart by Wellesley, who realised following further representations from Beresford how important the presence of sufficient British officers in the Portuguese army would be for the common cause, and the one step up provision was continued.[14] Later in the year Beresford and Wellington (for he had by then been created Viscount Wellington in August 1809), in a determined effort to prevent a drain of British officers from the Portuguese army, mounted a strong campaign which clearly persuaded the the government that British officers should not be allowed to leave the Portuguese service for the purpose of rejoining British regiments without the express permission of the commander on the spot, and any such decision was at his discretion.[15] As will be seen in ensuing chapters, British officers continued to apply to serve in the Portuguese army on the basis of a one step increase in rank there.

Promoted rank was only one of the problems facing Beresford in his effort to establish a committed officer corps in the Portuguese army. At the other end of the scale he had to deal with those whose primary interest was promotion rather than being part of the great drive to reform the Portuguese army, and he did not hesitate to refuse commissions.[16] The process whereby an officer might transfer from one service to another was straightforward, save that it depended on the preparedness of the commanding officer of the British regiment in question to agree that he could spare the man seeking to make the move. The correspondence is littered with requests where consent by Wellesley is followed by correspondence with regimental commanding officers resulting in agreement or refusal to let a man transfer.[17] This would seem to be indicative that the one step promotion in the Portuguese service only was sufficiently attractive to lure a considerable number of officers to transfer, for by the end of the war upwards of 300 had done so.[18]

The appointment of British officers to train and discipline the troops was only one facet of the challenge facing Beresford. He also had to remove Portuguese officers lacking in ability from causes such as incompetence and physical infirmity. At the outset there is little doubt that the British view of the calibre of many of the Portuguese officers was not complimentary. Warre expressed it thus: 'The officers for the most part, are detestable, mean, ignorant and self sufficient. It is incredible the little mean intrigues, the apathy, and want of military sentiment, the Marshal has had to work against. Nothing but a very severe discipline can overcome these, and which I hope he will follow.'[19] He did, however, acknowledge the promise of the young Portuguese officers.[20]

The testimony of Warre, while it may well reflect national prejudice, is important because he and his family spent much time in Portugal. He understood the language and was sympathetic to the cause. He was certainly not biased against the Portuguese nation, as is revealed by his complimentary remarks regarding their troops in general from an early date, recognising their potential:

> The Portuguese troops immediately under the instruction of British Officers are coming on very well. I could have wished we had been allowed more time, but even now have great hopes of some corps. The men may be made anything we please of, with proper management, and, wherever I have had authority, I have soon settled the little mean jealousies and tricks of the officers, and without, I hope, gaining much ill will. I will endeavour to combine inflexible firmness with politeness of manner. I know it is the only way to make these fellows respect you, and the mass of officers is miserable indeed. This, however, will in time be altered. Merit is the great recommendation with the General, not grey hairs and numbers of years service, however much to be respected, for these subalterns, some of whom should be anything but soldiers.[21]

The *reformado* (retired) Portuguese officers were replaced not just by British officers but by mostly young Portuguese now being trained by the British. Between the time of his appointment as Commander in Chief in March and the end of July 1809, at least 215 Portuguese officers were retired and replaced by a combination of British and Portuguese officers. While this caused disquiet in Portugal, critically Forjaz stood by Beresford. Though many of the newly appointed Portuguese were at the levels of lieutenant and captain, from the outset Beresford seems to have attempted to strike a balance in the upper echelons of each Portuguese infantry regiment; so that where the Lieutenant Colonel was British the Major would be Portuguese, or vice versa. Thus infantry brigades were commanded by those such as Ashworth, Bradford, Campbell and Pack, as well as Lecor, Fonseca, Palmeirim and Bernardim Ribeiros. The cavalry commanders were Hawker, Madden, Póvoa and Barbacena. The artillery was under the command of Colonel Alexander Dickson, who was later to play a pivotal role for Wellington in the liberation of Spain and the invasion of France. Major General John Hamilton was appointed Inspector-General of the army, and from early 1810 was to command the 'Portuguese' Division formed in late 1809. That division was made up of two or sometimes three Portuguese brigades and usually served with the 2nd Division. The Conde de Sampāio was appointed Inspector-General of the cavalry in April 1809.

The process of making appointments to the Portuguese army was a little cumbersome, for while in theory all promotions were in the hands of Beresford, as Commander in Chief, they were subject to the approval of the Regent, Prince Joāo. This meant that recommendations had to be sent to Brazil and then confirmed, a process which of necessity took a number of months. Until a confirmation was received the promotion remained conditional. The process also gave rise to another serious issue, for in August 1810 Beresford discovered that members of the Regency were making their own recommendations to Prince João without reference to Beresford. The Prince Regent having made appointments not sought by Beresford, the Marshal protested in the strongest terms against those advancements, requiring Forjaz to withdraw the recommendations in question and to undertake not to interfere in this aspect in future.[22] Further issues arose concerning appointments which Prince João was persuaded to make by those at Court, but Beresford brooked no opposition to his control of promotions; no more than he had on the question of discipline and the court martial process.[23]

Likewise, Beresford insisted that he, and he alone, should determine whether any Portuguese or British officer be allowed to resign from the Portuguese service. It was not merely a matter for the officer in question. When a specific issue arose in the shape of the attempt by Francisco de Mello to resign his commission, Wellesley supported Beresford's authority to determine the application. Forjaz also agreed that this was a matter within the Marshal's remit, but even then Beresford insisted on getting a ruling from the Prince Regent in Brazil. and his authority was confirmed on 17 May 1810, some five months after de Mello had sought to resign. This interval shows just how long it took to obtain a decision when a matter was referred to Rio de Janeiro, and of course consideration of an issue might mean it could be many months before a decision was made. However, on this occasion another issue fundamental to Beresford's authority over the army had been resolved in his favour.[24]

Relations between British and Portuguese officers varied, depending on the individuals involved. Although there were some serious incidents of both disobedience and personal antagonism, the records suggest that these were not widespread. Some of these stories involve merely personal disagreements; others breaches of discipline. Disobedience was not a one-way street and there are recorded instances of British officers being unwilling to submit to orders from Portuguese senior officers while training and in camp. One example of personal antagonisms (there is insufficient evidence to class it as a nationally motivated attack) and three examples of conflict in the course of training and on the battlefield will give a flavour of the sort of breakdown that might occur.

Edward Costello tells a most amusing story in his memoirs. He had gone to purchase rum at the headquarters of the 52nd Regiment when he fell in with a rather quarrelsome soldier from the 3rd Caçadores on his return. The Portuguese soldier threatened Costello with his bayonet whereupon Costello struck him hard. Other caçadores then approached Costello, allegedly yelling 'kill the English dog'. Just in time a party of men from the 52nd appeared and rescued Costello.[25]

The first example of a breakdown in discipline concerns the unfortunate Major James Warde Oliver, a Lieutenant Colonel attached to the 10th Portuguese Regiment of line, and who was to die later at the second siege of Badajoz. In October 1809 he was accused of abusing officers, tearing the epaulettes off the shoulders of one of them and striking soldiers in the Regiment. He denied abusive conduct, though agreeing that he might have spoken harshly in the field where necessary in order to gain the confidence and goodwill of the officers. Explaining the incident with the epaulettes, he indicated that he had spoken with an officer who was four paces out of line about ten or a dozen times as loud as he could, he then rode up to him, took him by the arm and put him in line during which time the epaulette came off and fell to the ground.

By May 1811 Oliver was with the 14th Regiment of line, then before Badajoz in the first Anglo-Portuguese siege of that city, when a controversy arose concerning the alleged mistreatment of Spanish lemonade sellers in the lines by a Major Lacerda (who apparently was already under arrest but clearly at liberty, presumably on parole). Lacerda refused to be questioned by Oliver on the incident whereupon Oliver struck him. For his own conduct Oliver was placed under arrest by General Fonseca, on the orders of Major General John Hamilton, the matter being referred to the Marshal. In the interim Oliver sought permission to return to the trenches with his regiment. His commitment to the cause was admirable but ended most unfortunately when poor Oliver died a month later of wounds received during the second siege of Badajoz and he is buried in the British Cemetery at Elvas.[26]

On another occasion, Lieutenant Colonel John Grant was deprived of command of a battalion of the Loyal Lusitanian Legion for striking a fellow officer. In imposing the sentence Beresford made it clear that he did not wish to lose Grant's services and he was requested to report to HQ. Baron Eben, in transferring the battalion to Lieutenant Colonel Hawkshaw, noted it had been much improved under Grant.[27]

A third incident involved George McGregor of the 8th Portuguese Regiment along with a Captain Marlay and Captain Charles Western and two Portuguese officers, the brothers João and José María Alferezes.[28] It resulted in a Court of Enquiry in Almeida with Lieutenant Colonel António de Lacerda Pinto da Silveira of the 11th Portuguese as President. As reported by McGregor to Beresford's military secretary, Robert Arbuthnot, it involved name-calling by the Portuguese resulting in João Alferezes being slapped by Captain Western. A campaign of harassment was then mounted by fellow officers of the Alferezes' over the next few days. McGregor confronted them on leaving Captain Marlay's house one evening and being certain they could not mistake him for Western, as McGregor was in English uniform, he threw down his sword and approached them with open arms. However, the Portuguese brothers drew their swords, one in front of him and the other behind. Western then arrived, picked up McGregor's sword and put them to flight. McGregor went to the Colonel (Vasconcellos) and asked him to put the two Portuguese under arrest which he agreed to do.

The British officers went in search of their Portuguese counterparts and broke down the door to a house, whereupon the Officer of the Guard arrived with soldiers and demanded McGregor give up his sword and go with him and a sentinel, claiming these were the orders of Colonel Vasconcellos. McGregor refused on the basis these could not be the orders. The Officer of the Guard told his troops to prepare to fire and a Mexican standoff ensued, with Western challenging them to shoot. The Officer of the Guard returned with another Major and the Guard was sent away. McGregor went before the Colonel, claiming he had been grossly insulted. In reply the Colonel claimed he should not be wearing a British uniform and that he should obey his orders. McGregor told him he considered himself a British officer and did not consider himself under arrest.[29]

Following a report from the President of the Court of Enquiry, Beresford determined to dismiss McGregor from the Portuguese service.[30] McGregor was a colourful character and by 1812 he was involved in the independence movements in South America, serving under Simon Bolivar and others. Later he was involved in a number of fraudulent schemes to entice settlers to Central America. This case exemplifies Beresford's preparedness to rely on the integrity of a Portuguese officer in a difficult case involving a British officer.

Whereas some of the British officers, and presumably likewise some of their Portuguese counterparts, found it hard to deal with these antagonisms, others merely regarded it as something which must be coped with and sought instead to emphasise their own sense of duty. Alexander Dickson in 1809 found his Portuguese commanding artillery officer extremely difficult but, rather than succumb, he determined to do all he could to help the common cause stating, 'I am determined to make no difficulties and to do all I can'; qualities that no doubt endeared himself to Wellington a few years later when he placed the young Lieutenant Colonel in charge of all the Allied artillery prior to the campaign in the Pyrenees.[31]

Beresford's emphasis on discipline extended not just to Portuguese officers and men but to the British officers in the Portuguese service. Not only did he seek to make promotions on merit, but he brooked no opposition to his authority as Commander in Chief, even when its source was a senior officer such as Lieutenant Colonel Robert Wilson, commander of the Loyal Lusitanian Legion. Beresford and Wilson had served together before. While they would have both briefly been in Egypt at the same time, in the summer of 1801, they do not appear to have met there. In 1805, however, they formed part of the army under General Sir David Baird which captured the Cape of Good Hope, and indeed Wilson and his dragoons landed with Beresford at Saldanha, thus missing the battle at Blaauwberg.[32] In 1808 it was Beresford who had inspected the newly formed Loyal Lusitanian Legion following their arrival in Portugal, and Beresford's correspondence leading up to and including the Porto campaign in the spring of 1809 contains a considerable number of letters to Wilson.

When Beresford arrived in Portugal, Wilson was harassing the French on the Spanish border with one of the battalions of the Legion. Cradock informed him of Beresford's arrival and appointment and that the British officers with him were getting one step up in rank, telling Wilson that he too should do so and that Cradock would support him. Wilson, with part of the garrison of Almeida, joined Beresford at Viseu on his march north in the campaign against Soult, which resulted in the scrambled French withdrawal from northern Portugal, but it was shortly afterwards when Beresford began in earnest the reform of the Portuguese army that matters reached an impasse which was to lead to Wilson leaving the Peninsula.

Beresford proposed to appoint Wilson a Brigadier, but made it clear that on promotion Wilson would not be in command of the Legion, but as a general officer and could not be restricted to any particular corps or place. Wilson, for his part, said that he had been appointed to raise, command and discipline the Legion and on 23 May first tendered his resignation. Beresford said while Wilson's departure would be a loss, he could not concede the principle, as it would be incompatible with all military systems. Wilson countered by saying that rather than retire he would prefer to join his regiment and hope to be relieved in due course. Beresford said that if he wanted to remain a Colonel then he would always serve with his corps, but he hoped Wilson would serve on the same principles as other officers of his rank served.

Wilson rejoined his regiment at Castelo Branco in early June but then unsuccessfully sought to enlist Castlereagh's assistance so that he could retain the Legion under his own direction. Wellesley backed Beresford's decision and in the autumn of 1809 Wilson left the Peninsula not to return; he was succeeded as Colonel of the Legion by Baron Eben.[33] Where British officers, such as Wilson and Colonel William Mayne, felt aggrieved that officers now joining Beresford in Portugal were receiving expedited promotion whereas those who had come to Portugal earlier were not able to avail of the same advantage, Beresford clearly sought to address that issue.

In reality, Wilson and Mayne wanted to remain independent of Beresford and the Portuguese command structure and instead sought integration in the British army. When that objective was frustrated, they left the Peninsula. Wellesley, noting that they were absent from the Portuguese service without leave, observed they could not be punished for their misconduct back in Britain because they were not in His Majesty's service. He was extremely critical of their conduct, suggesting they not be employed in future in England as Inspecting Field Officers or otherwise.[34] However, he warned Beresford to tread carefully, on the basis that Robert Wilson had friends at home spreading rumours that Wellington (as Arthur Wellesley had now become) had mistreated Wilson because of jealousy, observing 'he has many faults, but one above all others is that he cannot speak the truth'.[35]

Wellesley and Beresford were amongst the few field officers who did not go home at any stage prior to the conclusion of the war in 1814. They both became increasingly irritated by requests from officers to go home on leave, sometimes under the disguise of pressing business. There was no issue if the applicant was obviously ill, and a number of officers who went home because of illness returned later to the Peninsula.[36] In October 1809, Wellington told Beresford that the solution he had adopted with regard to officers in the British army going home was to oblige them to declare the nature of their business, fix the date of return and if they did not return by the due date court martial them for being absent without leave.[37]

Beresford was to prove equally intransigent, and when Brigadier General Miller sought leave to return to Ireland two weeks after his appointment as Governor of Minho in mid November 1809, Beresford responded that public service demanded sacrifice; stating that had he made the application prior to his appointment it might have been possible but that the Portuguese government needed the British officers. Beresford concluded, 'I don't doubt you will cheerfully occupy your post until a more favourable occasion.' All this despite the fact that Miller had said he understood that if he went he could not expect to retain the position of the Governor of Minho, and furthermore that if he was not in Ireland to sign some deeds for the sale of a property by 1 January, he feared foreclosure on a mortgage.[38] Miller chose to stay in Portugal, rendering valuable service there in the years ahead.

British officers who entered the Portuguese service but proved unsatisfactory were sent home, if this could be done without causing a political storm. One such was Brigadier General Robert MacLeroth, who only served in Portugal for a few months in 1809. Wellington was clearly of the view that MacLeroth should be sent home, but advised Beresford in October

Curraghmore, Co. Waterford, home of George de la Poer Beresford, 1st Marquis of Waterford and father of William Carr. Author's own collection.

Archway at Curraghmore, Co. Waterford. Author's own collection.

Curraghmore as it would have appeared in William Carr's lifetime. Reproduced from *Lord William Beresford V.C.* by Mrs Stuart Menzies, London 1917.

1st Marquis of Waterford by Gilbert Stuart. By kind permission of the Marquis of Waterford.

Commercial Regulations issued by William Carr Beresford as Governor of Buenos Aires, August 1806. Author's own collection.

Surrender of Buenos Aires by Major General Beresford 12 August 1806 by Charles Fouqeray. By kind permission of Museo Historico Nacional.

Freedom box awarded to Marshal Beresford by the City of London, 1811. By kind permission of the Museum of London.

Dress sword awarded to Beresford by the City of London following the capture of Buenos Aires. By kind permission of the Museum of London.

SERMON
DE ACCION DE GRACIAS,

QUE CON EL PLAUSIBLE MOTIVO DE LA restauracion de la Ciudad, y Plaza de Buenos-Ayres, Capital del Vireynato del Rio de la Plata, por las Armas Españolas, de que se recibió noticia con Extraordinario en esta Ciudad de la Plata, en dos de Setiembre:

DIXO

EN LA SANTA IGLESIA METROPOLITANA de Charcas el dia quatro del mismo, en la Solemne Misa que se celebró con asistencia de la Real Audiencia, Cabildos, Religiones, y numeroso Pueblo,

EL DOCTOR D.ⁿ MATIAS TERRAZAS,

DIGNIDAD DE TESORERO DE LA MISMA Metropolitana, destinado el dia antes para este efecto por el muy Venerable Dean, y Cabildo Sede Vacante de dicha Sta. Iglesia.

CON PERMISO DE LOS SUPERIORES.

En la Real Imprenta de Niños Expósitos.
Año de MDCCCVI.

'Sermon de accion de gracias': sermon preached in Buenos Aires in September 1806, following the recapture of the city from the British forces. Author's own collection.

Beresford's residence while Governor of Madeira, 1807–8, now the hotel Quinta Jardins do Lago. Author's own collection.

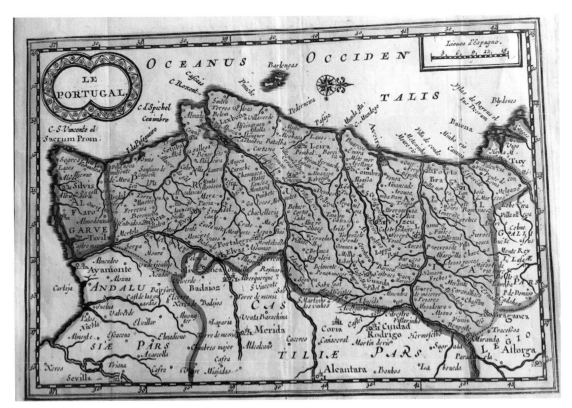

Eighteenth-century map of Portugal showing the territory lost to Spain following the conclusion of the War of the Oranges, 1801. Author's own collection.

Major General William Carr Beresford KB, Commander of the 88th Foot Connaught Rangers. By kind permission of The National Library of Ireland.

Marshal William Carr Beresford in Portuguese uniform, artist unknown. By kind permission of the Marquis of Waterford.

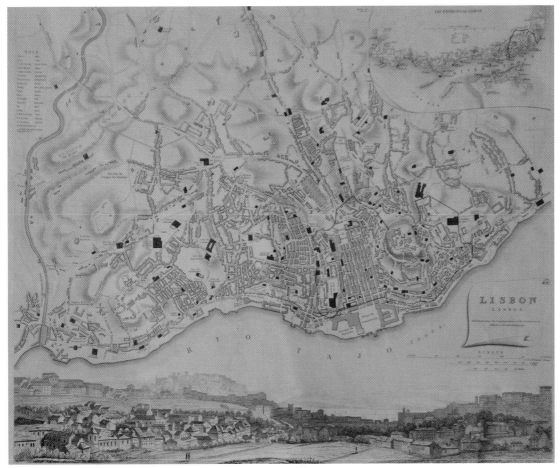

Lisbon and its environs, nineteenth century; drawn by W.B. Clarke and engraved by J. Henshall. Author's own collection.

Headquarters of Marshal Beresford at Lageoso do Mondego (Beira), 1810. Author's own collection.

Headquarters of Marshal Beresford at Trancoso, summer 1810. Author's own collection.

Headquarters of Marshal Beresford at Fornos de Algodres, May 1810. Author's own collection.

Casal Cochim, Sapataria (Lines of Torres Vedras), Headquarters of Marshal Beresford, October–November 1810. Author's own collection.

Headquarters of Marshal Beresford, Chamusca, early 1811. Author's own collection.

Plaque marking Marshal Beresford's Headquarters, Trancoso. Author's own collection.

General Junot's departure from Lisbon, September 1808. By kind permission of the British Library.

Marshal Beresford unhorsing a Polish lancer at the Battle of Albuera, 16 May 1811, by Franz Joseph Manskirch, engraved by M. Dubourg. Author's own collection.

Defeat of the French before Badajoz, 26 March 1811, by William Heath, engraved by J. Hill. By kind permission of Pedro de Avillez.

Capela Sao Joao de Corujeira, British Cemetery, Elvas where services are held each year to commemorate the battle of Albuera and those that fell there, by kind permission of The British Cemetery, Elvas.

1801 march of British army from Red Sea to Alexandria

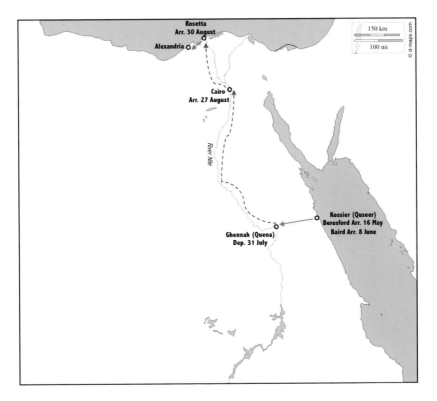

Buenes Aires, 1805–1806

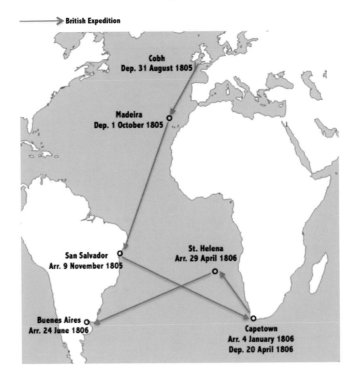

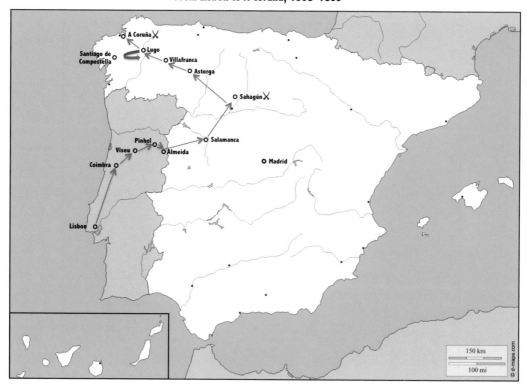

From Lisbon to A Coruña, 1808–1809

Beresford

A Coruña

Lugo

Santiago de Compostella

Villafranca

Astorga

Sahagún

Salamanca

Pinhel

Viseu

Almeida

Coimbra

Madrid

Lisbon

150 km

100 mi

© d-maps.com

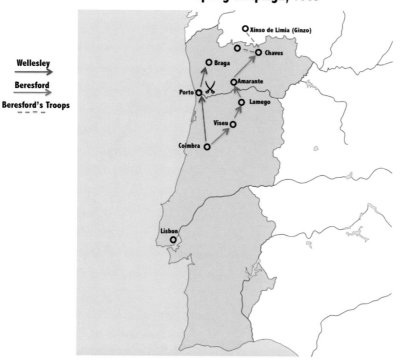

Spring Campaign, 1809

Wellesley

Beresford

Beresford's Troops

Xinso de Limia (Ginzo)

Chaves

Braga

Amarante

Porto

Lamego

Viseu

Coimbra

Lisbon

Summer Campaigns, 1809

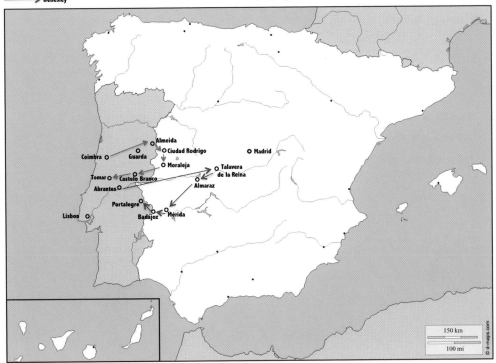

Portugal, 1810–1811

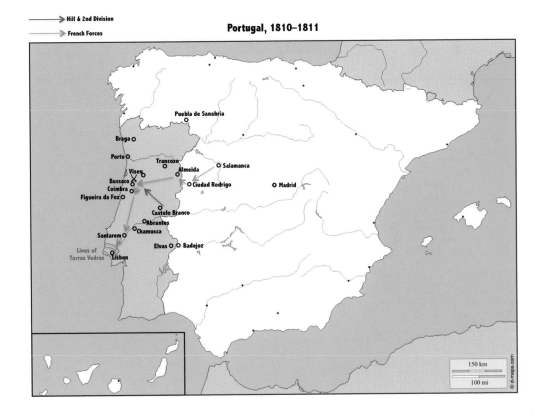

Lines of Torres Vedras, 1810–1811

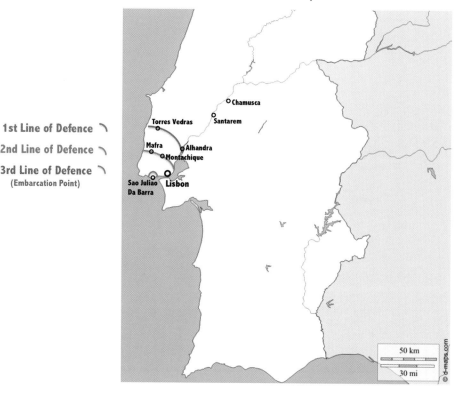

1st Line of Defence

2nd Line of Defence

3rd Line of Defence
(Embarcation Point)

Chamusca

Torres Vedras

Santarem

Mafra

Alhandra

Montachique

Sao Juliao
Da Barra

Lisbon

50 km

30 mi

© d-maps.com

Portugal & Spain – The Campaign of 1811

Wellington

Beresford

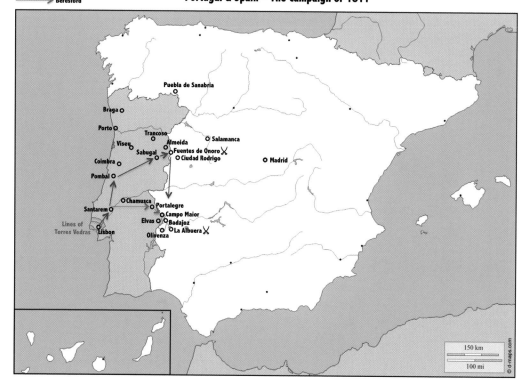

Puebla de Sanabria

Braga

Porto

Trancoso

Viseu

Almeida

Salamanca

Sabugal

Fuentes de Onoro

Coimbra

Ciudad Rodrigo

Madrid

Pombal

Chamusca

Santarem

Portalegre

Campo Maior

Elvas

Badajoz

Lines of
Torres Vedras

Lisbon

La Albuera

Olivenza

150 km

100 mi

© d-maps.com

1809 to proceed with caution by preparing the ground at Horse Guards before taking action to remove him. MacLeroth disappeared from Portugal shortly thereafter.[39] Of course, there were other officers that Wellington and Beresford would like to have sent away from Portugal, and later Spain, but it proved impolitic to attempt their removal.

It was Forjaz who implemented a recruitment policy which in turn enabled Beresford to put a well trained and disciplined army into the field. The efforts made by Forjaz to recruit in late 1808 and early 1809 have already been referred to, and Forjaz's own background and experience showed that he understood what was required. The arrival of Beresford and the allocation of British officers to train troops effectively gave Forjaz the impetus to introduce a more intensive and persistent system of recruitment. In doing so he broke with tradition and came into conflict with both the Regency and the magistrates at local level, but pushed by the determination and demands of Beresford, Forjaz proved a reliable colleague in this respect.[40]

The recruiting system in place at the beginning of 1809 involved the Superintendent of Police sending notices relating to recruitment to those responsible for recruiting in the individual provinces; the *capitães-mores*. There was a real problem in that initially so many privileges or exemptions from the obligation to serve were made, that it led to confrontation and delay in implementing decrees. The *capitães-mores* complained of the difficulties they encountered in recruiting, including emigration, concealment and the reception they received when recruiting. In response, the Superintendent directed the proper enforcement of the laws which included seizure of property and the sale of the goods of those avoiding recruitment and very severe penalties for those hiding a fugitive from recruitment.[41]

Insufficient numbers of recruits led to Forjaz taking further action. At his instigation the Regency issued decrees on 14 and 15 December 1809 providing the structure for increased recruitment. Recruiting was to be on a provincial basis with the responsibility for a determined number of recruits to be raised placed on the *capitão-mor* of the province in question. Within the provinces there were recruiting districts. Each district was required to raise one regiment of infantry and two regiments of militia. Two districts combined were required to produce a regiment of cavalry, while artillery recruits were drawn from all the districts. The number of recruiting districts in a province depended on population density.[42]

Single men between eighteen and thirty-five, with certain exemptions, were initially liable. The classes exempted were quite wide. Some of them are easily understandable, for they included certain agricultural workers and those involved in maritime commerce. Other groups exempted, such as students and those involved in the arts, are less comprehensible. In physical terms, men over 4-foot 10½-inches (1.49 m) were drafted, though this height requirement had to be reduced by an inch later.[43] Penalties were introduced for draft evaders, including loss of citizenship and possessions for those who left the country. When the age bracket for those liable for military service failed to produce sufficient recruits it was extended to the age of sixty. A system of provincial training depots was introduced with specific regiments allocated to particular depots. Peniche, Tomar and Viseu emerged as three of the most important training depots in the course of the war.

The effectiveness of this recruiting system depended on the commitment of the *capitães-mores* and the willingness of judges to enforce the rules in the case of evasion. The degree of commitment varied from province to province, but the end result was that in the spring of 1810 there were still insufficient recruits coming into the army. Beresford and Forjaz tackled the problem aggressively, devising a system which punished those harbouring fugitives and removing those *capitães-mores* who failed to recruit adequate numbers.

At Beresford's insistence, the filling up and training of the army rather than the militia was prioritised, and within the army the priority was the infantry, not least because of a shortage of horses to mount the cavalry regiments. Raising the cavalry component of the army to a state of full efficiency remained problematic throughout the war, despite some fine performances by individual units under leaders such as D'Urban and Madden. In March 1809, Beresford could at best field five of the notional twelve cavalry regiments. As one Portuguese author has pointed out, the number of horses reportedly existing in the different districts of the realm in 1808 was virtually the same number required to equip all the cavalry regiments, so inevitably mounting the cavalry was going to be a hard task.[44]

After the summer campaign Forjaz, at Beresford's request, ordered the military governors of the various provinces to provide 100 mares each for the 2nd Cavalry regiment but success was limited and on 12 December 1809 a decree was issued which restricted the ownership and use of horses for non-military purposes with a provision for swingeing fines to be imposed on transgressors.[45] Seizures were made, with hundreds of horses thus being acquired, though unsuitability as cavalry mounts, together with sickness and deaths of animals, meant the supply of horses remained a continuing struggle. Alongside appropriation Forjaz sought to obtain horses from the Barbary coast and suggested Beresford might do so from England. Wellington also issued an order to prevent British army officers buying Portuguese horses of the size required for the cavalry. When an allegation was made in 1810 that such a horse had been purchased, Wellington wrote to tell Beresford that while he thought this might be a false report, if proven the horse would be given up.[46] Despite all these difficulties, Beresford did manage to increase the numbers of cavalry in 1810, though the figure was to slip backwards a year later.[47]

The four regiments of artillery under the command of Dickson appear to have been well organised from an early date. Their problem, which they shared with the cavalry, frequently centred on a lack of feed for their animals.[48] Beresford did bring in a number of reforms in respect of the artillery, including the creation of a dedicated battalion of artificers in 1812. In the same year he created a battalion of dedicated artillery drivers. While Beresford appreciated the importance of the militia, their training was for him secondary to that of the army, though he did allocate regular army officers to assist with the training of officers of the militia.

So how successful was the enforcement of the Portuguese recruitment regulations? Certainly considerable numbers were recruited to the ranks and many of the regiments filled up from time to time, but losses, whether caused by injury, sickness or desertion, meant that regiments were rarely able to put their full complement in the field. When Forjaz reported to Beresford that between May 1809 and October 1810 29,796 men had been raised giving a total count of 56,217 men in the army, he also noted that losses over the same period amounted to 16,571 including 10,224 deserters. Beresford was not hugely impressed with the net increase of 13,221 men, clearly feeling that a nation of over three million people should have produced more than 29,000 recruits in eighteen months.[49]

On his arrival in Portugal, Beresford had written to Charles Stewart telling him the Portuguese army was no better than a mob with a dangerous proclivity towards mutiny.[50] He had immediately set to work with his original allocation of British officers training a number of Portuguese regiments, and he was encouraged enough after the Porto campaign to believe that the Portuguese could be welded into an effective and disciplined force given time and training. It did not look as if there was to be sufficient respite to undertake the necessary training, for shortly after the return from the Douro information was received in Portugal to the effect that Soult and Ney had met at Lugo and suggested, erroneously as it turned out, that the combined 2nd and 6th corps were about to reinvade northern Portugal. In fact, Soult's force was temporarily exhausted and a combination of confrontation in Galicia and poor relations between the French generals prevented their combining to present a coherent threat for the time being.

An initial decision in mid-June that Beresford should march for Porto with a force was subsequently abandoned when the position became clear.[51] Instead Wellesley divided the Allied resources in two, with the main British army marching to Spain via Abrantes in a campaign that was to culminate in victory at the battle of Talavera and the subsequent tactical retreat back to Portugal. He took with him only two Portuguese regiments, the Loyal Lusitanian Legion and the 5th Caçadores. Beresford suggested that the Portuguese would occupy Puerto de Baños and the area around Plasencia (mid way between Ciudad Rodrigo and Wellesley's army on the Tagus) because of the fertility of the location, but Wellesley declined the suggestion and instructed him to guard the northern and north eastern frontier with a view to defending Portugal from any French incursion.[52] Beresford's Quartermaster General, D'Urban, was quite critical of this decision, claiming that it later allowed Soult to come down into this area, depriving the British army of supplies.[53]

Wellesley's instructions meant effectively that for many of the regiments involved training was 'on the hoof' as Beresford moved to assemble the army at Almeida. The *Return of the Army* for the end of July suggests he had about 18,000 men available, made up principally of fourteen regiments of regular infantry together with five battalions of caçadores, the university regiment of volunteers from Coimbra, together with the Portuguese artillery and a scratch collection of cavalry.[54] Drilling took place daily on the basis that replication of manoeuvres based on British drill regulations would produce the required discipline and steadiness to face the enemy.[55]

The results of the training during the summer were mixed. There was no instant achievement of an objective standard and much seems to have depended on the officers of each regiment. While there was progress, what Beresford referred to as 'a little light begins to show on the chaos I found here', it is probable that much more was achieved in the autumn and winter of 1809 when the army was back in encampments.[56] Beresford had by then appointed Major General John Hamilton to the post of Inspector of Infantry of the Portuguese army.[57] His reports to Beresford show their determination to produce an effective fighting force. The introduction of firing live ammunition on a daily basis unsurprisingly improved accuracy and engendered a real feeling of *esprit de corps*.[58]

One of those to comment broadly on the training of certain Portuguese regiments was Lieutenant Colonel William Cox. In April 1809, Beresford had appointed Cox Commander of the fortress of Almeida. His correspondence with Beresford and Wellington both in that year and 1810 reveals a man who was not happy at Almeida and who worried about almost every aspect of his command, and it was to drive both the Marshal and the Allied commander to distraction.[59] His comments on the training of the regiments at Almeida may not be representative of the position elsewhere because of Cox's personal insecurity, but they are some of the most extensively recorded. The 12th and 24th regiments were stationed in Almeida in the second half of 1809, but by the end of October a despondent Cox reported:

> I am sorry to say that the two regiments of this garrison have made very little progress in discipline since you saw them, and particularly my own: the causes of this are various, but it is principally owing to the want of active and intelligent officers. Had the 12th regiment remained under the command of MacDonnell, I am convinced that in a short time it would have made a rapid advance from the state it is now in to very much better, but unfortunately just as he was beginning to establish a good system, of which he is very capable, and had made some progress in the first principles of Drill, with which he began *de novo*, he is superseded in the command by a man who, let his talents be what they may, cannot possibly have the necessary experience; having served but a few months as an officer of the line, and having passed at once from a cadet of cavalry to be Lieutenant Colonel of Militia: to do him justice I must say he is extremely active and intelligent and in time may make a very good officer; but it might perhaps have been better if he had not jumpt all at once into command.[60]

James MacDonnell, referred to here by Cox, had joined the Portuguese service only on 26 August 1809 from the 78th Foot. He was to go on to become one of the heroes of Waterloo, famously with his sergeant closing the gates at Hougoument after the French forced them open.

As early as September 1809, MacDonnell protested to Cox because of his frustration that his training regime was being stifled by the Colonel of the regiment.[61] In October 1809 he informed Cox he wished to resign from the Portuguese service, though his formal request to do so was not made until 8 December.[62] Eventually, he left the Portuguese service on 21 Aug 1810; but his case for doing so was very different to most others because he had been appointed a Lieutenant Colonel in the British army and would have had expectations of command of a British regiment.[63] In the interim Cox seems to have warmed to Lieutenant Colonel Silveira, (about whom he had so recently expressed reservations) of the 12th Regiment saying he was:

> one of the very few well educated men I have met with in Portugal, and his natural abilities are good, he has also a considerable share of military knowledge, acquired by a great deal of study and some experience. McDonnell [*sic*] seems to have no intention of remaining in the Portuguese service, so if he goes I hope you will give the regiment to Silveira.[64]

Of his own regiment, the 24th Regiment, Cox went on to say it was even worse than the 12th. At its head 'is placed a very good little bustling man, without a military idea in the world'. He cited jealousy and bickering between the Colonel and the Lieutenant Colonel and it only had one English officer, which he emphasised was totally deficient for drill purposes.[65]

One of the problems afflicting some of the British officers in their efforts to train the Portuguese was an inability to communicate because of a lack of knowledge of the Portuguese language. George McGregor, in his short term as a Portuguese officer, alluded to this in November. While claiming that the 8th Regiment stationed at Fundão had made good progress, and that he hoped in a short time it would be considered fit for service, he enclosed a memorial from the son of an Irishman living in Portugal who wanted to join the regiment, with McGregor saying he would be happy if this could be arranged as he would be very useful to him in translating orders and otherwise.[66]

Training was only one of the prerequisites to building an efficient fighting machine that faced Beresford. Other aspects included equipment, clothing and weapons, remuneration and the supply of provisions. Meeting these objectives would help inculcate a spirit of subordination and respect for leadership. Beresford tackled all of these challenges and largely succeeded, with the exception of the regular supply of provisions and the payment of the troops, which the Regency was never able to assure with regularity, notwithstanding the very substantial assistance supplied by the British government whether through the British army commissariat or through financial assistance.

On arrival in Portugal, the dearth of arms, uniforms and other equipment had been immediately apparent to Beresford, and he had written to Castlereagh even prior to his formal appointment seeking news of the clothing and arms for 10,000 men promised by the British government. In addition, he sought 2,000 rifles for light troops (caçadores) as the nature of the country was most suited to them.[67] With the British commitment revised to support 20,000 and ultimately 30,000 Portuguese, there was a continuous requirement for supplies from Great Britain. Beresford sought these from the British government, as did Wellesley demanding in June 1809 further supplies including 30,000 greatcoats, the latter clearly with his eye on the winter ahead.[68]

Major McGregor, during his short term with the 8th Portuguese, reported at the end of October 1809 that training was proceeding but there was 'much want of arms' with only eighty stand of arms for 700 men. There was also a lack of clothing, ammunition, drums and medicines.[69] It is probably indicative of the emphasis placed by Beresford on the usefulness of caçadores that these regiments were reportedly completely kitted out with arms and uniforms before the end of July 1809.[70] By the end of 1809 most, though not all, of the Portuguese troops were properly armed. In contrast, much of the militia may not have been armed until 1810 when Wellington advised Beresford that 30,000 stand of arms had arrived for the Marshal and that he should now 'arm your militia and whatever else you think proper'.[71]

The provision of proper clothing and other accoutrements on a regular basis, so as to refurbish the troops in respect of lost or worn-out items, took considerable organisation and some time to implement.[72] Having required regimental records which demonstrated dates of last supply, Beresford established a system whereby regiments would be refurbished on a rolling basis once every eighteen months. Provisioning the Portuguese army continued to be a frustrating experience. Uniforms supplied from England were found to be unsuitable both as to quality and their ability to denote Portuguese regiments. Furthermore, distribution by the arsenal from Lisbon was found to be unsatisfactory by Beresford. Problems were overcome by a number of means including the employment of civilian tailors in Portugal as well as those with the regiments.

Many items continued to be supplied direct from the United Kingdom and billed in such a way as to be set off against the financial grant to Portugal; a policy which suited Beresford who was all too aware of the pressure on funds to meet other Portuguese requirements. Thus we see that in January 1810, Stuart (who administered the funds coming from Britain) was invoiced for 1,355 saddles, and a month later 1,315 saddles are stated to be on the *Achilles* transport together with 10,000 greatcoats, 10,000 suits of clothing and 40,000 pairs of half stockings, all specifically for the Portuguese service.[73] Difficulties in supply were compounded by the requirement to go on campaign in the summer of 1809, which in turn meant that the re-clothing of the army was not completed until later in the year and early 1810.[74] The appointment of Major Robert Harvey as Assistant Quartermaster General in 1810 provided impetus to the programme with a new issue of shoes supplied to the infantry in July.[75] While Beresford frequently complained of the inefficiencies of the Arsenal, and issues regarding equipment did raise their head from time to time thereafter, the Portuguese army was largely well clothed and armed from 1810 onwards.

Financing the Portuguese army was to remain difficult throughout the war, notwithstanding the extent of the British monetary contribution. While it was not Beresford's job but that of the Regency Council, and more specifically Forjaz as Secretary of Foreign Affairs, War and the Marine, to ensure the soldiers were paid and that sufficient monies were available for provisions, the reality was that the army could not go on campaign unless adequately financed. A combination of factors made it impossible for Portugal to finance its own army. These included the consequences of repeated invasions, the removal of the Court to Rio de Janeiro, and the loss of maritime commerce; the latter the result of not just the physical confrontation taking place but because of the commercial treaty with Britain which effectively transferred the Brazil trade from Portugal to Britain. Perhaps the most far reaching of these causes was the commercial treaty.[76] The impact of the termination of the Portuguese trading monopoly with Brazil may be understood readily when it is realised it accounted for 65 per cent of the gross national product.[77]

In 1809, the Regency Council estimated that Portuguese State income would amount to 6,758 contos with expenditure running at 11,743 contos, a deficit of 4,985 contos. Income was calculated to cover only 57.55 per cent of expenditure.[78] That the income improved in 1810 was mostly due to monies sent from Brazil and the seizures of property owned by French supporters. It is suggested that overall military expenditure amounted to 81 per cent of total expenditure with the army taking some 70 per cent of that total. The situation was to become even more demanding in the following years.[79] Additional monies were raised by a special defence tax and by property sales, but these were insufficient to meet requirements and the State suffered an ever increasing fiscal deficit through the war, notwithstanding the very substantial British subsidy of the Portuguese military force.

The British subsidy was originally designed to support 10,000 men. It then grew to finance 20,000 men in February 1809 and finally 30,000 men in the Portuguese army. The grant was for £980,000 in 1810 and this only represented a small proportion of British expenditure in respect of the war. It did not include the cost of funding the British army in Portugal or elsewhere. It did, however, include a sum for the pay of the British officers in the Portuguese army and covered a pay rise insisted on by Beresford for the Portuguese officers. The mode of distribution was through the British Minister in Lisbon, first John Villiers and subsequently Charles Stuart. The subsidy did not cover the cost of 30,000 soldiers as it was based on a false premise that the Portuguese regiments had their full complement at the time of initial calculation.[80] In 1810, the British Minister in fact overpaid the subsidy by some £250,000 in view of the crushing need of funds to support the Portuguese army.[81] In 1811 the British grant was fixed at £2,000,000; a far more realistic figure.[82]

With Portugal short of money and British payments frequently in arrears it is hardly surprising that the pay of the soldiers was more often than not also behind schedule, sometimes for six months or even more. The financial situation was so bad that on occasion Beresford was forced to use monies designated for payment of the troops for provisions instead, in order to feed the army. When shortages of food became critical it was almost inevitable that discipline would break down, with foraging parties imposing themselves on local populations. From the time of his appointment, however, Beresford made it clear that such seizures were unacceptable.[83]

Pay arrears impacted not just on the rank and file of the army but on officers as well, and while they might have sufficient funds to tide them over, this was not always the case. They also suffered from repeated delays in adjudication and payment of claims for losses to the Board of Claims. It took even a man of Beresford's position many years to recover the prize money he was due from the Buenos Aires expedition, and claims were outstanding also in respect of losses suffered in the retreat to La Coruña.[84] In October 1809, Lieutenant Colonel John Campbell was clearly desperate when he wrote to Beresford seeking help recovering sums due from the Board of Claims as he explained he was in want of money.[85]

In the autumn of 1809 Wellington, in recognition that the retention of Lisbon was the key to maintaining a presence in Portugal, determined to build two defensive lines of forts and redoubts on the Lisbon Peninsula stretching from the Atlantic to the River Tagus. Additional defensive positions were constructed at São Julião and Almada on the north and south sides respectively of the Tagus estuary. Militia and other native workforces were utilised in this project and almost immediately difficulties arose as to how to pay the militia, as many of the members of that force were to help with construction of the Lines of Torres Vedras, as they became known. Lieutenant Colonel Fletcher corresponded with Beresford on this point, citing the grievances felt by the militia as expressed by their Colonel.[86] In a similar vein, Captain Peter Patton of the Royal Engineers, who was overseeing the upgrading of the fortifications at Abrantes, complained to Arbuthnot in November 1809 that the workmen had deserted through lack of funds to pay them. He sought to impress on Robert Arbuthnot the beneficial effect of prompt payment in terms of creating goodwill.[87] Means of payment were eventually found, though this may well have resulted in delaying payment elsewhere.

The Junta de Viveres was the Portuguese commissariat responsible for supplying the Portuguese army. Although the Junta de Viveres was clearly incapable of ensuring adequate supplies to the army from an early stage, both Beresford and Forjaz persevered with it, and in doing so they had the support of Wellesley, who rejected the suggestion that the British and Portuguese commissariats should be merged to increase efficiency and to avoid competition for provisions.[88] The problem had not arisen in the campaign to drive Soult out of northern Portugal, as in fact the British commissariat had supplied both armies for that short campaign, but the fundamental weaknesses of the Portuguese commissariat were fully exposed in the summer campaign of 1809.

The intendants and *feitors* (managers) in each province were responsible for procuring supplies, and the latter sought to purchase at the lowest price possible, an attitude which antagonised the farmers who were reluctant to sell to the Junta because it took too long to pay. The problem of obtaining provisions was exacerbated by an inability to transport them to the designated point at the required time.[89] Following a short power struggle when Beresford dismissed a number of intendants in 1809, his authority was acknowledged by the Junta, though the fact that it was often starved of funds continued to limit its ability to get provisions to the army. Beresford and Forjaz arranged to set up a number of depots, each with four months supplies, but their efficacy was limited by both finance and the fact that garrisons at the depots frequently had to break into the stores to feed themselves because of a general shortage of supplies.

In 1810, Villiers recommended (as the British government had previously suggested) that the British commissariat take over responsibility for supplying both armies and Forjaz supported the suggestion; but it was not to be implemented until 1811 when Wellington finally accepted that this would have to be done if the Portuguese were to be utilised for the campaign that year. Henceforth, Portuguese units serving with the British army were supplied by the British commissariat irrespective of whether or not they were part of the 30,000 subsidised troops. The Portuguese commissariat only had responsibility for those that remained operationally independent, perhaps a quarter of the Portuguese forces.[90]

The inefficiency of the Junta de Viveres, while evident to all but the most subjective observer, needs to be seen in the context of the inability of Portugal to grow enough grain to feed its own population in time of peace and the chronic shortage of specie with which to purchase provisions.[91] Great Britain was aware of the issue from the time of the original expedition to Portugal in 1808, when Wellesley had taken with him food and forage transports to provide for his own army.[92]

Training and discipline were at the heart of Beresford's work in reforming the Portuguese army. Military training itself requires discipline, but in the present context it is necessary to consider general discipline both on and off the battlefield. The willingness with which an order is carried out is likely to be directly related to the degree of respect in which the person giving the order is held by its recipient. Hence the importance of the calibre of the officers in the Portuguese army being rebuilt and reformed by Beresford, with the help of Forjaz and Wellesley. Discipline for infractions of orders was often severe and sometimes terminal. Beresford determined that both trial and sentence, if there was to be one, should also be delivered quickly. In doing so he had to overcome a system of justice which was subject to serious delay and which produced results which marked it out as inconsistent and ineffective.

Instilling discipline no doubt helped Beresford impose his authority on the army and ultimately helped create a force much admired by those in its British counterpart. Eyewitness accounts stress the importance that promotion on merit, the spirit instilled by encouraging emulation, the banning of unregulated physical abuse of men by officers, the regular feeding of troops (though there were some serious lapses), and the provision of a functioning medical service had on the process.[93] It was these factors combined with discipline that converted the force which Beresford had described in 1809 as 'no better than a mob with a propensity to mutiny' into Wellington's 'fighting cocks' of 1813.[94] Wellington himself placed greater emphasis on regular pay and sustenance rather than instruction as the cause of their proficiency; a suggestion which he based on the poor behaviour, as he saw it, of the Portuguese in 1812; a time at which discipline had also broken down in the British army on the retreat from Burgos.[95]

There were many ways in which a lack of discipline might manifest itself, including theft, a refusal to obey orders and desertion. All were regarded as serious infractions but desertion proved to be a particularly difficult problem in the Portuguese army in the course of the war. It drove Beresford to declare to Forjaz, in the autumn of 1809, that 'I can never hope of attaining perfect discipline, because with sickness and desertion there would be almost a complete turnover of the army within a year.'[96] The problem of desertion was augmented by the difficulties encountered in recruitment.[97] Many sought to escape recruitment by a variety of methods including flight to Spain or Brazil, mutilation of index finger and thumb, the sale of public positions, and registration as an employee of the navy arsenal. The latter two situations were amongst a number of the factors giving rise to exemption, and both Forjaz and Beresford realised that they were on occasions effected with the complicity of the authorities in order to avoid recruitment. It has been estimated that at any one time, in round numbers, those escaping recruitment may have reduced the effectives in the Portuguese army by between 4,000 and 10,000 men.[98] Avoidance of recruitment was so bad in Lisbon that the 22nd Regiment, which was raised there, could not be used on campaign due to lack of numbers and it was used repeatedly for garrison duties.

Above all, however, existed the 'enormous crime of desertion'.[99] While it is suggested this was no more widespread in the Portuguese army than in the foreign regiments in British service, nor more widespread than that encountered in the French or Spanish armies, Beresford and Forjaz exerted themselves strenuously to reduce the incidence of desertion.[100] In his report to Forjaz of 16 November 1809, Beresford suggested that the lack of zeal of officials and the lack of enforcement of measures to punish them for failing to recruit properly itself caused desertion, and he called for the implementation of penalties including a system of bounties to those who recovered deserters to be paid by those who sheltered them, as well as penalties imposed on authorities who were found wanting in their duty.[101] Additionally, he called for a population census on a regular basis. In order to tackle desertion by soldiers from their regiment, Beresford insisted on the introduction of a system of passports, without which it was prohibited for soldiers to travel during the war, and that all travellers and outsiders be examined by the police.[102]

Unsurprisingly, the problem of desertion had a variety of causes. The numbers of those going absent without leave seemed to be more widespread when the troops were in cantonment rather than on campaign, though when campaigns were going badly there was frequently an upsurge in desertion. Further, the more men were recruited, the higher were the numbers of deserters, meaning that even ignoring genuine illness regiments were almost never at full complement.[103] The pattern of desertion changed when the army fought in Spain in 1812 and 1813, depending apparently on whether the Allied force was advancing or retiring; the fact of desertion remained, although the reduction in incidence in 1813 may be explained by more regular pay and an adequate supply of food. Beresford reacted in a determined fashion to reduce it by indicating that the Spanish authorities would be notified of desertions, and deserters would be liable to be arrested by Spaniards who were able to claim a bounty for each arrest made.[104]

In 1809, as we have seen, Beresford successfully established that his, rather than the Regency Council or the War Council, was the ultimate authority for determining guilt or innocence and the appropriate sentence for any soldier guilty of a misdemeanour. This approach could not have been implemented had Forjaz not supported him by seeking to impose a more structured approach on recruitment and the apprehension of deserters. The seriousness of the issue is shown not only by the fact that one of Beresford's early Ordens do Dia, on 16 April 1809, sought to tackle the problem of desertion, but that in total over forty-five Ordens do Dia before the end of 1813 contained anti-desertion measures to which may be added a further forty-three Ordens setting out specific penalties for individuals guilty of desertion and other related misdemeanours, the first of these being dated 17 June 1809.[105]

Sometimes the authorities had to deal not just with individual desertion, but desertion en masse. This usually involved the militia, such as in July 1810 when Cox reported from Almeida that two companies of the militia of Guarda had deserted and he sought instructions from Beresford as to what to do. He had hoped that the policy of confiscating the property of soldiers who deserted was beginning to take effect. Cox, in fact, may well have analysed the problem correctly in this instance in stating that he had heard a report that the French had entered Nave de Haver, where most of these militia came from, and he thought they had gone to protect families or properties. He had sent a captain after them but was not hopeful of bringing them back. Cox claimed that the safety of Almeida was at stake unless an additional regiment of line was put into the town.[106] Wellington himself despaired of the desertion by militia, writing to Beresford: 'what can be done?' but fortunately on this occasion the Alcalde of a nearby town arrested a number of the deserters and returned them.[107] Beresford responded to Cox's query by telling him to use his discretion in dealing with these deserters and Cox ordered their court martial but reported this was likely to be delayed because of the illness of the Juiz de Fora (a magistrate who administered justice).[108] Later, in 1810 Brigadier General Blunt reported from Óbidos that he had apprehended upwards of fifty deserters, some with their accoutrements, who claimed they were going to join General Silveira. He obviously did not believe the story and reported he was sending them to Lisbon.[109]

The hapless Cox reported other instances of desertion amongst his troops at Almeida, including deserters from the 24th Regiment found guilty at court martial and in respect of which he looked for guidance as to sentencing from the Marshal; but not all deserters were sentenced and those who returned voluntarily were on occasions not court martialled but were punished in some other unspecified way, to be decided by Beresford. In another instance, a member of the Trancoso militia who allowed the whole of the draft he was escorting to escape was sentenced to four months imprisonment.[110] A further troubling practice was the encouragement to desert from one regiment to fill up another; itself amounting to improper conduct.[111]

Insubordination was a lesser crime but still carried harsh penalties. Major Lacerda of the 23rd Regiment was sentenced to be reprimanded in front of his fellow officers; his commanding officer, Lieutenant Colonel Stubbs, also requested Lacerda be removed to another corps in order to preserve discipline, given that he did not wish to remain with the 23rd Regiment.[112] Failing to return from sick leave or provide a medical certificate of continuing illness led Captain Hugh Eccles of the 6th Caçadores into trouble. His defence was that he was a British officer and refused to be attended by a Portuguese medical man. This defence, of dubious merit, does not seem to have impacted on Hugh's career for he was subsequently promoted to be a captain of the 61st Regiment of the British army.[113]

Conviction for desertion from the Portuguese army, as distinct to being absent without leave, frequently though not invariably led to execution by shooting. Curiously, when Lieutenant José Bernardino de Oliveira of the 6th Cavalry regiment abandoned his post at Peso da Régua in the face of the enemy on 10 May 1809 he was merely retired from the service.[114] One analysis over a short period of time suggests that over 50 per cent of the rank-and-file soldiers condemned to die for desertion were executed with an 11 per cent commutation, the comparable figures for officers were just under 15 per cent and just under 18 per cent, respectively.[115] Other sentences included prison, continued detention, exile and even forgiveness.

Desertion was a problem in all the armies involved in this conflict and the correspondence contains numerous orders and other references to execution by shooting for desertion.[116] The figure given for the British army by Oman shows only seventy-eight soldiers adjudged guilty of desertion being shot in the Peninsular War. This figure seems low given the length of the conflict but may be explained by the fact that the British army was non-conscript, unlike others.[117] Late in the war, the Judge-Advocate General to the British Army, Francis Larpent, was to offer a rather strange reason for the paucity of deserters from the British army. He attributed it to the fact that the troops at the front of the line were Portuguese and that this resulted in fewer British and Portuguese deserters.[118]

The percentage recovery of deserters improved between 1809 and 1812 as the systems became more efficient, before falling off slightly in 1813, though whether this decline is due to the army being in Spain and then France for much of the year is unclear. There were numerically many less deserters in 1813 compared with the three previous years. Nevertheless, whereas those recovered had risen from 25 per cent in 1809 to 39 per cent in 1813, some 61 per cent of deserters in the latter year were still not being apprehended.[119] Beresford and Forjaz succeeded in limiting desertion, but eradicating the problem proved as insoluble for them as it did for other armies engaged in the Napoleonic wars.

British officers were not necessarily or always harsh in their application of discipline of members of the Portuguese forces. In 1810, Lieutenant Colonel Elder (3rd Caçadores) looked for a way of avoiding a court martial in respect of two brothers, Captain Joaquim Ignácio de Araújo and Ensign José Marca de Araújo, whom he clearly felt were guilty of various breaches of duty. He said he would adopt any measures devised by the Marshal to deal with the matter.[120]

The reform of the Portuguese medical corps and the treatment of illness within the military was one of the great success stories attached to the creation of an effective Portuguese army. The Regency Council realised the situation current in 1809 was completely inadequate and reduced the ability to put an army in the field. It had determined on some steps, including the establishment of fourteen military hospitals in March 1809, as Beresford was arriving to take up his appointment. However, Beresford quickly realised that the system left much to be desired and he commissioned a report from the British Medical Corps on 21 April 1809. The report, prepared by William Fergusson, was produced in May and it did not mince its findings regarding Portuguese hospitals.[121] Typhus, typhoid, malaria, venereal disease and other illnesses were identified. Fergusson found care to be poor, cleanliness to be virtually non-existent, patients without beds lying on damp floors and a general perception that those who went into hospital did not leave alive.[122] The latter belief made matters worse because men remained with the regiment rather than go to hospital and this caused some of the healthy to become sick in turn.

One of the problems was that the service was made up of hired, non-military, physicians; men who would not march with the army and when Beresford led his force in to Spain in the summer of 1809, there was a lack of medical attendants. Those that were available were castigated by another British doctor who spent two years in the Peninsula prior to 1811. Andrew Halliday MD produced the invaluable *Observations on the Present State of the Portuguese Army, as Organised by Lieutenant-General Sir William Carr Beresford, K.B., Field marshal and Commander in Chief of that Army* ... in 1811 on his return to England. He observed: 'In Portugal the Physicians seem, in the practical part of their profession, to be about a century behind the rest of Europe.' He identified the need to improve standards of cleanliness including the washing of patients, shaving of beards, and what was then a modern practice of giving cold baths for fevers, as well as the use of calomel, antimony and stronger purgatives as some of the alleged failures of Portuguese medical attendants.[123]

With two campaigns in 1809, a full assault on the problem of the medical service, while obviously of the utmost importance, had to be deferred until the autumn, at which stage Beresford informed Forjaz that he could not take the army on campaign again without reform of the Portuguese medical service. In early November he received a report from Andrew Halliday MD, 'Surgeon to His Majesty's Forces', which advised the desirability of establishing a proper regimental hospital with each corps. Halliday inspected the troops of Blunt's brigade at Tomar and found a number of the soldiers unfit for duty and considerable mortality; unsurprising given the wretched accommodation there and the lack of clothing and blankets. He sought a chest of medicines and a complete set of surgical instruments as even these were lacking. Some weeks later Halliday wrote again to Beresford's military secretary, Arbuthnot, complaining of a lack of instructions and an inability to treat the sick and prevent abuses because of a lack of clarity surrounding his position.[124] Frederick Jebb, another British surgeon at Leiria, complained that the medical officers of three regiments quartered in the town were completely without surgical instruments and that the only medicines they could obtain were from the local apothecaries. He too sought a complete chest of medicines and portable instruments together with a mule and pack saddle in order to be able to take the field. Other surgeons wrote to Arbuthnot in a similar vein.[125]

Forjaz responded to Beresford's demands by making additional funds available, but the Marshal clearly felt a root and branch approach was necessary. Beresford had at first sought and obtained the services of James McGrigor to head up the hospital services, but the latter was then diverted to the disastrous British expedition to Walcheren, where army personnel were decimated by what was then referred to as Walcheren fever, but is commonly known as malaria. McGrigor had served with Beresford in Egypt at the beginning of the century and it seems clear Beresford hugely respected him. In the event, McGrigor did not come to the Peninsula until 1812 when he was appointed chief of Wellington's Medical Staff, an outstandingly successful appointment that certainly vindicated Beresford's earlier choice.

In McGrigor's absence William Fergusson, who had applied earlier for the post, renewed his application and was successful in his own appointment in February 1810.[126] Apparently, the intention of the Regency had been to appoint Fergusson Inspector-General of the Portuguese Military Hospitals to give him equality with the Physician-General, but when the commission arrived from Brazil it was found that he had only been appointed Inspector of Hospitals with no right to intervene with the Physician-General. However, he used the style Inspector-General of Portuguese Hospitals, so this deficiency in nomenclature was presumably remedied.[127]

Fergusson carried out a complete reorganisation of both the general and regimental hospital system, carrying all the hallmarks of Beresford's approach to other military organisational challenges; namely regular reports combined with instructions on specific courses to be followed, in this case on many aspects of medical care. By the end of February, Fergusson had established a medical depository; and in March 1810, with a view to ensuring the presence of military surgeons as well as adequate operating equipment, the regiments began to receive thirty sets of bed linen each, together with medicines, surgical kit and dedicated horse conveyances as well as mules.[128] Getting the surgeons to the regiments was the subject of some delay as they apparently refused to go without receiving at least some of their pay arrears, but the problem was largely resolved prior to the beginning of the campaign of 1810.

British medical officers were appointed to the Portuguese army and given the military rank of captain in order to give them authority. Historically, appointments to the medical service in Portugal had been made by the Physician-General, as a result of which appointments on occasion were the subject of political rather than medical qualification. With Forjaz's support, a system was put in place whereby henceforth all medical personnel were examined for competency. A Board was established, composed of the Physician-General, one British and two Portuguese surgeons, for the purpose of examining and appointing candidates and in the Spring of 1810 a number of British and Portuguese were appointed following examination to various regiments.[129] Twelve British surgeons were appointed on 11 March 1810 and a further eighteen British staff surgeons were appointed prior to 1812 as Assistant or Field Inspectors of Hospitals.[130] Halliday, who had been critical of the method by which appointments had been made previously in Portugal, made it clear however that there was plenty of potential amongst Portuguese men of science and by the time he left Portugal in 1811 he was able to express the view regarding them:

> the military hospitals under their management have risen to a degree of excellence seldom equalled; and I feel a pleasure in recording, as a conclusion to these remarks, that the general military hospitals in the city of Coimbra, under the direction of Dr Antonio d'Almeida Caldas, Substitute-professor of Medicine, are now as perfect as any institutions of the kind can possibly be made.[131]

No doubt the performance of the medical staff in the army was encouraged by the very sizeable increases in their pay secured by Beresford from Forjaz. The pay of a Surgeon-Major was raised from 12 to 30 mil-réis per month while that of the assistant surgeon went up from 6 to 20 mil-réis.[132] Halliday was in no doubt about Beresford's success in reforming the medical capacity of the Portuguese army: 'They [the hospitals] were infinitely more destructive to the army than the sword of the enemy, and they would have destroyed it much faster than it could have been recruited had it not been for the exertions of Marshal Beresford.'[133] The Marshal's determination to reform the medical services in the Portuguese army and his success in doing so must have greatly reduced the mortality of injured and sick soldiers.

At the outset of this chapter it was explained that following the successful conclusion of the campaign in northern Portugal in May 1809 and a short rest, the Portuguese army was put into the field again and that therefore, of necessity, training in the summer of 1809 was very much 'on the hoof'. The campaign restricted the training which could be undertaken logistically, but also because of the incessant shortages of clothing, equipment and food supplies, all of which required the attention of both field officers and regimental staff.

Wellesley took the British army, with just two Portuguese regiments, east into Spain in the campaign that ultimately ended in success against Marshal Victor, with Joseph Bonaparte in nominal command, at Talavera de la Reina on 27 and 28 July; a success which was qualified by a strategic withdrawal behind the Portuguese border following the defeat of the Spanish army some time later and the intervention of Soult, who belatedly moved south to the Tagus.[134] Wellesley, who was not impressed by either Cuesta or the Spanish army, realised that for the time being he would have to fight a defensive war, telling Beresford that maintaining the army in Portugal was now the priority. While Wellesley worried that the French might attempt to take the great Spanish border fortress of Ciudad Rodrigo, and he was at that time prepared to make every effort to prevent its capture, neither he nor Beresford felt the French would at this time make a determined attempt to invade Portugal. Nevertheless, Wellesley made contingency plans requiring Beresford to conduct a fighting withdrawal so as to give time for the British army in Estremadura to come to his relief.[135]

The Portuguese army's part in the summer campaign was to guard the northern and north eastern frontiers of Portugal and Wellesley's left flank against French attack, whether in the form of a rejuvenated Soult's 2nd Corps, Mortier's 5th Corps, Ney's 6th Corps, or a combination of these forces. Beresford dispatched Brigadier General Archibald Campbell with the 3rd, 13th and 15th regiments north of the Douro and then proceeded to assemble his main force near Almeida. Before he was able to do so, Beresford had to return from Abrantes, where he had met with Wellesley to determine the strategy for the campaign, to Lisbon to plead with the Regency for supplies and money required urgently for the Portuguese army.[136] This time-consuming task was to become a familiar scenario during the course of the war.

By the end of July Beresford had some 18,000 men assembled near Almeida. Before moving into Spain they engaged in an intense period of training under both British officers who were already embedded and those who continued to arrive.[137] At the same time, the Ordens do Dia reveal that Beresford promoted a considerable number of Portuguese officers in June and July, including four Lieutenant Colonels, six Majors, four Captains and fifty Lieutenants.

On 2 July, Soult had received Napoleon's orders placing him in overall command of the forces under Mortier and Ney as well as his own. He sought to draw the three corps together at Salamanca but was frustrated by Ney's unwillingness to cooperate and by Joseph Bonaparte's insistence that part of Mortier's command was required in central Spain. Soult's intention was to seize Ciudad Rodrigo, and Almeida if possible, but he then received instructions from Joseph to threaten the left flank of Wellesley's army, thus requiring him to move south. Meanwhile, at the end of July, Beresford had moved his force east towards Ciudad Rodrigo where he liaised with the Spanish army of the Left under the Duque del Parque. As Soult moved south towards Wellesley's army, Beresford did likewise in parallel. On 9 August he moved the troops to the mountains of Perales occupying the pass of Puerto de Perales. When Soult occupied Puerto de Baños on 12 August, having evicted Robert Wilson's force, part of Beresford's army was at Moraleja.

Three days later, Beresford's main force established itself in a good defensive position at Zarza la Mayor. By then his supply situation was critical. The Portuguese commissariat was not able to supply his force, and indeed the Regency suggested that once he had entered Spain it was for the Spaniards to feed it.[138] In spite of promises from del Parque, who did in fact place two Spanish liaison officers with Beresford, totally inadequate provisions were supplied. With his army starving, sickness and desertion on the increase, and discipline beginning to break down, Beresford told del Parque that he had no choice but to retreat into Portugal.[139] Indeed, Wellesley had told him to retire and defend the passes into Portugal. By 20 August Beresford's main force was in Castelo Branco, recuperating but still guarding the Portuguese frontier.[140] Food remained a real problem and Beresford corresponded almost daily with Forjaz on the subject well into the late autumn.

From Castelo Branco Beresford explained to Forjaz that he was liaising and cooperating with Wellesley in the retreat of the British army and that the movements of his own force were in effect dictated by those of the army under Wellesley.[141] By early September, many of the Portuguese troops were back in Tomar where further training began in earnest, continuing until late spring 1810. If the Portuguese army was suffering through lack of provisions, then so was that of Wellesley who ordered his forces back to Portugal on 19 August, being cantoned initially for the most part between Alcantara and Campo Maior with headquarters at Badajoz in Spanish Extremadura.

Thus ended the campaign of 1809. The French had been driven out of Portugal, but neither Wellesley nor Beresford were under any illusions that they would not return eventually given the massive forces at their disposal. Wellesley, writing to Beresford on 19 August, says:

> I agree with you in thinking that the enemy will not now invade Portugal; and I also agree with you in thinking that it is desirable that your troops should have rest and leisure; and that a serious endeavour should be made to organise, discipline and clothe them, for which indeed, there has hardly yet been time.[142]

With this in mind he approved Beresford's moving his forces back to between Abrantes and Leiria while asking Beresford to put his right wing on Tomar and not to occupy Abrantes as Wellesley wished to do so himself; for the position of his own army was now becoming critical through lack of provisions to feed it and a lack of horses for both the cavalry and artillery, notwithstanding assurances from Cuesta that Spain would help in this respect.

Wellesley subsequently established his own force along the Portuguese–Spanish border between Elvas and Abrantes. Aware of the lack of cooperation between the Spanish armies and fearing a lack of leadership, Wellesley impressed on Beresford that they must make arrangements for the defence of Portugal; a strategy which proved completely justified with the defeat of Spanish armies at Ocaña and Alba de Tormes that autumn. The Commander of the Allied forces showed his customary perspicacity when writing to Beresford saying that the British government had acted rightly when sending troops to save Portugal while the French were involved with the Austrians; but now Napoleon had defeated the Austrians the question became a very different one, and the government decision was likely to be influenced 'by the prospect which you may be able to hold out of the existence of a Portuguese military force'. The ensuing correspondence makes it clear that Wellesley and Beresford worked closely and in harmony, with Wellesley doing his utmost to assist Beresford in the task of improving the Portuguese army.[143]

Wellesley recognised the immense difficulties faced by Beresford; in particular the lack of time to train while on campaign.[144] Though he despaired privately to Wellesley that it would take at least a year to train it properly, Beresford now followed up with intensive and in-depth training of the Portuguese army.[145] Wellesley, who had been created Viscount Wellington of Talavera and Wellington on 26 August 1809, promised the Marshal his support vis-à-vis the Regency on 5 October saying that Beresford 'will find me disposed to do everything in my power'.[146]

It was not until October that Napoleon, following his decisive victory over the Austrians at Wagram, confirmed that he intended to conquer the Iberian Peninsula with overwhelming force. While the construction of the Lines of Torres Vedras continued apace, there was nervousness in both Portugal and England that Napoleon's destruction of the Fifth Coalition would ultimately lead to the return of the British army in Portugal to Britain in the face of overwhelming force. Beresford's agent in London, Angus McDonald, put it thus: 'The peace between Austria and France will render all your exertions to preserve Spain and Portugal to no avail. I wish you were ordered off before the numerous battalions of the enemy march against you.' He went on to express concern that the British officers in the Portuguese service might be left to their fate in the event of a French conquest, and suggested it would be a good idea to bring the Portuguese regiments off as well and use them to take possession of Montevideo and other Spanish possessions in South America to avoid these becoming part of Bonaparte's empire, as the loss of South America would be irreparable to British commerce.[147]

In a similar vein Lowry Cole, who received orders to join Wellington in the Peninsula in September 1809 and was to serve with Beresford for much of the war as commander of the 4th Division, wrote to his brother-in-law, Lord Grantham: 'In the opinion of most people my stay will not be long, as it is supposed Lord Wellington cannot resist the force against him. I cannot find out whether it is the intention of the government to send more troops there or not, but I hope that some of those returning from Flushing will go.'[148]

McDonald and Cole were far from alone in their concern that the Anglo-Portuguese army might be steamrollered by a much larger French force. The concern of the British government is evident in Liverpool's letter to Wellington of 20 October, in which he set out a set of questions ranging from the likelihood of a French invasion of Portugal to the ability to bring off the British army should it prove necessary. Notwithstanding Wellington's relatively upbeat response on 14 November, Liverpool directed Wellington in early December that if embarkation of the British army became necessary, only a very small proportion of the best horses should be brought home, and that there was no intention of bringing back the horses of either the cavalry or the artillery; a chilling reminder of the events surrounding the embarkation at La Coruña only a year earlier.[149]

8 THE PORTUGUESE ARMY, 1809–1810

Beresford returned from the summer campaign in the Spanish province of Salamanca concerned about the inability of the Portuguese administration to supply the army with the requirements for a campaign, but particularly its failure to feed or pay the troops properly. The consequences of these shortcomings were no different from other armies of the period: a breakdown of discipline leading to seizures while foraging, desertion and insubordination, and a corresponding lack of effectiveness as a fighting force.[1] A huge onus now lay on Beresford to produce an efficient fighting machine, for as Wellington wrote to Liverpool on 14 November 1809: 'I consider the Portuguese government and army as the principals in the contest for their own independence, and that the success or failure must depend principally upon their own exertions, and the bravery of their army.' A good start had already been made in Wellington's view for he felt able to tell Liverpool at this time:

> It is scarcely necessary to point out the alteration in their [the Portuguese officers] situation produced by the appointment of Marshal Beresford to command the Portuguese army. All the abuses which existed in the service have been done away; and a regular system of discipline has been established, requiring the attention and attendance of all the officers with their regiments ...[2]

Between September 1809 and late spring 1810 Beresford showed his characteristic determination both in respect of the further training of the regiments for the next campaign and with a view to ensuring their proper supply. In doing so, he was supported by Forjaz to a high degree, though the latter hesitated to take steps which would structurally alter the Portuguese supply system and this diminished the effectiveness of Beresford's reforms in some areas. It should be remembered that Forjaz and Beresford had to deal with a Regency Council which was on occasions hostile and intransigent to the proposals for reform. Where necessary, Beresford did not hesitate to call on Wellington's support and in the last resort he would appeal to Prince João in Rio de Janeiro, though conscious that any such exchange would take months to complete. From early 1810, the British minister plenipotentiary in Lisbon, John Villiers, attended on the Regency on occasions when military matters were being discussed. Later in 1810, his replacement Charles Stuart formally became a member of that body, in a year that witnessed the retirement from it of the Marquês das Minas and the appointment of the Principal Sousa as well as the Conde de Redondo and Dr Nogueras.[3] Described by Napier as always opposed to the British authorities in Portugal, the avowed enemy of Beresford, the contriver of all confusion and the most mischievous person in Portugal it was the appointment of José António de Meneses de Sousa Coutinho, most frequently referred to as the Principal Sousa, that was to provide both Wellington and Beresford with many and varied challenges in the prosecution of the war.[4]

Training of the infantry proceeded apace in Tomar and other depots such as Peniche. Recruits were sent to Peniche where the governor was Brigadier General Blunt, who oversaw the initial training of large numbers of men prior to their being forwarded to their regiments. The imposition of the rules and regulations applied to the British army by British and Portuguese officers produced a fighting force which was to impress repeatedly not only the British general staff, but on occasions would bemuse their French opponents who tended not only to be dismissive of the Portuguese but who referred (and still do) to this war as 'La Guerre d'Espagne' rather than 'the Peninsular War' as it was known in Britain or 'As Invasões Francesas' (or 'A Guerra Peninsular') in Portugal. The Spanish for their part call the war 'La Guerra de la Independencia Española.'

The training of the cavalry made progress, albeit slowly, under the Conde de Sampáio assisted by various British officers. These included Lieutenant Colonel John Campbell, Brigadier General George Allen Madden and Brigadier General Sir Henry Fane. On his arrival in Portugal, Beresford had initially concentrated on the infantry and was somewhat despondent about the ability to get the cavalry into a state of effectiveness which would allow it to go on campaign. The shortage of horses in particular meant that only some regiments were mounted and even these frequently had to use smaller horses than would be normal for heavy cavalry, though they were sufficient for guard and reconnaissance duties.

Though Beresford complained to Forjaz early in 1810 that Madden's cavalry brigade was rendered almost completely useless through lack of horses and equipment, progress was such as to enable two brigades of Portuguese cavalry, along with a number of infantry regiments, to be sent south of the Tagus with Major General Hill in the spring of that year.[5] Beresford felt more was required, and in April sought Wellington's assistance. The latter advised Beresford that he had spoken to Major General Payne and that as a result troops of the 13th Light Dragoons would be sent to teach the Portuguese light dragoons work exercise at Salvaterra.[6]

Brigadier General Fane was assigned the responsibility for this training, and was appointed to command the 1st, 4th, 7th and 10th regiments of cavalry in the Portuguese army formed into a brigade with the 13th Light Dragoons.[7] In June 1810, he expressed his opinion to Wellington saying they were properly equipped, mounted and armed; with the horses 'all in good condition'. While there was still room for improvement, a good deal had been achieved by way of discipline.[8] In a letter written in October to Beresford, Fane was critical of the great waste of horses by the Portuguese cavalry due to issues such as using young horses unable to bear the fatigue, lack of care, including failure to shoe horses, and lack of forage.[9] The move to use the 13th Light Dragoons to train the Portuguese cavalry was seen as successful, as later in the year Fane suggested to Beresford that he look again to the 13th for assistance with other Portuguese cavalry, as some of their members would know Portuguese from their time with the regiments under Madden.[10]

Fane's optimism was born out when the cavalry of the 4th Regiment surprised and captured sixty French dragoons without losing a single Portuguese horseman on 22 August at Escalhas da Cima near Castelo Branco.[11] While there were to be occasions later in the war when the Portuguese cavalry gave Wellington cause for concern, as indeed did its British counterpart, it contributed to the war effort and it would be incorrect to dismiss it as a force of little consequence.

The artillery arm of the Portuguese army was felt to be in better condition than either the infantry or cavalry in 1809. It was to prosper under Alexander Dickson, who ultimately became Wellington's commander of artillery with the Anglo-Portuguese army in 1813 on the long haul through northern Spain culminating with the battle of Toulouse in April 1814. With Wellington's support, Beresford introduced a number of reforms in late 1809.[12] This involved reforming the composition of the four existing regiments of artillery, providing specific companies of firemen, miners and pontooniers.[13] Later, having witnessed the deficiency at the siege of Badajoz, Beresford was to raise in 1812 a dedicated battalion of artificers. The training of the artillery must have been impressive for even General Picton, known for his bluntness and direct speech, confirmed to Beresford that he had inspected two brigades of Portuguese light artillery under Victor von Arentschildt attached to the 3rd Division on 15 July 1810 and found 'the mules in excellent condition and the general equipment in perfect state for active service'.[14]

The creation of an effective fighting force with an *esprit de corps* required more than training and an understanding of the regulations combined with a willingness to implement orders. It needed to be clothed, armed, fed and paid on a regular basis, but these four fundamentals were to challenge both Beresford and Forjaz in the winter of 1809 and early 1810. The difficulties encountered in these administrative areas were of such magnitude that they threatened to distract Beresford's attention from turning promising material into a well-tuned fighting force. It had not proved possible to attire the regiments in a consistent manner prior to the campaigns of 1809. In the normal course of events clothing would have been made up and distributed by the arsenal based in Lisbon. This required a degree of organisation to ensure that uniforms of a quality and quantity identifying each regiment could be produced and distributed on a regular basis so that as items became worn out or lost in service they could be replaced without delay. Beresford realised very quickly that the arsenal had neither the resources nor the commitment to supply the army on an efficient basis and he sought to enlist Forjaz's support to reform it.

In early 1809, a quantity of clothing including shoes and accoutrements had been received from England as part of the aid approved in the autumn of 1808. Though this initial shipping was only for 10,000 men, by early autumn further consignments brought the British contribution to over 20,000 uniforms and accoutrements. In the interim Beresford had arranged for regiments to be supplied with cloth from the arsenals, on the basis that it would be made up by men in the regiments with the requisite skills. However, once again the supply system of the arsenal foundered in that it failed to supply the thread to sew the uniforms and six months later both Cox and Beresford were fuming at the incompetence of the arsenal.[15] Beresford enlisted Wellington's support in dealing with the British cabinet, seeking clothing and equipment for 30,000 men in the autumn of 1809.[16] Those supplies, including 30,000 uniforms and shoes for 60,000 men, began to arrive from February 1810 onwards and by June of that year sufficient supplies of this nature appeared to exist in Portugal, though distribution remained an issue through lack of transport to get the goods to the regiments.[17]

In 1809 Beresford had tried to overcome distribution problems caused through a lack of horses, oxen and carts by arranging for regiments to collect clothing individually from the arsenal. That system had ended in chaos when commanding officers attended themselves with a view to prioritising their own regiment's demands, and Beresford accordingly issued an Order providing for none higher than lieutenants to be used for the collection of uniforms.[18] A few days later distribution from the arsenal was temporarily abandoned with a view to putting its affairs in order. Beresford railed against the inefficiency of the arsenal, but to little avail at this stage as Forjaz felt there were other priorities.[19] Whereas Beresford thought the arsenal incompetent and dishonest, Forjaz felt that distribution was the greater problem and after investigation rejected the accusations of dishonesty.

Beresford sought to address incompetency by requiring both the arsenal and the regiments to keep and use records to assist clothing the army, just as he had used records for recruitment to and retaining regiments. He sought to establish what stores were contained in the arsenal and what had been supplied to the regiments. At a regimental level commanding officers were required to make returns showing what they had received and when they had received such materials. While regimental officers did make returns, the disorganisation of the arsenal meant that records of disbursements by the arsenal remained unavailable.

Early in 1810 the reports coming from the regiments made it clear to Forjaz that Beresford's complaints regarding supply were completely justified. Some units were reportedly without not just blankets to keep out the cold, but so lacking in clothing that they were not in a position to go on campaign,[20] Forjaz's inquiries led him to recognise that the arsenal was not able to produce sufficient finished uniforms within the time requirements, for in March 1810 he moved to appoint civilian tailors in Lisbon to cut the uniforms from cloth available at the arsenal.[21] He then appointed twelve commissaries with responsibility to supply the regiments from the arsenal.

Beresford remained unhappy, and later in 1810 he provided for regiments to be supplied on a rotational basis so that each regiment would receive new clothing on a regular predetermined basis. Uniforms were expected to last one year and priority was initially given to the clothing of regiments as yet unclothed or who had received clothing early in 1809. A further tightening up of the system of supply was made by Forjaz and Beresford, reserving to themselves decisions on resupply.[22]

As if the problems of the arsenal were not enough, it transpired that one large consignment of uniforms supplied from England was not just the wrong colour (brown rather than blue) but they were so shoddily made up in some instances as to fall apart quickly.[23] The question of colour was easier to resolve than the issue of the quality of made-up uniforms received from Britain. This deficiency proved so extensive and enduring that ultimately Beresford persuaded the British government to send cloth out to Portugal to have it made up into uniforms locally. Beresford used a rather astute argument to advocate making up the uniforms in Portugal, namely the cost of clothing 30,000 men in England would clothe the entire Portuguese army if the goods were made up in Portugal from cloth sent from England.[24]

Neither Forjaz nor Beresford ever fully resolved the inefficiencies of the arsenal. There was a lack of political will on Forjaz's behalf to implement a root and branch reform and in any event shortage of finance and other demands meant that he did not regard such reform as a priority. Supply problems were alleviated by the changes introduced in 1809 and 1810 and by the use later of local depots to supply the troops, but shortages continued to occur from time to time throughout the war. Between them and with Wellington's help, Forjaz and Beresford created a functioning though less than perfect system of supply.

Arms and ammunition for the infantry and cavalry were plentiful in Portugal by 1810 due to their prodigious output in Britain. Transporting them to the regiments stationed at a distance from Lisbon still remained a problem on occasions, due to the perennial difficulty of securing carts and the beasts to draw them. There was no separate military department charged with transport and as a consequence the army was dependent upon civilian contractors. After a chaotic start for both the British and Portuguese army, regulations were introduced in September 1809 providing for the compulsory requisition of carts, animals and drivers with provision for seizure and fines if they were not forthcoming.[25] Nevertheless, supply problems still persisted and in July 1810, only weeks before the commencement of the French siege of Almeida, the governor, William Cox, wrote to Beresford stating that notwithstanding the assurances of Quartermaster General D'Urban that 3,000 new arms were on the way to the fortress from Lisbon he despaired of getting them from the arsenal. He went on to complain that the 24th Regiment was still without bayonet belts, they lacked 500 caps, besides also missing haversacks, canteens, greatcoats, straps and various other articles. The position was stated to be even worse in respect of the Arganil and Trancoso militia regiments, with the former having no accoutrements at all and the latter few but very bad.[26] In the same month, July 1810, Lieutenant Colonel William Stewart complained that he had been sent 100 recruits from Chaves without jackets or trousers, as a result of which they could not join the battalion as currently clothed. He had applied to the arsenal and to General Leite without success.[27]

Beresford took this and many other complaints up with Forjaz. Supplies continued to pour in from England, but there were delays even from that source leading to Colonel Bunbury at the War Office, when telling Beresford in April 1810 that 60,000 pairs of shoes had been shipped for the Portuguese army, that if there was a pressing need for shoes prior to the arrival of this consignment, these should be borrowed from the British stores and replaced later.[28] Lest it be thought that Beresford was overreacting in his criticism of the arsenal, Brigadier José António da Rosa, Commander-General of the Portuguese artillery, complained of his inability to get supplies of munitions and cartridges in July 1810. In despair, Beresford forwarded the correspondence to Forjaz warning of the consequences and saying that while he could give Rosa no answer, the position needed to be remedied as soon as possible.[29] Ultimately, with a view to tackling this supply problem, a separate supply service within the Portuguese army was created in 1811.

Clothing and arming the Portuguese army was a challenge, but nothing compared to the difficulties faced in feeding and paying the troops. Here again Beresford sought to base supply of foodstuffs on regimental record keeping. Actual supply, however, was often frustrated by a lack of transport and finance. To some extent supply was addressed by the establishment of forward depots, but that system tended to be subjected to immediate demands which prevented the building up of a reserve. [30] Supply of foodstuffs and drink to the Portuguese army was the responsibility of the Junta de Viveres, a commissariat receiving its funds from the State Treasury. The Junta operated through a system of intendants in the provinces with *feitors* (managers) appointed at local level. These latter would be contracted to obtain the supplies required, which were paid for on bills drawn on the Junta. Lack of funds led to delayed payments and an unwillingness to supply foodstuffs. The result was severe shortages amongst certain regiments.

The problem of feeding the Portuguese army was exacerbated by the fact that not only was the Junta seeking to purchase on credit, but that frequently it was competing with the British commissariat which was able to pay cash. The result was, unsurprisingly, that producers chose to sell to the cash buyer. Wellesley and Beresford resolved a number of potential sources of friction by the issue of a joint memorandum in 1809 setting out procedures for when the two armies were operating together, so that there would not be competition for supplies and transport. [31]

Wellesley initially resisted suggestions that the British Commisariat take over the supply of the Portuguese army in addition to its own duties. This decision appears to have been influenced by a belief that the Junta could be made to operate efficiently and a desire to ensure that Portugal contributed to the common cause to the best of its abilities. The huge difficulties and suffering caused to the Portuguese regiments, whether with Beresford or indeed Wellesley, in the summer of 1809 led to a realisation that the Junta was incapable of performing its duties. In a memorandum of 2 February 1810, Villiers suggested that there were three alternatives: expanding the Portuguese commissariat, turning over its responsibilities to its British counterpart or contracting entrepreneurs to supply the army. In his opinion the preferred alternative would be to place responsibility for the supply of both armies with the British commissariat, with a settling of debts due by the Portuguese on a regular basis. It was to be 1811, however, before Wellington formally accepted the necessity of the British commissariat supplying the Portuguese regiments with his army with a financial settlement taking place each month.[32] The independent

Portuguese forces still continued to suffer on an intermittent basis. Meanwhile in 1810 the problem of feeding the Portuguese army which had threatened its existence as a viable force when on campaign in 1809 remained, both when in cantonment but more especially when on campaign.[33] On occasions it was so bad that the officers had to use private funds to secure such food as was available. Beresford observed to Forjaz, 'never has a Commander in Chief had a worse commissary, which wants to command him'.[34]

In July 1809, provisions destined for the British troops but being stored in Guarda were embargoed and used to feed Portuguese brigades assembling there.[35] On other occasions the Portuguese resorted to seizing food convoys destined for the British army, such as in October 1809 when thirty-one bullocks were seized. Following a formal protest, twenty-one were returned some days later and the cost of the other ten, which had been consumed, was discharged by the Portuguese commissary.[36]

The campaign of 1810 was not even underway when Beresford was advised by Picton's ADC in April that the Portuguese regiments with the 3rd Division at Pinhel were experiencing great difficulties and were frequently without bread, principally because the commissary did not have funds to pay for it, the consequences being that people hid their grain rather than make it available. He went so far as to suggest Beresford defer sending additional recruits until regular subsistence could be provided.[37] Likewise, in April, Dickson complained that orders to move artillery without adequate provision for the supply of corn would cause the mules to starve, for they could not be kept in 'an efficient state' on 'green forage alone'. He too stated that the farmers and country people would not advance anything on credit and instead chose to conceal their stock; though he did not doubt that with money supplies would appear.[38]

By mid May 1810, D'Urban was incandescent with rage at the failure of the Portuguese government, accusing it of having deceived Beresford on the matter of provisions: 'there are not above 5 days consumption in hand and no hope of more when that's done. If there be no treachery in this, there is the most shameless imbecility, iniquity and sloth that ever disgraced an Executive Government'.[39] On 24 May Wellington agreed to supply rations of beef to Beresford for his troops in a number of locations, with receipts to be given by the Portuguese commissaries. A week later he was looking into the business of supplying the Portuguese with forage corn.[40]

Once the campaign of 1810 began the problems became more acute. Beresford expressed his concern to Wellington regarding the supplies at Almeida, which it was anticipated the French would besiege once they had captured Ciudad Rodrigo. Wellington accepted there was a problem stating:

> the state of the magazine at Almeida is a matter of serious concern, and I do not know how to remedy it. We cannot withdraw our troops, nor can we feed them without sometimes coming upon the magazine at Almeida and as for carriages to draw up more we are worse off than ever and I have not seen or heard of an effective remedy.[41]

He went on to suggest the evacuation of the inhabitants of the town but thought it should be delayed until the last moment prior to the arrival of the French army. Two weeks later Wellington again referred to the problem, stating that the shortage of provisions and means of transport meant the British army was drawing biscuit from Almeida reducing that stored there from 251,648 lbs to 196,000 lbs. Wellington remarked that if 'we cannot get provisions or carriages we must conserve the provisions which we have in store'.[42]

The shortages in a major depot such as Almeida were not unique and it is clear that on the ground the Portuguese regiments' suffering continued. In early July Picton told Wellington that the whole weight of supplying the Portuguese artillery with his division would fall on the commissary of that division unless some means could be resorted to which would make the Portuguese commissary more effective, given that it had indicated bluntly that it could not supply its own.[43] The position remained dire later in 1810. Brigadier General Francis Coleman, then stationed at Quinta Nova, advised Beresford that he was having difficulties with provisions of every sort. He wrote:

> I have not had one ration of bread delivered to the brigade this day and have made an application from General Sontag and the British Commissary at Torres Vedras, but without effect and we have not received either rice or salt fish for some time. I have with the utmost difficulty these last few days got the commissary to procure a few sheep and goats from our front which have kept us from absolute want but the trouble I have had with the commissary of the brigade since he joined us at Filiadoca [sic] I cannot describe, and I have now sent him to you with this, he is the most inattentive and lazy and good for nothing and unfit for his situation.[44]

Pay was closely linked with both performance and the ability to survive. Historically, the pay of junior officers in the Portuguese army had been low, perhaps because they tended to come from notable families of independent means. However, poor pay did not encourage devotion to the job and may account for a considerable degree of absenteeism. Reforms introduced by Beresford, with Wellington's support, led the British government to agree a subsidy whereby junior officers pay was doubled early in 1810 and that of more senior officers increased by more than 50 per cent.[45] Regular pay was important not least because the existence of specie enabled cash purchases to be made. However, it was always in arrears causing difficulties of many sorts. Much of the time the office of the Portuguese Treasurer General (Tesoureiro Geral) was short of funds, and even when it did have funds its dilatory approach caused huge distress. Wellington and Beresford both stressed the need for Portugal to raise more finance itself, notwithstanding the ever increasing British subsidy. Wellington's intervention early in 1810 seems to have improved the situation temporarily, but it was not long before Beresford was once again complaining to Forjaz in this respect.[46]

It was not just the pay of regular troops that was in arrears. Pay for the militia working on the Lines of Torres Vedras was frequently delayed resulting in an unavailability of units to work. Fletcher wrote imploring letters to Beresford both seeking more men to work on the Lines and to make representations on behalf of the militia as to the inadequacy of the amount of their daily pay and rations.[47] Captain Peter Patton of the Royal Engineers, charged with strengthening the defences of Abrantes, wrote to Beresford in November and December 1809 seeking skilled and unskilled men and money to pay them.[48]

Forjaz accepted the need to feed and pay the troops claiming that the army was in fact receiving priority in terms of income available, and Beresford was pushing an open door with the Secretary for War and Foreign Affairs when seeking the reform of the Portuguese treasury.[49] Steps were taken, including the appointment of additional paymasters with funds being forwarded to regimental bases on a more regular basis. While this resulted in a decrease in arrears in 1810, the problem was to resurface again when the Anglo-Portuguese army moved into Spain and ultimately France later in the war. The simple fact was that Portuguese income and British subsidy combined were insufficient to support the war effort and to sustain the army at the targeted level. The commercial treaties agreed between the British and Portuguese governments giving access to British traders to Brazil decimated Portugal's primary source of income, as was recognised by Wellington.[50] Furthermore, despite very substantial increases in the British subsidy, which was designed to support 30,000 Portuguese troops and their British officers, the mode of calculation of the subsidy meant that it in fact supported a lesser number. This again was recognised by Wellington.[51]

When it emerged that the Treasury was being particularly reticent in discharging the pay due to British officers in the Portuguese service in late 1809 and early 1810, Beresford dealt with the problem firmly and quickly. Whether by design or through inadvertence, the incomplete nature of the records of a number of foreigners in Portuguese service meant that either reduced or in some cases no payments were being made to a number of those officers. Beresford and his staff received an increasing number of complaints. A series of letters in October 1809 regarding the pay of British officers attached to the 11th Regiment made the claim that it would be impossible to go on unless the position was regularised.[52] Beresford adopted the simple expedient of arranging for the arrears of pay of British officers to be paid directly out of the British subsidy, but there continued to be incidents in 1810 where such officers complained they were not being paid because the *pagador* (paymaster) had allegedly not been notified that the man in question was a Portuguese officer.[53]

It should be noted that whatever the difficulties in securing payment of the British officers in the Portuguese army, substantial numbers still continued to apply throughout 1810. Each application was considered on its merits both by Beresford, who was being asked to take on the officer, and by the Commander in Chief, in consultation with the commander of the British regiment he wished to leave, albeit temporarily; the latter having to consider whether it would cause inconvenience in that quarter.[54]

In March, Captain William Beresford of the 31st Foot applied to join the Portuguese service, but having been approved decided to go to England to consult with friends as he had permission from Wellington to take this leave. Given Wellington's and Beresford's reluctance to allow officers to go home on leave, family connections may have played their part in securing this permission, though no evidence has been found that this William Beresford was a relation of the Marshal.[55] In July 1810, Bathurst advised Arbuthnot that Wellington could not give leave of absence to Lieutenant Robinson of the 32nd Regiment so as to enable him to join the Portuguese army, though this decision may have been revised subsequently as he appears on the strength of the 9th Portuguese regiment.[56] In the same month, Major Hill of the 3rd Foot sought a transfer which does not appear to have been granted [204/34]; and on 12 July Arbuthnot noted that eight British officers were joining the Portuguese service being allocated to cavalry, line regiments and caçadores.[57] At the same time he noted three resignations, including that of Brigadier General Sir Robert Wilson, who in fact had gone home the previous autumn following Beresford and Wellington's refusal to let him keep the Loyal Lusitanian Legion as an independent command.[58] A Lieutenant Watson applied in November 1810 with the observation he could be spared as there were then twenty-seven subalterns with the 23rd Regiment (Royal Welsh Fusiliers); an application which may have been motivated in part by a desire to gain promotion in circumstances where it was likely to be a lengthy process within the regiment.[59] British non-commissioned officers were also assigned to the Portuguese army, with Major McGeachy reporting that ten such NCOs had joined the 22nd Regiment in April 1810, remarking that they appeared to be attentive and steady men who he hoped would be a valuable addition to the corps.[60]

The continued secondment of British officers to the Portuguese army in 1810 and later meant a reduction in opportunity for Portuguese to advance; but it is clear that wherever appropriate Beresford promoted Portuguese officers, even at the expense of their British counterparts. In doing so, Beresford and his regimental commanders were careful to avoid promoting on the basis of seniority alone, trying to ensure that those of ability succeeded retiring officers.[61] When Major Alexander McGeachy did not get the command of the 22nd Regiment on the retirement of another officer, and a Portuguese officer, Major Silveira, was appointed in his place, he resigned his commission.[62] However, he seems to have accepted a transfer to the 17th Portuguese regiment subsequently, before being killed at the second siege of Badajoz in May 1811.[63] In a similar vein, Beresford made it clear that British officers must show the same respect to Portuguese officers as they would show to a British officer, instructing Major General Hamilton to give Lieutenant Colonel le Mesurier a dressing down for commenting on the conduct of Brigadier General Fonseca.[64]

In December 1809, a general return of the Portuguese army, excluding cavalry, showed the total number of effectives to be 42,352 including the Loyal Lusitanian Legion (1,582), the police Guard (1,006) and four regiments of artillery (4,250). Of these there were currently 17,718 in British pay drawn from twelve regiments of line and three battalions of Caçadores.[65] Details on paper were importantly supported by progress in training and discipline. Beresford, along with his Quartermaster General, Benjamin D'Urban, inspected the 4th and 10th regiments of infantry at Tomar on 14 December with D'Urban observing: 'I have never seen an English brigade move with more steadiness and precision.' He felt that their commanding officers, Colonel Archibald Campbell and Lieutenant Colonel Warde Oliver deserved the highest credit.[66]

Given all the issues faced in clothing, arming, feeding and paying the Portuguese army, when Beresford and Wellington set out on a tour of inspection of the regiments at the end of 1809 and early 1810, it is perhaps remarkable the findings were extremely positive. Setting out from Coimbra they visited a number of regiments including that of Vila Real (3rd Caçadores) at

Punhete on 30 December on which D'Urban remarked it was 'in a state of discipline altogether excellent'.[67] The following day they inspected the Algarve Brigade (2nd and 14th) at Torres Novas and Wellington was 'perfectly pleased'.[68] Over the next week they jointly inspected a number of other Portuguese regiments, Wellington reporting to Lord Liverpool (who in the autumn of 1809 had succeeded Castlereagh as Secretary of State for War and the Colonies) that he was impressed with the progress made in reforming the Portuguese army:

> In my progress through Portugal to this place [Coimbra], I have had opportunities of seeing fifteen regiments in the Portuguese service, and I have great pleasure in informing your Lordship that the progress of all these troops in discipline is considerable, that some of the regiments are in very good order, and that I have no doubt but that the whole will prove an useful acquisition ... The pains taken by Marshal Beresford and all the British officers serving under his command, to bring the Portuguese army to the state in which it now is, are highly deserving of his Majesty's approbation.[69]

When Wellington returned to Coimbra, Beresford continued his round of inspections noting some imperfections but being generally satisfied with progress.

It was not just Wellington that admired what Beresford had achieved with the Portuguese army in under twelve months. Alexander Gordon, who was one of Wellington's ADCs, wrote home from headquarters at Coimbra to his brother, Lord Aberdeen, on 3 January 1810:

> On our way here Wellington went to see the Portuguese army ... I assure you their improvement has been very great and rapid. They will have in two months 20,000 effective men, almost as well disciplined as any British troops, and I have not a doubt incorporated with them will fight ... Indeed General Beresford deserves the greatest credit for the manner in which he has already brought about the army of this country.[70]

Major General Henry MacKinnon, who was to die in January 1812 in the assault on Ciudad Rodrigo, commanded a brigade in Picton's 3rd Division. In March 1810 he observed:

> I have with Colonel S****, who commands one of the regiments, been able to form a tolerably good opinion of the character of the Portuguese troops. They are extremely tractable, patient, sober, and I am informed, there are few complaints of their dishonesty. The Portuguese officers very unlike their Castillian neighbours, are ready to grant the superiority of our countrymen, and to receive instruction from them; and I doubt not, when the opportunity presents itself, we shall see them fighting by our sides, in a very different manner from the army of Cuesta at Talavera.[71]

William Warre, then serving as ADC to Beresford and who had been responsible for translating the directions for regulating infantry and cavalry into Portuguese from English, was a close and constant observer. He felt the Portuguese had made real progress and writing from Lisbon on 17

February 1810 told his father: 'The Portuguese troops are in very high spirits and seem anxious to meet the enemy. They are in a very improved state of discipline, and promise well ... I never saw a regiment embark in better style or higher spirits than the 29th [*sic*] Portuguese regt. did for Cádiz a few days ago.'[72] He was even complimentary about the Portuguese cavalry by mid March, though he doubted the wisdom of mounting them on mares, a decision which was borne of necessity.[73] He thought the Portuguese would fight well when commanded by British officers, referring to the Herculean and indefatigable exertions of Beresford as, 'a very superior, strong minded, clever officer, and should his labours be crowned with the success they deserve, he will become one of the most eminent men in England, and have deserved more of this country than they can ever repay'.[74]

There were of course exceptions to the praise for the Portuguese regiments. Picton, some months later, grumbled about the state of the Portuguese brigade under Lieutenant Colonel José Champalimaud (9th and 21st) forming part of his (3rd) Division claiming it was not possible for that officer to conform to the regulations or to promote the discipline of the corps, mentioning also that the regiment was frequently unfed, an issue that needed to be addressed without delay. A few days later Picton said the Portuguese artillery with his Division would be incapable of accompanying him unless measures were adopted to feed their mules properly as they were not fit for service.[75] In both cases any issues must have been addressed for in July Picton told Beresford that the Portuguese units were in excellent condition and were ready to serve alongside their British counterparts; and both these regiments and the Portuguese artillery under von Arentschildt were complimented by Picton for their performance at Buçaco in September, only four months after he had expressed his concerns.[76]

Wellington too had some concerns, for in May he wrote to Beresford pointing out the 11th Regiment had only four out of ten captains present and that while the 12th Regiment was in a 'fair state of service' it was impossible to put it in operations with British regiments until supplied with blankets.[77] One should not overemphasise Wellington's concerns. He had seen enough results of the work being undertaken by Beresford to recommend to the British government in June 1810 that the same policy be applied to the Spanish army; namely training by British officers combined with a British subsidy. Liverpool did not endorse the idea, concerned as he and the cabinet were at the escalating costs of the war, a conflict in which there was a feeling in Britain to the effect that the Spanish could make a greater contribution.[78]

Wellington's inspection of the Portuguese regiments convinced him that with certain exceptions the troops were of a standard that could be brigaded with British regiments. He proceeded to implement this integration beginning by way of a General Order issued on 22 February, and in 1810 the 3rd, 4th and 5th divisions each contained a Portuguese brigade, and the Light Division incorporated two regiments of caçadores.[79] A specific Portuguese Division was created and placed under the command of General Hamilton on 5 March 1810, and this division served on a regular basis with the 2nd Division throughout the remainder of the war. Additionally, there were three independent Portuguese brigades fighting alongside the British army in 1810.[80] When the Spanish sought British assistance at the end of January 1810 following the French advance through Sevilla with Cádiz as their objective, Wellington not only sent British troops there from Lisbon, but also both battalions of the 20th Line regiment of the Portuguese army, notwithstanding that he was acutely 'aware of the mutual hatred of the Spanish and Portuguese people towards each other'.[81] The Portuguese cavalry was adjudged not to be sufficiently advanced to be brigaded with its British counterpart. While it remained detached for the time being, progress under Vane and Madden in particular during the year led to an increasingly well mounted and disciplined force which performed well during the year. Overall, Wellington expressed quiet confidence in the Portuguese army writing to Villiers in June 1810: 'The Portuguese army are in a good state. We have arms for the militia, and upon the whole we have an enormous military establishment at our command', though he added ominously, 'We only want money to put it in operation and to keep it up.'[82]

While Beresford and Forjaz strove to improve the Portuguese army, Wellington as overall commander sought to prepare for the French onslaught on Portugal anticipated to take place in the spring of 1810. The intention to invade Portugal had been signalled definitively on 7 October 1809, when Napoleon ordered that 100,000 troops be added to the forces already in the Peninsula. All through the winter of 1809 and the spring of 1810 French reinforcements were observed passing south through Bayonne and Irun to join the various corps in northern Spain. The contest in the Peninsula would soon reach a critical point.

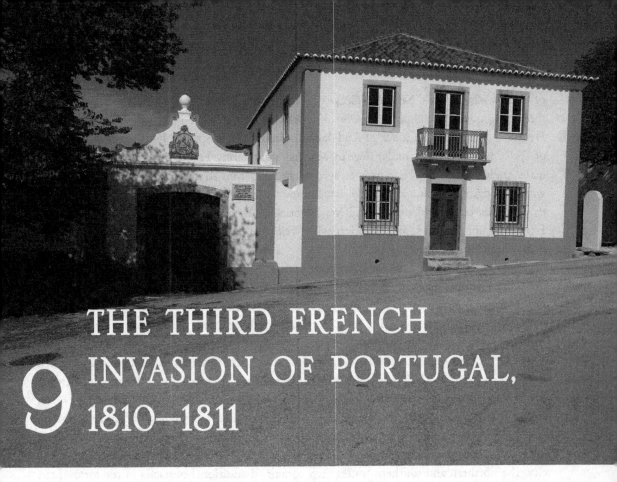

THE THIRD FRENCH INVASION OF PORTUGAL, 1810–1811

9

The French victory over the Austrians at Wagram in July 1809 not only forced the Austrians to sue for peace but freed up thousands of French troops with which Napoleon intended to finally subdue the Iberian Peninsula, driving the British from Portugal once and for all.[1] Napoleon initially intended to lead this massive force himself but his divorce from Josephine and marriage to the Emperor of Austria's daughter, Marie Louise, combined with other political imperatives led him to delegate this objective. The appointee was one of Napoleon's most experienced generals, André Masséna, recently created the Prince d'Essling. When informed that the Army of Portugal, the French forces in the Portuguese campaign, would be composed of the 2nd, 6th and 8th corps of the army of Spain Masséna expressed his reservations, based on the suggestion that he had yet to recover fully from the injuries received in the Austrian campaign, as well as expressing doubts of the calibre of the commanders of the 6th and 8th corps, Marshal Ney and General Junot. Napoleon was not prepared to change his mind and promised Masséna that he would not lack resources. On 17 April 1810, Masséna very unwillingly assumed this command.[2]

Masséna arrived in Valladolid on 10 May, and on 23 May William Warre reported the British and Portuguese general staff had just been informed of Masséna's arrival to take command of the Army of Portugal, then assembling between Salamanca and Ciudad Rodrigo. In the interim the French had begun to assemble in excess of 100,000 men in northern Spain, made up primarily of Reynier's 2nd Corps, Ney's 6th Corps and Junot's 8th Corps. This build up was all the more threatening given the comprehensive Spanish defeat at Ocaña in late 1809, which had enabled the French to take control of much of Andalucía and reduced the Spanish Junta to effective control of Cádiz, which was now under siege by Marshal Soult's army. Facing the Army of Portugal, the main Anglo-Lusitanian forces were arrayed over a long front stretching from Pinhel to Guarda, with Wellington's headquarters early that summer at Celorico and those of Beresford at Fornos de Algodres, both overlooking the River Mondego.[3] The ongoing preparations to receive the French did not prevent some relaxation, with Wellington and Beresford both hosting dinners in each other's honour in early June.[4]

Wellington's strategy for the defence of Portugal was clear, though dependent upon which invasion route the French pursued into the country. There were three practicable routes avoiding the mountainous provinces of Trás-os-Montes and Entre-Douro-e-Minho for a large force with Lisbon as its objective.[5] The most northerly route, guarded by the Portuguese fortress of Almeida, progressed down the Mondego valley towards Coimbra before turning south to Lisbon, a distance of just over 300 kilometres. A middle route, via Abrantes, which had in effect been followed by Junot in 1807, was some 200 kilometres long over much rougher terrain than the first option. Finally there was the southern route, via the massive fortress of Elvas. Quite apart from the virtual imperative to capture Elvas, this route posed a substantial difficulty in that to reach Lisbon the French would have to cross the river Tagus either by marching north to a point where it was bridged, or by obtaining sufficient boats to effect a water borne landing nearer the city. The northern and southern routes each contained additional obstacles in the form of the Spanish-held border fortresses of Ciudad Rodrigo and Badajoz, respectively, strong points which it would be prudent to reduce rather than leave to the invader's rear. While Wellington took the precaution of placing Hill's 2nd Division and additional troops to guard the southern entry point, he assumed correctly that the most likely point of attack would come through northeast Portugal requiring first the reduction of Ciudad Rodrigo and Almeida.[6]

Wellington and Beresford both realised that given the huge size of the armies the French could bring to bear, the defence of Portugal was going to be difficult, if not impossible. With only some 25,000 British troops available, much was likely to depend on the performance of the Portuguese army and the militia. In the event these Portuguese forces were to make up well over half the number of those defending Portugal in 1810. There was a general recognition that Wellington would have to fight a defensive campaign by choosing where and when to give battle. There was also an awareness that despite all the preparations the British might have to evacuate their army from the Peninsula once again, a prospect which if it dismayed the British government and army, caused apprehension and terror in Portugal. In this connection it should not be forgotten that despite various departures abroad of leaders and men, there remained a party in Portugal supportive of the French, as is evidenced by intercepted correspondence and by actions taken by the government in Lisbon, which included imprisonment and deportation.[7]

Richard Wellesley, then Secretary of State for Foreign Affairs, put the British view succinctly to Villiers, still British envoy in Lisbon at the beginning of 1810, when he said the government was determined to maintain the cause of the Allies in the Peninsula 'so long as the contest shall appear to afford any reasonable prospect of advantage against the common enemy, or of benefit to His Majesty's allies'.[8] Wellington for his part was able to advise Liverpool as early as 2 April 1810 that:

> All the preparations for embarking and carrying away the army, and everything belonging to it, are already made, and my intention is to embark it, as soon as I find that a military necessity exists for so doing. I shall delay the embarkation as long as it is in my power, and shall do everything in my power to avert the necessity of embarking at all.'[9]

In the autumn of 1809, Wellington, Beresford and Forjaz had determined that in the event of another French invasion of Portugal they should implement a policy designed to degrade the invading army to such an extent that it would no longer pose a sustainable threat by the time it reached the environs of Lisbon. The strategy involved laying waste to land, buildings, bridges and equipment before an advancing force, combined with a system of strong fortified positions in one or more arcs stretching from the Atlantic to the Tagus to protect Lisbon, and if necessary to cover an embarkation. It called for the removal of much of the population of the provinces of Beira and Estremadura to behind what came to be known as the Lines of Torres Vedras; an act which would require huge logistical support to feed and house people if unrest was to be avoided. This was not a policy that endeared itself to the entire Regency Council, some members of which wished to see the war fought on the frontiers of Portugal, but nonetheless the policy was adopted and substantially implemented with the assistance of Forjaz.

The practice of devastating the land before an approaching enemy was well known in Portugal and had been practised historically against invading Spanish forces. Neither was the construction of a system of fortifications north of Lisbon such as the Lines of Torres Vedras a novel idea. Proposals had been put forward in the 1760s for a line of fortifications to protect Lisbon and plans were resuscitated before the French invasion of 1807. Interestingly, they were known to Junot who failed to act on them in 1808 and it was only later in the same year that Major José Maria das Neves Costa of the Portuguese army completed a survey presenting his ideas for the protection of Lisbon to the Regency in the spring of 1809.[10] Prior to Wellesley's arrival in April 1809, work was already being undertaken by the Portuguese, with the assistance of British engineers, for the defence of Lisbon and some of the adjacent towns. Beresford had been shown the plans and was reportedly planning to start work on them straight away.[11] Neves Costa's survey was considered by Wellington, Beresford and Lieutenant Colonel Richard Fletcher of the Royal Engineers. Wellington gave the order for the construction of the Lines on 20 October 1809 and work continued on them until 1812, long after any immediate danger of French invasion.[12]

The plan called for the building of two lines to defend Lisbon and a third defensive line around São Julião to cover any embarkation of the troops should that prove necessary. Initially, the second line from the Atlantic to the Tagus had been envisaged as the main defensive line, but ultimately the first line proved so strong that it was never penetrated to any degree. That first line stretched from Alhandra on the Tagus via Monte Agraço to the mouth of the Zizandre, which was flooded by damming. It was some forty-six kilometres long and included the particularly strong point of Torres Vedras. A couple of kilometres behind the first line was constructed the heavily fortified line stretching from Quintela on the Tagus to a point north of Ribamar on the Atlantic where the Rio São Lourenço enters the ocean, via Cabeço de Montachique and Mafra; approximately thirty-eight kilometres in length. These two lines involved a chain of forts, redoubts and ravelins constructed in an interlocking sequence so that each could assist in the protection of its neighbours. Their construction was supervised by Lieutenant Colonel Richard Fletcher with the assistance of British, Portuguese and German engineers and was made possible by the engagement of upwards of 5,000 Portuguese labourers on a continuous basis for the first year.[13]

To these two lines was added a third ring of fortifications surrounding São Julião da Barra which guarded the entrance to the Tagus, and which it was envisaged would cover an embarkation should it prove necessary to evacuate the British army. In 1810 this was guarded by two battalions of British marines. Finally, a fourth line of defensive works was commenced south of the Tagus around Almada, and Setúbal was strengthened, both projects designed to cover an embarkation and to protect Lisbon against invasion through the Alentejo. Other strong points to receive additional attention included the fortress of Peniche, on a peninsula north of Lisbon, where the garrison was commanded by Blunt, and the town of Abrantes, the site of an important bridge crossing of the Tagus in mid Portugal.[14]

The possibility of a British withdrawal from Portugal was never far from the minds of the military and political representatives on the ground in Portugal throughout 1809 and 1810, and there was a mood of despondency at home as well. Fletcher himself had doubted the practicality of defending Lisbon to the last extremity and afterwards embarking the British troops.[15] Wellington was satisfied in March 1810 that with 45,000 tons of transports available in the Tagus Estuary he could embark the British and Portuguese armies if necessary, but it would not be possible to take off any Spanish regiments as well.[16] Writing to Beresford on 1 May 1810, Wellington declared, 'they are terribly alarmed about everything in England and I am advised on all fronts to do nothing'.[17] Beresford either did not share the widely expressed pessimism about a British army being able to remain in Portugal, or he was being diplomatic, for he maintained the view that it would be extremely hard for the French to force their withdrawal.[18] Wellington's ire against 'croakers', people who grumble or complain unreasonably, is well known, but there was considerable despondency within the army at times. Beresford's ADC, William Warre, while seeking to emphasise he was not a 'croaker' and that it was difficult to guess what the outcome of the contest might be, in July 1810 advised his father that prudence suggested the removal of all property from Portugal, given the superior numbers of the French army.[19]

Beresford, as one would expect as Commander of the Portuguese forces, was clearly involved in the planning and implementation of the construction of the Lines and the defence of Lisbon; frequently corresponding with Wellington on the topic and exhorting Forjaz to secure sufficient men to work on the demolition of roads and works which might assist the invader and the construction of works to repel him. On 5 February 1810 Beresford went to Torres Vedras to meet with Wellington, who had come from Viseu, and they inspected the works and field fortifications which were reportedly in a 'state of great forwardness'; doing 'infinite credit to Lieutenant Colonel Fletcher who traced, and Capt. Mulcaster who executed them'.[20] In all, 126 redoubts stretched across the length of the Lines north of Lisbon by late 1810, with further additions made in 1811 and 1812. The much vaunted telegraph system was only gradually being extended from Lisbon, and in May Beresford proposed to Forjaz a dedicated effective communications system to be implemented by volunteers based on a number of permanent posts. He went so far as to calculate the number of horses necessary and sent Forjaz a map showing the suggested location of the posts, though it is unclear if this suggestion was implemented for by July, though there was a telegraph in Trancoso, Beresford complained there was no dictionary such as would enable instructions to be given to General Cox in the fortress of Almeida in the event of a siege.[21]

The Allies were greatly assisted by French delays in assembling the army of Portugal. The reported incessant rain in late spring and early summer may have been partially responsible for the slow build up, giving the defenders additional time.[22] This not only allowed the substantial completion of the Lines of Torres Vedras prior to the invasion in late summer 1810, but also enabled further recruitment and training in the Portuguese army. Reports on the regiments were mostly positive. Following an inspection of the four Portuguese artillery brigades under von Arentschildt at Condeixa on 19 March, D'Urban reported they were in very high order and that nothing could be finer. However, the 1st and 2nd Chasseurs sent up to Craufurd on the Agueda were returned unfit for service, which did not surprise D'Urban as he described them as 'the worst in the army'.[23] Later that summer the 1st and 3rd Caçadores served with Craufurd with some distinction. By mid March, regiments were on the move to the frontier in anticipation of a French attack on Ciudad Rodrigo. That move did not develop, however, as at that stage Junot was moving instead to besiege and later capture Astorga.

D'Urban was surprised at the French delay, expressing the view in early April that if Portugal did not fall before autumn he didn't 'think it can fall at all'.[24] He was also outspoken regarding Wellington taking the best Portuguese regiments, saying that the Marshal would soon be without any division at all since all would be incorporated with the British. Because the Marshal remained in Lisbon (with periodic visits to Coimbra) undertaking administrative tasks, D'Urban felt he had lost his chance for an Advanced Command, which he would certainly have otherwise received from Wellington. There was probably some truth in this observation, for at the battle of Buçaco while Beresford is clearly involved as part of Wellington's staff, he did not seem to have a command specifically his own, apart of course being Marshal of the Portuguese army.[25] He did order the Portuguese Division to the front at the end of April, at Wellington's request, and this proceeded northeastward via Celorico. Beresford established his headquarters at Fornos de Algodres, some ten kilometres from Wellington at Celorico, and following discussions Wellington accepted that the British commissariat should support on an occasional basis the Portuguese troops, with the Portuguese Commissaries giving receipts on the basis that the expense would be settled between the two countries.

At the end of May, Wellington and Beresford inspected the Anglo-Lusitanian force commanded by Craufurd on the Agueda but it was early June before the French concentrated in strength before Salamanca, enabling further supplies to be brought up in the interim to the Allied army from Lisbon and Porto. This delay also permitted Fort Concepción, between Almeida and Ciudad Rodrigo, to be fortified on Wellington's orders.[26] In late June Beresford had moved his headquarters to Trancoso, some 25 miles from Almeida.[27] The 1st and 16th Portuguese regiments were stationed there and Wellington met him in Trancoso on 18 June to inspect them.[28]

It is noticeable that throughout the summer, and indeed at other times, there were almost daily communications between the two men, whether in person or otherwise. Much of that correspondence concerns the defence of Ciudad Rodrigo and Almeida, respectively. The mutual trust and respect between the two soldiers shines through in a letter written by Wellington to Charles Stuart in September 1810, where he stated: 'it is impossible for two people to understand each other better than Beresford and I. He is two miles from this [Gouveia] and I see him every day; and I believe that we take pretty nearly the same view of every transaction.'[29] Wellington went on to state that others in the Portuguese newspapers tried to suggest they had differences, based on their respective reports on events, which he attributed to the feverish state of the Portuguese government since Principal Sousa became a member of it.

Wellington, on the assumption the French would not determine to invade Portugal through Galicia, again left it to Beresford to organise the defence of the northern provinces, which he did under Generals Silveira and Baccelar, with Colonel/Brigadier General John Wilson serving as Chef de l'Etat Major.[30] In addition, Beresford did his best to secure the north of Portugal by appointing British governors of individual provinces and towns. Thus Brigadier General Nicholas Trant was Governor of Porto, Brigadier General Miller (1809–10) and John Wilson (1811–12) were both Governors of Minho during the period with headquarters at Viana, and General Thomas McMahon was proposed as Governor of Valença do Minho, an important border fortress, in 1810 though he subsequently declined to take up the post.[31]

The French had invested Ciudad Rodrigo on 5 June 1810, having begun a blockade of the city on 26 April. After a brave resistance, the Governor, Andrés Herrasti, surrendered on 10 July when it became clear that Wellington would not mount an attempt to relieve it. Criticised by some in Spain for his alleged failure, Wellington's decision would seem to have been sound for he had no intention of meeting a larger French force out in the open, but rather had determined to retreat into Portugal where he intended to use terrain and extended French communications as well as the Lines of Torres Vedras to his advantage. Following the capture of Ciudad Rodrigo, Masséna turned his attention to Almeida, but was delayed by reason of a need to build up supplies.

On 21 July, in the face of a French advance under Marshal Ney, Captain Burgoyne, on instructions, blew up the Spanish fort of Concepción, a star fortress some eight kilometres from Almeida. With the Light Division of some 3,500 infantry and 1,500 cavalry, Craufurd then formed a screening line east of the River Côa, shielding Almeida. Three days later, on 24 July Ney threw his entire corps of some 24,000 men against Craufurd's extended line. Craufurd's force, including the 1st and 3rd Caçadores, was driven back over the Côa with considerable loss, and nearly trapped by Ney in an engagement for which Craufurd was criticised by Wellington, not for the first time.[32] The engagement on the Côa preceded a general Anglo-Portuguese withdrawal, leaving Almeida to be invested by the French.[33]

The withdrawal was much criticised by members of the Portuguese Regency, but it led to an insurrection behind French lines almost as soon as they advanced into Portugal, because of their treatment of the population and the theft of the property of those subjected to abuse. In emphasising the importance of the Spanish guerrillas, the successes and sacrifices of their Portuguese counterparts are sometimes overlooked. Particularly following the second Portuguese invasion under Soult, a substantial fight back had taken place, formally in the guise of the army, militia and ordenança; but less formally in the shape of locals exacting retribution and revenge for hardships inflicted by the invader. D'Urban recites a number of examples in the summer and autumn of 1810, none more strange than that attributed to José Ribeira, Curate of Vila Maior, who is credited with killing an officer and twenty-five French dragoons in early August.[34]

At the same time, individual Portuguese commanders were securing successes, such as when Silveira forced the surrender on 10 August of a French battalion holed up in the castle of Puebla de Sanabria, a position which was north of Braganza but well within Spain.[35] The repeated interception of French despatches gave reason for further encouragement as they recited the 'wants and miseries' of the French army. Seen against the background of major battles, these sort of encounters and incidents may not appear significant, but they all played their part in eroding both the confidence and efficacy of the invading army and in providing invaluable intelligence to the Allies.

If some of these events were encouraging, the outcome of the siege of Almeida by Marshal Masséna was a bitter blow to the Allies, not because it succumbed, but because the actual siege, rather than the preparations, effectively lasted less than two days. Considerable effort and expense had gone into the preparations to withstand a French siege and expectations were that the town might hold out for a month, thus slowing any French advance into Portugal. The French began entrenching operations for the siege on 15 August but it was only on 26 August they began a sustained fire on the fort. When the main magazine exploded that evening, the first full day of the siege, it destroyed much of the town, and killed hundreds including many soldiers. Its Governor, Lieutenant Colonel William Cox, had little choice but to surrender on 28 August, but the nature of the fortress's fall and the events surrounding it were to cast a shadow over both the campaign and the reputations of some of those involved.[36]

Lieutenant Colonel William Cox was in 1810 an experienced if not particularly well known soldier. He had served under Baird in Egypt and been present at La Coruña. From an Anglo-Irish family established in County Wexford he was in all probability known to Beresford before he came to join him in the Portuguese service in 1809. He had performed services in Spain in 1807, for which he was made a Colonel in the Spanish army, and when he joined Beresford in Portugal he received the rank of Brigadier General and was appointed Governor of Almeida in early 1809.[37] This massive fortress, built in classic Vauban style in the shape of a twelve-pointed star, was like Elvas, which guarded the Portuguese–Spanish border 150 miles to the south, intended to guard the north eastern route into Portugal from invasion. Almeida and Elvas, respectively, stood opposite the Spanish fortresses of Ciudad Rodrigo and Badajoz, and any power aspiring to enter Portugal from the land side would ignore Portuguese occupation of these fortresses at their peril. The appointment of Cox as Governor in 1809 illustrates the importance attached to this defensive position. However, despite a year to prepare for the anticipated siege the preparations were far from smooth and Cox himself far from happy with arrangements prior to the commencement of the siege.

From the time of his appointment in 1809, Cox complained to both Beresford and Wellington about the failure to arm and clothe the garrison, the lack of British officers to train the regiments forming part of the garrison, the inadequacy of the size of the garrison; and the shortage of provisions. To this was added frequent unhappiness caused by pay arrears and the instability caused by that factor.[38] Initially, the defending force consisted of two Portuguese line regiments, the 12th and 23rd. In May 1809, however, the 23rd had been replaced by the 24th Regiment, of which Cox was appointed Colonel. In addition, Cox had a small detachment of cavalry drawn from the 11th Portuguese cavalry regiment. This consisted of sixty-one men under Captain Alexandre Pereira da Costa Cardoso. The fortress was well equipped, with guns of varying calibre manned by 222 men from the 4th Portuguese artillery regiment together with a number of volunteers. However, the 12th Regiment was withdrawn from the garrison prior to the commencement of the siege, leaving the 24th Regiment as the only line regiment serving there. The balance of the garrison was made up of militia regiments from Arganil, Guarda and Trancoso. By early July 1810 Cox claimed he had a garrison of 3,000, which in his mind was totally inadequate for the defence of Almeida, bearing in mind the make up of the troops. In a private letter of 1 July he complained that it was not fair that the Commander in Chief (Wellington) gave hints as to how he should act, as he would be criticised if he did not adopt those hints and likewise if he did adopt them and failed. This criticism appears to relate to Wellington's suggestions or comments made on a recent visit to Almeida.[39]

One of the problems Cox had to face was desertion by members of the militia, and he sought Beresford's advice on how to deal with it. On the very day Wellington attended at Almeida, some of the militia regiment of Guarda went missing, but they subsequently returned, it being discovered they had only gone to the fair there. A good many of the regiment of Trancoso were reported as having deserted, but subsequently returned following the completion of the harvest. Others went to protect their families or property and search parties sent out disappeared as well.[40] In early July, Cox unavailingly asked Beresford to replace two militia regiments with two regiments of line saying that Almeida was worth saving and it should not be entrusted to an inadequate garrison. If his request was granted he expressed the hope he could hold out for fifty days.[41] Later he suggested the garrison 'is scarcely sufficient for the common duties, not to talk of defence in case of serious attack'.[42]

Even before the siege began, while Cox appeared to be substantially happy with the armaments available he was bemoaning the lack of provisions claiming they only had a small reserve of biscuit and not one day's bread. He was trying to get grain from the magistrates in adjoining districts, but lack of transport was reported as a major hindrance.[43] This led Beresford to suggest that part of the civilian population should be sent away from the town, a move approved by Wellington.[44] Indeed, Wellington recognised the justness of some of Cox's complaints regarding provisions, as those intended for the siege were constantly being drawn upon to feed the Allied army in the vicinity.[45]

On 8 July, Wellington wrote in exasperation to Beresford telling him of a letter he had received from Cox that morning 'contradicting his former reports and saying that he is making some progress in replenishing his magazines. Any other officer would be ashamed of troubling his Commander in Chief with such little and unfounded complaints but he appears to think nothing of it'.[46] Two weeks later Wellington had had more than enough, writing again to Beresford enclosing another letter received from Cox requesting additional troops, and suggesting Beresford send to Elvas for General Picton and appoint him to command at Almeida if he should arrive before the commencement of the anticipated siege.[47] Wellington reversed that suggestion a day later, perhaps because he feared the French were going to move against Portugal further south in addition to Masséna's attack via Almeida.[48] Beresford therefore took probably the only course left to him, namely to reassure Cox before the siege began. He referred to Almeida being fully stocked with provisions but that if the fortunes of war should not smile on him, how important it was not to let ammunition, papers or provisions fall into the hands of the enemy. He felt there was even a chance Masséna might bypass Almeida, expressing the view that if he did do so, the army was pretty well prepared and that accordingly it might be an obstacle in the French retreat. He reproved Cox gently regarding his representations, writing:

I think you have been too pressing on them and that you mistake the nature and cause of responsibility. You cannot be exonerated because you think your garrison too small, or [sic] are you responsible should it be too little. The first is merely a matter of opinion of yours and the latter rests with us who have given that garrison and this whether you declared an opinion or not. Your honour is only committed in making the best possible defence with the means you have. This I am satisfied you will do, and I am under no unquietude for the event it will be I am sure everything that can be expected and beneficial to the public cause as honourable to the defenders in particular.

In closing Beresford wished Cox well, saying that in the event that the latter was made prisoner, he would not be forgotten.[49] In fact, poor Cox was sent as a prisoner to Verdun following the fall of Almeida; from whence he wrote numerous letters to British political and military leaders, none of which secured his release.[50]

Almeida was blockaded by the French from the end of July. Heavy cannon were moved up and entrenchments made, enabling a formal bombardment of the fort and town to commence early on 26 August. The cataclysmic nature of the explosion on the first evening of the full siege determined the futility of further resistance and the consequent surrender of Almeida on 28 August may have meant that better preparations would have been to no avail; but it is clear that Cox drove both Beresford and Wellington to distraction with his repeated complaints, requests and what they perceived as his lack of leadership. There was, however, further fall out relating to the massive explosion in the ammunition magazine, the way surrender negotiations were carried out and the subsequent actions of a number of Portuguese soldiers.

The generally circulated story regarding cause of the explosion was that while artillerymen were working in the magazine to bring barrels of powder by wagon to the expense magazines on the ramparts they left the doors to the magazine open. By chance a French explosive device landed in or rolled into a subsidiary magazine igniting 4,000 projectiles, which in turn detonated 150,000 lb of gunpowder and over 1,000,000 cartridges. An alternative version has the French projectile igniting a trail of gunpowder spilled from a barrel removed from the main magazine, leading back to the magazine which then exploded.[51] Cox, however, dismissed both these theories. Writing from Verdun in November, he said that while the cause of the explosion could never be truly ascertained, it was most probable that a heavy shell had broken through the doorway to the powder magazine, notwithstanding that he had had it covered with large beams of wood. He maintained there was no loading of wagons with ammunition taking place at the time, nor was the doorway to the magazine open. While there was the possibility it had been blown up by treachery he did not subscribe to that theory, notwithstanding the behaviour of the Portuguese commandant of artillery afterwards.[52]

Whatever the cause, the effect was devastating. The mediaeval castle, the town church, the governor's house and many other buildings were completely destroyed and few buildings retained their roofs. Over 500 people were reported to have died in the explosion, including many of the artillerymen and soldiers on the ramparts. Heavy guns were thrown from the ramparts and stone was reportedly thrown several hundred yards from the fortress, killing and injuring a number of the besiegers. While the outer walls were largely intact, it was impossible to move inside the town for debris. Movement was only possible along the ramparts. The gigantic explosion was heard in the Allied army and in Ciudad Rodrigo. One French witness stated:

> The earth trembled and we saw an immense whirlwind of fire and smoke rise from the middle of the place. It was like the bursting of a volcano – one of these things I can never forget after twentysix years. Enormous blocks of stone were hurled into our trenches, where they killed and wounded some of our men. Guns of heavy calibre were lifted from the ramparts and hurled down far outside them. When the smoke cleared off, a great part of Almeida had disappeared, and the rest was a heap of debris.[53]

The further defence of Almeida was now out of the question, yet to give Cox his credit he did not panic but rather determined to show the French that the garrison was still in a position to resist. He organised for the remaining guns to be manned and repeatedly fired at the besiegers and the garrison was put on standby to repel any attempted assault during the remainder of the night. The morning revealed the extent of the devastation inside the walls, themselves remarkably intact. Apart from the damage to person and property, an inventory of the powder and ammunition revealed the impossibility of any prolonged defence.[54] Cox decided he must give Wellington the chance to come to the aid of the stricken fortress. Therefore he conducted negotiations with the French with a view to delaying surrender if possible.

Masséna's aide-de-camp, Chef de Bataillon, Jean Jacques Pelet, was sent to demand the surrender of the town on the morning of 27 August.[55] Discussions followed with Pelet being admitted only to the intact casemates in the outer wall, so as not to enable him to ascertain the extent of the destruction, and Cox maintained he was still in a position to resist. Nevertheless, Cox agreed to negotiate and sent out two officers to do so. Unfortunately, the French were well aware of the extent of the damage from discussions between the garrison and Portuguese officers with the French who approached the walls. These included the Marquis d'Alorna and General Pamplona, Conde de Subserra.[56] Even worse was the decision of Major Fortunato José Barreiros, one of the officers whom Cox sent out to treat with the enemy, to defect to the French disclosing to them the full extent of the damage.[57]

Masséna was able to call Cox's bluff and declined to agree the proposed terms. The bombardment was resumed with Barreiros directing the French fire on the fortress.[58] The officers of the garrison led by the Lieutenant-Governor, Francisco Bernardo da Costa e Almeida, quickly impressed on Cox that further resistance was futile and if he did not surrender they would open the gates. Late that night terms were finally agreed providing for the regular troops to be sent to France as prisoners while the militia were to be allowed to return home on giving their commitment not to serve again in the present war.

On the morning of 28 August the garrison, now under 3,000, marched out, including Cox and five other British officers. It had barely done so when at the instigation of the Marquis d'Alorna and General Pamplona, Masséna agreed to raise a Second Portuguese Legion, described alternatively as a corps of pioneers or guides, under the command of Pamplona. Some 600 of the militia were coerced into joining it along with nearly the entire surviving members, including officers, of the 24th Regiment and a company of the 11th Dragoons. The remaining Portuguese artillerymen were placed under the command of Jean Baptiste Eblé, Masséna's chief of artillery. For many this was clearly a stratagem designed to avoid imprisonment in France, and over the next week substantial numbers deserted and returned to the Allied army.

While the return of men and officers of the 24th Regiment reassured both Wellington and Beresford that their concerns of potential large-scale defection were unfounded, Wellington expressed his disquiet regarding the officers having sworn allegiance to France, and Beresford, while lauding the behaviour of the militia, could not forgive the behaviour of the officers of the 24th Regiment for their defection.[59] Beresford and Wellington intended to make an example of them but this was forestalled when the Regency specifically approved the conduct of the deserters and restored them to the army.[60]

Wellington had made it clear that he would not risk the army to defend either Ciudad Rodrigo or Almeida.[61] The Allied army had been drawn back from Pinhel and Trancoso to the valley of the Mondego, where it was now concentrated. Observation posts were clearly able to see the damage to Almeida even before first-hand reports became available, for on 27 August D'Urban noted in his *Journal* that firing had ceased at 8 am that morning, and referring to the explosion of the previous evening, he remarked that the Church had been knocked down and the place was on fire.[62] Wellington ordered a further retreat, even though the army was not then pressed by the French, to ensure this could be carried out in good order; he moving his headquarters to Celorico while Beresford was at Lageosa and subsequently Cortiça. Under a flag of truce, Major Gordon was sent to propose the exchange of Colonel Cox for a French gendarmerie colonel and with money for the prisoners. Meanwhile, those of the militia not incorporated into the corps of pioneers began to straggle back to the Allied lines.

Cox clearly anticipated that he, along with a number of British officers, was to be allowed to return to England on parole.[63] It was not to be, however, and following the failure to effect an exchange they were sent back to France, where they were held in the great fortress of Verdun until released in 1814 at the conclusion of the war.[64] The Portuguese officers who defected to Masséna at Almeida were indicted, along with others who showed pro-French sympathies in a Tribunal which sat at Lisbon in the autumn of 1810. Found guilty of high treason they were given a death sentence, though only da Costa e Almeida and Mascarenhas were later executed.[65] Cox himself was later tried by a Portuguese court martial but acquitted of any wrongdoing and in 1815 awarded the Portuguese Order of the Tower and the Sword by Prince João. He was knighted in 1816.

The Allies were perhaps fortunate in that Masséna moved forward slowly following the fall of Almeida. While Napoleon had clearly indicated that Lisbon was to be the French objective, Masséna was given considerable discretion as to the timing of his operations, unlike Soult's strict timetable for the capture of Lisbon imposed by Napoleon in 1809. Indeed, his instructions were to besiege Ciudad Rodrigo and Almeida and then to pass into Portugal not before September, when the heat would have gone out of the day and the harvests would be in. Masséna's army only renewed its progress into Portugal on 15 September, after which it shortly became clear that Masséna intended to march on Coimbra via Viseu along the north bank of the Mondego rather than attempt to move along the southern side of the river, which Wellington had suspected initially might be their preferred route as it had better roads; Wellington, writing to Stuart that 'there are many bad roads in Portugal but the enemy has taken decidedly the worst in the whole kingdom'.[66] He altered his positions accordingly, preparing the ridge at Buçaco and drawing in his forces.[67]

Following skirmishes on the previous days, it was at Buçaco on 27 September that the Anglo-Portuguese army checked and then threw back Masséna's invading force with considerable loss. Accounts of the battle are plentiful, but what emerges from Wellington's and other dispatches is the steadiness and good performance of the Portuguese regiments, with Wellington reportedly clapping Beresford on the shoulder and shouting: 'Well, Beresford, look at them now!'[68] The result of the hard work of 1809 and 1810 was there for all to see and Wellington was full of praise in his report on the battle to Lord Liverpool. Along with a number of British regiments, the 8th, 9th, 19th and 21st Portuguese regiments, the 3rd Caçadores, together with Pack's Portuguese brigade (1st and 15th regiments together with 4th Caçadores) and Colman's Portuguese brigade were mentioned in this dispatch.[69] Wellington summarised the Portuguese performance thus:

> it has brought the Portuguese levies into action with the enemy for the first time in an advantageous situation; and they have proved that the trouble which has been taken with them has not been thrown away, and that they are worthy of contending in the same ranks with British troops in this interesting cause, which they afford the best hopes of saving.[70]

A military victory certainly, but equally importantly, as Wellington observed to his brother, 'the battle has had the best effects in inspiring confidence in the Portuguese troops both among our croaking officers and the people of the country'.[71] Beresford too praised the performance of the Portuguese.[72] Portuguese casualties in the battle were not dissimilar to those suffered by the British.[73] Before, during and after the battle, Beresford formed part of Wellington's inner circle and it must have been gratifying for him to witness the reformed Portuguese army come of age in this encounter. He praised his troops for their courage and bravery and ordered the release of all imprisoned soldiers.[74] For his part, Wellington made it clear that credit for rebuilding the Portuguese army was due to Beresford and to him alone:

> I should not do justice to the service, or to my own feelings, if I did not take this opportunity of drawing your Lordship's attention to the merits of Marshal Beresford. To him exclusively, under the Portuguese government, is due the merit of having raised, formed, disciplined, and equipped the Portuguese army, which has now shown itself capable of engaging and defeating the enemy. I have besides received from him all the assistance which his experience and abilities, and his knowledge of this country, have qualified him to afford me.[75]

While an Allied victory, Masséna's army still outnumbered that of Wellington after Buçaco, and his movement around Wellington's left flank ensured the continuation of the Allied withdrawal, via Coimbra and Leiria, towards the by now well prepared lines of Torres Vedras; all the time encouraging the Portuguese living in the line of march to withdraw precipitously while either destroying or hiding possessions and provisions. In this scorched earth strategy, the Portuguese were assisted on occasions by the British army, such as when a party under Major Cocks destroyed five mills at Castelo Mendo in mid August. The strategy had been agreed with the Regency, but it soon became clear that implementation was less than complete due to a lack of governmental commitment. It was more successful in Beira Alta than in either Beira Baixa or Estremadura, probably both because of the unwillingness of the Regency Council to support the policy on their doorstep and because of the speed of the Allied retreat following the battle of Buçaco; causing Cocks, a keen observer to remark:

> The enemy would have suffered much more considerably from the want of supplies had our commissioners been enjoined to buy up everything for ten leagues in front of the lines. General Blunt, the Governor of Peniche, asked the Capitao Mors [sic] some time ago what time would be necessary to remove all the grain between Leyria and the Lines. Their answer was six weeks but they had only a few days' notice when we fell back last month. It is clear vast quantities must have been left to the enemy.'[76]

Blunt himself was at Peniche, busy collecting provisions to prevent these falling into French hands, but as he observed, 'a great quantity remain in the neighbourhood for want of means to carry it away'.[77]

Just as it was difficult to get supplies to the army for lack of transports, so it proved difficult to bring in the harvests to central depots. More could have been done but there is no doubt of the degree of suffering imposed on the Portuguese people by the strategy, and it clearly played its part in depriving the French of provisions.[78] While it might be unwise to disregard the public relations purpose of the report, *Le Moniteur*, a Parisien newspaper, stated that the French in their march from Almeida to Alenquer 'found only towns and villages deserted, mills made useless, wine flowing in the streets, corn burned to ashes, and even furniture broke to pieces. They saw neither horse, mule, ass, cow or goat.'[79]

The plight of civilians in the path of the advancing army was described by Joseph Anderson, then a young officer with the 24th Foot, who wrote: 'most of the inhabitants leave their homes and property and falling back in thousands before us, rich and poor, men, women, and children, carrying little with them beyond the clothing on their backs, and halting and bivouacking in the open fields, a short distance before us, whenever the army halted for the night.' The retreat respected neither age nor wealth. Anderson went on: 'Before reaching Torres Vedras I remember seeing many of these noble patriots rich and poor, all barefooted and in rags. When we finally halted they went to Lisbon.'[80] The flight of civilians in front of the French advance may not have respected either age or wealth, but those with moveable assets in many cases managed not only to bring them to Lisbon, but to get them on board vessels which could remove them to safety, Admiral Berkeley observing: 'My ship is crammed with the valuables of the richest people, plate, money, and jewels.'[81]

The Allied army was better organised and the retreat was an orderly one, though Wellington had to resort to hanging a number of soldiers for looting in Tomar and Leiria.[82] A full ten days prior to the battle of Buçaco, Wellington had ordered Beresford to remove the stores and ammunition as well as the sick from Coimbra, a clear indication that barring an overwhelming victory in any contest he would be retreating to the Lines of Torres Vedras.[83] The main Anglo-Portuguese army retreated to the Lines via Coimbra, while Hill and Hamilton reached the Lines via Espinhal and Tomar without having to fight any rearguard action. Almost as soon as the Anglo-Portuguese army vacated each town it was entered by the French, causing massive destruction in search of provisions, for those carried with the French army were now becoming scarce and Masséna's efforts to prevent looting by his troops were largely ineffectual.[84] On 30 September, Beresford ordered the removal of all stores from Tomar and Santarém to Lisbon. A week later D'Urban was able to report that all the sick and wounded were safely arrived in Lisbon.[85]

The autumn of 1810 was a time of huge tension between Wellington and Beresford, on the one part, and the Regency (with the exception of Forjaz) on the other. Lisbon was restless, but Wellington was clear that the agitation in Lisbon was due to the conduct of the Regency and particularly the most recently appointed members of it, Principal Sousa and the Conde de Redondo, a relative of Sousa.[86] Not only was Wellington's policy of laying waste to the land not being properly implemented, with many sources of food left available for the enemy notwithstanding instructions to the contrary, but he feared the Regency were disturbing the population of Lisbon behind his back.[87] Principal Sousa and the Patriarch were continuously at odds with both Wellington and Beresford and during 1810 engaged in moves designed to undermine, discredit and ultimately remove Forjaz from power.[88]

Whether to better attack Forjaz or Wellington, or merely to remove someone who thwarted their own wishes, Sousa proposed in August that Beresford be replaced at the head of the Portuguese army by the Duke of Brunswick.[89] While it is unclear if the timing of this move was related to Beresford's rejection of military appointments made at the Court in Rio de Janeiro without reference to the Marshal, and contrary to the agreement that he should have sole control over such appointments, the episode is indicative of the difficulties Beresford faced. Beresford sought help to prevent these appointments from Wellington, citing his opposition to promotion other than on merit and the deleterious effect such would have on discipline and authority. He listed complaints regarding the proposed promotions of a number of named individuals. What upset Beresford most, however, was the prospect of army officers discovering (perhaps this should be rediscovering) that there were means of promotion other than on merit, or at the very least a fair attention to their duty.[90] Wellington supported Beresford and the proposals were at first suspended with the agreement of the Regency, pending further clarification from Rio.[91] Subsequently, Beresford's authority over promotions was confirmed.

The divide between some members of the Regency (in reality Principal Sousa and the Patriarch, though they received support from others on occasions) and the commanders of the British and Portuguese armies was far more than a struggle over promotions. It went to the very root of control of the Portuguese forces and the strategy to be followed in respect of the threatened and subsequently actual invasion. The Principal and the Patriarch demanded that Wellington stand and fight first on the Portuguese frontier and then on the open plains before the Lines of Torres Vedras. The Principal appears to have felt that notwithstanding the Regency's agreement in February 1810, the request to lay waste to the land and the destruction of property in front of the advancing enemy was an unreasonable request; and perhaps at the back of his mind lay serious concern that Wellington would ultimately embark the British army on the fleet of transports and warships sitting in the Tagus.[92] To pre-empt trouble, Wellington ordered the removal of two militia regiments from Lisbon, whom he understood had been spreading rumours of a British intention to embark and who were advocating a pre-emptive strike to prevent an embarkation, and replaced them with those considered more reliable.[93]

Further, notwithstanding the arrest and deportation of a number of Francophile Portuguese, there remained a pro-French faction. A considerable number of those deported appear to have been freemasons for whom the ideals of the French Revolution and liberalism in particular had a considerable attraction. Though very much a supporter of the monarchy, Beresford tolerated the masons and the lodges multiplied in Portugal at this time. Those deported were largely from the professional classes and neither he nor Wellington saw a need for deportation.[94]

Beresford was incandescent at Principal Sousa's persistent opposition to Wellington's plans. Writing to the the British Minister Plenipotentiary, Sir Charles Stuart (who had become a member of the Regency on 2 October) when the Allied army was retreating to the Lines of Torres Vedras after the battle of Buçaco, he did not pull his punches; complaining about the Principal's latest suggestion to the effect that while the British army should retire behind the

127

Lines, that of Portugal should stay without to defend the country, leading Beresford to dismiss the proposal as a silly idea, 'so truly absurd that it is impossible to consider a man in his right senses that he should propose such a thing'. Beresford perceived the Principal's threat to oppose the embarkation of the Portuguese army in the event of misfortune befalling the Allied army as more the actions of a partisan supporting the enemy than those of someone seeking to secure the protection of the Portuguese possessions beyond the Atlantic. Indeed, he felt that the end result would be to enable Napoleon to use the Portuguese army to increase the ranks of the French army, as had already happened in the case of the Portuguese Legion in 1808. He felt that the only alternative to viewing the Principal's conduct in a suspicious light was to consider him a madman, stating: 'Whether to deem him a fool, a rogue or a madman I really cannot determine.'[95] It was unfortunate that the Patriarch supported the Principal, but if the latter were removed from the Regency, then Beresford felt the Patriarch's opposition would not be of importance.

It was not that the Principal was pro-French, far from it, and the Patriarch had certainly shown his aversion to French domination in leading opposition to Napoleon's forces as early as 1808. A combination of horror at the likely effects of the scorched earth policy, concern over a possible British embarkation and a desire for power may explain their opposition to both Wellington and Beresford at this time.[96] While many in the Allied army were unaware of the full extent of the Lines, amongst the British officers who knew of their existence there was support for Wellington's gradual withdrawal combined with the scorched earth policy, with D'Urban calling the proposals of the Principal and the Patriarch foolish.[97]

When Wellington sought the extension of the scorched earth policy to the Alentejo, the Principal once again objected, causing Wellington to observe acidly, 'since that person has been in government, I have not made one proposition of any description in the execution of which he has not thrown difficulties, and has not opposed'.[98] Indeed, Wellington refused to deal with the Principal Sousa at all at this time, though he regarded the Patriarch as a necessary evil.[99] Wellington was so upset by the conduct of the Regency that he told the British Minister, Stuart, to inform the Regents, and above all Principal Sousa, that His Majesty and the Prince Regent had entrusted him (Wellington) with command of the armies and the conduct of military operations and he would not suffer any interference. He went so far as to instruct Stuart to make it clear to Principal Sousa that he would not remain in the Peninsula, once he had his Majesty's permission to resign, if Principal Sousa remained a member of the government or continued in Lisbon.[100]

Wellington wrote to the Prince Regent in Rio de Janeiro stating that either the Principal or he would have to leave the country. Not until late spring 1811 did a temporising response arrive back in Portugal, suggesting that the Principal would step down from the Regency if both Stuart and Forjaz did likewise.[101] Wellington did accept that Stuart should withdraw from the Regency, pending instructions being received from England, but he was appalled at the suggestion that Forjaz, whom he regarded as the most able Portuguese administrator, should also step down. Forjaz tendered his resignation, but he was subsequently confirmed in his position, probably as a result of Wellington's fulsome support conveyed directly to the Prince Regent in Brazil.[102]

Ultimately, a most difficult situation was overcome by military success with the expulsion of the French from Portugal in April 1811. This effectively enabled Wellington to ignore the attempted interference of the Principal in military affairs, though he remained an irritant until the culmination of the war.

Between 8 and 10 October, some ten days after withdrawing from the Serra de Buçaco, the Anglo-Portuguese army entered the Lines where it was augmented by newly arrived regiments from Britain. Wellington now had some 60,000 British and Portuguese regulars behind the Lines in addition to the militia and artillery regiments manning the redoubts and forts. Meanwhile, the Royal Navy controlled not just the estuary but the navigable part of the Tagus as far as Abrantes through heavily armed gunboats; though a seizure of other river vessels was only partly successful, much to Wellington's irritation.[103] Finally, the Marquis de la Romana, at Wellington's request, brought two Spanish divisions from Andalucía to Aldeia Galega on the south bank of the Tagus on 25 October from whence they were ferried across the river to occupy positions in and around Mafra.[104] Some 8,000 men in all, the question naturally arises whether their presence in Andalucía might have forestalled or prevented Soult's capture of Badajoz early in 1811? Certainly, Wellington's army now outnumbered that of Masséna, though he remained aware and concerned of a possible move by Soult to link up with the formidable French force facing the Lines. Wellington was now confident that he would be able to hold Portugal against the enemy.[105] Further, he felt the French were now 'in a scrape' and 'they will find their retreat from this country a most difficult and dangerous operation'.[106]

Incredible as it may seem, the existence of the Lines as a continuous chain of defence appears to have remained unknown, or at the very least the strength of the fortifications underestimated, to Masséna until his vanguard approached them on 11 October.[107] Indeed, their existence was unknown to many of the Allied officers and soldiers.[108] On the afternoon of 12 October, the French managed to expel pickets of the 1st Division from Sobral. In the presence of Masséna, Junot launched an attack from Sobral on 13 October, which was repulsed with no great difficulty; Colonel Harvey's Portuguese Brigade (11th and 23rd regiments), which formed part of Lowry Cole's 4th Division, distinguished itself.[109] Following a council of war that evening Masséna chose not to renew the attack, reporting to Napoleon that 'he had come to the conclusion that he would compromise the army of his Majesty if he were to attack in force lines so formidable, defended by 30,000 English and 30,000 Portuguese aided by 50,000 armed peasants'.[110]

Masséna initially sought to blockade the Allies, but shortage of provisions and broken communications, combined with few reinforcements, forced his withdrawal to Santarém in November. He was effectively cut off from Spain by the actions of detachments of Portuguese under Silveira around Almeida and Trant, who recaptured Coimbra on 7 October almost as soon as it was vacated by the main French army.[111] Contrary to a report in the *Gazeta de Lisboa* on 22 October, and repeated ad nauseam in French propaganda – notwithstanding a correction printed two days later in the *Gazeta* – it now seems clear that there was no massacre of French prisoners by the Portuguese when recapturing the city. The initial report had suggested 600–800 French had been killed, but on correction this was stated to be 6–8 people.[112] It seems clear this rumour resulted from a typographical error in the *Gazeta*. Trant took more than 5,000 sick and wounded French prisoners along with the French garrison, a serious blow to the wellbeing of Masséna's army and a fracturing of his line of communications. He distributed the huge number of captured arms to the Ordenença.[113] Masséna sought to justify to Napoleon leaving a weak garrison to guard his sick in Coimbra by suggesting he needed every fighting man possible. Meanwhile French efforts at foraging were hampered on the western seaboard by militia and recruits sent out from the fortress of Peniche.[114]

The Portuguese inhabitants played their role in frustrating the French, harassing foraging parties and capturing and often killing stragglers. The cause of this fierce retribution was remarked on by Masséna and also the Marquis d'Alorna, when the latter went to Pinhel: 'the few inhabitants left behind all say the same ... that they have been mistreated by the French soldiers.'[115] When Chef de Bataillon Delomme took five companies of infantry to the Douro to secure cattle in early August he was stopped by armed peasants from crossing the river, though he eventually managed to capture a flock of sheep before retiring.[116] Morale in the French army must have been sinking for there are numerous reports of deserters from that force giving themselves up to the Allies during the late autumn and winter.

Before Masséna retired to Santarém an important event for Beresford occurred at Mafra; the investiture of the Marshal as a member of the Order of the Bath (K.B., subsequently elevated to G.C.B). His knighthood was officially conferred by Wellington at the request of the King, Wellington himself already being a member.[117] He gave Beresford the insignia and medal on 3 November, and this was followed by a dinner for 200 and a ball for many more in the palace at Mafra four days later. This reception was attended by many army and navy officers, together with other notables.[118] The conferring of the knighthood and the subsequent party was a major social occasion. Joseph Anderson, then a young officer with the 24th Foot, has left a graphic account of the events.[119] He reported that Wellington had sent out a general order inviting one-third of the combined armies of England, Spain and Portugal to witness the ceremony of Beresford being knighted and announcing that he (Wellington) intended to return to his post early that night and wished other officers to do the same, while expressing confidence that those at their posts would do their duty if attacked by the enemy during the absence of those attending the ceremony. Anderson then continued:

> On our arrival there [Mafra] we found not only many hundreds of officers – English, Spanish and Portuguese – but also a great portion of the Portuguese nobility, all come to do honour to the occasion, Lord Wellington, and his brilliant staff amongst them; and, what was more remarkable, large masses of the French army not a quarter of a mile away from us, with their advanced picquets and sentries were looking quietly and coolly on at our gathering, and although our visitors from Lisbon advanced in crowds as near as possible to look and stare at them in turn, not the slightest attempt was made by our brave enemies to alarm or disturb them. The same consideration and courtesy was continued during the whole of that memorable occasion, so that I think to this day that the good feeling and understanding must have been previously arranged between Lord Wellington and General Masséna.[120]

Of the ceremony itself Anderson says relatively little, other than Wellington appeared in the hall of the palace with Beresford on his arm. When a circle had been formed Wellington read His Majesty's command, Beresford knelt, Wellington waved his sword over the General's head and said: 'arise, Sir William Carr Beresford'. Anderson is a little more expansive when he came to describe the festivities:

> Then was opened a folding door, displaying many tables laid out with a most recherché dinner and choice of wines for at least 500 people. I was one of the fortunate ones who succeeded in getting early admission. Then dancing was commenced and kept on without ceasing until daylight. Our popular commander danced without ever resting, and appeared thoroughly to enjoy himself though he retired at midnight, and many followed his example; but by far the greater number remained till morning, much to the delight of all the lovely and illustrious donnas and senoras of Lisbon. The night was very dark, and many officers going home lost their way and got into the enemy's lines, but on stating whence they came, were all treated most kindly, and at daylight were allowed with hearty good wishes to proceed to their respective quarters.[121]

The wandering officers were perhaps fortunate, though there were other incidents throughout the war when officers and soldiers fraternised. Sometimes this was when collecting water; on other occasions when recovering wounded comrades. On occasion relations could be more extensive, such as during the winter of 1810 when Anderson reported that British officers went to the theatre in Santarém at the invitation of their French counterparts with the sanction of the Commanders of both armies.[122] Wellington, however, was concerned that such fraternisation would lead to the unwitting disclosure of sensitive military information and he moved to prohibit casual contact, including unauthorised flags of truce; an order which he felt obliged to repeat in 1814 when the army was in France.[123]

The investiture and the ensuing celebrations had an important side effect. Giving the ball so close to the front line appears to have instilled considerable confidence at a time when there were still fears of a British withdrawal from Portugal. Samuel Broughton, a surgeon with the 2nd Life Guards, felt the occasion appeased the fears of those who had booked passage to England because of their terror of the French, and that many of them cancelled their bookings as a result.[124] That autumn Beresford was also honoured by the Prince Regent of Portugal, being invested with the Order of the Tower and the Sword; and in 1811 he was created the Conde de Transcoso.[125]

From Santarém, Masséna aspired to cross the Tagus, both to feed his army in the Alentejo and also to communicate and possibly link up with Mortier and Soult. To this end he engaged in bridge-building using pontoons. Hearing of this project from deserters Wellington sent a force of Portuguese caçadores and cavalry under General Fane to the left bank, where they were supported by ordenança from the north of the Alentejo.[126] This was followed by orders to Hill to cross the Tagus with the 2nd Division, Hamilton's Portuguese Division and the 13th Light Dragoons once news came in of a second bridge being thrown across the Zezere where the French had established a *tête de pont* at Punhete. Hill in turn was based at Chamusca, south west of Abrantes, which itself was well fortified and into which Fane now put his troops. On 24 November, Wellington, determined to starve out the French force, placed most of his army in winter quarters, leaving always men forward to deal with any movement, including French attempts to forage.

Beresford, for his part, was now back in Lisbon, for once again the Regency had failed to forward the means to pay the Portuguese troops, without informing either him or Wellington. D'Urban suspected that the money had been misappropriated and argued the only remedy was for the British to distribute the British subsidy.[127] Beresford's headquarters in the Lines had initially been at Casal Cochim (Sapateria, near Wellington's headquarters at Pero Negro), but following Masséna's retreat to Santarém he moved forward to Cartaxo. The difficulties in December regarding supply and finance led Beresford to go to Lisbon, but the move was temporary for on Christmas Day Wellington asked him to join him as soon as possible, and on 29 December he received orders to take command of the right division of the 'British and Portuguese army' due to General Hill's illness, which caused him to return to England.[128] Wellington explained to Hill and Beresford this was a temporary appointment pending Hill's recovery and rejoining the army.[129] Without delay Beresford crossed the Tagus on 30 December and proceeded to establish his headquarters at Chamusca. His corps, the right wing of the Allied army, occupied the left bank of the Tagus from Abrantes to Almeirim and as far as Salvaterra. Following an inspection of the area, which revealed French bridging preparations, he immediately ordered the reinforcement of positions opposite Punhete so as to command the mouth of the Zezere where it joins the Tagus. Not only did he have to guard against a full-scale French move across the Tagus, but also attempts to obtain supplies, on some occasions the subject of substantial raiding parties.[130] He still had to grapple with a shortage of supplies to the Portuguese troops, with D'Urban noting acidly that only such weak or criminal negligence would conquer Portugal, for not twice the present French forces would do so.[131]

Mortier was now reported to be moving north with a force which captured Merida and Medellin, both on the river Guadiana in Extremadura. It was generally assumed this was part of an attempt to effect a junction with Masséna and there was real concern if the result was to give the French possession of the Alentejo, a rich source of provisions for the Allies. The Regency was requested to order an evacuation in front of the anticipated French advance, but the required destruction of property and provisions was sporadic and ineffectual. Even Forjaz speculated as to whether the order to evacuate Alentejo was good for either the inhabitants or the army. He wondered whether the orders should be countermanded but said he would take no steps unless Beresford told him to do so.[132] However, the French did not attempt to come into the Alentejo at this point but instead occupied themselves with the sieges of Olivença (captured after a two-week siege on 23 January 1811) and then Badajoz.[133]

Wellington and Beresford met at Almeirim on 27 January; both of them clearly angered by the ongoing problems involving the Portuguese Regency and the difficulties in securing supplies for the Portuguese army because of the failure of the Regency to pay for them. One of the problems was that the Regency could not secure boats to deliver supplies as their owners were not prepared to make them available since they knew they had little prospect of payment. The Regency opted for seizure, which only made matters worse in Wellington's opinion as the boats would be hidden or leased to the British. Condemning what he felt was a 'system of violence' under 'the authority of the government' Wellington referred to the fact that the British Commissary for its part fed the Spanish army, and the Portuguese militia in the lines, besides the whole British army, and afforded not a little assistance to the Portuguese regular troops. He observed the problem would only get worse as the troops were moved further from the magazines.[134] He asked Stuart to make representations to the government about the distress of the Portuguese troops on the right-hand bank of the Tagus and threatened that if steps were not taken he would order the Portuguese army to Lisbon.[135] To Beresford he had indicated some days before their meeting at Almeirim:

> I don't know what to do about your means of transport, or indeed about anything for the Portuguese army. The government have not a shilling of money, and no credit; and although there are provisions in Lisbon now for a year, the Conde de Redondo cannot find out how to make biscuit, and wishes the Commissary General to supply him.[136]

In February 1811, an already bad situation became critical in some quarters with reports of Portuguese regiments not having received bread in certain instances for more than a week. Though clearly furious with the inaction of the Regency Council, Wellington sought to help by ordering the British commissary to supply Portuguese units with the British army, but problems persisted and the correspondence is littered with requests from Beresford to Forjaz for foodstuffs.[137] Forjaz did his best to supply these though Beresford observed in early March that 'the government troops are dying of hunger and the lack of food means they cannot serve as desired'. Regiments which had now been two or three days without rations could no longer advance. He railed against this treatment of an army that had served so well and said he would be making representations to the Prince Regent so that he was aware that the government let its troops die of hunger even though they voluntarily spilled their blood and gave their lives for the defence of the kingdom.[138] Forjaz felt Beresford was being somewhat unfair, at this stage in mid March, as Masséna's sudden retreat had taken the Regency by surprise, making it difficult for supplies to keep pace with the advance of the Allies.

None of these difficulties came between Wellington and Beresford. In late January, when making arrangements to meet him at Almeirim, Wellington referred to private letters Beresford had written him, obviously about the difficulties in dealing with the government, revealing at the same time the close cooperation and trust between the two men:

> Although the habit in which I am of opening my mind to you, upon all occasions and subjects, in the freest and fullest manner, may induce me to express my apprehensions in strong terms, you may depend upon it, not only that I am sensible of the real and cordial assistance which I have invariably received from you, but of the necessity that I should be

informed in time of all the difficulties which occur, in order that we may apply a remedy to them.[139]

While expressions such as these clearly indicate the strength of their relationship, there were clearly many occasions on which they chose not to put their thoughts in writing, and the correspondence between the two soldiers is full of tantalising but cryptic comments and suggestions on which they intend to converse.[140]

Wellington's confidence that the Lines would hold against any attack by Masséna increased as the winter wore on. Even when Drouet fought his way through from Spain to join Masséna in December with the 9th Corps and Gardanne's division, which had previously turned back at Abrantes due to guerrilla activity, Wellington does not appear to have been unduly concerned.[141] He remained vigilant at the prospect of either an attempt by Masséna to cross the Tagus and break into the Alentejo, whether in a strategic move in conjunction with Soult or Mortier, moving up from Andalucía, or on his own in order to feed his army – now stricken increasingly by famine. At the end of December there were reports that Soult had left the siege of Cádiz and Wellington instructed Beresford to ensure all boats on the Guadiana were either brought over to the right bank or destroyed, so that they might not be used by Soult in any attempt on the Alentejo.[142] Beresford had to be on a constant alert with his corps on the left bank of the Tagus in the first two months of 1811 prior to the sudden withdrawal of Masséna from Beira in early March; a retreat which was to culminate in the French abandonment of Portugal, with the exception of Almeida, by the end of April.

Reading Wellington's instructions, not only to Beresford but to the commanders of the other divisions, brigades and garrisons, one can only marvel at his encyclopaedic knowledge of the topography of the land and the available communications systems. By 10 January 1811 Wellington suspected that French intentions in the south were directed towards a siege of Badajoz, but he remained concerned that Mortier would try to link up with Masséna on the Tagus, coming through the Alentejo, and accordingly he did not send troops south at this time. Rather, his instructions to Beresford were to attempt to frustrate any juncture of Masséna and Mortier.[143] Wellington realised that Beresford could not take on both forces and if necessary he was to undertake a strategic withdrawal down the left bank of the Tagus. By mid January Wellington was aware of the French siege of Olivença and that they were scouting Badajoz. Accordingly, he did not feel they were intent on entering Portugal. He determined to keep Beresford's corps on the left of the Tagus for as long as possible, even if Masséna moved forward again on the right bank with his expected reinforcements. This decision was made with a view to saving the Alentejo, though Wellington recognised that a bold move might be made by the French to press southwards on both sides of the Tagus.

Meanwhile Romana, now very ill, agreed on 19 January to send the Spanish divisions of O'Donnell and Carrera back to Extremadura with a view to helping Olivença.[144] Wellington for his part swung between pessimism and optimism on the subject of Badajoz holding out. As time went on he became more confident that Badajoz would not fall providing the proper steps for its defence were undertaken.[145] Unfortunately the Governor, Mendizábal, was defeated outside the walls on 19 February, though he still retained upwards of 9,000 troops within the walls. Once Wellington realised on 6 March that Masséna was withdrawing definitively from Santarém, he moved to try to support Badajoz, directing Beresford on 9 March to move his corps south, but then thinking Badajoz was not pressed and that Masséna was making a stand at Pombal he called back Cole's division (4th) and the dragoons which had been designated to form part of Beresford's force.[146] At the same time he suggested that while Beresford set the remaining part of his force in motion, he himself should come to join Wellington with just his horses as he anticipated a battle on 11 March.

Wellington's desire to have Beresford with him for the anticipated battle probably reflects the good opinion he held of the Marshal's abilities. While there was an engagement at Pombal on 11 March it was not decisive, but part of a fighting retreat which also involved encounters at Redinha (12 March), and Sabugal (3 April). Masséna had entered Portugal with an army of some 65,000 in August 1810. In late 1810 he had received reinforcements of some 5000 men. Estimates vary but when he began his retreat from Santarém on 5 March 1811, he had some 45,000 soldiers with him; a loss of 25,000 men of which perhaps 1,500 had been lost through combat. Wellington's combined strategy of laying waste to the land and the building of the Lines of Torres Vedras had done their job and the third French invasion of Portugal had been beaten back to the Spanish border. On 20 March Wellington stood down the militia and ordenança manning the Lines of Torres Vedras. By mid April the only Portuguese territory still occupied by the French was a small piece of land around the Côa and the fortress of Almeida.

Lisbon and Portugal had been saved, but at great cost. The repeated devastation of the country resulted in its population being reduced by an estimated 10–20 per cent between 1807 and 1814, and it has been suggested that between 40,000 and 50,000 civilians died during the course of the third French invasion and the implementation of the scorched earth policy by Wellington.[147] Even allowing for possible animus, the descriptions of the condition of those still living in the areas laid waste by Masséna in his retreat are frightening. Children without parents were found barely alive in Santarém, wolves feeding off remains in the streets of Leiria, famine and disease rampant. Indeed, a French account described the breakdown of law and order in the French army during the winter of 1810–11 long before it began its retreat.

Subordinates disregarded superiors and went unpunished; those caught committing crimes were not penalised and the police turned a blind eye. Soldiers reportedly took to selling their women, or even gambling them against luxuries. By the time Masséna ordered the burning of the boats he had intended to use to cross the Tagus, reportedly one-third of the army was continuously out searching for subsistence.[148] Agriculture in Portugal took years to recover from the effects of this third invasion, and when victory was complete Portugal received only a small part of the reparations France was compelled to pay and representations went largely unheeded. There were impressive attempts by public grant and private subscription in the United Kingdom to alleviate hardship in Portugal, but the suffering was extensive in Beira and Estremadura in particular.[149] The relief took not just the form of food, but the means of future subsistence including cows, oxen, implements of agriculture and seeds. Commissioners were employed to administer the relief over a ten-month period.[150]

Masséna had begun his retreat on 5 March. Five days later Badajoz unexpectedly fell to the French. The relief force under Beresford could never have reached it in time to prevent the fall, but the nature of his assignment now changed, with the French position in the south of Spain having been considerably strengthened. The French now held three of the four great border fortresses guarding the border between Spain and Portugal. The Allies would have to turn their hand to a hitherto untried art, that of siege warfare. Starvation had driven the French out of Portugal, but the Imperial armies were still substantial and might well return until beaten decisively in battle or withdrawn from the Peninsula.

Forjaz, on behalf of the Regency, communicated to Beresford its praise for the army and the distinguished chief who disciplined and commanded that army saying: 'I have particular satisfaction in communicating the sentiments of the governors of the kingdom towards your excellency, being precisely those I have ever invariably entertained.'[151] Perhaps Forjaz was having a dig at the regents, who had so recently sought Beresford's replacement. For their part the French had learnt that the Portuguese soldier was a determined and brave opponent, once adapted to British discipline as instilled by Beresford. Masséna himself paid this tribute: 'the Portuguese soldier, intelligent, austere and an unflagging walker, commanded by British officers and subjected to British discipline, were as efficient as the Anglo-Hanoverians, and in some cases, better than them, because the Portuguese are often possessed of strong feelings of enthusiasm and honour'.[152]

Masséna's losses during the winter of 1810/11 and his subsequent retreat into Spain in the spring of 1811 did not ensure Portugal's independence or security. France still maintained over 200,000 men in the Peninsula. If the French armies could coordinate their activities, the Allies would face continued and substantial dangers, including the prospect of a further invasion of Portugal. Masséna's Army of Portugal still represented a serious threat and Joseph Bonaparte ruled in Madrid. For the time being Soult's *Armée du Midi* had the Spanish forces under the Junta penned in Cádiz; and Napoleon had ordered him to move to assist Masséna. In eastern Spain the *Armée d'Aragon* under General Suchet, and in northern Spain the *Armée du Nord* under Marshal Bessières, were distracted by Spanish guerillas as well as regular forces of varying calibre, but the existence of peace between France and her major European antagonists meant that should Napoleon chose to do so, France had the capacity to send additional forces to the Iberian Peninsula.

Both the security of Portugal and the ability of the Allies to push the French back in Spain required that the four great fortresses adjacent to the border between Spain and Portugal be in Allied hands. In the north the French held both Ciudad Rodrigo in Spain and Almeida in Portugal at the beginning of 1811. In the south the Spanish held Badajoz and the Portuguese were ensconced in Elvas at the beginning of the year. Thus while Soult and his lieutenants were present in Andalucía, with substantial bodies of French troops, Allied possession of Badajoz and Elvas meant the southern route into Portugal did not appear to be in imminent danger; enabling Wellington initially to develop a strategy designed to recover Almeida and Ciudad Rodrigo prior to launching any assault on the French armies in Spain.

In late 1810, the force in the Alentejo on the left bank of the Tagus under Hill was made up of the 2nd, 4th and Portuguese divisions together with a small cavalry arm. When Hill had first succumbed to a disabling fever, Wellington had placed William Stewart at the head of the 2nd Division. Stewart's impetuosity meant he did not enjoy Wellington's full confidence. The 4th Division was commanded by Galbraith Lowry Cole, a popular divisional commander, but again Wellington had reservations about his ability to command independently.[1] The Portuguese Division had been formally organised in 1810 and was commanded by John Hamilton. Throughout the war it served with the 2nd Division and the cavalry with this force consisted of one British cavalry brigade and de Grey's regiment of heavy dragoons, together with Otway's Portuguese cavalry (1st and 7th Portuguese cavalry regiments) and other small elements. At the end of December 1810, Beresford was appointed to lead this corps until 'General Hill's health shall be sufficiently re-established to enable him to resume the command.'[2]

Throughout the winter of 1810 and spring of 1811, Wellington and Beresford were in contact on a virtually daily basis, indeed often several times each day; additionally they held frequent meetings, even after Beresford had moved to the left side of the river. The Tagus does not appear to have interrupted Allied communications in any substantial fashion for the Royal Navy and Portuguese forces controlled the waterway between the ocean and Abrantes. The French were prevented from crossing the river in force by the construction of fortifications, gun emplacements, land and river patrols, though as has been seen, the failure to remove all boats left the French a capacity to move some troops and supplies as well as to mount raiding parties for provisions.[3] Initially, the objective of the force on the left bank of the river (the right wing of the Allied army) was to prevent the French crossing the Tagus and breaking into the Alentejo, whether to feed Masséna's army, threaten Lisbon from the left bank, or to attempt any merger of Masséna and Soult's armies if the latter marched north from Andalucía.[4] Additionally, this force was expected to curtail communication between Masséna and Soult.

At the end of December 1810, Wellington had become aware that Soult was moving from Sevilla towards the Portuguese frontier, and by early January Wellington apprehended a French siege of Badajoz, though he remained concerned that Soult's objective was to help Masséna.[5] Wellington requested the destruction of the bridges at Medellin and Merida, but the latter was not destroyed giving the French an easy crossing point of the Guadiana. On 22 January Olivença, garrisoned by a Spanish force, fell to Soult. Five days later, on 27 January, Soult had commenced the siege of Badajoz. Allied expectations were that the garrison could hold out for an extensive period and the town was in no immediate danger. This line of thought was reinforced when a Spanish corps under General Gabriel Mendizábal relieved the town on 6 February. Two weeks later, Marshal Édouard Mortier inflicted a crushing defeat of the Spanish army commanded by Mendizábal at Gebora on 19 February.[6]

Though he hoped Badajoz would hold out for a considerable time, this setback seems to have induced a sense of fatalism in Wellington concerning the likely fall of Badajoz, for with

Masséna still camped before the Lines at Santarém, Wellington could not contemplate the dispatch of part of his army southwards. His concern at that time was to instruct Beresford on how to meet Masséna's forces should they move into the Alentejo, though he signalled to Beresford that if Masséna retired from the Tagus an effort should be made to relieve Badajoz.[7] However, when Masséna began his precipitate retreat from Santarém on 6 March, Wellington's immediate reaction was to bring Cole's 4th Division and the brigade of heavy cavalry to join him on the right bank as part of the pursuit. A portion of Stewart's 2nd Division was also brought across the Tagus at Abrantes and Wellington additionally requested Beresford to let him have the brigade of dragoons as soon as possible.[8]

Wellington himself had been planning to attack Masséna in early March. In this enterprise he intended to use Beresford's force in an assault on Masséna's army by bringing him across the Tagus at Abrantes at the same time as Wellington launched his frontal attack on Masséna; but this was pre-empted by Masséna's retreat from Santarém towards the Spanish border. Wellington immediately set in motion a full pursuit of the retreating French and Beresford's command was at first designated part of that pursuit. The pace of Masséna's withdrawal was such, combined with the knowledge that Soult with *L'Armée du Midi* was threatening Badajoz seriously, that Wellington decided to divide his forces, ordering Beresford southwards on 8 March to guard the Portuguese frontier and with instructions to attempt the relief of Badajoz, now invested by the French. For this purpose Beresford was to take with him the 2nd and 4th divisions. He was to be joined by Hamilton's Portuguese Division and subsequently in April by the King's German Legion (KGL), recently arrived in Lisbon. A small cavalry force, made up of elements of the 13th Dragoons, de Grey's heavy cavalry and Otway's Portuguese horse, was added to the substantial force of infantry. General Fane, who had done so much to train the Portuguese cavalry, had returned to the United Kingdom and his replacement, Brigadier General Robert Ballard Long, only arrived in the Peninsula on 3 March.[9] Beresford would be joined on 30 March by 2,500 Spaniards under General Castaños, the remnant of the Spanish army of Extremadura crushed at Gebora.[10]

No sooner had Beresford been given the order to proceed to Badajoz than it was countermanded by Wellington on account of the Allied leader anticipating that Masséna might stand and fight in the region of Pombal or Punhete. He sent a message to Beresford saying that he had ordered General Cole and de Grey's Heavy Brigade to halt at Tomar on 9 March and he requested Beresford to send him the brigade of dragoons 'as soon as you can'.[11] This holding back of troops by Wellington emphasises the tightrope he had to walk at this time, for he did not have sufficient men to give him a meaningful superiority on one, let alone two fronts. On 9 March, in anticipation of Masséna forcing a battle on 11 March, Wellington requested Beresford to join the Allied army on the right bank of the Tagus, telling him about new dispositions for Cole's division and the dragoons as Wellington needed to strengthen his own position and 'as Badajoz is certainly not hard pressed and as at all events it would be desirable that you would not commence your operations there till the boats will have arrived at Elvas'.[12] It was only on 12 March that Beresford was ordered to resume his way south (and some regiments were in fact held back by Wellington until 16 March), by which time Badajoz had fallen to the French.[13]

On 13 March Wellington learnt of the capitulation of the city two days earlier. He expressed both surprise and anger at the suddenness of the surrender of Badajoz and felt the Spanish could have done more when aware that a relieving force was on its way. The Portuguese semaphore system meant that the garrison commander at Badajoz, General Imaz, knew of Masséna's retreat prior to his own surrender in circumstances where Wellington had advised him a relief force was on the way and requested he hold out.[14] Wellington felt the surrender was not just an act of treason but one which endangered the Peninsula; and suggested to his brother Henry in Cádiz that he could do no more than protect the Alentejo.[15] The loss of Badajoz was a serious setback for Wellington's strategy to secure Portugal and threaten the French hold on Spain. With the exception of Elvas the French now held the great fortresses guarding both sides of the frontier.

Marshal Soult returned to Sevilla with part of his army after the fall of Badajoz. He was concerned about a possible rising in the capital of Andalucía, a concern amplified following the Allies tactical and morale-boosting victory under General Graham at Barrosa on 5 March; a victory from which no advantage was obtained due to a failure of the British and Spanish forces to cooperate before, during and after the battle. Soult had left Mortier behind in Extremadura with a force of some 11,000 men.[16] Mortier garrisoned Badajoz with 3,000 men under General Philippon and then sent General La Tour-Maubourg with a force to capture the small and ill-equipped Portuguese fortified town of Campo Maior. The town succumbed on 21 March after a heroic six-day defence by a small Portuguese force.[17] The nearby town of Albuquerque was subsequently overcome. Wellington, for his part, continued his pursuit of the French which was to lead to the attritional battle of Fuentes de Oñoro over three days beginning on 3 May. Beresford, meanwhile, assembled his forces at Portalegre on 22 March.

Beresford's campaign in 1811 took place in the Portuguese province of Alentejo and its neighbouring Spanish province of Extremadura. The campaign was dominated by a number of events:

1. The performance of the Allied cavalry on the recapture of Campo Maior and in other engagements prior to the battle of Albuera, leading to the replacement of General Long as its commander;
2. The conduct of the first siege of Badajoz;
3. Beresford's decision to fight the French at Albuera and the conduct of both Beresford and the Allied army at that battle.

Each of these topics will be examined in turn.

While at Portalegre, Beresford learnt of the fall of Campo Maior. His first objective was to recapture the recently overrun town just under fifty kilometres away, followed by other small fortified towns such as Olivença, which was preparatory work for the siege of Badajoz. His arrival before Campo Maior on 25 March took the French by surprise. They were in the act of evacuating the town with the heavy guns captured there, in order to use these to bolster the already impressive armoury at Badajoz. Beresford's force managed to secure the town before the French could destroy the defences, but was frustrated in its attempt to recover the heavy artillery.[18] Initially the Allied cavalry, under Brigadier General Robert Long, routed the French cavalry commanded by General Chamorin, who lost his life in this encounter.[19]

Facing odds of at least 2:1, the Allied cavalry had to this point performed well, but it overextended itself in a wild pursuit with consequent heavy losses. In that pursuit Long's cavalry (Beresford had held de Grey's heavy cavalry in reserve) recaptured the guns being taken by the French from Campo Maior to Badajoz under an escort commanded by La Tour-Maubourg. The British and Portuguese pursuit went all the way to the glacis of Badajoz, where the light cavalry came under fire from the walls and was then subjected to a charge by fresh French horse, which not only drove the Allied horse away, but ensured the recovery by the French of all bar one of the sixteen Campo Maior heavy cannon which were then brought into Badajoz. Beresford, meanwhile, had been pursuing the retiring French infantry with de Grey's heavy cavalry and some guns, but had halted this force because he had been given an erroneous report that his light cavalry had been surrounded and had possibly surrendered in its entirety.[20] In his own report he mentioned that since the French infantry retired in good order he felt he could not risk de Grey's heavy cavalry (3rd Dragoon guards and 4th Dragoons) not knowing what fresh force might be sent out from Badajoz.[21]

Such a decision is completely understandable when one considers Wellington's own strictures to Beresford while the latter was marching south. Not only was he advised to keep his troops *en masse* but he was counselled: 'the cavalry to be the most delicate arm that we possess. We have very few officers who have a practical knowledge of the mode of using it, or who have ever seen more than 2 regiments together.' Having warned Beresford of the propensity for all the troops to get out of order in battle, Wellington added: 'the defeat of, or any great loss sustained by, our cavalry, in these open grounds, would be a misfortune amounting almost to the defeat of the whole; and you will see the necessity of keeping the cavalry as much as possible en masse and in reserve, to be thrown in at the moment when an opportunity may offer of striking a decisive blow.'[22]

Beresford was upset. He had given Long an order not to endanger his force, probably based not solely on Wellington's strictures but also on concerns which had arisen following earlier lack of discipline in the cavalry at the battles of Vimeiro and Talavera. When he reported the event to Wellington, he did so in terms which while regretting the impetuosity of the cavalry were supportive of their commanders. Having commended the steadiness of the heavy brigade he went on:

> Brig. Gen Long manoeuvred with knowledge, and used every effort to moderate the over ardor of the cavalry and to regulate its movements. The gallantry of all was conspicuous, particularly of Colonels Head and Otway, and the squadrons with them; and the only thing to be regretted, which is usual with our troops on their first meeting with the enemy, was too much impetuosity.[23]

Wellington was furious at the lack of discipline shown and indicated that if the 13th Dragoons were guilty of this type of conduct again, he would take their horses from them and send the officers and men to do duty in Lisbon.[24] Long and his fellow officers felt this criticism unjustified and to his brother he expressed the view that if Beresford understood cavalry as he undoubtedly understood infantry he would not have lost the opportunity of striking such a severe blow.[25] However, not only did Beresford have Wellington's orders ringing in his ears but British cavalry had something of a reputation in the Peninsula. There is no doubt it proved itself on many occasions in Portugal and Spain but it had a real problem with control at times and the issue was to reoccur a year after Campo Maior at Maguilla, when following the rout of Slade's force, Wellington observed: 'Our officers of cavalry have acquired the trick of galloping at everything. They never consider the situation, never think of manoeuvring before an enemy, and never keep back or provide for a reserve.'[26] There was no doubting their bravery, but the impetuosity of the British cavalry was to raise its head again at Waterloo.

Notwithstanding his recognition of Long's expertise and the commitment of other cavalry officers, Beresford's criticism of the cavalry at Campo Maior rankled with Long who felt, probably with some justification, that Beresford did not trust him thereafter. In early April the 13th Light Dragoons were involved in a further incident when a squadron including Major Redmond Morres was captured in circumstances for which Beresford felt Long was at least partially accountable.[27] Certainly their relationship took a turn for the worse when Beresford removed Long from his cavalry command following further incidents preceding the battle of Albuera, and Long for his part had begun to criticise Beresford in correspondence after the engagement at Campo Maior. He also waged a campaign of attrition against Beresford and his staff seeking a full explanation of each order received in a manner which led them to question his suitability for command. However, his replacement by General Lumley at the head of the cavalry before the battle of Albuera may not have been entirely based on Long's behaviour prior to the battle. The background to Long's removal was the subject of both contemporaneous and subsequent argument and comment and it is worth seeking to draw together those views in order to ascertain exactly what prompted his being replaced by Sir William Lumley.

Long's precipitous retreat in front of the army before the battle of Albuera was the subject of discussion, centering on whether or not Long was responsible for that withdrawal of the cavalry under his command from Santa Marta across the river Albuera on 15 May, or whether he was acting under orders. Certainly retiring suddenly had a not inconsiderable impact on Beresford's state of knowledge of the whereabouts of Soult's forces prior to the battle. The evidence suggests that Long was certainly not solely responsible for the speedy retreat of the cavalry; but surviving documents, while not putting the matter beyond doubt, indicate that even prior to that development, Beresford had already determined to replace Long as commander of the Allied cavalry. This was probably not just because of the disappointment at Campo Maior and upset at some additional incidents over the next few weeks involving Long and the cavalry. The decision may have been influenced by the politics and precedents involving combined commands.

Beresford's replacement of Long with Lumley at the head of the cavalry prior to the battle of Albuera has usually been cited as due to Beresford's perception of Long as a weak commander. Certainly it did not take long for Beresford to form an unfavourable view of Long's abilities. In

November 1811 the Marshal summarised those views which had left him in no doubt Long's performance justified his removal:

> he was fully aware of what he himself merited and from his own disposition would have no idea of the forbearance, or allowance that another would make for a theorist, just come out, and totally ignorant [sic] of actual service and expecting that his conduct would be precisely detailed ... his friends have been such fools as to show his letters publickly in the business of Campo Maior though he positively disobeyed my orders in the matter and was the cause of the escape of the French detachment. I only told him that it was the first time & the business was over & could not be helped. For the business of Los Santos, it was so bad that I could say nothing in his excuse and yet though he was again the cause of the escape of two regiments of cavalry, I did nothing more than simply omit mentioning his name in my report. His retiring from Santa Martha to Albuhera [sic] was so shocking that I could no longer even trust with that arm of the service and indeed to the security of my army leave him in command of the cavalry & I superceded him, yet I chose to do this in a manner that had no occasion to hurt his feelings, as I make a point of never hurting the feelings of any officer beyond what is absolutely necessary for the good of the service.[28]

At Los Santos (Los Santos de Maimona), a small town south east of Albuera, there had been an opportunity to trap a column of French cavalry but the operation was only partially successful because of Long's failure to obey orders with expedition, orders which had to be repeated by Beresford. Lieutenant Colonel José Luis de Vasconcelos, commander of the 23rd Portuguese Regiment of Line at Albuera (and later the 10th Cavalry) leaves us in no doubt that Long was at least pedantically slow in making his dispositions.[29]

Beresford and his staff were certainly frustrated with Long's inability to act within general orders and his repeated requests for more precise direction in the weeks preceding Albuera. Whether he clearly lacked confidence in himself or his repeated requests for clarification of orders were intended to pressurise Beresford, the result not only irritated Beresford and his staff but gave the impression that he lacked a firm grasp of what was required, and raised the spectre of his suitability for independent command. D'Urban, writing in 1833, disclosed that even though Beresford felt a lack of trust in Long after the three incidents at Campo Maior, Los Santos, and the precipitous retreat from Santa Marta, he was reluctant to supersede him with Lumley; but Long had himself raised with Beresford the prospect of Penne Villemur commanding the Allied cavalry, and this was used as the reason for appointing Lumley whether to avoid hurt to Long's feelings or otherwise. Beresford and others would seem to be wrong in suggesting that the manner of the retreat from Santa Marta could have been a factor in Long's removal from the command of the cavalry, for Long was told by D'Urban on 14 May, two days prior to the battle and before the retreat from Santa Marta, that he was being replaced by Lumley in terms which at least outwardly adopted Long's own reasoning regarding the desirability of a British commander: 'the Marshal further begs me to acquaint you, that to obviate the evils of undefined rants and claims of command averted to in your letter of last night, he has directed Major General Lumley to assume the command of the cavalry of the army.'[30]

Long had not got off to a great start when he arrived at Lisbon on 3 March 1809. He met up with Wellington at Santarém a few days later and Wellington apparently suggested an appointment to command an infantry brigade. Long expressed his dissatisfaction as he had anticipated a cavalry appointment, and his complaint probably did not endear him to the 'Hero of Talavera', as he repeatedly refers to Wellington in his correspondence.[31] When he was summoned to Horse Guards by Colonel Torrens on 16 January 1811 prior to taking up his appointment to the army in Portugal in 1811, Long, who had very fixed ideas of right and wrong, told his father that he would not consider any offer unless 'proper to be accepted' and that he would not have 'anything to do with Marshal Beresford and his Portuguese heroes'.[32] Why he held this attitude is unclear. Beresford and Long do not appear to have served together prior to 1811 save that Long arrived at La Coruña in January 1809 shortly before the battle and subsequent evacuation of the British army. That short association seems unlikely to have given rise to any antagonism, as Beresford's conduct of the rearguard during the evacuation was regarded as exemplary. When Wellington sent him to meet Beresford at Tomar in mid March 1811, Long was initially impressed by the Portuguese troops whose appearance he felt was 'in every respect equal to our own'. Likewise, his first impressions of Beresford were positive, notwithstanding his earlier reservations, for he wrote in his diary for 16 March: 'From the three days intercourse I have had with Marshal Beresford I am inclined to like him most exceedingly.'[33] Long was then confirmed in his command of Beresford's cavalry.

Clearly it only took a short time for Beresford to form a poor impression of Long's abilities. Likewise, Long's initial view of Beresford was to change. However, it seems likely that there may well have been another reason for Long's replacement by Lumley. The Marshal may have wished to ensure that a British rather than a Spanish general officer commanded the cavalry, just as Wellington manoeuvred to ensure Beresford had overall command of the army. Indeed, there may have been a further factor at play for Brigadier General Madden, with a brigade of Portuguese cavalry, was due to join Beresford at Albuera (though ultimately he did not do so prior to the battle). Had he joined the Allies, Madden rather than Long would have had claims to command that wing of the army.

Whether at Beresford's instigation or otherwise, Wellington had determined to remove Long from command of the cavalry prior to the battle of Albuera. By late April Wellington had offered Beresford Sir William Erskine as a replacement for Long, stating that even though Erskine was very blind, he was cautious and 'you will find him more intelligent and useful than any body you have'.[34] The timing of this offer subsequent to Wellington's visit to Beresford at Elvas from 20 to 22 April seems to suggest they must have discussed Long's performance during their meeting. Initially it looked as if General Erskine would replace Long, but presumably this intention was overtaken by events.

In a slightly convoluted and perhaps uneasy fashion, Wellington had written to Long on 11 May explaining that his original intentions regarding the disposal of his cavalry forces had not worked out and that as a result of Madden being in Extremadura he must have commanded there but for the fact that Erskine had requested the command. He went on to say that he had intended the command of a good brigade of cavalry for Long but the Prince Regent had appointed Alten to command the hussars of the German Legion, with the result there was currently no appointment available. He therefore requested Long to remain with Beresford for the time being.[35] The correspondence suggests therefore that Long's replacement had been determined some time before the battle, not just by Beresford but by Wellington. Conveniently, a reshuffle of appointments allowed Beresford also to ensure that a British officer commanded his cavalry in the event of a major battle; as William Lumley was senior to Penne Villemur, the Spanish cavalry commander. Lumley did have experience as a cavalry officer, albeit earlier in his career.

Long was understandably upset. Whatever the merits of the criticism of his conduct at Campo Maior, the bridgehead at Juromenha, and Los Santos, the allegation that Long's conduct in withdrawing to Albuera precipitously was contrary to expectation is harsh, in the light of D'Urban's order that day for him to retire 'immediately' on Albuera. Contemporary witnesses leave us in no doubt that the retreat was sudden with Colonel Hardinge reporting the horses to be distressed. Indeed French evidence suggests the retreat was conducted without attempting to hold up the advance by resistance at Santa Marta.[36] There was a second aspect to that retreat for which Long does not appear to have been responsible, namely bringing the cavalry over the bridge at Albuera instead of remaining to monitor the French on its right bank for as long as possible. The evidence points to this being the subject of an order from Beresford's Assistant Adjutant-General, Colonel Rooke. Indeed D'Urban later noted that it had been the intention to post infantry amongst the trees on the far side of the river Albuera and that would have been a far more effective method of preventing the French advance guard approaching, or at least slowing it down. He gives no explanation as to why this was not in fact done.[37] Notwithstanding his replacement by Lumley, to his credit Long performed well at Albuera and later that year, under Hill, was to distinguish himself at Arroyo dos Molinos.

The delay in Lumley assuming the command until the morning of the battle of Albuera arose simply because Lumley was part of the force at Badajoz on the far side of the Guadiana and had to detour via Juromenha to join Beresford. As it was there were difficulties with Penne Villemur during the battle, so appointing Lumley turned out to be a good move by Beresford. Colonel William Napier, who was to later emerge as a critic of Beresford, approved of the decision to appoint Lumley.[38]

Long did have a history of implacable opposition to perceived wrongs and these had led repeatedly to his falling out with superiors. These incidents involved him in disputes concerning regiments in which he had served as well as military expeditions on which he had been employed. He became embroiled in arguments relating to the 2nd Dragoon Guards and the 15th Light Dragoons as well as the conduct of the Walcheren expedition and fell out with such august and important persons as the Duke of York and his brother the Duke of Cumberland. Nonetheless, he was not without friends prepared to fight his corner. Long was a professional soldier. He was also a person who abhorred bloodshed and suffering. He had railed against the loss of lives at Walcheren in 1809 and was appalled by the desolation, destruction and killing of men, women and children which he saw on the French retreat from the Lines. It was not therefore surprising that, like Beresford, he anguished over the loss of life at Albuera.

Following Albuera and his removal from the command of the cavalry, Long remained for another two years in the Peninsula, during which time, while serving with Erskine's cavalry Division, his correspondence is critical of both Hill and Wellington. It is also frequently extremely pessimistic in respect of British and Allied prospects, symptomatic of the 'croakers' of which Wellington complained. He was criticised by Lumley for his failure to support Penne Villemur in the pursuit of the French after Albuera.[39] Neither did his relations with Wellington improve, for the latter reprimanded Long for his conduct of a skirmish near Elvas in June.[40]

Long did not miss an opportunity to continue his campaign against Beresford in his letters home. He had a further disagreement with Beresford in 1811, when the latter complained that Long had appropriated two Portuguese ADCs without Beresford's permission, before giving them sick leave and leave of absence. Beresford, to whom he refers as 'the great Marshal', was understandably concerned at the impact such moves might have on discipline and when Wellington backed up Beresford, Long railed against the commander in chief of the Allied forces in the Peninsula.[41] Given his views one can understand why Long was particularly sickened when Beresford was granted the title of Marquês de Campo Maior. Ultimately his complaints against the various commanders did him no good for in 1813 Wellington did not oppose the recall of Long and his replacement by Colquhoun Grant; and Long did not serve again in the war or in the Waterloo campaign.

The conduct of Long and the cavalry may have been worrying for Beresford but he could not let it distract him from his prime objective, the recovery of Badajoz. Beresford faced a tricky problem if he was to besiege Badajoz for the French controlled not only the bridge at Badajoz but that upstream at Merida. The lack of bridges downstream of Badajoz meant that if Beresford was to invest the city he would need to cross the river Guadiana with his army at a time when part of it might be exposed to the French before he could get a critical mass across the river. A lack of supplies and boats, and a flooding river, combined to hinder the investment of Badajoz. Wellington himself advised Beresford to cross at Juromenha, but no pontoon bridge was available on Beresford's arrival because the only one which might have been available locally had been captured by the French at Badajoz, where it had been stored.[42] Boats to form a pontoon arrived at Elvas on 23 March, but they were too small and too few. As a result an ingenious trestle bridge was built from each bank with the pontoon in the middle, but disaster then struck when the river flooded due to rain and part of the bridge was washed away. It was only on 7 April that Beresford had the greater part of his army on the left bank. Once across the Guadiana he forced the retirement of La Tour-Maubourg's force towards the Sierra Morena, leaving Philippon in Badajoz with 3,000 men and a further garrison in Olivença. Beresford ordered Cole to besiege the latter town with the 4th Division on 9 April, while he moved with the remainder of his force to occupy Valverde and Albuera (11 April). Following the capture of Olivença on 16 April the army reunited and Beresford, while waiting for a siege train to arrive at Badajoz from Elvas, used the time to drive La Tour-Maubourg further out of Extremadura.[43] Beresford was the subject of some contemporary criticism for the time it took him to commence the siege of Badajoz, but he clearly felt it desirable to mop up other resistance points while waiting for siege equipment. Nor was he responsible for delays, the result of the weather and the absence of a pontoon bridge. Alexander Gordon, an ADC to Wellington, having written critically to his brother, Lord Aberdeen, on the subject of Beresford's alleged delay on 8 April, fully recanted when writing again two weeks later. On the latter occasion he formed part of Wellington's party, which had ridden south to Elvas following the expulsion of Masséna from Portugal and his retreat to Salamanca. Gordon then wrote: 'I must take occasion to say that since we have been here and seen things in their true light, it does appear that Beresford has done as well as he could do, and has not lost much time.'[44]

Wellington visited Elvas on 20 April. Beresford was then at Almendral, returning from Santa Marta and Los Santos where the 13th Light Dragoons had been engaged in a small cavalry action in respect of which he praised their conduct; notwithstanding his criticism of Long whom he blamed for the escape of two regiments of French cavalry.[45] Wellington and Beresford conducted a reconnaissance of Badajoz on 22 April, in circumstances where Wellington seems to have disregarded his personal safety, proceeding without waiting for his guard detail and risking capture by the French. Wellington then issued instructions to Beresford in respect of the siege and the campaign in Extremadura which effectively governed his conduct there. These detailed instructions also called for Beresford to fight at Albuera if challenged by the French in circumstances which might enable Beresford to resume the siege.[46] Wellington had picked the ground for battle.

In the event that it appeared to Beresford that the enemy was likely to be too strong for him, taking into account the assistance he might receive from such Spanish troops as were available, he was instructed to retire across the Guadiana taking the position of the Caia and Portalegre successively. He was authorised 'to fight the action if he should think proper, or to retire if he should not'.[47] Wellington hoped that Beresford's chances of success in any battle against the French would be materially improved in the event of Spanish cooperation. Apart from the force under Castaños, which had already joined Beresford, there were two other Spanish forces available, the Third Army under Ballasteros and the much larger Fourth Army under Captain-General Joachim Blake, which it was hoped would join Beresford.[48] To this end Wellington wrote a Memorandum to the three Spanish Generals, and perhaps foreseeing that Blake might place difficulties in Beresford's way he advised Beresford on 6 May not to commence the siege until the General had agreed to the proposals outlined there: 'If Gen. Blake does not positively agree to everything proposed in my memorandum, and does not promise to carry it strictly into execution, I think that you ought not to be in a hurry with the siege of Badajoz.'[49]

Those who criticised Beresford for his delay in commencing the siege may not have been aware he was merely following these orders.[50] It was to be 8 May before Beresford received the necessary confirmation of cooperation from Blake. In the interim, Castaños, with whom Beresford got on well, had reportedly acted a l'Espagnol by going off for 6–8 days with part of Morillo's force which was meant to be available for the siege.[51] A huge logistic effort had been made in April and early May to find and bring up materials to Badajoz. The investment of the town was taking place from 4 May onwards and on 8 May work on the trenches was begun. Three days later the guns opened fire on the fort. Criticism of Beresford for alleged dawdling would seem to be misplaced, as not only was he following Wellington's orders, but there was a shocking lack of guns and other equipment required for a major siege.[52] Some of the stores only reached the army from Elvas on 12 May. Allied to the suggestion that Beresford delayed it was suggested he was over cautious in his campaign, but the French had 70,000 men in Andalucía and Drouet D'Erlon was known to be on his way south with a further force in excess of 10,000, so caution was appropriate.[53]

Badajoz was the first siege of consequence conducted by the British or combined Allied forces in the Peninsular War. The lack of British siege artillery in 1811 arose because it had not been envisaged that the Allies would be besieging Badajoz at this time. Beresford's mission was incepted to relieve Badajoz, not invest it. When the task changed because of the fall of the town to the French, the Allies did not have the wherewithal to implement a proper siege. Beresford had to make do with what could be supplied by the Portuguese. The cannon brought from Elvas to Badajoz were not only insufficient in number and calibre, but also in many cases almost 200 years old. A lack of sappers and miners did not help the situation. Beresford did have the services of Dickson as head of artillery and those of John Squire of the Royal Engineers to advise on how to conduct the siege, but there was a limited amount they could do in the absence of cannon, sappers and artificers. Following representations, Beresford assigned troops as artificers but this ad hoc arrangement is indicative of the general state of unpreparedness for a siege due to a lack of training and experience in such matters.[54] In any event, such efforts as were made were of no avail for within a week of investing Badajoz's strong fortifications the Marshal had to lift the siege, following receipt of news on 12 May that Soult's army was approaching from Sevilla.[55] In the interim a French sortie from the besieged city on 10 May destroyed some of the siege works, further delaying progress.[56]

Wellington's timetable of sixteen days for the capture of Badajoz was unrealistic in circumstances which were totally different to those that pertained nine months later at Ciudad Rodrigo. For the siege of the northern fortress, Wellington brought up a properly equipped siege train from Lisbon over a period of at least four months, and there would be no French army marching to the relief of Ciudad Rodrigo. Richard Fletcher, who had ridden south with Wellington to inspect Badajoz, and John Squire both felt that the timetable of sixteen days was insufficient and further time would be required. It should not be forgotten that the successful French siege had taken six weeks. Furthermore, a twenty-one day siege of Badajoz in May–June 1811, with almost four times as many guns as enjoyed by Beresford, failed to produce the desired result. The news that Soult had left Sevilla on 9 May with a substantial army led Beresford to lift the siege on the night of 12 May, in the knowledge that he did not have a sufficient body of men both to continue the siege and fight Soult. Suggestions were made that he should have persisted with the siege, but such a course would have been to risk being caught between Soult's advancing army and the French in Badajoz. Even Colonel W.F.P. Napier, who emerged as Beresford's sternest critic of the conduct of the battle of Albuera, supported the view that to have tried to maintain the siege would have been to invite disaster and that the decision to raise the siege saved the army.[57]

Soult, who had left Sevilla with 20,000 infantry, 3,000 cavalry and perhaps 30 cannon, had hoped to meet up with Drouet d'Erlon's corps coming south from Masséna's army as well as with the corps under La Tour-Maubourg already in Extremadura. In the event the body under Drouet d'Erlon was retained further north, but on 13 May Soult's forces joined with those of La Tour-Maubourg at Fuente Caños, and by 15 May the combined force was at Santa Marta, only twenty kilometres from Albuera. Soult's army had covered 200 kilometres in six days, a distance normally taking four days longer.

11 THE BATTLE OF ALBUERA AND ITS AFTERMATH, MAY–JUNE 1811

Peace to the brave who nobly died,
Albuera, on thy marshy side,
When carnage scattered far and wide
Had strewn thy fields with dead. Anon.[1]

The decision to fight the French at Albuera and the conduct of the battle by Beresford has been the subject of considerable controversy. This chapter will summarise events and then proceed to analyse the issues in dispute in greater detail.

Wellington apprehended that when he sent Beresford to besiege Badajoz, Soult might seek to intervene. Based on information received he initially had some hopes that Soult was concentrating on building works designed to reinforce Sevilla. Nevertheless, he directed Beresford to be prepared for a French attempt to interrupt the siege, giving him orders which allowed him to retreat or fight a battle should circumstances offer a reasonable prospect of victory. Wellington's orders required Beresford to ascertain whether he could be joined prior to any engagement by the Spanish forces under Ballasteros and Blake; and if so, would he have a substantial numerical superiority such as enable him to face a battle with confidence.[2]

Before Badajoz, Beresford had already been joined by General Castaños and a force of about 2,500 Spanish. On 12 May, Beresford received intelligence from Blake that Soult had left

150

Sevilla on 10 May and later that night he heard from Blake again to the effect that Soult was now approaching at speed with a considerable force. Beresford prepared to lift the siege and proceeded to near Valverde with the 2nd and Portuguese divisions. Here again he was following Wellington's suggestion, because at this stage he could not be sure whether Soult would attempt to reach Badajoz through Albuera or by way of a more westerly route. Wellington had also proposed that the Spanish withdraw to Valverde in the face of a French advance, an indication of the extent to which he sought to micro-manage strategy. Beresford's numbers were reduced by the fact that he had left Cole with the 4th Division to cover the withdrawal of the siege equipment from Badajoz, albeit with instructions to join Beresford as soon as possible. Leaving Cole at Badajoz resulted in all of the siege equipment and the stores being removed without loss, a tribute to Beresford's organisational abilities.[3] Additionally, Kemmis's brigade had been cut off on the wrong side (the right bank) of the river Guadiana by rising waters and like Madden's Portuguese cavalry was not available to Beresford immediately. In the circumstances, Beresford was clearly concerned for the safety of his army and expressed those concerns to Wellington in a letter of 14 May.[4]

Ballasteros had some 3,500 men in Extremadura, and Blake had landed with his forces amounting to about 8,000 men (Zayas and Lardizabal's Divisions together with the cavalry of Loy) at the mouth of the Guadiana on 25 April. Beresford met Blake with Castaños on 13 May at Valverde, and Blake who had brought his army up from the South to Almendral, a short march from Albuera (12 kilometres/7.7 miles), was reportedly particularly keen to fight. Beresford hesitated, still considering the option of a retreat into Portugal, but Blake indicated he would fight Soult with or without the Anglo-Portuguese army. Notwithstanding the numerical advantage of the Allies, it was with considerable unease, reflected in his correspondence with Wellington, that Beresford made the decision to stand and fight the French.[5]

The issue of who should command the combined Allied army in Extremadura was a difficult one for Wellington. While he ordered that for the purposes of the siege of Badajoz each nation should operate under its own 'chiefs', he recognised that 'for the purpose of giving battle to the enemy, it will be necessary that the whole should be under the orders of the officer of the highest military rank'.[6] As things stood, this would mean that Captain-General Francisco Javier Castaños would lead the Allies in any battle in Wellington's absence, being of a senior rank to Beresford. Wellington out of a sense of duty offered Castaños the command, but having pointed out the relative contribution in men, Castaños chose to step aside in a move of cooperation not always evident between the Allies. This action, which gave command to Beresford, was much appreciated by Wellington who praised Castaños for what he referred to as an honourable act of self denial.[7]

When it became clear to Beresford that Soult intended to use the route through Albuera to attempt the relief of Badajoz, he moved the 2nd and Portuguese Divisions to that village on 15 May, having arranged with Blake (who had previously linked up with Ballasteros) that the latter should join him at Albuera with his army by noon on 15 May. Beresford placed the 2nd Division with its right across the Valverde road and its left across the road to Badajoz. Left of this position he positioned the Portuguese, and the King's German Legion were placed in the greatly ruined village. Blake did not appear at midday or during the afternoon as arranged. Given the short distance between Almendral and Albuera, the failure of Blake to arrive that day is difficult to explain, and indeed contemporary British sources do not offer an explanation.[8] Accordingly, when the British cavalry came in at about 3 pm, Beresford placed them temporarily to the right of the 2nd Division, where he had intended to place the Spanish forces.

It was only during the night of 15/16 May that Blake's forces joined with those of Beresford on the gentle slopes above Albuera. Accounts differ but if the advance guard of Blake's force was with Beresford by about 11 pm on 15 May, it appears that the final troops of Blake's army were only arriving at about 3 am on the following morning, and that because of difficulties with dispositions they were still forming up when the French began their preliminary moves at 8 am. Castaños only came up with his force at the same time, as did Cole with part of the 4th Division. Whether because of the direction from which they had come, through battle order precedence, or because the Spanish force (totalling some 14,000 men, including those of Castaños) was an unknown quantity and he felt the main French attack would come straight across the river, Beresford placed the Spaniards on his right. His own testimony later suggested the Spaniards were placed there because it was his strongest position and because they came from that direction.[9] The Allied centre was composed of the 2nd Division under Stewart (the brigades of Abercrombie, Colborne and Hoghton) while the 1st and 2nd battalions of the King's German Legion occupied the village of Albuera. On Beresford's left were placed Hamilton's Portuguese (1st Brigade, commanded by Brigadier-General Luis da Fonseca; 2nd Brigade under the command of Colonel Archibald Campbell) with Collins' Independent Brigade in reserve. Insofar as it was possible given the shallow nature of the hills about Albuera, Beresford followed Wellington's practice by seeking to place Blake's forces along with the 2nd Division on the reverse slope so as to render them protected from the French artillery.[10] Guarding the flanks on each side were the cavalry, much inferior in number to its French counterpart. The 4th Division formed the reserve in an oblique line to that of the main army. Part of the 4th Division, Kemmis' brigade, only reached the scene the morning after the battle, as it had been on the right bank of the Guadiana at Badajoz and could only reach Albuera via the pontoon bridge at Juromenha.[11]

When General Briche, commander of the advance guard of the French cavalry, reported the retirement of the Anglo-Portuguese cavalry from Santa Marta on the afternoon of 15 May, Soult himself had gone to inspect the reported concentration of the Allies on the other side of the river 'on the plateau of Albuhera'. Up to that time Soult had apparently been inclined to believe that Beresford was seeking to avoid a decisive confrontation and would instead recross the Guadiana.[12] Having undertaken this reconnaissance, Soult determined to mount his major assault by way of a left hook designed to get behind the Allied right. This was to be masked by a powerful feint directly against the Allied front through the village of Albuera. Soult, for his part, alleged he was unaware when implementing his plan of action early on 16 May that Blake had managed to join up with Beresford during the night, and his decision to launch his main attack on Beresford's right was predicated upon a desire to interpose himself between the two Allied forces. Soult's assertion on this point, whilst making strategic sense, is strange as Blake's Spaniards, due to their arrival during the night, were in some confusion and were reportedly on the front of the slope facing the streams and thus visible to the French, at least early in the morning. Many, though probably at this time not all, the Spaniards would have been in national uniform with much white and yellow in evidence.[13] Penne Villemur, commanding the Spanish cavalry, refers to coming under fire from English infantry which he attributed to their being 'without a regular uniform'.[14] In his post-battle report, Soult suggests he only became aware of Blake's involvement from a Spanish prisoner taken after Girard's attack on Beresford's right flank.[15]

Irrespective of whether Soult was aware of the arrival of Blake's army, he had another very good reason for trying to outflank Beresford's right wing. The purpose was quite simply to capture the road to Olivença from Albuera via Valverde, with a view to preventing Beresford's retreat in that direction, a strategy which was designed to throw him back on Badajoz and catch him between two French forces.[16] Prior to launching his main attack on Beresford's right, Soult launched the strong feint against the village. This was resisted successfully by the King's German Legion supported by nine Portuguese cannon, but the sharpness of the fight may have contributed to Blake's conviction that rather than the developing attack on the Allied right, this remained the primary contact point, thus creating an unwillingness in the Spanish General's mind to follow Beresford's order to bring about substantial numbers of his troops, so as to face the French divisions which crossed the river on the Allied right.

It is not proposed here to give a blow-by-blow account of the battle, which was to prove one of the most sanguinary of the Peninsular War. D'Urban felt that 'it has been desperately fought for and brilliantly achieved' but not everyone agreed.[17] The controversies that subsequently broke out concerning the conduct of the battle by both the French and Allied commanders means that the course of the battle has been well aired and there are many good analyses in existence drawing on contemporary records and recollections.[18] In brief, there is no dispute that whereas the opposing armies initially faced each other across the Albuera river (in fact it divided into two streams – the Nogales and Chicapierna – above the village), Soult sought to turn the Allied line by bringing his main force around the Allied right. Beresford responded by ordering Blake to face his Spaniards against the new threat, but not persuaded that the flank attack was the main one, and only after further discussion, Blake allocated just a small part of his force to meet this new threat.

At the commencement of the battle the Spaniards on the right flank were the divisions of Ballasteros and Lardizabal, with that of Zayas in the second line. Beresford seems at this stage to have visited Stewart and perhaps Hamilton on the Allied centre and left, respectively, with a view to getting them to close up on Blake. Hearing of Blake's failure to bring his force about to face the French he rode back to remonstrate with the Spanish Captain-General. Even when Beresford had ridden to Blake to remonstrate in person, the latter initially persisted in his refusal to face his regiments about, ultimately doing so late and with difficulty. Beresford became so frustrated that he himself began to direct the change. To meet the flanking threat the brigade led by General José Zayas, which included two battalions of the Guardias Reales de España together with the 2nd and 3rd battalions of the Regiment d'Irlanda and the Voluntarios de Navarra, was moved up so that it was placed in a 'hammer shape' resting its left flank on the right side of the line.[19] Ultimately, Zayas was backed up by Ballasteros' Division on his left and Lardizabal's Division on his right; but in the meantime Zayas, with some 2,000 infantry, had to face the combined weight of first Girard's and then Gazan's Divisions, with Soult holding the Division of Werlé in reserve.

The Spaniards performed heroically and it is important not to underestimate their contribution to the victory, but it was achieved at a heavy price. Beresford requested Stewart to move the 2nd Division to support the Spaniards, but rather than letting them form into squares before advancing, elements were rushed forward in column by Stewart (presumably because of perceived urgency and danger) and they were carved open by the French cavalry, including the Vistula Lancers. It was only when Lumley launched a counter attack by two squadrons of the 4th Dragoons together with two squadrons of Spanish cavalry that the French horse retired with heavy losses. The British brigades of the 2nd Division in turn stood their ground in a war of attrition with the French which Beresford attempted unsuccessfully to resolve by personally bringing forward Spanish regiments not hitherto involved. In doing so it is suggested he manhandled a Spanish officer in an attempt to get him to advance his men. There is a suggestion that these were regiments which had been so badly mauled by the French at Gebora that they were unwilling to fight. The incident was witnessed by Colonel Henry Hardinge, Beresford's Deputy Quartermaster General.[20]

While Abercrombie'a brigade was covering the British left in this second stage of the battle, the right was seriously exposed by the refusal of the Spaniards to move up. Beresford went to bring forward the Portuguese but in desperation Hardinge rode to Cole. After a discussion with senior staff, Cole ordered the advance of the 1st Brigade of the 4th Division and the Portuguese Brigade forming part of that Division and it was this advance that turned the battle in the Allies favour.[21] Whether that advance was at the suggestion of Colonel Hardinge or Major General Lowry Cole itself became a cause for dispute later, but in any event Cole took the decision and implemented a complicated manoeuvre, which finally caused Soult to abandon the field of battle and withdraw.[22]

British losses in the battle meant that Beresford's leadership was the subject of contemporary comment, some of it critical; but it was the criticism of William Napier nearly twenty years after the event that was to ignite a controversy that rumbled on for some years. Napier's *History of the War in the Peninsula and in the South of France from the year 1807 to 1814* was published from 1828 onwards. It is beautifully written, but extreme caution is necessary when considering Napier's statements on the topic, for not only is there clear evidence of animus but Napier was not at the battle and indeed Oman concluded he had never visited its site. Apart from conceding that Beresford demonstrated personal courage and bravery, combined with an ability to lead from the front on the day, Napier has little good to say concerning many aspects of Beresford's military career. Furthermore, it is telling that when Wellington formed his administration in 1828 and it was reported that Beresford and other named officers were to be preferred, Napier displayed prominently his Whig colours, stating: 'The report goes that Beresford, Murray and Sir H. Taylor are to be in commission; this will be destruction to the army and to my prospects. The dispute at present is whether the Duke is a damned idiot or only a common idiot.'[23]

Interestingly, this comment was made when Napier had written the first volume of his book but before its publication. Even before Beresford's inclusion in Wellington's administration Napier had condemned Beresford, and was as a result concerned for his own advancement. Additionally, the historian needs to bear in mind Napier's friendship with and admiration for Marshal Soult.

Napier criticised the conduct of the entire campaign undertaken by Beresford in 1811, including events surrounding the recapture of Campo Maior, the handling of the campaign in Extremadura, as well as the preparations and implementation of the siege of Badajoz. His most severe criticism, however, was reserved for Beresford's decision to fight Soult when the French General marched north from Sevilla in an attempt to relieve Badajoz, and of Beresford's handling of the Battle of Albuera. In order to consider this accusation, that Beresford should not have fought the battle, it is necessary to have regard for the background to the decision. Beresford, when initially he received news of Soult's departure from Sevilla with the army, was unsure of Soult's intentions. Once he felt sure the objective was to relieve Badajoz, Napier does concede that Beresford was right to suspend the siege, but he felt that the circumstances were such that rather than fight a battle which he deemed unnecessary, Beresford should have retired into the Alentejo.[24] It will be recalled that Wellington's instructions of 23 April to Beresford were specific. If he thought the French too strong for him he should retire across the Guadiana, and thence if necessary towards Portalegre, taking the position of the Caia and Portalegre successively; having first ensured that the ordnance and stores used in the siege were removed from Badajoz and returned to Elvas which would then be exposed to the French. Wellington went on:

> If Sir W. Beresford should think his strength sufficient to fight a general action, to save the siege of Badajoz, he will collect his troops to fight it. I believe that, upon the whole, the most central and advantageous place to collect his troops will be at Albuera. If the enemy should attempt to turn his left, in order to march upon Badajoz by Talavera, he has his choice, between attacking them in that operation, or marching by his own left, along the Talavera rivulet. If they attempt to turn his right, he has the same choice, or to march by his right upon Valverde, and place his right upon the Valverde rivulet. All this must of course be left to the decision of Sir W. Beresford. I authorize him to fight the action if he should think proper, or to retire if he should not.[25]

Napier claimed that Beresford fought at Albuera for a number of reasons. He maintained Blake and Castaños warned Beresford that the Spanish army would disintegrate and desert if a retreat was ordered into Portugal. He added that Beresford for his part did not wish to abandon (other than temporarily for the purpose of giving battle) the prospect of bringing the siege of Badajoz to a successful conclusion. Further, he did not wish to endanger Elvas or open up the Alentejo to the French by a retreat, and fighting a battle in the Alentejo with less troops if the Spanish disappeared in whole or in part would be to place himself at a considerable disadvantage vis-à-vis Soult. Napier claimed, however, that these entirely plausible reasons 'were but a mask' and that the real reason behind Beresford's decision to fight was the pressure he was put under by his British troops (presumably officers) who were upset that they had not fought and had therefore been denied an opportunity for glory at Buçaco in 1810 and on the pursuit of Masséna in March 1811. The last point does not come through in contemporary records and Beresford makes no such suggestion. Nor does the point feature in Beresford's Quartermaster General's 'Report of the Operations of the Right Wing of the Allied Army' written some years prior to Napier's history igniting the controversy.[26] However, D'Urban specifically rejects the allegation in the preface to the Report before it was published in 1831.[27] D'Urban explained that the result of the conference at Valverde was agreement to assemble the army at Albuera and to give battle to the enemy. Beresford, in response to Napier, qualified that statement only to the extent of saying 'but that the enemy would there give battle, Lord Beresford was at least very uncertain'.[28]

Beresford's Quartermaster General, Benjamin D'Urban, makes clear that Beresford's decision to give battle should Soult chose to do so was predicated on a number of considerations, including knowledge that Blake's Spanish army could not retreat by the way it had come, combined with Blake's assertion that it would disperse and desert if he retired into Portugal. He doubted whether in fact it could have been induced to cross the Guadiana and if left alone it would have been 'infallibly sacrificed'. Beresford was also conscious that retreat would mean giving up the siege of Badajoz, so important to the Commander in Chief and the common cause. Other criteria listed by D'Urban for Beresford's decision include those quoted by Napier that to abandon Extremadura would be to open up the Alentejo and endanger Elvas, not to mention the prospect of having to fight Soult after a dispiriting retreat. Beresford himself suggested that weather also played a part in his decision to stand his ground. His experiences of the Guadiana over the preceding two months meant he was right to be concerned that in the event of that river rising because of rainfall he could be trapped against its banks in a situation where even if his bridge survived he might have to sacrifice either his stores or part of his force in order to get the remainder of the army to safety.[29] D'Urban wrote that all these difficulties were weighed against the advantages of defeating Soult; and the conclusion that a successful battle would destroy the army of Andalucía and enable the resumption of the siege of Badajoz.[30]

D'Urban's report has the advantage of being composed by someone who was not only at the battle but also intimately involved in relevant events before and after this contest with the French; someone moreover who would have been present at the important meetings which resulted not just in the decision to fight, but the subsequent deployment of the army. Critics will no doubt point to his friendship with Beresford as a reason for discounting D'Urban's testimony, but while they are right to scrutinise it, D'Urban was a professional soldier who himself achieved high command in due course. Indeed, one does not need to rely solely on D'Urban for in his initial report on the battle, Beresford made it clear he was horrified at the slaughter on the day and stated he had doubts as to whether he should have fought the battle both before and after the encounter. This report, which Wellington requested be rewritten, made it clear that Beresford had fought the battle even though he disliked the ground and against his own 'most decided opinion' because of Blake's refusal to retire across the Guadiana and on the basis of information received that the French army did not exceed 20,000 men, whereas it had turned out to be between 22,000 and 24,000 men. In conclusion, Beresford stated that by beating Soult the Allies had escaped destruction, but he went on: 'I am very far from feeling happy after our triumph.' He was distraught at the suffering of the British regiments in particular.[31]

Beresford chose to give battle, notwithstanding his own preference for a withdrawal and notwithstanding the uncertainty as to how the Spanish would perform on the day.[32] Prior to the battle he expressed his doubts to Wellington on whether the circumstances warranted giving battle. He set out these concerns in a series of letters written to Wellington on 12, 13, 14 and 15 May, making it clear during the correspondence that his hand had been forced as Blake 'would not listen to crossing the Guadiana'.[33] He was particularly concerned at the French superiority in cavalry, which 'terribly outnumber us and this will create difficulties in this country'.[34] In the aftermath of the battle Beresford was critical of himself for risking the encounter, but that criticism should be viewed in the context of Beresford being appalled at the number of men lost, whether dead or wounded, and he went on to note that Blake left him little option but to fight.[35] He could not reasonably leave Blake to fight Soult's well-trained cohesive force alone and with an inferior sized army. The result would in all probability have been the destruction of Blake's force. In fighting, however, Beresford was conscious of the risk he was taking and that defeat would put at risk that which it had taken Wellington so long to gain.[36] Napier's criticism of Beresford's decision to stand and fight fails to take into account the full circumstances or even Beresford's own preference to retire across the Guadiana without giving battle, while waiting for Wellington. At no stage subsequently did Wellington criticise Beresford's decision to fight.

Wellington in fact was sufficiently alarmed by Beresford's reports from the Extremadura to decide that he himself should return to the south, no doubt with a view to making a decision himself as to whether to fight and if so, where and when to do so. Prior to making that decision he assessed both the dangers to Beresford's army and his own situation post the battle of Fuentes de Oñoro. He formed the opinion that the French were not in a position to move against him in the north and that even if they did do so, it should be possible to fight a defensive war with less troops. He was also concerned as to the number of men Soult might bring against Beresford. Accordingly, the 3rd and 7th divisions were sent south to assist Beresford on 14 May, with the 2nd Hussars following a day later.[37] Spurred on by Beresford's letters of 12 and 13 May, Wellington set out for the Alentejo himself on 16 May, telling both Beresford and Charles Stuart he would be there on 21 May, absent any developments.[38] Receiving en route Beresford's letter of 14 May indicating 'he did not like his situation', Wellington determined to leave his baggage behind and moving as fast as possible he reached Elvas on 19 May, three days after the battle.[39]

When preparing for the potential battle Beresford clearly considered taking up position at Valverde, which he regarded as stronger than Albuera, but he rejected this possibility as it would open the way to Badajoz for Soult without forcing a battle.[40] Further, he was conscious of Wellington's suggestion that he choose Albuera, though as he put it, this involved taking up 'a position (such as could be got, in this widely open country) at this place, thus standing directly between the enemy and Badajoz'.[41] The advantage of Albuera was that there were no less than seven roads by which Soult might march on Badajoz. Wellington clearly understood

Albuera was at the centre of the arc covering these routes and Beresford could thus move in either direction should Soult move left or right instead of proceeding through Albuera.

Having castigated Beresford for his decision to fight Soult rather than withdraw, Napier then criticised the decision regarding the placement of the Allied army at Albuera. However, that location had effectively been chosen by Wellington after he and Beresford had been over the ground. Because of the confluence of roads, the village and the streams, the location was at first glance a good one, but it was not a strong defensive position even though it gave the opportunity to deploy on the reverse side of a shallow ridge. Soult was able to expose the weakness of the location because in reality the ridge was over seven kilometres long, with higher hills as it went south from the village. Beresford had insufficient troops to guard both the roads and the hills to the south of the village, as well as the village and the bridge over the Albuera leading into it. The result was that Soult was able to capture the southern knoll and then overlook the Allies on their partially-exposed flank. Furthermore, while the right bank of the river was reportedly wooded in 1811, thus enabling Soult to screen his intentions, the left bank and the countryside beyond it was open country and perfect for cavalry in which the French had a marked superiority of numbers.

The opening phase of the battle involved Soult's masterful plan to attack the right flank of the Allied army while successfully leading Beresford and the Allied command to believe that the main thrust of attack would be through the village of Albuera, or at least directly across the stream in the vicinity of the built-up area and the bridge. The precipitate withdrawal of the entire British cavalry from the right bank (east) of the Albuera River on the previous day meant that this flanking attack through woods and olive groves went unnoticed until the French crossed the river. Much has been made of the retreat of the Allied cavalry on 15 May with the result that it ended up on the left bank (west) of the river. However, one must wonder whether this would have made any difference in terms of ascertaining Soult's tactical movements the following morning, for presumably any Allied picquets would have been pushed in and forced to cross the river prior to Soult declaring his hand. D'Urban and others did not believe Soult did not know of Blake's arrival prior to the battle, but he did feel Soult's decision to attack the Allied right by way of a left hook might well have been based on Soult's reconnaissance of the evening of 15 May, which would have shown the Allied right guarded by cavalry without adequate infantry support.

Contemporaries and historians have generally agreed that Soult was a clever strategist and his performance after Talavera, when he nearly cut Wellington off from his retreat into Portugal, is sometimes cited as evidence of his tactical adroitness. While Napoleon would on occasions be critical of Soult, he recognised his qualities: 'Marshal Soult is the best of all the generals of Europe, the most capable of manouvering great masses, of taking the major role on a field of battle, of doing wonders at the head of the French army.'[42] The events of 1813 and 1814 were to show Soult also as a master of defensive preparation. Beresford was perhaps fortunate that if a good strategist, Soult lacked flexibility in the heat of battle.

Napier alleged Beresford failed to act expeditiously when he first received reports from the 13th Light Dragoons to the effect that Soult was massing his forces and crossing the river for an attack on the Allied right flank. Beresford may have taken time to react to this threat, but he did so because he wanted to be sure where the main offensive would take place. Beresford apparently left Blake after telling him how to make the new dispositions, but Blake deferred taking action and it was only when Beresford returned from instructing Stewart and Hamilton respectively on where to move the 2nd and Portuguese divisions that the Spanish regiments were placed by Beresford himself. When he did act, there was still time to meet the threat on the flank but the army was put in extreme peril through Blake's failure to obey Beresford's orders.[43]

Witnessing the decimation of Zayas's 4th Spanish infantry division, Beresford ordered Stewart to assist on the right flank with the 2nd Division. The redeployment of Colborne's, Hoghton's and Abercrombie's brigades took longer than it might otherwise have taken because Colborne's brigade (1/3rd, 2/31st, 2/48th and 2/66th), normally positioned on the right of the Division, had been on its way to reinforcing the King's German Legion in the village when it was redirected to the right. Rather than bring Colborne's troops into the left of the 2nd Division, Stewart, perhaps mindful of custom and practice, waited while they made their way back to the right prior to advancing to support the beleaguered and exhausted Spanish troops. He then sent the brigade forward without giving them the opportunity to form up either as a defensive unit or in line behind the Spanish, so that the latter could withdraw through the British line as it advanced. Colborne sought permission of Stewart to pause and reform in such a way as to protect his flank, but this was refused by Stewart with devastating consequences. Initial success, when his brigade poured volley after volley into the French left, turned to disaster when Colborne's brigade was then cut down by the French cavalry while in the act of undertaking a bayonet charge.

Stewart's refusal to allow the 2nd Division to form up properly, for which he was roundly condemned by Napier later, may have been because that General could see the seriousness of the situation, though others have blamed him for aspiring to achieve glory by breaking the French himself.[44] With the various disagreements regarding the conduct of the battle there is surprisingly little evidence of acrimony regarding Stewart's decision, though a contemporaneous letter from Colborne made it clear that he had nothing to do with the arrangement but merely obeyed the orders of General Stewart.[45]

The French cavalry charge by the Vistula Lancers and the supporting hussars, which caused horrendous losses for Colborne's brigade (the 2/31st Regiment escaped relatively unscathed because it was able to form a square), resulted in such a breakthrough that Beresford and his general officers were directly threatened and became involved in hand-to-hand fighting. It was at this stage that Beresford, when attacked by a lancer of this Polish regiment, managed to unhorse him in an incident that was much celebrated afterwards by painters. When the dismounted lancer persevered, he was apparently dispatched by one of the Marshal's bodyguard.[46] Poor weather, including substantial rainfall, had apparently obscured the arrival of the Vistula Lancers and their uniforms were such that some mistook them for Spanish cavalry. Ultimately, de Grey's heavy cavalry charged and despite losses forced back the French horse, but it is less clear whether the Spanish cavalry under Penne Villemur, which Lumley also ordered forward, did engage the enemy.[47] The Spanish Brigadier's account of the battle has his cavalry fulfilling Lumley's orders and he takes some credit for forcing the French to withdraw, lamenting the fact that his cavalry were fired on by the English though this did not 'disturb this cavalry's good dispositions'.[48] Likewise, D'Urban makes no distinction between the efforts of the English and Spanish horse stating, 'these troops fell upon the lancers and hussars with so much fury, that the greater part of them were cut to pieces'.[49] D'Urban's liaison officer with Penne Villemur was not impressed, claiming the Spaniards pulled up in front of the enemy and refused to go further.[50] The success of lancers in French service on this and other occasions led to a number of British regiments being equipped as lancers after the conclusion of the war.[51]

Three out of four of the battalions in Colborne's brigade were decimated. It is unfair to attribute that disaster to Beresford, who was entitled to rely on an experienced general who would have been fully au fait with the custom and practice of moving regiments in battle; rather it was due to Stewart's impetuosity. Hoghton's brigade then replaced that of Colborne and for over an hour faced the might of both Girard's and Gazan's Divisions in a war of attrition.[52] Beresford appreciated that Hoghton required assistance, and in the absence of Spanish support he looked for Hamilton's Portuguese, who had at least in part moved from the left to fill the gap behind the village vacated by the 2nd Division. However, there was some delay in getting this message through to Hamilton, and there have been suggestions that Beresford may have set off himself to find Hamilton. Beresford then appears to have ordered Alten to withdraw the King's German Legion from the village, either with a view to their defending the Valverde road in case a retreat proved necessary, or alternatively with a view to replacing them with Spanish troops who he hoped would prove more cooperative defending the village.[53] If the Spanish secured the village then the King's German Legion would have been available to attack the French on the Allied right.

There were suggestions later by Sir Julius Hartman, who commanded a brigade of guns at the battle, that Beresford had ordered a retreat, but Beresford and his staff denied these allegations, which Hartman seems to have made on the basis that General Baron von Alten of the King's German Legion and Major Dickson, in command of the Portuguese artillery, had claimed that Beresford had ordered them to quit the village and to retreat; on enquiry there was found to be no substance to either claim.[54] Von Alten had said: 'Meanwhile the engagement on our right had become very serious and doubtful for the allies; and it was at this time that I received Marshal Beresford's orders to get loose of the village with my brigade, with the ultimate view of taking up a position in rear of it, covering the Valverde road.' Dickson, for his part, pointed out: 'I was not posted at the village of Albuera during the battle, nor were the guns under my immediate orders there.'[55] Beresford always denied he had ordered a retreat and even Napier conceded the importance of controlling the conical hill and the Valverde road, and he suggested that Beresford was contemplating retreat.[56] The move to relocate the King's German Legion (assuming they were not to be replaced in the village) should arguably be seen in the light of an intelligent and prudent precursor to such an eventuality.[57]

Napier complained that Beresford failed to organise support for the 2nd Division. It seems to be widely accepted that he intended the Portuguese Division to provide that reinforcement, and this would have made good sense both from the fact that it had operated with the 2nd

Division for over a year, as well as its proximity to the action. No satisfactory explanation has been offered as to why Hamilton and the Portuguese could not be found. The order may have been delayed, perhaps because one and possibly two of Beresford's ADCs were injured either in the *melée* with the Vistula Lancers or in conveying the message. Alternatively it is suggested that Major Arbuthnot could not locate Hamilton because the latter had already moved nearer the village of Albuera, having been earlier given discretion to do so by Beresford. Hamilton's Division consisted of some 5,000 troops and Collins' Independent Brigade a further 1,385.[58] It is difficult to understand how Arbuthnot or anyone else could have failed to locate a force of this size in the relatively small area of the battlefield, even allowing for bad weather and smoke. The suggestion that Beresford himself rode to find Hamilton, if correct, could arguably be indicative of a lack of ability to delegate while himself remaining with his staff at a central point to control all his troops.

Beresford indicated that he was considering using Cole's 4th Division, but he did not take the decision to advance this force which turned the flow of the battle. Beresford seems to have been determined to maintain a critical mass which would secure his retreat if necessary, and his order to Alten to pull out of the village if a precursor to a general withdrawal would have been sensible. Beresford maintained he did not order a retreat and quoted Lumley, Cole and the by then deceased Stewart in his support in his correspondence with Napier.[59] While von Alten suggested that pulling the King's German Legion out of the village of Albuera was because Beresford intended a retreat, and Tomkinson of the 16th Light Dragoons says Beresford ordered a retreat, D'Urban suggests that pulling the Germans out of the village was to use them in a final push against the French, and Beresford intended replacing the Legion with Spanish regiments, an unlikely step had he intended to retreat. Tomkinson is frequently judgmental in his diary and it should be noted that neither Tomkinson nor the 16th Light Dragoons were present at the battle. [60]

In conclusion, Beresford was intent on maintaining a line of retreat through Valverde, Olivença and across the Guadiana utilising the strong *tête de pont* he had caused to be established at Juromenha. The withdrawal of the King's German Legion from the village is consistent with both the suggestion that he intended to replace it with Spanish troops, using the Germans to support the 2nd Division, and with a move preparatory to ordering a retreat. On balance it is extremely doubtful that Beresford in fact ordered a retreat at any stage during the battle.

Lowry Cole's decision to bring up the 4th Division to assist the 2nd and the Spanish, notwithstanding Beresford's orders not to move unless he received a command to do so, determined the outcome of the battle. It would appear that Cole had already sent an officer to Beresford to seek instructions, but that officer, Major de Roverea had been badly wounded while at Beresford's request seeking to bring up the Guardias Walonas, a Spanish brigade, to assist the 2nd Division. Roverea in his memoirs states he received no instruction from Beresford prior to that time in respect of the 4th Division. Meanwhile, two of Beresford's general staff, Hardinge and Rooke, had both reached Cole and urged him to move against the French left, which he determined to do. Cole orchestrated a difficult advance in echelon without losing cohesion, though in doing so the Fusilier brigade and Harvey's Portuguese brigade suffered heavily. The movement of the 4th Division prompted Beresford to order the Legion to re-enter the village. Even though Soult himself then brought up reserves under Werlé, the French Marshal was unable to stem the tide. The French retreated across the stream under the cover of La Tour-Maubourg's cavalry and artillery fire. The British cavalry was insufficient in numbers to contemplate a follow up, and the serious fighting ended at about 2 pm, though a cannonade and a certain amount of musketry persisted until nightfall.[61]

The outcome of the battle was that the French failed in their attempt to relieve Badajoz, and after collecting and treating a number of his wounded on 17 May, Soult retreated towards Llerena and Sevilla. An Allied victory had been secured and the Allies were enabled to resume the siege of Badajoz. The result may also have played its part in stiffening the resolve of the Cortes of Cádiz, which the French clergyman and diplomat Abbé Dominique du Pradt claimed was preparing to recognise Joseph as King when news of the French defeat at Albuera reached that city. [62]

The battle of Albuera was a singularly sanguinary affair. In the four hours of the most intense fighting it seems probable some 14,000 soldiers were killed or wounded; perhaps over 8,000 on the French side and just under 6,000 (of which 1,000 were killed) on the side of the Allies. Soult's report of the battle was self-serving and not accepted as accurate by his own generals. In the first place he reported a mere 3,000 casualties, but this was quickly corrected by his own Chief of Staff Mocquery, who listed 5,936 casualties. An intercepted letter from General Gazan to Soult written three days after the battle refers to 4,000 injured with the army being attended by only five surgeons, and that assessment ignored the dead and those injured left on the field of battle. In all he estimated French losses as about 8,000.[63] La Tour-Maubourg's Chief of Staff later put French losses at 10,000.[64] Oman's research of the French archives a century later led him to conclude that French casualties were in the region of 7,900 casualties and perhaps more.[65]

Whereas Soult's initial report on the Battle of Albuera portrayed it as a successful attempt to free the Province of Andalucía (presumably from the threat of invasion) rather than an attempt to ensure the security of Badajoz, in a letter of 27 May he admitted to Marmont that he had failed in his objective of relieving Badajoz, and this was the entire object of the battle.[66] Perhaps naturally he dressed up the defeat by referring to the capture of five guns and a number of colours. Soult's account failed to mention the huge losses suffered by both the Lancers and Hussars, nor did he avert to the loss by the Lancers of a flag or guidon to the Spanish troops.[67]

While French casualties greatly exceeded those of the Allies, the latter had suffered terribly, the British regiments in particular suffering some 4,159 casualties (dead, wounded or missing), causing Castlereagh when seconding the vote of thanks to Beresford, the officers and the army in the House of Commons to compare the losses to those suffered at Assaye.[68] Over a quarter of these were suffered in the disaster involving Colborne's brigade, which would in all likelihood not have suffered to this extent had Stewart followed the battle practice of the time. The Spanish losses were measured at 1,368 and the Portuguese losses only 389. Over half the Spanish losses were suffered by Zayas' regiments in their heroic stand against Girard's division. Portuguese losses were relatively small, because apart from Harvey's independent brigade which formed the right flank of Cole's advance, the Portuguese forces were not substantially involved.

The Allied victory had been achieved at a huge price in terms of men killed and wounded. The number of wounded was so large that when Soult abandoned many of his own wounded (reportedly 900–1,000) on the field of battle the British medical teams already trying to cope with their own losses struggled greatly to help the French.[69] Beresford ordered that French combatants be given such assistance as was possible, just as Mortier had done in reverse following Wellington's retreat after the battle of Talavera, but British losses were such that they could not easily offer assistance; and Beresford sent a messenger to the French Commander at Badajoz inviting him to send medical assistance to the French wounded, an offer which was not taken up. Beresford also asked the Spanish to assist in treatment of the British wounded. Rather bizarrely, the reported response was that it was the responsibility of each nation to look after its own.[70] On learning of the nature of the battle, Wellington ordered hospital stores and supplies from Lisbon.[71]

The day after the battle Beresford gave thanks in a General Order to the entire army. He expanded on his recognition of their bravery four days later when he singled out British and Portuguese officers by name and in praising the cavalry gave credit to Lumley, Long and Colonel de Grey. In his report to Wellington he mentioned many others, but though he mentioned Cole positively, he was not over effusive, and this may have led to a certain coolness between the two men later.[72]

Beresford now ordered his cavalry under General Lumley to follow Soult without risking a major engagement. Some days later it performed well at Usagre when Soult sent La Tour-Maubourg against it. While of little consequence in the overall scheme of things, the defeat of the French cavalry at Usagre must have boosted morale further. While the French lost 170 killed or wounded and eight prisoners were taken, Allied losses were put at three killed and four wounded. Of more concern to the French commander may have been the contrasting performance of the French cavalry at Albuera, where it had performed well, with its poor achievements at three other engagements, Campo Maior, Los Santos and Usagre.

Beresford sent his virtually unused Portuguese Division under General Hamilton back to invest Badajoz on 19 May, and the garrison reaped little or no benefit from the temporary abandonment of the siege.[73] The 3rd and 7th divisions reached Campo Maior on 23 May and shortly afterwards moved to join the Portuguese in the second British siege of Badajoz. Remarkably, when the siege had been lifted on 12 May Beresford had been able to secure all the guns and supplies present with the army outside Badajoz, sending these back to Elvas. In this respect he paid tribute to the zeal and commitment of Lieutenant Colonel Fletcher of the Royal Engineers and Major Dickson of the Artillery, as well as Lieutenant General Leite, the Governor of the Alentejo.[74]

On his arrival in Elvas on 19 May Wellington received Beresford's report of the battle. In it Beresford was so dispirited and dwelt on his losses to such an extent that Wellington had it altered to give a more upbeat message before sending it on to Britain. At the same time Wellington was most supportive to Beresford, telling him that: 'You could not be successful in such an action without a large loss, and we must make up our mind to affairs of this kind sometimes – or give up the game.'[75] Even then Beresford responded that he could scarcely forgive himself for risking battle and he felt he had been unwise to 'have done it', a brutally honest statement that was seized upon by his critics.[76]

On 21 May Wellington was at Albuera. The following days were taken up with the organisation of the second British siege of Badajoz and Wellington returned to Elvas on 26 May. On his way to join him there, Beresford undertook a tour of Santa Marta, Valverde and Olivença. At Valverde and Olivença he visited the wounded, and he met Blake at Santa Marta and urged him to pursue the French more vigorously.[77] On 27 May, Wellington merged Beresford's force with his own army and reassumed overall command of the combined force now besieging Badajoz. The second British attempt to capture Badajoz did not last long. On 10 June, with intelligence coming in that Marmont, who had replaced Masséna, was approaching at the head of the French Army of Portugal with the objective of joining Soult, Wellington raised the siege and prepared to engage this new threat. He was faced with a combined French force of 60,000 infantry and 7,000 cavalry, which he could oppose with only 44,000 infantry and some 4,300 cavalry. He considered giving battle at Albuera again, and indeed a substantial part of his army was there on 15 June, but no contact was made with the French and Wellington withdrew the Anglo-Portuguese army west of the River Caia between Elvas and Campo Maior. When the French were thought to be moving down the Tagus at the end of July, Wellington moved his main army further north to meet the threat. However, the threat failed to materialise and by the end of July much of the army was in summer cantonments, though a force maintained a loose blockade of Ciudad Rodrigo in the north.

At the end of 1811, after three years of fighting, Portugal and its long-suffering people were rid of Napoleon's armies. Though at the time it was far from certain that their expulsion was permanent, Wellington was able to report great progress.[78] D'Urban noted in his *Journal* that a campaign of fifteen months had witnessed four pitched battles, Buçaco, Barrosa, Fuentes de Oñoro and Albuera, and many affairs that in 'common periods' would have been called battles. Wellington had been outraged at the escape of the French from Almeida after the hematic battle of Fuentes de Oñoro, and there is evidence of a certain sensitivity regarding those two events. The costly victory of Albuera, however, caused at least one observer to remark that it might make people forget about Fuentes de Oñoro and Almeida.[79] The successes of 1811 were the turning point which enabled Wellington to carry the war into Spain in 1812 and thereafter into south west France culminating in the defeat of Soult at Toulouse in the spring of 1814. At Fuentes de Oñoro and Albuera the Portuguese had once again fought with distinction, enabling D'Urban to assert: 'that the painful labours of Marshal Beresford had not been thrown away, that the troops he had formed were steady, and could be relied on, and from that instant Lord Wellington was confident of his ultimate success.'[80]

With the return of General Hill from England to the command of the 2nd Division, in June Beresford went back to Lisbon to resume the dual task of training the Portuguese army and securing practical Portuguese support for the war. Shortly after the battle he had expressed to Blake his wish to be released from his command, 'as I have an abundance in my hands now for arranging the Portuguese army which after the campaign requires a little repairing'.[81] This was something of an understatement for Wellington had complained that a number of the Portuguese regiments were seriously under strength, whether due to illness or otherwise.[82]

Beresford's preparations for and handling of the battle of Albuera was subsequently the subject of considerable discussion and comment, so it is important to review any criticism in the context of the achievements of the campaign and in the context of subsequent events. Between arriving in the Alentejo and Extremadura in late March and the battle of Albuera, Beresford had cleared a large area of the French and regained a number of towns, including Campo Maior and Olivença. Soult's purpose in bringing his army back into Extremadura was to relieve Badajoz. At Albuera Beresford succeeded in preventing Soult from reinforcing Badajoz and Soult clearly failed in his objective. Badajoz was not even resupplied in the week when Beresford lifted his siege and immediately after the battle the city was reinvested. Beresford had achieved the objective of saving the siege of Badajoz, which had been established by Wellington as one of the criteria justifying fighting a battle with Soult. The subsequent failure of the second siege of Badajoz was due to a lack of engineering expertise and artillery, combined with the emergence of a new threat in the shape of the combined armies of Portugal and the Midi/Andalucía. That the second siege had to be abandoned on 10 June is no reflection on Beresford.

Albuera, like a number of other Peninsular War Allied victories, gave the Allies a temporary advantage until met by a concentration of French forces, often in overwhelming numbers. Each battle sapped the strength of the French in the Peninsula, but given British and Allied numeric inferiority, it was not until Napoleon withdrew troops for his Russian campaign in 1812 that substantial advances into Spain and ultimately France became possible. However, Beresford's advance through the Alentejo and into Extremadura was responsible also for the abandonment of another French objective in March 1811, which was for Mortier with his force to enter the Alentejo and even move against Elvas, the sole remaining border fortress of any great consequence in the hands of the Allies.[83] It was therefore not without significance when combined with the frustration of Soult's attempt to relieve Badajoz. At the time Wellington opined to Hill that he hoped the battle will 'enable us to obtain possession of Badajoz, upon which we are busily employed'.[84]

The battle of Albuera took place over a period of some five hours between 9 am and 2 pm on 16 May. Initially there was some skirmishing, but the heaviest fighting took place between 10 am and 2 pm.[85] Much of the battle was fought in bad weather, making conditions even more difficult for both sides. It was arguably the most ferociously contested battle of the Peninsular War. Benjamin D'Urban, who had been Quartermaster General of the Portuguese army under Beresford since April 1809 and who was present at Albuera, described it thus:

> the contest was bloody and obstinate, it lasted from 10 am till 2 pm. An uninterrupted fire of artillery and musketry, the latter frequently at 20 paces asunder, varied at short intervals by partial charges of the Bayonet continued for the four hours. From 12 till 2 it was the hottest action of the Peninsular war and unequalled in the memory of the oldest soldier.

The enemy brought up reserve upon reserve, but at 2 he could make no further efforts, he was turned by both flanks.

D'Urban went on to praise the valour of the British and Portuguese troops and the gallantry of the Spanish, whom he felt however suffered from a serious lack of discipline.[86]

From a British perspective the performance of the Spanish on the day was a mixed one. General Blake initially disregarded Beresford's order to manoeuvre half his force to meet the massive French flanking attack on the Allied right, endangering the entire Allied army. Instead, after repeated urging he merely moved the battalions making up the Division of Zayas to meet this threat, though these were aided in time by the troops of Ballasteros and Lardizabal. Zayas' men behaved heroically. On the other hand, Carlos de España's brigade allegedly refused to move forward when ordered to support their countrymen, leading to the widely reported incident of Beresford attempting to frogmarch one of their officers to the front line in the hope of setting an example. These reports are puzzling in the light of Beresford commending the corps in his report of 18 May 1811. This brigade had suffered badly at Gebora, which may have contributed to its unwillingness to fight. Furthermore, as we have seen, the Spanish cavalry of Penne Villemur, which had also been at that battle, were reportedly reluctant to get involved, though again Beresford singled them out for praise in his report of 18 May 1811.[87]

In his dispatches after the battle, Beresford spoke of Blake's goodwill and courage, but that may well have been for the sake of political expediency and in order to maintain a united front. Later, in his *Refutation* Beresford was to say that he never saw Blake from the commencement of hostilities until after the conclusion of the battle.[88] Further, Wellington in a letter to his brother Henry wrote: 'Beresford tells me it would be a great point gained if Blake were to return to the Regency as he is not very accommodating, although he adhered strictly to the letter of everything I laid down for his guidance.'[89] Beresford mentioned Ballasteros, Zayas and España and the corps under their command as having shown conspicuous gallantry, and recognised the contribution of General Castaños.[90] Overall he felt the Spanish fought well but observed, 'had they had discipline, and in some instances better officers, they would have done everything that was wished'.[91] Whether it was this observation or private views expressed to Wellington by Beresford or others, Wellington expressed rather faint praise when telling Lieutenant General Brent Spencer that 'the Spanish did not behave ill'.[92] He was even less enthusiastic writing privately to England: 'Beresford's was a terrible fight; but he would have succeeded without much loss, if the Spaniards could have moved; nevertheless there they stood like stocks, both parties firing upon them, and it was necessary to apply the British everywhere.'[93]

D'Urban, Beresford's Quartermaster General, was not quite so fulsome. He wrote in his diary that the 'Spaniards behaved gallantly but were so devoid of discipline that they stood in the way and did more harm than good'.[94] However, in his report D'Urban singles out the Spanish and Walloon Guards and the Regiment d'Irlanda, all from Zayas's 4th Division, as being particularly distinguished; and he gives credit to Generals Ballasteros, Zayas, Don Carlos de España and Penne Villemur. Blake, on the other hand, is unequivocally condemned by D'Urban.

The British Cemetery, in the bastion of the fortress of Elvas, Portugal, by kind permission of the British Cemetery, Elvas.

Portuguese officers' military uniforms by H. Michel. Author's own collection.

Captain Mathew Latham defends the colours of the 'Buffs' at the Battle of Albuera, by J.A. Atkinson. Author's own collection.

Major General Benjamin D'Urban, Beresford's Quartermaster General during the Peninsular War, by Thomas Mogford. Author's own collection.

Robert Arbuthnot, who was with Beresford as ADC in southern Africa and Buenos Aires, and with Beresford in Portugal as ADC and military secretary; artist unknown. By kind permission of anonymous owner.

Marshal Beresford portrayed by Henri L'Eveque. By kind permission of Suzie Pack-Beresford.

Marshal William Carr Beresford, artist unknown. By kind permission of Suzie Pack-Beresford.

Marshal William Carr Beresford, artist unknown. By kind permission of Mrs Mindy Maclean.

Battle of Toulouse, 10 April 1814, published in *France Militaire*.

General Sir Denis Pack by Joseph Saunders. By kind permission of Suzie Pack-Beresford.

Gravestone of Lieutenant John Theophilus Beresford, mortally wounded in the capture of Ciudad Rodrigo, 19 January 1812. Author's own collection.

Monument to General Maximilien Sébastien Foy at Orthez where he was severely wounded during the battle on 27 February 1814. Engraving from France Militaire in author's own collection.

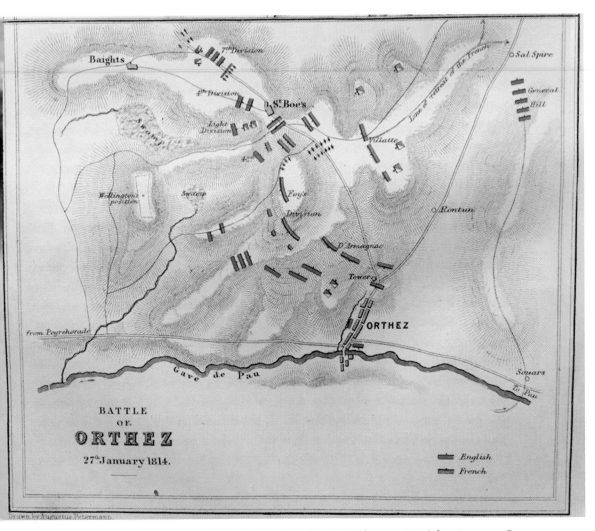

Placement of armies at the outset of the Battle of Orthez, 27 February 1814, by Augustus Petermann. Author's own collection.

John Poo Beresford, brother to Marshal Beresford, by Sir William Beechey, engraved by Thos Hodgetts. By kind permission of the Marquis of Waterford.

Cameo of Marshal Beresford. By kind permission of Suzie Pack-Beresford.

Louisa de la Poer Beresford, daughter of 1st Lord Decies, wife of Marshal Beresford, by Sir M.Archer Shee. Author's own collection.

Detail from the scabbard of the sword presented to Marshal Beresford by officers of the Portuguese army, 'showing the de la Poer Beresford crest. By kind permission of the Marquis of Waterford.

Marble bust of Marshal Beresford by Humphrey Hopper. By kind permission of the Marquis of Waterford.

The Peninsular Heroes assembled at The United Services Club by J.P. Knight; Marshal Beresford seated at extreme right. Author's own collection.

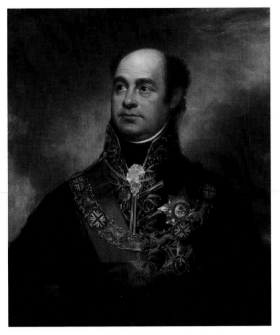

Marshal Beresford by Thomas Beechey. By kind permission of the National Portrait Gallery, London.

Marshal Beresford by Thomas Lawrence. By kind permission of Historic England.

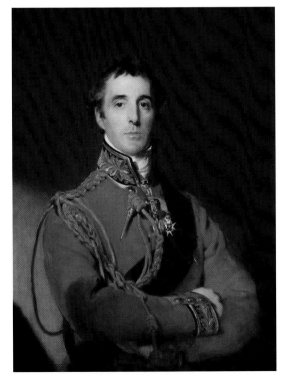

The Duke of Wellington by Thomas Lawrence. By kind permission of Historic England.

William Carr Beresford by Thomas Heaphy. By kind permission of the Marquis of Waterford.

Guilherme Carr Beresford, Conde de Trancozo, painter Henrique José da Silva. By kind permission of the Marquis of Waterford.

Marshal William Carr Beresford's medal case. By kind permission of the Marquis of Waterford.

Marshal William Carr Beresford's Connaught Rangers (88th) Peninsular War medal. By kind permission of the Marquis of Waterford.

Palacio de Ega, Beresford's HQ and home in Lisbon after the conclusion of the Peninsular War. Photo by Carlos Pombo; by kind permission of PT Arquivo Historico Ultramarino.

Campaign of Marshal Beresford, Spring 1811

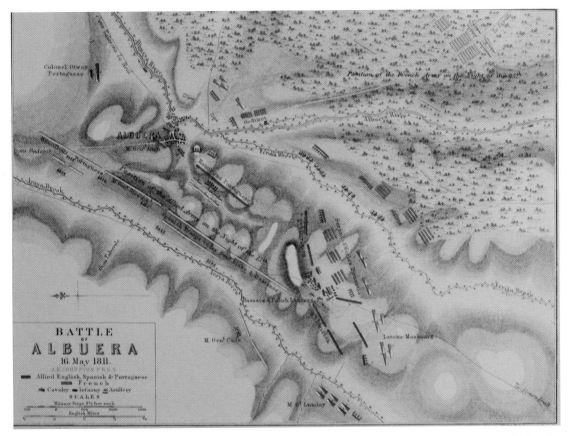

Battle of Albuera, 16 May 1811: position of the Allied and French armies before and during the battle, by A.K. Johnston. Author's own collection.

No. 21.

THE PORTUGUESE FRONTIER, for operations of Wellington & Beresford, April-August, 1811

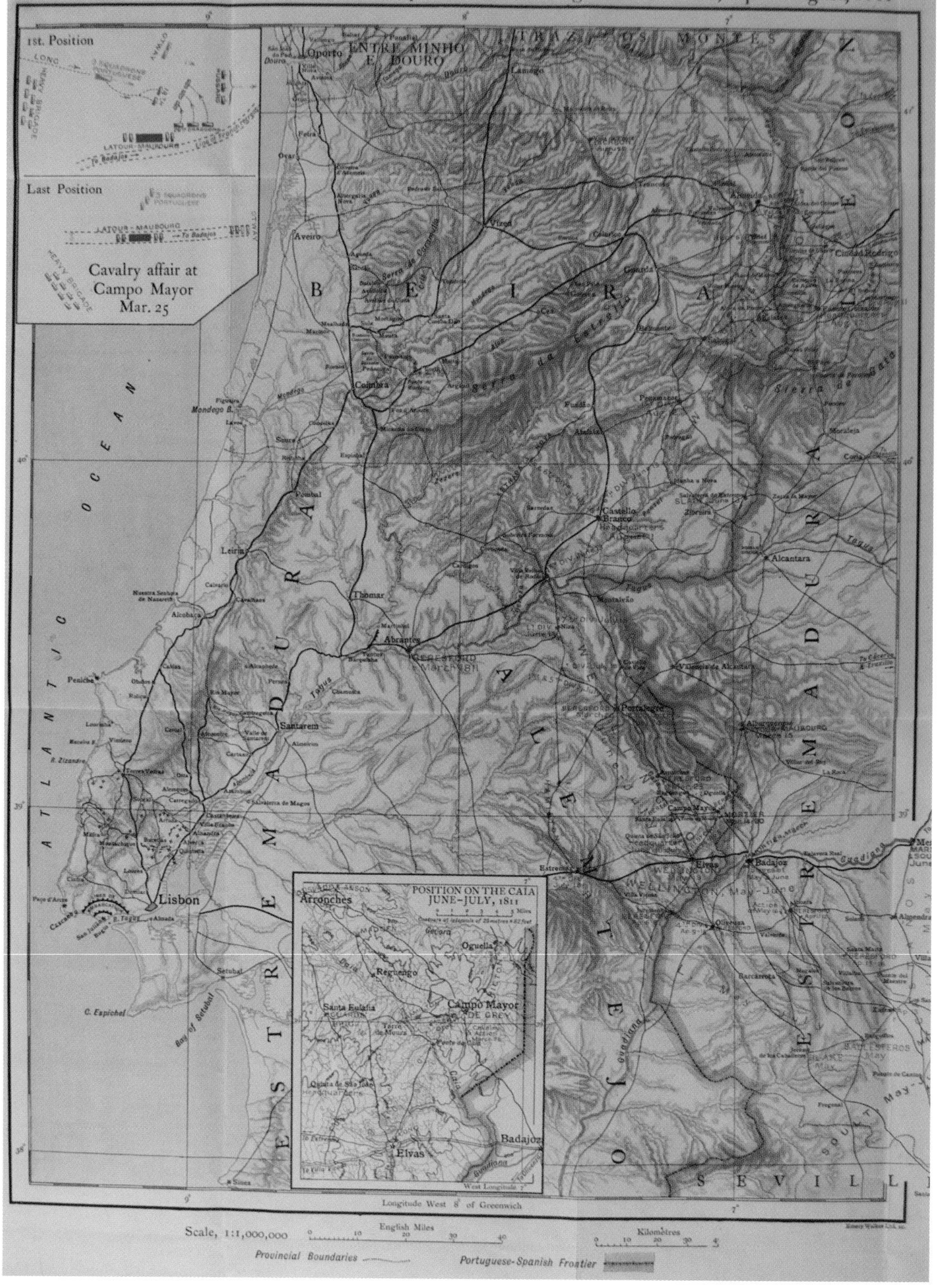

1st. Position
Last Position
Cavalry affair at Campo Mayor Mar. 25
LATOUR-MAUBOURG
HEAVY BRIGADE
To Badajoz
ENTRE MINHO E DOURO
TRAZ OS MONTES
Oporto
Lamego
Aveiro
Vizeu
Guarda
Almeida
Ciudad Rodrigo
Coimbra
Mondego R.
Pombal
Leiria
Thomar
Abrantes
Castello Branco
Alcantara
Santarem
Portalegre
Albuquerque
Campo Mayor
Elvas
Badajoz
Estremoz
Olivenza
Lisbon
Setubal
C. Espichel
Bay of Setubal
Peniche
Alcobaça
Torres Vedras
Tagus
Guadiana
ATLANTIC OCEAN
B E I R A
E S T R E M A D U R A
A L E M T E J O
E S T R E M A D U R A
S E V I L L
L E O N
POSITION ON THE CAIA JUNE-JULY, 1811
Arronches
Reguengo
Ouguella
Santa Eulalia
Quinta de São João
West Longitude 7°
Longitude West 8° of Greenwich
Emery Walker Ltd. sc.

Scale, 1:1,000,000 English Miles 0 10 20 30 40 Kilomètres 0 10 20 30 40

Provincial Boundaries *Portuguese-Spanish Frontier*

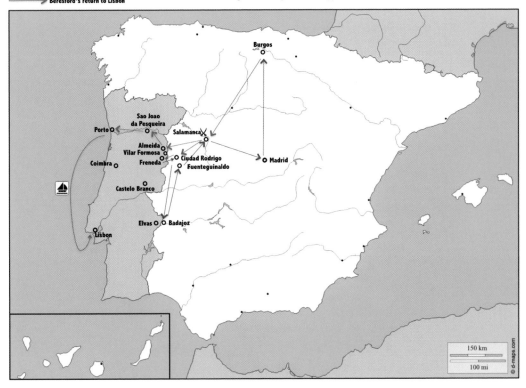

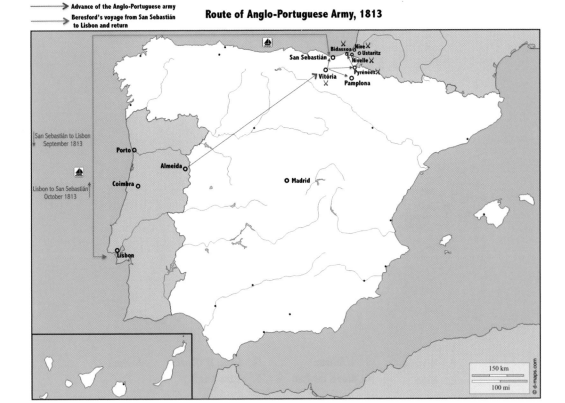

Allied Positions before Nivelle (10 November 1813) and Nive (9–13 December)

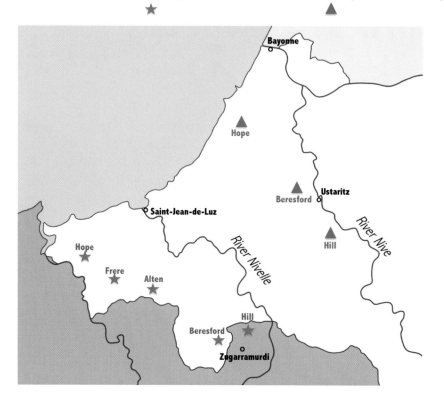

The Allied Conquest of South-West France, 1814

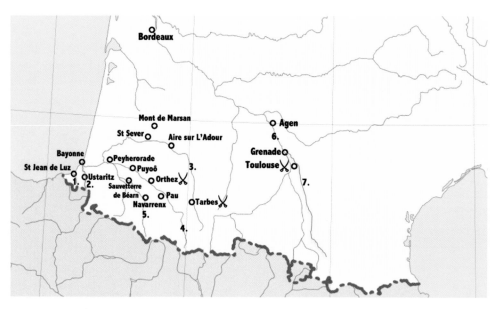

Rivers
1. Nivelle
2. Nive
3. L'Adour
4. Gave de Pau
5. Gave D'Oloron
6. Garonne
7. Hers

When discussing Beresford's decision to face Soult's forces on the right and his orders for new dispositions, D'Urban observed:

> These dispositions were promptly and precisely carried into effect, with the exception of that of General Blake, whose delay in executing it had very nearly led to the most fatal consequences, for so much time had been lost, that instead of being prepared upon the ground he was to hold, his troops had scarcely placed themselves there when the enemy fell upon them.

He goes on to detail how Beresford himself had to post the troops in the absence of proper orders from Blake.[95]

The Spanish report on the battle of Albuera prepared by Adjutant-General António Burriel, with subsidiary reports by Marshals Lardizabal and Zayas as well as General Ballasteros and various more junior officers, does not throw light on the instructions Beresford gave to Blake and their interpretation. While individual officers paid tribute to the bravery of the British soldiers, the references to Beresford are limited to the build up to the battle, giving no indication that Blake put Beresford under any pressure to stand and fight. Having told the reader of the position taken up by the army of Marshal Beresford in anticipation of the battle he receives no further mention in Burriel's report, which is largely an acclamation of the performance of the various units within the Spanish army.[96] While not all the British officers present praised the Spanish infantry as Beresford did after the battle, the encounter at Albuera did have important consequences, not least of which the British had seen the Spanish stand and fight and secondly that cooperation on the field of battle was possible, wiping away some of the doubts which had existed at least since Talavera.[97] Castaños, in his own dispatch on the battle, chose to stress the harmony amongst the generals and the most fraternal union amongst the soldiers, who gave each other mutual aid and assistance.

What of the performance of Marshal Soult in the spring of 1811? His initial success in capturing Badajoz was substantial, but he was unable to build on that achievement. In May, having assembled a substantial force, Soult marched from Sevilla to relieve the siege of Badajoz and failed in his objective; retiring back to Sevilla with the remnant of his force including many wounded, with more left on the field of battle. His report on this ferocious encounter to Marshal Berthier, the Imperial Chief of Staff, dated 21 May 1811 is revealing for what it does not say as much as for the suggested turn of events. Notwithstanding that he had made it clear to Berthier on 4 May that he was assembling an army to go to the relief of Badajoz, he now presented his expedition as one to clear the British out of Extremadura, claiming his march had freed the province and forced the enemy to recall all his corps to Albuera, conveniently failing to mention that subsequent to the battle the Allies had again moved forward into Extremadura, reoccupying many towns and villages and resuming the siege of Badajoz.[98] Soult presents the end of the battle as a stalemate, with the French occupying the positions they had taken during the battle. That, of course, was not the case as the French had retired (fled in many British accounts) back across the streams forming the Albuera river. It is likely his army was only saved due to very good work by his cavalry and artillery in covering the retreat, and indeed Soult praised both La Tour-Maubourg and Ruty for the performance of the cavalry and artillery respectively.

Having substantially misrepresented his losses, Soult concludes his report with the suggestion that once he had sent his wounded and the prisoners back to Sevilla, he manoeuvred to join up with other troops to complete the defeat of the enemy. It is unclear what he meant by that claim, since it was to be several weeks before he joined Marmont, who had then moved south from Salamanca in force. He states that it was Beresford's receipt of reinforcements from Elvas that prompted him to make a movement (note he does not retire or retreat) on Solano on 18 May. During that retreat he was to lose further men and materials. Where the two commanders did agree was that this encounter was hard-fought *le combat fut des plus terribles* and it is clear from other contemporaneous accounts and the losses that this was one of the most vigorously contested actions of the Peninsular War. While Soult did not manifest Beresford's horror at the carnage, he was certainly aware of the horrendous losses, however much he tried to hide them from Berthier and Napoleon.

Were there any grounds for Soult to claim a victory? Soult was able to send regimental colours captured at Albuera to Napoleon.[99] Perhaps, however, any claim to victory rests not so much on the outcome of the battle itself, but on the fact that fighting the battle delayed the siege of Badajoz with the result that three weeks later Wellington was forced to abandon the second siege of that city in the face of the coming together of Marmont's and Soult's forces. When Badajoz was eventually relieved by the French in mid June, Soult made even greater claims regarding Albuera suggesting that 20,000 Frenchmen had beaten an Allied army of 45,000; while even then continuing to maintain that French losses at the battle had been only half those of the Allies. While Major William Brooke, a British officer taken prisoner, wrote that the French army was very dispirited on the day after the battle, Soult was not backward in taking credit for himself and his army for the relief of Badajoz in June and linked it to the French performance at Albuera which had he said brought them twenty days grace in which he had effected a junction with Marmont's Army of Portugal.[100]

Soult was a very clever strategist but it is arguable that like Beresford he was not good at adapting to changed circumstances during a battle. At Albuera his method of sending Gazan to support Gerard was clumsy and resulted in confusion, and when he did ultimately throw his reserve under Werlé into the fray to support Gazan in turn, it was after an overlong delay and with little hope of success in the formation employed. Soult was not immune to criticism for his performance. Even Napoleon, who greatly admired him, felt he could have done better.[101] Soult had now seen British infantry in action on three separate occasions: before La Coruña, at Porto and now at Albuera. He was to face them again in 1813 and 1814 and was well placed to warn Napoleon of their effectiveness prior to the battle of Waterloo; only to have his warning dismissed. In 1811, in the absence of specific instructions from Napoleon, it is clear that neither Marmont nor Soult had any appetite for a further invasion of Portugal on anything like equal terms with their protagonists.

Beresford and his army received the thanks of both houses of parliament following the battle. In June 1811 he was appointed a Captain-General of Spain.[102] Of course, Beresford was replaced by Hill on his return to Portugal from England in June 1811, but that was an event that was predetermined, as Beresford's appointment in December 1810 had been stated to be temporary. Notwithstanding that after Albuera he had joined Wellington in the second British siege of Badajoz, Beresford seems to have been unwell, and he was certainly deeply effected by the losses sustained at Albuera. He spent a considerable part of the summer organising and directing the Portuguese army from Sintra where he had gone for his health. It was winter before he rejoined Wellington at the front line. He then served with distinction throughout the rest of the Peninsular War.

At this remove it is difficult, if not impossible, to opine with certainty on the nature of Beresford's ill health following the battle. His correspondence shows that he suffered intermittently from what he called 'my bilious complaint'.[103] He also suffered from erysipelas, but it seems clear that some other ailment was now afflicting him. It is possible that he was suffering from what in the twentieth century was identified as post-traumatic stress disorder (PTSD). He told Wellington immediately after the battle, when sending on his dispatch with Arbuthnot, that he was glad Wellington was coming to join him as he was not very well.[104] A week later he apologised to his friend Charles Stewart, Wellington's Adjutant-General, for not having spoken to him in more detail at Albuera, noting that he had been against risking a battle and after the engagement was:

> very much out of spirits from the conviction of having acted unwisely in risking so immensely as would have been the consequence of misfortune. However Wellington's usual kindness and assurances have a little tranquilised me on that head, and I have only now to regret our great loss, which also at that time much weighed upon my mind.[105]

Beresford himself alluded to his situation again when writing to his good friend Brigadier General Denis Pack from Elvas on 1 June. He put it that he was not well, and although not in pain and not unwell he found himself weak and languid.[106] He raised the possibility that he might go to Lisbon, though that would depend on the circumstances. Just over a week later an unidentified correspondent, who may have been Major General Henry Cadogan, wrote to Pack from Talavera la Real on 9 June, prior to the raising of the second siege of Badajoz. Having observed that Wellington looked well but had a cold, he went on: 'The Marshal looks dreadfully worn and nervous beyond belief.'[107]

Shortly thereafter Beresford returned to Lisbon, where he based himself initially at Sintra. By mid October he was back in the city where he continued his work of reorganising the Portuguese army.[108] As late as November D'Urban reported, 'relapses of a lingering feverish affection and great debility' which prevented the Marshal joining the army though he then intended to proceed to Vilar Formoso where he would be near Wellington at Freneda.[109] Wellington wrote to Beresford on 13 December with compassion, for while he stated: 'I am very anxious to see you, as there are many subjects on which I wish to converse with you' he went on to say that it would 'be better to take the trouble of setting them in writing than that you should have a serious illness from coming here in the middle of winter'.[110] Further relapses prevented him joining Wellington until the beginning of 1812.[111] Beresford himself, writing to Torrens on 1 November, referred to having been laid up for many days but getting better and the doctors were now allowing him to eat again, and that he hoped to be well enough to join the army in ten to fourteen days. It clearly took somewhat longer for him to recover.[112] Wellington urged him to join him for some fox hunting, but it was to be the New Year before he returned to anything like his former self.[113]

A lot has been made of Wellington not giving Beresford independent command again of a separate Allied army, but not too much should be read into that fact. Wellington was loathe to appoint a formal second in command at any stage, or indeed give others independent command.[114] The command he was given in the Alentejo was so circumscribed with specific instructions that it was not in reality an independent command. Wellington gave detailed instructions not just for the siege of Badajoz, but also for any major battle which might take place, down to the desired venue and dispositions. He dictated what was required of the Spanish armies and ensured their support of Beresford in the first siege of Badajoz. He was in daily (and sometimes more frequent contact) with Beresford and personally travelled south to give his input on the siege and battle plans.[115] He even sent him a list of materials required for building a bridge over the Guadiana, apologising for the delay in doing so.[116] He did, of course, leave Beresford with discretion as to whether or not to give battle. After the battle had been fought and won he remained supportive of Beresford. Irrespective of whether or not Beresford was a lateral thinker, those instructions would have made it difficult for him to be innovative.

Throughout the rest of the war, Beresford not only remained in command of the Portuguese army, which became an increasingly effective fighting force, but he commanded wings of the Allied army at many of the important battles in the years 1812–14.[117] He remained a close confidant of Wellington, who fully appreciated Beresford's importance to the wellbeing of the Portuguese army, a factor which may have played a part in Wellington's use of Beresford in the next three years. We have seen how in 1810 the latter had written to Sir Charles Stuart, the British plenipotentiary Minister to Portugal: 'It is impossible for two people to understand each other better than Beresford and I. He is two miles from this [Gouveia] and I see him every day; and I believe that we take pretty nearly the same view of every transaction.'[118] The question as to who should succeed Wellington as Commander in Chief of the Allied armies in the Peninsula in the event of his incapacity was to raise its head on a number of occasions as the war continued, and the topic will be further explored in Chapter 13. Throughout these exchanges, whether with politicians or with those in the higher echelons of the army, Wellington remained steadfast in his view that Beresford was the best person to succeed him as the only one of his generals 'capable of conducting a large concern'.[119]

High praise indeed from the outstanding military leader of his generation. In the context of the Battle of Albuera it is worth noting that Wellington recognised that there might be more talented military strategists amongst his other generals but Beresford had other attributes which Wellington reportedly summarised to members of his staff ... 'If it was a question of handling troops some of you fellows might do as well, nay better than he, but what we want now is some one to feed our troops and I know no one better for the purpose than Beresford.'[120]

Wellington was so certain that this was the right course that he stood firm in the face of the strongly expressed views of the Duke of York, Commander in Chief. The Duke expressed those views not because of any animus against Beresford but because there was a long-standing tradition in the British army that no field officer should have to serve under an officer more junior than himself.[121] When against tradition the Earl of Moira had been appointed to command in the Netherlands in 1794, a number of officers had refused to serve under him and the impasse had only been resolved with Moira's resignation. Further, the difficulties concerned with Beresford's appointment to command in Portugal in 1809 we have seen caused problems.[122] In early 1813, Wellington wrote to Bathurst concerning Beresford: 'I never doubted about the succession of that officer to the command when I should be gone.'[123] The question of who should command the Allied army in the event of Wellington's absence reared its head again in September 1813, in circumstances where although the French were now pushed back to the Pyrénées there was the possibility that Wellington would have to go to Catalonia, where his recent success had not been matched by the Allies against the French.[124]

Beresford's performance at Albuera, while arguably lacking in confidence, was not the sole cause of the British losses. To suggest that this was so fails to recognise the many and complex factors which faced him on the day. While there are a number of aspects of the battle that still remain unclear, it is evident that Beresford had reservations about fighting Soult at Albuera but these were overcome by consideration of the alternatives. During the battle itself, while brave and courageous Beresford appears to have reacted only slowly to the unfolding situation. He is certainly not immune to criticism that he failed to show innovative or original qualities, or an ability to think 'outside the box'. Napier suggested that at crucial moments Beresford was indecisive. Clearly he did not give the order for the 4th Division to advance and that advance when made ensured the battle was won, but is that evidence of indecision? Cole's ADC, Major Roverea, who attended on Beresford for part of the engagement, certainly found it strange that orders were not sent to Cole to get involved, but it seems clear Beresford was not only determined, almost to the point of obsession, to keep open a safe line of retreat, but also seeking an alternative solution to the use of the 4th Division, namely the involvement of the hitherto unused Portuguese Division and possibly also the King's German Legion.

Some criticism may be justified, but other complaints lack substance. Beresford could not have occupied all the heights south of Albuera without either abandoning the town and the bridge over the river, or rendering his line so thin as to be incapable of resisting a major attack at any particular point. The whole point in centering the army on Albuera was to enable Beresford to move left or right in the event of Soult choosing an alternative route to Badajoz. Even before the battle there was an element of confusion when Blake's army only arrived during the previous night and it became difficult to place. It is difficult to see how Beresford could be blamed for the late arrival of Blake's army. Nor can he really be criticised for failing to follow up more vigorously following Soult's withdrawal. The Allied army was exhausted and had many injured men. When

Wellington arrived he approved Beresford's caution in the pursuit of Soult. The fact was that Extremadura was in many respects perfect cavalry country and both before and after the battle Soult had substantially more cavalry than that possessed by the Allies.

It should also be remembered that Beresford commanded an army made up of a number of nationalities including British, Portuguese, Spanish and Germans. Barely one quarter of that force was British (including the King's German Legion), and there were not just communication difficulties.[125] While the Spaniards fought bravely on the day, this was the first occasion they were to show the British that they could withstand French columns. Prior to the battle the British commanders had serious doubts about the effectiveness of Spanish military forces; and Beresford must have had his worries as to the level of Spanish commitment to the battle and the possibility he would be left fighting a superior force in the difficult circumstances of a retreat. D'Urban himself had voiced this concern in February 1811, when he referred to their panics, confusions and flights.[126] Further, D'Urban himself thought that Beresford had probably overestimated the ability of the Spanish to manoeuvre.

Beresford was undoubtedly let down by some of his senior generals, such as Blake and Stewart. He did not blame them in his initial report, perhaps seeking to maintain Allied and indeed British cohesion. No evidence has been found that he blamed Stewart for the latter's disastrous mode of deploying the 2nd Division but within days of the battle Beresford made it clear that while Blake had done what he had agreed with Wellington he would do, there was literally no managing the man and the best thing Beresford felt Blake could do would be to return to the Regency. He felt clearly some things were better not reduced to writing, telling Wellington: 'I have much to say to you regarding our Spanish friends and particularly Blake. We are very good friends but I think it would be impossible to long act with him. He should lose no time returning the way he came to annoy the enemy in the Sierra Morena.'[127]

Many years later, when argument arose relating to the conduct of the battle, he and others were more critical. Furthermore, as we have seen, D'Urban was extremely critical of Blake in the aftermath of the battle. An interesting aspect of both the failure of Blake and Stewart is that both acted or failed to act on Beresford's orders in his absence. In each case the Marshal had moved on having given the order. It is certainly arguable that Beresford should himself have insured his orders were properly carried out instead of moving off to undertake another task, though one might equally make the case that his generals should have implemented his orders in a proper and timely fashion. One is left wondering whether Beresford should have been moving around the field of battle to the extent that occurred; rather he might have been better advised to have remained in a central commanding position, or at the very least not spread himself so thinly on the ground. It is noteworthy that while Beresford had manoeuvered with large forces in 1808, 1809 and 1810, he had never previously had the responsibility of leading a large force in battle.[128]

Perhaps Beresford was overcautious and even uncertain as a commander at the battle of Albuera. If so, this was in marked contrast to his performance on other occasions, albeit when under Wellington's overall command.[129] Wellington's ADC and military secretary, Lord Fitzroy Somerset, while not at the battle, summarised Beresford's performance by suggesting Allied losses would not have been so severe had Beresford shown more skill in managing the battle.[130] Twenty-five years later Wellington, in conversation with Earl Stanhope, reflected on the events which had led up to the battle and its development. He related to Stanhope the fact that shortly after the battle of Fuentes de Oñoro, the French garrison under General Brenier had escaped from Almeida having blown up the fortifications. Wellington was very critical of the performance of a number of British officers for this mishap and attributed his own wait for an assessment of the damage there as having prevented him being at Albuera in time for the battle. He confirmed to Stanhope his, 'this won't do, write me down a victory' statement on receipt of Beresford's initial report on the battle, remarking at the same time:

> Had I been there we should have made a great thing of it. Marshal Beresford had not as much as myself the habit of responsibility and chief command, nor of course, in the same degree, the confidence of the troops. He therefore could not do so much. I remember he wrote me word that he was delighted I was coming, that he could not stand the slaughter about him and the vast responsibility. His letter was quite in a desponding tone ... Afterwards they grew very proud of the battle, and with full reason. There is no doubt they had completely got the better of Soult.[131]

Allowing for any error in transcribing the conversation by Stanhope, it is notable that this statement was made post the exchanges brought on by Napier's criticism of Beresford. Wellington, while feeling he would have made a better job of winning the battle, remained supportive of the Marshal and the achievement on the day, while putting Beresford's difficulties down to lack of experience and not having the same relationship with his troops as did Wellington.

Clearly mistakes were made by both commanding officers at Albuera. Those who argue that Beresford should have delegated more and not attempted to control personally all aspects of the battle need to recall that when he did delegate to Blake and Stewart, performance was mediocre. However, it is arguable that his personal involvement in many aspects of the battle led to a temporary loss of control of events. He was the first to admit that it was probably good fortune rather than his own merit that had won the battle, though he did make the point that consideration might be given to the materials he had to work with.[132] From an historical perspective, Beresford's misfortune was to make an enemy of both Sir William Napier, an ardent admirer of Marshal Soult, and to be assailed by the family of Ballard Long, who felt he had been harshly treated at the time of Albuera. Napier's later criticism was fed by the Long family taking up the baton on behalf of the then deceased Ballard Long in the 1830s.

Before judging Beresford too harshly on Napier's evidence it would be as well to remember that Napier was contradicted and refuted by a number of those on whom he wrote so eloquently.[133] Wellington for his part continued to show trust in Beresford's abilities and judgment, and the greatest historian of the Peninsular War, Sir Charles Oman, felt that Napier had erred and been unjust in his assertions regarding Beresford's performance at Albuera.[134] Moreover, there was clearly a body of opinion that felt, irrespective of any weaknesses in Beresford's performance at Albuera, his contribution to the cause was a substantial one requiring not just recognition but condemnation of Napier's one-sided approach to the topic. The *United Service* magazine attempted to sum up on the subject in 1834 as follows, claiming that it had gone minutely as well as reluctantly into the subject of the controversy:

Yet we would not have our readers suppose that we approve of all Lord Beresford's dispositions, either during or subsequent to the battle; far less that we account him a rival to his and our master, with whom, we venture to pledge ourselves, he never, even in thought, contrasted himself. We are not unaware of the prejudice which prevailed against Lord Beresford in the Peninsular army, nor of the feeling which pervaded it respecting the battle of Albuera; neither are we blind to the errors which he committed, both in the field and elsewhere; but were Beresford's demerits ten times greater than we believe them to have been, Colonel Napier would still be without excuse for the tone which reigns throughout his strictures.[135]

12 THE PORTUGUESE ARMY GOES FROM STRENGTH TO STRENGTH, 1811–1812

Beresford arrived back in Lisbon on 4 July 1811 and initially resumed residence in the Palácio Sobral at Calhariz, where he had started his reform of the Portuguese army in 1809. However, he was clearly not well and his health took him to Sintra on 15 July. A short interlude by the sea at the end of September and early October meant he did not resume his residence in Calhariz until 16 October, where he stayed until early in the New Year.[1] Throughout this period he suffered intermittent colds and fevers,[2] nonetheless the records show him pursuing with diligence the further improvement of the Portuguese army and the reform of its civil departments. He dealt with staff transfers, retirements, regimental reorganisation, the reorganisation of the engineers, the supply of provisions, deserters, complaints of those who claimed to have suffered at the hands of the military, prisoners and the need for further recruits for the work of fortifying the Lines around Lisbon and the city itself; an indication that Wellington did not regard Portugal as definitively secure from a further French attempted conquest and occupation.[3] In his endeavours he was greatly assisted by Forjaz, but others played an important part. The sustained support and encouragement of Wellington and the British Minister Plenipotentiary at Lisbon, Charles Stuart, was supplemented by many others including Beresford's Portuguese Military Secretary, Lemos de Lacerda and his Adjutant-General, Manoel de Brito Mozinho; along with Beresford's ADCs such as William Warre, and William Henry Sewell. Meanwhile, D'Urban and Hardinge continued to work hard with the army alongside the commanders of the individual regiments.[4]

The Portuguese army had served with distinction in three major engagements, Buçaco, Fuentes de Oñoro and Albuera, along with a host of lesser encounters by the end of 1811.[5] It was now well drilled, armed and for the most part adequately clothed. However, there remained a number of serious threats to its wellbeing, any one of which could gravely affect it as a fighting force. Difficulties with recruiting were compounded by desertion; but above all the inefficiencies of the Arsenal and the chaotic performance of the Junta de Viveres repeatedly threatened the very ability of the army to go on campaign.

In the autumn of 1811 Beresford persevered with the creation of six new regiments of caçadores, bringing the total number of such regiments to twelve.[6] The backbone of three of these new regiments was to be made up of the former battalions of the Loyal Lusitanian Legion, which Beresford determined to integrate fully into the Portuguese army. Three additional regiments were also raised in northern Portugal, thus enabling a regiment of caçadores to be placed with each brigade.[7] Prior to implementing this proposal, in April Beresford sought Wellington's advice, observing that to make anything of the move it was necessary to deprive the Legion of its name, a reference probably to the earlier attempts of Sir Robert Wilson to persuade the British and Portuguese governments that the Legion should effectively amount to a separate command. He felt that the establishment of these additional light infantry regiments would add force and experience to the army, and that while providing for them would be a challenge, the additional finance coming from England should make the move feasible.[8] Wellington supported the move, which proceeded to implementation and the six new regiments were ready for the upcoming campaign in early 1812.

The addition of the new regiments placed further stress on the recruitment of soldiers, but whether because Forjaz now had a well-oiled machine in place, or because of Allied success, Portugal produced increasing numbers of recruits in the second half of 1811.[9] The increase, which ensured well over 1,000 new recruits each month, probably owed something to Beresford's continual pressure and his complaints as well.

New training facilities were opened at the palace of Mafra on Beresford's request.[10] In 1812, recruiting to the infantry fell off, running at an average of 459 men per month, with August providing only twenty-six men. Whether because of Beresford's inaction due to injury in July or otherwise, such as the harvest, is not clear.[11] This figure for recruits to the infantry may seem small, but at the same time Beresford and Forjaz pursued an aggressive policy towards deserters, which was markedly successful in reducing losses from that source. Having previously introduced the system whereby those absent from their regiment required a passport, Forjaz followed up in 1811 with a requirement for regimental commanders to furnish lists of those missing, and these in turn were published in the offenders' home towns and regions along with a promise of reward for information leading to capture. Irrespective of whether a deserter was a member of a front line or a militia regiment, the reward for the apprehension of a deserter was increased to 4,800 reis at the end of December 1811.[12] Nonetheless, the Marshal found himself compelled to introduce even more draconian rules in 1812, directing the execution of every deserter, and the Ordens do Dia reflect the implementation of that decision with thirty-three soldiers being executed in June and July 1812.[13] Desertions from the Portuguese army now dropped from an average of 600 to well under 300 per month and on occasion less than 200 per month.[14]

Both Beresford and Forjaz were their 'own man', not afraid to express an opinion, but throughout the war they worked well together to resolve difficult issues. Each respected the view of the other even if not in agreement. Thus, while both understood that financial constraints meant that for much of the war the theoretical sixteen batteries of artillery attached to the Portuguese army could not be maintained in battle readiness, when that number declined to four active batteries in 1812, Forjaz agreed with Beresford that funds needed to be allocated from the military chest to resupply three additional batteries, on the basis that monies could be saved by dismounting others. In 1812, at Beresford's suggestion, there was added a battalion of artificers and a battalion of drivers. Nevertheless, it was a bit like robbing Peter to pay Paul and a combination of shortage of finance and animals (oxen, horses and mules) meant that at the beginning of 1813 there were only six batteries available for deployment.[15]

A further area of friction with the Regency appears to have arisen over Beresford's reorganisation of the engineers, which had been 'long in his contemplation'. In November 1811 he writes to Wellington complaining that though he thought the military questions with the government had been fully settled it was still difficult to make the Regency leave go their hold. He reported that the plan was settled with Forjaz and General Azado, the chief of the engineers, and that he would send on the plan to Wellington as soon as it was finalised. The difficulty seemed to be Beresford's determination to make the engineers a military corps subject to the Commander in Chief rather than anyone else.[16] Wellington responded that it was obvious that matters were not yet right with the Portuguese government 'and probably never would be as long as de Souza remains'; noting that his own correspondence with the Regency went unanswered.[17] Clearly there was no love lost between the different camps but Allied successes made it difficult for Principal Souza to interfere.

Finance dictated that economies had to be made elsewhere as well. Throughout the war the lack of horses had made it impossible to mount completely the twelve nominal regiments of Portuguese cavalry. A census of horses in Portugal had shown clearly the inability to supply these at home. Efforts to acquire horses in north Africa, England, Ireland and even north America had only partially alleviated the problem. In late 1811, Beresford and Forjaz considered the issue from the standpoint of both the need to economise and the lack of horses. Whereas the Regency Council was reluctant to reduce the number of cavalry regiments, the preserve of the ruling class, Forjaz had no such reservations, himself proposing to close the cavalry school and transfer the cadets there to the infantry. Between December 1811 and late spring 1812 Beresford dismounted six of the cavalry regiments (2nd, 5th, 7th, 8th, 9th and 10th) on the basis that the men could be recalled from the infantry as and when funds and animals became available. The dismounted cavalry included the brigade of George Madden, which had behaved badly by failing to follow its commander at Gebora and which inexplicably failed to rally to the army prior to the battle of Albuera. It had been in the field for over nine months, and according to Wellington was 'worse than useless'. Initially, in the autumn of 1811 it was sent north of the Douro to recuperate and train, but in 1812 Beresford selected the brigade for disbandment, with

Madden being placed in command of an infantry brigade in the 6th Division. The reduction in the number of cavalry regiments led to additional funding and horses being made available for the remaining regiments, though Beresford complained that these were still inadequate.[18]

For Beresford, the outfitting, feeding and payment of his troops was crucial. Time and again he made the point that without resolving these issues the troops could not go on campaign. Furthermore, discipline would, and on occasions did, break down. His response to indiscipline was predictably harsh, but at the same time he persistently sought clothing, provisions and funds on behalf of the army. The necessity to do so was both wearing and time consuming, time which could have been spent honing his fighting force. Where a course of action failed to remedy a situation it was changed. One such example had been the decision in 1810 to manufacture uniforms for the army in Portugal from imported cloth because of the perceived inadequacy of those manufactured in England. This experiment was adjudged unsuccessful in early 1812, when a decision was made to revert to the importation of ready-made uniforms from the United Kingdom.[19]

The most persistent challenges to the creation of an efficient fighting force arose from a lack of finance. Frequently the pay of the troops was up to six months in arrears leading to unrest and having a knock-on effect for those who wished to buy food or luxuries, such as they were. Even more serious was the inability of the commissariat to feed the troops, so that on occasion they could not march, or after a few days were reduced to semi-starvation. Beresford's correspondence remonstrating on these points shows his deep level of frustration with the Regency Council and his anger that those other than the men defending the kingdom were obtaining preferential treatment. In early 1811 Wellington had recognised the necessity of the British commissariat to feed the Portuguese regiments serving with the Allied army, but even then it seemed to be an insurmountable task for the Junta de Viveres to cater for those left outside this situation.[20]

In the autumn of 1811 Beresford finally won his long-running battle to abolish the Junta de Viveres, though it took the intervention of Wellington and the support of Prince Regent João to do so.[21] It was abolished with effect from 1 January 1812 and replaced with a Commissary General, Domingos José Cardoso, and deputies reporting to him. This commissariat now had responsibility for both supplies and their transport, replacing the two previous organisations which had divided such responsibility between them. Initially the new commissariat appears to have had some success, but in spite of all Beresford's efforts, and those of Forjaz, problems of supply persisted until the end of the war to a greater or lesser degree, even on occasions requiring Beresford's return to Lisbon while the army was on campaign. The reason was simple; lack of finance. Even such extreme measures as the virtual abolition of the Portuguese navy (that part of it left behind following the departure of the court for Brazil), and the closure of the Arsenal at Porto did not rectify the position. Nor did the British grant resolve matters, and the government continued to run a monthly deficit of in excess of £80,000 into 1813.[22]

Wellington hoped, and Beresford had expected, the latter would leave Lisbon for the frontier in late November or early December 1811, but repeated setbacks to his health, as much as the administration of the Portuguese army, prevented his departure until the New Year.[23] That Wellington desired the Marshal's presence at or near his own base at Freneda is clear, both as a sounding board and as a companion to ride out with whether following the hounds or otherwise.[24] In early November Wellington wrote to Beresford from Freneda expressing the hope he would soon join him: 'I mean to have a comfortable house prepared for you in one of the neighbouring villages as soon as I hear that you are about to set out. I hope you bring up good horses as the hounds go at the devil of a rate.'[25] Beresford responded, expressing the hope he would soon join Wellington and that he thought he was 'pretty well mounted and I shall be glad to join the chase.'[26] Beresford's family, on the other hand, felt he should go home to recuperate, but he made it clear that while he would love to do so, duty would not permit such a move, even for a short visit. Writing to his half-sister, Anne, on 6 December he stated:

> nothing but a sense of duty prevents me, as independent of my health I should be most happy in a little quietness and the enjoyment of my friends society. But the machine I have got to wield I am afraid of losing sight of it for a moment, it goes pretty well now, but still requires the Master's hand, and to tell you the truth, if once I give up even for a short time the command of the Portuguese army I think I should not like to resume it. I fear it would be in some degree to begin again, for unfortunately I have no second, nor if I went could I be certain that the same system would be adhered to.[27]

Duty is a theme that runs through Beresford's career but here we also see his evident concern that if he should absent himself even for a brief time, it would affect the efficiency of the military machine created through his efforts and those of others.

It was only on 6 January 1812 that Beresford left Lisbon. Passing by Abrantes, where he inspected the garrison, and from there to Tomar and Coimbra. When Beresford finally joined up with Wellington at Galegos, the siege of Ciudad Rodrigo was under way. The conditions were demanding to say the least. General Henry MacKinnon observed that on the march to the town the snow was in many places knee deep. They were obliged to sleep out and a number of men died.[28] It was perhaps not surprising that the French command were not prepared for Wellington's move against Ciudad Rodrigo. In the autumn and early winter, Wellington had caused the first proper British siege train in the Peninsula to be brought to Almeida from Lisbon. Having concentrated his forces in early January 1812, he commenced the siege on 8 January with the town being stormed only twelve days later on the night of 19 January.

Beresford joined Wellington on or about 16 January but there is no evidence of his playing any major role in the siege of Ciudad Rodrigo.[29] The storming of the city caused the Marshal further personal trauma through the loss of a young cousin, John Theophilus Beresford, the circumstances of which clearly shook the Marshal to the core; demonstrating a very human side to this brave man, sometimes presented as cold, gruff and uncaring.[30] The 88th Regiment (the Connaught Rangers), which he had led for so long and of which he was Colonel, participated in the successful capture of the town.[31] The Connaught Rangers formed part of Picton's 3rd Division, charged with attacking the principal breach prior to which Picton reportedly declared: 'Rangers of Connaught! It is not my intention to expend any powder this evening. We will do this business with the cold iron.'[32] John Beresford, then aged twenty and a Lieutenant in the regiment, had been appointed ADC to General MacKinnon but also commanded the sap at the principal breach, a task for which he had volunteered.[33] John's story is told elsewhere but in brief, while the 88th was clearing the ramparts MacKinnon ordered Beresford to accompany him.[34] Shortly afterwards, the French detonated a mine within the bastion killing MacKinnon and others and injuring John Beresford.[35] At first his injuries were not thought to be life-threatening, though clearly he had serious burns. On 20 January, the Marshal wrote to his brother Poo telling him that 'John has become very much burnt in the face, and all his hair, he will be in great pain for some time and though this wound may be called severe yet there is nothing in the least dangerous in it. He goes tomorrow to my house in Villa Formosa. He volunteered for the service he was on which was a very perilous one.'[36]

John was brought to the Marshal's house in Villa Formosa, some thirty kilometres from Ciudad Rodrigo, where he received the best treatment available. However, even the Marshal's accommodation was not of a high standard. He described the house as having no windows or doors though he had had the apertures filled up and installed a fireplace. In addition, the roof had been repaired. Writing to his sister Anne on 28 January 1811, Beresford recognised the wound was indeed much more serious than at first thought:

> Poor John Beresford is in the room next to me and in just such a one as my own, only it does not leak from above he is as far as accommodation goes comfortable enough, but poor fellow he has had a most dreadful wound, much worse than I had imagined it, he has been delirious until yesterday, however he is now calm and all fever has left him, but the burns are dreadful, and he will be long before he recovers. I trust however he is out of danger & which the doctors think, though from such a wound it is difficult for a long time to be certain. He has taken a good deal of nourishment today & as he can now want for nothing & there is a medical gentleman only to take care of him, I have every hope that all will go well, but I am very anxious about him.[37]

The Marshal was right to be anxious for young John passed away the following day. He is buried on the walls of the great fortress of Almeida with a gravestone engraved in both Portuguese and English. The Marshal was so distraught that he could not bring himself to write to John's mother for several months, for as he later explained he had given her and others false hope of John's recovery.

On 20 January the Marshal had written to John's mother, Lady Frances, saying John, 'an amazing fine spirited lad', had distinguished himself the previous night by his gallantry but that he had been wounded. He did not wish her to read about it first in the newspapers which might cause distress. He described the wounds as superficial 'being scorched with powder on the face and two or three other places', which might leave a few grains of powder in his face but he expected him to recover in two or three weeks.[38] Even worse from the point of view of raising expectations was a further letter written to John's mother on 29 January, only hours before John's death, telling her the doctor had just pronounced that John was not in any danger and the medical men had never had any apprehension for his life. It was too soon to say if he will 'have any marks on his face from his wounds but at present rather thought that he will not. His eyes are quite safe.'[39] That night the Marshal wrote to his half-sister, Lady Anne, advising her to prepare Lady Frances for the worst as John was sinking fast and that he was gradually though rapidly declining.[40] It was only when preparing for the renewal of the siege of Badajoz (third Allied siege) in March 1812 that the Marshal wrote to Lady Frances, having received her letter of 7 February after his arrival at Elvas. The Marshal referred to his own sadness at the loss of 'your lamented son' and the fact that he, the Marshal, had not had the courage to write directly. He explained that John had not uttered any complaint during his illness. He added, 'I told him I was writing to you and he asked me to tell you he could not write and to give you his love.'[41]

Beresford was very much involved in the campaign whereby Wellington now took the war against France into Spain. The situation had changed dramatically from that pertaining early in 1811. Now the Allies held three of the four great border fortresses on the border of Spain and Portugal with only Badajoz remaining in French hands. Marmont had been forced to send troops both to eastern Spain, to assist Suchet, and more importantly some of the most seasoned regiments had been summoned to assist Napoleon's invasion of Russia. Nevertheless, Joseph still reigned in Madrid, Soult controlled much of Andalucía, and Marmont's Army of Portugal was only one of a number of significant forces. Following the surrender of Ciudad Rodrigo, the investment of which had taken Marmont by surprise, Wellington moved south with the siege train to tackle Badajoz. Marmont sought to go to the relief of Badajoz but was hamstrung by long-distance directives emanating from the Emperor; orders which often bore no relation to reality by the time they were received in the Peninsula.

Involvement with the campaign did not mean that Beresford escaped from his responsibilities vis-à-vis the Portuguese army and he continued his campaign to remedy a lack of supplies and finance, complaining repeatedly to Forjaz about the inadequacy of supply of clothing and feedstuffs. He returned to Lisbon in mid February to secure money for the payment of troops, and in this respect he appears to have worked with Stuart to ensure compliance. His dealings with the Regency were further strengthened, for when his military secretary, Colonel Lemos Pereira de Lacerda, returned from Rio de Janeiro in February 1812 he brought with him enhanced powers for Beresford. Lemos had been sent to the Brazils by Beresford in the summer of 1811 because of the problems Beresford was encountering vis-à-vis the Regency. Beresford was now named a Councillor of War giving him specific control over the civil departments of the army.[42] Further, the Regency was directed to defer to Wellington and Beresford in military matters, even to the extent of not requiring referral of reforms to the Prince Regent in Brazil prior to implementation.[43] Notwithstanding these new powers, Oman suggests the visit to Lisbon was a short and stormy one with Beresford harrying the Regency on financial matters.[44]

At the end of February he took his leave of the Regency, and the Marshal was back in Elvas on 6 March where he met Wellington on the eleventh of the month.[45] Five days later Wellington directed Beresford to invest Badajoz, which he did with the Light, 3rd and 4th divisions (Craufurd, who had commanded the Light Division, had been killed at Ciudad Rodrigo) and one troop of the Portuguese 3rd Cavalry Regiment on the left bank. On the right bank he placed the Algarve Brigade and one troop of light cavalry.[46] Since the expedition against Soult in

Porto in 1809, Beresford had commanded mixed forces of Portuguese and British troops. While his command of the Portuguese army continued throughout, and indeed beyond the war, it is noticeable that from the time he was appointed to his 'temporary command' on the left bank of the Tagus right through to the end of the conflict, Wellington used Beresford to command forces in which British rather than Portuguese troops dominated.

Badajoz was stormed on 6 April with the Allies suffering some of the heaviest losses of any engagement in the war. Wellington reported 1,035 Allied killed and 3,787 wounded with a further 63 missing. Perhaps as a result, when they entered the town a number of British regiments went on the rampage and control was not re-established for three days, much to Wellington's chagrin. Wellington complimented Beresford on keeping the Portuguese regiments intact, which may in part have been due to the strict discipline insisted on by Beresford. While it was Wellington's approbation that perhaps mattered, recognition of the fruits of the labours of Beresford and the other British officers continued to pour in from all sides. George Hennell, a young gentleman volunteer with the 94th Regiment, paid tribute to the Portuguese soldiers saying they improved very fast. At a more senior level, Picton wrote to Lord Hastings: 'There was no difference between the British and the Portuguese, they were equal in their exertions and deserving of an equal portion of the laurel.'[47] Reporting to Liverpool on the outcome of the siege of Badajoz, Wellington declared: 'Marshal Sir W. Beresford assisted me in conducting the details of this siege; and I am much indebted to him for the cordial assistance which I received from him, as well during its progress, as in the last operation which brought it to a termination.'[48]

Following the fall of Badajoz, Wellington was still threatened by both Soult in the south and Marmont in Beira Baixa. Wellington prepared to take up a position at Albuera, but Soult retired into Andalucía enabling Wellington to send much of his army north to ensure Marmont's withdrawal. Marmont, who had invaded Portugal with the view to getting Wellington to abandon the siege of Badajoz, had proceeded south to the environs of Castelo Branco. He now withdrew to near Salamanca in Spain, deciding to avoid an encounter at this time.

Wellington then prepared to march into Spain, but before doing so engaged in extensive preparations which required Beresford to ensure that the Portuguese army designated to serve with Wellington (perhaps 17,000 out of a total of 43,000 infantry) was properly equipped and provisioned. He exhorted Forjaz to provide money for salaries, which were again six months in arrears, with limited success. More successful was the re-fitting of the regiments with new clothes and shoes, though here again the Arsenal and Forjaz felt Beresford's ire when a consignment of shoes was shipped to India rather than being supplied to the army in Portugal.[49]

The Anglo-Portuguese army under Wellington advanced on Salamanca in June, taking the city when Marmont retreated northwards. On 22 July, Wellington achieved one of his most famous victories when overwhelming Marmont's army at the Battle of Salamanca (Los Arapiles). Had the follow up been sustained the French defeat might have been even more devastating. At Salamanca Beresford commanded the centre of the Allied army, on this occasion composed of the Light, 4th and 5th divisions, all of which contained Portuguese brigades.[50] In a situation where Cole's 4th Division was engaged in a desperate musketry duel with the French who were bringing up reserves, Beresford personally led Brigadier General Winfried Spry's Portuguese brigade to attack the French. This decisive action enabled the 4th Division to regroup and prevented the French from breaking the Allied line.

Beresford's conduct was not without personal cost. He had lately reported to his sister Anne that 'he was never so well since coming to Portugal' but was now injured for the second time in under a week.[51] He was showing his customary bravery, and was reported to be about twenty yards in front of the colours when struck by a musket ball.[52] On this occasion, the ball tore into the left-hand side of his chest but apparently without breaking any bones. William Warre told his father that it was near sunset when the Marshal was injured and that he had accompanied Beresford to the rear, and later that evening into Salamanca, where they did not arrive until 11 pm, having had Beresford's wounds dressed on the road. A Portuguese account of Beresford's injury is more graphic. When he was struck a Portuguese officer (perhaps one of his escort) shouted for an English surgeon and an unnamed English medical officer attached to one of the Portuguese regiments came immediately. Beresford by this stage was lying in a wagon, together with a wounded sergeant. There was a stream of blood flowing from the left-hand side of the Marshal's blue uniform near his decorations, where there was a small black hole. The Marshal's eyes were half closed and he had a ghastly white pallor.[53]

Two days after the battle Warre was able to declare that Beresford was 'quite free from fever, and doing as well as possible'. He explained: 'The ball entered the side near the left breast, and, slanting round the external part of the ribs, was cut out at the back about 4 inches below. The bone is not supposed to be injured at all, and it is thought that the ball went round it thro' the muscles.'[54] Taken to Salamanca, Beresford convalesced there for a month before making his way back to Lisbon. Unfortunately, the wound did not heal properly with the result that an operation was required in early 1813 to remove a piece of material which had become lodged under the skin. Retention of clothing leading to infection was a not infrequent complication of musket ball wounds, sometimes with fatal consequences.

In at least one account of the battle Beresford was reported as dead, though Wellington understood that the wound, while serious, was only likely to deprive him of the Marshal's 'counsel and assistance for some time'.[55] Reading his report of the battle, it is clear that Wellington placed a special value on Beresford's presence: 'I am much indebted to Marshal Sir W. Beresford for his friendly counsel and assistance, both previous to and during the action.' For the second time in this report he refers to the importance of the Marshal's 'counsel and assistance', and he distinguishes Beresford's contribution from his praise for the commanders of the various divisions involved in the battle.[56]

This was an occasion on which Wellington was unstinting of his praise for the performance of both the British and Portuguese cavalry. He was so impressed he supplicated Bathurst to seek an award for Sir Stapleton Cotton, the commander of the cavalry, saying: 'I don't know where we should find an officer that would command our cavalry in this country half so well as he does.'[57] Of the Portuguese cavalry he declared: 'the troops were supported in the most gallant style by the Portuguese cavalry under Brig. Gen. D'Urban'.[58] Both at Badajoz and Salamanca, Beresford and his staff were clearly involved in the thick of the action. There is substantial evidence of integration not just of the Portuguese regiments but of Beresford and his team at staff level; and whenever Beresford is present, Wellington pays tribute to Beresford's contribution. At the same time Wellington clearly recognised the vital importance of Beresford being able to give his time and expertise to the running of the Portuguese army, and made it clear that this was the reason he did not employ him more extensively in leading the Allied troops.

When the question of who should command the army in the event of Wellington's incapacity arose at the end of 1812, he explained to Beresford that it was only because Beresford had too many duties of a general nature to perform, and it was necessary to refer to him too often, that he had not charged him with 'the details of command; and excepting on the occasion on which I requested you to take the command in the Alentejo in 1811, (which Hill had held) during his absence, I have not desired you to take upon you such details'.[59] Wellington clearly realised there was a balancing act involved between his desire to have Beresford with him at the front and the need to keep the Portuguese army at a high level of readiness. This combination of factors, it is suggested, needs to be taken into account when measuring Beresford's contribution to the various aspects of the war effort. Insofar as Beresford's performance at Albuera was the subject of adverse comment in some quarters, it did not cause a measurable decline in his performance or standing. Wellington continued to trust him and he continued to contribute hugely to the war effort, whether through his dealings with the Regency, his leadership of the Portuguese army or otherwise.

Beresford described his own wound as 'pretty severe yet there is not anything of the least danger in it to life or limb. It only requires a little patience. It is in the upper part of the side but took so favourable direction, that there is now little doubt that no bone is even hurt. I had been slightly wounded in the thigh 4 days before.' However, he was 'a good deal weakened' and was advised to leave Salamanca because of fevers prevalent there and to go to the seaside. As soon as he felt able he proposed to go to Lisbon, though the wound meant he was not able to travel by land, and he planned to go down the Douro to Porto and from thence by sea to Lisbon. He was deeply frustrated at having to leave the army but hoped it would be for no more than two months.[60]

Beresford remained in Salamanca when the army moved on towards Madrid and his recovery was slower than he hoped. On 3 August he told Wellington that while every appearance was favourable the doctors did not think he would be out of doors for a month. Two days later there was a setback and he advised Wellington that 'some of the bone has come away so that contrary to our expectations founded on the symptoms and appearances of the wound, it appears the ribs are injured and this accounts for the appearance of the ball when extracted'.[61] Then, on 24 August he advised Wellington that the doctors had advised him to leave Salamanca where he had contracted a slight fever and where fever was rampant; and to convalesce by the sea. While disappointed to leave the army he would go to Lisbon where he could attend to unfinished business, though he would leave his horses at Almeida and planned to return as soon as possible.[62] In a further note to his half-sister Anne he advised her the wound was healing well, but he was a good deal weakened. He had tried an outing in a carriage for the first time on 25 August and it was painful, but he was going to repeat it with a view to getting used to the movement.[63]

The time spent at Salamanca was not wasted, with Beresford continuing to correspond with Wellington, Forjaz and others on current issues. He was greatly vexed by the performance of elements of the 1st, 11th and 12th regiments of Portuguese cavalry at Majadahonda, when part of an Anglo-Portuguese force under Brigadier General D'Urban. In this affair, on 11 August D'Urban's force, part of the Allied advance guard, was surprised by the French cavalry. D'Urban led the Portuguese cavalry in a charge against the French, but to his surprise found himself and a few officers alone in the French ranks when the Portuguese failed to push home the attack. D'Urban extricated himself but the Portuguese were routed with the loss of three cannon. Ultimately, the French were forced to retreat into the town of Majadahonda by the determination of the dragoons and infantry of the King's German Legion; behind whom the Portuguese then rallied.

Reporting on the battle, D'Urban sought to exculpate the officers of the Portuguese dragoons, blaming their mounts and equipment and the absence of British officers.[64] In particular, he felt that the absence of Lieutenant Colonel Watson and Captain Owsen, respectively commandant and riding master of the 1st Regiment of cavalry, had led to a falling off of discipline and alertness as well as riding performance. Beresford initially wondered whether the 12th Regiment of Portuguese cavalry should not be sent back to Lisbon, but he authorised D'Urban to communicate to the corps 'my opinion and strong dissatisfaction at their shamefull [sic] conduct', leaving it to D'Urban to decide any further decision which might have the desired effect. Subsequently, he modified his opinion based on D'Urban's reports on the conduct of all three Portuguese regiments, suggesting he would like to give them another chance to demonstrate their prowess if there was any likelihood of an opportunity presenting itself 'in a short time'. If that was not likely, he thought Wellington might let them go back to Portugal where he hoped at least to get the 1st and 11th regiments in respectable order.[65]

Wellington said it would not be possible to send the cavalry to the rear at the moment as 'we are worse provided with cavalry than our neighbours and a body commanded by such a man as D'Urban even though they won't fight, are better than none'. However, he went on to pass a damning judgment on them: 'In fact they behaved infamously and they must not be employed again alone or with our cavalry who gallop too fast for them, but as they were on 22nd July in support of our infantry and with English dragoons with them.'[66]

Another issue which needed to be addressed by Wellington and Beresford was the question of who would command the Portuguese Division in Major General John Hamilton's absence, as he was very unwell in August and September 1812. Normally sensitive to Wellington's proposals, on this occasion Beresford does not seem to have adopted the latter's suggestion that General Silveira, Conde de Amarante, might be temporarily given the command; though it is unclear whether this was because Beresford had reservations about Silveira's suitability, the need to keep him in Trás-os-Montes, or otherwise.[67] Ill health did eventually force Hamilton to temporarily give up command in February 1813, at which time Silveira did hold the command until it was resumed by Hamilton the following November. However, less than a month later Hamilton again had to give up command of the Division and from 18 November 1813 until the end of the war it was commanded by Major General Carlos Frederico Lecor.

It was not until 3 September that Beresford was fit enough to make the journey back to Lisbon, after making a few short journeys outside Salamanca to test his fitness for the journey.[68] William Warre explained that the Marshal would make his way overland to San [sic] João de Pesqueiria on the Douro. There they would embark on a river vessel travelling downstream to Porto. When the time came for departure Beresford's wounds had improved to such an extent that he was able to ride on horseback for 6–8 miles for two days prior to reaching Lamego, where he embarked for Porto on 9 September reaching that city two days later.[69] Beresford described his journey as annoying and sometimes painful but being of benefit to his health and that he found himself 'rather strong'. Clearly the wound to his chest was to be kept open 'for some time yet', though that to the leg was healed up.[70]

In Porto he was feted by the civil and military authorities and it was to be 14 September before he was able to set sail for Lisbon, where he disembarked on 18 September and where he spent the remainder of the year based in Calhariz and Sintra. He wrote to the 2nd Marquis of Waterford on his arrival at Lisbon describing the journey, describing Porto as 'nothing can be more magnificently beautiful' and giving his half-brother details of his wound. He hoped to be back with the army in six to eight weeks though his wound, which he described as a long one, was not yet closed. He said he would have liked to use the time to visit Ireland but he feared the army would be injured if it passed out of his hands and that his presence was most necessary in Lisbon. If he left the command of the Portuguese army he did not think he would ever resume it, unless circumstances should change. He even suggested that he was contemplating resignation from that command, perhaps indicative of his frustration at the difficulties encountered with the Regency Council at almost every turn.[71] A month later he declared to the same correspondent that he was remarkably well in health and with a consequent appetite. His wound was making progress, though part of it was being treated with caustic soda. He still had considerable stiffness but hoped to be with the army at the end of the month if business did not detain him in Lisbon.[72]

Thus Beresford missed the occupation of Madrid, the siege of Burgos and the retreat from Burgos to the Portuguese frontier. Wellington kept him closely informed of developments at Burgos, going from heady optimism on 26 September, when he thought that with luck the Allies would take Burgos in two days, to a much more dismal report on 5 October reflecting both his dissatisfaction at the lack of progress and recording the deterioration of discipline in the army.[73] The retreat witnessed scenes of indiscipline in the Allied army not seen since the retreat to La Coruña nearly four years earlier. While Wellington castigated his own officers and hanged a number of men for misdemeanours on the retreat, he was well aware of problems in the Portuguese regiments. Writing in the spring of 1813 Wellington attributed ill behaviour by the Portuguese troops in the campaign of 1812 to arrears of pay, a view which had been explained to him by their officers.[74] While recuperating at Salamanca, Beresford had expressed his concerns about both arrears of pay and lack of provisions.[75]

Unsurprisingly there were reports on the retreat from Burgos of the by-now customary breakdown in supply of provisions, which reduced the Portuguese brigade attached to the 2nd Division to near starvation.[76] Beresford suggested to Wellington that the Portuguese government troops in Spain might be supplied from Spanish resources, only to be told that Wellington had already made such an arrangement with the Intendant of Salamanca, but then the latter had been dismissed and not replaced with the result that the Allies were reaping no advantage, because the Spanish 'numerous but useless troops eat up everything'.[77] Lack of provisions and arrears of pay contributed to desertion. Prior to the battle of Salamanca, Beresford had made an example of a number of deserters by condemning these to death, but deprivation meant that on the retreat from Burgos, this course of conduct raised its head again, with losses in the Portuguese regiments exceeding those in the British army in percentage terms.[78] As late as January 1813, Beresford in his Ordens do Dia was dealing with issues arising from desertions on the retreat from Burgos.[79] A number of officers in different regiments were involved and morale seems to have suffered in the autumn of 1812.

By the end of November Wellington had the troops in winter quarters behind the Agueda. The process of re-equipping both British and Portuguese for 1813 was soon underway with Beresford, on the one hand, imposing discipline and on the other castigating the Regency for failing to ensure adequate provision for the army. From his headquarters in Freneda, Wellington urged Beresford to have the troops ready by the middle of March, as if not disturbed he proposed to take the offensive in April 1813. Beresford, in conjunction with Forjaz, set about further recruitment to fill the gaps created by the campaign of 1812. There are some suggestions that Portugal was now running out of men eligible for service and new measures were certainly implemented in late 1812 and early 1813 to ensure that those chosen by lottery were apprehended and sent to the army. Additionally, Beresford dismissed those in the militia eligible for army service, subsequently taking them into the army, and instituted a new lottery for those eligible for militia service only.[80] At the urging of Stuart, Wellington and Beresford, Forjaz managed to reduce the arrears of pay due to the army so that these were almost on a par with the British army.[81] Wellington, however, was clearly concerned that once he went on campaign in 1813, the arrears would swell again with unfortunate consequences. Wellington had long felt that the Regency was not taking the steps which it could take to raise additional revenue in Portugal, and this failure contributed to the frequent arrears of pay suffered by the troops.[82] In April 1813 Wellington himself was moved to write to Prince João because of the unwillingness of the Regency to tackle the issue.[83]

If relations with the Regency were sometimes fraught, Beresford seems to have established a good relationship with Prince João from an early stage, a friendship that was to stand the test of time and the machinations of various ministers. In early 1811, João had created him Count of Trancoso, though at the time Beresford had felt erroneously the British Prince Regent might not allow him to assume the title.[84] Now, on 17 December 1812, he was elevated to the Marquisate of Campo Maior. Additionally, he and a number of other British officers were knighted with the Portuguese Order of the Tower and the Sword (*Ordem Militar da Torre e Espada*); an Order revived by Prince João in May 1808 to enable the Portuguese Crown to reward both Portuguese and foreigners who were ineligible to be appointed to other Portuguese orders by virtue of their religion.

The award was made at three ascending levels of Knight, Commander and Grand Cross. The initial appointees were Royal Navy officers who had escorted the Portuguese royal family to

Rio de Janeiro in 1807–8 but during the Napoleonic conflict a considerable number of British army officers and some civilians also received the Order.[85] Beresford was awarded the Grand Cross in 1811 and he along with Wellington was authorised to wear it in the same year.[86] At one stage in 1812 Wellington fulminated to the effect that he would not wear his Order of the Tower and Sword if so many were being issued.[87] The award did not entitle the recipient to be called 'Sir' in the United Kingdom.[88] A further friendship was in the making, for the Conde de Palmela was appointed Portuguese ambassador to the Court of St James in the winter of 1812. Writing to the 2nd Marquis of Waterford, Beresford asked him and Lady Waterford to welcome the Count and Countess telling Waterford: 'I am much interested as well personally as that on general considerations he should be received well by my friends', and requesting Waterford 'to be as civil as you can'.[89] Palmela was to become one of the most influential Portuguese politicians of the first half of the nineteenth century.

Throughout the winter of 1812–13 Wellington and Beresford remained in constant contact, with letters flowing on an almost daily basis between the two soldiers. Wellington spent nearly three weeks in Cádiz, energising the Spanish war effort and at the same time being placed in overall command of the Spanish army.[90] The remainder of the winter he was based in Freneda while Beresford prepared the Portuguese army from his base in Lisbon. By May 1813 Wellington had some 77,000 British and Portuguese troops at his disposal, in addition to the four main Spanish armies and substantial guerrilla forces. His preparations for the forthcoming campaign must have been bolstered by the knowledge that Napoleon's Russian campaign had ended in disaster, combined with the French withdrawal from Andalucía. When all was said and done, however, France still appeared to be the dominant military power on the European continent at the close of 1812. With up to 200,000 men still in Spain, France was unlikely to abandon its position there without a contest.

PREPARATION FOR AND PARTICIPATION IN THE CAMPAIGN OF 1813, LEADING TO THE INVASION OF FRANCE

13

Back in Lisbon during the winter of 1812–13, Beresford worked hard to maintain and improve the Portuguese army. Whether because of a charm offensive vis-à-vis members of the Regency, or because of the single-minded support of Forjaz, Beresford was able to have the penalties for those chosen by lottery for the army who failed to enlist not only increased but enforced against defaulters.[1] The Provincial Governors were ordered to imprison draft dodgers until they could be brought to the training depots.[2] This stratagem, while resulting in a further stream of recruits, was clearly not sufficient for in mid 1813 Forjaz further limited exemptions from armed service and threatened to extinguish these altogether if sufficient numbers of men were not forthcoming.[3] The latter move, in August 1813, is relevant for the Regency was frequently accused of failing to properly support the war once it had left Portugal's borders; but here we have Forjaz at least taking decisive action to support the cause at a time when the army was in the Pyrénées.

Throughout the winter of 1812–13 Beresford and Forjaz worked not only to fill up the Portuguese regiments but to ensure they were properly clothed and equipped for the forthcoming campaign.[4] By early April, not only had new clothing and shoes been issued to those regiments entitled to them under the procedure established by Beresford, but arrangements had been made to provision the army while on campaign.[5] In the spring of 1813 arrears of pay to the Portuguese army became an issue once again, and these were only reduced when Wellington threatened to give the British monthly subsidy directly to the paymaster of the army should there be no reduction of arrears to the level of arrears in the British army.[6]

On his return from Cádiz, Wellington, now overall commander of the Spanish as well as the Anglo-Portuguese armies, visited Beresford in Lisbon, arriving there on 16 January before proceeding to Freneda on the nineteenth of the month. While in Lisbon it is likely that Wellington discussed the question of succession with Beresford. The issue of second in command and succession, in the case of Wellington's incapacity for whatever reason, had been a topic of correspondence and discussion since at least the previous summer, and it was shortly to be resolved. Wellington's choice of Beresford caused huge difficulties at Horse Guards and with the Commander in Chief, where the position taken was that seniority in the British army should be the deciding factor. We have already seen that there was some unease at Beresford's promotion ahead of others in 1809, but there was considerable disquiet about the potential consequences in the event of Beresford's appointment to succeed Wellington four years later.[7]

Wellington expressed the view to the government and to Beresford that he regarded the position of second in command as pointless. He wrote: 'It has a great and high sounding title, without duties or responsibility of any description', giving rise to pretensions.[8] While the title of second in command might have been useful in the days of 'councils of war' and might look well in a newspaper, Wellington felt that there could be no one who must not see that in a modern army there was nothing for such an appointee to do.[9] If it had been just a question of second in command, it would be easy to attribute Wellington's choice to a desire to have someone he could trust and who clearly supported him in every way possible, rather than run the risk of a new arrival with whom it might be difficult to build the same relationship.

Furthermore, for all their contests with the Regency, Beresford and Forjaz were clearly a most impressive team. Between them, they had rebuilt the Portuguese army almost in its entirety, and Beresford with his officers had ensured it could be fully integrated with its British counterpart. However, Wellington was being asked to advise on his successor in the event of the Marquis, as he then was, being knocked out of the equation. He could have taken the easy way out and left it to the Commander in Chief to appoint a senior general, or he could have put forward another of the generals serving with him, but Wellington followed neither course. Instead, he advocated strongly for the appointment of Beresford. His correspondence makes it clear that it was not just Beresford's position vis-à-vis the Portuguese army that directed his choice, but that he supported him on the basis of Beresford's perceived abilities, notwithstanding the challenges the Marshal had experienced at Albuera and his ill health thereafter.

The position of the Commander in Chief appeared straightforward to the British government. The government's stance was based on historical precedent which dictated that the senior man on site should command the forces and that no senior field officer could be expected to serve under his junior abroad. The implication if that policy was pursued would be for Lieutenant General Sir Thomas Graham (the hero of Barrosa) to assume command in the event of Wellington's unavailability. Additionally, Sir Rowland Hill and Sir Stapleton Cotton were both nominally senior to Beresford. Furthermore, at one stage the government had sent out Sir Edward Paget with a view to him being second in command to Wellington, but he had been captured by the French on 17 November during the retreat from Burgos. Wellington regarded Beresford as the ablest man in the army and justified his choice to Bathurst accordingly:

> All that I can tell you is that the ablest man I have yet seen with the army, and the one having the largest views, is Beresford. They tell me that, when I am not present, he wants decision: and he certainly embarrassed me a little with his doubts when he commanded in Estremadura: but I am quite certain that he is the only person capable of conducting a large concern.[10]

Writing to Beresford Wellington stated: 'I have always felt that you were ready to take upon you any duty which might be imposed upon you, whenever it should be necessary' and that the only reason he had not exercised command, save in Hill's absence, was that he had too many other duties.[11]

Wellington expressed his concern to Lord Bathurst, Secretary for State for War and the Colonies, that Beresford himself would be put in a difficult position and could well resign his appointment in Portugal in the event of someone else being appointed to succeed Wellington.[12] He cleverly used British government precedence against those who argued on seniority by pointing out that as a Marshal in the Portuguese army, Beresford carried precedence in the Allied army over British lieutenant generals, which could only be overcome by the appointment of a different successor to Wellington to the position of Marshal-General; the position held by Wellington.[13] The British government attitude to such a suggestion was that foreign service rank did not count, but that conflicted with previous practice such as when Castaños had been offered command of the Allied army before Albuera but had declined the suggestion. York appreciated the dilemma, telling Bathurst that either Beresford would have to be recalled, or if Wellington maintained his preference for Beresford it would require the recall of all the British lieutenant generals in the Peninsula senior to Beresford.[14] Wellington was at pains to stress that he and Beresford sought a decision on the point, not necessarily in Beresford's favour but so that Beresford should not be placed in an awkward predicament. He felt Beresford should command the Allied army and that would not be inconsistent with a British lieutenant general being appointed to command the British army in the Peninsula.

The outcome of these discussions was far from certain while they were ongoing. In early February Beresford expected to be called home and he asked Wellington to return D'Urban, who had been sent to Trás-os-Montes to assist there, back to Lisbon, presumably to take at least temporary charge of the Portuguese army as Quartermaster General. Beresford felt humiliated at the idea that he should be recalled to facilitate the appointment of another lieutenant general as second in command, and as Wellington's heir apparent in the event of the latter being unable to carry on in command. He went so far as to say he wished he had gone home because of his injuries, as this would have been less humiliating.[15] When Beresford wrote of resignation, Wellington urged him not to take any such step. Wellington thought the ministers in the British government supported his own stance that Beresford should succeed to the command and he was proved right.[16]

Ultimately, the question was resolved in Beresford's favour with the consent of the increasingly blind Graham. He had returned home late in 1812 and talked with Bathurst on the topic. He agreed with Bathurst that his health would not allow him to take on the position of Commander in Chief should the issue ever arise and that he would decline the position if offered. He pointed out that in fact he had served as junior to Beresford at the outset of his military career, but his obligation to the service bound him not to sacrifice the rights of British officers from a spirit of purely personal accommodation. The stratagem agreed with Graham was that since he would decline the post in any event, no precedent would be created and that the arrangement was temporary.[17] Cotton was then somewhat unwillingly persuaded to agree on the same basis.[18] Graham returned to the Peninsula for the 1813 campaign but departed for home following the battle of Vitória, hoping to retire. However, he was prevailed upon to lead a poorly conceived operation to the Low Countries in early 1814.[19]

The correspondence on the issue of Wellington's successor does throw light as to why Hill had been placed in command of the force operating in the south along the Portuguese–Spanish border in the first place and how he came to be replaced by Beresford when ill in late 1810. In a lengthy letter dated 12 February 1813, Beresford recollected that when the corps to guard the southern gateway to Portugal was first formed (1809) Wellington had offered Beresford the command but that given the state of the Portuguese army and his desire to give it his personal attention, he had felt it his duty to refuse. Hill was then named to lead this corps and it was to avoid difficulties when Hill left that Beresford accepted command on a temporary basis. Those difficulties were clearly outlined by Beresford in his letter, and it was because of a concern that if a senior general was appointed to Hill's command he might be unwilling to vacate it on Hill's return that led Beresford to offer his services, specifically as the locum tenens of Hill.[20]

Portugal may have been rid of the French invader for over a year, but the toll of in excess of five years warfare was visible almost everywhere, a factor which needs to be taken into account in any commentary on the Portuguese war effort. There are many accounts of the physical destruction of Portuguese towns and villages, particularly those in Beira; but the destruction of crops, and lack of animals for breeding, working and feeding the populace was extensive. The countryside was a dangerous place with *banditti* roaming even areas frequented by the Allied army. To combat this threat Beresford had infantry patrols on the road to Nisa and Villa Velha, and in January 1813 had a friend organise a *chasse* on the left bank of the Tagus to keep the *banditti* away.[21] It is likely that such moves only offered temporary relief, for having returned from Lisbon to his headquarters at Freneda towards the end of January, Wellington, in thanking the Marshal for looking after his own security, sent Beresford a report of the murder of a sergeant and a soldier of the 9th Light Dragoons by *banditti* on the road from Abrantes to Alter do Chão.[22] Beresford, having discussed the threat caused by the *banditti* with the Regency, determined that the only way to inhibit them was to allocate cavalry regiments to take responsibility for the area as the *banditti* were themselves mostly mounted.[23]

Beresford's efforts to prepare the Portuguese army for the campaign of 1813 were successful.[24] Following his own second operation to alleviate the wound suffered at Salamanca, he made a rapid recovery and was able to join Wellington at his headquarters at Freneda on 1

May.[25] While he led the Portuguese army in the campaign, Beresford was closely involved with Wellington's strategy and its implementation, not because he was now 'second in command' but because Wellington respected his views and wished for his input. Wellington confided his plans for the year to Beresford on 24 April, three weeks before informing the government.[26] Notwithstanding the withdrawal of French forces to fight in northern Europe, Wellington still faced French armies numbering some 90,000, with the prospect of Suchet sending further help from eastern Spain. To counter the French under Jourdan and Joseph, Wellington had between 77,000 and 81,000 men, made up of 52,000 British, 29,000 Portuguese; to which must be added the increasingly effective Spanish guerrilla forces operating behind French lines in the Asturias and Navarre. In due course he was also joined by the Spanish Fourth Army, a force of some 25,000 men now commanded by General Giron.[27]

Wellington deceived the French into believing his main army was retracing its steps to Burgos via Salamanca, while he despatched Graham with a powerful left wing over the Douro in Portugal, a force which was to continuously threaten to get behind the French right as it retreated hastily to the Ebro and from there to Vitória, where it was routed on 21 June 1813. With the exception of San Sebastián, Santoña and Pamplona, French resistance in northern Spain was now at an end, though Suchet continued to dispose of considerable forces in Catalonia until virtually the end of the war.

Wellington paid tribute to the performance of the Portuguese troops at the battle of Vitória, praising in particular those serving with the 3rd and 4th divisions under the command of Brigadier General Power and Colonel Stubbs, who 'led the march with steadiness and gallantry never surpassed on any occasion'.[28] Praising Graham and Hill for the manner in which they led the two wings of the army, he did not forget to mention Beresford, who though he lacked a specific role was commended for 'the friendly advice and assistance which I have received from him upon all occasions during the late operations'.[29] Wellington's attention to detail on this as on other occasions was impressive. When preparing a return of the officers for the Vitória medal, he enquired of Beresford whether his Portuguese Adjutant-General and Secretary had been in the action and would therefore be entitled to be honoured accordingly.[30] A copy of Beresford's reply has not been located.

The importance of the destruction of the largest French army in Spain was quickly appreciated in Britain, where Wellington was appointed Field Marshal in early July. Torrens thought there had never been an English baton and rather intriguingly stated to Wellington he would get one prepared to present to 'each of our Marshals'.[31] Napoleon's reaction to the disastrous rout of the French army at Vitória was to appoint the experienced Soult to command the army facing Wellington. Soult, who had been recalled from Spain in late 1812, travelled from northern Europe at speed and reached Bayonne on 11 July. With characteristic energy he set about rebuilding the forces available to him. Rather than attempt to form a defensive line on the Pyrénées, his first thoughts were to attempt the relief of both Pamplona and San Sebastián, the two major fortresses still in French possession in northern Spain. In a series of punishing engagements, the French at first forced the Allies back, recapturing the passes at Maya and Roncevalles, before the Allied army rallied at Sorauren, only kilometres from Pamplona.

Following these very testing exchanges in the Pyrénées, Wellington sent a lengthy report to Bathurst during which he again gave prominent mention to Beresford and the Portuguese troops:

> Marshal Sir W. Beresford was with me throughout these operations; and I received from him all the assistance which his talents so well qualify him to afford me. The good conduct of the Portuguese officers and troops in all the operations of the present campaign, and the spirit which they show on every occasion, are not less honourable to that nation than they are to the military character of the officer who, by his judicious measures, has re-established discipline, and renewed a military spirit in the army.[32]

There was no equivocation in Wellington's praise for Beresford's rebuilding of the Portuguese army. Of that army, the Judge-Advocate General, Francis Larpent, reported in July 1813: 'Lord Wellington talking of the Portuguese, said that it was extraordinary just now, to observe their conduct; that no troops could behave better; that they never had now a notion of turning; and that nothing could equal their forwardness now, and willing, ready tempers.'[33]

Wellington hesitated to invade France, even though he told Bathurst on 8 August that he did not doubt he could do so and reach the River Adour (this river flows into the Atlantic at Bayonne, having risen in the Pyrénées flowing north before turning westward to the sea). The reason for his hesitancy was his concern that if the 'Powers of the North' made peace with Napoleon to the exclusion of Britain and those in the Peninsula, the Allied army would of necessity have to withdraw into Spain and he feared a very difficult retreat. The concern that one or more parties might do a deal with Napoleon which would leave him on the throne of France was one which was to haunt British statesmen and military leaders until virtually the end of the campaign. Wellington was merely being prudent at a time when in fact a ceasefire was in place in northern Europe, and indeed had just been renewed with a view by at least some to negotiating peace.

Beresford and Wellington both suffered some ill health in August but both were improving by the middle of the month. However, Beresford was no sooner recovered than it became necessary for him to return to Lisbon to cajole the Regency into making greater efforts to support the Portuguese army, now encamped on the French border nearly 1,000 kilometres from Lisbon. In mid September he returned there, arriving on 18 September after a sea passage of seven days from San Sebastián. Beresford had to address the perennial problem of funds for the army, though it was hoped the introduction of an income tax would ameliorate the situation. At this time he was having his 'new house' in Lisbon prepared, but was disappointed to find it was not yet ready and he was obliged to stay in the centre of the city. He wrote to his sister Anne, telling her he was determined to visit England during the winter unless unforeseen circumstances intervened, though the government did not like the idea of a lengthy absence, even after five years service. In the event no more was heard of the proposal to leave the Peninsula even for a short while and on his birthday (2 October) Beresford headed back to France on an available frigate.[34]

The British government was at this stage already putting forward the suggestion that the Portuguese royal family and court return to Lisbon. Wellington supported the proposal and the British Minister at Lisbon, Charles Stuart, felt a return was likely.[35] However, on this as on other future occasions, Prince João was not to be moved from Rio de Janeiro. Before Beresford left for Lisbon that autumn, Wellington had suggested he be granted a pension for his services to the crown and Bathurst supported the suggestion, noting that if peers for military services should be made at the close of the campaign, Sir William's name should not be omitted; and that with a peerage would come an entitlement to a pension.[36]

No sooner had Beresford departed for Lisbon than the spectre of Wellington's 'second in command' raised its head again. On this occasion it arose by virtue of the appointment of Sir John Hope to Wellington's staff. Hope was considerably senior to Beresford in the British military hierarchy and rumours were circulating that he was being appointed Wellington's second in command; rumours which Colonel Torrens, as Military Secretary to the Commander in Chief, moved to quell. He informed Wellington that he had written to Sir John to the effect no such term was applied to his appointment on Wellington's staff, but that he would be next in seniority, with the command of a division. Hope had replied that he would not have wished any such vague appointment as that of second in command without the charge of troops.[37] The appointment of Wellington as a Field Marshal in the British army following the battle of Vitória meant that Hope, a Lieutenant General senior to Wellington, could serve under Wellington without having to be concerned about issues of seniority. His position vis-à-vis Beresford was full of uncertainty and when Wellington was considering going to Catalonia in October he observed: 'How I am to settle the rank and pretensions of the gentlemen left behind I am sure I do not know.'[38] In the event he never had to make that decision as Wellington did not go to Catalonia.

Beresford had to face a further effort by the Regency to dislodge him as Commander in Chief of the Portuguese army in the autumn of 1813, though this does not seem to have been a factor in his visit to Lisbon. Once again the move was led by Principal Sousa, who was promoting the notion that General Silveira should replace Beresford. Anti-British sentiment had emerged again once the Allied army had moved into Spain, and on this occasion Forjaz appears to have supported Sousa while rejecting the notion that Silveira should be appointed as Beresford's successor, even on a provisional basis.[39] Wellington was having none of it, summarily dismissing both the proposal and Silveira's abilities stating: 'He possesses not one military quality; and he has been repeatedly guilty of courting popularity with the common soldiers, by flattering their vices, and by impunity from their misconduct. Such a man will not do in this army!'[40]

By mid October Beresford was back in Navarra with the Allied army having spent a mere two weeks in Lisbon. On his return he was based at Errazu; mid way between Wellington's headquarters at Bera and the French frontier fortress of Saint-Jean-Pied-de-Port. He had missed the crossing of the Bidasoa on 7 October when the Allied army moved into France, but now in command of the 3rd, 4th and 7th divisions he was at the front of Wellington's plans for a further push into southwest France.[41] By the end of the month he was about to undertake Wellington's request to move more to the centre (westwards), on the basis that Hill would be moving north to Beresford's right following the anticipated surrender of Pamplona.[42] Pamplona surrendered on 31 October, removing the last serious French stronghold in Spain other than those in Catalonia.[43] This opened the way for the campaign, which took the army to the gates of Bayonne before the weather became impossible for forward manoeuvres in late December. That campaign was to witness two important battles, the first the crossing of the River Nivelle on 10 November, the second the crossing of the River Nive a month later on 9 December.

The crossing of the Nivelle was in fact postponed from early November because of inclement weather, including early snow in the mountains. When it did take place, on 10 November, the Allied left comprising the 1st and 5th divisions was commanded by Hope. Beresford commanded the centre, including the 3rd, 4th and 7th divisions, which descended from the heights of La Maya, Zugarramurdi and Etxalar; while the right under Hill, including the 2nd Division, the Portuguese division and the Spanish corps under Pablo Morillo, came north from the valley of Baztan.

Beresford's advance following the capture of La Petite Rhune took him to the small village of Ibarren de St Pé (Saint-Pée-sur-Nivelle) about fourteen kilometres inland. For their part in the advance, the 11th Caçadores, and the 9th and 21st Portuguese regiments received honourable mention along with a number of British regiments. Beresford and Hill were highlighted in Bathurst's congratulatory letter to Wellington after the engagement, based of course on Wellington's report.[44] The French still fought well, but the troops were now becoming dispirited, and morale cannot have been helped by the news which reached Bayonne the day before that Napoleon had suffered a major reverse in Germany at the battle of Leipzig.[45] The French lost a reported fifty-two guns at the battle of La Nivelle, a huge number though dwarfed by the 150 guns lost at Vitória.[46] Following the battle, the Allies were welcomed by residents into Saint-Jean-de-Luz, a large fishing port where the river enters the sea.[47] Here Wellington set up his headquarters.

From mid November Beresford was based in or near Ustaritz, a small town at the navigable limits on the River Nive at the foot of the Pyrénées.[48] Some thirteen kilometres from Bayonne, then under partial blockade, Ustaritz is double that distance from Saint-Jean-de-Luz, a journey that was no trouble to either Wellington or Beresford, which they made frequently during the winter. Wellington reportedly spent the night before the battle of the Nive at Beresford's château at Ustaritz.[49] The French were always close by, calling for defensive alertness as well as preparations for moving forward when the weather and circumstances would permit. Bridges were built and taken down and troops were continuously on the move.

The battle of the Nive, which resulted in the Allies reaching the outskirts of Bayonne, was fought on 9 December. Hope led the left wing of the army and reported to Wellington that:

> the conduct of the Portuguese troops on this occasion is particularly deserving of commendation in common with the British troops, they having maintained their ground under disadvantageous circumstances; and when hard pressed or forced to retire before superior numbers, they rallied with great readiness, and in spite of all opposition re-occupied their ground.[50]

Beresford's command was in the centre of the line at the battle of Nive and he pointed out himself that while he began the movement, his troops faced little or no resistance given that the French attacked the two wings. He was full of praise for Hill, telling Lady Anne Beresford: 'Rowland Hill cannot be praised enough. I brought up my troops to support him but he did the business right well himself.'[51]

When the French attempted a breakout from St Pierre, a suburb of Bayonne, on 13 December trying to force the Allied centre, the Portuguese again received favourable mention in the report on the encounter, with specific individuals receiving mention in the 14th and 18th regiments of line in addition to those in the 6th Caçadores.[52] Beresford added his own praise of the Portuguese to that of others: 'the Portuguese are praised by all and nothing could be finer than their conduct, it would be injustice to praise them above the British or the British above them.'[53] While the two armies then went into winter quarters, there was a certain amount of skirmishing along the River Adour, which flows into the Atlantic at Bayonne; important because of the use of the river for bringing in supplies. The engagements resulted in the seizure of islands and barges. Soult for his part had a number of dykes broken to cause flooding in the area.

From his winter quarters in Ustaritz, Beresford targeted both the lack of finance and the failure of the Regency to forward recruits to replace losses. Arrears of pay were now running at eight months for many Portuguese regiments. Beresford wrote furiously to Forjaz, and the situation was only partly ameliorated because while 200,000 dollars was sent from Lisbon (presumably part of the British subvention), further funds were supplied in Portuguese paper money, which was not acceptable to many as it could only be redeemed in Portugal.[54] With the assistance of Stuart in Lisbon, 1,000 recruits were sent to France in January 1814 from the depot at Mafra, where they had received initial training under General Blunt. A further 2,600 men were dispatched in March 1814, though these must have arrived too late to partake in the fighting.[55]

The campaign of 1813 had been a truly remarkable one. Within eight weeks of leaving Portugal the Allied army was on the French frontier. By Christmas it was ensconced in southwest France, having recovered the last strongholds in northern Spain in French hands and having beaten Soult's forces in the Pyrénées and crossed the rivers Bidasoa, Nivelle and Nive. It was poised to launch itself further into France once winter receded and subject to being resupplied. The latter task was now much easier logistically, given Allied control of the ports along the coast of northern Spain and its possession of Saint-Jean-de-Luz. Beresford had played his part in the advance of 1813, but 1814 was to give him the opportunity to show his talents once again. Before Wellington could move forward, however, he needed to find sufficient funds to pay both the British and Portuguese armies. He chose to leave most of the Spanish forces available in Spain, partly because they too were not fed or paid properly, but more so because of their inclination to plunder – caused by these problems – and by a desire to exact revenge for years of mistreatment at the hands of Napoleon's armies. His determination to forbid plunder, and the harsh retribution exacted on those involved in such actions, meant that the Allied army was largely welcomed in France by a populace who could hardly believe their luck at receiving payment for goods from foreigners when they had been plundered by their own armies.

When the Allies paused for two months before advancing forward in a meaningful way, it gave the opportunity for relaxation for those who could escape the rigours of the Pyrenean winter. Wellington held a ball in Saint-Jean-de-Luz which Beresford attended, along with local notables. Officers and men organised shoots and there may have been hunting, for the Pau Hunt can trace its evolution back to that winter, though the Allies did not occupy Pau until March 1814.[56] Wellington and others had hunted extensively during the winters at Freneda, and there were several packs of hounds sent out from the British Isles to Portugal. Additionally, there were probably regimental theatricals as these had been a feature at the times when the army was resting in the Peninsula.[57] Morale was now high and Beresford's observation that 'Bonaparte's building must now fall and peace is at hand' must have been one shared by many of his colleagues.[58] Beresford was on horseback each day from before daylight until after dark. He was fatigued but reported that his health was good.[59] Beresford was keen to leave the Pyrénées, which had now been in the army's sight since June, observing 'it is impossible that even we Irish people could have had a conception of the eternal rain that drenches this country. The only difference I see between it and the monsoon in India is that there the rain is periodical, here continual.'[60]

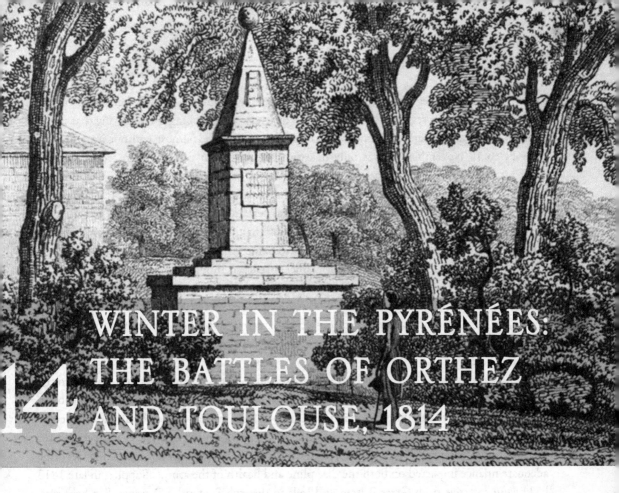

WINTER IN THE PYRÉNÉES: THE BATTLES OF ORTHEZ AND TOULOUSE, 1814

14

'Ah Messieurs, pourquoi n'êtes vous pas venus plutot,
we have long anxiously looked for you'[1]

Two substantial challenges faced the Allies in southwest France at the beginning of 1814. These were the weather and finance. The first Wellington could do nothing about, but the winter of 1813–14 was a particularly bad one in northern Europe. In the British Isles it was one of the five coldest on record, with the Thames freezing over in London and so much snowfall in Dublin that people were trapped in their houses for days.[2] For an entire month, from 27 December 1813 to 28 January 1814, there were sub-zero temperatures in much of the United Kingdom and the situation in France was clearly not much better. The diaries and letters of Allied officers in south west France are full of comments on the weather, and it is clear that both before and after the new year meteorological conditions hindered Wellington's plans. He himself, in his correspondence with Bathurst, referred 'to the impossibility of marching in this country in the rainy season' and after the battle of the Nivelle, the British commissariat had difficulty in supplying the Allied army, with the result that the advance was inhibited.[3]

Wellington had intended to advance and cross the Nive after the battle of the Nivelle but 'was prevented by the bad state of the roads, and the swelling of all the rivulets occasioned by

199

the fall of rain in the beginning of that month' (November).[4] Indeed, the weather was so bad by 18 November that the regiments were placed in quarters, with Wellington observing that it was impractical for any general movement of troops as it had rained 'almost without intermission' from 11 to 19 November.[5] It was only in early December that conditions improved enough to let him move forward. Then, later in December, the weather closed in again. For much of January Beresford operated from his base in the château at Ustaritz, ensuring that the French did not break out south of the Adour. His comfort was certainly not shared by all, with Sir George L'Estrange reporting that men were sleeping out in tents in the snow.[6] There were amusements for officers, such as the ball held by Wellington in Saint-Jean-de-Luz on 11 February, and food seems to have been in adequate supply for officers at least, though Beresford was to complain later at the price of provisions.[7] There was some sport to be had, with quail and other birds being shot in the Pyrénées. In February 1814, Wellington decided to advance after a few dry days, but no sooner had he put the army in motion than sharp frosts and heavy snow were reported in the foothills of the Pyrénées and as late as 3 March, when the Allied army was at Aire, there was snow and sleet.[8]

Finance, or the lack of it, greatly exercised Wellington at this time. He put it bluntly to the British government: 'It is vain to expect to be able to continue to carry on our operations through the winter, unless we should be supplied with money from England, and should be enabled to bring round from Cádiz and Lisbon the sums which we may get at those places respectively, for bills upon the Treasury.'[9] Wellington acted decisively for he knew from experience that securing adequate finance impacted on both the discipline and health of the army.[10] Supplies in late 1813 had begun to arrive from Great Britain and Ireland through Santander, Passages, San Sebastián and Saint-Jean-de-Luz using a sea route much shorter than that to Lisbon or Porto. However, French and American privateers continued to intercept some of these vessels and Wellington railed against the inadequate support he felt was being supplied by the Royal Navy. Indeed, supplies meant to come up from Cádiz and Lisbon by sea could not be moved for a lack of warships. The pay of both British and Portuguese troops was now many months in arrears. On 8 December, Wellington complained to Bathurst about the lack of money, noting that the pay of the troops was six months in arrears; and that the Spanish and Portuguese were equally unprovided with money.[11] It was with the greatest difficulty that suppliers were prepared to procure provisions of all sorts on foot of bills drawn either on the British or Portuguese treasuries.

The Spaniards that remained with Wellington were no better off, with the Allied commander having to provision them from time to time.[12] By mid December the situation was so bad that Wellington complained to Bathurst that he was overwhelmed with debts and he went on: 'I can scarcely stir out of my house on account of the public creditors waiting to demand payment of what is due to them.'[13] The situation was somewhat relieved with the arrival of $200,000, part of the British subsidy, from Lisbon for the Portuguese army; but the extremity in which Wellington found himself is clearly shown by his having to borrow $50,000 of that sum to 'keep the Spaniards together' and a further $10,000 'to keep the British cavalry from perishing'. Wellington claimed he could push the enemy to the Garonne in the winter if he had money, but that he could not move at all and that British credit was already destroyed in France.[14] Later in the month, when money arrived from England on the *Garland*, Wellington had to allocate some of it to the Spanish and Portuguese to honour British commitments.[15] It was a juggling act in which Wellington was restricted to looking after the most pressing claims.[16]

The British government was stung into action by Wellington's complaints. A senior officer, Colonel H. Bunbury, then Under-Secretary for War, was sent out to Saint-Jean-de-Luz in order to explain to Wellington the government's difficulties and with instructions to listen to Wellington's views so as to enable a more certain and streamlined financial provision to be made in the future. In the second week of January the *Medina* arrived with $482,000, which equated to approximately £106,000. However, Wellington understood he was to send some of that to the army in Catalonia. He reminded Bathurst that even if he was to receive the entire amount it would only pay the British troops for one month.[17] At the end of the month $400,000 dollars arrived from Cádiz for the Spaniards, money which should have arrived on 1 November 1813.[18] Then the *Desirée* arrived at Passages on 3 February with £400,000, enabling Wellington to declare that he would begin to move as soon as he got the money up to Saint-Jean-de-Luz, by which time he hoped the rain would have ceased a little.[19]

Wellington was now able to release a further $50,000 to Beresford for the Portuguese army, telling him he proposed to move as soon as they had two or three days fair weather.[20] The distribution to the benefit of the Portuguese army was sorely needed, for the paper money sent by the Regency, which had only been accepted with reluctance in Portugal, was of no use outside the country, causing Beresford to state in early January: 'that by reason of the absolute lack of means that the army finds itself, it will not be able to maintain itself any longer.'[21] Orders for movement of part of the army involving both Beresford and Hill's divisions were then issued by Wellington on 10 February, with the intention of opening the campaign.[22] While there were still arrears, the crisis had passed. It was further ameliorated by monies procured by Nathan Meyer Rothschild on behalf of the British government, though these sums only began to arrive towards the end of the campaign.[23]

Notwithstanding the shortage of money and the inevitable delays in bringing up supplies, the Anglo-Portuguese army had wintered well.[24] In November 1813, Wellington had written to Bathurst stating that 'although the army was never in such health, heart and condition as at present; and it is probably the most complete machine for its numbers now existing in Europe, the rain has so completely destroyed the roads that I cannot move'. He went on to praise the troops but stressed that everything depended on their moderation and discipline. He observed that 'hitherto these have behaved well, and there appears a new spirit among the officers, which I hope will continue, to keep the troops in order'. One reason the army had wintered so well was that Wellington continuously emphasised the need to treat the inhabitants of France with respect, paying for goods and services. He was able to report back to the Minister for War that:

> the natives of this part of the country are not only reconciled to the invasion, but wish us success, afford us all the supplies in their power, and exert themselves to get intelligence for us. In no part of Spain have we been better, I might say so well, received; because we really draw more supply from the country than we ever did from any part of Spain.[25]

Likewise Beresford informed his half-sister Anne, 'it is not easy to describe the good will we are everywhere received with, and the efforts of the inhabitants to be useful to us even against their own army'.[26] There were exceptions to this welcome, particularly at Bidarry and Baïgorry (two communities close to the Franco-Spanish border and adjacent to the Maya valley). In late January Beresford reported to Wellington their hostility. Wellington ascribed this development to the rapacity with which the Spaniards had treated the natives when they had been plundered by Mina's troops. Nonetheless his reaction was severe, composing a letter to the inhabitants in both French and Basque telling them that they were acting differently to others, their conduct was unacceptable and if they wanted to wage war they should join the army. In a side note to Beresford, Wellington authorised him to send an even tougher message with the officer chosen to deliver the letter; namely that if there was any further reason for complaint: 'I will act towards them as the French did towards the towns and villages in Spain and Portugal; that is, I will totally destroy them, and hang up all the people belonging to them that I shall find.'[27]

Though in fine order, the army was suffering from a lack of men to replace those lost in battle and those who had deserted. Wellington was particularly critical of some of the German replacements sent out from England who deserted when in France, though many of these may have been men previously in the French service who had been captured and sent to England as prisoners. Of the Portuguese he observed that they did not desert to go over to the enemy, but to return home, a feature which may be indicative of war fatigue, for many had now been fighting for six years and the rationale for continuing to do so was weakened the further they advanced from their own frontier. Their government, in the form of the Regency, appeared to be suffering from a lack of enthusiasm for a now distant war, though the delay in sending recruits to the Portuguese army in France, referred to in the previous chapter, may have reflected a degree of discontent with the lack of credit given to the Portuguese army for the advance through Spain and into France by the British government and media, as well as a desire to save costs.[28] There was also irritation at the unwillingness of Spanish suppliers to accept bills drawn by the Portuguese commissary, notwithstanding an agreement with the Spanish government that goods supplied would be paid half in cash and half by way of such bills.[29]

There were over 9,000 Portuguese recruits reportedly ready to travel from Lisbon in January 1814, but despite Wellington sending eight transports for them to Lisbon, Forjaz did not give the necessary orders for embarkation. Indeed, there were now so many recruits that even though a new military school was established, they caused concern in Lisbon and conscription was stopped. At the end of the month Forjaz weakened his stance sufficiently to order 1,000 recruits who had been trained at Mafra go on board the transports destined for France.[30] In February, Beresford requested a further dispatch of recruits be sent by land if sea transport was not available; but transports arrived in Lisbon and Stuart was able to report that 2,600 had gone on board and sailed in mid March, though of course these can have played only a limited part in the final weeks of the campaign. At the same time, the training school in Mafra was relocated to Lisbon to allow for the refurbishment of the palace at Mafra in anticipation of the return of Prince João from Rio de Janeiro.[31]

Loss of men, whatever the cause, threatened to disrupt Wellington's plans. Some idea of the scale of the problem may be gleaned from his assertion in January 1814 that 30,000 had been wounded since June 1813 and thousands of these were still in hospital or on convalescent leave. Further, he was battling with the Spanish local government in Santander, who were claiming that the British hospital there should be closed down due to an alleged epidemic of fever. Nevertheless he still felt able to state to his brother, Sir Henry Wellesley, on 14 January that 'during the five years I have commanded the army, I have never known it so healthy as it is, and has been since the month of May last'.[32]

Soult, in contrast, had fought four major battles on both sides of the Pyrénées resulting in a French withdrawal on each occasion, including three defeats in October, November and December 1813 when the Allies crossed the Bidasoa, the Nivelle and the Nive respectively. The Allies now controlled much of the left bank of the Adour above Bayonne and could intercept supplies to the beleaguered city. In addition, Soult had been required to send further troops north to assist Napoleon. Thus in January he was deprived of 12,000 of his best infantry, half his cavalry and thirty cannon, all of which made their way northward.[33] In theory Soult was to be be assisted by the Army of the Reserve, that Napoleon had decreed should be established in November 1813. It was intended to be comprised of forty battalions raised in cities across the south of France including Bordeaux, Toulouse, Montpellier and Nîmes. Fresh recruits were to prove no match for Wellington's veterans.

Napoleon had released Ferdinand of Spain having agreed terms, the Treaty of Valençay, with the Spanish King which if approved by the Cortes would remove Spain from the war. Those terms were not approved but in a moment of supreme optimism the Emperor suggested at one point that Soult leave only a screening force in the south and march with his army to the Loire.[34] The Army of the Pyrénées was chronically short of money, and while living off the land had been the norm for the French abroad, forced requisition with paper money caused huge antipathy at home.[35] The effect on French army morale must have been adverse. In danger of being outflanked, he left a large garrison in Bayonne and moved the remainder of his army westwards along the right bank of the Adour, and from there south into the foothills of the Pyrénées so as to protect the fertile district of the Béarn and Departments further north and east.

Soult moved his own headquarters to Peyrehorade on the Adour before Christmas. Some idea of the natural defensive qualities of the Adour may be gleaned from the fact that it is tidal as far as Peyrehorade, nearly forty kilometres from the sea.[36] The French Marshal fully realised the importance of holding the line of the Adour; and to this end he flooded areas of land adjacent to the river. To the south of the Adour, Soult's forces held Saint-Palais and Saint-Jean-Pied-de-Port at the outset of 1814, and a number of rivers that flowed north from the Pyrénées before joining the Adour offered defensive positions. If Wellington breached this line it would be hard to create a new defensive line south of the Garonne. It was through this ring that Wellington would have to break out if he was to advance further into France. Throughout January Soult remained aggressive, pushing the Allies back around Port-de-Lanne and Hasparren, while forcing the Spanish out of the Ossau Valley.

Wellington determined to threaten the French left with a view to forcing Soult to reinforce that area and to reduce his ability to cover Bayonne, which Wellington left Sir John Hope to invest. When fine but cold weather arrived on 10 February, orders were given to Beresford to defend the area between the Nive and the Adour with the 4th, 6th and 7th divisions while Hill was designated to move on Hasparren supported by Cotton and the cavalry.[37]

Wellington's instructions were conveyed in the form of simultaneous written orders by Quartermaster General George Murray to Hill, Beresford and Cotton, so that each knew not only what was expected of him, but also the directions given to the others. On 14 February, the long awaited advance commenced with Hill now being supported by Morillo's Spanish division, which had been quartered in the Baztan Valley. In all Hill had about 28,000 men. Wellington was close by, with his headquarters in Hasparren, and it was he who directed the successful attack on Garris the next day. Earlier that afternoon, from the heights above Isturits, Wellington had sent Beresford orders to tighten up the line, as he was concerned that even though the French were retiring, it was over extended.[38] Wellington had reports that the enemy intended to stand on the Bidouze, but himself felt that the Gave was a more likely point for them to attempt to hold the Allies.[39] On the night of 15/16 February the French evacuated Saint-Palais, crossing the Gave de Mauléon the following day. On 16 February, Beresford with the 4th and 7th divisions crossed the Joyeuse, occupying the heights above La Bastide-Clairence. Care was needed, for D'Armagnac's division was pushed forward from Peyrehorade on the left bank of the Adour. While Hill pressed on, Beresford's force was in effect used to prevent Soult acquiring reinforcements from his right, now tenuously maintaining contact with Bayonne.[40]

For eleven days from 14 February Soult's divisions retired, crossing a series of rivers and then holding these against the Allies for a short time before resuming the retreat. In this way the Allies crossed the Joyeuse, the Bidouze, the Saison and the Gave d'Oléron. In vain the French destroyed the bridges after crossing the rivers. Soult realised that the move to outflank his left was Wellington's intention and to combat this threat he moved continuously to the east. This had the desired effect of drawing his forces away from Bayonne, leaving that city to its own devices. He wrote to the Minister for War, correctly analysing Wellington's intention 'to turn my left with General Hill's corps, whilst that of Marshal Beresford will move on the Bidouze to attack the divisions which I have allotted to the defence of that river'.[41] Soult's pleas for reinforcements went unheeded, as did his warnings that he would have to concentrate his army as he could no longer keep an extended line. Having passed over the river Saison he formed a line on the Gave d'Oléron and the Adour from Navarrenx to Peyrehorade.

Wellington made a fast return trip to Saint-Jean-de-Luz from 19 to 21 February, to oversee progress designed to put the Allies across the Adour between Bayonne and the sea so as to complete the encirclement of that city. Late on 21 February he arrived back at Garris, from where he planned the next advance. With a view to forcing Soult's left flank he brought the Light and 6th divisions east to join Hill, leaving Beresford to threaten, but essentially to hold, the French from Urt on the Adour upstream to perhaps ten kilometres beyond Peyrehorade. Part of this deception involved the collection of boats on the Adour for a putative crossing. Soult's new defensive line was quickly breached. Between Navarrenx and Sauveterre-de-Béarn, the Gave d'Oléron was forded in several places on 24 February.[42] Leaving the Spanish to invest Navarrenx, Hill forced the French to abandon Sauveterre-de-Béarn on 24 February.[43] Soult meanwhile had left Sauveterre on 22 February for Orthez, a small town on the right side of the Gave de Pau with steep hills facing the river and several means of retreat behind it, whether northwards to Dax and Bordeaux or to Saint-Sever and eastwards towards Toulouse. While the French began to prepare positions for the defence of Orthez, Soult remained concerned that the Allies might continue to move to their right towards Pau and Tarbes, threatening all the while his own left wing.

Prior to Hill's force mounting the offensive across the Gave d'Oléron on 24 February, Wellington ordered Beresford to distract the French by threatening their right wing. With the 7th Division he overran the French advance posts south of the Adour at Hastingues and Oeyregave on 23 February, obliging them to retire within the *tête de pont* at Peyrehorade before retreating across the river. The retreating French then blew up the bridge at Peyrehorade. Meanwhile Beresford pushed the 4th Division towards Sorde-l'Abbaye, covering his own right flank with Vivian's cavalry. Simultaneously, Hope was moving his forces across the mouth of the Adour to invest Bayonne and all these movements formed part of Wellington's overall strategy, which was designed to shock and force back the French all along their extended line, preventing any part giving succour to the other. The advance was Wellington at his strategic and tactical best.

The French army then passed to the right bank of the Gave de Pau, concentrating on Orthez. There were only two bridges over the river in the locality, one at Orthez and the second at Bérenx. The latter was successfully blown up by the retreating French, but that at Orthez was only partially damaged due to its solid construction. The tower on it approaching the right bank was then fortified. Between the two bridges the land rises steeply on either side of the river, which narrows and deepens which would have made fording it a considerable challenge in winter. On 26 February, however, the 3rd Division and the Hussars crossed at a ford below Bérenx.

Beresford, meanwhile, with the 4th and 7th divisions preceded by Vivian's cavalry, had crossed both the Gave d'Oléron and the Gave de Pau above where those two rivers join before emptying into the Adour just below Peyrehorade. For some days prior to 25 February, his scouts had been testing the fords on the Gave d'Oléron. These had been fortified by the French with stakes and with upturned harrows. The crossing of the Gave de Pau was at Cauneille, where an unguarded ford was shown to Beresford by a local man.[44] An early morning crossing was followed by a rapid march up the right bank through Puyoô before reaching Baigts that evening. Reports vary, but Beresford probably reached Baigts between 3 pm and 5 pm. Wellington now had Beresford's force, together with Somerset's cavalry and the 3rd Division of his army together with their artillery, on the right bank of the Gave de Pau. Beresford's pontoon bridge men were sent to Bérenx where they laid down a bridge to enable the 6th and Light divisions to cross over on the morning of 27 February. Only Hill's 2nd Division and the Portuguese Division then remained to menace Orthez on the left bank of the river in front of the town and threatened to outflank Soult by moving to cross upstream.

Beresford suggests that his success in crossing the Gave de Pau with the 4th and 7th divisions prompted Wellington to pull his own forces from the right using the passage of Bérenx to bring across the remainder of the army to face Orthez, the implication being that had Beresford not crossed the Gave de Pau, Wellington might himself have crossed it with the main army above Orthez, once again threatening to get in behind Soult's left.[45] Wellington does not appear to mention this point, but of course it was the success of the Allied right that caused Soult to withdraw his divisions on the Adour to Orthez, thus rendering Beresford's crossing unopposed. In any event, Beresford was delighted, for as he put it to his half brother, John Poo Beresford, 'this from being in the rear threw me into the front'.[46]

While Wellington prepared for battle the following day, both he and Beresford felt it more likely that Soult would retreat once again.[47] Beresford's advance along the right bank of the Gave de Pau had been so rapid that when he had stopped to consolidate his forces after pushing the French out of Puyoô, he had had time to write to his half-sister Anne. After explaining that he was without baggage or servants (presumably because of the speed of the march), he noted the location of the French army 'as about 6 miles from where I am, but it will be undoubtedly off in the night and there will be no chance of catching it this side of the Garonne'.[48] Despite being urged by Clausel, one of his corps commanders, Soult had missed an opportunity during the afternoon of 26 February to attack Wellington when only part of the Allied army was across the Gave de Pau. Soult in fact determined to fight the following day and placed the right of his army on the heights at Saint-Boès covering also the Dax road. The centre, including the divisions of D'Erlon, Foy and d'Armagnac, stretched from there to Orthez with Clausel on the left. His cavalry, under Pierre Soult, covered the road from Orthez to Pau. While he prepared to fight, Soult had one eye on withdrawal. He established a reserve artillery park at Aire and moved part of his administration to Saint-Sever.

The structure of the battle of Orthez involved Beresford with the 4th and 7th Divisions supported by Vivian's cavalry making the initial attack on Saint-Boès as Wellington deemed this to be the key to forcing the French back.[49] The 3rd and 6th divisions were for the time being held on the Bayonne–Orthez road just below the town, while the artillery and Light Division were placed on a height to support Beresford. Hill was instructed to cross the river above Orthez. The initial attack under Beresford was made by Cole's 4th Division. They had to cover extensive marshy ground before climbing steep hills to achieve the plateau west of Saint-Boès. Fighting probably commenced about 9 am. Ross's brigade, being part of the 4th Division, gained control of Saint-Boès after a stiff encounter and when the 7th Division moved up Beresford ordered an attack on the main French position.[50] This faltered and the French counter attacked, regaining possession of some of the houses in Saint-Boès before in turn being driven back leaving the Allies holding the village. However, judicious placing of the French artillery enabled it to cause serious destruction, preventing further advance on the French right for the time being, notwithstanding several further attacks and counter attacks.

Given this stalemate, Wellington ordered forward the 3rd and 6th divisions against Soult's centre. Here too the Allies found progress difficult and reputedly Soult even felt confident of victory at one point, exclaiming *enfin, je les tiens*. However, it was not to be; General Foy, whose corps held part of the centre, was badly injured and the line began to buckle.[51] Hill crossed the river above Orthez with the 2nd Division, meeting little resistance. In spite of being reinforced from the French right, the French centre did not hold and began a withdrawal. Beresford's force, though it met heroic resistance from Taupin's corps, was now able to advance and by about 2 pm had joined Picton's 3rd Division on the heights. Endangered on all sides, the French retreat – which had commenced in an orderly manner – turned to flight.[52] That evening Soult reformed his army on the right bank of the Luy de Béarn at Sault-de-Navailles, a spot he had chosen in the event of being forced to retire. Once again the bridges over the river were destroyed to prevent pursuit.

Soult conceded he had lost some 4,000 men in the battle whereas Wellington reported the loss of 2,267 British and Portuguese.[53] While Soult had escaped encirclement, this was another crushing defeat leaving him with no offensive capacity and separated from the large French garrison at Bayonne. His position was now dire, for he had to choose between either retiring north to Bordeaux or east to Toulouse. He could not cover both cities. Beresford paid tribute to the courageous resistance of the French, telling his sister: 'I have not seen them fight so well for these two or three years, but they were most completely beat, and their loss is very great, and the consequence will be nearly fatal to that army, as vast part of it will desert & which they are now daily doing in great numbers.'[54] Of his own efforts, Beresford observed laconically that his 'Division had something to do in this affair as they were the principally engaged, and I had had the good luck the day before to secure to the army the passage of the river'.[55] He was full of praise for Wellington on this 'glorious day' at the end of which the enemy 'was in full as great confusion as after the battle of Victoria [sic]' stating that he had 'seldom seen Wellington attempt a more daring thing'.[56]

When news of the battle reached London a vote of thanks to the Marquis of Wellington was moved in the House of Commons, during which a proposal was made to build a house for Wellington in Ireland since one had been built in England for Marlborough; thus drawing parallels between the two great generals, even prior to Wellington fighting the battle of Waterloo. Another Irish MP pointed out that the country which had given birth to this great hero had also produced Beresford, Ponsonby and Cole.[57]

But why did Soult fight the battle? He had rejected Clausel's advice to attack the Allies as they crossed the Gave on 26 February; though according to Foy, Clausel was the only one of his generals present who favoured such a move.[58] According to general Foy, Soult hoped that the sight of his massed army in a commanding defensive position would cause 'the English' to pause. Foy claimed that he was critical of the decision to fight at Orthez and that Soult should have retired during the night of 26 February beyond the Luy de Béarn, some twelve kilometres distant.[59] It is suggested Napoleon had ordered Soult to fight Wellington, but the letter to Soult containing this directive did not reach him until after the battle.[60] A more likely factor in bringing about Soult's decision to engage Wellington at Orthez was that the terrain offered some advantage to a defensive position on the heights, providing a natural concave circle stretching from the Dax road to the town of Orthez. Secondly, Orthez was an important crossroads and once captured would offer the Allies several alternatives for advance further into France. Thirdly, the speed of the Allied approach up the right bank of the Gave de Pau clearly took Soult by surprise and he himself expressed the view that on 26 February the armies were too close together to avoid a battle.[61] On the outcome Soult declared, 'La bataille d'Orthez est honorable pour les armes de l'Empereur', which was perhaps as much as he could say. Soult was criticised by Napoleon for his performance at Orthez, though later in Saint Helena, he was to revise that opinion. The French performance on the day was perhaps all the more creditable given the widely reported fall in morale.[62]

Soult now engaged in an orderly, perhaps masterly, retreat to Toulouse over a four-week period with frequent sharp exchanges with the Allied army in pursuit. Initially Soult retired to Saint-Sever, but he abandoned that town on the night of 28 February heading east towards Aire-sur-l'Adour. On 1 March Beresford crossed the Adour with the 4th and 7th divisions. However, he was diverted from the Allied pursuit for Wellington had another role in mind for him.

The way to Bordeaux was now open by virtue of Soult's decision to retire towards Toulouse. Moreover, there had for some time been reports of a growth in royalist sentiment in Bordeaux and Wellington determined to move to secure this important port and commercial city. With the outcome of any negotiations in the north still uncertain, Wellington remained resolute in his determination not to acclaim the Bourbons. His own proclamations did not refer to the Bourbons but merely what was necessary to preserve the peace. The Duc d'Angoulême had been in the south west of France since early in the New Year in the guise of the Comte de Pradelles, but Wellington, while studiously polite, kept his distance.[63] Two days before the battle of Orthez, he advised Angoulême that he (Wellington) was still convinced that it was in the interests of the Royal family neither to seek to influence nor advance public opinion.[64] A few days later he wrote to him again, advising that while there was royalist support in both Saint-Sever and Mont-de-Marsan, and the appearance of the white cockade and the fleur-de-lis had not caused any unrest, the town council of the latter had indicated it would not recognise any authority other than that of the Commander in Chief.[65]

On 3 March Beresford was at Mont-de-Marsan, some fifteen kilometres north of Saint-Sever. Wellington decided to send him to Bordeaux with a substantial force made up of the 4th and 7th divisions together with Vivian's Hussars and Ross's troop of horse artillery; at the same time seeking naval support to blockade the estuary of the Garonne.[66] His instructions, issued on 7 March, were to take possession of the city if possible, but not to encourage the flying of Bourbon colours or to recognise the Bourbons in any formal capacity. He was to establish 'our authority' in Bordeaux.[67] If asked to proclaim Louis XVIII, he should merely state that the British nation and the Allies wished him well and while if public peace was maintained Wellington would not stand in the way of any party opposed to Bonaparte during the war, when peace was concluded he (Wellington) could not give them any help, and the inhabitants should bear that in mind.[68] Notwithstanding this warning, if Bordeaux should hoist the white standard and proclaim Louis XVIII, Beresford should not oppose such a move. Wellington did not expect resistance of any substantial nature, but warned Beresford to keep a close eye on the Garonne and in the direction of Agen. At Langon, Beresford could decide the size of the force he should take to the city. He was to issue similar proclamations to those used by Wellington to date, calling for the authorities to determine whether they would continue or not their duties as before, and if they declined to do so they should be required to withdraw from the areas occupied by the army.

Beresford set out for Bordeaux on 8 March with the 7th Division and Vivian's cavalry. He was followed a few days later by Cole and the 4th Division. Wellington sought to fill the vacuum caused by the loss of Beresford's force by calling up General Manuel Freire's Spaniards, who were part of the army besieging Bayonne which he deemed surplus to that objective. He also ordered up his heavy cavalry, which had been of limited use in the Pyrénées. Even before the Marshal had reached Bordeaux, Wellington was writing to tell him he was anxious to have him and the 4th Division back with him and that he should leave Lord Dalhousie and the 7th Division to finish the business on the Garonne.[69] Travelling via Roquefort (8 March), Captieux (9 March) and Bazas (10 March) Beresford reached Langon on 11 March; Beresford's march was largely unopposed though a group of gendarmes had 'the impudence' to attack an advance piquet of cavalry before he reached Langon.[70] The British troops were cheered at different points by the populace, and harking back to earlier times, he told John Poo that the peasants on the road referred to the fact that Aquitaine had once been English.[71]

On the night of 11 March the remaining troops loyal to Napoleon withdrew from the city of Bordeaux, crossing to the right bank of the Garonne where the French continued to occupy the fortress of Blaye and other locations. The next morning Beresford was met by the Mayor and civil authorities outside the city, who following an address expressing joy at their delivery from slavery stripped the tricolour and other insignia of the Empire before donning a white cockade. In one of those quirks of history, the Mayor, Jean-Baptiste Lynch, was another Irishman, or perhaps more properly of Irish descent.[72] At about 12.30 pm Beresford entered the city to the acclaim of about 60,000 inhabitants. Beresford sent out troops to secure various points and to make contact with the fleet. That evening Beresford attended the opera, to thunderous applause.[73]

He reported immediately to Wellington, advising him that he understood the Duc d'Angoulême was entering Bordeaux and that in accordance with Wellington's instructions he would give him every assistance possible.[74] He did so, however, without committing the British government to support the house of Bourbon, for when he determined on 13 March to send a patrol to the fort of La Teste, still held by the French, Angoulême requested that he be allowed to send an officer to summons it in the King's name. Beresford told Wellington that his response had been that while he had no objection to any person accompanying the patrol, his own purpose was merely to ascertain the state of the force in the place.[75]

Beresford's deliverance of Bordeaux resulted in the liberation of a number of members of the Portuguese nobility who had been imprisoned there since being sent to France by Junot in 1807 and 1808. Junot's ostensible object in dispatching some of those subsequently imprisoned in France had been to offer the crown of Portugal to Napoleon, but they had been incarcerated for upwards of six years. Those imprisoned included the Marquis of Penalva, Viscount Barbacena and the Portuguese Inquisitor-General.[76]

Beresford did not tarry long in Bordeaux. Leaving Lord Dalhousie in charge of a quiet city he departed on 17 March and the following day was in Roquefort. The 4th Division under Lowry Cole and most of Vivian's cavalry followed, as requested by Wellington, and by 22 March was in Trie (sur-Baïse) with Beresford in the nearby village of Castelnau. As soon as the news of the capitulation of Bordeaux had been received from Beresford, Wellington had sent it on to

Toulouse, no doubt in the expectation it might encourage royalists there, and correspondingly discourage Soult's army. However, following sharp actions at Vic-en-Bigorre and Tarbes on 19 and 20 March Soult himself fell back on Toulouse, hoping that Suchet or at least part of the army of Catalonia would join him there. He proceeded to reinforce the existing fortifications of the city and the Allied army now converged again. Coming down the road from Auch, Beresford was in Lombes on 24 March and in Sainte-Foy (de-Peyrolières) on 25 March, while Hill was coming up to Toulouse from Saint-Gaudens with Wellington between the two of them with the rest of the army.[77] The Allied forces converged near Toulouse.[78] Writing to John Poo Beresford, the Marshal expressed the view that Bonaparte was near the end and that while Soult might seek to place the Garonne between his own army and that of the Allies, he did not think the Allies would have much difficulty crossing it.[79]

In fact, crossing the Garonne did not prove quite as easy as Beresford had anticipated. As Wellington's Quartermaster General put it to Hill, he expected the whole army to be pretty well connected on 26 March and the noose on Toulouse was tightening.[80] As the Allies approached Toulouse on 28 March, the French retired into the suburbs which they had fortified. The problem was that it had rained extensively and the Garonne was flooding. There was too much water to lay a bridge below the city, so Wellington attempted to put Hill across the Garonne at Roques and at Pinsaguel, where the Ariège joins the Garonne between Muret and Toulouse, but despite reaching Villefranche-de-Lauragais on the Toulouse–Narbonne road, the move proved impracticable and his force was ordered to return to the left bank of the Garonne.

On 3 April, Wellington directed that an attempt be made to cross the Garonne at Grenade, downstream from Toulouse, directing Beresford to send the 4th and 6th divisions, together with Vivian's cavalry, to the point where it was planned to lay down a pontoon bridge the following day. Hill was advised to do nothing which might alarm the enemy, and to warn Wellington if there was any sign of a French attack.[81] The bridge made up of seventeen boats was laid on the morning of the 4 April, but after the 3rd, 4th and 6th divisions and three brigades of cavalry had crossed over it was found necessary to take up the planks of the bridge as the waters continued to rise.[82] Wellington was now in a dangerous position, with Beresford's force isolated on the right bank, but Soult failed to take advantage of the situation, just as he had failed to do so at Orthez. The French were fully aware of the crossing and sent down trees and at least one barge loaded with stones in an ineffective effort to destroy the pontoon bridge, as the boats themselves had now been taken out of the water leaving only the cables across the river, under which the barge passed on its way downstream.[83]

A flying bridge was established, though it is not clear whether Beresford and Wellington used this or a small boat to cross to and from the right bank.[84] Wellington took the precaution of placing his guns on the left bank so that they could rake any French advance from the city towards the Allies on the right of the river. It was not until the evening of 8 March that Wellington was able to re-establish a pontoon bridge over the Garonne, this time closer to Toulouse by the Château de Gagnac.[85] Further troops, including Freire's 4th Spanish army, were now brought across the river, and Quartermaster General George Murray informed Hill that Wellington intended to move against the enemy the next day. Hill was requested to undertake a diversion only so as to draw off French troops on his side of Toulouse (the suburb of Saint-Cyprien).[86]

The battle of Toulouse was fought on Easter Sunday 10 April. Wellington determined to launch his main attack on Toulouse from the north of the city, providing for Picton (3rd) and Hill (2nd and Portuguese) to demonstrate at the north west and south of the city, respectively, in order to keep the French guessing for as long as possible and to prevent them from bolstering the strong French force on the heights of Calvinet and Mont Rave, towards which Beresford was directed to march with the 4th and 6th divisions.[87] On these heights the French had erected five redoubts connected by lines of entrenchments. The attack involved the crossing of the Hers river at Croix-Daurade, followed by a dangerous march in three columns across marshland on the left of the Hers and under the French guns on the heights; with the intention that when Beresford's force was parallel with the great redoubts on the hill it would then swing right and attack these.[88] Simultaneously, Freire's Spanish division was designated to attack the hill from the north end.

Beresford's march took longer than planned because of the terrain. He had to abandon his cannon at Montblanc and there was a severe setback when Freire, contrary to instructions, failed to wait for Beresford's advance on the heights and launched his own forces against the French. The Spanish were routed and forced back in disarray, and the situation was only rescued when a part of the Light Division moved to the Spaniards assistance. After an extremely hotly contested engagement, lasting for perhaps six hours, Beresford with Cole's 4th Division and Clinton's 6th Division carried the redoubts on the heights with the French retiring across the Canal du Midi into the city of Toulouse during the afternoon, covered by cannon on the walls of the city.[89] In the early part of the action Beresford, in the absence of his artillery, had relied on Congreve's rockets, which caused considerable discomfort to the enemy. Each redoubt was fiercely defended and the fighting desperate and often hand to hand.[90] While the combat was hard, on occasion great kindness was shown such as when John Malcolm was wounded and captured. He was taken into Toulouse and there operated on by a French surgeon, before being placed in a ward with injured Frenchmen. He was treated in a friendly manner, with Toulousains giving him various soups and fruits.[91]

Allied losses were considerable, and it is noticeable that these included senior officers in Beresford's command.[92] Lieutenant Colonel Robert Coghlan of the 61st lost his life in the attack on the heights while Major General Pack was wounded and Colonel James Douglas lost his leg while leading the Portuguese brigade, including the 8th Portuguese regiment.[93] Wellington paid tribute to both the soldiers and to Beresford's conduct of the attack and capture of the heights, while Beresford himself praised the conduct of his Quartermaster General, Benjamin D'Urban, and his Adjutant-General, Brito Mozinho, amongst others.[94] Of his own performance, Beresford observed: 'I had command of 4th and 6th divisions by whom all the business was done – indeed no others ordered for the attack save the Spanish Division under General Freire of about 9,000 men and they fled and really disbanded which placed the army in a perilous position.'[95] Beresford had enough confidence to depart from Wellington's final instructions on the mode of attack, reverting to his leader's original plan, for as he put it 'therefore I followed but the spirit of your orders in reverting to your first arrangements.'[96]

The Allies now controlled three sides of Toulouse, but Soult was not finished yet. A good defensive position had meant he had lost less men than the Allies in the battle. However, he would either be bottled up in Toulouse or he had to escape with his remaining forces. On the night of 10 April, he sent some of the wounded by canal boats to Castelnaudary. Wellington sent a cavalry detachment to close off the remaining coach-worthy road to the east, but on the night of 11 April Soult made his escape leaving 1,600 wounded in the city, including a number of field officers. Soult headed towards Castelnaudary and from there to Carcassonne. On the morning of 12 April, Wellington entered Toulouse to a tumultuous welcome; but Beresford did not participate in the festivities that evening, which included a visit to the theatre. Instead, at Wellington's request he went in pursuit of Soult accompanied by the 4th Division and followed by the 6th Division, in addition to Colonel Arenschildt's cavalry.

Occupying the Toulouse–Revel road, he had Hill on his right on the main Carcassonne road. Beresford's orders were to prevent the French stopping in or near Bazrège but not to attack them save in concert with Hill's column.[97] On 12 April, Beresford was at La Bastide, about twenty-two kilometres east of Toulouse.[98] While he was back in Toulouse on 16 April, Soult's refusal to surrender on being told of the abdication of Napoleon meant that Beresford was preparing to march on him, though he did not anticipate a march of more than three or four days, as other generals were now surrendering and he was confident he would soon be able to travel to England on the conclusion of the war. He wished they had known of the situation (Napoleon's abdication) before the battle on 10 April, noting that it would have saved many lives.[99]

Sadly, the battle for Toulouse was unnecessary. The Allies had entered Paris on 31 March and Soult was aware of that development before the battle, but unaware that Napoleon had abdicated on 6 April. News of his abdication did not reach Toulouse until the evening of 12 April, whereupon Wellington sent this news on with a French officer to Soult. However, when the latter caught up with Soult at Naurouze on the 13 April he refused to accept the veracity of the news for some days and it was only on 19 April that a suspension of hostilities was agreed. Suchet, who had been moving northwards from Spain with his own army, likewise signed a cessation of hostilities and with some small exceptions the war was now concluded.[100]

Having obtained leave of absence from the Portuguese Regency, Beresford headed for London via Paris, perhaps in ignorance that the Prince Regent of Great Britain had decided to create him a peer of the realm.[101] Arriving in London on 30 April, he was delighted to discover that his half-brother John Poo had been responsible for transporting the returning French monarch, Louis XVIII, across the Channel. In London the Marshal was feted extensively, finally receiving on 11 June the Freedom of the City voted back in 1806 for the capture of Buenos Aires, together with the gift of a fine sword and a gold freedom box, being an additional gift in recognition of his services in the Peninsula.[102] He had been away from the British Isles for much of the last twenty years and had been absent for the entire of the last five years.

As soon as he could he hurried home to see the family in Ireland, though by mid August he was on his way back to Lisbon to resume command of the Portuguese army. To his confidant, John Poo, he expressed the view that he did not expect to stay long in Portugal after Prince João's return, noting that if the Prince's ministers' views were the same as those of the Regency regarding the

British officers in the Portuguese army it would be impossible to stay, unless it was for pleasure, as he would not be able to prevent the army from falling to pieces.[103] Having brought Louis XVIII back to France, John Poo was now designated to secure the return of the Portuguese royals from Rio de Janeiro to Lisbon. Beresford asked John Poo to tell the Prince that had it not been for the Prince's anticipated return the Marshal would not have himself returned to Portugal.[104]

The colossal nature of the contribution of Portugal in terms of fighting men during the war needs to be recognised. A country with a population of some three million, devastated by three French invasions in the space of four years produced an army under Beresford of in excess of 50,000 men, together with a militia and ordenança. True, it was largely financed by Great Britain, but the achievement was nonetheless remarkable. When Beresford arrived in Lisbon in March 1809, the army, such as it was, was in no position to fight the French. Disbanded in late 1807, with its prime regiments sent to fight for Napoleon, the army was substantially rebuilt and trained within a year of Beresford's appointment to lead it. While its contribution in battle was well recognised by contemporaries, its numerical contribution to Wellington's battle force is sometimes overlooked. The returns by Wellington's recently appointed Adjutant-General, Edward Pakenham, during the winter of 1813 and spring of 1814 tell the story:

	British	Portuguese	Total
19 November 1813			
Cavalry present	7,239	1,206	8,445
Forces present	37,922	21,666	59,588
14 December 1813			
Cavalry present	7,347	1,206	8,553
Forces present	39,065	21,233	60,298
27 January 1814			
Cavalry present	7,307	1,219	8,526
Forces present	37,208	20,334	57,542
17 February 1814			
Cavalry present	7,315	1,210	8,525
Forces present	36,934	20,219	57,153
22 March 1814			
Cavalry present	6,892	1,220	8,112
Forces present	35,673	18,310	53,983

These figures are for rank and file only, they do not include officers, sergeants, trumpeters or drummers. The full returns are published in Wellington's Supplementary Despatches.[105] While only approximately one-eighth of the Allied cavalry was Portuguese, between a third and two-fifths of the infantry was Portuguese throughout the campaigns of 1813–14. The extent of this contribution may be readily understood by virtue of the fact that there were twenty-one out of a total of twenty-four Portuguese line regiments and eleven of twelve caçadore regiments serving with the Allied army in France in early 1814.[106] All British divisions, with the exception of the 1st and Light divisions, contained a Portuguese brigade; and in the Light division there were Portuguese battalions in the two brigades (1st and 3rd caçadores and 17th Line). In addition there was Hamilton's Portuguese brigade and the two independent Portuguese brigades of Bradford and Campbell.

With the war over, the troops of Great Britain, Portugal and Spain returned home, though in the case of the British troops a number of regiments were shipped straight from France to the United States, with whom Britain remained in conflict. The British infantry for the most part embarked at Bordeaux while the Portuguese marched home through northern Spain, with the injured being carried by sea from Passages to Portugal.[107] In Beresford's absence they were led by General Lecor, and reportedly only lost two men out of some 20,000 on the homeward march; a remarkable feat taking into account that the distance from Toulouse to Lisbon even today is in excess of 1,250 kilometres.[108] Strong bonds of friendship had been formed between entire regiments of the two nations as well as individuals, and there are many reports of emotional farewells during the march home, which for some distance was the same route whether to Bordeaux or Lisbon.[109]

For Beresford it was a triumphant end to five years of continuous warfare. With justification he was able to say:

> It has been a glorious termination of the war, I was not myself a little fortunate in having had (under Lord Wellington) the principle [sic] part, and share in this last battle [Toulouse]. The whole was gained by the two divisions under my orders; the Spaniards which were the only troops intended to cooperate in the direct attack failed almost immediately and their conduct was bad.[110]

Wellington agreed, praising Beresford: 'I cannot sufficiently applaud the ability and conduct of Marshal Sir W. Beresford throughout the operations of the day.'[111]

15 FAMILY, FRIENDS, FINANCE AND POLITICS

Throughout the Peninsular War and in later life, William Carr Beresford was a regular correspondent with his extended family. Correspondence extant reveals that subject to the vagaries of his life and those of his correspondents, he was in frequent touch with his siblings as well as more remote relations.[1] He may have been an equally good correspondent in earlier days, while serving in North America, Corsica, Egypt, the Cape of Good Hope, South America and Madeira, but for that period, with few exceptions, only official correspondence has come to light. Staying in touch with the family was evidently important for him as he frequently refers to his desire to see individual members, and it must have been hard for him not to have seen them, with the exception of John Poo, for over five years while in the Peninsula. William's correspondence as revealed includes letters to his half-brothers, Henry, the 2nd Marquis of Waterford, and John George, later Archbishop of Armagh; his half-sisters, Anne and Elizabeth, as well as his uncle, also named William, Archbishop of Tuam.[2] In terms of sheer volume and in what it has to offer us, it is his letters to his half-brother John Poo, the naval officer, which stand out.[3]

William frequently chided the 2nd Marquis for failing to respond to letters, such as in 1808 when writing to him from Salamanca to say that his ADC (William Sewell) has arrived from England with letters, but 'not one from the noble Marquis'.[4] Nonetheless, they were clearly on good terms with William sending him horses, sheep and various wines from the Peninsula.[5]

When the time came, Henry fully supported the Marshal's candidacy to become a member of parliament. Henry's severe gout appears to have been offered as a reason for his failings as a correspondent, and indeed at times it does appear to have kept him at the family home of Curraghmore in County Waterford rather than enjoying the social season in London. On occasion he also pleaded the demands of parliamentary business and dealing with lawlessness as reasons for being a poor letter writer.[6]

John George was Bishop of Raphoe while William was in the Peninsula. Waterford had striven to get John George appointed to that Bishopric with a view to maintaining Beresford influence in the northern counties of Ireland. Their correspondence reflects the political situation in Ireland, the military position in Portugal and deals with family concerns.[7]

On his infrequent visits to London, William obviously relished the company of his father's widow, Elizabeth Monck. The 1st Marquis had died in 1800. Beresford and Elizabeth were clearly on good terms, and these visits to Hampstead, where she resided when in London, may reflect claims that she had nurtured William and John Poo when they were young.

William's relationship with his uncle, the Archbishop of Tuam, shows the high regard in which William was held by the family. Not only were the two of them nominated as guardians of the young children of the 2nd Marquis, should the latter die while they were minors, but William along with the 1st Marquis was also given a power of attorney to act on behalf of John Poo Beresford.[8] William spent little time in Ireland in the war years, but he was there in 1803–5 and returned in 1814. In due course, in 1832 he was to marry his first cousin, Louisa, the youngest daughter of the Archbishop of Tuam.

William was friendly with both his half-sisters, Anne and Elizabeth (Bess), but the correspondence located to date for the years of the Peninsular War is predominantly with Anne, whereas that with Elizabeth is slightly later. It covers a large range of topics, from reporting on military training, campaigns and battles to personal challenges and illness. He laments the fact that he does not have the opportunity to go to see Anne and other family members in Ireland after returning to England from La Coruña, because of his appointment to command in Portugal – an appointment which he could not refuse – and on arrival in Lisbon, the first letters (of a non official nature) are to Anne and to the 2nd Marquis of Waterford.[9] To her he expresses his concern about the dangers being faced by Poo when the French squadron escapes from Lorient into the Atlantic, and his relief when he hears the French have put back into Rochefort.[10] In general terms he writes about the training and discipline being instilled into the Portuguese troops and he gives Anne an account of various encounters with the French.

Not only does he give us some insight into his medical condition at various times, but he deals with his wounding at Salamanca and the ensuing difficult trip back to Lisbon.[11] William grumbles in his letters to Anne about the 2nd Marquis's failure to respond to letters, expresses his desire to be in Ireland and repeatedly explains that he dare not leave the army for any period of time, partly because of his concern that no one else will drive it with his determination, but also because of the government in Lisbon, which he feels is determined to mortify him.[12] He had signalled his hopes of visiting home in the winter of 1813 (presumably on the basis that the armies would be in cantonments due to the weather in the Pyrénées) but that was not to be.[13] Instead we find the Marshal encamped in the not-uncomfortable quarters of the château at Ustaritz, complaining of the Pyrenean weather.

When he returned to Lisbon in September 1813, to iron out problems with the Regency and to secure men and money for the army, we learn of his disappointment that the house in the country he is having decorated is not complete and that accordingly he has to stay in the centre of town, ending the letter rather morbidly that the house will be ready next time 'I return, if I ever return'.[14] Anne must have kept a close eye on Wellington's official dispatches as published, for in response to her remarks William tells her not to be angry if his name is not conspicuous following the battle of the Nive in December 1813, as he commanded part of the army (the centre) not particularly engaged: 'for though I began the movement and attacked the enemy on the 9th crossing the river twice in his face, and that we might have expected the brunt of the business, he made little or no resistance, and has not since thought fit to direct his attack against my positions, but against the extreme right and left of the army.' He goes on to commend Rowland Hill, who 'cannot be praised enough. I brought up my troops to support him but he did the business right well himself'.[15] The warmth of William's relationship with Anne is suggested in his address, which is invariably 'My Dearest Anne', whereas correspondence with other siblings, male and female, tends to commence with the expression, 'Dear'.

One of William's most regular correspondents was his slightly older half-brother, Poo. This is perhaps surprising in that they were frequently hundreds if not thousands of miles apart, both engaged in trying to make their way without the benefit at the outset of personal wealth. Of course, they had been together at school in England and had clearly bonded during that time, with Poo allegedly being the daredevil and William the uncertain younger brother. In their letters from the time of the Peninsular War their affection for each other shines through, and they are mutually delighted when Poo finds himself on the Lisbon station in the winter of 1810. William, of course, provides Poo with accommodation in Lisbon. It is striking that whereas the 2nd Marquis addresses Poo (his half-brother) as 'My Dear Beresford' or 'My Dear Captain', William's letters to Poo begin 'My Dear Poo', 'My Dear Fellow' or even, 'My Dearest Friend'.[16]

In this correspondence William discloses both his fondness for Poo and his concerns relating to his own fluctuating fortunes, whether because of criticism of his handling of the Allied army at Albuera, his battles with the Regency, or indeed his own health. Their friendship is obvious, with William being declared Poo's residual legatee under wills made before and after Poo's marriage to Mary Anne Molloy in 1809, with a codicil providing for the payment of all Poo's debts to William as a first charge; Poo is sure William will look after his children in the event any accident befalls him.[17] In the event, it was a different accident that changed Poo's life, as the death of his beloved Mary Anne occurred in 1813, just four years after their marriage. Two years later William was able to congratulate Poo on his second marriage, to Harriet Peirse of Bedale in Yorkshire.

William corresponded with Poo about each major battle in which he fought, including Albuera, Salamanca, Orthez and Toulouse, providing useful detail of his own involvement on each occasion.[18] He confides in Poo, just as he does with Anne, the reasons for not being able to leave the army in the winter of 1813, stating it would be impossible, not least because it requires daily urging to keep the Regency awake to the necessities of the army, now at a distance from Portugal, which itself is no longer threatened. His own task he compares to that of Sisyphus, stating that the latter has a better chance of getting to the top of the hill and there take a rest.[19] He feels able to tell Poo some things regarding his own health that he seems hesitant to tell Anne. Thus, at the end of January 1814 he tells Anne that he has not seen Wellington for three weeks without explaining to her, as he does to Poo, that he has had 'abominable biles' (from the context probably piles) which prevent William from riding. Luckily these cleared up in time for the campaign begun in mid February.[20] Clearly it was not a one-way correspondence, though little has been found to date of Poo's writings to William. The correspondence continued throughout the rest of their lives, encompassing personal as well as state affairs.

Beresford corresponded with his wider family, including John Claudius Beresford, the banker and politician, and of course Lady Frances, the mother of John Theophilus Beresford, who lost his life from wounds received at Ciudad Rodrigo in January 1812. Evidently, he took a real interest in John Theophilus, for he corresponded with the young man's mother even before the sad event.[21]

Beresford's Portuguese military secretary was António Lemos Pereira de Lacerda Delgado, later Viscount Juromenha.[22] António married Maria da Luz Willoughby da Silveira in 1802 and for some twenty years Beresford and Maria conducted an affair, as a result of which it is thought she bore him at least two children. These were William Lemos Willoughby and Maria Efigenia Willoughby, born on 30 November 1812 and 19 December 1816, respectively. A further baptismal certificate shows that Beresford had another daughter, also called Maria, of mother 'incognita', whom he acknowledged as his on 13 May 1818. This may well have been Maria Guilhermina, referred to in correspondence by the Viscountess Juromenha in 1822.[23] While Beresford was clearly fond of the Viscountess, they did not marry on the death of Viscount Juromenha in August 1828, resulting in an understandable cooling of the relationship.[24] Sir Robert Wilson met Maria Juromenha in Lisbon in 1809, at which stage she was already reportedly Beresford's mistress. Wilson described her as 'certainly the handsomest woman in the country, and what is more pleasing, very clean but still much inferior to any moderate handsome woman.'[25] During the war and long afterwards Lemos remained a trusted confidant of the Marshal, and he and his wife lived for extended periods with Beresford in what seems to have been an amicable *ménage à trois*. On several occasions Beresford dispatched Lemos to make representations to João in Brazil both, when Regent and subsequently as King.[26] Lemos was clearly a friend and confidant.

Beresford made other friendships in Portugal but the nature of the job seems to have caused him to keep many fellow officers at arms length. In reforming the Portuguese army Beresford, as has been stated, was careful to preserve a balance between the number of British officers appointed and their Portuguese colleagues, and there were good practical reasons for doing so. National sentiment demanded it but organisational efficiency dictated such a policy as well, not least because many British officers spoke little or no Portuguese on arrival. There were of course exceptions, such as the talented William Warre who was appointed one of the Marshal's ADCs and whose contribution included translation of the military manuals necessary for the training of the troops: 'a tiresome undertaking but most necessary, and for the appearance of which I am much hurried'.[27]

Warre's family was an important one in the Anglo-Portuguese wine trade and while he had been brought up in Porto, he was educated at Harrow. A career soldier, Warre was fluent in both English and Portuguese and was present at Roliça and Vimeiro, where he had been ADC to General Ronald Ferguson. From 1809 to 1812 he was one of Beresford's ADCs, arriving with Beresford in Lisbon on 2 March 1809. Unfortunately for the historian, recurring illness meant that Warre was absent from both Buçaco and Albuera and the reader is thus deprived of his insights on these battles. Back with the army in 1812, Warre accompanied the wounded Beresford on his return to Lisbon following the battle of Salamanca. His letters home are highly informative.

High minded and conscious of the desperate financial state of Portugal, Warre refused to accept the pay of a Portuguese officer in addition to British pay, unlike many of his contemporaries.[28] He shared the prejudice of many of his countrymen regarding the likely conduct of the Spanish armies, though he admired the 'naturally brave Spaniards'. Warre was unsparing in his criticism of the Portuguese commissariat and many of the officers in place in the Portuguese army in 1809.[29] Beresford weeded out the inefficient and uncommitted and sought to promote on the basis of merit. Warre was delighted by that and by the end of 1809 was able to report that there were 'many very promising young Officers, and the old ones have in great measure been got rid of'.[30] Later he would remark repeatedly and admiringly on the achievements of the Portuguese regiments.[31]

Warre applauded what Beresford was doing in Portugal. Citing his unremitting exertions and his Herculean labour, Warre continued:

> There exists not a more honourable, firm man, or a more zealous Patriot. His failings are mere foibles of a temper naturally warm and hasty, and a great zeal to have everything right, without much patience. Those who accuse him of severity are either those who have felt it because they deserved it, their friends, or people wilfully ignorant of the state in which he found the army. And of how much he has foreborne, as to myself, I declare I do not know of one instance of severity, and do know numberless ones of his mercy, and goodness of heart, where others would have been less lenient.[32]

Later, on writing to his father in 1810, Warre declared of the Marshal: 'I cannot sufficiently admire the firmness and understanding with which he has overcome difficulties, which would have disheartened and overturned the plans of most, even very superior men. He is just the man for this particular service.'[33]

Beresford acquired a substantial staff and in 1810, apart from Warre, he had by his own account seven other ADCs, both Portuguese and British, as well as 'about' fourteen secretaries.[34] They included the Marquis of Angeja, the Count of Alva, Don José de Sousa, the Count of Lumiares, Captain William Henry Sewell and Captain Molloy.[35] The most important Portuguese members of his staff were his Adjutant-General, Manoel de Brito Mozinho, and his Military

Secretary, António Lemos, but each of these was backed up by a rake of assistants and deputies.[36] There were British counterparts, including Colonel Robert Arbuthnot, who was appointed his British Military Secretary and who was to remain with Beresford until 1817. Arbuthnot had been with Beresford in South America, where they were imprisoned together, and was present at La Coruña and most of the subsequent major battles of the war in the Peninsula, rendering extensive and valued service.[37] Like so many on Wellington's own staff, Sewell, Molloy and Arbuthnot all had an Irish background or relations.[38] A further example was Denis Pack, who had also shared in Beresford's adventure in South America where he commanded the 71st Regiment. Pack went on to command the Independent Portuguese Brigade of Porto in the defeat of the French in Spain and at Toulouse, before later commanding the 9th Brigade as part of Picton's division at Waterloo. In 1816 he married Beresford's half-sister, Lady Elizabeth, and the families were to be closely connected thereafter.[39]

Wellington, of course, has a claim to be the person most supportive of Beresford's undertaking to rebuild and reform the Portuguese army. Forjaz too, at personal risk to his career and reputation, was an integral part of the machine that produced such a fine army in a relatively short period of time. Without in any way demeaning those claims, it would be wrong to fail to recognise the enormous contribution made by Beresford's own Quartermaster General, Benjamin D'Urban, in the performance of the army, since logistics threatened time and again to derail Beresford's efforts. D'Urban had previously gained experience as Assistant Quartermaster General in Ireland, and had been involved in the same capacity with Sir David Baird's supporting force when Sir John Moore led the British army into Spain in 1808. Left behind in Spain when the British retreated to La Coruña, D'Urban spent time in both Spain and Portugal, with Cuesta and Sir Robert Wilson, before joining Beresford on his return to the Peninsula. He was appointed Quartermaster General of the Portuguese army on 14 April 1809 and established a distinct Quartermaster General's department in that army, at Beresford's request, using both British and Portuguese officers.

On the march north leading to the defeat of Soult and the recapture of Porto in May 1809, D'Urban was with Beresford when he encountered the then Major Henry Hardinge. He was highly impressed with him and as a result persuaded Beresford to offer Hardinge the post of Deputy Quartermaster General with the Portuguese army. The development of the department proceeded so well that in 1811 D'Urban and Hardinge could be released for other duties, with D'Urban being appointed to command a brigade of Portuguese cavalry which performed heroically at Salamanca before disappointing at Majadahonda, both in 1812.[40] Uniquely qualified by virtue of serving with Beresford over many years, D'Urban was to participate in his defence when the Marshal's conduct of the Battle of Albuera was subjected to hostile scrutiny by Napier. He kept a diary and was a good correspondent throughout the war, both of which give valuable insights on the campaigns and the workings of the Anglo-Portuguese alliance.[41] He was one of the British officers who remained on in Portugal with Beresford at the conclusion of the war, not returning to the United Kingdom until 1817.

At the end of his life Beresford died a wealthy man, but it is difficult to ascertain the degree that this was due to the accretion of wealth from his wife Louisa, who pre-deceased the Marshal, for she had married into substantial wealth in the shape of Thomas Hope in 1806.[42] Beresford was certainly given a start on the ladder of life by his father. Thereafter, no evidence has been found of financial support and to a large extent Beresford seems to have acquired wealth through his army salaries and through prize money. To this must be added some generous gifts by individuals, corporations and the governments of Great Britain and Portugal, including pensions.

During the Peninsular War he did not live ostentatiously, though he did maintain certain comforts, including a base in Lisbon.[43] He drew a salary both as a British and Portuguese officer, but he clearly felt this more than met his own needs, for while he doubted the financial prudence of Poo, he was quick to offer him assistance remarking that he did not think he himself would need the money. Beresford's generosity extended to the 2nd Marquis, to whom he sent both Merino sheep and wines on a number of occasions; advising Waterford of the need to house the sheep in Ireland in winter. The traffic was not all one-way; a request to the Marquis to send cider to Portugal via either Cork or Waterford was acted upon.[44]

Beresford's share of the prize money from the expedition to the Cape of Good Hope and the River Plate was threatened by litigation instigated by Sir Home Popham against Sir David Baird and Beresford, claiming that they had entered into agreements with him regarding the division of any entitlement. Their defence was simple, namely that the agreement was based on Popham's assertion that he was a Commodore with a Captain under him and therefore a flag officer, which subsequently turned out to be false. Nevertheless, while the litigation ensued Beresford remained concerned at the unpredictability of court proceedings, even though Popham had admitted to Beresford that the latter must have entered into the agreement on the basis put forward in the defence, as Popham thought this was the case himself.[45] In the short few weeks Beresford was back in England after La Coruña he had to attend to this affair, and it raised its head repeatedly in correspondence with his agent in London, Angus McDonald, during the next few years while he was back in the Peninsula.

In essence, so far as the expedition to Buenos Aires (as distinct from that to the Cape) was concerned, Popham had made a private agreement with Baird for the division of the eighth of the prize money reserved for the commanding officer.[46] He then proceeded to make agreements with Beresford and with the ships' captains involved in the expedition. Popham's first reversal in terms of prize money came when the appointment by Baird of Beresford as a Major General was disclosed to Popham when they arrived off South America. This promotion entitled Beresford to a larger share of any prize money obtained.[47] After the termination of the expedition, Baird repudiated the agreement with Popham on the basis that the latter had misrepresented his situation. Popham felt aggrieved that this resulted not only in Baird increasing his share, but Beresford receiving twice the sum allocated to Popham. He unsuccessfully sought redress from the Privy Council.[48] Captain Donnelly of the *Narcissus* also sued Popham. In that action, in the High Court Mansfield Ch. J., held against Popham on the basis that he was a captain and not a commodore.[49] Popham was unsuccessful in seeking a retrial again of Donnelly's action, just as he failed ultimately in his claims against Baird and Beresford.

Until the litigation was determined, however, Beresford was hugely agitated concerning its potential outcome because of events much nearer home. In November 1808, Beresford had written to the 2nd Marquis of Waterford requesting that his money be invested in landed securities. Beresford used Angus MacDonald for the purpose of making some investments.[50] The request made to Lord Waterford was more likely related to the fact that he had placed some of his money with the Beresford Bank in Dublin, in which his nephew John Claudius Beresford was a senior partner.[51] John Claudius was also a member of parliament, one of a number of Beresford members.[52] The Beresford Bank was one of many small private banks established in Dublin in the late eighteenth century.[53] These banks proliferated and many of them issued notes in excess of their assets, as a result of which the Bank of Ireland determined to refuse to accept any notes of private banks, including those previously reputable. There were several 'runs' on the Beresford Bank, and in 1806 John Claudius, a Tory supporter, had to seek extended credit, even going so far as to support the Ministry of All the Talents in the hope of reciprocity from the government.[54]

John Claudius handled considerable investments on behalf of the Marshal. As early as the autumn of 1808, Beresford had asked Waterford to withdraw monies from John Claudius (presumably a reference to the bank) so that it might be invested in landed securities. He had written to the banker but had received no reply. Beresford did not want to embarrass John Claudius by withdrawing it all at once, as he believed it was considerable, though he conceded he did not know exactly how much was lodged with the banker.[55] On returning to Portugal Beresford obviously received reports which alarmed him, and by early 1810 he was complaining to Poo that he was in the dark as to how his affairs were being looked after and that he was waiting to hear from John Claudius. Because of the Popham litigation the Marshal was particularly anxious as:

> in the case of any accident happening to my money with John Claudius, I should not have enough to pay what might be claimed, which would place one in a situation very different from losing the whole sum if it was all my own, and I would wish some steps to be taken to secure this money and on which I would wish you to consult with the Bishop.[56]

The Marshal was right to be worried about the embarrassment which might be caused by a default for the bank failed later in 1810, and in 1811 John Claudius was personally declared bankrupt.

The extent to which creditors were ultimately satisfied from the collapse of the Bank and John Claudius's own bankruptcy is not clear. There is a suggestion that creditors of the Bank were paid in full, but only following the sale of John Claudius' home and contents; other reports are far less positive. However, Beresford's personal finances and his difficulties were obviously the subject of common knowledge in 1811. When Prime Minister Perceval moved, and Castlereagh seconded, the parliamentary vote of thanks to Beresford for the victory at Albuera, supporting speeches were made by a number of others including the sitting member for Tipperary, General Montague Mathew. In his speech Mathew alluded to Beresford's perilous financial situation caused by the failure of a family member, and urged that some pecuniary award might be added to his honours. Mathew was no friend of the Tories, being a Whig and an ardent supporter of

Catholic emancipation, but clearly personal friendship and/or admiration enabled him to cross party lines.[57]

John Claudius' bankruptcy presented a further problem for the Beresford family, which controlled a number of parliamentary seats in Ireland.[58] Since January 1806, John Claudius had been the member for County Waterford in succession to his father, who had died late in 1805. His impending bankruptcy caused much discussion in the family as to whether he was bound to resign from parliament, and if so who should be put forward to succeed him.[59] In the event it was accepted that a bankrupt could no longer remain a member of parliament (though he could and did remain an alderman of Dublin city) and in consequence he resigned his seat in June 1811.[60] There was unanimity amongst the family at a suggestion which was probably first made by the Archbishop of Tuam, Waterford's uncle and William's great-uncle, that William Carr Beresford be asked to fill the position.[61] Notwithstanding the 2nd Marquis's customary lethargy, the subject of considerable correspondence, the Marshal was returned unopposed on 28 June 1811.[62] While this move may be regarded as the beginning of a political career for Beresford in the United Kingdom, he cannot have made any parliamentary contribution as MP for County Waterford, for he resigned the seat on his being created Baron Beresford of Albuera and Dungarvan in May 1814 and he was not in the United Kingdom between June 1811 and May 1814.

16 BERESFORD'S CONTRIBUTION TO ALLIED SUCCESS IN THE PENINSULA

'A braver man or a better man I never served'[1]

In February 1809 William Carr Beresford, a relatively junior Major General in the British army, had been commanded by his sovereign to take command of the Portuguese army on the heels of a request from the Regency struggling to restore law and order in Portugal – a country devastated by occupation and threatened with further invasion. His role was to rebuild the army so that it could play its part in the common cause, namely the defeat of Napoleon. He had not sought the position, and indeed the Portuguese had sought a Lieutenant General, with a preference for Sir Arthur Wellesley, the victor of Vimeiro. In order to meet the requirement for a Lieutenant General, Beresford was made up as such for the duration of his Portuguese appointment. The Portuguese then made him a Marshal, as he was told this was imperative if he was to command the army and avoid a situation where he would be outranked by other Portuguese lieutenant generals. Beresford neither sought nor wished to be made a Marshal, but the combination of these various promotions was to make life difficult for him and for the Commander in Chief of the Allied army in the Peninsula, Sir Arthur Wellesley, later Viscount and then Duke of Wellington.

Beresford's brief was the reconstruction of the Portuguese army, so that it would become an effective fighting force which could operate and cooperate with the British army. In Britain and in Portugal it was agreed that he had done a wonderful job. There were those he had disciplined and those whom he had retired who perhaps did not agree, but Beresford had shown in Portugal that the organisational and administrative skills manifested in the rebuilding of the 88th Regiment, the march across the Egyptian desert, the capture of Buenos Aires and his administration of Madeira were capable of being translated onto the bigger stage. He had created an army which could stand with and against the best in Europe. Of course he had substantial help. In Portugal, Wellington, Forjaz and Stuart had all played their roles; along with D'Urban, Harvey, Mozinho, Blunt, Pack, Lemos de Lacerda, Lecor, Bacelar, Silveira, Trant, d'Avillez, Warre and a host of other British and Portuguese officers.

The Portuguese infantry regiments and caçadores had proved themselves time and time again. The artillery, reformed by Beresford, performed well throughout under the overall leadership of Commandant-General de Rosa, who had been appointed by the Marshal in 1809. In the field the artillery was commanded by Alexander Dickson, who proved so effective that he became overall commander of the Allied artillery at Wellington's behest in 1813.[2] It would be harsh to blame Beresford or the cavalry regiments if they did not reach the heights of their colleagues. They never acquired either enough, or even suitable, horses to be other than a useful reconnaissance force combined with escort and piquet functions. Nevertheless it did acquit itself well on occasions under Madden on the Portuguese Spanish frontier and more so under Lumley at Usagre and D'Urban at Salamanca; before a dismal performance at Majadahonda.

How had Beresford turned 'a mob with a propensity to mutiny' into Wellington's 'fighting cocks'? He had addressed each facet required to create an army in a methodical and determined manner, and ensured these requirements were fulfilled to a remarkable degree. In doing so he had addressed the need to clothe, equip, provide for and pay the force while overseeing the creation of a medical and hospital function which could look after the injured while on campaign. Pay was always in arrears, but it was not Beresford's function to procure funds, merely to ensure they were distributed when available and to raise objections when they were not forthcoming, and he was assiduous in doing so. He did not succeed in reforming the Portuguese commissariat to a degree where it could feed the Portuguese army, the greater part of which ended up relying on the British commissariat. As a result, despite all his efforts troops did go hungry intermittently throughout the war, usually but not exclusively while on campaign. Even the merger of the provisioning and transport components of the army failed to address this difficulty; a predicament that was enhanced by the lack of finance, a lack of food within Portugal, a country dependent on imported foodstuffs even in peacetime; and an unwillingness of farmers to accept Portuguese paper money or give credit to a bankrupt government.

Under the officers appointed by Beresford the troops were expected to train on a daily basis when not on campaign and the introduction of British regulations enabled them to integrate fully with their British counterparts. He introduced a strict discipline from the moment he assumed command in 1809. This involved the execution of deserters on occasion and the imprisonment of those who refused to obey orders expeditiously or at all. In doing so he was determined to apply the rules without favour to any particular group, as was witnessed by his abolition of arbitrary punishment of men by their officers. His regime was no harsher than that of the successful continental armies.

In building an *esprit de corps*, Beresford insisted that the soldiers were properly dressed and presented, to such effect that the British Judge-Advocate General Francis Seymour Larpent observed in the summer of 1813:

> Nothing can look in a higher state than the Portuguese troops. They are cleaner than our men; or look so, at least. They are better clothed now by far, as they have taken the best care of their clothes: they are much gayer, and have an air, and a je ne scais [*sic*] quoi, particularly the Caçadores both the officers and the private men, quite new in a Portuguese. This is curious to see the effects of good direction and example, how soon it tells.[3]

The Portuguese army did not just look good. The transformation effected by Beresford turned it into a respected fighting force on the European stage. There were occasions even late in the war, such as at the combat on the Aire on 2 March 1814, when Portuguese individuals and groups of men did not perform as expected, but these were few and far between, and Beresford dealt with them accordingly.[4] Further, in this respect the Portuguese were not alone. Those of other nationalities on occasion performed in a less than acceptable manner. However, the overall performance of the Portuguese army was such that it won the plaudits of British officers and soldiers and the grudging admiration of the French. Wellington, in one of many laudatory expressions, said of the Portuguese after Buçaco: 'they have proved that the trouble which has been taken with them has not been thrown away'. Of Beresford he said on the same day: 'To him exclusively, under the Portuguese government, is due the merit of having raised, formed, disciplined, and equipped the Portuguese army, which has now shown itself capable of engaging and defeating the enemy.'[5]

Without Beresford's Portuguese army, it is uncertain whether Wellington would have been able to defend the Lines of Torres Vedras. Beresford had been in charge for just eighteen months at that stage, and had managed to produce a rejuvenated army which went on improving right up to the end of the war in April 1814. Other British officers agreed that by the end of the war the Portuguese were every bit as good as their British counterparts.[6] For their part, Generals Foy and Marbot, two of the most experienced French commanders who saw extensive service in the Peninsula, both acknowledged the importance of the Portuguese in Wellington's army.[7] Beresford, understandably was very proud of what the Portuguese had achieved, even before the battles of Orthez and Toulouse: 'the Portuguese are praised by all and nothing could be finer than their conduct. It would be injustice to praise them above the British or the British above them.'[8] His own part in building the army had been at least in part due to his own foresight in declining to take up the appointment to command until his sole responsibility for all aspects of its organisation and discipline, including all promotions, had been confirmed by the Regency.[9]

Beresford's performance on the field of battle was for long dominated by William Napier's views to the effect that he should not have fought the battle of Albuera and that on the day of the battle he failed to make the right decisions; leading to a victory, albeit with huge British losses. Sir Charles Oman, in his magisterial work *A History of the Peninsular War*, certainly believed that Napier had treated Beresford unfairly and he had access to materials not available to Napier. There is a strong case for arguing for a different interpretation of events leading up to the battle and its subsequent development which differs from that of Napier. First, it is clear that Beresford did not particularly wish to fight that battle, but Blake's insistence that his Spanish army would not retreat into Portugal and would fight with or without the Anglo-Portuguese force, which in Beresford's judgment would have led to its annihilation, clearly swayed his decision. Wellington had given Beresford discretion in deciding whether to fight, but if he did not do so at Albuera, it would enable Soult to relieve Badajoz.

Secondly, it is equally clear that on the day Beresford was let down by a number of his commanders who either temporised or even ignored orders, or who failed to follow standard battle procedure of the time for effecting an advance. Thirdly, while the Allied cavalry arguably performed well, it was heavily outnumbered with a consequent limitation on what it could do. Finally, it needs to be remembered that this was the first major encounter with the French of an Anglo-Hispanic-Lusitanian force under a single commander. On the day the heroics of Spanish, Portuguese and British soldiers overcame the deficiencies in command structures. Beresford's talents as a general do not bear scrutiny, and nor is it suggested they should do so, alongside Wellington; but with the possible exception of Hill, he was Wellington's most successful lieutenant in the war. On the occasion of Albuera he appears to have been determined to secure his line of retreat, and while claims that he had decided to retreat are easily disposed of, it would appear that it was certainly in his contemplation when Lowry Cole took the momentous decision to bring forward part of the 4th Division which in effect saved the day. It has been suggested that Beresford panicked at the critical moment, but once again the evidence is meagre. He may have prevaricated at crucial moments in the battle but there are arguments for suggesting that he was more unfortunate than blameworthy for the huge losses, casualties which he regretted and for which he did blame himself because he felt he should not have fought the battle, but rather retired. He was deeply shocked and it seems likely that his subsequent illness was at least in part due to what we now call post-traumatic stress disorder.

Beresford's determination was such that he persevered both with the command of the Portuguese army in the face of continued opposition, and in his role as a general commanding multiple divisions in the Allied army. He distinguished himself at Salamanca, where he was wounded twice. Having recovered, he participated fully in the campaigns of 1813 and 1814, taking part in the Allied victories at Vitória, the Pyrénées, the Nivelle and the Nive, before going on to lead the principal attacks in the two final battles of the war at Orthez and Toulouse. All those achievements were made possible by the unswerving support of Wellington, who expressed his positive views of Beresford's capabilities on numerous occasions. Beresford's great strengths were his single-minded determination and his organisational abilities. He proved to be an excellent motivator even if not a great tactician. He was the right arm and long-term friend of the Duke of Wellington, and although they did have disagreements, those did not impair either their friendship or their working relationship. The differences which emerge in correspondence seem to have occurred in 1809 and to have been resolved without any fallout.

The first of these differences was caused by the awkwardness created by Beresford's appointment as a Lieutenant General in the British and Portuguese armies in February 1809. The appointment leapfrogged him over a number of senior officers, and was exacerbated by his appointment as Marshal on arrival in Portugal. In 1809 Tilson, Mackenzie and John Murray were unhappy to serve under him, all on the basis of seniority in the British army. Initially Wellington suggested that the matter would be resolved if Beresford resigned from the British army, a step Beresford was not prepared to contemplate. Perhaps realising that as a Marshal of Portugal Beresford would out rank those British officers in any event when serving together, Wellington did not press the point. Later in the war, when the issue of a potential successor to Wellington arose there was a hiatus, with on one side those, including the Commander in Chief and the Duke of York, insisting on following the precedent of seniority based on promotion date, and on the other side Wellington, again firm in his support for Beresford. Wellington was without doubt concerned as to what would happen to the Portuguese army if Beresford should retire, but it is difficult to believe the outstanding military commander of the time, and arguably Britain's greatest military leader, would have insisted on Beresford as his successor had he not believed he was the right man to lead the Allies in the Peninsula should Wellington be incapacitated.

The second identifiable topic of disagreement, which arose in 1809, was when Wellington queried whether inserting British officers into Portuguese regiments was a worthwhile investment, given that it involved a lot of junior officers who he felt did not have the requisite knowledge and experience to train the Portuguese properly. Instead, Wellington suggested a smaller number of highly qualified officers in a supervisory or staff capacity. In this instance Beresford responded not by refuting Wellington's argument, but by pointing out that the inclusion of British officers in the Portuguese regiments had proceeded to such an extent that the changes suggested were not practical. In any event, he felt that the system implemented had begun to show dividends and this Wellington accepted, indicating his recognition of what had been achieved when making his tour of inspection of the Portuguese regiments in late December 1809 and early January 1810.[10] Further, he was so impressed by what had been achieved with the Portuguese army that as we have seen he recommended a similar policy vis-à-vis the Spaniards, though for financial reasons this was not pursued by the British government. At the same time Beresford clearly took the hint of the benefit of experienced British officers being placed on the staff of Portuguese generals, and John Wilson was subsequently sent to assist Silveira in northern Portugal.

Fortescue, in his *History of the British Army*, refers to some discord between the two men in December 1809, but does not elaborate further.[11] Surviving letters to Beresford's family throw no light on the suggestion, nor does reference to D'Urban's diary give any clues either, as there are no entries between September and early December 1809. Wellington had been with the British army and in Badajoz for much of the autumn, and it was only at the end of the month he joined Beresford at Punhete, before going on the tour of inspection. Wellington's appointment by the Regency as Marshal General of the Portuguese forces in April 1809 was confirmed by Prince Joao in Rio de Janeiro in July, though the notice of such confirmation was only promulgated in Lisbon in November. It is unlikely that Beresford's nose was put out of joint by this event as Wellington had been commander of all the Allied forces since his arrival in Portugal in the spring, and there is no evidence to suggest that Beresford was other than happy to serve under him. Further, Beresford made it clear to Wellington in the autumn of 1809 that he welcomed the authority given to Wellington by the Prince Regent, writing:

> I must admit I have long wished that an authority such as given to you should be placed in some one's hands who will be free from the feelings, and prejudices, and intrigues inseparable from any of the great persons of this kingdom; and I need not say that in my opinion the person could not have been better chosen.[12]

In any event, whatever their differences both men were clearly able to put these behind them and Wellington fully recognised Beresford's abilities, which outweighed any weaknesses he may have exhibited as a battlefield commander.

What of Beresford the person? In his diary Schaumann, the Deputy Assistant Commissary-General with the British army, describes an incident in November 1808 where he both sought assistance from and offered gratuitous advice to Beresford. The latter reportedly looked Schaumann up and down: '"I don't want your advice Sir; mind your own business and take yourself off this instant!" he snorted angrily, showing his enormous face and squint-eyed glance; and I quickly rushed from the room.'[13] The 'squint-eyed glance' is presumably a reference to Beresford's appearance following the shooting accident in which he had lost an eye as a young man. Some twenty years later, Thomas Creevey, the MP and diarist, described Beresford when he met him for dinner in August 1827:

> I can safely say that in my life I never took so strong a prejudice against a man. Such a low-looking ruffian in his air, with damned bad manners, or rather none at all, and a vulgarity in his expression and pronunciation that made me at once believe that he was ignorant, stupid and illiterate as he was ill-looking. Yet somehow or other he almost wiped away all these notches before we parted. In the first place, it is with me an invaluable property in any man to have him call a spade a spade. The higher he is in station the more rare and entertaining it is. Then I defy any human being to find out he is either a marshal or a lord; but you do find out that he has been in every part of the world, and in all the interesting scenes of it for the last five and thirty years.[14]

Creevey was a Whig and a political opponent of Beresford, but this looks like an attempt to make a fair assessment. He was clearly entertained by Beresford and impressed by Beresford's refusal to adopt airs and graces; though he was not too enthusiastic about his manners.

Physically, Beresford may not have been attractive but he attracted great loyalty from those who knew him. Apart from Wellington, he was clearly a friend of Sir David Baird, Benjamin D'Urban, and many others who served with him including William Warre, who had great battles with the Marshal which never lasted long and who told his mother: 'There exists not a more honourable, firm man, or a more zealous Patriot. His failings are mere foibles of a temper naturally warm and hasty, and a great zeal to have everything right, without much patience.'[15] It is also noticeable that many of those who elected to serve with Beresford in Portugal had served with him either in his days with the 88th Regiment or in the other theatres of war covered here. They included Denis Pack, Robert Arbuthnot, Robert Patrick, and others, a testimony to the high regard in which he was held by those who had observed him at close quarters.[16]

Not only did Beresford call a spade a spade, but he was a man of integrity. He insisted on promotion on merit, and where disputes arose between British and Portuguese officers he would back the Portuguese man if he felt he was right. The common soldier, notwithstanding the famous comment of 'whore's our Arthur?' attributed to one at Albuera, seems to have liked him and he probably had the common touch, as intimated by Creevey. Rifleman Harris approved and Andrew Pearson not only applauded Beresford's bravery but also noted Beresford's herculean strength and that he was terrible to look upon at all times. The latter may be a further reference to the squint he had in one eye.[17] Beresford's bravery was never in doubt, he led from the front on many occasions, including the battles of Salamanca and Toulouse. In Albuera he was in the thick of it, which would suggest he was not over cautious, at least when it came to his own life. A general, however, has to be able to oversee the entire battle, and it must be hard to keep track of developments if the commander is particularly involved in close contact with the enemy.

Beresford apparently also had a good sense of humour, even if his table was not known for its gourmet dishes.[18] Lady Anne Barnard referred to him as 'good humoured and conversable' when she met him in 1799.[19] Towards the end of the war Richard Henegan, who was a commissary with the Field Train and later an ordnance commissary, was brought before Beresford at Saint-Pé after the battle of Nivelle, having sought to prevent a Portuguese commissary taking forage on the basis that this act had not been approved by the French municipal authorities. The Mayor of Saint-Pé was produced to confirm that approval had been given, whereupon Henegan received a roasting from the Marshal, after which he was no longer cross. Henegan observed that Beresford was a well known joker and in the 48th Regiment was known as 'The Joker'.[20] He apparently never lost his Irish accent, alluded to by Creevey, and Lady Barnard is helpful in forming a picture of him with her description of Beresford as 'having but a small portion of the Irish Housemaid along with the manners of the noble blood of the Marquiss [sic] father'.[21]

One of the most fascinating relationships to emerge out of the war was that between Prince João and Beresford, who in due course became an adviser in whom João placed great confidence. They would not meet until 1815, when Beresford was in Brazil for some eleven months, however Beresford was clearly trusted by João long before that visit, though it is difficult to get a flavour of this trust from the formal correspondence between them. Presumably João was given a good report by Strangford, the British emissary to Rio, and at this stage of their relationship Forjaz would probably also have been supportive. Forjaz's strong support of reform in the army enabled him and Beresford to work together throughout the war. Likewise, when Lemos de Lacerda was sent to Rio by Beresford he would have been able to brief the Prince Regent and his ministers.

The Chamberlain of the Common Court of the Council of the City of London, when awarding Beresford the Freedom of the City, was effusive in stating his admiration for Beresford's success:

in an attempt where even great Pompey failed. He boasted he had only to stamp his foot in any part of Italy, and numerous armies would spring up to his aid; but you my Lord, without boasting, succeeded in calling into action the latent powers of a friendly Nation, and, by adding discipline to their native valour, enabled them nobly and powerfully to co-operate in the great cause of Europe's Deliverance.[22]

Here again we see evidence of Beresford's modesty, which had been referred to by Creevey. This achievement was the essence of Beresford's contribution to victory in a conflict where he had done more than any other individual to assist Wellington in the Peninsula.[23]

Beresford had his difficulties, caused in part at least by adherence to a strict hierarchical system in the British army. He also had his admirers. In *Wellington's Army in the Peninsula 1808–1814*, Michael Glover quotes an unnamed British officer writing of Beresford:

He is a very brave officer and with a greater share of talent than our generals probably average, and the spirit with which he embarked, and the firmness which he displayed in this nation's service cannot be too highly commended. Faults, grievous faults, it cannot be denied that he possesses, of which ungovernable temper and obstinacy are the most prominent. These are two traits which would even lead one to doubt the goodness of his heart, which on the other hand is manifested by many examples of his private kindness and unsolicited benevolence.[24]

Beresford was not without his supporters in Portugal either. The *Gazeta de Lisboa* on 23 June 1814 reproduced a panegyric of Wellington and Beresford in which it stated of Beresford:

Son of Portugal honed in fine stone
O Illustrious Beresford, acclaimed Hero;
Commanding wisely and in accordance with the law,
Showing rare valour in the field.[25]

A newspaper might reflect public opinion or it might have another agenda, such as to seek to curry favour. Others did not have the same imperative. Father Frade Fortunato, a Cistercian who later became Bishop of Evora, wrote biographical accounts of a number of the leading players in the Peninsular War. Beresford, he opined, combined diplomacy with discipline, punishing delinquents in proportion to their crimes, and in doing so persuaded the Portuguese nation that many of the practices hitherto considered acceptable were in fact inadmissible.[26] Perhaps even more important is the evidence of Ricardo Raymundo Nogueira, a contemporary who lived through the wars. A professor of law at Coimbra University, and a politician who served as a member of the Regency Council from 1810 to 1820, he would have known Beresford well, and certainly in later years was generally one of the Marshal's opponents. Of Beresford he said:

> He is a brave soldier and a great officer for disciplining the army. Portugal owes him a great deal in this respect and his ability in getting the military laws observed brought our troops to a state of perfection that in a short space of time placed them on a par with the best in Europe. A lot of this was due to his inflexibility of character and to his being a foreigner ... I believe that one of the great benefits we owe to providence was that of having employed the Duke of Wellington in command of the Allied army and Beresford in the organisation and instruction of our troops, which he commanded under the orders of Wellington. If the duties had been reversed I am persuaded things would have gone badly because the Duke of Wellington did not have the character to enter into the details of supervising the observance of military discipline, nor was Beresford as skilled as he was in directing a battle and forming a plan of campaign. However, these good qualities of the Marshal were counterbalanced by great defects. He is extremely ambitious for power, obstinate and imprudent.[27]

Beresford's return to Portugal in the late summer of 1814 would open another chapter in his life. He was to find that with the defeat of the French some of his erstwhile strongest supporters in the Portuguese Regency not only no longer felt the need to back him, but on occasion sought to attack his authority both covertly and openly. Portuguese politics over the next six years were to test the Marshal as Commander in Chief of the Portuguese army to a degree he had not hitherto experienced, in circumstances where after Napoleon's final defeat at Waterloo, the threat from France was replaced by Spain, Portugal's traditional enemy.

17 PORTUGAL AND BRAZIL, 1814–1820

These years are the story of Marshal Beresford's struggle to maintain the authority of the Portuguese crown and the strength of the Portuguese army in the face of almost relentless opposition from the Portuguese Regency. Driven by a desire to restore Portugal's – and their own – fortunes, which had been substantially eclipsed by the removal of the Court and administration to Rio de Janeiro in 1807, part of that process of restoration involved making economies by reducing the size of the army, while at the same time removing Beresford and the British officers in the army so that Portuguese individuals might be advanced in their place.

The Regency pursued defence cuts notwithstanding internal and external threats to the country. It had, of course, been a thorn in the sides of both Wellington and Beresford during the Peninsular War, but at that time Forjaz, Secretary for War and Foreign Affairs, had for the most part been their supporter while the Principal Sousa (a member of the powerful Sousa Coutinho family) had frequently opposed their schemes. Beresford after the end of the war had to face the opposition of both men, and his position was made all the more difficult by their success in ensuring that other members of the Regency who were more pro-British no longer frequented that body (The Monteiro-mor – Marquis of Olhão – and Ricardo Raymundo Noguiera). On occasion the Principal did support Beresford, but this was probably with a view to checking Forjaz's power and position.

Beresford returned to Lisbon to resume command of the Portuguese army in August 1814. He returned as Baron Beresford of Dungarvan and Albuera, which carried with it the handsome pension of £2,000 p.a. for life. While his duty took him back to Portugal, he was not at all optimistic for the future, for with the danger of French invasion gone, he appeared to have lost his trump card in dealing with a recalcitrant Regency. It is clear that his purpose in returning to Portugal was to welcome back Prince João on his return from Brazil, and that he did not expect to stay long afterwards. In writing to his brother John Poo (then a naval captain), who had been sent to Brazil to escort the Portuguese royals to Lisbon, he indicated not only that he felt his stay would be of a short duration, but that if the King's ministers were of the same view as the Regency it would be impossible for British officers to remain in Portugal unless it was for pleasure. For his own part he requested John Poo to tell João that had it not been for the Prince's anticipated return, the Marshal would not himself have returned to Portugal.[1] That Beresford remained in Portugal for the next six years was due to the strong support he received from Prince Regent (soon to be King) João and some of the ministers in Brazil, as well as from the British government.

Beresford returned to a Portugal devastated by war and the loss of Brazilian trade – now open to all following the treaties with Great Britain giving the merchant subjects of George III preferential status over other nations. The absence of the royal family and much of the nobility in Brazil combined with the emergence of liberal thought to produce a ferment of unrest in Portugal reflecting events elsewhere in Europe. Events in Portugal and Beresford's role in them in the period 1814–20 should not be viewed in isolation for they are only explicable in terms of what was happening elsewhere in Europe and the Americas.

The Portuguese army arrived back in Portugal after its long march through south west France and northern Spain in early August, the sick and wounded having been sent back by boat from Passages in northern Spain. Beresford's first move on his return was to organise a victory parade for the Portuguese army. In his Order of the Day (Ordem do Dia) just after his arrival in Lisbon on 27 August he stated he would forever recall the sacrifices they had made, noting they had proved themselves the equal of the best soldiers in Europe. The Marshal's sentiments were not reflected in the actions of the Regency. The regiments retired to barracks where they were soon to learn their fate. Volunteers were the first to be let go, even though Beresford's Quartermaster General, Benjamin D'Urban, felt they were in many instances the best troops.[2] The result impacted particularly on the cavalry regiments, many of which were 'reduced to nothing'.[3] More drastic was the decision to reduce the pay of those in the ranks, which D'Urban attributed to a desire by the Regents to reduce the army to its 'former state of wretchedness and nonentity'. He was disgusted, noting on his arrival in Lisbon a few days after Beresford:

His [Beresford's] reception by the government pretty well indicated their feeling towards him and the line of conduct they had in view to adopt. The General who had formed their army from worse than nothing to be the second in Europe in the scale of Excellence, who had raised their military character from the Dust, from something beneath Contempt, to the praise and admiration of the Military World, and had thus placed security within the grasp of Portugal, by giving her Martial Reputation of Renown, who had more than once shed his Blood, – who had a hundred times risked his life, who had sacrificed his fortune and his Health, nay staked his Character as a soldier to serve and save her, – This General, – (will Posterity believe it?) after Six Campaigns of Glory, returning from the last of these, in which he had led her Triumphant Legions into the Heart of France, and left the Terror of her Bayonets under the walls of Toulouse, – This General was suffered to land in the Metropolis of the Country he had thus served, and saved, and lifted into notice, and proceed to his house like an humble individual unhonoured, unvisited, unregarded.[4]

D'Urban speculated that some of the nobility might even aspire to deliver the kingdom of Portugal to be a province of Spain, a most perceptive remark given the events that were to follow. He claimed that the Government now proceeded to put in place a plan that it had long meditated over and of which he had warned Beresford when the latter had indicated an intention to return to Portugal. This involved a dual strategy of getting rid of the Marshal, combined with clearing the army of British officers.

The attack on the Marshal was to be achieved by intrigue in Portugal and Brazil, with a view to severing Beresford from Prince João's support, removing British officers involved, refusing to implement appointments, and the non-payment of salaries. D'Urban cited history and the treatment of former foreign commanders such as Marshals Schomberg and La Lippe as precedent for his prediction, warning Beresford that if he stayed his reputation was likely to suffer, unless he secured the full backing of both the British Government and the Prince Regent of Portugal.

The desire of the Regency, and undoubtedly some officers, to terminate British involvement in the Portuguese army clearly did not reflect Beresford's standing amongst the officer class in general. In 1815 he received a ringing endorsement from the officers, who chose to subscribe to a fund which resulted in the creation of a stunningly beautiful ceremonial sword and scabbard designed by the Portuguese royal painter Domingos António Sequeira. It bore the inscription:

'Beresford do valor a insignia empunhe'
(Beresford who has the courage to wield it);

and on the reverse,

'Heróe votado á Glória Lusitana'
(Voted a hero to Lusitanian glory).

It bore his family crest and was complemented by a chest plate and shoulder strap with a fitting for the Grand Cross of the Order of the Tower and the Sword.[5]

The conduct of the Regency in wishing to reduce the size of the army was understandable from a purely economic perspective, notwithstanding D'Urban's condemnation. The country had been ruined by the war and was continuing to run a considerable budgetary deficit. Almost immediately, pressure was exerted on Beresford to dismiss and replace the British officers in the Portuguese army. In the short term these were reduced by about fifty to 117 and these were placed on full British pay in January 1815.[6] D'Urban felt Beresford should not have agreed to this reduction as it would only undermine the army, both physically and morally; an objective the Regency sought to achieve by failing to feed it properly and by generally neglecting that body. The Regency had known since April of the impending return of the Portuguese army, yet no plans had been made to quarter the regiments and the barracks were unfit for their reception. Beresford made representations, but in the first instance – in the manner frequently adopted by governments who do not wish to address a problem – the Regency appointed a Commission of Inspection, a commission which D'Urban claimed was of little or no use, remaining under various pretences in the same place for months on end.[7] As a result, men were forced to spend a severe winter in inadequate barracks without the benefit of blankets, mattresses or articles of 'barrack furniture'. D'Urban was critical of Beresford's forbearance, wondering why he did not take immediately the step he was to pursue later of going to Brazil to seek the support of the Crown and an enhancement of his own powers.

Matters improved somewhat in early 1815 with the arrival of clothing and equipment from England, enabling D'Urban to re-equip some regiments, though he fulminated against the continuing practices of the Regency, which he felt Beresford only tolerated because of his expectation of the arrival of Prince João from Brazil. Meanwhile some 12,500 men were discharged from the army.[8]

The electrifying report that Napoleon had escaped from Elba was followed by news that Wellington had requested a Portuguese contingent be sent to the Low Countries to join the Allies in the struggle to be renewed against Napoleon. Wellington wrote to Beresford in March seeking 12,000–14,000 men and his request was endorsed by the Count of Palmela (as he then was), the Portuguese envoy to the Congress of Vienna.[9] Beresford readily acquiesced and ordered D'Urban to prepare a force for embarkation, though he already perceived that the Regency were looking for an excuse not to comply with the request, reporting that the news from France had thrown Forjaz into despondency and that Beresford was so out of favour with the Regency that he had no influence.[10] The Portuguese contribution as envisaged by Beresford and D'Urban was to be composed of 12 regiments of the line, 6 regiments of caçadores, 4 brigades of artillery and a few squadrons of cavalry. D'Urban designated officers from his own staff to accompany the expedition and furnished a detailed plan of the clothing and equipment required. British transports began to arrive in the Tagus towards the end of April, but in early May Beresford advised Wellington that the Regency had determined not to decide on the request to furnish troops until they had the approval of the Regent. He anticipated delay and felt the Regents would never send 'this force', as all they were doing was preparing to send the assembled force to the Brazils.[11]

The force for 'the Brazils' had been requested by João before Napoleon escaped from Elba. It was required because for the Portuguese crown another dynamic was at work, based on a desire to take advantage of Spanish weakness in the Americas in the face of widespread independence movements. The chance to expand and secure Brazil's southern frontier by extending Portuguese territory to the Banda Oriental bordering the River Plate (modern-day Uruguay) was too good an opportunity to miss in an area that had been the subject of historic dispute between the two Iberian nations. As recently as 1811 Portugal had sent armed forces into the area.

In attempting the conquest of the Banda Oriental, João was not just attempting to overthrow Spanish rule but resist the attempts of the Rio de la Plata (Argentina) to impose its will on the left bank of the river centred at Montevideo, and the desire of some of the inhabitants for full independence. With that in mind he sought 5,000 troops from Portugal, together with the best officers possible. Beresford expressed his dismay to Wellington in early May, indicating this move would impact negatively on the force which he still aspired to send to Flanders.[12] By early June he was writing despondently, 'I am doomed I fear for this campaign to be a spectator when I would rather be an actor.'[13] Even a proposal put forward by the Spanish government to send a composite British–Portuguese–Spanish force under Beresford to invade south west France came to nothing. Beresford expressed his view of the Regency succinctly: 'I have been also quite disgusted with the refusal of these people to enter into the common cause of Europe.'[14]

George Canning, now the British Minister Plenipotentiary in Portugal, was so incensed at the refusal of the Regency to allow the embarkation of the force for either Flanders or Bordeaux without the specific order of the Prince Regent that he declared that if the Spanish invaded Portugal there would not be a voice raised in England to save the country.[15] Beresford, for his part, was bitterly disappointed. Writing to Wellington after receiving the news of Waterloo he congratulated the Duke while regretting the loss of so many of his 'family'. He went on to express his displeasure because the Regency had determined, 'to have no part in the war but done everything possible to continue to destroy the army and their object was to avoid entering into the war should it have been continued'. He declared he would not put up with the attitude of the Regency and would leave, but before making a final decision he intended to travel to Brazil to ascertain the views of the Regent, proposing to be back 'whether in or out of Portuguese service by December'.[16]

In fact, notwithstanding Wellington and Beresford's enthusiasm for Portuguese troops, the British government doubted whether such an expeditionary force to the Netherlands was the answer to the requirement for manpower. Bathurst made the point forcibly to Wellington, suggesting that it would take too long to get the detachment to Ostend and in any event twice as many Germans could be obtained for the same money. However, he chose to leave the final decision to Wellington.[17]

In early June 1815 the Regency refused to ratify Beresford's promotion of British officers in the Portuguese army and, as D'Urban put it, 'this brought the affair to a crisis and rendered it impossible to proceed'.[18] The proposed promotions included Colonel William Cox, the former military commander of Almeida who had surrendered that fortress to the French in 1810 following an explosion in the fort's magazine which rendered the castle virtually indefensible. For the way in which the fort had been surrendered, Almeida e Costa (the Portuguese Governor of the town) had been tried and executed. Now the Portuguese wished to court martial Cox, who had spent the balance of the war imprisoned in France. As a result he was court martialled by a mixed Court of Portuguese and British army officers but acquitted in March 1815.

The Regents sought to obstruct Beresford's departure for Rio, obviously fearing that he would obtain royal support.[19] For rather different reasons, the security and safety of Portugal, Viscount Santarém, a strong supporter of the monarchy, also wished him to remain, but on 10 August Beresford sailed from Lisbon on the *Fama*, a ship of the Portuguese navy. He fully intended his visit to Brazil to be a short one, but it was to be September 1816 before he returned.

On leaving Portugal, D'Urban tells us that the Marshal was attended by all the officers in or near Lisbon, notwithstanding the intrigues of the Regency. Certainly at this time Beresford seems to have commanded the full support of the army. He left in his place a number of trusted officers in crucial commands throughout Portugal, none more so than Sir Archibald Campbell, commanding the Lisbon division. On arriving in Brazil, Beresford was provided with a substantial residence in Rio, along with a carriage and horses. His initial reaction was to be impressed by the country, writing to Canning, still British Minister in Lisbon: 'the country is most beautiful. No part of the world I have seen exceeds it. It is magnificent, the soil most fertile, and verdure is here the whole year round. It is a magnificent country and capable of anything.'[20]

The first test Beresford had to face in Brazil was a suggestion by the Regents that he be replaced as Commander in Chief by a German with German officers replacing their English counterparts. Neither Prince João nor António Araújo, now Minister for the Marine and the Colonies (and in 1815 created the Conde de Barca), supported the Regents' suggestion, for notwithstanding difficulties – including Britain's attempt to prohibit slaving operations – the Prince not only trusted Beresford but was keen to maintain the British connection. In Araújo we see again one of the conundrums of Portuguese politics, for here was a Minister who in the previous decade had been so pro-French that he had allowed the army to wither through neglect, and who had been so hated that he had had to board the vessels for Brazil in 1807 in disguise, but who was now supporting the pro-British faction in politics.

Beresford wished to avoid any repetition of the scenario which had precluded the dispatch of Portuguese troops to the Low Countries to assist Wellington earlier in 1815 on Napoleon's escape from Elba. Writing home, he proposed that the Portuguese military establishment be maintained at 54,000 together with a militia. This would enable 15,000–20,000 men to be available to serve abroad if subsidised. The danger of the Regency once again saying that it had no authority to send troops abroad could be overcome by a series of treaties providing for mutual aid. Meanwhile, Canning had departed Lisbon when it became clear that João would not be returning there. While Canning's posting there is viewed as his return from political exile following his falling out with Castlereagh, it also serves to demonstrate the importance Britain attached to the Portuguese connection.

The Marshal's visit to Rio de Janeiro once again demonstrated the difficulties under which Beresford laboured attempting to serve two masters, Great Britain and Portugal, and within the Portuguese political system demonstrated his desire to serve Prince João in preference to the Regency in Portugal, a position that was unsurprisingly repeated later in the Portuguese civil wars between João's sons; where Beresford, a committed Tory in British politics, steadfastly opposed liberalism.

In December, in a further sign of royal support, Beresford was created Marshal-General of all the armies of the Crown in both Europe and the Americas, the appointment being made symbolically on Queen Maria's eighty-first birthday.[21] In the same month, one of Beresford's most trusted Portuguese advisers, Lemos de Lacerda was created Viscount Juromenha. Beresford was now increasingly anxious to return to Portugal, but on 20 March 1816 Queen Maria died and João at last succeeded to the throne. In a signal sign of his high standing, Beresford was selected as one of the pallbearers at Maria's funeral, the only non-Portuguese to do so. However, the Court then went into a full year's mourning and Beresford found it impossible to depart for some months.

Towards the end of 1815, the first part of the Portuguese expeditionary force destined for the Banda Oriental arrived in Rio de Janeiro. In January 1816, the Division 'the Royal Volunteers of the Prince' under General Lecor embarked from Portugal for Brazil. In total this Division numbered nearly 5,000 (3,632 infantry, 894 cavalry and 282 artillerymen). Beresford was on hand to welcome the arrivals from Portugal, and it was not until after the departure of Lecor's division to join other Portuguese and Brazilian troops to create a force of 10,000 men at Santa Catarina (an island forming a natural harbour in the Province of the same name north of the Banda Oriental), in preparation for the invasion of the Banda Oriental that Beresford was able to sail for Lisbon on the Portuguese frigate *Principe Dom Pedro*.

The importance of the invasion and capture of the Banda Oriental to the development of both Brazil and Portugal is that it diverted precious resources in terms of finance and men while increasing enmity with Spain. Beginning in January 1817 with the capture of Montevideo, the Portuguese extended their grip over the area which became known as the Province of Cisplatina, only to lose it to those in favour of independence in 1828 after Brazil itself became independent of Portugal in 1822.[22] The invasion brought further deterioration in Anglo-Portuguese relations, already suffering due to Britian's resolve to end slaving and its enforcement of a treaty to that effect on the Portuguese, for Britain had arranged an armistice between the Portuguese and the Spanish in 1812 in order to protect Spain's possessions. Efforts to persuade Portugal to withdraw from the area in 1817 were unsuccessful.

Life did not get any easier for those in charge of the Portuguese army in Portugal while Beresford was away. D'Urban's journal discloses the rejection of the report on the condition of barracks by Dom Miguel Forjaz, Secretary of State for War and Foreign Affairs, and the Quartermaster General's struggle to ameliorate the position of the troops so that they did not have to bear the misery of another winter in uninhabitable barracks without the necessaries to support them. Forjaz stated that very little could be done, ostensibly due to a shortage of finance. Some troops were ordered to be moved to new quarters, though D'Urban could do no more than express the hope that some little good might result, 'for this Gallant and Unfortunate Army, which has little merited that these lives which escaped the Fire and Sword of the Enemy in the Battles of Six Years should be extinguished by the hardships and misery to which their own Government so coolly consigns them.'[23]

Early in the New Year, D'Urban received the welcome news from Rio de Janeiro that all the promotions proposed by Beresford in 1815, including those of the British officers in the

Portuguese service, had been approved by Prince João, though the Regency failed to promulgate these notwithstanding their publication in the Court Gazette. He deplored the continued degradation of the army, which he feared would lay the country open to Spanish intervention. With the decision in 1816 that they should now be paid by the Portuguese government, the situation of the British officers in the Portuguese service became less attractive and less secure. A number, including D'Urban and Robert Arbuthnot, two of those who had served longest with Beresford, now prepared to depart.

The ministers of the new King had not been entirely lacking in strategy, however, for they had secured the agreement whereby the two Portuguese Princesses (Maria Isabella and Maria Francisca) would marry Ferdinand VII, king of Spain, and his brother Don Carlos. The two Princesses arrived in Cádiz on 5 September. Two weeks later, on 18 September after an absence of over one year, the Marshal-General himself disembarked at Lisbon after a two-month voyage. Although welcomed with smiles by the Regency, it was not long before he was at loggerheads again with its members as they determined to resist Royal orders on the basis that they would increase the expenses of the State.

Following Beresford's return to Portugal, matters again reached a crisis point when the Regency attempted to address arrears of army pay by allocating two-thirds of this in paper money, contrary to what had been agreed previously.[24] The position was exacerbated because Lecor's division in South America was still maintained on the Portuguese payroll. Beresford recognised that he still faced a difficult situation, observing to his good friend General Sir Denis Pack that on his return he found the Regency cowed but not beaten.[25]

Beresford was now seriously concerned at the state of unrest in Portugal, writing to Wellington on 7 November 1816 to warn him of the growth of a pro-Spanish party and his concerns of a developing conspiracy to overthrow the King. Wellington in turn warned Beresford that the Supreme Council of Spain had urged Ferdinand to reject the Portuguese Princesses and instead declare war against Portugal, using armies ostensibly prepared for campaigns in the conflict between Spain and Portugal in South America. In fact, Ferdinand shunned this advice marrying Maria Isabella; but the reality remained that Spain now had a number of armies available to invade Portugal, should it choose to do so, while the Portuguese army had both been degraded and part sent to Brazil, rendering the kingdom largely defenceless in the conventional sense. Spain protested repeatedly to the British government at the Portuguese intervention in the Banda Oriental, with the result that the Portuguese were informed in December 1816 that unless that government could give a satisfactory explanation Britain would have to consider that Portugal had forfeited her claim to compensation in respect of slaving vessels illegally seized by British cruisers, a claim recognised under secret clause 3 of the Treaty between the two nations dated 22 January 1815.[26]

Beresford expressed his concern that Lecor's mission to the Banda Oriental would lead to Spanish intervention in Portugal in the event of the capture of Montevideo by the Portuguese, an event that did occur on 20 January 1817. With reports of a Spanish invasion imminent, Beresford sought orders from Forjaz at the end of December 1816 to fill up the regiments of the line with transfers from the militia. The Regency took fright, permitting the appointments ordered in Rio the previous February. However, while the Regency then authorised Beresford to prepare for the defence of Portugal, his instructions were shrouded in secrecy in the hope that the Spanish would not feel these moves were linked to Lecor's achievement. Only 16,000 troops were available to take the field in defence of Portugal, with the Spanish under O'Donnell having an estimated 20,000–30,000 men available in Andalusia alone. Beresford's position was made more difficult by the less than lukewarm support for Portugal emanating from Britain.

Beresford set off on a tour of the Alentejo in February 1817, returning to Lisbon later that month appalled by the state of ruin of the fortresses, amid fresh rumours of an impending Spanish invasion. Spain used the Portuguese invasion of the settlements on the River Plate (Banda Oriental) as an excuse to demand of Great Britain that Beresford be withdrawn from the Portuguese service. The Regency, in an act which is difficult to explain in the context of their desire to be rid of him, then requested Beresford to take such steps as were necessary for the defence of the Kingdom. Probably the only explanation is that while the nobility in Portugal wished to weaken the crown and increase their own strength, they did not – or at least most of them did not – contrary to D'Urban's view desire a Spanish occupation of the country.

Beresford now lost his right-hand man in Portugal, for D'Urban was promoted Colonel of the Royal Staff Corps and Deputy Quartermaster General of the British army; a move which required his return to England after eight years at Beresford's side. D'Urban endeavoured to continue to support his former commander from England in the struggle to defend Portugal from Spanish intervention. However, during 1817 help for Beresford was to come from another quarter.

In early April 1817, Beresford became aware of rumours of an alleged intended coup. His informant was an army officer and the information available initially was scanty in the extreme.[27] The information pointed to a plot involving a number of Portuguese freemasons and others, but it was so nebulous that Beresford determined to seek to uncover more rather than bring a report to the Regency. This he proceeded to do, through persuading his informant to get further involved with those planning a rising. By 23 May Beresford was in possession of sufficient detail to be reasonably sure that some attempt was imminent, but he faced a problem in that his informant was being sent by the plotters to Beira to enlist further support. He determined therefore to go public, even though the identity of all the leaders remained unclear. In the first instance, he approached a number of high-ranking individuals he trusted to discuss with them whether he should hold off telling the Regency until he discovered more, or whether the anticipation of an almost immediate attempt to overthrow the regime meant he should inform the Regency of what he knew without delay.[28] They strongly advised him to act without waiting further, and on the same day he sought out Dom Miguel Pereira Forjaz, the Minister for War, and gave him details and papers.

In discussion with Forjaz and the other members of the Regency present he sought ten days grace in which to make further enquiries, but the Regency were so alarmed at the prospect of a coup that it determined to proceed with the arrest of the identified personnel as quickly as possible. With admirable speed the Marshal's erstwhile enemies in the Regency had become

Beresford's supporters for the purpose of saving their own positions. On 25 May, thirty alleged conspirators were arrested in successful raids, though Beresford appears to have felt that had this move been delayed he might have uncovered others who were never indicted.[29] Many of those arrested were masons. Alarmingly, but perhaps unsurprisingly for Beresford, a number were middle-ranking officers in the army; mostly captains but with a smattering of majors and one colonel. At the top of the pyramid of those arrested was General Gomes Freire de Andrade, a soldier who had served Napoleon from 1808 until 1814 before being allowed to return to Portugal in the latter year. Yet the army as a whole remained loyal, which greatly strengthened Beresford's standing.

The accused were put on trial during the summer and on 18 October twelve of the convicted were executed, while three or four were exiled to the African colonies and two were reported acquitted. The bodies of the executed, including General Gomes Freire de Andrade, were burned afterwards.[30] Because of delays in the hangings, these were still going on after nightfall, giving rise to the famous – or infamous – comment attributed to Forjaz: 'felizmente há luar' (fortunately there was moonlight).[31]

Beresford played no part in the prosecution of the conspirators, though he did reportedly interview at least one of the prisoners. He sought to ensure that Gomes Freire enjoyed at least a comfortable imprisonment before and during his trial, though his efforts were on occasions frustrated by the Regency.[32] Apprehending that executions would create martyrs, Beresford sought a deferment of the implementation of the death sentences passed down, in order that they might be confirmed or commuted by King João, but this was refused by the Regency, whether through concern for their own authority or otherwise. Indeed, there was some speculation that the plotters had a connection with a member of the Regency or other powerful members of the nobility, though if this was the case it does not appear to have been disclosed.[33] Beresford himself felt that Gomes Freire was a pawn being used by others and later suggested that the executed General had revealed names after his arrest which were suppressed by the Regency.

One of the most interesting military figures involved in the plot was Frederick, Baron von Eben, a Prussian officer who served in the British army before joining the Loyal Lusitanian Legion to serve in Portugal in 1808. Eben served with the Portuguese army throughout the Peninsular War. A General in the Portuguese service and a Colonel in the British army by the end of the war, he felt aggrieved at what he perceived to be Beresford's failure to promote him further in 1815, and a personal animosity had developed when his commission in Portugal was terminated. Nonetheless, with the Prince Regent's permission Eben stayed on in Portugal. Beresford had to tread carefully for Eben was a personal friend of many members of the British royal family and was Aide-de-Camp to the Prince Regent (later George IV). That he was a foreigner resulted in his escaping a death sentence but led to him being banished from Portugal under pain of execution if he ever returned to any Portuguese possession. His close friendship with the royal family did not save him from condemnation in Britain, where he was dismissed by the Prince Regent from the service of the King and his name removed from the army list.[34]

In fact, Beresford's correspondence with his half-brother John Poo clearly shows he had doubts as to Eben's guilt, noting that although his consorting with Gomes Freire was suspicious, there was no hard evidence of his involvement, and Beresford thought the Regency might just send him to England on the mail packet when he was first arrested. Indeed, he expressly wanted to avoid prejudicial opinion being formed in Britain against Eben on the basis the Prussian might be perfectly innocent; evidence that notwithstanding any personal animosity Beresford wished Eben to be treated fairly.[35] Eben went on to lead a colourful life in South America, where he joined Simon Bolivar in the wars of independence against Spain, ultimately dying in Bogota in 1835.

The objectives of these revolutionaries of 1817 remain unclear, though it would appear they were both anti-Regency and they sought the removal of Beresford as Commander in Chief of the army and the dismissal of the British officers remaining with the army. Some commentators have suggested they were also anti- the monarchy in the form of the distant João, whose reluctance to return from Brazil to Portugal was causing serious discontent in circumstances where the mother country was now almost the colony of its former dependency. Economically, Portugal had been devastated not just by three French invasions between 1807 and 1810/11 but by the liberalisation of Portuguese and Brazilian trade to the advantage of Great Britain, which deprived Portugal of its base as an entrepôt for goods coming from its colonies. There seem to have been suggestions in 1817 that João might be replaced as King by the Duke of Cadaval, who belonged to a cadet branch of the House of Braganza.[36] It is clear that a majority of the plotters were masons influenced by liberal philosophy, extolling both individual freedoms and nationalism; principles which led them to seek to curb absolutism and substitute a constitutional type of monarchy. A few may have been republicans, certainly Beresford viewed them as Jacobins, but they were almost certainly in a small minority. Spanish armies on Portugal's frontiers and the supply of arms to the revolutionaries were designed to exert pressure on João and the Portuguese government so as to cause João to desist from the attempted expansion of his dominions in South America. It is extremely unlikely that however much he wished to frustrate João's ambitions in South America that Ferdinand VII wished to promote a radical or liberal government in Portugal. However, annexation of Portugal was an enticing prospect.

Beresford survived 1817 and for a time had consolidated his own position vis-à-vis the Regency, for that body had been seriously shaken by the Gomes Freire conspiracy and realised not only that the causes of the plot were more than a desire to remove Beresford and the British officers in the Portuguese army, but that the Regency's own survival might depend on the army. However, it was not long before the tensions mounted again between the Regency and Beresford, and though the evidence suggests he played no part in the prosecution and trial of the plotters he was inevitably associated in the public mind with the execution of men who came to be seen as martyrs in Portugal. On this occasion few senior officers had joined the conspiracy, but Beresford must have been concerned at the number of junior officers who showed their disloyalty and who were condemned for treason. His correspondence with D'Urban, now in London, reflects Beresford's anxiety even towards the end of 1817 that Spain might intervene in Portugal and the difficulties, nay inability, of the army to prevent that intervention. Beresford

243

lamented that including every man on paper he would only be able to put 21,000 men in the field if Spain should invade, and he apprehended that just as they had done in 1810 the Regency would seek to defend the country from 'Chaves to Lagos' rather than draw a defensive ring around Lisbon.[37] He was concerned that other 'traitors' would gravitate to the 'Spanish party' and that Portugal surrounded by Spanish armies could with luck survive one campaign but no more. Indeed, D'Urban himself was so troubled by this correspondence that he suggested to the Prime Minister (Liverpool) that he might be allowed to return to Portugal 'should matters proceed'.[38]

Absent a successful coup with or without Spanish intervention, or an assassination, Beresford's position remained secure as long as he retained the confidence of João. His stay of nearly one year in Rio in 1815–16 had cemented an already strong relationship, which had prospered in the absence of any personal meeting up to that point, and in spite of the attempt by some politicians in both Portugal and Brazil to secure his downfall. Beresford had served João well in the war, and thereafter had enabled the King to seek to extend the boundaries of the influence of the Portuguese crown by sending some of the best battle-hardened troops from Portugal to Brazil, even though he personally disapproved of the invasion of the Banda Oriental because he feared it might lead to conflict with Spain, for which the remainder of the Portuguese army was unprepared. The crucial role played by the Marshal in terms of the survival of the House of Braganza was further emphasised by a rebellion in the Brazilian province of Pernambuco in the spring of 1817, a rebellion brought on by gross dissatisfaction amongst the Brazilian settlers who perceived the Portuguese arrivals since 1807 getting jobs and preferment at their expense, combined with a disastrous collapse in sugar prices. That rebellion was forcibly put down by loyal troops, many of them Portuguese.

These two events (the rebellion in Brazil and conspiracy uncovered in Portugal) made it clear that the House of Braganza was no longer inviolable and its absolutist powers might be the subject of attack, notwithstanding the failure of the movements on both sides of the Atlantic in 1817. The genie had escaped from the bottle and though it had been re-corked, the years ahead were to prove challenging for the Portuguese royal family. Those who held power in Portugal felt they were neglected and disadvantaged by João ruling from Brazil, while the settlers long established in Brazil felt ignored and demeaned by the new arrivals from Portugal. Beresford had repeatedly urged João to return to Portugal once the war had ended. He made the case not just to João but to his ministers in Brazil.[39] Those urgings were not just to reflect British government policy but arose because he believed that such a move was necessary to save the kingdom for the House of Braganza. Beresford's political nous was not always beyond criticism, but in this belief he was constant and was to prove correct. In May 1819, there were rumours in the Correio Braziliense of the impending return to Portugal of the royal family, but these proved once again to be unfounded. Portugal was rapidly descending into a state of crisis, with the army unpaid and frequently unfed, but it was rebellion in next door Spain in 1820 which was to ignite the fires of revolution again in Portugal. Unfortunately for João, and indeed perhaps for Beresford, the Marshal's warnings and exhortations to João to return to Portugal, frequently reported in his letters home, went unheeded.

The shifting sands of Portuguese politics are hard to follow both during the Peninsular War and afterwards. Families were split between pro-British and pro-French factions and sometimes positions became reversed. The Principal Sousa, who had been such a thorn in both Wellington and Beresford's sides during the war at a time when Forjaz supported their efforts, became openly more pro-British afterwards, whereas Forjaz became an almost constant opponent of Beresford, ostensibly with a view to making economies in the army but also with the objective of replacing Beresford and the British officers with Portuguese. Beresford's struggle with Forjaz became more obvious after 1817, when Sousa died, and in the following year he considered resigning his position, even though the British government felt that his presence there was important to the stability of Portugal.[40]

During 1818, Portugal was so calm that Beresford felt it safe to make a trip to both England and Ireland, but not before a meeting with the Regents to discuss defence which, he observed, revealed such disarray in the country's finances that he might as well not have attended. Later in the year he visited Waterloo with John Poo. Together they attended the Grand Review of the Allied armies at Valenciennes. Arriving back in Lisbon in February 1819 he received a good reception, though he noted that the pay of the soldiers (with the exception of those in Lisbon) was in arrears from January.[41] All seemed well and it was at this time Beresford applied to Castlereagh for King George's permission to allow him to take out Portuguese nationality, perhaps in the hope it would secure his position as Commander in Chief, a permission which was granted on 23 April.[42] It is unclear whether he did in fact act on this permission, but it seems unlikely, even though on his return Beresford made an extensive and triumphal tour of central and northern Portugal, staying with members of the clergy in Coimbra, Porto and Braga.

His staff included 'young Cradock', the son of the man whom Wellington had replaced back in 1809 as commander of the British forces in Portugal, surely giving the lie to the suggestion that Cradock and Beresford had not seen eye to eye during their brief time together before Wellington's arrival. Beresford wrote to his half-sister Harriet in praise of the countryside and the people of Portugal but condemning the government, even though he found its attitude towards him much changed, giving no ground for complaint.[43] The Marshal was further gratified when he made a tour of inspection of troops north of the Tagus in July to be able to report that he had been very well received and that the troops (or what are left of them) were in a most excellent state.[44]

Revolution in neighbouring Spain clearly had the Marshal worried. A large Spanish army destined to attempt to reimpose Spanish rule in South America was being assembled in Andalusia with the object of sailing from Cádiz when it rebelled under General Rafael del Riego. It was followed by revolts elsewhere in Spain, resulting ultimately in the restoration of the liberal Constitution of 1812. Even prior to the outbreak of hostilities within Spain, the Marshal advised John Poo Beresford in the autumn of 1819 that he planned to go to Rio to take leave of the King with a view to returning to Ireland, a desire he repeated in early 1820. By December 1819 there were again substantial arrears in army pay, which had only been made to April, and although the Regency had resolved to sell some Crown lands, he was conscious of the fact that there were other demands which might preclude the payment of arrears. He advised Wellington in January that events in Portugal were hindering his departure for Rio, though he reported the country quiet for the present. The problem as he saw it was that the system of government in Portugal was so like Spain that Portugal could never be safe 'and the string that is so stretched must be in momentary danger of breaking'.[45] Though the Regents now behaved well towards him, he felt he could not go on working with Forjaz and he indicated a desire to resign his situation.[46] Wellington urged him to stay on until at least Beresford could see what the relations between the two governments of the Peninsula were likely to be after the mutiny of Spanish troops had been defeated.[47] Wellington's confidence proved to be misplaced, for Ferdinand was forced to accept again the liberal constitution of 1812. It was only when the French invaded Spain in 1823 that Ferdinand was able to restore absolutism.

Beresford feared that the loss of Spain's South American colonies made it all the more likely she would turn her attention to Portugal. In this respect his concerns may have been fully justified, for there is evidence that amongst an element of Ferdinand's advisers there was an extensive strategy which envisaged using the Portuguese invasion of the Banda Oriental as an excuse to invade and conquer Portugal; and that further those involved were prepared if necessary to forfeit Spain's South American colonies if the result was the permanent annexation of Portugal to the Spanish Crown.[48] Spanish intelligence deriving from Rio clearly indicated that the Braganzas were not keen to return to Portugal and that instead they preferred to seek to expand their New World empire. That Spain did not invade Portugal was partly due to the dysfunctional nature of the Spanish government, where some ministers were unaware of policies and actions being followed by others, and partly due to the fact that a large radicalised army was kept in Extremadura for nearly four years while waiting for a decision as to its destination; the end result being the revolt of 1820.

In early March 1820, fed up at the failure to tackle abuses, Beresford confirmed to the Regents his intentions to travel to Rio which caused 'a great ferment'. He was doubtful he would succeed in either curbing the abuses, bring about reforms or be able to persuade João to return to Portugal, but felt he should try for the sake of preserving the kingdom.[49] In addition, he was determined to secure monies to pay the army. He thought that even if the liberals were to gain ground it would be some time before it 'affected us' and 'at all events I shall have time sufficient to go and return from Rio'.[50] Wellington and Palmela urged Beresford against going to Brazil at a time when matters in Spain were in such flux and with increasing unrest in Portugal, but it is clear the Duke's missive of 28 March to this effect did not reach Beresford before he sailed for Rio.[51] By now Beresford was more concerned at the possibility of an internal rising than external invasion in his absence, and in April, notwithstanding the Regents protests, he sailed for Rio on the Frigate *Spartan* fully fearing that 'Portugal must now go through the same crisis as Spain is now suffering'.[52]

He arrived in Rio on 2 May carrying letters from the Regents seeking royal intervention in Portugal. Beresford's sometimes fragile health did not trouble him and he reported that he had never felt better in his life. In early June he inspected a brigade of his Portuguese troops only to lament at their 'falling off' since their arrival in South America. Relations with João were excellent, but the discussions aimed at achieving his objectives of reforms and the return of the royals to Portugal were proving testing, and he felt that though it was not for want of trying, neither João nor the Prince Royal (Pedro) would travel to Portugal. He was forthright in his view that if João did not return to Portugal he would lose that kingdom and that Brazil would not be far behind. He even contemplated resignation once again, but ultimately determined this was not the moment and he owed it to João to soldier on. While his hopes of removing Forjaz from the Regency were not realised, João further promoted Beresford to Marshal-General 'a pessoa real' giving him the right to deal with João directly, bypassing the Minister for War. Further, he was granted a seat on the Regency.

Beresford left for Lisbon on HMS *Vainqueur* on 13 August with £80,000 to pay the army, but revolution broke out in Porto while he was returning to Portugal.[53] It spread to Lisbon, where the Regency caved in to the rebels in mid-September despite the attempt of Beresford's Adjutant-General, Brito Mozinho, to rally loyal troops. Wellington, who had felt Beresford should have remained in Portugal rather than travel to Brazil, was fiercely critical of the pusillanimity of the British officers remaining for not calling out the troops; but Sir Archibald Campbell did try to do so unsuccessfully, and when Brigadier General Sir Maxwell Grant attempted to intervene he was arrested and imprisoned in Porto. When Beresford arrived in the Tagus in mid-October, the Junta now controlling Portugal refused to allow him to land, and after handing over the monies for the army on foot of a signed bond, and having resigned his commission, he left for England arriving in Falmouth on 28 October. After residing at a family home for a number of weeks he spent Christmas and New Year with Castlereagh at his home in North Cray, a sign of his standing in political circles in Britain.[54]

After eleven years at the helm of the Portuguese army, Beresford came back to the British Isles with few regrets. On a number of occasions since the conclusion of the war he had expressed the view that he would shortly return, and that he felt there was no future for him in Portugal. Yet he had remained on, partly at the urging of the British government and indeed with the encouragement of the Duke of Wellington; but perhaps more surprisingly because of the strong bond he had formed with João, a bond which remained in place when the King returned to Portugal in 1821 and which was to lead Beresford to some involvement in Portuguese affairs for a further decade. A liberal constitution modelled on that adopted by Spain was succeeded by a reversion to absolutism before Portugal descended into civil war, pitting two of João's sons against each other.

Beresford had probably saved the Regency when he uncovered the Gomes Freire plot in 1817, but its members were unable to see Beresford's importance other than in the short term to their own survival, and in Beresford's absence the Regency was swept away in 1820 with the demand being made for a liberal constitution. Beresford like others had failed in his repeated attempts to get João to return to Portugal before the crisis erupted. Lest it be thought that Beresford commanded in Portugal without support there, that was clearly not the case. Offsetting the animosity of some of the Regency he clearly enjoyed the backing of a considerable number both within and outside the administration and army, including the Conde de Santarém, Cipriano Ribeiro Freire (President of the Junta de Comércio), José António de Barros (Auditor

General of the Army), Lemos de Lacerda, Brito Mozinho and most importantly the Conde de Palmela. The latter had succeeded Araújo as Minister for Foreign Affairs. An astute diplomat who had represented Portugal at the Congress of Vienna in 1815, he corresponded regularly with Beresford from his base in London, obtaining from the Marshal information on current affairs in Portugal.

During the years between 1814 and 1820, Beresford corresponded continuously with not just his half-brothers but also his half-sisters. This correspondence discloses that notwithstanding his difficulties with the rulers of the kingdom, he had a considerable affection for both the country of Portugal and its people. However, these letters tell us nothing about a matter which must have been of considerable importance in his personal life, which involved the continuation of his affair with Maria da Luz Willoughby, the wife of Beresford's military secretary and one of his closest confidants, António Lemos Pereira de Lacerda. The *ménage à trois* was by all accounts a happy one, with all three living under the same roof at the Palácio da Ega (now the Museo Ultramarino), a gift from João to the Marshal following its confiscation from the Count of Ega, a supporter of the French.[55]

The years between 1814 and 1820 saw Portugal stagnate. The Regency agreed on little save a desire to reduce or be rid of British influence in the army, and when danger threatened even that modicum of agreement was jettisoned overboard. Major decisions could not be made in Portugal but continued to be referred to Rio de Janeiro, which resulted in delays of months or even years. To many it appeared that Portugal was dominated by Britain in the person of Beresford, who commanded the only functioning instrument of government, the army, but the reality was very different for the exercise of that command depended upon João, and in the final analysis the subjects of João's kingdoms on both sides of the Atlantic. Portugal's ruler never deviated from his support of Beresford, even when faced with a *fait accompli* in the shape of the liberal revolution of 1820; and in the next decade he consulted Beresford repeatedly, clearly continuing to think highly of him.

Beresford for his part had for many years addressed the challenge of having two masters. He liaised throughout his period at the helm of the Portuguese army with Liverpool, Castlereagh and Wellington, ascertaining British views on the challenges faced by Portugal, whether at home, in the wider Peninsula or in South America, yet at the end of the day he took his orders from João, not from the British government. This created difficulties for him when Britain expressed its disapproval of João's attempt to seize the Banda Oriental in South America and in relation to the slave trade, precisely because his own views on these two topics mirrored British government policy. Overriding all was the shared view of Beresford and the British government of the need for João to return to Portugal, if that country was to be resurrected from the ashes of the French invasions. Ironically, it took the revolution of 1820 to secure that return, by which time it was too late to save the Portuguese empire. The transfer of the Court to Brazil in 1807, and its failure to return following the conclusion of the Peninsular War, left a political vacuum that was filled by the liberals, who set about frustrating the centralisation of power desired by absolutists. Rioting, land wars and the refusal to discharge taxes ultimately led not just to the termination of Beresford's appointment as Commander in Chief of the Portuguese army, but to the downfall of the Regency and the installation of a liberal constitution.

Beresford himself was arguably partly responsible for the move from absolutism to the establishment of a constitutional monarchy in the 1820s, not because he desired it but because from the time of his taking charge of the Portuguese army in 1809 until the date of his demission in 1820 he was a strong and consistent proponent of promotion on merit rather than class and privilege in the armed forces, a policy which enabled and produced an entirely new cadre of officers, many imbued with the ideas of the liberals and even the revolutionaries of eighteenth-century America and France.

BRIEF CHRONOLOGY OF THE WARS WITH FRANCE, 1793–1814

(A) denotes an allied victory
(F) denotes a French victory
(GB) denotes a British victory

1793

21 Jan.	Execution of Louis XVI.
1 Feb.	France declares war on Great Britain. Henceforth the latter subsidises a number of alliances against revolutionary and imperial France.

1799

1 Nov.	Napoleon overthrows the Directory and establishes the Consulate.

1801

9 Feb.	End of the War of the Second Coalition in that Austria and Russia make peace with France leaving Great Britain to fight alone.

1802

25 Mar.	Peace Treaty of Amiens between France and Great Britain.

1803

18 May	War recommences between Great Britain & France, ending only with Napoleon's abdication on 6 April 1814.

1805

21 Oct.	Battle of Trafalgar (GB)
2 Dec.	Battle of Austerlitz (F)

1806

8/9 Jan.	British capture Cape of Good Hope under General David Baird. William Carr Beresford commands brigade.

1806

27 June	Beresford captures Buenos Aires with a force of 1,400.
12 Aug.	Beresford surrenders Buenos Aires and is held under house arrest in various locations in the Viceroyalty of Rio de la Plata.

1807

Feb.	Beresford and Denis Pack escape with the help of Portenos and reach Montevideo on 22 February. Beresford then returns to England.
14 June	Battle of Friedland (F)

1807

27 Nov.   1st French invasion of Portugal. Departure of Royal Family from Lisbon for Brazil where it remains until 1821.

1807

24 Dec.   Beresford arrives at Madeira and takes possession of the island.

1808

Aug.   Insurrections in Spain and Portugal against French rule. British landings in Portugal and defeat of French at Rolica (A) and Vimeiro (A) followed by Convention of Cintra to secure French evacuation. End of 1st French invasion. Beresford arrives from Madeira with 3rd regiment.

1808

Oct./Dec.   Sir John Moore leads army from Lisbon into Spain, subsequently retreating to La Coruña.

1809

16 Jan.   Battle of La Coruña (A).

1809

17/18 Jan.   British army evacuated from La Coruña and returns to England.

21 Jan.   Soult captures the Spanish naval base of Ferrol.

Feb.   2nd French invasion of Portugal under Soult.

2 Mar.   Beresford arrives in Lisbon to take command of the Portuguese army.

29 Mar.   Soult captures Porto (F)

12 May   Wellesley recaptures Porto (A); Beresford pursues French to Chaves.

5/6 July   Battle of Wagram (F): Napoleon defeats Austrians.

28 July   Battle of Talavera (A).

19 Nov.   Battle of Ocana (F).

28 Nov.   Battle of Alba de Tormes (F).

11 Dec.   Gerona falls to French (F).

End of 1809   Wellesley & Beresford inspect reformed Portuguese army.

1810

10 July   Ciudad Rodrigo surrenders to French (F).

24 July   Engagement on the R.Coa (F) 3rd French invasion of Portugal under Marshal Massena.

28 Aug.   Almeida surrenders to French (F).

27 Sept.   Battle of Busaco (A).

8/10 Oct.   Anglo-Portuguese army enters Lines of Torres Vedras.

11 Oct.   Massena's vanguard arrives before the Lines.

3 Nov.   Beresford knighted at Mafra by Wellington on behalf of George III.

15 Nov.   French army retires from Lines of Torres Vedras to Santarem

30 Dec.   Beresford assumes temporary command of corps on left bank of Tagus, replacing General Hill who returned to England to recuperate from illness.

1811

19 Feb.	Battle of Gebora (F).
5 Mar.	Massena's army commences retreat from Portugal. Battle of Barosa (A).
10 Mar.	Badajoz falls to French (F).
3/5 May	Battle of Fuentes de Onoro (A).
6 May	Beresford commences 1st allied siege of Badajoz.
10 May	French abandon Almeida.
12 May	Beresford lifts siege of Badajoz.
16 May	Battle of Albuera (A).
18 May	2nd siege of Badajoz commenced.
10 June	Wellington abandons 2nd siege of Badajoz (F).

1812

8 Jan.	Wellington commences siege of Ciudad Rodrigo. French capture Valencia (F).
19 Jan.	Wellington captures Ciudad Rodrigo (A).
7 April	Wellington captures Badajoz (A).
22 July	Battle of Salamanca (A).
12 Aug.	Allies enter Madrid (A).
7 Sept.	Battle of Borodino (F).
19 Sept.	Siege of Burgos commenced.
21 Oct.	Siege of Burgos lifted (F).
Nov.	Allied army back in Portugal in winter quarters.
26/29 Nov.	Battle of Berezina (A): retreat from Moscow.

1813

21 June	Battle of Vitoria (A).
28 June	San Sebastian besieged.
28/30 July	Battle of Pyrenees (A).
31 Aug.	San Sebastian captured (A).
7 Oct.	Allied army crosses R. Bidassoa onto French territory (A).
16/19 Oct.	Battle of Leipzig (A).
31 Oct.	Pamplona surrenders after 4-month siege (A).
10 Nov.	Battle of Nivelle (A).
9/10 Dec.	Battle of Nive (A).

1814

27 Feb.	Battle of Orthez (A).
12 Mar.	Beresford takes surrender of Bordeaux (A).
6 April	Napoleon abdicates.
10 April	Battle of Toulouse (A).
27 April	Surrender of Bayonne (A).

Definitive Convention For The Evacuation
Of Portugal By The French Army

August 30, 1808

The Generals commanding in chief the British and French armies in Portugal, having determined to negociate and conclude a treaty for the evacuation of Portugal by the French troops, on the basis of the agreement entered into on the 22d instant for a suspension of hostilities, have appointed the under-mentioned officers to negociate the same in their names; viz. —on the part of the General-in-Chief of the British army, Lieutenant-Colonel Murray, Quarter-Master-General; and, on the part of the General-in-Chief of the French army, Monsieur Kellermann, General-of-Division to whom they have given authority to negociate and conclude a Convention to that effect, subject to their ratification respectively, and to that of the Admiral commanding the British fleet at the entrance of the Tagus.

Those two officers, after exchanging their full powers, have agreed upon the articles which follow:

I.   All the places and forts in the kingdom of Portugal, occupied by the French troops, shall be delivered up to the British army in the state in which they are at the period of the signature of the present Convention.

II.   The French troops shall evacuate Portugal with their arms and baggage; they shall not be considered as prisoners of war; and, on their arrival in France, they shall be at liberty to serve.

III.   The English Government shall furnish the means of conveyance for the French army; which shall be disembarked in any of the ports of France between Rochefort and L'Orient, inclusively.

IV.   The French army shall carry with it all its artillery, of French calibre, with the horses belonging to it, and the tumbrils supplied with sixty rounds per gun. All other artillery, arms, and ammunition, as also the military and naval arsenals, shall be given up to the British army and navy in the state in which they may be at the period of the ratification of the Convention.

V.   The French army shall carry with it all its equipments, and all that is comprehended under the name of property of the army; that is to say, its military chest, and carriages attached to the Field Commissariat and Field Hospitals; or shall be allowed to dispose of such part of the same, on its account, as the Commander-in-Chief may judge it unnecessary to embark, In like manner, all individuals of the army shall be at liberty to dispose of their private property of every description; with full security hereafter for the purchasers.

VI.   The cavalry are to embark their horses; as also the Generals and other officers of all ranks. It is, however, fully understood, that the means of conveyance for horses, at the disposal of the British Commanders, are very limited; some additional conveyance may be procured in the port of Lisbon: the number of horses to be embarked by the troops shall not exceed six hundred; and the number embarked by the Staff shall not exceed two hundred. At all events every facility will be given to the French army to dispose of the horses, belonging to it, which cannot be embarked.

VII.   In order to facilitate the embarkation, it shall take place in three divisions; the last of which will be principally composed of the garrisons of the places, of the cavalry, the artillery, the sick, and the equipment of the army. The first division shall embark within seven days of the date of the ratification; or sooner, if possible.

VIII.   The garrison of Elvas and its forts, and of Peniche and Palmela, will be embarked at Lisbon; that of Almaida at Oporto, or the nearest harbour. They will be accompanied on their march by British Commissaries, charged with providing for their subsistence and accommodation.

IX.   All the sick and wounded, who cannot be embarked with the troops, are entrusted to the British army. They are to be taken care of, whilst they remain in this country, at the expence of the British Government; under the condition of the same being reimbursed by France when the final evacuation is effected. The English government will provide for their return to France; which shall take place by detachments of about one hundred and fifty (or two hundred) men at a time. A sufficient number of French medical officers shall be left behind to attend them.

X.   As soon as the vessels employed to carry the army to France shall have disembarked it in the harbours specified, or in any other of the ports of France to which stress of weather may force them, every facility shall be given them to return to England without delay; and security against capture until their arrival in a friendly port.

XI.   The French army shall be concentrated in Lisbon, and within a distance of about two leagues from it. The English army will approach within three leagues of the capital; and will be so placed as to leave about one league between the two armies.

XII.   The forts of St. Julien, the Bugio, and Cascais, shall be occupied by the British troops on the ratification of the Convention. Lisbon and its citadel, together with the forts and batteries, as far as the Lazaretto or Tarfuria on one side, and fort St. Joseph on the other, inclusively, shall be given up on the embarkation of the second division; as shall also the harbour; and all armed vessels in it of every description, with their rigging, sails, stores, and ammunition. The fortresses of Elvas, Almaida, Peniche, and Palmela, shall be given up as soon as the British troops can arrive to occupy them. In the mean time, the General-in-Chief of the British army will give notice of the present Convention to the garrisons of those places, as also to the troops before them, in order to put a stop to all further hostilities.

XIII.   Commissioners shall be named, on both sides, to regulate and accelerate the execution of the arrangements agreed upon.

XIV.   Should there arise doubts as to the meaning of any article, it will be explained favourably to the French army.

XV.   From the date of the ratification of the present Convention, all arrears of contributions, requisitions, or claims whatever, of the French Government, against the subjects of Portugal, or any other individuals residing in this country, founded on the occupation of Portugal by the French troops in the month of December 1807, which may not have been paid up, are cancelled; and all sequestrations laid upon their property, moveable or immoveable, are removed; and the free disposal of the same is restored to the proper owner.

XVI.   All subjects of France, or of powers in friendship or alliance with France, domiciliated in Portugal, or accidentally in this country, shall be protected : their property of every kind, moveable and immoveable, shall be respected: and they shall be at liberty either to accompany the French army, or to remain in Portugal. In either case their property is guaranteed to them; with the liberty of retaining or of disposing of it, and passing the produce of the sale thereof into France, or any other country where they may fix their residence; the space of one year being allowed them for that purpose. It is fully understood, that the shipping is excepted from this arrangement; only, however, in so far as regards leaving the port; and that none of the stipulations above-mentioned can be made the pretext of any commercial speculation.

XVII.   No native of Portugal shall be rendered accountable for his political conduct during the period of the occupation of this country by the French army; and all those who have continued in the exercise of their employments, or who have accepted situations under the French Government, are placed under the protection of the British Commanders: they shall sustain no injury in their persons or property; it not having been at their option to be obedient, or not, to the French Government: they are also at liberty to avail themselves of the stipulations of the 16th Article.

XVIII.   The Spanish troops detained on board ship in the port of Lisbon shall be given up to the Commander-in-Chief of the British army; who engages to obtain of the Spaniards to restore such French subjects, either military or civil, as may have been detained in Spain, without being taken in battle, or in consequence of military operations, but on occasion of the occurrences of the 29th of last May, and the days immediately following.

XIX.   There shall be an immediate exchange established for all ranks of prisoners made in Portugal since the commencement of the present hostilities.

XX.   Hostages of the rank of field-officers shall be mutually furnished on the part of the British army and navy, and on that of the French army, for the reciprocal guarantee of the present Convention. The officer of the British army shall be restored on the completion of the articles which concern the army; and the officer of the navy on the disembarkation of the French troops in their own country. The like is to take place on the part of the French army.

XXI. It shall be allowed to the General-in-Chief of the French army to send an officer to France with intelligence of the present Convention. A vessel will be furnished by the British Admiral to convey him to Bourdeaux or Rochefort.

XXII. The British Admiral will be invited to accommodate His Excellency the Commander-in-Chief, and the other principal officers of the French army, on board of ships of war.

Done and concluded at Lisbon this 30th day of August, 1808.

  [Signed] George Murray, Quarter-Master-General.

   Kellermann, Le Général de Division.

We, the Duke of Abrantes, General-in-Chief of the French army, have ratified and do ratify the present Definitive Convention in all its articles, to be executed according to its form and tenor.

  [Signed] The Duke Of Abrantes.

   Head-Quarters-Lisbon, 30th August, 1808.

Additional Articles to the Convention of the 30th of August, 1808

I. The individuals in the civil employment of the army made prisoners, either by the British troops, or by the Portuguese, in any part of Portugal, will be restored, as is customary, without exchange.

II. The French army shall be subsisted from its own magazines up to the day of embarkation; the garrisons up to the day of the evacuation of the fortresses.

a. The remainder of the magazines shall be delivered over, in the usual form, to the British Government; which charges itself with the subsistence of the men and horses of the army from the above-mentioned periods till they arrive in France; under the condition of their being reimbursed by the French Government for the excess of the expense beyond the estimates, to be made by both parties, of the value of the magazines delivered up to the British army.

b. The provisions on board the ships of war, in possession of the French army, will be taken in account by the British Government in like manner with the magazines in the fortresses.

III. The General commanding the British troops will take the necessary measures for re-establishing the free circulation of the means of subsistence between the country and the capital.

Done and concluded at Lisbon this 30th day of August, 1808.

  [Signed] George Murray, Quarter-Master-General.

   Kellermann, Le Général de Division.

We, Duke of Abrantes, General-in-Chief of the French army, have ratified and do ratify the additional articles of the Convention, to be executed according to their form and tenor.

The Duke of Abrantes.
  (A true Copy.)
  A. J. Dalrymple, Captain, Military Secretary.

ENDNOTES

Introduction

1 The family name appears in a number of guises including Le Poer, de la Poer, La Poher and Power. James' father, Richard, the 1st Earl, had himself been implicated in the so-called 'Popish Plot' of 1678. Later released, he served as a Colonel in the army of James II until the surrender of Cork, whereupon he was imprisoned and died in the Tower of London in 1690. James managed to convince the government of William of Orange (William III) that he had supported the Jacobites under family duress.

2 Curraghmore is still the family home of the Marquis of Waterford. Sited adjacent to the village of Portlaw in the beautiful valley of the River Clodagh, it is periodically open to the public.

3 The Earl of Tyrone was created Marquis of Waterford in 1789. The Monck family owned extensive lands at this time in and around Dublin, including Charleville, Enniskerry, County Wicklow. Elizabeth's father had married Lady Ann Isabella Bentinck, daughter of the 1st Duke of Portland.

4 Earl Fitzwilliam was Lord Lieutenant of Ireland in 1794–5. One of his first acts was to remove John Beresford from his post as Revenue Commissioner. Whether it was the removal of Beresford or the introduction by Fitzwilliam of a bill for Catholic emancipation, the result was the removal of Fitzwilliam as Lord Lieutenant in 1795, less than two months after his arrival. Fitzwilliam felt that Beresford was 'filling a situation greater than that of the Lord Lieutenant himself'.

5 John Poo Beresford (1766–1844) was the older of the two boys. He entered the Royal Navy in 1772, becoming a Captain in 1795, Rear Admiral in 1814 and ultimately a full Admiral in 1838. Knighted in 1812 and created a baronet in 1814, he played a prominent part in naval actions on both sides of the Atlantic during the wars against France and the war of 1812 against America.

6 John's (the Commissioner) son, John Claudius, was to become a banker whose bankruptcy severely threatened the finances of his relations. Another son of the Commissioner, Marcus, was the father of John Theophilus Beresford who was to serve and die in the Peninsular War. Ultimately William Carr was to marry Louisa, the youngest daughter of the 1st Lord Decies.

7 Herbert Maxwell (ed.), *The Creevey Papers: A Selection From the Correspondence & Diaries of the Late Thomas Creevey, M. P.* (London: John Murray, 1903) vol. II, p. 127 stated the brothers were 'still in ignorance of who their mother was, or whether they had the same; but from the secrecy upon this head, from their being sent from Ireland, and above all, from Lady Waterford having seemed always to show more affection to them than to her own children, there is a notion they were *hers* before her marriage.' See also, Bernardo Almazán, *Beresford, Gobernador de Buenos Aires* (Buenos Aires: Editorial Galerna, 1994), which suggests that William's mother was called Luisa Carr. However, that assertion is referenced to another source which in turn gives no reference. While no one in the family is known to have been called Carr before William's birth in 1768, it is noteworthy that in 1858 the son of his half-brother John Poo Beresford, Sir George de la Poer Beresford, called one of his own sons William Carr de la Poer Beresford. This second William Carr survived a mere two years. It seems probable

that he was named after his recently deceased uncle, who had died in 1854. Carr is a name found today in Waterford and in the village of Piltown, County Kilkenny, a mere seven kilometres from the Curraghmore estate, the home of the de la Poer Beresfords. William Carr and John Poo Beresford were always close, as witnessed by their extensive correspondence now in the North Yorkshire Archives (ZBA collection), but *Creevey* is the only source to suggest they might have been full brothers.

8   See Beresford to Fitzroy, 18 November 1821 (WP1/685). Some of Beresford's Papers (referred to as some 400 letters) were sold by Messrs E. & H. Lumley in August 1899. The newspaper report states they were unpublished letters between Wellington and Beresford. The report in *The Times*, 1 August 1899, states many of the letters are of a less formal and more friendly type 'for between the two generals – Irishmen both – there was a great sympathy; Beresford, indeed, as these letters show, was one of the Duke's few real personal friends.'

9   National Army Museum (NAM), manuscript number 2007-03-83.

10   Samuel E. Vichness, 'Marshall of Portugal: the military career of William Carr Beresford, 1785–1814' (Unpublished PhD thesis, Florida State University, 1976).

11   Francisco A. de la Fuente, *Dom Miguel Pereira Forjaz: His early career and Role in the Mobilization of the Portuguese Army and Defense of Portugal during the Peninsular War, 1807–1814* (Lisbon: Tribuna da Historia, 2011). Hereafter '*Forjaz*'.

12   Almazán, *Beresford, Gobernador de Buenos Aires*; John D. Grainger, 'The Royal Navy in the River Plate 1806–1807' *Navy Records Society*, vol. 135; Ian Fletcher, *Bloody Albuera: The 1811 Campaign in the Peninsula*; Mark S. Thompson, *The Fatal Hill: The Allied Campaign Under Beresford in Southern Spain in 1811* (Sunderland: Mark Thompson Publishing, 2002); Malyn Newitt and Martin Robson (eds), *Lord Beresford and British Intervention in Portugal 1807–1820* (Lisbon: Imprensa das Ciências Sociais, 2004).

13   British nomenclature normally asserts this title of nobility as 'Marquess'. In the present instance the initial publication of the grant of the patent of George de la Poer Beresford is specific in referring to 'The Marquis of the County of Waterford', though the actual patent refers to 'The Marquess of the County of Waterford.' The title holders have accordingly used 'Marquis' and this is the rendition followed throughout this work. A number of other peerages were also created using 'Marquis' rather than 'Marquess'. The reference to 'The County of Waterford' rather than 'Waterford' was an important one at the time. A title taking its name from a county was more prestigious than one taken from a city or town. Subsequently the reference to the county has been often disregarded as in the present case. The granting of the patent was published in *The London Gazette* and is dated 12 August 1789. See also *Burke's Peerage and Baronetage*, 106th edition (1999), xxx.

Chapter 1

1   Margaret Lenta and Basil Le Cordeur (eds), *The Cape Diaries of Lady Anne Barnard 1799–1800* (Cape Town: Van Riebeeck Society, 1999); 2 April 1799, Lady Anne encountered Beresford at Capetown on his way to India in 1799, having both him and his half-brother, Lord George Beresford, to dinner on 1 April. The quotation uses the words 'the old Lords' rather than 'the old Lord'.

2   There were four boys and two girls born to George and Elizabeth (see family tree). The eldest boy, Lord Le Poer, died young. His next brother George succeeded to the titles and was created Marquis of Waterford in 1789. A third brother, Lord John George, was to rise to become Archbishop of Armagh. The fourth boy, Lord George, was to become a soldier and Privy Councillor. Finally, the two daughters, Lady Anne and Lady Elizabeth, were both regular correspondents with their half-brother and were clearly devoted to him. In the case of Lady Elizabeth, she married Major General Sir Denis Pack, who served for much of his military career with William Carr Beresford. George (the Marquis) had two brothers, John and William.

John (the Commissioner) was the First Commissioner of the Revenue for Ireland, a position from which he exercised so considerable an influence that he was on at least one occasion referred to as 'the king of Ireland'. The youngest of the three boys, William, became Archbishop of Tuam and was created Lord Decies. His daughter, Louisa, was later to marry William Carr Beresford. The first Marquis thus had six children to survive childbirth, John had no less than twelve such children and Archbishop William had seven children surviving childbirth. With their dynastic alliances and acting often collectively as a family, they formed a powerful faction.

3   The 1st Marquis of Waterford in correspondence addressed his brother, the Commissioner, as 'Dear Beresford', not 'Dear John'. They were on very good terms. See North Yorkshire Archives (NYA; NYA/ZBA 21/9, f. 3, microfilm 1275).

4   On 22 March 1811, Henry 2nd Marquis of Waterford consented to the continuation of William's use of the name Beresford. The licence is dated 1 April 1811 and is recorded on 2 July 1811 (NYA/ZBA 21/10, f. 7). Military and Court papers refer to him in the 1780s and 1790s variously as William Beresford, Carr Beresford and William Carr Beresford. See *The Royal Kalendar 1796* which lists William as 'Lieutenant Colonel Carr Beresford' as of 3 May 1795. In the case of 'Poo', this name appears as 'Poer' in some later documents contained in the North Yorkshire Archives. By 1786 he was certainly signing himself 'Poo Beresford' to his father (NYA/ZBA/21/9, f. 2 microfilm). A power of attorney of 30 March 1798 describes him as John Poo Beresford and William as William Carr Beresford (NYA/ZBA 21/1, f. 1).

5   The Beresford Pierse manuscripts located in the North Yorkshire Archives contain an undated memorandum which refers to a boarding school in Catterick kept by a Mr Kirby, where William Carr and John Poo were educated, and the source for this information may have come from the *York Herald* of 15 January 1805 (NYA/ZBA 20/5, f. 19).

6   Mary and Catharine Morrits were left legacies by John Poo in his Will of 1808 (NYA/ZBA 21/1, f. 4).

7   E.A. Beresford, W. Beresford and S.B. Beresford, *Beresford of Beresford: Eight Centuries of a Gentle Family* (London: W.H. Eaton, 1895). Part III, 2 includes an account of a story of how John Poo, having left the school in York in 1782, returned to visit William and friends (presumably in 1783 or early 1784). They all climbed the Minster and went out on to the battlements whereupon John started jumping from one battlement to the next, terrifying the younger William.

8   There was no academy in Great Britain for the non-technical training of officers prior to the French Revolution. At that stage the Royal Military College was formed under general Le Marchant. The Royal Military Academy for training artillery officers had existed since 1741 at Woolwich. In France there were seven artillery schools by 1789, including Strasbourg, Brienne (where Napoleon studied) and La Fére. Wellington studied at the Royal Equitation School in Angers. There was also an engineering school at Mézières as well as the École Royale Militaire set up in 1751.

9   The 1st Marquis of Waterford died in 1800 and was succeeded by Henry, 2nd Marquis, a half-brother to William Carr.

10   Thomas Molyneux later rose to the rank of Major General. He was the third son of Sir Capel Molyneux, MP for the University of Dublin.

11   Clarke (ed.), *The Georgian Era: Military and Naval Commanders. Judges and Barristers. Physicians and Surgeons* (London: Vizetelly, Branston and Company, 1833), p. 111.

12   Beresford was appointed Colonel of the 16th Regiment on 15 March 1823. This regiment had been raised in 1688 as Archibald Douglas's Regiment of Foot.

13   Curiously enough, Beresford was also Colonel of the 69th Regiment (11 March1819–15 March 1823). Both the 16th and 69th regiments were stationed in Ireland at various times in the 1780s and 1790s. Admiral Lord Hood, 1st Viscount Hood, was Commander in Chief in the Mediterranean (May 1793–October 1794).

14 Monthly returns for the 124th Regiment of Foot. Beresford's half-brother, Captain Lord George Beresford, was also a member of the regiment, though listed as recruiting in Ireland in August 1795. He too transferred to the 88th on the dissolution of 124th Regiment; National Archives (NA; NA, WO 17/227).

15 Waterford to John Poo Beresford, 28 July 1795. Quoted in Hugh de la Poer Beresford, *The Book of the Beresfords* (London: Phillimore, 1977), pp. 150–2.

16 The 88th Regiment (the Connaught Rangers) was initially raised in Connacht by John Thomas de Burgh, Earl of Clanricarde. The rank and file came predominantly from the counties of the west of Ireland, though following the merger with the 124th Regiment (Waterford), names from that county feature extensively.

17 Sir James McGrigor, *The Autobiography and Services of Sir James McGrigor* (London: Longman, Green, Longman and Roberts, 1861), ff. 42.

18 Regimental return for 88th Regiment, 1 April 1796 (NA, WO 17/209).

19 Three companies of the 88th ultimately reached the West Indies, being those of Captains Shadwell, Trotter and Vandeleur; all of whom were to play a part in Beresford's later life. They returned to Ireland in late 1796.

20 Richard Wellesley (1760–1842) was the eldest son of the Earl of Mornington. Created Marquess Wellesley in 1799, he later served as Ambassador to Spain during the Peninsular War and Foreign Secretary (1809–12). In 1821 he was appointed Lord Lieutenant of Ireland, where he generally supported Catholic emancipation. He served a second term as Lord Lieutenant of Ireland in 1833.

21 See Rory Muir, *Wellington: The Path to Victory, 1769–1814* (London: Yale University Press, 2013) for a good recent account of Wellington's time in India.

22 Marquess Wellesley to Beresford, 4 December 1800. In which he indicated he was very happy to gratify Beresford's wish to serve under Colonel Wellesley and that he was 'always happy to prove my respect for Lord Waterford'; and Beresford to Marquess Wellesley, 24 December 1800; British Library (BL; Add MS 13,712).

23 Arthur Wellesley was not happy at the prospect of serving under Baird and he let his brother Richard know that to be the case. See Muir, *Wellington: The Path to Victory*, pp. 96–9.

24 Baird reported that the army marched by night but sleep was almost impossible by day as the temperature in the tents registered from 110 to 115 degrees. British troops, including the 88th Regiment, numbered 3,234. while 'native' troops, by which he meant Indian, numbered 3,201; W.H. Wilkin, *The Life of Sir David Baird* (London: G. Allen, 1912), pp. 134–5.

25 Robert Thomas Wilson, *History of the British Expedition to Egypt* (London: C. Roworth, 1803), p. 167, suggests that Baird acquired 5,000 camels at Kosseir before crossing the desert.

26 According to the French historian and artist, Vivant Denon, who accompanied Desaix on his march into Upper Egypt, there were only four wells between Ghennah and Kosseir, and one of these was only suitable for camels. Vivant Denon, *Travels in Upper and Lower Egypt During the Campaign of General Bonaparte* (London: T.N. Longman, 1803); vol. 2, p. 49.

27 The cannon were drawn by bullocks reportedly brought from India, See Wilson, op cit., p. 168.

28 Piers Mackesy, *British Victory in Egypt, 1801: The End of Napoleon's Conquest* (London: Routledge, 1995), p. 201, suggests that losses were somewhat greater than three. He notes that in the British contingent the Paymaster and twelve soldiers died of sunstroke and that two sepoys shot themselves; James Bruce, *Travels to Discover the Source of the Nile, 1768–1773* (Edinburgh: G.G.J. and J. Robinson, 1790).

29 Beresford, in his statement of service, states that he was nearly two years in Egypt until the final evacuation of the country (NA, WO 25/744).

30 Beresford to Major General Sir Charles Asgill, 13, 14, 15 and 16 December 1803 (BL, Add MS 35,704. Hardwicke Papers). Others taken by the militia at that time included William O'Brien, Brian Morris and

Hugh Byrne. Beresford was based at Saunders Grove, near Baltinglass, County Wicklow, some twenty kilometres from Hollywood.

31 Beresford to Major General Sir Charles Asgill, 16 December 1803 (BL, Add MS 35,704. Hardwicke Papers).

32 It is only possible to speculate as to why the union might have been prevented. Consanguinity of first cousins was not necessarily a bar to marriage, but if there was a friendship between William and Louisa at this stage in their lives, his illegitimacy and/or lack of prospects might have caused the family to be reluctant to allow the matter to go forward.

33 Louisa Beresford and Maria Edgeworth corresponded with each other extensively, and Maria visited her in England on a number of occasions. Some of that correspondence exists in the Edgeworth Manuscripts in the National Library of Ireland (NLI), in particular MS21740. Amongst Maria's most popular works were *Castle Rackrent* (1800), *Belinda* (1810) and *Harrington* (1817). Thomas Hope was influential as a designer of furniture and himself a well-known author. His published works include *Household Furniture and Interior Decoration* (1807) and *Anastasius;or Memoirs of a Greek Written at the Close of the Eighteenth Century* (1819).

34 Louisa was reportedly born in 1783 so would have been twenty years old in 1803. The most likely other relevant occasion on which Beresford might have been in Ireland would have been 1797–8 when Beresford and the 88th Regiment was stationed in Jersey. At that stage Louisa would have been only fifteen. She died aged sixty-eight in 1851. See *The Gentleman's Magazine and Historical Review*, vol. 195, p. 314.

Chapter 2

1 General Manuel Belgrano (1770–1820) was a politician, military leader and one of those most associated with the fight for independence leading to the foundation of Argentina. Creator of the Argentine flag. Bartolomé Mitre, *Historia de Belgrano y de la Independencia Argentina*, sixth edition (Buenos Aires: Felix Lajouane, 1913).

2 Great Britain claimed justification for the attack because it had learnt of a secret agreement between France and Spain whereby the latter would pay to the former 72 million Francs per annum until Spain declared war on Great Britain. The Spaniards viewed the attack on their fleet off Cape Santa Maria as an act of piracy and declared war on Great Britain on 14 December 1804, with Britain responding with a formal declaration of war in January 1805.

3 Castlereagh to Cornwallis, 10 September 1805. Enclosed with Castlereagh to the Lords of the Admiralty, 10 September 1805 (NA, Adm 1/4200).

4 The Treaty of Amiens was a peace treaty signed on 25 March 1802 by Marquess Cornwallis, on behalf of Great Britain, and Napoleon's brother Joseph Bonaparte, on behalf of France. The parties had already begun to extract themselves from some territories designated for withdrawal prior to the signing of the documentation, but other provisions were never implemented and by May 1803 France and Britain were at war again. This period, of just under fourteen months, was the only time of peace between the two nations between 1793 and 1814. In Ireland, Amiens Street in Dublin was named in honour of this short-lived treaty.

5 La Grande Armée was assembled from 1803 onwards on the northern coast of France near the port of Boulogne, with the declared objective of the invasion of Great Britain. In the event it was used to destroy both the Austrian and Russian armies in 1805 at the battles of Ulm (16–19 October) and Austerlitz (2 December), respectively; having marched at speed (it left the Boulogne area on 27 August) across Europe so as to enable Napoleon to intercept each component part of the coalition's forces before they could unite.

6 The expedition numbered some 6,000 soldiers, including three companies of Royal Artillery. It included seven regiments of foot: 24th, 38th, 71st, 72nd and 83rd, as well as the 59th and 93rd destined for India. In addition, 200 light dragoons were dispatched with the force. The first battalion of the 71st Regiment, which was that sent to the Cape, was commanded by Lieutenant Colonel (later Sir Denis) Pack. The second battalion, which did not serve there, was commanded by Lieutenant Colonel Lord George Beresford, a half-brother of William Carr Beresford. The 71st Regiment contained a number of Irish officers and men (see below). After the close of the Peninsular War, Pack married Elizabeth, sister of George Beresford and half-sister of William Carr Beresford.

7 Baird to Gordon, 12 January 1806. Refers to having obtained 60–70 horses in São Salvador before sailing on 26 December 1805; 'Military Transactions of the British Empire from the Commencement of the Year 1803 to the Termination of 1807', compiled by Lt Col. J.W. Gordon (London: Luke Hanfard & Sons, 1808). The biography of the late Captain Dugald Carmichael states the fleet left São Salvador on 26 November 1805; *The Edinburgh Philosophical Journal*, vol. 13, p. 96.

8 Sir John Fortescue, *A History of the British Army*, thirteen volumes (London: Macmillan, 1899), vol. 5, p. 306.

9 Baird to Castlereagh, Capetown, 12 January 1806 (NA, WO 1/342). Saldanha Bay is named after the Portuguese naval captain António de Saldanha who visited what is now South Africa with the explorer and statesman Afonso de Albuquerque on his way to India in 1503.

10 In Beresford's absence, Baird himself commanded the 1st Brigade at the battle of Blaauwberg. The landing at Leopard's Bay was not without incident. While organised resistance was slight, forty-one privates in the 91st Regiment were drowned in the surf. See Thomas Fernyhough, *Military Memoirs of Four Brothers engaged in the service of their country, as well as the New World and Africa and on the Continent of Europe* (London: William Sams, 1829).

11 The Commandant of Capetown, Lieutenant Colonel Hieronymus Casimir von Prophalow, surrendered to Baird on 9 January 1806. The terms of capitulation, which were approved by Janssens on 18 January, provided for the repatriation of Dutch officers and men to the Netherlands. Under the terms private property was respected and the privileges of the inhabitants confirmed. Capetown remained in British hands until 1814, when it was formally ceded to Great Britain.

12 Baird to Castlereagh, 12 and 26 January 1806 (NA, WO 1/342). Beresford was sent after Janssens with the 59th and 72nd regiments accompanied by a detachment of artillery comprised of four six-pounders and two howitzers.

13 Castlereagh to Baird, 25 July 1805. Quoted in its entirety in Wilkin, *Life of Sir David Baird*, pp. 168–74. The Azores were ruled then, as now, by Portugal which was attempting to follow a policy of neutrality between the warring European powers.

14 Sir Home Popham had presented a memorandum to Lord Melville (Henry Dundas, 1st Viscount Melville; First Lord of the Admiralty) on the topic of an expedition to the River Plate on 16 October 1804. The combined objectives of such an expedition were to cut Spain off from exports from South America and to open up trade in that part of the world to British merchants. See *Correspondence of Castlereagh*, vol. III, pp. 290–2. Francisco de Miranda (1750–1816) from Venezuela had been a General in the Spanish army.

Having failed to get assistance from either the United States of America or France to support a rising in Venezuela against Spanish rule he had turned to England, where his plans were not without support, and he received at least some encouragement from Lord Melville. Further plans for intervention in South America were put forward both by recent settlers and by those who had been in South America for some time. Long-term settlers aspiring to change the status quo appear to have included the Alzaga and Casamayor families, while more recent arrivals included those of Irish extraction, such as Tomas O'Gorman and James Florence Burke. Tomas O'Gorman (a relative of the well-known medical doctor in Buenos Aires, Miguel [Michael] O'Gorman) was married to Ana (otherwise Anita) Perichon from a prosperous merchant family of French extraction; he also was a merchant who threw in his lot with Beresford.

Burke was a very colourful character. Of Irish descent, he served initially with Dillon's regiment in France. Following the revolution this became the French 87th regiment of the line and it was sent to Haiti to combat the rebellion there. After the defeat of the French in Haiti, Burke transferred his services to the British government, becoming a spy in South America. As such he built up contacts with those in Rio de la Plata aspiring to independence. He later served with the second regiment of foot in the Peninsula, rising to become a Lieutenant Colonel.

15 Home Popham to William Marsden (First Secretary at the Admiralty), 30 April 1806. Quoted in Wilkin, *Life of Sir David Baird*, p. 159. See also Alexander Gillespie, *Gleanings and Remarks: Collected During Many Months of Residence at Buenos Ayres, and Within the Upper Country* (General Books Reprint), Ch. II, p. 5, which refers to information obtained from Captain Wayne, an American slave trader.

16 The expedition was augmented by some 180 officers and men from the Saint Helena regiment under Lieutenant Colonel Lane along with a small detachment of the Saint Helena artillery and two 5.5 inch howitzers.

17 Baird to Castlereagh, 14 April 1806 (NA, WO 1/342).

18 The 71st had augmented its numbers by recruiting some of the Waldeck Chasseurs, though it is doubtful they were of great assistance subsequently due to desertion.

19 *United Service Magazine*, 1836, vol. 2, p. 195. Quoted in Ben Hughes, *The British Invasion of the River Plate 1806–1807* (Barnsley: Pen and Sword, 2013). Unfortunately the regiment favoured by Popham is not identified in the *United Service Magazine*.

20 *United Service Magazine*, 1836, vol. 2, pp. 195–6.

21 The 71st Regiment comprised 889 officers and men. In addition there were 340 marines, the picket of the 20th Light Dragoons, some Royal Navy Engineers, and commissary officers. This small force was augmented by those taken on at St Helena and sailors from the fleet. Popham's squadron for the River Plate expedition consisted of the *Diadem* (64 guns), *Raisonable* (64 guns), *Diomede* (50 guns), *Leda* (48 guns), *Narcissus* (32 guns) and *Encounter* (12 guns), together with transports. The total force available including officers, ranks, engineers, artillerymen, surgeons, marines and seamen would appear to be have been less than 1,650; Gillespie suggests 1,645 and *The English Naval Chronicle* 1,638. Beresford's own figure was 1,635 (Beresford to Windham, 2 July 1806).

22 Baird, when congratulating Beresford on the capture of Buenos Aires, referred to the unpleasant situation where Popham and Beresford had disagreed as to their first objective, complimenting Beresford on his forbearance while pointing out that without harmony between the two services nothing could be done. Baird to Beresford, 13 August 1806 (University of Southampton Library, MS 296, Pack Papers, folder 14).

23 Lieutenant Colonel Denis Pack to James Butler, 6 July 1806. In Denis R. Pack Beresford, *A Memoir of Major-General Sir Denis Pack, KCB* (Dublin, 1908), Pack says that he supported Popham, but had he been aware of the difficulties in navigating the river, he would have voted with the General. Gillespie also admitted that the choice of Buenos Aires involved a sacrifice of national interests. Op. cit., Ch. VI, p. 11.

24 Details of this commission are contained in Baird to Castlereagh, 14 April 1806 (NA, CO 324/68).

25 The guards in the fortress of Santa Teresa on the 'Uruguayan' side (Banda Oriental) of the River Plate reported the sighting of HMS *Leda* on 20 May. This vessel, under Captain Honeyman, had been sent

ahead by Popham to undertake reconnaissance of the River Plate and its defences; Jorge Fortin (ed.), *Invasiones Inglesas* (Buenos Aires: Colección Pablo Fortín, 1967), p. 149.

26 See, the 'Diary of William Gavin' in *The Highland Light infantry Chronicle* (1920–1921) for an eyewitness account of the landing, conquest and subsequent surrender of Buenos Aires, though his figures are at times at odds with other commentators. Hilarión de la Quintana was a career military officer who having surrendered Buenos Aires in June to Beresford was in August 1806 one of the leaders of the army of the Reconquista. De Liniers was later to describe de la Quintana as a friend of Beresford; see De Liniers to Beresford, 7 November 1806; quoted in Ernestina Costa, *English Invasion of the River Plate* (Buenos Aires: G. Kraft, Ltda, 1937). See also Carlos Roberts, *Las Invasiones Inglesas del Rio de la Plata (1806–1807) y la Influencia Inglesa en la Independencia y Organizacion de las Provincias del Rio de la Plata* (Buenos Aires: Talleres gráficos, S.a. Jacobo Peuser, ltda., 1938).

27 Denis Pack to James Butler (later 19th Earl of Ormonde), 6 July 1806. Puts the total number of British troops, marines and seamen landed at 1,400; Pack Beresford, *A Memoir of Major General Sir Denis Pack*, p. 11.

28 Report of Beresford, 30 April 1806, received in London 24 June refers also to having received from Governor of St Helena 139 men of the St Helena regiment together with 91 artillerymen (NA, CO 324/68).

29 Beresford to Windham, 30 April 1806, and Beresford's report, 11 July 1806 (NA, CO 324/68). Rafael, Marques de Sobremonte (1745–1827) was Governor of Córdoba del Tucuman and Viceroy of the Virreinato de la Plata (modern-day Argentine, Chile, Uruguay, Paraguay and Bolivia). Sobremonte had warned the Spanish authorities in 1805 that Buenos Aires would be difficult to defend and that troops should be concentrated in Montevideo in order to defend that more defensible city. His justification for leaving Buenos Aires was that he was attempting to save the treasure of the State. He established his temporary capital in Córdoba following his retreat from Buenos Aires. The treasure was left at Luján because of difficulties in transporting it in the southern hemisphere winter. In Córdoba he gathered a force of some 3,000 together with the objective of recovering Buenos Aires. However, when de Liniers, together with Pueyrredón and el Alcalde Álzaga, recovered Buenos Aires on 12 August, the Cabildo nominated de Liniers to overall command. In 1809 Sobremonte retired to Spain.

30 On 12 August, Colonel Lane of the Saint Helena Company arrived in Capetown with the news of the capture of Buenos Aires. In response to Beresford's report (in which he had referred to his disagreement with Popham over whether to attempt to capture Montevideo or Buenos Aires first), Baird wrote on 13 August 1806:

> From my heart and soul, I congratulate you and your fine fellows on your great success. I have great satisfaction in assuring you, that I most fully approve, not only of what you have done, but what you have left undone, it would have been the height of madness to have attempted dividing your small force in the situation you were in.

He went on to detail the preparations he was making to dispatch reinforcements, with which he hoped Beresford would be able to attack Montevideo. Interestingly, he was prepared to take these steps even though he had received orders to hold every infantry soldier in readiness to proceed to India. See Beresford to Baird, 2 July 1806, and Baird to Beresford, 13 July 1806 (NA, WO 1/342).

31 Both Popham and Beresford corresponded with the authorities in London (see Beresford's report to Windham of 2 July 1806 of the landing and taking of Buenos Aires) and that correspondence, which is now in the National Archives in Kew, was widely published at the time in the *London Gazette* and the *Gentleman's Magazine*.

32 Beresford refers in his letter of 11 July 1806 to Baird having authorised him to draw the salary of the Spanish Governor, which he said was $40,000 per annum. He went on to say, however, that this sum was insufficient to meet his expenses (NA, C0 324/68/2).

33 Between 29 June and 4 August 1806 Beresford issued seven Proclamations as well as many subsidiary orders. The seven Proclamations were:

i.   29 June 1806 – A proclamation stating that the organs of government and church would continue to function as hitherto with the same personnel and under Spanish laws; the only change was that of Viceroy where Beresford replaced Sobremonte, subject to the sovereignty of George III.

ii.   30 June 1806 – Return of previously arrested local trading vessels and cargos to their owners.

iii. 2 July 1806 – Spanish officials who did not wish to go to England as prisoners might remain in Buenos Aires subject to swearing loyalty to King George III; guarantee of security of private property and that of the church. For the purpose of taking the oath Beresford fixed the date of 7 July before Popham and himself. Further opportunities for declaring allegiance were available before Gillespie.

iv.   4 July 1806 – Slaves to continue in the ownership of existing owners.

v.   5 July 1806 – All arms issued by the government to be given up to the mayors of localities by 12 July, with a penalty of $200 per weapon not surrendered.

vi.   19 July 1806 – Death penalty for those persuading or encouraging English soldiers to desert.

vii. 4 August 1806 – Commercial regulations; see text of this article.

34 Beresford to Castlereagh, 16 July 1806 (NA, WO 1/161).

35 Captain Robert Arbuthnot, later General Sir Robert Arbuthnot, born in Rockfleet, County Mayo 1773. He joined the army in 1797 (20th Light Dragoons). He went from the Cape to Rio de la Plata with Beresford as his ADC. His imprisonment in South America only ended with the general release of prisoners in 1807. He joined Beresford again in Madeira and served with him through most of the Peninsular War, including the retreat to La Coruña. In 1809 he was seconded to the Portuguese army and he became one of Beresford's military secretaries. He was selected to carry home the news of the victory of Albuera. Note, William Gavin suggests that the party sent out to recover the treasure was under the command of Captain Charles Graham (see diary entry 27 June 1806) though he would only have been a Lieutenant in the 71st Foot in July 1806. He was one of the party under Arbuthnot, but Beresford makes it clear that Arbuthnot was in command (Beresford to Windham, 2 July 1806).

36 Luján is 68 km north west of Buenos Aires. Gillespie, op. cit., p. 13, agrees there were thirty men in the party sent to Luján.

37 Beresford to Castlereagh, 11 July and 16 July 1806 (NA, WO 1/161). See alternatively *Gentleman's Magazine*, 76, 2. It is clear that the prize money ultimately received by participants in the expedition was made up of much more than just a share of the 'treasure' brought back from Luján. It included the value of vessels and their contents seized during the course of the expedition.

38 *The Times*, 22 September 1806 reported:

> On Saturday, September 20th, at seven o'clock in the morning, the Loyal Britons Volunteers mustered in St James's Square, and after firing three rounds, proceeded to Clapham, to escort the treasure landed from the *Narcissus*, at Portsmouth, to town. On their arrival at Clapham they found the cavalcade, consisting of eight waggons each drawn by six horses, adorned with flags, pendants and blue ribbons, On the flags was inscribed the word TREASURE. They were preceded by a brass field-piece taken from the enemy.
>
> ... the procession was accompanied by a band playing stirring tunes. The procession stopped at the Admiralty and then at Colonel Davidson's [*sic*] house in St James's

Square where Mrs Davidson presented colours to the convoy stating 'Buenos Ayres, Popham, Beresford, Victory'. It then passed through the City of London to the Bank of England.

Lieutenant Colonel Alexander Davison commanded the Loyal Britons Volunteers and in addition was Popham's agent in London. With Davison's house being in St James's square, it is not difficult to imagine the stage management of this event.

39   See *The Times*, 11 June 1807. When Popham failed at trial to augment his share of the prize money, he sought a retrial which was denied. He then unsuccessfully petitioned the Privy Council on the basis of an alleged entitlement as a flag officer. He also attempted to resist payment of a share to Baird, but he had induced Baird to give him the troops for the expedition by the promise of a share. In fact Baird had secured Popham's agreement that Baird would receive a two-eighth share of captured property as against a one-eighth share for Popham before endorsing the expedition. Baird renounced that agreement on the basis of Popham's misrepresentation of his status as a Commodore. See *The Times*, 21 July 1807.

40   *The Court of Common Council Records*, 2 October 1806.

41   Beresford's sword is now on display in the Guildhall, London. His freedom box is displayed in the Museum of London.

42   Sir Samuel Auchmuty (1750–1822) was born in New York City. He supported the loyalist cause in the Amercan War of Independence, joining the army. In the Rio de la Plata his command was superceded by the appointment of Lieutenant General Whitelocke. At the end of his life Auchmuty succeeded Baird as Commander in Chief, Ireland in 1822.

43   See Beresford to the secretary of State for War & the Colonies (William Windham), 11 July 1806 (NA, CO 324/68). Beresford reportedly sent gifts to Casamayor. The 71st Regiment sent a number of gifts to the Bethlemite fathers. See end note 56 below.

44   From 10 July, Beresford opened an office in Buenos Aires manned by Captain Alexander Gillespie for the purpose of administering the oath of allegiance to George III. It is suggested fifty-eight people swore the oath and according to Gillespie six of these were members of the Primera Junta, the name given to the first independent government of Argentina, created in 1810. The book in which the names of oath takers were inscribed was allegedly later destroyed by Canning, though the reason for this is not clear. See Gillespie, *Gleanings and Remarks*.

45   One of those who tricked Beresford was Santiago de Liniers, who indicated he wished to cease the military way of life and become a merchant, an assertion supported by his father-in-law, Martin de Sarratea, who was a well-respected merchant. He was released from his parole and then absconded to Montevideo. Beresford to Gordon, 6 and 10 May 1807; Gordon, op. cit.

46   See the 'Journal of Captain Pococke', *Highland Light Infantry Chronicle*, 1899. Pococke served with the 71st in South America and refers to the attempts of the Spanish to get men to desert, as does Gillespie in *Gleanings and Remarks*, op. cit., p. 89. Fernyhough (op. cit., p. 98) tells us that the deserter recaptured on 1 August at Perdriel had been manning one of the guns used against the British there, and he was shot on 9 August following his court martial. A rather different case involved a cadet from the Saint Helena regiment who converted to Catholicism, married a Creole and chose to stay in South America after release in 1807, joining de Liniers' army.

47   Juan Martín de Pueyrredon was the son of a Béarnais (French) merchant who had settled in Argentina. His mother, Rita O'Doghan (Duggan) y Martinez, was of Irish descent. Sent to Spain after the recovery of Buenos Aires as a representative of the city, he was there during the French occupation. He later became one of the instigators of Argentine independence and was a member of the triumvirate that ruled

Buenos Aires in 1812. Subsequently in 1816 he was elected Supreme Director of the United Provinces of the Rio de la Plata at the Congress of Tucuman. At Perdriel, Gavin says there were 1,500 horsemen with Pueyrredon. 'Diary of William Gavin', 1 August 1806. Pack says Pueyrredon had 1,600 men with him; Pack to Sir John Cradock (then Colonel of 71st Regiment), August 1806, quoted in Pack Beresford, *A Memoir of Major-General Sir Denis Pack*, p. 14.

48 Denis Pack to Sir John Cradock, August 1806; *A Memoir of Major-General Sir Denis Pack*, p. 15.

49 Santiago (Jacques) de Liniers y Bremond was of French origin but served in the Spanish navy, being sent in the capacity of Captain to the Rio de la Plata command in 1788. His popularity as the perceived architect of Beresford's defeat led to his appointment as Viceroy in the place of Sobremonte, and in that capacity he defended Buenos Aires against the much larger British attack of the city in 1807. In later life he supported the royalist cause in Argentina and when captured by those seeking independence he was executed without trial in 1810. Pascual Ruiz Huidobro was civil and military Governor of Montevideo from 1803. Taken prisoner at the battle of Montevideo in 1807, he was sent to England, but released when England and Spain became allies the following year.

50 Beresford to Gordon, 6 and 10 May 1807; Gordon, *Military transactions of the British Empire*, ff. 173.

51 The Return shows 2 officers killed with 8 wounded, and 43 rank and file killed with 92 wounded and 9 missing. It is not clear how many of the wounded subsequently died (BL, Add MS 32,607, f. 41).

52 The Recova was at that time a recently built market and warehouse complex on the banks of the river with a large arch (the Arch of the Viceroys) as its centrepiece. It looked towards the Cabildo (Government House) which is now the National Museum.

53 Costa, op. cit., p. 60.

54 Pococke, op. cit., p. 254.

55 Popham to the Governor General of Montevideo (Huidobro), 17 August 1806 (BL, Add MS 32,607, f. 20).

56 Beresford to Castlereagh, 12 May 1807 (NA, WO 1/162).

57 Huidobro, when faced with the written evidence of the terms, attempted a different argument, namely that de Liniers had no power to agree those terms because he only derived his commission from the chiefs of the Province, rather than the Viceroy. Popham dismissed this argument on the basis that de Liniers could not have been expected to wait for orders from the Viceroy to engage in treaty discussions. Popham to Huidobro, 27 August 1806 (BL, Add MS 32,607).

58 BL, Add MS 32,607. This manuscript contains extensive correspondence on the terms of surrender, including copies of the agreement in both English and Spanish.

59 See Hughes, op. cit., pp. 90–1.

60 The hospital (on a site now occupied by the Colégio Nacional in front of San Pedro Telmo church) was run by the Bethlemite Order. Major Alexander Gillespie attested to the kindness of this Order. Subsequently, the 71st Regiment donated two clocks (a grandfather and a mantle clock) to the Bethlemite Order in Buenos Aires in April 1809 in recognition of their services and kindness. These were inscribed 'fugit irrevocabile temous, Beneficiae haud fugit memoria' (time flees irrevocably, the benefits received will never be forgotten). The grandfather clock now stands in the church of San Pedro Telmo.

61 Pack to Sr Don Luis-----, 16 July 1809 (University of Southampton Library, MS 296 Pack Papers 296/1/2).

62 While those in the ranks killed in the retaking of Buenos Aires were buried in a ditch outside the fort, more compassion was shown to a number of dead officers. Captain Kennet, who had died at Beresford's side, and Lieutenant Mitchell were buried in El Retiro, as being Protestants they were not allowed to be buried in consecrated ground. Liniers attended this joint funeral, and authorised his own troops to fire a salute.

63 The other estancias included those of Felipe Otalora, José António Otalora and Marcos Zavaleta, in the Province of Buenos Aires. Captain Gillespie was sent to 'Santa Rosa' where he received a visit from Spanish officials who wished to obtain from him the book signed by those declaring loyalty to George III, but Gillespie reportedly had buried it, and he told them he did not have it. The British rank and file were distributed far from Buenos Aires with 400 in Córdoba, 200 each in Mendoza, Tucuman and San Juan, and 100 each sent to Santiago del Estero and San Luis.

64 See Gillespie, op. cit., Ch. VIII, p. 40. Gillespie refers to horse racing and cricket, 'for which we always carried the materials'. Cricket has continued to thrive in Argentina under the auspices of the Argentine Cricket Association.

65 Roberts goes so far as to suggest that Peña, whose ultimate aim was independence, sought at a meeting on 7 February 1807 to persuade Martin Alzaga, the Mayor of Buenos Aires, that Beresford could be used as a go between to achieve a bloodless solution to the threatened second British invasion of Buenos Aires as Peña felt resistance would be unsuccessful; op. cit., p. 222.

66 The other procurator may have been Dr Pedro Andrés Garcia, though in some accounts Garcia is listed as the officer in charge of the escort taking the British officers to Catamarca. Garcia was a military man (Lieutenant Colonel) and an explorer and was subsequently involved in the independence movement. As soon as the Cabildo of Buenos Aires learnt of the fall of Montevideo on 5 February 1807, the order was given to seize Beresford's papers; see Roberts, *Las Invasiones Inglesas*, p. 221. There is a story which claims Arbuthnot hid the original of the surrender terms in a tree to keep it from falling into the hands of the Spaniards, a story which would certainly have a reason, namely the preservation of the original terms which, in British eyes, had been fundamentally flouted. The papers taken from Beresford comprised both correspondence and bills reflecting commercial transactions, which were later referred to by Roberts; see in particular op. cit., pp. 165–6.

67 San Fernando del Valle de Catamarca is in the north west of present-day Argentina, some 200 km south of Tucuman. Even today it is remote from Buenos Aires.

68 Pack to Sir Samuel Auchmuty, 27 January 1807; Pack Beresford, *A Memoir of Major-General Sir Denis Pack*, p. 23.

69 Roberts suggests that the commanding officer of Beresford's escort from Luján to Catamarca, Captain Martinez, was in fact a relative of Peña and that Olavarria, a bother of Peña was in the escort party. Both Martinez and Olivarria were subsequently arrested but later released by de Liniers; op. cit., p. 223.

70 Peña and Padilla accompanied Beresford to Montevideo. Roberts, op. cit., p. 223.

71 HMS *Charwell* was a former 16-gun French corvette, *L'Aurore*, captured in 1801. The vessel that took them out to HMS *Charwell* was reportedly the *Flor del Cabo*, a Portuguese smuggler's boat commanded by António Luis de Lima. At least two other officers escaped subsequent to the escape of Beresford and Pack. In March 1807, Major Henry Dunbar Tolley and Lieutenant Adamson of the 71st Regiment escaped from St Ignatia.

72 Peña and Beresford's relationship is discussed in Roberts, op. cit., ff. 220.

73 The Court of Inquiry consisted of two senior navy and two senior army officers, with Brigadier General Lumley as President. See Beresford to Gordon, 10 May 1807 quoted in *Military Transactions*.

74 Lucas Munoz y Cubero to Auchmuty, 21 March 1807, and Beresford to Castlereagh, 12 May 1807 (NA, WO 1/162). Munoz y Cubero had emerged in Buenos Aires during the opposition to Beresford in August 1806, and at the end of August he was named by Sobremonte as Superintendente de Ejercito y Real Hacienda (Superintendant of the Army and Royal Finances). The reference here is to Captain Robert Patrick, who was to serve with Beresford again in Portugal (see Chapter 6, below).

75 *United Service Magazine*, 1836, III, p. 212.

76   See Costa, *English Invasion of the River Plate*, p. 37.

77   An examination of the dividend lists for Buenos Ayres [*sic*] details prizes from seizures on land and at sea. These include members of Beresford's staff: Honourable Major Deane 38th Foot, Honourable Captain A. Gordon 3rd Footguards, and certain 'servants': Privates Will Cox (88th), William Basbrook (38th) and Thomas Trickett (54th). In addition, Thomas Forbes, surgeon (paid the same rate as a captain) and Richard Halliday, hospital mate received dividends. Those who had died in South America had their dividends paid to their next of kin. All of this took time, and the third dividend was not certified until 1813. From the lists it is evident that there were a large number of soldiers with Irish names (Burke, Coyle, Cowan, Samuel Curran, Neil Develin [*sic*], Patrick Dogherty, Fitzgerald, Fleming, Gill, Dan Gorman, Hogan, Leary, Timothy Lynch, O'Neil) in the 71st Regiment and that a not insignificant number of these (147 listed in the first dividend) chose to remain in South America. As such they forfeited their dividend. Of course, one should not jump to conclusions as to the origin of those with Irish sounding names, but given that the 71st had been stationed in and actively recruited in Ireland in the years before the expedition it is likely that there were many Irish who chose to stay in South America and who subsequently formed the nucleus (though by no means the earliest) of the Irish diaspora there. Some of these later fought in the war of independence in the Rio de la Plata (NA, WO 164/517, 518, 519 and 520).

78   Popham became involved in litigation with some of his own captains, including Donnelly of the *Narcissus*, in relation to prize money.

79   *The Times*, 16 March 1807.

80   Fernyhough, op. cit., p. 83.

81   For Beresford's views on the difficulties faced by Spain in re-establishing control over the Rio de la Plata see NA, CO 324/68. The quotation is from Grainger, 'The Royal Navy in the River Plate'.

82   Castlereagh Correspondence, vol. VII, pp. 385–9.

83   William Windham (Secretary for War and Colonies) to Baird, 26 July 1806, quoted in Wilkin, *The Life of Sir David Baird*.

84   See, 'A full and correct report of the trial of Sir Home Popham' (London: J. and J. Richardson, 1807).

85   Windham to Beresford, 24 September 1806 (NA, WO 1/161), in which he makes it clear to Beresford that the government did not hold him accountable for disobeying orders, and which congratulated him for the measures he had taken in Buenos Aires and which also promised reinforcements.

86   Denis Pack to Sir John Cradock, August 1806; Pack Beresford, *A Memoir of Major-General Sir Denis Pack*, p. 16.

87   Reverend Herbert Randolph (ed.), *The Life of General Sir Robert Wilson*, vol. 1 (London: John Murray, 1862).

Chapter 3

1   Queen Maria I of Portugal (1734–1816). Married her uncle Pedro in 1760. He died in 1786 and two years later the death of their eldest son seems to have induced serious melancholia, with the Queen suffering not just depression but insomnia and repeated fevers. She was declared insane in 1792, but her son, João, initially declined to be named Regent even though he took over the reins of government. João officially assumed the role of Prince Regent in 1799 and held this position until his mother's death in 1816. See Jenifer Roberts, *The Madness of Queen Maria* (Chippenham: Templeton Press, 2009).

2   The Continental System, or *Blocus Continental* as it was called in France, was Napoleon's response to the British naval blockade of France introduced on 16 May 1806. The Continental System was brought about by the Berlin Decree of 21 November 1806 banning the import of British goods to all countries

allied to or dependent on France. In a tit-for-tat move Britain then forbade French trade with Great Britain, its allies or neutrals, and France in a further response by virtue of the Milan Decree provided that neutrals using British ports were to be regarded as British and seized. Initially the Continental System applied to all of continental Western Europe bar Portugal, but support for it was at best half-hearted in some countries and ultimately countries such as Russia and Sweden determined to break from the system.

3 See Thomas Munch-Petersen, *Defying Napoleon: How Britain Bombarded Copenhagen and Seized the Danish Fleet in 1807* (Stroud: Sutton Publishing, 2007).

4 Throughout the summer and early autumn of 1807, Portugal had struggled to maintain neutrality while the court made preparations to leave the country in the event of a French invasion. Work on the repair of the Portuguese fleet began in August but Prince João remained non-committal about a departure in the face of French threats, hoping to satisfy both protagonists in September, October and even early November. There was a suggestion by Minister Araújo that the Portuguese might engage in a simulated war on Great Britain (Strangford to Canning, 8 September 1807; NA, WO 63/55). As French pressure grew greater concessions were made to Napoleon, including the expulsion of Britons and the seizure of goods. At the same time agreements for assistance were being negotiated with Great Britain.

In early November, the Marquis of Marialva was sent to France to capitulate, but he was incarcerated in Madrid where his passport was seized. In early November, realising his predicament, João had moved from the palace at Mafra to the Ajuda Palace on the Lisbon docks. On the night of 24/25 November the decision to embark for Brazil was taken following the receipt of news that Junot had crossed the frontier.

5 NA, FO 63/58 contains at f. 13 a *Projet* for the removal of the Portuguese seat of monarchy and fortune to Brazil in the event of unjust French demands and threats. The Portuguese preference was to try and remain neutral by virtue of an increasingly difficult balancing act. To appease the French it envisaged closing Portuguese ports to British shipping but recognised the fact that this might lead to British reprisals, including a naval blockade and bombardment of Lisbon and the occupation of Madeira. Article I of the Treaty signed in London on 22 October 1807 provided that there would be no British expedition against Madeira or other Portuguese possession without notifying the Portuguese Minister in London and in arrangement with him. In return the Portuguese agreed not to reinforce Madeira with troops from Brazil or Portugal and undertook not to allow any French officer on the island whether in the service of France or Portugal. Secret orders were to be sent to the Governor of Madeira not to resist a British landing. These were sent on 14 November 1807. Article 2 of the Treaty provided for British assistance to help the Court move to Brazil.

6 When Prince João succumbed to French demands and expelled the British from Portugal there followed a massive exodus, with sixty vessels leaving Lisbon on 17 October and reportedly another forty-six from Porto. See Christopher D. Hall, *Wellington's Navy: Sea Power and the Peninsular War* (London: Chatham Publishing, 2004), p. 14.

7 See Kenneth Light, *A transferencia da capital e corte para o Brasil*, (Lisbon: Tribuna, 2007). See also Pereira J. Rodrigues, *Campanhas Navais (1793–1807): A Marinha Portuguesa na Época de Napoleão*, vol. I (Lisbon: Tribuna, 2005), pp. 171–84. The British squadron escorting the royal family and court included twelve ships of the line, two frigates and two corvettes. The squadron, which was commanded by Sir Sidney Smith, included HMS *Theseus* (seventy-eight-guns) commanded by Captain (later Admiral) John Poo Beresford, a half-brother of William Carr Beresford. The Portuguese navy involved included eight ships of the line, four frigates, one corvette, four brigs and two schooners. The fleet became separated on a number of occasions, but a number of vessels were off Madeira on 9 and 10 December and off the Cape Verde Islands 17–20 December 1807. Some vessels made landfall at Rio de Janeiro but the royal party arrived at São Salvador (now Bahia) on 22 January 1808 and did not reach Rio unti 7 March of that year.

8 Four of the British ships of the line escorted the Portuguese to the Brazils, the remaining eleven ships sailed with the fleet as far as Madeira and then returned to Lisbon to enforce the blockade of that port. Wisely, the Portuguese royal family was split between a number of vessels to avoid catastrophic loss in the event of any mishap.

9 Those strategies involved a proposed phony war on Great Britain designed to delay a French invasion, and ultimately the closure of Portuguese ports to British shipping. When the latter move failed to appease Napoleon, the Marquis of Marialva was ordered to Paris to capitulate, but in the event his passport was confiscated in Madrid. In a desperate move José Oliveira de Barreto, a leading merchant, was sent to meet Junot to persuade him of Portuguese compliance. They met on the banks of the Zezere river but by then the die had been cast and Napoleon's decision to remove the house of Braganza from the throne of Portugal was common knowledge. Moving the court and government to Brazil had been suggested previously post the destructive earthquake of 1755, during the Seven Years War and more recently during the War of the Oranges.

10 See Patrick Wilcken, *Empire Adrift: The Portuguese Court in Rio de Janeiro 1808–1821* (London: Bloomsbury, 2005). The royal treasury was loaded along with a cache of Brazilian diamonds, but much of the royal library was left on the docks as were fourteen carriages of church silver.

11 Treaty of Fontainebleau, 27 October 1807. France's main interest at this stage, apart from denying Britain access to the continent, centred around securing Lisbon and the strategically important Tagus estuary for its own forces, together with the Portuguese fleet to help replenish its own maritime losses. This dependency in central Portugal was seen as disposable on a general peace, with Napoleon looking to exchange it for Gibraltar.

12 9 November 1807 (NA, WO 1/354).

13 Castlereagh to Beresford, November 1807 (NA, WO 6/68).

14 Gordon, *Military Transactions*. Lieutenant Colonel Gordon was at this time Military Secretary to the Commander in Chief, the Duke of York. The officers taken by Beresford to Madeira included Captains Murphy and Penderleath, of the 88th, Lieutenant W. Sewell of the 16th Light Dragoons, and Major John Austin of the 58th Regiment. Austin was to serve with Beresford in Portugal as Deputy Adjutant-General and rose to be a Lieutenant Colonel in 1829. Sewell later served as Beresford's ADC in Portugal. See *Royal Military Calendar*, 4, pp. 441–2.

15 The other regiments forming part of this show of force were the 25th and 63rd, which were destined for Barbados following the taking of Madeira; Castlereagh to Beresford, 14 November 1807 (NA, WO 6/68).

16 A number of the vessels from the fleet carrying the royal family and court, which had left the Tagus on 29 November, had called into Madeira between 8 and 10 December 1807, so the Governor of Madeira was clearly aware of the departure of the administration from Portugal.

17 Beresford to Castlereagh, 29 December 1807 (NA, WO 1/354). Murphy carried back to England the news of the taking of Madeira.

18 The Terms of Capitulation of the island of Madeira and its dependencies signed 26 December 1807 were executed by Pedro Fagundes Bacelar d'Antas e Menezes, Sir Samuel Hood and Major General Beresford. The Portuguese copy is held at TT-TRT-GB2-8. It clearly provides for the return of these islands to Portugal when the sovereignty of Portugal shall be emancipated from the control or influence of France (Clause II). A further copy is reproduced in *The Naval Chronicle* (1807–1808), vol. 19.

19 The Quinta was subsequent to Beresford's term purchased by the Blandy family of Madeira. It is now a hotel, and some of the dining furniture is that of General Beresford, which he left there on his departure from the island.

20 Officials in Funchal were required to attend at twelve noon to take the oath of allegiance at the Palace of São Lourenço on 1 January 1808. Those residing in the interior were required to do so as soon as was convenient (NA, WO 1/354).

21 Castlereagh to Beresford, 30 November 1808 (NA, WO 6/68).

22 Beresford to Gordon, 3 January 1808; Gordon, *Military Transactions*. Gordon's correspondence regarding the British occupation of Madeira is on pp. 318–27.

23 Castlereagh to Beresford, 20 February 1808 (NA, WO 6/68).

24 Beresford to Castlereagh, 2 January 1808 (NA, WO 1/354).

25 An amount of £20,000 in dollars had been provided for the use of the troops in charge of Deputy Commissary Spilla. Two victuallers, one laden with pork and the other with flour sufficient for the garrison for more than six months were designated but seem to have been delayed. See Castlereagh to Beresford, November 1807 (NA, WO 6/68).

26 See 'Day Books of Cossart Gordon & Co.', 10 July 1808. They refer to a large transport being sent to the Western Islands to bring a load of cattle. The entry refers to the great scarcity of meat in Madeira and states none of the troops have tasted fresh meat since they arrived there. The Day Book also states 'everything goes smoothly now under General Beresford's government'.

27 Beresford to Castlereagh, 2 January 1808 (NA, WO 1/354, f. 37) includes a list of the artillery on the island;

28 Castlereagh to Beresford, February 1808 (NA, WO 1/354).

29 Castlereagh to Beresford, 20 February and 24 March 1808 (NA, WO 6/68).

30 Beresford to Castlereagh, 24 April 1808 (NA, WO 1/354).

31 Beresford to John Poo Beresford, 9 June 1808 (NYA/ZBA 21/10, f. 1) expressed his concern at being detained in Madeira and thus missing out on expeditions to either South America or Portugal.

32 Castlereagh to Beresford, 16 July 1808 (NA, WO 6/68).

33 See 'Madeira Factory Records'. The piece of plate was a wonderful centrepiece by Paul Storr of London, described as a three female figure silver gilt George III Dolphin centrepiece with basket and glass top, which disappeared in the course of the Second World War. British merchants occupied a pivotal position in the economy of Madeira in the eighteenth and nineteenth centuries. The British Factory was essentially their Chamber of Commerce, acting both as agents for British merchants and as revenue collectors to forward projects such as the building of an Anglican church.

34 'Day Books of Cossart Gordon & Co.', 6 September 1808.

35 Holy Trinity Church, Funchal, Madeira.

Chapter 4

1   The flag was hoisted on the castle with a twenty-gun salute. In the following disturbances at least thirteen French soldiers were killed on 13 and 14 December, together with a number of Portuguese. William Jarvis, the US consul in Lisbon, reported on the growth of opposition to Junot when writing to James Madison (then Secretary of State) on 21 December 1807, noting that it was the people who rioted and that the Portuguese soldiery played no part with the people and were subsequently put on the same pay as the French. On this occasion he commended General Junot for his moderation (University of Virginia, DNA:RG 59-CD-Consular Dispatches, Lisbon).

2   The Portuguese Legion, or *Légion Portugaise*, when formed initially under Pedro de Almeida, Marquis d'Alorna in early 1808 consisted of some 9,000 men. In the spring of that year the *Légion* was marched through Spain to Bayonne in France, and some units participated in the siege of Pamplona. On the

way some 5,000 men deserted, and on returning to Portugal many re-enlisted in the Portuguese army reformed later by the combined efforts of Marshal William Carr Beresford and Dom Miguel Forjaz. The *Légion* served with considerable distinction until the end of the war, particularly at Wagram and Smolensk, where it suffered severely as it did again on the retreat from Moscow. When it was disbanded at the end of the war it contained perhaps less than 1,000 Portuguese. D'Alorna himself played an interesting role, being present at the siege of Almeida with Masséna in 1810 before dying at Königsberg in 1813 following wounds received in the retreat from Moscow. In his absence from Portugal he was tried for treason and sentenced to death. His second in command, General Gomes Freire, Grand Master of the French-leaning Freemasons, was found guilty of conspiring to lead a revolution that failed in 1817 for which he was condemned to death and executed.

3   The militia was dissolved on 11 January 1808 and the ordenança on 10 February 1808.

4   Having lured the Marquis of Abrantes (President of the Regency Council) to France where he was imprisoned, Napoleon created Junot the Duke of Abrantes on 6 April 1808.

5   Napoleon's decree was in fact dated 23 December 1807 and provided also for the sequestration of all the property of the Queen and Prince Regent. In addition, all those who had followed them into exile were to lose their property if they had not returned to Portugal by 15 February 1808. Further, Junot directed that all gold and silver from all churches be brought to the mint within fifteen days of 1 February. On 15 February, a draconian decree was issued by Junot forbidding the carrying of firearms in Portugal with a proviso that any non-military personnel found in possession of a firearm was to be treated as an assassin. This step arose because of a number of assassinations (BL, 594, f. 24. Portuguese Proclamations).

6   The original appointees as Governadores (Conselho de Regência) in 1807 were Conde de Castro Marim (President), Marques de Abrantes (a cousin of Dom João), Francisco da Cunha e Meneses, Principal Castro (Dean of the Lisbon Patriarchate), Pedro de Mello Breyner (Presidente do Real Erário), Luis de Vasconcellos e Sousa, and Dom Francisco Javier de Noronha. The Secretariat consisted of the Conde de Sampāio, Dom Miguel Pereira Forjaz and/or João António Salter de Mendonça. Junot replaced the Governadores with a council of his own appointees, some of whom had served as appointees of Prince João. The new Council comprised Dom Pedro de Mello Breyner (Conseiller de Gouvernement pour l'Interieur), M d'Azevedo (Conseiller de Gouvernement des Finances), M. Lhuitte (Secretary of State for War and the Navy), Conde de Sampāio (Conseiller de Gouvernement for the War and the Navy), Principal Castro (Conseiller de Gouvernement for Justice and Religion, with title of Regedor), M. Viennez-Vaublanc (Secretary General). Portuguese nominees were in effect shadowed by French appointees (for instance a Monsieur Hermann, previously French consul in Lisbon, was appointed Administrator General of Finance alongside de Mello Breyner), but the cooperation of the Conde de Sampāio and Pedro Mello de Breyner with Junot was to taint them as collaborators when the country was liberated in 1808. Interestingly, Principal Castro was appointed Minister of Religion by Junot but managed to escape condemnation later. See Paul Charles Dieudonné Thiébault, *Relation de l'Expédition du Portugal*, pp. 99–101.

7   Six soldiers of the No. 2 Porto Regiment and three civilians were executed allegedly for ridiculing and making fun of French soldiers.

8   Carlos IV abdicated on 19 March 1808 in Bayonne.

9   The Generals heading the three Spanish divisions were Solano in southern Portugal, Caraffa in Lisbon and Taranco in Porto. Taranco died on 25 January 1808 and was succeeded by Belesta.

10   There were risings in many parts of Portugal but most effectively in the north and in the Algarve. Chaves, Braga, Bragança, and Trancoso all rose in the north where Junot's attempt to subdue the Portuguese

was ineffective. One of the earliest and most effective manifestations of Portuguese resistance to French rule took place in the northern Province of Trás-os-Montes where Colonel Silveira (later Conde de Amarante) with a scratch collection of previously disbanded soldiers and militia defeated a French force under the much feared and detested General Loison following a running engagement over nearly three days at Padrões de Teixeira (north of the river Douro) from 21–23 June 1808. Loison then retired to Almeida before receiving orders to join Junot at Lisbon.

11   The Bishop of Porto declared for the Prince Regent on 19 June. The following day he proclaimed José Monteiro Guedes de Vasconcellos Mourão Military Governor of the city.

12   Castlereagh to Lieutenant General Sir Arthur Wellesley, 21 June and 30 June 1808 (NA, WO 1/228).

13   Castlereagh to Lieutenant General Sir Arthur Wellesley, 30 June 1808 (the quote in the text is from this letter) and 15 July 1808 (NA, WO 1/228). In the later letter Wellesley was told, 'the attack upon the Tagus should be considered as the first object to be attended to'. It also envisaged that up to 10,000 of the expeditionary force might be used to cooperate with the Supreme Junta of Seville, without prejudice to operations on the Tagus.

14   Wellesley stated at the Inquiry into the Convention of Cintra that he had about 9,064 men, including the Fourth Royal veteran Battalion, 275 artillery and drivers, and about 300 cavalry, of which 180 were mounted. He sailed on HMS *Bengal* but subsequently transferred to a fast frigate, as instructed, HMS *Crocodile*.

15   Wellesley to Castlereagh, 26 July 1808 (NA, WO 1/228).

16   The Spanish were commanded by Joaquim Blake and Gregorio de la Cuesta.

17   The Russian fleet under Dmitri Seniavin had exited the Black Sea and been operating in the Mediterranean with a view to preventing French advances in the Balkans. Following the treaty of Tilsit in 1807, Russia effectively changed sides and much to Seniavin's discomfort Russia gave up its hard-earned gains in the eastern Mediterranean. Seniavin determined to return to Russia through the Straits of Gibraltar and then via the English Channel. Putting into Lisbon, which he understood to be a neutral port, he had been trapped there by the English fleet.

18   The Spanish force under General Castaños had caused the French under Dupont to surrender at Bailén, and were given terms allowing the French army to return to France. See, House of Commons, 'Copy of the Proceedings upon the Inquiry relative to the Armistice and Convention made and concluded in Portugal in August 1808, between the Commanders of the British and French Armies' (London: War Office, 1809).

19   Castlereagh to Wellesley, 15 July 1808 (2 letters); NA, WO 1/228. See also, WSD 4, 17–18.

20   This meeting was also attended by Manuel Pinto de Bacelar, whose Portuguese forces (mostly militia) were operating in the Beira Alta.

21   Manuel Amaral; 'The Portuguese Army and the Commencement of the Peninsular War', in Adelino de Matos Coelho (ed.), *O Exército Português e as Comemorações dos 200 Anos da Guerra Peninsular*, vol. I (Lisbon: Exército e Tribuna da História, 2008).

22   Nicholas Trant came from a Roman Catholic family long established in south west Ireland. He went to military college in France and subsequently served in the regiment of Walsh (sometimes referred to as Walsh Serrant) in the Irish brigade in the French service. On the outbreak of the revolution he transferred to the 84th Regiment in the British service. He served in Egypt under Sir Ralph Abercrombie in 1800–1 but subsequently retired from the army. He later re-enlisted, transferred to the Portuguese service and raised a regiment, the backbone of which was made up from students at Coimbra University. He served with his force at both Roliça and Vimeiro, but is perhaps best remembered for his recapture of Coimbra in October 1810 at the head of a militia brigade when he secured a large number of French sick

and wounded left there by Masséna, protecting them from an enraged crowd. Knighted by Dom João he was appointed Governor of Porto. See, Wellesley to Castlereagh, 16 August 1808.

The Portuguese force was made up of 1,000 regular infantry, 400 caçadores and 250 cavalry. Note, however, that in *A Logística do Exército Anglo-Luso na Guerra Peninsular: Uma Introdução (An Introduction to the Anglo-Portuguese army logistics in the Peninsular War)*, p. 42, Gabriel Espirito Santo and Pedro de Brito suggest a stronger Portuguese contingent joined Wellesley at Alcobaça: 1,514 infantry, 569 caçadores, 299 cavalry and 201 gunners.

23   There is a lack of clarity as to the numbers on each side at Vimeiro. Oman calculated the French had some 13,000 men and the British and Portuguese force combined was about 19,000. At the Inquiry into the convention of Cintra it was suggested Wellesley disposed of a force of 18,000 infantry and 500 cavalry whereas Junot possessed 14,000 infantry and 2,500 cavalry. Following Roliça, Wellesley had been joined by Anstruther on 19 August with 3,000 men. On 20 August he was joined by Ackland with further reinforcements.

24   Sir Harry Burrard had served under Cornwallis in the American War of Independence. In the wars against France he served with the Anglo-Russian force operating in the Netherlands in 1799 and later he commanded the 1st Division under General Cathcart at Copenhagen.

25   In this decision Burrard was supported by both Brigadier General Henry Clinton and Lieutenant Colonel George Murray; See Captain Thomas Hamilton, *Annals of the Peninsular Campaigns (1808– 1814)* (London: T. Cadell, 1829), p. 323.

26   See, 'Inquiry into Convention of Cintra, 1808'. 25,747 French were transported home of which 20,900 were under arms. At Vimeiro, Wellesley stated he had some 470 mounted men which included 260 Portuguese. He thought Junot had some 1,200–1,400 cavalry at that battle. Sir John Moore referred to the French as having 'superior cavalry unbroken' (2 October 1808); J.F. Maurice (ed.), *Diary of Sir John Moore*, 2 volumes (London: Edward Arnold, 1904).

27   Sir Hew Dalrymple was commissioned in 1763 and subsequently moved up the ranks without seeing much active service. He did serve under the Duke of York in Flanders in 1793. In 1806 he was appointed Governor of Gibraltar. Sir John Moore recognised his limitations when he wrote of Dalrymple, 'who seemed to be completely at loss in the situation in which he was placed' and 'he was never able to determine any point whatever'. Maurice, *The Diary of Sir John Moore* vol. II, ff. 259.

In contrast, Moore sympathised with Burrard's situation and felt he had behaved correctly in allowing Wellesley to remain in command until Burrard ascertained the military position. Further, he found Burrard's decision not to pursue the French after the battle of Vimeiro entirely logical in the circumstances, when French reserves were of an unknown quantity combined with a strong French cavalry presence. Ibid. p. 268.

28   See evidence given to the Inquiry into Convention of Cintra, 1808.

29   It is suggested in evidence this was at about 2 pm.

30   Section 5 of the Suspension of Arms.

31   See sections 6, 7, 8 and 9 of the Suspension of Arms.

32   A good recent account of the Convention of Cintra is that of Michael Glover, *Britannia Sickens: Sir Arthur Wellesley and the Convention of Cintra* (London: Leo Cooper Limited, 1970).

33   Ayres Pinto da Souza later served in the Portuguese army under Beresford, and in June 1811 was appointed Brevet Brigadier General. His correspondence with Dalrymple was exhibited at the subsequent Inquiry into the terms of the Convention of Cintra.

34   Lieutenant Colonel George Murray (later Sir George) was Quartermaster General to Wellesley's army for much of the Peninsular War. Later in life he succeeded Marshal Beresford as Lieutenant General of

Ordnance (1824–5) and later still was appointed Master General of Ordnance (1834–6 and 1841–6), a post previously held by Marshal Beresford.

35 The separate Convention between Admiral Sir Charles Cotton and Vice Admiral Dmitri Seniavin was signed on 3 September 1808. It provided for the surrender of the Russian naval vessels to Cotton, on the basis these would be taken to England and restored to Russia six months after peace between Great Britain and Russia. The convention further provided for Seniavin, his sailors and marines to be repatriated to Russia at Britain's expense.

36 Those in attendance on 29 August were Sir Harry Burrard, Sir John Moore, Hon. John Hope, Mackenzie Fraser and Sir Arthur Wellesley.

37 These alterations were of a minor nature. They concerned the timing of the surrender of the forts of Cascais, São Julião da Barra on the right bank and Bugio on the left bank of the Tagus estuary.

38 The terms of the Convention are set out in full in the published documentation of the House of Commons; supra end note 18.

39 It is suggested that Junot took the title of Duc d'Abrantes not so much with a view to humiliating the Marquis of the same name, then imprisoned in France, but to reflect the town where he had first entered Portugal. Either way it created resentment, as did the fact that the British failed to secure the release of Portuguese prisoners from the French as part of the terms of the Convention.

40 Lieutenant Colonel Lord Proby (John); Assistant Quartermaster General in 1809 and later commander of the British garrison in Cádiz (1811).

41 The full text of the Convention is set out in Appendix A hereto: 'Definitive Convention for the Evacuation of Portugal by the French Army'.

42 De Souza to Dalrymple and Dalrymple to de Souza, 1 and 2 September 1808 (NA, WO 1/243, ff. 33 and 76).

43 Bernardim Freire to Dalrymple, 2 September 1808 (NA, WO 1/416).

44 Proby to Dalrymple, 3 September 1808 (NA, WO 1/416); See also, House of Commons papers. Dalrymple had rejected a suggestion by Junot even prior to the finalisation of the Convention that he was entitled to take a number of Portuguese naval vessels with him including the *Vasco de Gama*. Dalrymple to Lt Col. George Murray, 26 August 1808 (NA, WO 1/416).

45 William Beresford had been promoted Major General on 25 April 1808 while Military Governor of Madeira. He left Madeira on 23 August (some reports suggest 16 August) on HMS *Amazon* and HMS *Undaunted* with the 3rd Regiment, arriving off the Portuguese coast shortly before the end of the month. Thus he missed the battle of Vimeiro. Wellesley had been advised that Beresford would be joining him with the 3rd Regiment by letter from Castlereagh, dated 15 July 1808 (NA, WO 1/228). Captain T.J. Maling of the *Undaunted* was awarded £102-2-0 (9 June 1809) for conveying Beresford and his suite from Madeira to Lisbon. See, *Journals of the House of Commons*, vol. 65, p. 554. Six years later, HMS *Undaunted* was to convey Napoleon to Elba.

46 Dalrymple to Proby, 4 September 1808 (NA, WO 1/416).

47 Article 12 provided for the handover of São Julião, Bugio and Cascais forts on ratification of the Convention.

48 Beresford to Wellesley, 5 September 1808 (WSD 6, 130).

49 Fernand Calmettes (ed.) *Mémoires du General Baron Thiébault*, vol. IV (Paris: Libraries Plon, 1893), p. 196.

50 Over twenty-five of these letters were submitted to the Court of Inquiry and are exhibited in the Appendix to the account of the Inquiry (they are contained within letters 65–94).

51 The French sought to take with them a number of Portuguese vessels including the *Vasco da Gama*, a Portuguese naval frigate that had been left behind when the Court left in November 1807 because it had not been fitted out for sea. They were not permitted to take them (NA, WO 1/416).

52 Beresford and Proby to Dalrymple, 4 September 1808 (NA, WO 1/416).

53 Beresford and Proby to Dalrymple, 5 September 1808 (NA, WO 1/416).

54 *House of Commons Papers*; Appendix 55.

55 Quoted in Adam Neale, *Letters from Portugal and Spain: Comprising an Account of the Operation of the Armies Under Their Excellencies Sir Arthur Wellesley and Sir John Moore from the Landing of the Troops in Mondego Bay to the Battle at Corunna* (London: Richard Phillips, 1809). See in particular pp. 43 onwards, which is a transcription of part of a friend's journal but which starts with a landing at Figuera. Possibly the diarist may have been an ADC to Wellesley as he refers to dining with Wellesley and Junot, and is seated next to the latter's ADC. The Duke of Sussex (sixth son of George III) had spent time in Lisbon between 1801 and 1804 under the name of Count of Diepholz. He may have become involved in assisting to recruit for Baron de Rolls regiment stationed in Gibraltar.

56 Dalrymple to Beresford and Proby, 7 September 1808 (NA, WO 1/416). Dalrymple here was at the very least opening the door in support of the French keeping gold and silver bullion melted down from church plate or other items.

57 See *House of Commons Papers*, appendices 75 and 76.

58 Quoted in Anon., *A History of the Campaigns of the British Forces in Spain and Portugal* (London: T. Goddard, 1812), vol. II, pp. 336–7. Atreu Campos was a Judge.

59 Ibid. ff. 336.

60 Castlereagh had stated to Dalrymple on 16 August 1808 (though not in his official dispatch) that he should consider himself in Portugal as Commander of a force acting in alliance with the sovereign of that country (NA, WO 6/47).

61 *Memorial on the Principal Inconveniences which are found in the Convention agreed on between the English and French armies for the Evacuation of Portugal, wherein is stated minutely those Circumstances of the worst Consequences to this Country*, 3 September 1808; Anon., *A History of the Campaigns of the British Forces in Spain and Portugal*, vol. II, ff. 319.

62 Op. cit. 4 September 1808, quoted in vol. II, ff 334.

63 These protests are contained in (NA, WO 1/416).

64 Dalrymple to Castlereagh, 6 September 1808 (NA, WO 1/416).

65 Dalrymple to Beresford and Proby, 8 September 1808 (NA, WO 1/416).

66 Charles Stewart to Castlereagh, 8 September 1808 (PRONI, D3030/P/210).

67 Neale, *Letters from Portugal and Spain*, p. 72. The *Napoléon d'Or* was a twenty franc piece in gold issued by Napoleon from 1803 and used in France until World War I. It contained 5.8 grammes of pure gold.

68 Nicholas Trant (1769–1839), see note 22 above. St António Rodrigues de Oliveira was a Portuguese lawyer. A commissaire de guerre was an administrative post within the French army involving inspectors of various categories, such as Duplier. Apart from financial responsibilities they would also take part in military reviews.

69 The Committee for Receiving Reclamations sat at Largo do Loreto No. 8, being the house of António Rodrigues de Oliveira (NA, WO 1/416).

70 Beresford and Proby to Kellerman, 9 September 1808 (NA, WO 1/416).

71 Beresford and Proby to Dalrymple, 11 September 1808 (NA, WO 1/416). See also Schedule 5, Part B to the 'Report of General Officers to Inquire into the Causes that led to the Convention of Cintra', *Journals of the House of Commons*, vol. 91, p. 198.

72 Because of the danger to the French, they were camped on heights and in some of the squares with cannon guarding the entrances.

73 Schedule 5 Part B to the 'Report of General Officers', *Journals of the House of Commons*, vol. 91, pp. 88 and 92. See also, *The Annual Register*, 1808 and 1809.

74 Dalrymple to Castlereagh, 27 September 1808 (NA, WO 1/234, f. 217).

75 The figure given to the Inquiry stated that 24,735 men, 213 women, 116 children and 759 horses were embarked at Lisbon. The garrison of Elvas (1,400) together with released French prisoners from Badajoz were embarked at Aldeia Gallega (opposite Lisbon) on 7 October. The garrison of Almeida was brought to Porto and ultimately returned to France with their colleagues from Elvas.

76 Dalrymple to Castlereagh, 29 September 1808 (NA, WO 1/234).

77 Anon., *Advantages of the Convention of Cintra, briefly stated in a Candid Review of that Transaction and of the circumstances under which it took place* (London; Richardson, 1809).

78 Beresford to Forjaz, 21 September 1808 (Arquivo Histórico Militar (AHM; AHM-CLFFTV-TT-IGP-019). The letter was co-signed by Gregório Gomes da Silva. It is interesting that Beresford was insisting on rearmament of the Spanish given the shortage of arms available for the Portuguese, but then the Spaniards were going to have to march through potentially hostile territory.

79 W.H. Maxwell, *Life of Field-Marshal His Grace the Duke of Wellington* (London: A.H. Baily and Co., 1840), pp. 362–3; See also, C.W. Vane, *Narrative of the Peninsula War from 1808 to 1813* (London: Henry Colburn, 1828), p. 167.

80 Dalrymple officially decreed the reinstatement of the Council of Governadores on 18 September. The original appointees as Governadores in 1807 are listed in end note 6 supra. In September 1808, the Marques de Abrantes was imprisoned in France. Breyner and Sampāio were *persona non grata* as they had collaborated. Those that remained (Francisco de Mello da Cunha, Principal Castro [who though appointed to Junot's Council had resigned shortly afterwards], and Francisco de Noronha) together with Montéiro-mor (he had been nominated by Dom João for the first vacancy) were invited to assume the reins of government. They in turn elected the Bishop of Porto and the Marques de Minas. Forjaz and Salter de Mendonça were joined by Cipriano Ribeiro Freire.

81 Hope was sent into the Alentejo to ensure the peaceful surrender of Elvas, which the Spanish were besieging in contravention of the terms of the Convention. See, Sir Hew Dalrymple, *Memoir*, (London: Thomas and William Boone, 1830). p. 97. Dalrymple stated in this *Memoir* that 'I established Major-General Beresford in Lisbon, as a channel of communication between the Commander of the British forces and the Portuguese Government.' Sir John Moore in his diary also refers to the appointment, 'Camp at Quelus, 24th September'. See, Maurice, *The Diary of Sir John Moore*, vol, II, p. 267.

82 Beresford to Forjaz, 22 September 1808 (AHM-Div-1-14; CX 16).

83 *The Morning Chronicle*, 2 September 1808 was headlined 'Most Glorious News from Portugal, Complete Defeat of General Junot and Proposals for the Surrender of His Army.' Note the *Chronicle* was a Whig publication. Other publications to attack the government included William Cobbett's *Political Register* and the *Edinburgh Review*. In addition, provincial papers throughout the United Kingdom carried critical articles and calls for an Inquiry into the terms of the convention. See *The Northampton Mercury*, *The Norfolk Chronicle* or the *Norwich Gazette*, *The Lancaster Gazette* (12 November 1808), *The Chester Courant* (31 January 1809), *Kentish Gazette* (18 November 1808), *Leeds Mercury* (29 October 1808) to name but a few.

84 As to the place of signing of the 'Convention of Cintra'; it would appear that Junot signed it at his headquarters in Lisbon, Largo de Barão de Quintela, while it was ratified by Dalrymple at Torres Vedras. It owes its name simply because Dalrymple's correspondence home following the execution of the Convention was headed as coming from Cintra, whence he had moved his headquarters.

85 William Wordsworth, *Concerning the Convention of Cintra* (London: Longman, Hurst, Rees and Orme, 1809); Two letters of Wordsworth, 1811; Lord Byron (George Gordon) *Childe Harold's Pilgrimage*.

86 See for example poems contained in *The Morning Chronicle*, 20 September, 19 October and 7 November 1808.

87 *The Political Register*, 10 September 1808. An excellent account of the newspaper reports is contained in Wendy Hinde, *George Canning* (London: Collins, 1973).

88 Ibid. pp. 201–5.

89 Robert Ker Porter, *Letters from Portugal and Spain Written During the March of the British Troops Under Sir John Moore* (London: Longman, Hurst, Rees and Orme, 1809). It is interesting to see the use of the word 'electric' in this context at such an early date.

90 Lord Lowther, a local Tory, may have been instrumental in preventing the proposed meeting in Cumbria. Byron was to reflect the mood regarding the unwiseness of the Convention in *Childe Harold* when he wrote:

> 'Here folly dashed to earth the victor's plume
> And policy regained what arms had lost.'

91 See Hinde, op. cit., p. 204.

92 George Cruikshank, 'Whitlock the Second or Another Tarnish for British Valor'; 29 September 1808. This caricature shows the three British Generals, Dalrymple, Burrard and Wellesley, genuflecting before Junot while presenting him with the terms of the Convention, while a miserable looking Portuguese officer reflects that they (the Portuguese) thought the British had come to drive out the (French) thieves, not protect those thieves and their stolen goods, and asking the question 'is this British honour, is this British valour?'; British Museum (BM; Collection no. 1862, 1217.390).

93 Castlereagh to Dalrymple, 17 September 1808 (NA, WO 1/234, f. 59).

94 Wellesley had taken leave of absence from his post as Secretary to the Lord Lieutenant of Ireland in order to go to Portugal.

95 Wellesley to Castlereagh, 22 August 1808, *Dispatches of Field Marshal the Duke of Wellington* (WD 4, 115).

96 The full text of the King's Order, the various addresses and narratives, the Report of the Board of Inquiry dated 23 December 1808 – together with the documents set out in the Appendix, the letter requiring further clarification of the findings dated 25 December and the further findings of the Board dated 27 December 1808, together with the King's declaration of His Majesty's Disapprobation may be found in 'Copy of the Proceedings'.

97 Lieutenant General O. Nicholls, Lieutenant General Sir G. Nugent, General Lord Heathfield, General Craig, Lieutenant General the Earl of Pembroke, General the Earl of Moira made up the Board of Inquiry with General Sir David Dundas.

98 'Copy of the Proceedings'.

99 The Lieutenant Generals involved were Sir Harry Burrard, Sir John Moore, Lieutenant General Hope, Lieutenant General McKenzie Fraser, and Sir Arthur Wellesley; see 'Copy of the Proceedings', p. 43.

100 Wellesley to Castlereagh, 6 October 1808 (NA, WO 1/228).

101 Beresford was not called to the Board of Inquiry as a witness; he was then in Spain with Sir John Moore. However, his correspondence with Dalrymple and others was exhibited with a view to showing that there had been vigorous and responsible implementation of the Convention.

102 Many of those in Dupont's army and in Vedel's Division which surrendered some days later were to spend the next six years incarcerated, first in hulks moored in the harbour of Cádiz and later as prisoners on the desolate island of Cabrera off Mallorca, where substantial numbers died of disease and/or starvation.

Initially the Junta in Cádiz had looked for ways to repatriate the French force, with the assistance of the Royal Navy. Admiral Lord Collingwood had sought instructions from Castlereagh, the Minister for War, and Castlereagh's response reveals why the British Government were so concerned with the arrangements made at Cintra. On 19 August, just a few days prior to the battle of Vimeiro, Castlereagh wrote, 'it is impossible not to feel, and to regret, that an army of sixteen thousand men, nearly half of them fully equipped, is thereby permitted to return to France, in order possibly to recommence, within the space of a few weeks a fresh attack on Spain', prophetic words indeed, for within months many of Junot's troops were back in Spain with their commander; Castlereagh to Collingwood, 19 August 1808 (NA, FO 72/60).

Of Dupont's army only some 180 officers were repatriated in the autumn of 1808, while a further convoy of officers and sergeants was ultimately brought to England from Cabrera in 1810. There the officers were placed on parole and the sergeants imprisoned in Porchester Castle until the end of the war in 1814. Some of the enlisted men did escape from Cabrera, while others (mostly non French) chose to join the Spanish army. Denis Smith, *The Prisoners of Cabrera: Napoleon's Forgotten Soldiers 1809–1814* (Toronto: Macfarlane Walter & Ross, 2001).

103 General Robert Anstruther died at La Coruña (before the battle) and is buried alongside Sir John Moore by the latter's request.

104 The letters furnished by Castlereagh to the Board of Inquiry are set out in a number of schedules. Schedule 5, Part B lists the correspondence with the Commissioners. It lists thirty-one papers of which at least twenty-two are letters to or from Beresford (NA, WO 1/415).

105 The Earl of Moira was the only dissenting voice regarding the advisability of the Armistice. Nicholls, Pembroke and Moira disapproved of the Convention, 27 December 1808.

106 See Articles 15, 16, 17, 18 and 19 of the Convention in particular.

107 Denis Arthur Bingham, *A Selection From The Letters And Despatches of The First Napoleon* (London: Chapman and Hall, 1884), p. 414.

108 Ibid. p. 415.

109 Junot and 3,000 of his men were disembarked at La Rochelle on 11 October and the remainder at Quiberon, being just about the furthest point under which they could be landed under the terms of the Convention which provided for their landing between La Rochelle and Lorient.

110 By the Convention entered into on the surrender of Genoa on 4 June 1800, the French troops were allowed to return home to France. On the surrender of Malta by the French in September 1800, the French were allowed to withdraw to Marseilles, but had to ground their arms on departure. They were embarked at the expense of His Britanic majesty; wagons and shallops were supplied for personal belongings; and the French were reported to have left without payment of debts. When those monies were sought from France after the peace of 1814, the Maltese were told it was a matter for Great Britain with whom all had been settled. Indeed, the Maltese had submitted a memorial on the subject to George III in 1801 so the government clearly knew about the matter and it was still the subject of applications in the 1830s. Interestingly, the Maltese were not consulted prior to the agreement of 1801.

The French had sought agreement for a provision for the non-molestation of any person in respect of their actions while Malta had been under French rule, but this had been turned down with the assurance that such people would be treated with justice and humanity. Under the arrangements entered into in Egypt, the French army was allowed home and transported there in British vessels. There were disputes about the possessions they could take with them, and the British insisted on retaining the Rosetta stone. The arguments regarding plunder in Egypt involved some of the same personnel from the French Institut de Sciences as were involved in Portugal, and it was Beresford who was attributed by some French as being difficult on both occasions.

The Treaty of Yorktown of 19 October 1781, whereby Lord Cornwallis had surrendered, allowed officers and soldiers to keep their private property of every kind, but noted: 'It is understood that any property, obviously belonging to the inhabitants of these states, in the possession of the garrison, shall be subject to be reclaimed' (see Article IV). Furthermore, a proposal that there should be no punishment of those who had supported the defeated power had not been agreed to as it was a provision of 'civil resort' (Article X). Other treaties which provided for soldiers to return home included those following the capture of the Cape of Good Hope and Bailén (see above).

111 Beresford's small force had also been granted this right on surrender in Buenos Aires in 1806, though the terms were not honoured subsequently on the basis that the General involved, de Linieres, did not have the power to grant such terms.

112 General Sir John Moore had arrived at British headquarters after the battles and indeed after the initial Armistice. He clearly thought little of Dalrymple's abilities and in his diary wrote of Dalrymple: 'Sir Hew Dalrymple was confused and incapable beyond any man I ever saw head an army. The whole of his conduct then and since has proved him to be a very foolish man ... Sir Hew being our commander, I am quite convinced that the best thing to do was to treat on almost any terms.' Maurice, *The Diary of Sir John Moore*, vol. 2, p. 270.

113 One of the results of Cintra was that effectively dozens of elderly generals were never again employed by Britain. There was a clear out of dead timber.

114 *The Morning Chronicle* of 28 and 31 January 1809 bemoaned the fact that charges had been brought against the Duke of York, as it was felt to be a distraction from the Government's misconduct of the Spanish war and the Convention of Cintra.

115 It is difficult to know how much 'plunder' was salvaged by the actions of the commissioners, though one source put it at up to £200,000 of private and public wealth. See, Porter, *Letters from Portugal and Spain*.

116 Junot did lose a number of Swiss troops, who took the opportunity to go over to British employment, in addition to the losses at the battles of Roliça and Vimeiro, as well as lesser engagements.

117 The topic of the impact of international capital flows in the Napoleonic Wars is addressed in Larry Neal, *The Rise of Financial Capitalism* (Cambridge: Cambridge University Press, 1990), Chapters 9 and 10. Donald D. Horward, 'Wellington and the Defence of Portugal', *The International History Review*, vol. 11, p. 40 estimated that as much as 50 per cent of the portable wealth of the kingdom had been removed to Brazil in 1807.

118 There was a system of permits and baggage allowances to allow for orderly embarkation. Thus the Royal Treasury was loaded along with a cache of Brazilian diamonds, the printing press and government files. The royal archivist, Cristiano Muller, was told to pack the archival records and preparations were made to place thirty-four crates of these records on the *Medusa*. The 60,000 volume library from the Ajuda Palace was taken to the docks but not loaded due to lack of space. Araújo's personal library was also prepared for embarkation. The royal family went on board (split between various vessels) on 27 November leaving fourteen carriages full of Church silver on the docks. The fleet sailed on 29 November when the wind permitted it to do so, passing the Russian fleet at anchor in the river. See Wilcken, *Empire Adrift*.

119 Hew Dalrymple was created a Baronet on 6 March 1815. This title was extinguished on the death of his son, Sir Adolphus Dalrymple, on 3 March 1866.

120 Porter, *Letters from Portugal and Spain*.

121 Dalrymple had noted that Portuguese ire was directed almost as much against the English as against the French for the latter's depradations (supra). The Rev James Wilmot Ormsby, the Chaplain on the Staff, while noting the success of Beresford and Proby, stated that the Portuguese were accusing the English not just of dereliction of duty but partisanship against them. A few weeks later, on the restoration of Portuguese government, Ormsby found the sentiment towards the English improving. See Rev. J.W. Ormsby, *An Account of the Operations of the British Army: And of the State and Sentiments of the People of Portugal and Spain, During the Campaigns of the Years 1808 & 1809*, two volumes (London: James Carpenter, 1809), vol. 1, letter V, 14 September 1808 and letter IX, 17 October 1808.

Chapter 5

1 Henry Curling (ed.), *The Recollections of Rifleman Harris* (London: H. Hurst, 1848), p. 149.

2 Beresford to Dalrymple, 30 September 1808 (NA, WO 1/416) on an interview he had with Forjaz on the points Dalrymple wished to make to the Regency Council; Burrard to Castlereagh, 15 October 1808 (NA, WO 1/235).

3 Bernardim Freire de Andrade had been appointed commander of the forces in northern Portugal by the Supreme Junta of Porto. Having met Wellesley at Leiria in the run up to the battle of Roliça, he successfully prevented forces under Loison from joining General Laborde in time for that battle. In March 1809 he was lynched by the mob at Braga because of his failure to defend that town against Soult's army (the second invasion of Portugal). General Burrard formed the view that Bernardim Freire de Andrade did not wish England well (Burrard to Castlereagh, 15 October 1808). Beresford sent his report to Bernardim Freire de Andrade in October 1808 and a copy to Burrard in November of the same year (NA, WO 1/235).

4 While Beresford did attempt the experiment of training away from home towns in 1809, he soon abandoned the concept on the basis that it caused a loss of morale. See, Beresford to Forjaz, 10 June 1809 (AHM 1-14, CX18).

5 Burrard to J.W. Gordon, 15 October 1808 (BL, Add MS 49,485).

6 Beresford to Cooke, 30 September 1808. See, C.W. Vane (ed.), *Correspondence, Despatches and Other Papers of Viscount Castlereagh, Second Marquess of Londonderry* (London: William Shorbell, 1851), vol. VI, p. 459.

7 The Bishop may have been stirring up trouble on his own account, but Burrard's analysis suggested the riots in Porto were at least partly the result of the Regency Council decision to lower rates of army pay (NA, WO 1/235).

8 The Regency Council as first constituted in November 1807 was made up of the Marques de Abrantes (President), Francisco de Melo da Cunha 1st Marques de Olhão, Principal Castro, Pedro de Mello Breyner, Francisco de Noronha, Conde de Sampáio (First Secretary) with Miguel Pereira Forjaz and João António Salter de Mendonça as alternates. This Council was dissolved by Junot on 1 February 1808. When Dalrymple reconstituted the Regency Council, he excluded those deemed to have collaborated with the French. These were Pedro de Mello, Principal Castro, the Conde de Sampáio and the Marques de Abrantes (the latter in fact being a prisoner of Napoleon in France). Those added to the Council were the Bishop of Porto, the Conde das Minas and Cipriano Ribeiro Freire.

9 Beresford's troops consisted of elements of the 9th, 43rd and 52nd regiments.

10 Burrard to Castlereagh, 15 October 1808 (NA, WO 1/235). Burrard was so concerned at the turn of events in Porto that he selected three further battalions of infantry and one 3-pounder brigade of artillery under General Stewart to follow Beresford.

11   The creation of the force that was to become the Loyal Lusitanian Legion was the suggestion of the Chevalier Domingos Sousa Coutinho, the Portuguese Ambassador to the Court of St James. It was designated to be composed of three battalions of chasseurs and one battalion of artillery to be made up of Portuguese officers and other Portuguese refugees. The original concept appeared also to provide for a cavalry regiment. Only two battalions of infantry and one of artillery were in fact raised. The British government gave permission for three serving British officers to join the Legion. They were its commander, Sir Robert Wilson, Lieutenant Colonel Count George de Perponcher (a Dutch general of Huguenot extraction) who had joined the British service in 1799, and Major Baron von Eben. Wilson's orders were in some respects vague. On arrival in Portugal he was to report to whoever commanded His Majesty's troops there, but to take such actions as the Chevalier de Sousa and the acting governor of Porto shall approve. See Castlereagh to Sir Robert Wilson, 4 August 1808 (NA, WO 6/47). While relations with Wilson were cordial at this stage, Beresford was to have difficulties with him later in the war. Further, in 1817 Eben was to be involved in a plot generally referred to as the Gomes Freire conspiracy, a plot shrouded with controversy as to its objectives. Eben's role resulted in his expulsion from Portugal.

12   See Maurice, *The Diary of Sir John Moore*, vol. II, ff. 324.

13   The composition of this brigade was 1/9th, 2/43rd and 2/52nd with a total complement of 2,297. In addition there were five companies of the 60th, along with the Fane's Brigade (2,320) under Beresford's command. See Maurice, *The Diary of Sir John Moore*, vol. II, p. 277.

14   Beresford to the 2nd Marquis of Waterford, 22 and 29 November 1808 (Beresford family papers).

15   Beresford to 2nd Marquis of Waterford, 16 December 1808 (Beresford family papers).

16   Made up of 12,298 infantrymen, 1,027 artillerymen and 3,100 cavalry.

17   Moore envisaged first a retreat to the Portuguese border, but if it proved impractical to defend the country re-embarkation from Lisbon. He instructed General John Randoll Mackenzie to load the stores on transports in preparation for evacuation. Moore to Mackenzie, 29 November 1808 (NA, WO 1/233).

18   The 15th Hussars received a battle honour for Sahagún, one of only two occasions such an honour was granted to a single corps in the war, and the only one to a cavalry regiment. The contest at Sahagún was with Debelle's light cavalry brigade (8th Dragoons and 1st Provisional Chasseurs) which was screening Soult's army based on Carrion.

19   'During the march to Villa Franca, the rain came down in torrents, men and horses sinking through fatigue, covered the roads, and soldiers whose strength still enabled them to proceed, maddened by the continued suffering of cold and hunger, were no longer under any subordination.' Sergeant Anthony Hamilton, *Hamilton's Campaigns with Moore and Wellington During the Peninsular War* (New York: Troy, 1847), p. 43; Ormsby, *An Account of the Operations of the British Army*.

20   Ormsby, op. cit., 4 and 6 January 1809, letters XXI and XXII.

21   'Bembibre exhibited all the appearance of a place lately stormed and pillaged. Every door and window was broken; every lock and fastening forced. Rivers of wine ran through the houses and into the streets, where lay fantastic groups of soldiers (many of them with their firelocks broken), women, children, runaway Spaniards and muleteers, all apparently inanimate except when here or there a leg or an arm was seen to move while the wine oozing from their lips and nostrils seemed the effect of gunshot wounds.' Julian Sturgis (ed.) *A Boy in the Peninsular War: The Services., Adventures And Experiences of Robert Blakeney* (London: John Murray, 1899), p. 50.

An extraordinary story is told by Captain MacCarthy of the 50th Regiment about an event on the morning of the battle on 16 January. An Irish woman, the wife of a soldier in the light company of the 50th regiment, came from the enemy's line on that morning having been attended in childbirth by the French doctors, supported at the expense of Marshal Soult. She was sent back with Soult's compliments, that he should soon visit the 50th Regiment! Presumably she had been left behind on the retreat. See *Recollections of the Storming of the Castle of Badajos by the Third Division under Lieutenant General Sir Thomas Picton, A Personal Narrative by Captain MacCarthy late of the 50th Regiment* (London, 1836), p. 81.

22 Beresford to the 2nd Marquis of Waterford, 22 November 1808 (Beresford family papers), and *General Orders Spain and Portugal*, vol. 1, p. 198.

23 Journal of Lieutenant Colonel George MacGregor, 78th Regiment.

24 During the retreat, part of the army consisting of the light brigades under Craufurd and Alten had been directed to Vigo, up to that time part of the Reserve Division. Leaving the main army on 31 December, they marched to Vigo via Ourense.

25 Beresford had now served with Baird in Egypt, the Cape Colony and Spain. He counted Baird a friend as well as a colleague. Beresford to 2nd Marquis of Waterford, 14 January 1809 (Beresford family papers).

26 Even prior to the arrival of Moore's army at La Coruña, the difficulties likely to attach to an embarkation were readily recognised. Major General Broderick, based in La Coruña, had written to Castlereagh on 3 January 1809 lamenting the likelihood that there would be a deficiency of transports for 10,000 infantry and at least 4,000 horses. In the event, part of the army retired to Vigo, but many of the horses were put down prior to embarkation (NA, WO 1/235). According to one contemporary source each regiment was restricted to taking thirty horses on embarkation. Taking the case of the 15th Hussars, who had arrived at La Coruña in November with 682 horse, the extent of the loss must have been considerable even allowing for campaign losses. Gareth Glover (ed.), *From Corunna to Waterloo: The Letters and Journals of Two Napoleonic Hussars 1801–1816* (London: Greenhill, 2007).

27 The victory of the French army is engraved on the Arc de Triomphe, as Bataille de La Corogne along with a number of other disputed victories, including Fuentes de Oñoro and Albuera.

28 Beresford to Lady Anne Beresford, 5 January 1809 (Beresford family papers).

29 The embarkation was not without incident. The wife of Corporal Riley allegedly drowned because of the quantity of gold in her clothing when she fell between the boat carrying her from the shore and the transport ship which she was trying to board (Hamilton, *Hamilton's Campaigns with Moore and Wellington*, p. 42). However, in *The Story of the Oxford and Buckinghamshire Light Infantry* Newbolt says the unfortunate was the wife of one Maloney, tailor to the 52nd.

30 The Heights of St Lucia were where Beresford had been stationed on 16 January before withdrawing that evening to the town. For an eyewitness account of the embarkation see Rear Admiral Michael de Courcy (HMS *Tonnant*) to William Wellesley Pole, 17 and 18 January 1809 reproduced in a Supplement to the *London Gazette Extraordinary* 24 January 1809. French cannon fire forced some transports to slip their anchors and a number were lost on the shore. Embarkation from the town was abandoned and instead undertaken from a beach beside the lighthouse. Having lost transports a substantial number of troops had to be embarked on warships.

31 Anon., *A History of the Campaigns of the British Forces in Spain and Portugal*, vol. III, p. 464.

32 Beresford's brigade consisted of 1/6th, 1/9th, 2/23rd and 2/43rd.

33 Warre refers to the French approach to the town on 17 January and the ensuing artillery duel, paying tribute to the part played by the Spaniards. He also notes that the remaining forces were in some trepidation as they were only just enough to man the works, the boats being only able to take off 500 men at a time and the weather being very bad. In Edmond Warre (ed.), *Letters from the Peninsula, 1808–1812 by Lieut.-Gen. Sir William Warre* (London: J Murray 1909), p. 50–1. Beresford's rearguard amounted to 2,000; see Anon., *A History of the Campaigns of the British Forces in Spain and Portugal*, vol. III, p. 453.

34 The exchange of fire on 17 January was quite intense and the Spanish artillery assisted the English in what was becoming an increasingly critical situation. Captain William Warre, who had initially gone to Portugal as ADC to Major General Sir Ronald Craufurd Ferguson, had become attached to Beresford's staff (Ferguson having returned to England) and was present with him on the retreat to La Coruña. Warre stated that in what is obviously a reference to 17 January: 'We were very weak, just enough to man the works, and dreaded an assault, the boats being able to take only 500 at a time, and weather very bad. However, we not only got ourselves but most of the wounded into safety, though all most overcome with fatigue.' There is a tradition that Beresford and Warre were the last British soldiers to leave the quay for the ships but no corroboration has been found to date. Both Warre and Beresford returned to England on the *Barfleur* (98-guns, commander Sir Edward Berry) See Warre, *Letters from the Peninsula 1808–1812* (Spellmount edition published 1999 with comments by William A. Warre, hereafter referred to as 'Warre'). Also Beresford to 2nd Marquis of Waterford, 18 and 27 January 1809 (Beresford family papers).

35 A number of women and children were apparently left at La Coruña; MacCarthy, op. cit., p. 82.

36 Hope to Baird, 18 January 1809 (reproduced in full in Cobbett's *Political Register*, pp. 154–9).

37 Beresford to Lady Anne Beresford, 18 January 1809 (Beresford family papers).

38 Beresford to 2nd Marquis of Waterford, 14 January 1809 (Beresford family papers). Romana, whose army was retreating into Galicia at the same time, was very critical of the English (Romana to A. Cornel, 18 January 1809, quoted in Charles Esdaile, *The Peninsular War: A New History* (New York: Palgrave Macmillan, 2003), p. 153).

39 A vote of thanks to Lieutenant General Baird and the other returning generals – including William Carr Beresford – who served under the late Sir John Moore for their distinguished conduct and exemplary valour in their repulse and defeat of the French was passed by the House of Commons on 25 January 1809 (House of Commons Debates, *Hansard*, vol. 12, cc 144–5).

Chapter 6

1 Allan R. Millett, 'Captain James H. Hausman and the Formation of the Korean Army, 1945–1950' *Armed Forces and Society*, 23, 4 (Summer 1997), p. 503.

2 Beresford to Lady Anne Beresford, 20 February 1809 (Beresford family papers).

3 Ibid.

4 The royal party did not reach Rio de Janeiro until 7 March 1808.

5 Ordem, 2 January 1809 (TT, Ministério do Reino, livro 380).

6 Cradock to Castlereagh, 14 December 1808 (NA, WO 1/232). See also Castlereagh to Cradock, 28 January 1809, and Cradock to Admiral Berkeley, 9 February 1809 (ibid.).

7 There was outrage when British messengers were stopped by the Portuguese guard outside Lisbon in February 1809 and forced to disclose letters. See Brigadier General Langworth to Cradock, 1 February 1809 (NA, WO 1/232).

8 Ormsby, *An Account of the Operations of the British Army* (letter of 17 October 1808).

9 De la Fuente, *Forjaz*. Forjaz was ultimately created Count of Feira by João VI when he retired from public affairs in 1820.

10 Burrard to J.W. Gordon, 15 October 1808 (BL, Add MS 49,485).

11 Dom Miguel Pereira Forjaz Coutinho Barreto de Sá e Resende ('Forjaz'). Born 1769, Forjaz joined the Portuguese army in 1785 and fought in the Roussillon campaign against revolutionary France in 1793–5, for which the Portuguese forces were manifestly unprepared. Further disappointment for Portugal

followed with defeat by Spain in the War of the Oranges in 1801. A Commission was established in late 1801, with Forjaz as Secretary, to make reccommendations for the reform of the Portuguese army. Unable to agree on final recommendations, a report was presented but only minor reforms were implemented prior to the first French invasion in 1807, as a result of a combination of inertia, disagreement and French pressure on Portuguese ministers.

12 Karl Alexander von der Goltz was a Prussian General who had served under Frederick II of Prussia. He was appointed on the recommendation of the Portuguese Ambassador to Prussia, Visconde d'Anadia.

13 For an account of developments between 1801 and 1807 see *Forjaz*, pp. 29–38.

14 General Bernardim Freire de Andrade was the brother of Gomes Freire de Andrade who commanded the Portuguese Legion from 1810. Gomes Freire de Andrade was to figure substantially in Beresford's life in 1817 in the Gomes Freire conspiracy.

15 18 October 1808, Torre de Tombo (TT; Reino, Cx. 324, f. 4).

16 The Portuguese Legion (Legião Portuguesa) was commanded by the Marquis d'Alorna (1808–10), José Carcomé Lobo (1810) and Gomes Freire de Andrade (1810–14).

17 The Loyal Lusitanian Legion was founded in Great Britian by Carlos Federico Lecor and José Maria Moura with the support of Domingos de Sousa, the Portuguese Minister at the Court of St James. When it became fully integrated in the Portuguese army, its battalions became the 7th, 8th and 9th caçadores.

18 Decrees of 14 October and 21 November 1808.

19 See Oman, *A History of the Peninsular War*, vol. II, p. 213. Baron Frederick von Decken had served in George III's Hanoverian army before Napoleon's conquest of Hanover. In exile in England he was one of the founders of the King's German Legion (KGL).

20 NA, WO 1/234. See also Fernando Dores Costa, 'Army size, Military Recruitment and Financing During the Period of the Peninsula War – 1808–1811', *e-Journal of Portuguese History*, 6, 2 (Winter 2008). Available at: http://www.scielo.mec.pt/scielo.php?script=sci_arttext&pid=S1645-64322008000200003 (accessed 23 April 2018).

21 Brigadier General Charles Stewart to Cradock, 15 December 1808 (NA, WO 1/232) lists the requirements of the Portuguese army, from which it is clear that it was in need of complete re-equipping. He requested 51,703 muskets, 73,763 bayonets, 2,134 swords and 13,176 pistols.

22 Cradock to Castlereagh, 9 January 1809 (NA, WO 1/232).

23 Cradock to Villiers, 20 December 1808 (NA, WO 1/232). Cradock had arrived in Lisbon on 13 December 1808.

24 General MacKenzie to Castlereagh, 5 December 1808 (NA, WO 1/233).

25 Villiers to Canning, 3 January 1809 (NA, FO 63/75).

26 'Estado actual do Exercito Portuguez', furnished to Prince João on 10 March 1809 (TT, MNE CX 885) quoted in Fernando Dores Costa, 'Army size, Military Recruitment and Financing During the Period of the Peninsula War', pp. 4–5.

27 Wellesley to Castlereagh, 1 August 1808 (WD 3, 46–7).

28 Canning to Villiers, 22 November 1808 (NA, FO 63/74).

29 Cipriano Ribeiro Freire to Villiers, 26 December 1808. Cipriano Ribeiro Freire was a Portuguese diplomat, previously first Portuguese Ambassador to the United States, who served as a Secretary to the Regency. In a covering note to Canning, Villiers expressed the view that the request for a British officer to command the Portuguese army probably originated with Forjaz; 27 December 1808. On 3 January 1809, Villiers expressed the view that 'this part of the peninsula will fall whenever it is attacked, unless measures for its defence are immediately taken. In itself at present it may be considered as defenceless' (All NA, FO 63/75).

30 Request dated 26 December 1808 enclosed with letter of 27 December, Villiers to Canning (NA, FO 63/75)

31 Earl of Munster, *An Account of the British Campaign in 1809 under Sir A. Wellesley in Portugal and Spain* (London: Henry Colburn and Richard Bentley, 1831).

32 Villiers to Canning, 26 December 1808 (Canning Papers 48/12, quoted in Muir, *Wellington: The Path to Victory*, fn. 21 to Chapter 17). Napier also suggested that Wellesley was favoured by the Portuguese. See, William F.P. Napier, *History of the War in the Peninsula and the South of France from the year 1807 to the year 1814* (London: Constable, 1828–40), vol. I, p. 450 (hereafter, '*History*') and William Carr Beresford, *Strictures* (London: Longman, Rees, Orme, Broen and Green, 1831), 11–12.

33 Castlereagh to John Stewart, 22 September 1809 (PRONI, D3030/3295) quoted in Rory Muir, *Britain and the Defeat of Napoleon, 1807–1815* (London: Yale University Press, 1996), p. 84.

34 George Canning, born in Ireland in 1770; Foreign Secretary in the Portland administration, 1807–9. See Canning to Villiers, 17 February 1809 (NA, FO 63/74).

35 See Chapter 5 above. This plan was sent by Burrard to Sir J.W. Gordon on 15 October 1809 (BL, Add MS 49,485).

36 Oman, *History*, vol. II, p. 217; Wellesley to Castlereagh, 27 April 1809, vol. 3, pp. 193–4.

37 See WD 6, 552 for 26 January 1811 and Fortescue, *History of the British Army*, vol. 7, p. 420.

38 Wellesley to Castlereagh, 1 August 1808 (WD 3, 46–7).

39 Oman, op. cit., vol. II, pp. 216–17.

40 See, Introduction.

41 Canning to Villiers, 28 January 1809 (NA, FO 63/74) suggests Castlereagh has offered Beresford the post.

42 Beresford, *Strictures*, p. 5 and Napier, op. cit., Book VI, p. 162.

43 Beresford, *Strictures*, pp. 8–12.

44 The only prolonged period Beresford had spent in Ireland between 1793 and 1809 was on his return from Alexandria in late 1803, prior to his departure on the expedition to capture Capetown in the second half of 1805. Save for the few weeks spent in England in late January and early February 1809, he was not to return to the British Isles until peace was concluded in 1814. Beresford expressed his disappointment in not being able to go to Ireland in a letter to the 2nd Marquis of Waterford written from Horse Guards shortly before his departure for Portugal, 16 February 1809 (Beresford family papers).

45 Beresford to Lady Anne Beresford, 20 February 1809 (Beresford family papers).

46 NA, FO 63/74.

47 Beresford and his suite were conveyed to Lisbon on HMS *Amazon*, under Captain William Parker, for which the Captain was awarded $152-2-0; *Journals of the House of Commons* (9 June 1809), vol. 65.

48 Beresford to Lady Anne Beresford, 3 March 1809 (Beresford family papers). In this letter he reflects a concern for his half-brother, John Poo Beresford. At this time 'Poo' (HMS *Theseus*) was in command of three ships of the line blockading Lorient, and he was successful in preventing vessels leaving that port joining another French fleet under Admiral Willaumez. Later he was to become an Admiral and was created 1st Baronet Beresford of Bagnall in 1814. Their correspondence makes it clear William Carr and John Poo remained close for their entire lives.

49 Beresford to Charles Stewart, 9 March 1809 (NA, WO 1/239). See also Villiers to Canning, 9 March 1809 (NA, FO 63/75). Villiers also reported Beresford's wish to be a General rather than a Marshal, perhaps a sign of sensitivity on Beresford's behalf to potential resentment. However, Villiers reported that the term 'General' was not a rank as such in the Portuguese army. One could be a General of cavalry

but would still be liable to be commanded by a Lieutenant General (NA, FO 63/75). See also Beresford, *Strictures*, p. 18.

50   Forjaz to Villiers, 15 March 1809 (NA, FO 63/75).

51   Enclosure with letter: Canning to Villiers, 17 February 1809 (NA, FO 63/74).

52   NA, FO 63/75 f. 184 is a note from Forjaz to Villiers confirming that subject to the law, Beresford will have authority over discipline in the army as [well as] approbation of all recommendations for filling the posts of officers, reform and dismissal, and the ability to approve or exclude the men who would compose the army.

53   Beresford to Forjaz, 21 September 1809 (AHM, 1-14 CX 17).

54   Beresford, Ordens do Dia, 15 March 1809, 1 and 2.

55   The duality of Beresford's allegiance may be exemplified by the fact that he drew a salary as a British Lieutenant General as well as one for a Portuguese Marshal. In this respect he was no different to other British officers who frequently had the British part of their British salary paid at home.

56   An undated list of Beresford's Staff in the Portuguese archives gives some clues as to who these were. It lists Lt. Col. Wilson [probably Lt. Col. John Wilson, who served in the LLL and then Portuguese army throughout the war], Robert Arbuthnot (Major/Lt Col), W. Warre (Captain/Major), William H. Sewell (Lt/Captain), George Gore 9th Light Dragoons (Captain/Major), Carroll [presumably William Parker noted as in Spain], Roche (in Spain), Hardinge (Major), Hawkshaw (Major – with Brigadier General Campbell), Smith (Captain – with Brig. General Coleman), B. D'Urban, (Lt. Col.), and Robert Henry (Captain) [note where two ranks given they reflect British and Portuguese ranks but where one rank is given it is the British rank] (TT, MNE CX 204).

57   Ordem do Dia, 22 March 1809, 3.

58   Manuel de Brito Mosinho (b. *c*1763, d. 1832) was Major at the time of the French invasion of 1807. After the dissolution of the Portuguese army he entered the Portuguese Legion under the Marquis d'Alorna. Disillusioned, he returned quickly to Portugal probably soon after crossing into Spain. He rejoined the nascent Portuguese army and served under José de Miranda Henriques in late 1808. In 1809 he was appointed Adjutant General by Beresford; promoted to Major General on 11 February 1818. António Lemos Pereira de Lacerda (1761–1828) was a Lieutenant in 1789, served in Catalunya and Roussillon against the French, a Major in the caçadores and subsequently Lieutenant Colonel. Was military secretary to Marshal Beresford until 1820; Lieutenant General 11 February 1818; 1st Viscount Juromenha. See *Gazeta de Lisboa*, 18 May 1818.

59   'Estado Actual do Exercito Portuguez' (TT, MNE CX 885).

60   A very full account of recruiting and the finances of doing so is given by Dores Costa in 'Army size, Military Recruitment and Financing During the Period of the Peninsula War' .

61   Fernando Dores Costa, op. cit., p. 6. These figures include infantry, caçadores, cavalry, artillery and policemen.

62   There were a number of British officers already involved with the Portuguese army, including Sir Robert Wilson, Lieutenant Colonel William Mayne and Colonel Nicholas Trant, an Irishman who having served in the French army under the Ancien Regime (Walsh's regiment) joined the British army in 1794 (84th Regiment and subsequently Royal Staff Corps). Appointed to the Portuguese army in 1808, he became a noted leader of militia and led these part-time forces with considerable success from 1808 onwards. His exploits included the capture of Coimbra in October 1810 (see Chapter 9) and the exclusion of Masséna's army from the territories north of the Mondego in 1811, with much smaller and inexperienced forces compared to the French army. Trant's leadership amounted on occasions to guerilla warfare and he was much appreciated by both Beresford and Wellington. Following the recovery of Porto in 1809 he

was appointed Commandant of that city on 13 May by Wellesley. A number of English officers were also embedded with the Spanish army.

63 Treaty of Badajoz, 6 June 1801.

64 Beresford was to add a further six battalions of caçadores to the Portuguese army in the years ahead, and the integration of the Loyal Lusitanian Legion into the army in 1811 further strengthened this aspect of the armed forces.

65 Andrew Halliday, *Observations on the Present State of the Portuguese Army as Organised by Lieutenant-General Sir William Carr Beresford K.B.* (London: John Murray, 1811). Note, however, that Foy and Maxwell both felt the Portuguese army might amount to some 17,000.

66 One of these officers was Major Robert William Patrick of the 57th Regiment and subsequently Lieutenant Colonel of the 12th Portuguese Line. Patrick was to die of natural causes in Lamego on 10 May 1810.

67 Beresford to Brigadier Charles Stewart, 17 March 1809 (NA, WO 1/239).

68 The extent of Portuguese resistance to Soult's invasion in 1809 is sometimes not fully appreciated. Captain Victor von Arentschild, a German officer in the British army (King's German Legion) but serving with permission in Portugal, reported on 26 March to Beresford the extensive preparations made in Porto to resist Soult, including the mounting of 180 guns, but expressed his concern at the lack of regular troops. Arentschild to Beresford, 26 March 1809 (NAM 1995-09-87). His fears were soon realised due to the lack of organisation and insubordination.

 French losses were substantial, not just at the capture of Porto but at Ponte de Amarante, Ponte de Lima, Ponte de Mizarela, Mesão Frio and Guimarães. Loison's force also suffered considerably. De Naylies in *Mémoires sur la Guerre d'Espagne pendant les années 1808, 1809, 1810 et 1811* (p. 62) even remarks that many women, including nuns, were involved at the defence of the Minho. See also Oman, op. cit., vol. II, pp. 223–72 for an account of the second French invasion of Portugal.

69 Beresford to Cradock, 29 March 1809 (NA, WO 1/239). Beresford was receiving reports from British officers in Porto. Major Robert Patrick described the anarchy in Porto, and could not himself attempt to leave for fear that his own life would be in danger if he did so (BL, RP 5296, 23 March 1809).

70 Luis de Oliveira and fourteen other presumed traitors were taken from the prison in Porto before being killed.

71 Apart from receiving a sizeable number of stragglers back after the retreat to La Coruña, Cradock received reinforcements from England in March 1809, including a force under Sherbrooke, and he may have had 15,000 men available. William Napier suggested that Beresford urged Cradock to use the British army to attack Soult in Porto, but while Beresford clearly recognised the value of defeating French armies in turn (a policy endorsed by Wellesley later in the spring and summer of 1809), rather than letting them join together, he does not appear to have advocated an immediate march on Porto, but rather a gradual move north which would still enable a return to Lisbon if it was threatened from the east by General Victor. Napier, *History*, vol. II, pp. 25–9.

72 Following Cuesta's defeat and retreat, Wilson was ordered to the neighbourhood of Ciudad Rodrigo or Almeida (Beresford to Wilson, 24 March 1809. BL Add MS 30,106, quoted in Sir Robert Wilson, general correspondence, vol. II).

73 Major Robert Patrick to Beresford, 7 April 1809 (BL, RP 5296).

74 Trant to Beresford, 29 March 1809 (BL, RP 5296).

75 Trant to Beresford, 5 April 1809 (Rice University Digital Scholarship Archive, Coimbra 4-5-1809).

76 Trant to Colonel Benjamin D'Urban, 19 April 1809; Trant to Beresford, 22 April 1809 (BL, RP 5296).

77 Extract from letter of Colonel Trant, 1 May 1809 (WP1/259/2).

78 Report to Beresford, 29 April 1809 (BL, RP 5296).

79 Wellington to Liverpool, 9 May 1810 (WD 4, 58).

80 Benjamin D'Urban (1777–1849) was a professional soldier who joined the British army in 1793. He served in Portugal and Spain in 1808–9 before being appointed Beresford's Quartermaster General in the Portuguese army in 1809. Later in the war he was to lead Portuguese cavalry with success at Salamanca, but was badly let down at Majadahonda. In 1813 he was promoted Major General in the Portuguese army (Colonel in Great Britain). He returned to Portugal after the war and remained there until 1816 when he was promoted to Colonel of the Royal Staff Corps.

81 Ordem do Dia, 18 April 1809, No. 24.

82 William Warre ('Warre') to his father James Warre, 27 April 1809 (*Letters from the Peninsula*).

83 The 4th and 19th regiments were placed under the command of Brigadier General Blunt. This was followed in April by the 3rd and 15th being placed under the command of Brigadier General Alexander Campbell, while the 1st and 13th were given to Brigadier General António Marcelino da Vitória. See Ordens do Dia.

84 Sir David Dundas to Wellesley, 13 May 1809 (WP1/260/5). Dundas had replaced the Duke of York as Commander in Chief in 1809 following the scandal of the sale of commissions by the Duke of York's mistress. As of 13 May 1809 a total of twenty British officers had already been appointed to the Portuguese army, in addition to those who travelled to Portugal with Beresford. These were Lt. Cols Cox, McMahon, and Burghersh and Majors Brown, Oliver, Patrick, Douglas, Burke, Doyle, Waters, McBean, Hill, Campbell, Arbuthnott [*sic*], Carroll, Harding, Le Mesurier, Roche, Elder and McCreagh.

85 Castlereagh to Cradock, 15 February 1809 (NA, WO 1/232). The early appointments by Beresford referred to in the Ordens do Dia suggest that Henry Belson, Richard Blunt, Richard Bushe, Archibald Campbell, William MacBean and August Waddington may have arrived with Beresford. See Beresford to Castlereagh, 8 March 1809 (NA, WO 1/239). Another early appointment was John MacDonald of the 88th Regiment (Connaught Rangers), of which Beresford was Colonel. MacDonald arrived as a Lieutenant in March 1809 and was shortly thereafter appointed Captain. On 15 November 1809 he was promoted Major of the 2nd Infantry Regiment, and Lieutenant Colonel on 14 April 1812. He fought in many of the major battles including Buçaco, Campo Maior, Albuera, Vitória, and Toulouse, and participated in a number of sieges including the first and third sieges of Badajoz.

86 Beresford to Brigadier Charles Stewart, 16 April 1809 (NA, WO 1/239). Later Beresford was to try unsuccessfully to get Charles Stewart to join the Portuguese army.

87 See, 'History of Parliament online' (http://www.historyofparliamentonline.org); entry for John Hobart Cradock. General Cradock's own father had been Bishop of Kilmore and subsequently Archbishop of Dublin in Ireland, so the Beresford and Cradock families may have known each other in Ireland.

88 Progress was uneven. While substantial progress was made with a number of infantry regiments (see text), Colonel Mayne (LLL) reported on 11 May that the cavalry at Almeida 'are most wretched and worse accoutred' while Brigadier General Fane a day later said the two squadrons of cavalry at Goligao (Golegã) were in poor condition, not being able to turn out above 120 horse and some of them would 'never reach Abrantes' (a distance of some forty kilometres). Mayne and Fane to Mackenzie, 11 and 12 May 1809 (BL, Add MS, 40,722).

89 Major Robert Patrick (who was Beresford's eyes and ears in Silveira's corps) to Beresford, 8 April 1809 (Woodson Research Center, Fondren Library).

90 Ordem do Dia, 9 April 1809, No. 17.

91 Beresford to Forjaz, 19 April 1809 (AHM, 1-14 CX 18).

92 Decree of 6 October 1809; Forjaz to Beresford, 14 November 1809 (AHM, CX 39).

93   José António de Oliveira Leite de Barros was Chefe da Auditoria Geral do Exército (appointed 15 April 1809, see Ordem do Dia No. 20) throughout the war and later a much feared and hated Judge supporting the Miguelist side in the Civil War.

94   Vichness, op. cit., pp. 163–4.

95   Beresford, 11 January 1811, confirmation of sentence handed down 29 December 1809 (AHM 1-14-019-01-0096).

96   See de la Fuente, *Forjaz*, Chapter V; in addition Vichness, op. cit., Chapters 8 and 9; Fernando Dores Costa. All excellent accounts.

97   Ordem do Dia, 6 April 1809, No. 14.

98   Ibid.

99   Ordem do Dia, 23 March 1809.

100 Ordens do Dia, 8, 12 and 15 April 1809.

101 Major John Leslie (ed.), *The Dickson Manuscripts: Being Diaries, Letters, Maps, Account Books, With Various Papers of the late Major General Sir Alexander Dickson* (Woolwich: Royal Artillery Institution Printing House, 1908). See entries inter alia for 2, 7 and 9 April 1809.

102 Cradock to Beresford, 18 April 1809 (Arquivo Municipal de Mafra [AMM]; PT/AMM/CFLLTV/TT, MNE 022).

103 The official notice of Arthur Wellesley's appointment to command in Portugal is dated 2 April 1809, but he had clearly been told of the appointment in late March; see Wellesley to the Duke of Richmond, 28 March 1809; (WD 3, 184).

104 Wellesley to Castlereagh, 1 August 1808 (WD 4, 43).

105 Wellesley to Castlereagh, 5 September 1808 (WD 3, 113–17 at 115).

106 Memorandum on the defence of Portugal (WD 3, 181–3).

107 Cradock was not enamoured by this move. He served as Acting Governor of Gibraltar only between May and August 1809. From 1811 to 1814 he served as Governor of the Cape Colony.

108 Wellesley to Beresford, 23 April 1809 (WD 3, 186–7).

109 Beresford to Cradock, 29 March 1809 (Beresford, *Strictures*, p. 83) referring to the previous day's meeting.

110 Oman, op. cit., vol. II, p. 314 notes that Beresford had ten Portuguese regiments at Tomar and Abrantes including three newly raised battalions of caçadores. He had previously placed Wilson and the Legion on the Portuguese–Spanish border as an observation force and this force had successfully rebuffed an attempt by General Lapisse to move towards Almeida.

111 Wellesley to Villiers, 4 May 1809 (WD 3, 209–10).

112 Warre, 27 April 1809.

113 Wellesley to Beresford, 6 May 1809 (WP1/262/19). Major General J.R. Mackenzie to Sir Arthur Wellesley (WP1/259, f. 11; 3 May 1809) noted that while he could say nothing of the efficiency of the Portuguese troops yet, the British regiments were placed in such a manner as to be able to drill them.

114 Beresford to Wellesley, 7 May 1809 (WP1/259/31).

115 Julia Page (ed.), *Intelligence Officer in the Peninsula: The Letters and Diaries of Major the Hon. Edward Charles Cocks, 1786–1812* (Tunbridge Wells: Spellmount, 1986).

116 Munster, *An Account of the British Campaign in 1809*, pp. 13–14. 'Without going into further detail it will be sufficient to remark that the arrangement and system of the Marshal were so good and improvement so rapid in the Portuguese army, that within two months from the date of his first order, a battalion of the 16th regiment was brought into collision with the enemy, and if it did not distinguish itself as much as it did on so many subsequent occasions, it evinced neither confusion nor dismay.'

117 Wellesley to Villiers, 11 May 1809 (2 letters; WP1/262/41 and 42).

118 Beresford to Mackenzie, 2 May 1809 (BL, Add MS 40,722) enclosed a return of Portuguese troops (10,021 fit for duty) which would work with Mackenzie's British troops; Mackenzie listed the force under him as including part of the Loyal Lusitanian Legion based at Alcantara together with some militia; one battalion each of the Portuguese 1st, 3rd, 13th, 15th and two battalions of the 4th Portuguese regiments, two further militia regiments at Santarém and part of the Regiment of Porto. He estimated he had 6,500 Portuguese infantry and 4,500 militia. In addition he had elements of British infantry and dragoons. All of these were spread in a wide arc along the River Tagus. Mackenzie to Wellington, 3 May 1809 (WP1/259/11).

119 It is sometimes overlooked that Silveira's force held up Loison at Amarante from 20 April to 2 May 1809. That prevented Loison from clearing the way east before Beresford arrived on the scene. Soult was unaware of Loison's exact whereabouts or circumstances, which may well have impacted on his own planning.

120 Louis de Saint-Pierre and Antoinette de Saint-Pierre, *Mémoires du Maréchal Soult: Espagne et Portugal* (Paris: Hachette, 1955).

121 Beresford's initial force included five battalions of the Portuguese army (1st Regiment, one battalion; 7th Regiment, two battalions; 19th Regiment, two battalions), two squadrons of Portuguese cavalry and two batteries of artillery. He was later joined by elements of the Legion under Wilson and by Tilson's brigade and linked up with Silveira's force.

122 Beresford to Wellesley, 9 May 1809 (WP1/259/38).

123 Wellesley to Beresford, 7 May 1809 (WD 4, 309).

124 Wellesley to Beresford, 11 May 1809 (WP1/262/40).

125 Tilson had been promoted to Major General on 25 April 1808; Beresford had been promoted to Major General on the same date, which may have caused Tilson to resent having to serve under the Marshal.

126 Beresford to Wellesley, 11 May 1809 (WP1/259/49).

127 Beresford to Wellesley, 17 May 1809 (WP1/260/34).

128 Major General Sir John Murray also objected to the possibility of serving under Beresford at this time, observing that he had nearly had to obey his orders and would have had to do so had they met. Murray had been created Major General in October 1805 so was considerably senior to Beresford. Murray requested Wellesley's permission to resign his situation on the staff, and Wellesley acquiesced, perhaps not that impressed with Murray's performance on the Douro in any event. Murray to Wellesley, 25 May 1809 (WP1/261/10).

129 Wellesley to Beresford, 29 May 1809 (WP1/263/46); Tilson to Wellesley, 22 June 1809 (WP1/264/27).

130 Beresford used here the informal brigades he had previously established, led by Bacelar, Brito de Mosinho, Silveira and Lopes de Sousa (Ordem do Dia, 11 May 1809).

131 D'Urban, noting that the artillery and cavalry arrived at Lamego on 11 May, pointedly refers to the fact that the British brigade failed to reach the town on that day. Benjamin D'Urban, *The Peninsular Journal 1808–1817*, edited by I.J. Rousseau (London: Greenhill Books, 1990), p. 52.

132 Soult's army spent the night of 12 May largely camped at Penafiel and Baltar.

133 Page, op. cit., p. 28. Cocks says that it was only on 13 May that Wellesley learnt of Beresford's capture of Amarante.

134 Beresford again makes reference to Tilson's delay, implying that it delayed the crossing of the Tamega, in his letter to Wellesley of 13 May 1809 (WP1/260/3).

135 Robert S. Rait, *The Life and Campaigns of Hugh First Viscount Gough* (London, Archibald Constable & Co. Ltd., 1903) gives a good account of these events.

136 Ibid. Gough says that Beresford only halted for twelve hours in three days; with the 88th suffering terribly having lost 550 troops sick and exhausted on the march out of a total of 700; on 17 May the body of troops were too exhausted to move.

D'Urban reported that Beresford received instructions from Wellesley on 15 May directing him to proceed to Chaves, by which time he was well on the way there. (TT, MNE CX 204).

137 Montalegre is referred to as Monte Alegre in Beresford's correspondence; Beresford to Wellesley, 17 May 1809 (WP1/260/35).

138 The greater part of the British troops straggled into Chaves on 18 May, many without shoes; Beresford to Wellesley, 18 May 1809 (WP1/260/49).

139 Mackenzie to Wellesley, 15 May 1809 (2 letters; WP1/260/15 and 17). On 16 May he went so far as to write, 'nothing can save the capital but the immediate presence of the force under your command' (WP1/260/28). On 18 May Mackenzie wrote to say he was immediately retiring behind the river Zezere with his British troops stating, 'I am sorry your progress should be interrupted but I conceive the safety of the capital immediately depends on your return' (WP1/260/43).

This correspondence reflects a level of panic by Mackenzie, but also a considerable information supply line via Portuguese spies or information officers. However, the intelligence was not always reliable, for Mackenzie erroneously thought the French had captured Castelo Branco which caused him to retreat precipitously. On 19 May Wellesley informed Beresford that as a result of Mackenzie's communications he was moving south immediately (WP/1 263/5).

140 See Vichness, op. cit, p. 192. Vichness relies on the published diary of Brigadier General Silveira. *Lagarde Portuguez ou Gazeta para depois Jantar* (Lisbon), 10 July 1809; *Correio Brazilense ou Armazen Literario*. See also Wellesley to Villiers, 17 May 1809 (WD 3, 238–9). This shows that in fact Beresford had anticipated Wellesley's order to proceed to Chaves with a view to cutting of Soult there. See Wellesley to Beresford, 14 May 1809 (ibid. 234).

141 Beresford to Lady Anne Beresford, 26 May 1809 (Beresford family papers).

142 Rait, *The Life and Campaigns of Hugh First Viscount Gough.*

143 Wellesley to Castlereagh, 18 May 1809 (WD 3, 239–41).

144 Ordem do Dia, 27 May 1809.

145 Wellesley to Mackenzie, 21 May 1809 (WP1/263/13).

Chapter 7

1 Beresford to Forjaz, 21 September 1809 (AHM, 1-14, CX 162, f. 43) quoted in Vichness, p. 261.

2 Castlereagh to Beresford, 15 February 1809 (NA, WO 1/239).

3 Castlereagh to Cradock, 15 February 1809 (NA, WO 1/232).

4 Beresford to Castlereagh, 5 April 1809 (NA, WO 1/239), which gives a list of those joining the Portuguese service from the British army in Portugal. A later list, dated 31 October 1809, is located at TT, MNE CX 204, f. 167.

5 Beresford to Brigadier Charles Stewart, 16 April 1809 (NA, WO 1/239).

6 In January 1810, Lieutenant Colonel Henry Bunbury at the War Office confirmed to Lieutenant General Hamilton that the British pay of British officers was liable to income tax, though this was not the case in respect of forage and other allowances. Bunbury (Under Secretary at the War Office) to Hamilton, 13 January 1810 (NA, FO 342/11).

7 Beresford to Castlereagh, 5 April 1809 (NA, WO 1/239). The number of 150 must have been reached by reference to the twenty-four regiments of line and six regiments of caçadores.

8   Wellesley to Castlereagh, 7 April 1809 (WSD 6, 215).

9   Beresford to Lady Anne Beresford, 23 April 1809 (Beresford family papers).

10 Beresford to Castlereagh, 18 April 1809 (NA, WO 1/239).

11 Beresford to Forjaz, 21 September 1809 (AHM, 1-14 CX 162).

12 Dundas to Wellesley, 13 May 1809 (NA, WO 1/238) and Wellesley to Villiers, 19 May 1809 (WD 3, 241). See also, Wellesley to Villiers, 30 May 1809 (WP1/263, f. 47).

13 Dundas to Wellesley, 10 July 1809 (*The Dickson Manuscripts*, vol. II, p. 179. Quoted in Vichness, p. 215).

14 Beresford to Wellesley, 12 June 1809 (WP1/264, f. 14).

15 Liverpool to Wellington, 7 November 1809 (TT, MNE CX 207, f. 40).

16 For a good discussion on this topic generally, see Vichness, ff. 207. For instance, Vichness has calculated that between 14 June and 1 August 1809 there were twelve new appointments and eleven resignations of British officers.

17 See, for example, Major Lewis Newman to Lt Col Bathurst, 4 October 1809 (TT, MNE CX 204). An example of Wellington refusing a transfer on the grounds it would not leave a regiment with enough officers is that involving Lieutenant Newport of the 39th Regiment (Somerset to Arbuthnot, 13 May 1810; Ibid CX 206, f. 129).

18 Lionel S. Challis's 'Peninsula Roll Call' gives the names of many of the British officers who served in Portugal in the Portuguese army. See, 'Lionel S. Challis's "Peninsula Roll Call"' (*The Napoleon Series*, 2009). Available at: https://www.napoleon-series.org/research/biographies/GreatBritain/Challis/c_ChallisIntro.html (accessed 24 April 2018).

19 William Warre to his father James, 6 September 1809 (*Letters from the Peninsula*, p. 49).

20 Ibid. 31 December 1809, p. 61.

21 Ibid. 27 April 1809, p. 41.

22 Beresford to Wellington, 10 August 1810 (AHM 1-14, Cx 12 and NA, WO 1/400).

23 Charles Stuart referred to the promotions authorised from Rio in the summer of 1810, 'with little attention to any other recommendations than favour and interest at Court', as being highly prejudicial to the arrangements of Marshal Beresford since they would involve the removal of officers responsible for reorganisation of the army, which would produce a relapse and the reintroduction of the old and inveterate bad habits. Beresford had suggested a suspension of the execution of these appointments and Stuart thought this suggestion would be accepted and the appointments would not go ahead. Stuart to Wellesley, 20 August 1810 (NA, WO 1/400).

24 AHM-DIV-1-14-019-1 and 39-1, quoted in Vichness pp. 279–80.

25 Edward Costello, *Adventures of a Soldier: Written by Himself. Being the Memoirs of Edward Costello* (London: Colburn and Co., 1852).

26 TT, MNE CX 204 and CX 205 ff. 493.

27 TT, MNE CX 207, ff. 396 and 398.

28 Challis lists three officers by the name of Marlay serving in Portugal. This incident probably involves Stephen Edward Marlay, who transferred from the 82nd Foot to the 8th Portuguese, since the report is by Major McGregor of the 8th Portuguese. Charles Western served with the 16th and 29th regiments before joining the Loyal Lusitanian Legion and ultimately the 8th Caçadores. The denomination of the two Portuguese brothers as 'Alferezes' may merely reflect their rank rather than a surname, for 'alferes' is a rank in the army equivalent to Second Lieutenant or Ensign.

29 George McGregor of 8th Portuguese (TT, MNE CX 204, f. 982); Court of Inquiry, January 1810.

30 Ordem do Dia, 10 April 1810. In fact Captain McGregor (as he was in British service) had only received Wellington's blessing to join the Portuguese service on 1 October 1809. Wellington to Beresford, 1

October 1809 (TT, MNE CX 204, f. 65). Interestingly, McGregor was experimenting with what he referred to as a new telegraph system which would not be costly. McGregor to Arbuthnot, 19 December 1809 (TT, MNE CX 206, f. 179).

31 Dickson to Major General John Macleod, 3 July 1809 (*The Dickson Manuscripts*, vol. I, p. 44).

32 Randolph, *The Life of General Sir Robert Wilson*, vol. 1, pp. 254–5 and 296. Randolph makes it clear that Wilson was introduced to Beresford at a dinner while the British fleet was anchored off Madeira on 30 September 1805. Wilson did not go on the 1806 expedition to the Rio de La Plata, and indeed appears to have been chastised by Home Popham for expressing doubts to Beresford about the project.

33 See correspondence between Beresford and Wilson, 23, 25, 29 May, 1 and 2 June 1809, and Wilson to Castlereagh, 5 June 1809. All contained in Sir Robert Wilson general correspondence, vol. II (1 February 1809–31 December 1812); BL, Add MS 30,106. See also NA, WO 1/230.

34 Wellington to Castlereagh, 20 October 1809 (WD 3, 560).

35 Wellington to Beresford, 23 April 1810 (TT, MNE CX 206, f. 258). Beresford was perhaps fortunate in that Wilson relied greatly on Canning for support, but the latter was now out of office following his duel with Castlereagh.

36 Such as when Major General Rowland Hill had to go home in the winter of 1810 for some six months. In the case of Captain G.M. Hodges, the medical certificate of Surgeon John Griffith read: 'I certify that Captain G.M. Hodges of the 1st company of grenadiers of the 7th Portuguese regiment is afflicted with a complaint, resembling the Venereal Disease, by which his health is so materially impaired that for the reestablishment of which, I am of the opinion that it is absolutely necessary for him to go to England for a period of not less than three months' (TT, MNE CX 207, f. 605).

37 Wellington to Beresford, 3 October 1809 (TT, MNE CX 204).

38 Correspondence, Miller and Beresford, 15 and 27 November 1809, 27 December 1809 (TT, MNE CX 206, f. 226 and CX 207, ff. 92 and 152).

39 Wellington to Beresford, 3 October 1809 (TT, MNE CX 204). Macleroth had been on the summer 1809 campaign with Beresford.

40 See de la Fuente, *Forjaz* for a comprehensive discussion on the means and results of the Portuguese recruiting policy.

41 See Dores Costa, 'Army size, Military Recruitment and Financing During the Period of the Peninsula War'.

42 Anthony Gray, *The French Invasions of Portugal, 1807–1811: Rebellion, Reaction and Resistance* (MA thesis, University of York, 2011) is a detailed account of recruiting policy in the Peninsula War. See also Victor Cesar, 'A Evolução do Recrutamento em Portugal: Desde 1809 até 1901', *Revista Militar* 2, 9 (Setembro 1909), pp. 577–92.

43 De la Fuente, *Forjaz*, p. 124.

44 Dores Costa, op. cit., p. 6.

45 Forjaz to Beresford, 8 November and 16 December 1809 (AHM, 1-14, CX 527).

46 Wellington to Beresford, 10 July 1810 (TT, MNE CX 204, f. 505).

47 Dores Costa, op. cit., p. 6.

48 Picton to Beresford, 10 May 1810 (TT, MNE CX 206, f. 105) for example states that having inspected the Portuguese artillery attached to the division he had found their forage was so irregular and inadequate that the mules were not fit for active service requiring any exertion and that they would shortly be incapable of accompanying the division on any movement unless measures were adopted. Da Silva's and Freire's batteries were both attached to the 3rd (Picton's) Division.

49 Forjaz to Beresford, 11 December 1810 and Beresford to Forjaz, 25 December 1810 (AHM, 1-14, CX 39 and CX 20).

50 Beresford to Charles Stewart, 19 March 1809 (NA, WO 1/239).

51 Wellesley to Forjaz, 18 June 1809 (WD 3, 306) envisaged Beresford with all available Portuguese troops marching to the Douro to meet the French threat.

52 Wellesley to Beresford, 1 July 1809 (WSD 6, 302).

53 D'Urban wrote an account covering the period June–August 1809 (TT, MNE CX 204, ff. 1021–1025).

54 Ibid. D'Urban gives details of the location of the various Portuguese regiments including those serving with Wellesley. See also Oman, *History*, vol. II, p. 600, which gives details of the regiments present with Beresford as follows: 2nd, 3rd, 4th, 6th, 7th, 9th, 10th, 11th, 13th, 14th, 15th, 18th, 19th and 23rd (all bar 15th Regiment, two battalions strong), together with the 1st, 2nd, 3rd, 4th and 6th caçadores. In addition the 2nd Battalion of the Loyal Lusitanian Legion and the 'Voluntarios Academicos' of Coimbra were with Beresford for this campaign together with a force under Lieutenant Colonel Archibald Campbell, who had joined the Portuguese service from the 88th Regiment where he had served under Beresford. Note the 16th Regiment was left in Tomar for recruiting and training after its exertions in the spring campaign (see Chapter 6, above).

55 Harvey to Arbuthnot, 28 July 1809 (TT, MNE 170/2).

56 Beresford to 2nd Marquis of Waterford, 27 June 1809 (Beresford family papers).

57 Major General Sir John Hamilton from County Tyrone served first in the army of the East India Company before transferring to the British army in 1788. He may well have been enticed to join the Portuguese army by Beresford, for he was married to Emily Monck, a daughter of Lady Araminta Beresford, herself a sister of the 1st Marquis of Waterford. Wellington referred to Hamilton as a 'madman', but he was very effective in training the Portuguese; Wellington to Fane, 3 November 1810 (WD IV, 387). In 1813, however, Hamilton was so 'unwell' that Wellington requested Beresford to remove him from the command and he did so, Hamilton returning home and the Division afterwards being commanded by Francisco Lecor. Wellington to Beresford, 5 October and 16 November 1813 (WD 7, 38 and 142–3). Later in life Hamilton, who had been created a baronet in 1814, was made Colonel of the 69th Regiment, of which the previous colonel was Marshal Beresford.

Francisco Lecor had declined to go to France with the Portuguese Legion. He served with the Loyal Lusitanian Legion and subsequently commanded the 12th Regiment of Line before commanding the Portuguese Division and subsequently the 7th Division. He was later central to Prince João's attempts to extend his power in South America.

58 Ordens do Dia, 9 and 20 November 1809.

59 In July 1810, Wellington caustically remarked to Beresford that Cox exaggerates 'the real difficulties of our situation and teaze me with his trifling complaints'. Two days later he observed: 'Any other officer would be ashamed of troubling his Commander in Chief with such little and unfounded complaints but he appears to think nothing of it.' Wellington to Beresford, 6 and 8 July 1810 (TT, MNE CX 204, ff. 397 and 448).

60 William Cox was Lieutenant Colonel of the 24th Regiment of Line of Portugal.

61 MacDonnell to Cox, 14 September 1809 (TT, MNE CX 169/1).

62 McDonnell to Robert Arbuthnot, 8 December 1809 (TT, MNE CX, 206, f. 60).

63 Wellington to Castlereagh, 20 October 1809 (WD 3, 560).

64 Cox to Beresford, 19 November 1809 (TT, MNE CX 207, f. 107).

65 Cox to an unidentified General, 25 October 1809 (TT, MNE CX 204). Cox had been commander of the 24th Line but presumably must have ceded command at this time, given the reference to bickering

between colonel and lieutenant colonel. Vichness, in analysing the allocation of British officers to Portuguese regiments, suggests that Beresford concentrated on those regiments which could be soonest brought up to a state of preparedness and allocated a disproportionate number of British officers to those regiments, which did not include the 12th and 24th regiments. See Vichness, op. cit., pp. 223–4.

66 George McGregor, 17 November 1808 (TT, MNE CX 207, f. 102).

67 Beresford to Castlereagh, 8 March 1809 (NA, WO 1/239).

68 Beresford to Wellesley, 16 June 1809 (NA, WO 1/238); Return of Arms Required for the Portuguese Service, 30 June 1809 (NA, WO 1/239). Wellesley to Castlereagh, 19 June 1809 (WD 3, 307).

69 McGregor to Arbuthnot, 27 October 1809 (TT, MNE CX 204).

70 AHM, 1-14, CX 37, f. 1.

71 Wellington to Beresford, 3 April 1810 (TT, MNE CX 206, f. 11). There were forty-eight militia regiments based on districts within each province.

72 Cox to D'Urban, 6 December 1809 (TT, MNE CX 206, f. 41) complained he was still waiting for armament for the 24th Regiment promised long ago, but that only 500 muskets without accoutrements had arrived in August at which stage he had been given to understand the rest would follow immediately.

73 Richard Wellesley to Stuart, 31 January and 6 February 1810 (Stuart de Rothesay Papers, NA, FO 342/11).

74 For further information on the equipping of the Portuguese army see de la Fuente, op. cit., ff. 134. Once again Lieutenant Colonel Cox at Almeida is a source of information, complaining to D'Urban in December 1809 that the delays in getting both clothes and armaments from the Arsenal in Lisbon is causing far-flung regiments serious problems. He instanced the greater part of the clothing being detained at Barquinha (40 or 50 leagues distant) or Abrantes for two months, and when they arrived little progress had been made due to lack of thread. As of 6 December the clothing for the 12th Regiment had arrived at Barquinha, but the commissary wanted Cox to find carts and an escort to bring the cargo to Almeida. He advised the setting up of a depot at Barquinha and use of the militia to escort the delivery of goods. Cox to D'Urban, 6 December 1809 (TT, MNE CX 206, f. 41).

75 Captain Robert Harvey served initially in Portugal with the 53rd Foot. He transferred into the Portuguese army in 1810, receiving the one step promotion to Major and being appointed Assistant Quartermaster General. In 1811 he became based at Wellington's HQ acting as a liaison officer between Wellington and Beresford. Later he was appointed Colonel commanding 14th Light Dragoons.

76 Treaty of Commerce & Navigation between Great Britain and Portugal (19 February 1810), Treaty between Great Britain and Portugal for the abolition of the slave trade north of the Equator (19 February 1810). The quid pro quo was an arrangement whereby Portugal could suspend remittance of payments of loans agreed in 1809. Lewis Hertslet (ed.), *A Complete Collection of the Treaties and Conventions, and Reciprocal Regulations, at Present Subsisting between Great Britain and Foreign Powers*, vol. II (London: Butterworth, 1840). Hereafter, Hertslet's *Commercial Treaties*.

77 António Alves Caetano, *A Economia Portuguesa no Tempo de Napoleão* (Lisbon: Tribuna da Histórica, 2008).

78 See Dores Costa, op. cit., pp. 13–16.

79 Ibid. pp. 14–15.

80 For an account of Portuguese revenues and the British subsidy see de la Fuente, op. cit., pp. 153–60.

81 Stuart to Wellesley, 25 November 1810 (NA, FO 342/23) and Wellington to Stuart, 20 February 1811 (WD VII, 279) quoted in de la Fuente, *Forjaz*, p. 159; Wellington to Richard Wellesley, 26 January 1811 (WD 4, 553–6).

82 House of Commons Debate, 18 March 1811 (*Hansard*, vol. 19, cc 387–415).

83 See Ordens do Dia, 11 May 1809, which refers to seizures of hay, grain and other rations and forbade such practices unless authorised by the Commissariat.

84 In fact, in 1810 Beresford was called upon to help his commissary from the Buenos Aires expedition, Captain Alexander Gillespie (Royal Marines). Gillespie had looked after the British prisoners of war following their surrender at Buenos Aires four years earlier, purchasing them meat, greens and other articles on a daily basis, expending his own funds in doing so. All expenses had been entered each day in a book and totalled over $1,000.00. See Gillespie to Beresford, 17 April 1810 (TT, MNE CX 206, f. 191). For further information on Gillespie and the attack on Buenos Aires see:, Marcus de la Poer Beresford, 'William Carr Beresford: The Capture of the Cape Colony and the Rio de la Plata Expedition of 1806', *The Irish Sword* XXIX, 117 (2012), pp. 241–62.

85 Campbell to Beresford, 29 October 1809 (TT, MNE CX 204, f. 156).

86 Fletcher to Beresford, 10 November 1809 (TT, MNE CX 207, f. 68).

87 Patton to Arbuthnot, 13 November 1809 (TT, MNE CX 207, f. 82).

88 Wellesley to Huskisson, 22 June 1809 (WD 4, 449).

89 De la Fuente gives one example of an appalling piece of carelessness when 30,000 lbs of biscuit which was meant to be sent forward from Almeida to Beresford's army outside Ciudad Rodrigo (47-kms/30-miles) in the summer of 1809 was in fact sent to Sevilla (450-kms/280-miles); de la Fuente, op. cit., p. 145.

90 Ibid. ff. 142 for a comprehensive discussion on the topic of the performance of the Junta de Viveres.

91 Adrien Balbi, *Essai Statistique* (Lisbon: Imprensa Nacional Casa da Moeda, 2004), quoted in Espirito Santo and de Brito, op. cit., p. 30.

92 Espirito Santo and de Brito, op. cit., p. 13.

93 See Halliday, *Observations on the Present State of the Portuguese Army*.

94 Beresford to Brigadier General Charles Stewart, 19 March 1809 (NA, WO 1/239).

95 Wellington to Liverpool, 25 July 1813 (WD 10, 569).

96 Beresford to Forjaz, 21 September 1809 (AHM, 1-14, CX 17).

97 A most useful piece of research on recruitment and desertion in the Portuguese army in the Peninsula War is contained in a paper given by José Nogueira Rodrigues Ermitão ('Ermitão') to the *XX Colóquio de História Militar, 2011*; 'A Desercão Militar no Periodo das Invasões Francesas/Guerra Peninsular.'

98 Ibid. p. 2.

99 Ordem do Dia, 21 July 1813.

100 Ermitão, op. cit., pp. 6–7.

101 Simão José da Luz Soriano, *História da Guerra Civil e do estabelecimento do governo parlamentar em Portugal comprehendendo a história diplomática, militar e política da este reino desde 1777 até 1834*, vol. V, pt. II, doc. 104 (Lisbon: Imprensa Nacional, 1893).

102 Colonel Robert Wilson refers to an ingenious Portuguese sergeant who before the introduction of formal passports stole an officer's sash to serve as a passport. He seduced fifteen men to leave with him but was captured, court martialled and sentenced to death. Wilson; general correspondence, 30 March 1809 (BL, Add MS 30,106). Beresford on 3 August 1809 ordered that no soldier should be absent without a passport (Ordem do Dia, 3 August 1809).

103 Ermitão, op. cit., pp. 7–9.

104 Ibid. p. 9.

105 Ibid. p. 5.

106 Cox to Beresford, 18 July 1810 (TT, MNE CX 204, f. 624).

107 Wellington to Beresford, 19 July 1810, and Cox to Beresford, undated (ibid. ff. 647 and 653).

108 Cox to Arbuthnot, 20 July 1810 (ibid. f. 673). One wonders whether the court martial ever took place given that the siege and surrender of Almeida took place a short time later. Cox was most concerned that Wellington and Beresford appeared to blame him for allowing the desertion (ibid. f. 683).

109 Blunt to Arbuthnot, 19 December 1810 (TT, MNE CX 207, f. 576).

110 Cox to Beresford, 13 April 1810 (TT, MNE CX 206, f. 144).

111 Cox to Beresford, 19 July 1810, referring to an unnamed officer commanding the 3rd Caçadores.

112 Stubbs to Beresford, undated (TT, MNE CX 206, f. 314). Perhaps this was the same Major Lacerda who had the confrontation with Major James Warde Oliver of the 14th Regiment at Badajoz in 1811.

113 *Royal Military Chronicle*, 20 April 1813. Indeed Hugh Eccles was to lose an arm fighting in the Peninsula. At the time of the reported incident he was a Captain in the Portuguese army.

114 Beresford, Ordem do Dia, 12 May 1809.

115 Ermitão, op. cit., p. 14.

116 See Pakenham, General Order 23 January 1811, stating four Brunswick Oels to be shot for desertion and two others to be given 200 lashes each for being absent from quarters after hours (TT, MNE CX 207, f. 337). Wellington may have pardoned these. On the other hand, Conrad Buttles of 7th Line Battalion KGL was sentenced to 1,000 lashes on 29 December 1810 for the same offence (ibid. f. 667).

117 Sir Charles Oman, 'Courts Martial of the Peninsular War 1809–14', *Royal United Services Institution Journal* 56, 418 (2009), pp. 1,699–1,716. Of the 78 shot for desertion, 52 were described as British while 26 (half the previous number) were listed as foreigners.

118 Francis S. Larpent, *The Private Journal of F.S. Larpent, Judge-Advocate General of the British Forces in the Peninsula attached to the headquarters of Lord Wellington during the Peninsular War from 1812 to its close*, two volumes (London: Richard Bentley, 1853), vol. 2, p. 303

119 Ermitão, op. cit., p. 11.

120 Elder to Arbuthnot, 10 July 1810 (TT, MNE CX 204, f. 507).

121 William Fergusson (1773–1846), one of the first physicians to understand that insects were responsible for the transmission of disease. In 1810 was appointed Principal Medical Officer of the Portuguese army. See his *Notes and recollections of a Professional Life* (London: Longman, Brown, Green and Longmans, 1846) edited by his son James. Fergusson served with Wellesley's army at the capture of Porto and the Battle of Talavera. He applied to Beresford to join the Portuguese army in 1809 looking for an appointment 'with rank' but at that time he was not successful, perhaps as Beresford was seeking the appointment of James McGrigor. Fergusson to Beresford, 21 March 1809 (BL- RP 5296).

   Fergusson was appointed to the Portuguese service in 1810 (sometimes described as Principal Medical Officer and sometimes as Inspector-General of Hospitals or Inspector of Hospitals). He served with the Portuguese army at Buçaco, Albuera and on the campaigns in Spain and France. For his report entitled 'Memorandum on Portuguese Hospitals' see TT, MNE Maco 170/2.

122 Cox to Beresford, 20 May 1809 (TT, MNE Maco 170/2) suggested that virtually no one left the hospital alive.

123 Halliday, op. cit., p. 93. Halliday describes the dearth of physicians when Beresford moved his army into Spain at p. 258. A hospital mate, Halliday had accompanied Beresford to Buenos Aires in 1806, though it is not clear if this is the same person as Andrew Halliday in Portugal.

124 Halliday to Arbuthnot, 1 and 29 November 1809 (TT, MNE CX 207, ff. 7 and 175).

125 Jebb to Arbuthnot, 1 November 1809 (Ibid. f. 9). Thomas (Coimbra) to Arbuthnot, 6 November 1809 (Ibid. f. 35). The requisition for a medical chest by Thomas is set out as follows: 'A regimental chest for one thousand men including linnens, flannel rollers, lint, linnen [*sic*], sponges, etc. One complete set of instruments for hospital use, one small ditto for field service, field tourniquets No. 20.'

126 Fergusson to Arbuthnot, 3 November 1809 (TT, MNE CX 207, f. 22).

127 Halliday, op. cit., p. 262, and see Fergusson to Arbuthnot, 3 April 1810 (TT, MNE CX 206, f. 16).

128 Beresford to Forjaz, 20 March 1810 (AHM 1-14, CX 19, no. 1). Fergusson claimed some days later that the Marshal had agreed to five mules per brigade for the carriage of the medicine chest, hospital bedding and surgical panniers but these were slow in forthcoming though several regiments had received two mules for the surgeon and assistant surgeon's private baggage. Fergusson to Arbuthnot, 7 April 1810 (TT, MNE CX 206, f. 85).

129 Fergusson to Arbuthnot, 3 April 1810 (TT, MNE CX 207, f. 16); Halliday, op. cit., pp. 88 and 89.

130 Beresford, Ordem do Dia, 11 March 1810; Halliday, op. cit., p. 437.

131 Halliday, op. cit., p. 273.

132 Halliday, op. cit., pp. 263–4.

133 Halliday, op. cit., p. 258.

134 The Portuguese with Wellesley were the Loyal Lusitanian Legion and 5th Caçadores, though the Legion was not at Talavera but seeking to threaten Madrid in a flanking movement. It later retreated and fought heroically against the VIth Corps under Marshal Ney at Puerto de Baños on 12 August 1809, but suffered very severely there before ultimately fleeing the field. In his letter to his father of 25 July 1809 Cocks put British losses at Talavera at about 3,000 and French losses at some 8,000; Wellesley put overall British losses at a higher figure of 5,423 (including 653 missing). Page, *Intelligence Officer in the Peninsula*; Wellesley to Castlereagh, 29 July 1809 (WD 3, 371 at 375).

135 Memorandum – Plan of Operations, 12 August 1809 (WD 3, 412–13).

136 D'Urban suggests that Beresford proposed to Wellington that he might place the Portuguese army around Plasencia, fortifying the Puerto de Baños; on the basis that this was not only a strategic area south of Ciudad Rodrigo, but also a very fertile one which could help feed the army. Wellesley did not adopt the suggestion and later Soult was able to benefit by foraging his army there. Account of the campaign by Benjamin D'Urban (TT, MNE CX 204, ff. 1021–1025).

137 It will be recalled that Beresford had a target number of 179 British army officers for the Portuguese army. By the end of October 1809 there were eighty-four British officers attached to the Portuguese army. This figure rose to 107 by May 1810. António de Lemos Pereira de Lacerda (Beresford's Portuguese Military Secretary), Return of British Officers, 31 October 1809 (TT, MNE CX 166/2). See also, Beresford, Ordem do Dia, 13 April 1810.

138 José Vital Gomes de Souza (War Office) to Beresford, 13 August 1809 (AHM 1-14, CX 17, f. 1)

139 Beresford to del Parque, 17 August 1809 (TT, MNE CX 204, f. 252).

140 Beresford to Forjaz, 20 August 1809 (AHM 1-14-017-04-0074/76) complains of the difficulty he had in securing provisions notwithstanding the assurances received from del Parque. Beresford also complained of the quality of the Portuguese commissariat, 21 August 1809 (AHM 1-14-017-0083).

141 Beresford to Forjaz, 26 August 1809 (AHM 1-14-017-0091).

142 Wellesley to Beresford, 19 August 1809 (WD 3, 430). When there was a scare that the French would turn their attention to Portugal in October 1809 Wellington indicated to Beresford that while he would put his army across the Tagus with the right on Guarda and the left on Viseu with the Portuguese in the second line. This probably reflects a recognition that the Portuguese were in no position yet to fight in the front line. See Wellington to Beresford, 20 October 1809 (TT, MNE CX 204, f. 92).

143 Wellington to Beresford, 19 August 1809 (WD 3, 429–30); Wellington to Beresford, 26 and 30 August (2 letters), 15 and 17 September (2 letters each) and Wellington's correspondence with Castlereagh reflecting his concerns (all in WD 3).

144 Wellesley to Beresford, 19 August 1809 (WD 3, 430).

145 Beresford to Wellesley, 3 September 1809 (WSD 6, 345).

146 Wellington to Beresford, 5 October 1809 (TT, MNE CX 204).

147 McDonald to Arbuthnot, 4 November 1809 (TT, MNE CX 207, f. 26).

148 Cole to Grantham, 5 September 1809; Maud Lowry Cole (ed.) and Stephen Gwynn, *Memoirs: Sir Lowry Cole* (Uckfield: The Naval & Military Press, 2011), p. 56. Grantham was married to Lady Henrietta Cole.

149 Liverpool to Wellington, 20 October, and Wellington to Liverpool, 14 November 1809 (WD 3, 583–8) and Liverpool to Wellington, 15 December 1809 (Stuart de Rothesay Papers, NA, FO 342/11).

Chapter 8

1 One only has to look at the British retreat to La Coruña, the French retreat from Porto and the later Anglo-Portuguese retreat from Burgos. A review of Beresford's Ordens do Dia reveals that he had to address repeatedly the issue of illegal seizure of provisions by Portuguese troops and even officers. On 11 May 1809 he forbade the taking of articles unless it was done by the commissariat, stating he had learnt that officers and soldiers had seized hay, grain and many types of rations from both magistrates and other people. He reissued the order on 25 May, directing it be read on three consecutive days to the troops on parade. On 20 August 1809 he ordered soldiers not to seize carts and beasts of burden. All Ordens do Dia.

2 Wellington to Liverpool, 14 November 1809 (WD 3, 583–8).

3 Charles Stuart, later 1st Baron de Rothesay, was appointed British Minister Plenipotentiary to Portugal and Brazil in 1810 and continued in that position until 1814. George III gave permission for Stuart to join the Regency in July 1810. His daughter, Louisa, was to marry Henry, 3rd Marquis of Waterford. The Prince Regent of Portugal had previously given Stuart's predecessor John Villiers permission to attend the Regency when matters concerning the army were to be discussed. See Soriano, *História da Guerra Civil*, Segunda Epoca, I, p. 606.

4 Napier, op. cit., vol. III, p. 293.

5 Beresford to Forjaz, 9 January 1810 (AHM 1-14-50-52).

6 Wellington to Beresford, 17 April 1810 (TT, MNE CX 206, f. 187).

7 Sir Henry Fane (1778–1840) arrived in Portugal in 1808 as part of Wellesley's army and fought at Vimeiro. Retreated with the army to La Coruña and returned to Portugal. On 13 May 1810 he was appointed to command a brigade of 13th Light Dragoons and four Portuguese cavalry regiments. They guarded the right flank at Buçaco but were not engaged. Fane went home ill before the end of 1810 but returned to the Peninsula in 1813 and fought at Vitória that year and Orthez in 1814. He was present at the final battle of the war, Toulouse, but the cavalry were not utilised there to any degree.

8 Fane to Wellington (TT, MNE CX 204, Maco 169, f. 1).

9 Fane to Beresford, 24 October 1810 (TT, MNE CX 041, copy in Arquivo Municipal de Mafra). Fane also criticised the ability of the horsemen as riders and suggested the creation of a riding school, or if that was not possible a depot healthy for both men and horses. The cavalry commander needed to be able to speak Portuguese, which Fane observed ruled him out.

10 Fane to Beresford, 15 November 1810 (TT, MNE CX 204, f. 904).

11 Fane to Hill, 22 August 1810 (*The Dickson Manuscripts*, vol. II, p. 246).

12 Wellington to Forjaz, 14 October 1809 (AHM 1-14-010-14).

13 João Centeno, 'Portuguese Artillery of the Napoleonic Wars' (*The Napoleon Series*, undated). Available at: https://www.napoleon-series.org/military/organization/portugal/c_portugalarty1.html (accessed 24 April 2018).

14 Picton to Beresford, 15 July 1810 (TT, MNE CX 204, f. 601). Major Victor von Arenschildt commanded the 2nd Portuguese artillery regiment.

15 Cox to D'Urban, 6 December 1809 (TT, MNE CX 204); Beresford to Forjaz, 30 December 1809 (AHM 1-14, CX 17). Note there was in fact a second arsenal at Porto which supplied some equipment and clothing.

16 Beresford to Wellington, 16 October 1809 (NA, WO 1/242).

17 The correspondence contains many references to the supply of items to Portugal for both the British and Portuguese armies. See John Trotter (Storekeeper's Office) to George Harrison (Colonial Office), 15 January 1810 (NA, FO 63/137) enclosing a statement of the stores required for the Portuguese forces, demanding 5,000 saddles, 5,000 saddlebags, 10,000 greatcoats, 10,000 suits of clothing, 10,000 caps and plumes, 40,000 pairs of half stockings, 40,000 knapsacks, 40,000 shirts and 20,000 blankets, and observing some to be shipped that day and others contracted for. On 6 February 1810 Richard Wellesley advised Stuart that 1,315 saddles, 10,000 greatcoats, 10,000 suits of clothing and 40,000 pairs of half stockings were being shipped on the *Achilles* for the Portuguese forces (NA, FO 342/11). Presumably this was part of the consignment referred to by Trotter. Because of the urgency to supply the Portuguese, Harrison advised Colonel Henry Bunbury, Under-Secretary at the War Office, on 16 January 1810 that they were disregarding the normal mode of contract by public tender (NA, FO 63/137). This correspondence shows shipments continuing through the spring and summer of 1810.

18 Ordem do Dia, 21 September 1809, no. 116.

19 Beresford to Forjaz, 21 November, 7 and 19 December 1809 (AHM 1-14, CX 17).

20 James Douglas to Arbuthnot, 22 April 1810 (TT, MNE CX 204). Colonel James Dawes Douglas (later Major General Sir James Dawes Douglas, 1785–1862) was one of the first officers to follow Beresford to the Peninsula. As a captain he had been in Buenos Aires in 1806 and in that capacity he volunteered to go with Beresford to Lisbon, availing of the two-step promotion which made him a Major in the British army and a Lieutenant Colonel in the Portuguese army. He commanded initially the 16th Regiment of Line, then the 8th Regiment, and later still the 7th Brigade in the Portuguese Division. Present at the crossing of the Douro in 1809, Buçaco 1810 – for which the Regiment received Wellington's praise – and most of the other major battles of the Peninsular War, including Toulouse, where he was badly wounded, losing a leg. Wellington held him in high regard: 'He is one of the best and most intelligent officers that I have seen.' Wellington to Torrens, 14 October 1814 (WD 7, 580).

21 Forjaz to Beresford, 27 March 1810 (AHM 1-14, CX 38).

22 Beresford to Forjaz, 23 April 1810 (AHM 1-14, CX 19).

23 Gomes da Silva to Forjaz, 25 September 1809 (AHM 1-14 CX 37) referred to in Vichness, op. cit., p. 302. Gregório Gomes da Silva was Conselheiro to Forjaz. The quality of clothing remained a problem for Colonel Campbell. Acknowledging receipt of uniforms for the 4th and 10th Portuguese line in July 1810 he stated to D'Urban on 1 July 1810, with regard to the consignment, that 'in the course of a week's wear it would all fall to pieces' (AHM-14-020-0027-30).

24 Wellington to Liverpool, 27 June 1810 (WD 4, 141).

25 'Regulations and Plan establishing the Manner of Proceeding to the Embargo of the Necessary Transports for the Portuguese and English Armies Services, 5 September 1809' (AHM 1-14, CX 194, No. 5). Note a further decree issued 16 November 1809 (ibid. CX 268, No. 27).

26 Cox to Beresford, 11 July 1810 (TT, MNE CX 204, f. 523). It is difficult to know why Cox emphasised a lack of greatcoats as in July temperatures regularly exceed 30° Centigrade in Almeida and do not normally fall below 15° at night. Giving him the benefit of the doubt and considerable optimism (which he did not normally display), he may have been looking ahead to winter.

27 William Stewart to D'Urban, 9 July 1810 (AHM 1-14-020-14-82/85).

28 Bunbury to Beresford, 26 April 1810 (TT, MNE CX 029 in Arquivo Municipal de Mafra).

29 Beresford to Forjaz, 12 July 1810 (AHM-14-020-14-0061/62/63). Note: Rosa's name is sometimes spelt Roza. There is substantial correspondence in AHM on the lack of all sorts of provisions and the delay in supplying them.

30 Forward depots were established at Abrantes, Coimbra, Figueira, Leiria, Santarém, and Sobreira Formosa in addition to the depot at Lisbon. Additional magazines were established at Almeida, Elvas and Valença de Castela.

31 Memorandum for an Arrangement for the Portuguese Commisary, 10 June 1809 (WD 4, 450). Notwithstanding these arrangements, there was still some friction and in 1810 Wellington wrote to Beresford on the topic when disputes arose between the respective commissaries, complaining the Portuguese commissaries were breaching the 'articles'. Wellington to Beresford, 22 April 1810 (TT, MNE CX 206, f. 248).

32 Wellington to Stuart, 5 March 1811 (WD 7, 342).

33 There are numerous references to a lack of provisions when on campaign in 1810 (TT, MNE CX 204, ff. 299, 320).

34 Beresford to Forjaz, 26 July 1810 (AHM 1-14-20-0117-0123).

35 Mathew O'Meara to Arbuthnot, 23 October 1809 (TT, MNE CX 204, f. 112).

36 Brigadier General Francis Coleman to Arbuthnot, 16 October 1809 (TT, MNE CX 204, ff. 67 and 71).

37 Alexander Gordon to Beresford, 21 April 1810 (TT, MNE CX 206, f. 228). Gordon wrote on Picton's behalf as the latter had an inflammation of the eyes. The Portuguese regiments with Picton were the 9th and 21st regiments of line.

38 Dickson to Major General Hamilton, 22 April 1810 (TT, MNE CX 206, f. 250).

39 D'Urban, 19 May (op cit., pp. 106–7).

40 Wellington to Beresford, 24 May 1810 (two letters) and 28 May 1810 (WD 4, 88).

41 Wellington to Beresford, 6 July 1810 (TT, MNE CX 204, f. 397).

42 Wellington to Beresford, 20 July 1810 (TT, MNE CX 204, ff. 665–668).

43 Picton to Wellington, 7 July 1810 (TT, MNE CX 204, ff. 434 and 438).

44 Coleman to Beresford, 30 November 1810 (TT, MNE CX 204). Coleman commanded the 6th Independent Portuguese brigade made up of the 7th and 19th regiments (two battalions each), and the 2nd Caçadores. This brigade played a notable role in the defence of the ridge at Buçaco.

45 Wellington to Liverpool, 14 November 1809 (NA WO 1/242). See Vichness, op. cit., pp. 282–3 for salary scales. See also Maria Cristina Moreira, 'Portuguese State Military Expenditure: British support of the Peninsular War efforts of the Erário Régio (Royal Treasury) from 1809 to 1811', in Stephen Conway and Rafael Torres Sánchez (eds), *The Spending of States, military expenditure during the long eighteenth century: patterns, organization, and consequences, 1650–1815* (Saarbrucken: VDM Verlag Dr. Müller GmbH & Co. KG, 2011).

46 Wellington to Forjaz, 5 January 1810 (AHM 1-14-11-04); Beresford to Forjaz, 1 May 1810 (AHM 1-14-19-1).

47 Fletcher to Beresford, 10 November 1809 (TT, MNE CX 207, f. 68), seeking inter alia 800 additional men. On 12 November he wrote again suggesting he had been given to understand that pay of half a dollar a day for a captain and a quarter a dollar for a subaltern in the militia would suffice. Wellington had, he said, asked him to give an opinion on the subject but he would not pay these sums without approval. He further stated that in England subalterns received four shillings for superintending a party of more than fifty men (ibid., f. 73).

48 Patton to Beresford, 9 December 1809 (TT, MNE CX 206, f. 70) citing earlier letters.

49 FO 342/26.

50 In 1808 Brazilian ports were opened to trading vessels of friendly foreign nations (Decree of Prince João, made at Bahia, 28 January 1808). This was followed by the Treaty of Commerce and Navigation between Great Britain and Portugal, 19 February 1810; Treaty between Great Britain and Portugal for the abolition of the slave trade north of the Equator, 19 February 1810; See Hertslet's *Commercial Treaties*, vol. II.

51 See de la Fuente, op. cit., pp. 153–60 which deals with Portuguese finances at some length. An estimated £675,000 was the subsidy for 20,000 troops in 1809. This was increased to £980,000 for 30,000 troops in 1810. Forjaz was quick to point out that the increased subsidy would not cover the cost of keeping 30,000 troops in the field, because it was based on the erroneous assumption that the earlier subsidies would cover the cost of 10,000 and 20,000 troops respectively. That for 20,000 troops was based on a calculation where regiments were incomplete, numbering only some 17,000 men, whereas they were represented at full strength. Furthermore, the Portuguese had understood that Britain was going to assume the entire cost of financing 10,000, then 20,000 men whereas Britain provided a fixed sum only. In recognition of the deficiency, the British Government paid a further £250,000 by way of Portuguese subsidy in 1810 and in 1811 the subsidy was increased to £2,000,000.

52 William Chartres to Lieutenant Colonel McDonald, McDonald to Coleman, Coleman to Arbuthnot, 24 October 1809 (TT, MNE CX 204, ff. 116, 118 and 120).

53 Lieutenant Colonel Arthur William Chichester Crookshank to Arbuthnot, 2 July 1810 (TT, MNE CX 204, f. 318). Crookshank was then serving with the 15th Line, but subsequently served with the 12th Caçadores.

54 Thus Wellington refused to let Lieutenant Newport transfer out of the 39th Regiment as he felt it was short of officers; Somerset to Arbuthnot, 13 May 1810 (TT, MNE CX 206, f. 131).

55 Captain Beresford to Arbuthnot, 4 and 15 April 1810 (TT, MNE CX 206, ff. 43 and 162). Captain Beresford obviously determined to remain in the British army for in 1812 he was promoted to Major in the 31st Regiment (*Royal Military Chronicle*, vol. IV, p. 337). It is unknown if this William was any relation to Marshal Beresford. The 2/31st (Huntingdonshire) was at Albuera, being part of Colborne's brigade in Stewart's 2nd Division. It also participated in many other Peninsular battles, including Orthes [*sic*] for which it was granted a battle honour.

56 Lieutenant Robert Robinson, see Challis's 'Peninsula Roll Call'. However, he is noted by Arbuthnot as resigning from the Portuguese service on 12 July 1810 (see below).

57 John Hill is shown as having remained with the 3rd Foot (Challis's 'Peninsula Roll Call').

58 Robert Arbuthnot to unidentified recipient, 12 July 1810 (TT, MNE CX 204, ff. 549–551). The officers were Captain White to be a Major in the 10th Cavalry, Captain Will Vance to be a Major in 10th Cavalry (not listed in the Challis index), Captain Peter Fearon to be a Major in the Loyal Lusitanian Legion (later 7th Caçadores), Lieutenant Thomas Monaghan to be a Captain in the 5th Caçadores, Lieutenant Will Cotton to be a Captain in the 9th Regiment (not identifiable from the Challis index), Lieutenant Wiliam Cheslyn to be a Captain in the 13th Regiment, Lieutenant Samuel Hawkins to be a Captain in the 6th Cavalry, and Ensign Campbell to be a Lieutenant in the 4th Regiment (possibly John Campbell who per the Challis index was with the 4th Portuguese cavalry).

59 8 November 1810 (TT, MNE CX 204, f. 949).

60 McGeachy to Arbuthnot, 10 April 1810 (TT, MNE CX 206, f. 118).

61 See Lieutenant Colonel Charles Sutton to Brigadier General Campbell, 1 November 1809 (TT, MNE CX 207, f. 11) suggesting that the senior Major of the Regiment Evelijno Pereira was unsuitable by

reason of age, bad eyesight and other incapacities and he therefore recommended Captain João Leandro de Macedo Valladar, being 'at once zealous, able and active and an officer from whom the regiment will derive the greatest advantage'. See also Cox to Beresford, 5 November 1809 (TT, MNE CX 207, ff. 31 and 96).

62 McGeachy to Beresford, 22 April 1810 (TT, MNE CX 206, f. 283).

63 McGeachy's widow, Sarah, received an annual pension of £300 from the Portuguese government until her own death in 1876; See James Brandow (ed.), *Genealogies of Barbados Families* (Baltimore: Genealogical Publishing Co., 2001).

64 Arbuthnot to Major General Hamilton, 29 November 1810 (TT, MNE CX 204, f. 979). Haviland Le Mesurier had served with the 21st Foot before being seconded to the 14th Portuguese regiment.

65 Abstract from General Return of the Portuguese army excluding cavalry, 17 December 1809 (TT, MNE CX 206, f. 147). On 16 December, Beresford had advised Forjaz that the training of troops was coming on well. See Forjaz to Beresford, 19 December 1809 (TT, MNE CX 206, f. 177).

66 D'Urban, *Journal*, p. 77.

67 Ibid. p. 78.

68 Ibid. p. 78. Wellington was so pleased that he made Lieutenant Colonel Campbell a Colonel on the staff.

69 Wellington to Liverpool, 4 January 1810 (NA, WO 1/243). Wellington was based at Tomar on 30 and 31 December 1809, Leiria on 1 January 1810, Pombal on 2 January, Coimbra 3–10 January. He set up his headquarters at Viseu on 12 January. While Beresford did not move his headquarters to Beira Alta until mid March it is clear that he and Wellington were in virtually daily contact with each other.

70 Rory Muir, *At Wellington's Right Hand: The Letters of Lieutenant-Colonel Sir Alexander Gordon, 1808–1815* (Stroud: Sutton for Army Records Society, 2003), p. 77.

71 Henry MacKinnon, *A Journal of the Campaign in Portugal and Spain, Containing Remarks on the Inhabitants, Customs, Trade and Cultivation of those Countries from the year 1809 to 1812* (London: Longman, Hurst, and Co., 1812). Colonel S**** may refer to Colonel Charles Sutton who commanded the 9th Portuguese (Vianna) regiment, one of the Portuguese regiments brigaded with British regiments in the 3rd Division.

72 Warre to father, 17 February 1810 (*Letters from the Peninsula*, p. 71). It was in fact the 20th Regiment that was sent to Cádiz.

73 Warre to father, 21 March 1810, ibid. p. 74.

74 Warre to his sister Emily, 9 May 1810, ibid. p. 80.

75 Picton to Beresford, 8 and 10 May 1810 (TT, MNE CX 206, ff. 79 and 105). José Champalimaud enjoyed a successful career in the Portuguese army becoming a Marshal in due course as well as Governor of Elvas.

76 Picton to Beresford, 15 July 1810 (TT, MNE CX 204); Halliday, op. cit., p. 339.

77 Wellington to Beresford, 10 and 30 May 1810 (TT, MNE CX 206, ff. 125 and 235). This regiment (Chaves) was not present at Buçaco.

78 Memorandum of the Marquess of Wellesley, June 1810 (WSD 6, 550–2).

79 Wellington Supplementary Dispatches, vol. 6, p. 477.

80 The three independent Portuguese brigades were each commanded by British officers, namely Brigadier Generals Denis Pack (1st, 16th and 4th caçadores), Alexander Campbell (6th, 18th and 6th caçadores) and Francis Coleman (7th, 19th and 2nd caçadores). Between them they mustered in excess of 8,000 men. Well in excess of 20,000 Portuguese troops (out of an Allied total of some 51,000) fought at Buçaco.

81 Two battalions of 20th Portuguese sent to Cádiz, numbering about 1,300 men. Wellington to Major General Stewart and Bart Frere, 9 February 1810 (WD 7, 728 and 729). See Ordem do Dia, 10 February

1810. The 20th Regiment was commanded by Manoel Pereira Campos and Major Richard Bushe until the latter was killed from injuries suffered at the battle of Barrosa (5 March 1811). The Anglo-Portuguese force was under the command of Major General William Stewart until he was superseded by Lt General Thomas Graham in March 1810. See also Wellington to Liverpool, 30 March 1810 (WD 5, 610).

82 Wellington to Villiers, 5 June 1810 (WD 4, 103–4).

Chapter 9

1   Napoleon announced his intention to assemble a massive force to subdue the Iberian Peninsula on 7 October 1809. Napoleon to Clarke, 7 October 1809; Joseph Bonaparte, *The Confidential Correspondence of Napoleon Bonaparte with his brother Joseph*, two volumes (London: John Murray, 1855), pp. 72–3.

2   Decree 17 April 1810 created the Armée de Portugal. Masséna left Paris on 29 April arriving in Spain a week later.

3   In late June, in response to the French investment of Ciudad Rodrigo, Wellington moved his headquarters briefly to Almeida, then Alverca before returning to Celorico. Meanwhile Beresford had moved his own headquarters to Trancoso where were stationed three Portuguese brigades.

4   Warre to father, 20 June 1810 (*Letters from the Peninsula*, p. 83).

5   The route through northern Portugal would have been extremely difficult in that following the retreat of Soult in May 1809 the French had lost control of Galicia and much of the Asturias.

6   Wellington directed Beresford to employ a small Portuguese force to guard the River Zezere, which combined with the garrison of Abrantes was intended to preserve communications with Hill in the south.

7   See Cox intercepts (TT, MNE CX 207, ff. 28–33 and 150). In September 1810, with Masséna inside Portugal, a group of doctors, lawyers, journalists and others deemed French supporters were shipped on the *Amazon* to Terceira in the Azores. Known as Setembrizados, they soon mixed with the local population and it is not surprising that later in the century liberal ideas found great support on the islands.

8   Marquess Wellesley to Villiers, 5 January 1810 (NA, FO 342/11). In fact, John Villiers' tenure of the position of British envoy ceased on 10 January 1810 when he was succeeded by Charles Stuart.

9   Wellington to Liverpool, 2 April 1810 (WD 3, 810).

10 Neves Costa had in fact been responsible for drawing up the plans in 1806. In 1808 an engineer, Colonel Charles Vincent serving in Junot's army, had presented the idea to Junot. In doing so he had been assisted by Neves Costa (see PRONI, D3030/2662/1, 'Translation of the Plan of Defensive Operations for the French army in Portugal', 28 June 1808, signed by Colonel Vincent). Junot did not act on the suggestion of building fortifications to the north of Lisbon. José Maria das Neves Costa (1774–1841) studied at the Academy of Fortification, Artillery and Design and subsequently the Naval Academy. An accomplished cartographer, he was appointed in 1802 as part of a team to study and make recommendations regarding the strong places on Portugal's frontiers. Promoted Major in the Royal Engineering Corps in 1807, he received instructions to triangulate the area between Lisbon and Peniche with particular reference to Cabo da Roca and Peniche. In March 1809 he submitted his report to Forjaz, a report seen later by Wellington, Beresford and Lieutenant Colonel Fletcher. Neves Costa rose to be a Brigadier and in 1823 was appointed Minister for War by the liberals, though he did not take up the position due to the return to power of the absolutists. For an account of his life and achievements see, Colonel José Custódio Madaleno Geraldo, 'José Maria Das Neves Costa e as Linhas de Torres Vedras' (José Maria das Neves

Costa and the Lines of Torres Vedras), *Revista Militar* (February/March 2015). Available at: https://www.revistamilitar.pt/artigo/530 (accessed 24 April 2018).

11   Captain Stephen Chapman to Lieutenant General Robert Morse, 22 March 1809 (NA, WO 55/958).

12   Wellington Memorandum to Lieutenant Colonel Fletcher, 20 October 1809 (WD 3, 556–60). Wellington was later dismissive of the impact of Neves Costa's plans on the Lines as ultimately built, but the correspondence of the engineers on the ground makes it clear that works to strengthen the defences around Lisbon were already being undertaken from the autumn of 1808 and were gathering pace in 1809 prior to Wellington writing his memorandum. All Wellington acknowledged was that Forjaz had given him a plan of the country and a Memoir by Neves Costa. He maintained, however, that both were so inaccurate that no reliance could be placed on them. Indeed he went further and said that in 1810 he had been obliged to destroy some of the works previously undertaken. See Wellington to Forjaz, 24 April 1812 (WD 9, 81).

13   The standard work on this topic is, Sir John T. Jones, *Journals of Sieges carried on by the Army under the Duke of Wellington in Spain*, three volumes (London: John Weale. 1846). See also, John, Grehan *The Lines of Torres Vedras: The Cornerstone of Wellington's Strategy in the Peninsular War, 1809–1812* (Staplehurst: Spellmount, 2000). The topic of the Lines of Torres Vedras is also well covered in Mark S. Thompson, *Wellington's Engineers: Military Engineering in the Peninsular War 1808–1814* (Barnsley: Pen and Sword Books, 2015).

14   D'Urban even expressed the view that the British could continue to hold Peniche following an evacuation of Portugal. He also viewed it as a possible site for embarkation of the British army (op. cit., p. 74).

15   Fletcher to Morse, 28 August 1809 (NA, WO 55/958) quoted in Thompson, *Wellington's Engineers*, p. 44.

16   Wellington to Stuart, 10 March 1810 (WD 3, 775).

17   Wellington to Beresford, 1 May 1810 (TT, MNE CX 206, f. 1; WD 4, 41).

18   Beresford to Anne Beresford, 13 June 1810 (Beresford family papers).

19   Warre to father, 10 July 1810 (*Letters from the Peninsula*, p. 93).

20   D'Urban, op. cit., pp. 87–8.

21   Beresford to Forjaz, 16 May 1810 (AHM 1-14-020-12, ff. 3, 4, 5); Beresford to Forjaz, 14 July 1810 (AHM 1-14-20-14, f. 76). The reference to a dictionary may relate to a simple signals code rather than any attempt to encrypt.

22   Warre to Eleanor Warre, his sister, 23 May 1810 (*Letters from the Peninsula*, p. 82).

23   D'Urban, op. cit., p. 93. The 1st and 2nd Chasseurs were ordered back to Coimbra where they received further training.

24   D'Urban, 1 and 10 April 1810, op. cit., pp. 95 and 97.

25   D'Urban, 10 April 1810, op. cit., p. 97. The Portuguese Division at Buçaco was commanded by Major General John Hamilton. While Spencer and Hill were both senior to Beresford, he would have been senior to Cole, Craufurd, Leith and Picton, though of course his early promotion as Lieutenant General in 1809 had caused friction in the British army which might have weighed against him.

26   Fort Concepción was subsequently abandoned and partly destroyed by mines during the French advance in July 1810, as Wellington then deemed it indefensible.

27   Beresford's headquarters on the square in Trancoso are still standing.

28   D'Urban 18 and 23 June 1810, op. cit., pp. 114 and 118.

29   Wellington to Stuart, 11 September 1810 (WD 4, 273).

30   John Wilson, Lieutenant Colonel in the Royal York Rangers and Brigadier General in the Portuguese army. Francisco da Silveira was the General in command of Trás-os-Montes with headquarters in

Braganza. His corps was intended as one of observation, working on the flanks of the invader. Manuel Pinto Bacelar was the General commanding Beira with his headquarters at Lamego.

31 D'Urban 11 and 15 July 1810, op. cit., pp. 125 and 127.

32 Craufurd had arrived too late to participate in the battle of Talavera, notwithstanding an impressive forced march from Lisbon with his troops. Subsequently, in August 1809, desperate for action, he had contacted Beresford to indicate his desire to participate in any move Beresford might make, and with a view to making himself available Craufurd moved from positions designated by Wellington, for which he incurred the Commander in Chief's ire. See Bathurst to Craufurd, 13 August 1809 (TT, MNE CX 204, f. 288), in which he was reminded of the importance for officers to obey orders strictly, and having obeyed them he should wait patiently for further orders. His attention was drawn to the orders given and that his actions had now put the detailed plan for the defence of Portugal in doubt. It is perhaps a reflection of Craufurd's high standing with Wellington that there were no further recriminations. The 1st and 3rd Caçadores conducted themselves well at the Côa, though the 1st Caçadores was criticised for its precipitous initial retirement. Alexander Gordon, one of Wellington's ADCs, wrote to his brother Lord Aberdeen criticising the caçadores; see Muir, *At Wellington's Right Hand*, pp. 98–100. Beresford commended their valour afterwards to Forjaz, citing in particular that their commander 'Lt Colonel Jorge d'Avillez was admired by all for his personal conduct.' Beresford to Forjaz, 31 July 1810 (AHM 1-14-020-149 and 150).

33 The 3rd Caçadores under Colonel Elder were reported to have performed very well and a number of officers were singled out for praise by a number of commentators. Wellington in his report to Liverpool referred to the steadiness of the 3rd Caçadores, 25 July 1810 (WD 4, 184). However, he was obviously concerned at the initial reports (including a letter from Beresford of 24 July) he received on the performance of the 1st Caçadores for Wellington initiated inquiries which enabled him to tell Beresford on 29 July that this battalion had not quit its post on the right of the Côa until ordered to do so, they had no orders to halt before the bridge, and they reformed thereafter. He concluded reports of their poor conduct were exaggerated and every report raised the opinion which he had formed of their commanding officer (WD 4, 192–3). Craufurd, in his report to Wellington of 25 July 1810, makes no specific mention of either caçadores regiment.

34 D'Urban, 6–7 August 1810, op. cit., p. 131.

35 Silveira was aided by a small Spanish force under General Taboada, who had previously been driven from the town by the French on 29 July. There was concern at Silveira's headquarters, and indeed amongst Wellington's staff, that the French move leading to the town's capture heralded a further invasion of northern Portugal, but the capture of Puebla de Sanabria by General Serras was never intended as more than a diversionary tactic and he had withdrawn from the town before Silveira and Taboada arrived there, leaving only a garrison of one battalion behind.

36 Colonel William Cox had served under Sir David Baird in the expedition to Egypt in 1801, so would presumably have been known to Beresford since at least that time. He served with Moore on the retreat to La Coruña and was appointed Brevet Lieutenant Colonel of the 16th Regiment of Foot in February 1809. On his arrival in Portugal to join the Portuguese army under Beresford, Cox was a made a Brigadier General in the Portuguese army, being sent to command the fortress of Almeida, a position he held from April 1809 until its surrender on 27 August 1810. He had hoped to be exchanged (indeed he told Beresford that he, Major Hewitt and Captain Foley of the 24th Regiment were to be allowed by Masséna to return to England – see Cox to Beresford, 30 August 1810; AHM 1-14-011-72), but remained a prisoner of France until the end of the war in 1814, being held in the fortress of Verdun; though he had sought to be allowed to go to Paris on parole. Returning to Portugal he was tried and acquitted at court

martial of misconduct at Almeida. He was appointed a Major General in Portugal in 1815, while in 1819 he rose to be a Brevet Colonel in the British service. He was knighted in 1816 (*Royal Military Calendar*, vol. 4, p. 249 and WD 4, 257-258).

37   In 1809 with the King's consent, Cox was appointed a Brigadier General in the Spanish army as well on condition that he would continue to serve in Portugal. This was perhaps a reward for his having acted as an intelligence officer in Spain (both at Sevilla and Cádiz) in 1808. Torrens to Lieutenant Colonel Bunbury, 9 November 1809, and Torrens to Wellington, 14 November 1809 (TT, MNE CX 207, ff. 64 and 88).

38   As late as 17 July 1810, Cox reported having to send a sergeant and twelve men to Porto to collect money for the payment of the troops, noting that he did not expect them to return before the commencement of the siege. At the same time he sent another sergeant and ten men to Peniche with French prisoners, bemoaning the fact that he could well do without the loss of these men. Cox to Beresford, 17 July 1810 (TT, MNE CX 204, ff. 615 and 616).

39   Cox to Beresford, 1 July 1810 (TT, MNE CX 204, ff. 299 and 306).

40   Cox to Beresford, 18 July 1810 (ibid. f. 624).

41   Cox to Beresford, 8 July 1810 (ibid. f. 458).

42   Cox to Beresford, 21 July 1810 (ibid. f. 699).

43   Cox to Beresford, 4 July 1810 (ibid. f. 344).

44   Cox to Beresford, 9 July 1810 (ibid. f. 499).

45   Wellington to Beresford, 20 July 1810 (ibid. ff. 665–668), refers to the returns from Almeida, the dramatic reduction of biscuit in store, the fact that he cannot say what will be drawn from Almeida as it depends on ability to obtain supplies from other quarters, ending with the statement that if 'we cannot get provisions or carriages we must conserve the provisions which we have in store'.

46   Wellington to Beresford, 8 July 1810 (ibid. f. 448).

47   Wellington to Beresford, 21 July 1810 (ibid. f. 708).

48   Wellington to Beresford, 22 July 1810 (ibid. f. 726) enclosing yet another letter from Cox.

49   Beresford to Cox, 24 July 1810 (ibid. f. 746).

50   See, for example, Cox to Lord Liverpool, 27 November 1810 (TT, MNE CX 204, f. 831).

51   There are a number of French accounts, including those by Jean Jacques Pelet in 'Campagne de Portugal' and Jacques-Louis Hulot 'Souvenirs'. Of course, they suffer from the fact that they were not present within the fortress at the time of the explosion, but were presumably dependent on those of the garrison whom they subsequently talked to. See *The French Campaign in Portugal 1810–1811, An Account by Jean Jacques Pelet*, Edited, translated and annotated by Donald D. Horward (Minnesota: University of Minnesota Press, 1973). Soriano records a similar account in his *História da Guerra Civil* which it is claimed came from an eyewitness, João de Sousa Moreira (2 epoca, vol. III, p. 73, fn. 1).

52   Cox to Liverpool, 27 November 1810 (TT, MNE CX 204, f. 831).

53   Colonel Emmanuel Frederic Sprunglin, *Souvenirs*, pp. 444–5, quoted in Oman, *History*, vol. III, p. 273. Sprunglin was an ADC to Masséna.

54   Cox to Beresford, 30 August 1810 (letter enclosed with Beresford to Wellington, 4 September 1810; WD 4, 257–8) describes the cataclysmic events of the evening of 26 August leading to the surrender of Almeida. The inventory of the remaining ammunition and powder revealed some made up cartridges in the expense magazines and thirty-nine barrels of powder which had been deposited in the laboratory.

55   Jean Jacques Germain Pelet-Clozeau (1777–1858) was Aide-de-Camp to Masséna during the campaign of 1810–11; a close confidant trusted by Masséna who relied on his advice.

56 Pedro de Almeida, 3rd Marquis d'Alorna. Having fought against the French in the War of Roussillon 1793–4, d'Alorna espoused the cause of Napoleon. He subsequently commanded a corps of light infantry and cavalry (Legião de Tropas Ligeiras), which formed the backbone of the Portuguese Legion formed after the First French invasion of Portugal in 1807, and commanded that Legion in the French service. In April 1810 he was assigned to the staff of Masséna and accompanied him on the Third French invasion of Portugal. Died at Königsberg in 1813 during Napoleon's retreat from Moscow.

General Manuel Pamplona, subsequently 1st Count of Subserra, was an officer in the Portuguese army and a mason. A friend of d'Alorna, Pamplona also participated in the Roussillon campaign. Colonel of the 9th Cavalry Regiment at the time of Junot's invasion, he too joined the Portuguese Legion on the disbanding of the Portuguese army. He survived the retreat from Moscow, and remained in France following the restoration of the Bourbons until amnestied in 1821. Returning to Portugal he served in several governments before being imprisoned by Dom Manuel and dying in the fort at Elvas in 1832.

57 Cox to Liverpool, 27 November 1810 (TT, MNE CX 204, f. 831) claimed that Masséna informed him that Barreiros had given him perfect information of the state of the place, told him exactly the quantity of ammunition which remained after the explosion, and directed his fire to the spot where it was deposited; Captain Pedro de Melo, who had been sent out with Barreiros to negotiate with the French, returned to Almeida following negotiations. Barreiros was rewarded by the French by being made a colonel in the French army.

58 Donald D. Horward, *Napoleon and Iberia: The twin sieges of Ciudad Rodrigo and Almeida, 1810* (Tallahassee: University Presses of Florida, 1984), ff. 306.

59 Beresford to Wellington, 4 September 1810 (AHM 1-14-011-72). See also Ordem do Dia, 6 September 1810.

60 Wellington to Stuart, 11 September 1810 (WD 4, 273). The 24th Regiment was to make considerable amends for this episode when, under the command of Silveira, it halted General Gardanne and reinforcements reaching Masséna in November 1810 (D'Urban, *Journal* 25 November 1810, p. 165).

61 Wellington to Liverpool, 27 June and 11 July 1810 (WD 4, 140 and 161). There are many other references to his decision communicated to British and Spanish commanders, based on an assessment that he did not wish to meet Masséna in the open given the unfavourable odds.

62 D'Urban, *Journal* 27 August 1810, p. 135.

63 Cox to Beresford, 30 August 1810 (WD 4, 258).

64 Along with Cox, Major Isaac Henry Hewitt (24th Portuguese Regiment), and Captain John Foley (7th Portuguese Regiment) were sent to Verdun; See Steve Brown, 'Register of British Officer Prisoners held at Verdun 1804–1813' (*The Napoleon Series*, March 2013) and taken from a list kept by POW John Hopkinson. Available at: https://www.napoleon-series.org/military/organization/Britain/ Miscellaneous/c_POWsatVerdun.html (accessed 24 April 2018).

65 Mascarenhas was in fact captured by ordenença while carrying a report on the battle of Buçaco from Masséna. Sent to Lisbon he was executed on 22 December 1810 following trial. Wellington thought it a mistake to execute him, though the Portuguese were entitled to do so for spying. His suggestion was that if convicted he should be sent to Brazil for Prince João to deal with. Wellington to Liverpool, 8, 10 and 12 November 1810 (WD 4, 404, 407 and 416), and 14 February 1811 to Stuart (ibid. 598). Cox's evidence regarding Costa e Almeida was to the effect that while the Governor had acted with zeal prior to the siege, he had locked himself up following the explosion and then moved to counteract Cox's wishes to hold out; Beresford to Wellington, 4 September 1810 (AHM-14-011-72).

66 Wellington to Stuart, 18 September 1810 (WD 4, 289).

67 Wellington had an alternative point prior to the Lines at which he proposed to confront Masséna if the latter avoided the Serra de Buçaco. This was Coimbra. See Wellington to Stuart, 26 September 1810 (WD 4, 300).

68 William Grattan, *Adventures with the Connaught Rangers from 1808 to 1814* (London: H. Colburn, 1847), p. 37.

69 The 8th Regiment praised by Wellington was one which at the commencement of the year he had dismissed as one which would be of no use in the current campaign. Wellington to Beresford, 23 January 1810 (WD 3, 692).

70 Wellington to Liverpool, 30 September 1810 (WD 4, 304–8 at 307).

71 Wellington to William Wellesley-Pole, 4 October 1810 (WSD 6, 606–7).

72 Ordem do Dia, 28 September 1810.

73 Wellington reported 1,269 killed, wounded or missing of which some 620 were Portuguese (WD 4, 308). The performance of the 8th Portuguese regiment under Lieutenant Colonel James Douglas was regarded as somewhat mixed; its bravery in assisting the British repulse Reynier's second assault was remarked on. Later, however, the 8th and 9th Portuguese were broken by Foy's assault (Reynier's third attempt) when vastly outnumbered, though they did reform. The French, who had hitherto been contemptuous of the Portuguese troops, began to revise that opinion with Pelet observing 'the Portuguese were interspersed with the British; they acted perfectly, serving in the covered positions' (Pelet, op. cit., p. 181).

74 D'Urban in his *Journal* makes it clear there was close contact between Wellington and Beresford, ff. 145. The order for release of imprisoned soldiers is Ordem do Dia, 28 September 1810, pp. 109–11.

75 Wellington to Liverpool, 30 September 1810 (WD 4, 303–4).

76 Page, op. cit., p. 93.

77 Blunt to Beresford, 9 October 1810 (TT, MNE CX 048, found in Arquivo Municipal de Mafra).

78 Masséna's army had to stop repeatedly to allow food wagons to catch up. Thus he delayed three days at Viseu, giving Wellington additional time both to collect his troops and to encourage the inhabitants to flee having destroyed goods and structures. Pelet, op. cit., p. 169.

79 *Le Moniteur Universel* and *Journal de Paris*, 11 December 1810.

80 Lieutenant Colonel Joseph Anderson, *Recollections of a Peninsular Veteran* (London: Edward Arnold, 1913), pp. 41, 45.

81 Berkeley to Bathurst, 10 October 1810 (Historical Manuscripts Commission, *Report on the Manuscripts of Earl Bathurst*, pp. 150–1).

82 General Orders (GO), 3 October 1810 (WD 4, 311. See also GO; 1810, 172–5).

83 D'Urban, op. cit., 17 September 1810, p. 143.

84 *Mémoires de Massena*, 8 October 1810, Tome 7, p. 220.

85 D'Urban, op. cit., 8 October 1810, p. 155. The influx of evacuees placed severe pressure on the Lisbon hospitals, as a result of which Forjaz advised Beresford on 6 October 1810 that he was establishing an additional hospital in the convent at Mafra (TT, MNE CX 038, copy in Arquivo Municipal de Mafra).

86 Wellington to Stuart, 9 September 1810 (WD IV, 270).

87 In fact while the Principal opposed the scorched earth policy demanded by Wellington, it was not overtly opposed by the Patriarch. See Wellington to the Prince Regent of Portugal, 30 November 1810 (WD 4, 439–42).

88 The Sousa faction in both Rio de Janeiro and Lisbon pressed hard for Forjaz's dismissal, suggesting that he and Stuart were more intent on promoting British power than the interests of Portugal and Prince João. Wellington, who had earlier sought Forjaz's resignation, had by 1810 come to realise that he was the most able of the Portuguese Ministers, and the British commander now sought the removal of Principal

Sousa. The Prince Regent countered with a suggestion that both Principal Sousa and Forjaz should step down. Ultimately, Prince João did agree to the removal of Principal Sousa from office but Wellington chose not to seek the enforcement of that decision, believing that it might cause more trouble than good and end up making a martyr of Sousa. Forjaz did seek to resign in 1811 but his position was secure when Prince João indicated Forjaz was completely restored to royal favour. Following the defeat of the third French invasion, the lessening of tensions within the Regency meant it was possible for both Sousa and Forjaz to continue in office. See de la Fuente, op. cit., pp. 87–106.

89   Frederick William, Duke of Brunswick (1762–1815). Bitter opponent of Napoleon who fled to England after Battle of Wagram. His sister Caroline was unhappily married to the Prince Regent, later George IV. He was killed at the Battle of Quatre Bras, 16 June 1815.

90   Beresford to Wellington, 11 August 1810 (AHM-14-011-65-09). Amongst those named were Lt Col. Felix Alvares de Andrade, the 2nd Marquis of Sabugosa, who Beresford said had continually declined to serve; Brigadier Rosa, whose performance at court martials was called into question, suggesting that at such events there was a tacit agreement between officers not to punish each other; and Lieutenant Colonel Louis Machado de Readores of the 16th Regiment, who Beresford felt had done nothing further to merit promotion other than win Wellington's praise for his actions at Grijó in 1809 (for which he had already been promoted) being subsequently absent from his regiment due to ill health. The unsuitability of other promotions were referred to collectively by ranks in Beresford's letter but he attached for Wellington a copy of the list emanating from the Court at Rio de Janeiro which is at ff. 029 and 030. Beresford was also upset that promotions he had recommended in June 1809 had not yet been confirmed as of July 1810. See Beresford to Forjaz, 4 July 1810 (AHM 1-14-020-14-0002).

91   In supporting Beresford, Wellington suggested that where possible Portuguese rather than British officers should now be promoted, though if the effect of a Portuguese promotion would place a Portuguese over a British officer previously the senior of the Portuguese Wellington suggested both should be promoted to preserve the hierarchical status quo. Wellington to Beresford 12 February 1811 (WD 4, 594. See also WD 4, 225).

92   From 1809 until 1812 the Royal Navy squadron in the Tagus was commanded by Admiral George Berkeley. He left an undated account, 'The role of the Royal Navy in the Peninsular War' (National Maritime Museum, Greenwich AGC/B/3), which shows the extensive role it played in guarding Wellington's right flank when the allied armies occupied the lines of Torres Vedras. The Royal Navy used battery ships and gunboats to patrol the river and was responsible for securing Portuguese vessels on the river to positions behind the lines. In addition it conveyed Fane and later Hill's troops across the Tagus to the left bank, before transporting Romana's army there on 7 January 1811 in the first leg of its return to Extremadura. However, in early 1810 Wellington was far more concerned about the possibility of having to re-embark the British and possibly a large part of the Portuguese army in the face of overwhelming French superiority on land. To this end he sought and obtained some 45,000 tons of transports and calculated that with this tonnage and the ships of the line present he could evacuate the British army and those of the Portuguese who wished to leave, but would not be able to embark the Spaniards with the army. See Wellington to Liverpool, 31 January 1810 and Wellington to Stuart, 10 March 1810 (WD 3, 722–3 and 773–6).

The Regency for its part viewed the presence of this fleet with alarm, worried that the British would depart leaving the Portuguese to face the wrath of the French invader. To counter this prospect Principal Sousa even suggested the British fleet should quit the Tagus, a stratagem designed to ensure there was no general embarkation.

93   Wellington to Stuart, 9 September 1810 (WD 4, 270). It had been intended to use the regiments to garrison Setúbal and Palmela.

94 The masons were first lodged in the tower at Belém before being conveyed to the Azores. Note there were rumours of Beresford's contacts with the masons in South America during his time there. José San Martin, one of South America's liberators, served for a while with the Spanish army and was present at the battle of Albuera with Beresford. The Viscountess Juromenha, mother of a number of Beresford's children was also reportedly admitted to the Freemasons, primarily with a view to try to influence Beresford. Gomes Freire de Andrade became Grand Master of the Portuguese Freemasons (Grande Oriente Lusitano) in 1815, and was executed two years later for his alleged involvement in a plot against the Regency, though Beresford thought it was a mistake to execute him. Gomes Freire de Andrade had supported France in the Napoleonic wars. There is no suggestion that Beresford was a mason, though it is the case that a number of members of the family were such, and his grandfather, the Earl of Tyrone, had been Grand Master in Ireland. As a young man Wellington had been a mason, though he let his membership lapse. Freemasonry presented both men with a contradiction in that many British regiments had associations with masonic lodges, whereas in Portugal it was associated with French ideas of liberalism. However, when British masons paraded from the citadel to the British Factory in Lisbon at Christmas 1809, resulting in protests from the Catholic Church and government, Wellington ordered that such manifestations should cease while the British army was in Portugal. Wellington to Colonel Peacocke (Commandant of Lisbon), 4 January 1810 (WD 3, 675).

95 Beresford to Stuart, 6 October 1810 (Beresford family papers).

96 Wellington was not taking any chances and was prepared to evacuate Portugal if necessary. By mid June baggage was being loaded on board some vessels which had been allocated to individual regiments, such as the *Arethusa* and another being allocated to the 71st Regiment. See John Vandeleur to his mother, 1 November 1810; John Vandeleur, Andrew Bamford (ed.), *With Wellington's Outposts: The Peninsular and Waterloo Letters of John Vandeleur* (Barnsley: Frontline, 2015).

97 D'Urban, op. cit., 6 October 1810, p. 154. In which he stated of the Principal and Patriarch 'These wretches are beyond belief.'

98 Wellington to Stuart, 25 October 1810 (WD 4, 354).

99 Wellington to Stuart, 26 October 1810 (WD 4, 357).

100 Wellington to Stuart, 6 October 1810 (WD 4, 320). See also 99, 379 and 382.

101 Linhares to Wellington, 11 February 1811 (quoted in Oman, *History*, vol. III, p. 418) received in April. Of course Linhares, who was Chief Minister in Brazil, was also the Principal's brother.

102 Wellington to Prince João, 7 May 1811 (AHM, 1-14, CX 186). For a full account of the difficulties between the Regency of the one part and Wellington, Beresford and Forjaz of the other part, see de la Fuente, op. cit., Chapter IV.

103 Some forty boats were reportedly still at Santarém when the French occupied that town. On 16 October, Admiral Berkeley was ordered to use gunboats to secure the islands of Lyceria and Alhandra in the Tagus but to Wellington's irritation he found on 28 October there were still cattle on the island of Lyceria, which became a target for French raiding parties. Nevertheless, Allied control of the river was maintained throughout the winter (WD 4, 309).

104 These were the divisions commanded by Charles O'Donnell and Martín La Carrera. D'Urban refers to them as 'altogether undisciplined', op. cit., 2 November 1810, p. 161.

105 Wellington to Vice Admiral G. Berkeley, 3 October 1810 (WD 4, 312).

106 Wellington to Henry Wellesley, 3 October 1810 (WD 4, 313).

107 There is a suggestion that Abbe José Bernardino Silveira had told the French at Viseu on 23 September 1810 of the existence of the fortifications surrounding Lisbon but the significance of this information

was not then realised. Pelet suggests that the French became aware of the Lines on 7 October but were not at that stage unduly concerned; Pelet, op. cit., p. 222.

108   See Anderson, *Recollections*, p. 45.

109   Wellington to Liverpool, 13 October 1810 (WD 4, 331).

110   Maurice Girod de l'Ain, *Vie Militaire du Général Foy* (Paris: E. Plon, Nourrit et cie., 1900), p. 343.

111   Trant had arrived in the neighbourhood of Coimbra on 6 October, anticipating that he would be joined by further Portuguese levies under Miller and Wilson so that they could make a combined attack on the city. When they were not forthcoming he determined to move himself, and in a surprise attack on 7 October captured the town together with some eighty French officers and a reported 4,000–5,000 men. These surrendered 'at discretion' but on the basis that Trant would protect them from the Portuguese. Protection proved difficult when the destruction wrought by the French became evident. The Bishop of Coimbra claimed the French soldiers had killed 3,000 people and torched some 1,100 homes, but this report is likely exaggerated. However, feelings were running high on the city's recovery and Trant decided to move the prisoners to Porto without delay. Against this background the small number of French deaths (6–8 according to Portuguese sources) is a remarkable testament to the discipline of Trant's troops. Trant also recovered about 3,500 firelocks which were distributed to the ordenanca, 53 horse, 60 oxen as well as 200 sheep. The latter were returned to their owners, but the horses were sold and in a humane touch, which Beresford pointed out was contrary to orders, part of the proceeds given to the impecunious brother of a Portuguese sergeant killed in the fighting; the balance being deposited for safekeeping with the Dean of Porto cathedral. See Trant to Arbuthnot, 20 November 1810 (2 letters, TT, MNE 204). For a good account of the alleged massacre at Coimbra see, General Rui Moura, 'Um erro repetido mil vezes torna-se "realidade" O "massacre" de Coimbra, 7 de Outubro de 1810', *XX Colóquio de História Militar* (18 November 2011).

112   *Gazeta de Lisboa* issues 253 and 255, 22 and 24 October 1810 (reproduced by Hathi Trust). See also Trant to Beresford, 7 October 1810 (WD 4, 345–6).

113   Trant to Beresford, 7 October 1810 (WD 4, 345–6). The prisoners included some eighty officers, most of which were shipped north to Porto for onward transmission to England.

114   Peniche was commanded by Lieutenant Colonel Blunt. His detachments also took a considerable number of French prisoners, principally from foraging parties. See Wellington to Liverpool, 20 October 1810 (WD 4, 345–7).

115   D'Alorna to Masséna, 14 August 1810 (Archives de Masséna, Carton C7 20, LVI 327–28) quoted in Horward, *Napoleon and Iberia*, p. 253.

116   Ibid. p. 256.

117   Beresford's patent is dated 16 October 1810, so the King must have determined the appointment immediately on hearing from Wellington after the battle of Buçaco, if not beforehand. Wellington had been appointed on 28 August 1804.

118   Wellington to Beresford, 3 November 1810 (WD 4, 387).

119   2/24th, commanded by Colonel Lord Blantyre was in the 2nd Brigade of the 1st Division under Major General Brent Spencer at Buçaco.

120   Anderson, *Recollections*, pp. 48–9.

121   Ibid. p. 50. Wellington apparently paid for the dinner himself: Wellington to Stuart, 12 August 1811 (WD 5, 212).

122   Anderson, *Recollections*, p. 52. It does seem slightly puzzling that they were permitted to go to the theatre in Santarém given the aversion commanders would have had to letting enemies see their defences, a reason used on occasions for refusing or delaying the release of a prisoner being exchanged. Perhaps just

as surprising in the twenty-first century is the fact that coffee and other luxuries were traded through the lines. See Wellington to Stuart, 6 February 1811 (WD 4, 583).

123   GO, 20 January 1814 (WD 7, 277).

124   Samuel Daniel Broughton, *Letters from Portugal, Spain and France written during the campaigns of 1812, 1813 and 1814* (London: Longman, Hurst, Rees, Orme and Brown, 1815), p. 80.

125   Created Conde de Trancoso 13 May 1811. The Prince Regent was of course acting in the name of his mother, Maria I.

126   Wellington sent some of Congreve's rockets with Fane, though he confessed he had never seen them used and their deployment was clearly experimental. Wellington to Berkeley, 1 and 3 November 1810 (WD 4, 381, 387, 402 and 411). The intention was to use the rockets to destroy the French depot and boats at Santarém. Captain (later Sir John) Poo Beresford was carrying them on the *Poictiers*, a 74-gun ship of the line.

127   D'Urban, op. cit., 23 December 1810, p. 170.

128   Hill's illness had been reported to Wellington on 1 December when Major General W. Stewart temporarily assumed command of the 2nd Division. See Wellington to Stewart, 2 December 1810 (WD 4, 447). See also Wellington to Beresford, 25 December 1810 (WD 4, 477). Hill's fever may have been malaria complicated by jaundice. See, Joanna Hill, *Wellington's Right Hand Man* (Stroud: The History Press, 2011), pp. 79–80.

129   Wellington to Hill, 30 December 1810 (WD 4, 486). On 8 January 1811 Wellington suggested to Hill he move to Cintra for the air (WD 4, 509).

130   These raids included attempts to seize cattle on the the Isla dos Ingleses, Lyceria (Mouchão da Póvoa) and Ilha da Boavista. See Wellington to Beresford, 24 February 1811 (WD 4, 634). D'Urban in his *Journal* also makes reference to these raids (pp. 183–4). See also, André Masséna and Général Koch (ed.) *Mémoires d'André Masséna, Duc de Rivoli, Prince d'Essling, Maréchal d'Empire* (Paris; Jean de Bonnot, 1966), p. 169 which recites a raid on Boavista in February 1811 involving Captain Parmentier and thirty soldiers of the 47th Regiment where they discovered a huge amount of grain, pigs, cattle and even horses before they were driven off by a superior force.

131   D'Urban, op. cit., 6 January 1811, p. 173.

132   Forjaz to Beresford, 19 March 1811 (TT, MNE CX 065, copy in Arquivo Municipal de Mafra) in response to a series of requests by Beresford on army supply. Forjaz said he had made representations to government but it was impossible to furnish all the provisions requested. The letter is apologetic and Beresford's achievement in keeping the army together needs to be seen in the light of regular shortages.

133   Olivença surrendered on 23 January.

134   Wellington to Stuart, 23 January 1811 (WD 4, 544–6). The practice of seizure by the Portuguese government was a continuous irritant to Wellington, notwithstanding all his and Beresford's efforts to ensure that agreed arrangements covering procurement and payment were adhered to. On 14 May 1810 Wellington had written to Beresford to complain about the Portuguese practice in and around Guimarães, stating the result was that the British commisaries could get nothing (WD 4, 66).

135   Wellington to Stuart, 25 January, 1811 (WD 4, 551).

136   Wellington to Beresford, 25 January 1811 (WD 4, 552).

137   Wellington to Charles Stuart, 26 February 1811 (WD 4, 637).

138   Letters between Forjaz and Beresford, 8, 12 and 16 March 1811 (TT, MNE 062–064, copies in Arquivo Municipal de Mafra).

139   Wellington to Beresford, 26 January 1811 (WD 4, 553).

140   For instance, Wellington to Beresford, 22 May 1810 (WD 4, 84).

141 Lieutenant General Jean-Baptiste Drouet, Comte d'Erlon (1765–1844) had a distinguished record in the Peninsula, and during the French retreat of 1813 his corps defeated General Rowland Hill's divisions at the Maya Pass. Served again with Napoleon during the Hundred Days in 1815.

142 Wellington to Beresford, 31 December 1810 (WD 4, 487).

143 Wellington to Beresford, 12 January 1811 (WD 4, 515–17).

144 Romana died on 23 January 1811. Wellington had expressed confidence to his brother Henry as early as 13 December 1810 that he could do without the Spanish divisions (WD 4, 458). He turned down a request to furnish British officers to train a Spanish Legion being raised by Colonel Downie in the same month. Wellington to Liverpool, 15 December 1810 (WD 4, 461–2).

145 Wellington to Mendizabal, 30 January 1811 (WD 4, 565). See also Wellington to Beresford, 12 February 1811 (WD 4, 594–5).

146 Wellington to Beresford, 9 March 1811 (WD 4, 661). In fact Wellington also decided at this time to hold Hoghton's brigade and some of Beresford's Portuguese troops at Tomar in case of need.

147 David Gates, *The Spanish Ulcer: A History of the Peninsular War* (New York: W. W. Norton, 1986), p. 225.

148 Pierre Guingret, *Relation historique et militaire de la campagne de Portugal sous le Maréchal Masséna, Prince d'Essling* (Paris: Chez Bargeas, 1817), pp. 123–6. Guingret served with the 6eme Légère.

149 The United Kingdom parliament in 1811 voted a sum not to exceed £100,000. On foot of this resolution a parliamentary committee visited Portugal gathering information, pursuant to which grants were made. 'Report of the Committee Appointed to Direct the Distribution of the Grant voted by Parliament of the United Kingdom for the relief of the Inhabitants of the Districts of Portugal, Laid Waste by the enemy in 1810' (Lisbon: Na Impressão Regia, 1813). In addition, the wife of the Lord Mayor of London together with a number of ladies collected for a fund to give relief to women and orphans, a development which was highlighted in the *Gazeta de Lisboa* of 4 July 1811 (Noticias de Londres de 12 de Junho).

150 The Philanthropic Society established a fund. On 24 April 1811, the Society held a meeting in the City of London with John Whitmore in the chair, and appointed a committee made up of both Portuguese and British persons. The list of subscribers as of 3 May 1811 is impressive, with over 1,000 listed having raised in excess of £20,000. Subscribers included A.T. Sampayo (a supplier to the British army in Portugal)–£300, The Portuguese Ambassador–£200, Brigadier T. Mazzaredo (Spanish)–£100, John N. Vizeu–£315, Spencer Perceval (Prime Minister)–£100, General W. Picton–£100, Ship Builders of the Port of London–£525 and George Canning–£50. *Subscription for the Relief of the Unfortunate Sufferers in Portugal, who have been plundered and treated by the French armies with the most unexampled Savage Barbarity* (London: The Philanthropic Society, 1811).

151 Forjaz to Beresford, 19 April 1811 (AHM, 1-14-012).

152 Masséna, *Mémoires*, p. 95.

Chapter 10

1 General Sir Galbraith Lowry Cole (1772–1842). Son of the Earl of Enniskillen, he joined the army in 1787 and was a career soldier, serving in Egypt and then Italy before being promoted to command the 4th Division in Portugal in 1810. He served at Albuera, Salamanca and the battles leading to and during the invasion of France in 1813–14.

2 Wellington to Major General William Stewart, 29 December 1810, and Wellington to Hill, 30 December 1810 (WD 4, 483 and 485).

3 Wellington to Berkeley, 16 October 1810 (WD 4, 331).

4   Wellington to Stuart, 16 January 1811 (WD 7, 147–9). Masséna in his *Mémoires* indicated that his intention had been to bridge the Tagus and get into the Alentejo with a view to feeding his army (vol. 7, pp. 249–50).

5   Wellington to Beresford, 10 January 1811 (WD 4, 651).

6   The Spanish army at Gebora was defeated by a much smaller French force under Marshal Mortier. The Spanish army was that previously brought to help defend Lisbon by General Romana. It had been sent back to help meet the French threat in Extremadura, though Romana had died shortly before its departure from Lisbon. Serving with it was Madden's Portuguese cavalry. Madden expressed his unhappiness with the conduct of the Spanish in his correspondence with Beresford (TT, MNE CX 207, ff. 254 and 259) and show that in January 1811 Madden wished to withdraw his troops from the Spanish army but Beresford indicated that he must stay and strive to influence and conciliate as much as possible.

7   Wellington to Beresford, 5 March 1811 (WD 4, 651).

8   Wellington to Beresford, 7 and 8 March 1811 (WD 4, 656 and 662).

9   Wellington informed Beresford of Long's appointment to command the cavalry on 8 March. Wellington to Beresford, 8 March 1809 (WD 4, 659).

10   General Castaños had been appointed to command the Army of Extremadura subsequent to the death of Romana in January 1811, but he had not reached that army prior to the Battle of Gebora. Castaños was also appointed Captain-General of the Army of Galicia. He got on well with both Wellington and Beresford. Long, however, felt Castaños 'to be a perfect old woman, whose sole occupation is powdering his hair, and patrolling about his country with a suite of servants and soldiers from 50 to 60 in number, at which the common people gaze with admiration and cry out "Viva"'.

See T.H. McGuffie (ed.), *Peninsular Cavalry General 1811–1813: The Correspondence of Lieutenant-General Robert Ballard Long* (London: George G. Harrap & Co., 1951), p. 96. The English press was rather more impressed by Castaños' modesty and the fact that he praised the 'cool and steady conduct' of the British and their allies. His account of the battle of Albuera tallied with that of Beresford. See *The European Magazine and London Review*, vol. 59, and 'Extract from a Despatch of Castaños', 19 May 1811 in Cobbett's *Political Register*, vol. 19, p. 1,501.

11   Wellington to Beresford, 8 March 1811 (BL, Add MS 36,306).

12   Wellington to Beresford, 9 March 1811 (BL, Add MS 36,306). It is clear Beresford did join Wellington; see Wellington to Liverpool, 14 March 1811 (WD 7, 348). The request to join came when Wellington was at Perucha, north of Tomar. Beresford may have accompanied him as far north as Ceira, just south of Coimbra.

13   On 9 March, the Commander of Badajoz, General Imaz, had been informed by telegraph from Elvas that Beresford's relief force was on its way. When discussions with his own lieutenants took place on 10 March following the creation of a practical breach in the wall, Imaz did not disclose that a relief force had been despatched by Wellington. The fortress surrendered on 11 March with over 7,000 Spanish troops becoming prisoners and Soult securing a fortress which it would take a year and three sieges to recover.

14   Wellington to Liverpool, 14 March 1811, and Wellington to Marquis of Wellesley, 16 March 1811 (WD 7, 349 and 356).

15   Wellington to Marquis Wellesley, 16 March 1811 (WD 5, 674 and 686).

16   Mortier returned shortly afterwards to Paris where he became involved in the planned invasion of Russia. He did not participate in the Battle of Albuera.

17   A strong defence of the town was mounted in the circumstances, given its condition and lack of equipment. It was commanded by Major José Talaya with only 800 Portuguese militia and fifty old

cannon. Jones, in *Journals of Sieges* (vol. I, p. 1), felt that to mount an efficient defence of Campo Maior would have required a garrison of 5,000 men.

18   Belmas states that the Anglo-Portuguese army were visible on the Portalegre road at 10 am on the morning of 25 March, at which time the remainder of the artillery being sent to Badajoz was half a league down the road to that fortress, guarded by the 100th Regiment of infantry commanded by Colonel Quiot and protected by La Tour-Maubourg's cavalry. J. Belmas (ed.), *Journaux des Siéges faits ou soutenus par les Français dans la Péninsule de 1807 a 1814*, four volumes (Paris: Chez Firmin Didot Fréres et Co., 1836–1837).

19   This cavalry force consisted of two squadrons of 13th Dragoons and two squadrons of 1st Portuguese cavalry regiment. See *Royal Military Chronicle 1820*, p. 102 and WD 4, 659. Further units of Portuguese cavalry must have joined the army prior to the battle of Albuera (see Appendix XV in Oman, *History*, vol. IV); indeed, while he does not identify them, Long in a letter to his brother Charles of 17 March 1811 refers to his command as being three British and two Portuguese regiments. In his diary the entry for 16 March lists the regiments as 3rd Dragoon Guards, 4th Dragoons, 13th Light Dragoons and '2 Regiments of Portuguese'. McGuffie, *Peninsular Cavalry General*, pp. 64 and 68.

20   Beresford to Wellington, 26 March 1811 (WSD 7, 90–2) explains he had told Long that if he found the opportunity he could charge the enemy cavalry but not to risk the light cavalry. The pursuit to the gates of Badajoz led to their losing contact with Beresford until he received reports assuring him the four squadrons which had participated in the charge must be prisoners. Beresford, with the heavy cavalry, felt he should pause for his own infantry to come up which gave the French infantry time to escape. McGuffie, in editing Long's correspondence, suggests Beresford wrongly claimed Long was the source of this information, and that Baron Tripp was responsible. McGuffie, *Peninsular Cavalry General*, p. 72. Ernst Otto, Baron Tripp (Netherlands) commanded the Nassau Brigade at Waterloo.

21   Beresford to Wellington, 26 March 1811 (WSD 7, 89–90; this is his official report).

22   Wellington to Beresford, 20 March 1811 (WD 4, 681).

23   Beresford to Wellington, 26 March 1811 (WSD 7, 89–90).

24   Wellington to Beresford, 28 and 30 March 1811 (WD 7, 412 and WD 5, 710–11).

25   Long to Charles Long, 28 March 1811 (McGuffie, *Peninsular Cavalry General*, p. 80).

26   See Oman, *History*, vol. V, p. 524.

27   Beresford to Wellington, 7 April 1811 (WP1/327/27).

28   Beresford to Torrens, 1 November 1811 (NYA/ZBA 21, f. 10).

29   See Edwards, op. cit., pp. 76–7. Vasconcelos was later created Conde de Vila Real, and he served as Portuguese Minister at the Court of St James.

30   D'Urban to Long, 14 May 1811 (TT, MNE CX Maco 166, ff. 406–7).

31   McGuffie, *Peninsular Cavalry General*, p. 61.

32   Ibid. pp. 44–5.

33   Ibid. p. 69.

34   Wellington to Beresford, 24 April 1811; WD 4, 770–1. Erskine was in command of the Light Division in Robert Craufurd's absence. He led it in some extremely controversial circumstances during Masséna's retreat but Wellington could not dismiss him because of his influence at Horse Guards. One must wonder at Wellington's motives in offering him to Beresford since Wellington considered Erskine a madman. Subsequently he commanded the cavalry with Hill's corps operating south of the Tagus until forced to relinquish this command due to increasing mental health problems. He died in 1813, having jumped from a window in a house in Lisbon.

35   Wellington to Long, 11 May 1811 (WD 5, 4).

36 See Édouard Lapène, *Conquête de l'Andalousie, Campagne de 1810 et 1811 dans le Midi de l'Espagne* (Paris: Chez Anselin et Pochard, 1823), p. 150.

37 Benjamin D'Urban, *Further Strictures on those parts of Col. Napier's History of the Peninsular War which relate to the military opinions and conduct of General Lord Viscount Beresford* (London: Longman, Rees, Orme, Brown, Green & Longman, 1832), p. 119.

38 Napier, op. cit., vol. III, p. 556.

39 Lumley to Beresford 21 May 1811 (TT, MNE CX 205, f. 603).

40 See McGuffie, *Peninsular Cavalry General*, p. 111. Wellington sent the note of reprimand to Long through Sir William Erskine, then commanding Wellington's 2nd Cavalry Division of which Long's brigade formed part.

41 Ibid. pp. 145–57.

42 See Oman, *History*, vol. XXX, p. 267, notwithstanding Wellington's request that the pontoons be moved to Elvas when Badajoz was first threatened by Soult.

43 For the siege of Olivença, Cole had six twelve-pounders from Elvas which only arrived on 14 April. The Portuguese 11th Regiment was also in attendance.

44 Gordon to Aberdeen, 23 April 1811 (Muir, *At Wellington's Right Hand*).

45 Beresford to Wellington, 18 April 1811 (WD 4, 775) and see also Beresford to Torrens, 1 November 1811 (NYA/ZBA 10, f. 12), which is quoted later in this chapter. The French 2nd Hussars suffered considerable losses at Los Santos and over 100 prisoners were taken, but Beresford felt more could have been achieved.

46 Wellington to Beresford, 23 April 1811 (WD 4, 763).

47 Ibid.

48 Joaquin Blake was a Spanish General of Irish ancestry. At the outset of the Peninsular Wars he was given the command of the army of Galicia. Notwithstanding a number of setbacks, in 1811 he was placed in command of an expeditionary army which landed at Ayamonte (from Cádiz) in April 1811 with a view to joining Castaños' army of Extremadura. After Albuera he participated in operations allied to the second siege of Badajoz before being sent to Valencia, which he surrendered to the French in January 1812 after a short siege. He became a prisoner in France and was not released until the end of the war in 1814.

49 Wellington to Beresford, 6 May 1811 (WD 4, 785). Wellington's memorandum to the Spanish Generals is dated 23 April 1811 (WD 4, 766–7). In the memorandum he set out his suggestions as 'proposals'. He concluded by saying the entire army, including all those who had joined, should be commanded by the officer of the highest military rank and requested the Spanish general officers 'to state to Sir W. Beresford whether they will, or will not, co-operate with him in the manner above proposed in carrying on the siege of Badajoz'.

50 Napier (op. cit., vol. III), having criticised Beresford for his tardiness (p. 527) acknowledges that the delay before he invested Badajoz 'was unjustly attributed to him' (p. 548).

51 Beresford to Wellington, 3 May 1811 (WP1/330/5). Castaños was nothing if not positive. On 1 May he proposed to Beresford a three-pronged strategy involving the blockade of Badajoz, fighting Soult and forcing Victor to abandon the siege of Cádiz; though he did admit it would need Wellington's army as well as those of Beresford and Blake (TT, MNE CX 205, Maco 166, f. 453).

52 A good account of all three allied sieges of Badajoz is contained in Thompson, *Wellington's Engineers*.

53 Napier, *History*, vol. III, p. 528.

54 Napier, in his *History* savages the British Government for its lack of preparation for the siege of Badajoz: 'no army was ever so ill provided with the means of prosecuting such an enterprise' (vol. III, Book XII, p.

525). Whether or not the lack of artificers available at the first British siege of Badajoz was the prompt, in 1812 Beresford added a battalion of artificers to the establishment of the Portuguese army.

55 See D'Urban, op cit., p. 213. See also Beresford to Wellington, 16 May 1811 (WD 5, 34); though Fortescue suggests Beresford knew Soult had left Sevilla as early as 9 May. This cannot be right as Soult only left Sevilla on 10 May at about midnight; Lapène, *Conquête de l'Andalousie*, p. 148.

56 Wellington to Liverpool, 15 May 1811 (WD 7, 564–5).

57 Napier, op. cit, vol. III, p. 529.

Chapter 11

1 John Gwilliam, *The Battle of Albuera, A poem: With An Epistle Dedicatory to Lord Wellington* (London: Gale and Curtis, 1811).

2 Wellington to Beresford, 23 April 1811 (WD 4, 763–5).

3 Beresford to Wellington, 16 May 1811 (WD 5, 35).

4 Beresford to Wellington, 14 May 1811. See Wellington to Brent Spencer, 17 May 1811 (WD 7, 557).

5 Beresford to Wellington, 14 and 15 May 1811 (WSD 7, 125–6).

6 'Memorandum to the officers in command of the corps in Estremadura', 23 April 1811 (WD 4, 766).

7 Wellington to Castaños, 13 May 1811 (WD 5, 8); Wellington to Liverpool, 22 May 1811 (WD 5, 37); Wellington to Wellesley, 22 May 1811 (WD 5, 30). See also Castaños' Dispatch after the battle of Albuera, below at end note 69.

8 See Napier, op. cit., p. 529. Beresford, in his letter to Wellington of 18 May, refers to Blake making a forced march, which makes the late arrival of the Spanish army all the more inexplicable. Castaños' troops were with Cole but on arrival were placed with Blake's Spaniards.

9 D'Urban, *Further Strictures*, p. 112.

10 Guy Dempsey, *Albuera 1811: The Bloodiest Battle of the Peninsular War* (London: Frontline Books, 2008), points out that sunrise was at 4.20 am on 11 May 1811.

11 The Allied army at Albuera was made up as follows (from Oman, *History*, vol. IV, Appendix XV. In Oman there is also detail regarding effectives and losses):

British
2nd Division (Colborne's Brigade 1/3-2/31-2/48- 2/66 regiments; Hoghton's Brigade 29-1/48-1/57 regiments; Abercrombie's Brigade 2/28-2/34-2/39 regiments; 3 companies 5/60).
4th Division (Myers' Brigade 1/7-2/7-1/23 regiments; Kemmis' Brigade [one company of each 2/27- 1/40-97 regiments; Alten's Independent Brigade, 1 and 2 Light Battalions KGL).
Cavalry (de Grey's Brigade; 3rd Dragoon Guards; 4th Dragoons).
Artillery (2 batteries British and 2 batteries KGL).

Portuguese
Harvey's Brigade: 11 (2 batteries), 23 (2 batteries), LLL (1 battery).
Hamilton's Division: 2 (2 batteries), 14 (2 batteries), 4 (2 batteries), 10 (2 batteries).
Collin's Brigade: 5 (2 batteries), 5th Caçadores (1 battery).
Cavalry (1st, 7th, 5th (1 Squadron); 8th (1 squadron).
Artillery (2 batteries).
Total for Beresford's Army 20,358

Spanish

Blake's Army (Vanguard Division, Murcia (2 batteries), Canarias, 2 León, Campo Maior).

3rd Division (1 Catalonia, Barbastro, Pravia, Lena, Castropol, Cangas de Tineo, Infiesto).

4th Division (2 and 4 Spanish Guards, Irlanda, Patria, Toledo, Estranjera, 4 Walloon Guards, Ciudad Real).

Cavalry (Santiago, Húsares de Castilla, Granaderos, Instrución).

Artillery (1 battery).

Castaños Army (Carlos de Espana Infantry (3 batteries); Penne Villemur Cavalry; detachments from seven regiments; Artillery (1 battery)).

Total Spanish armies 14,634.

For the arrival of Kemmis's Brigade see D'Urban, op. cit., vol. VI, 17 May 1811.

12   Lapène, *Conquête de l'Andalousie*, p. 149. Captain Lapène was an artillery officer with Girard's 5th Corps at Albuera.

13   England was supplying Spain with material for uniforms just as it supplied Portugal. This was one reason why troops would not necessarily have been wearing their appointed uniform.

14   See 'Report of Penne Villemur' in Mark S. Thompson, *The Spanish Report on the Battle of Albuera* (Sunderland: Mark Thompson Publishing, 2015), p. 45.

15   Soult to Berthier, 21 May 1811, quoted in WD 5, 770–1.

16   Lapène, *Conquête de l'Andalousie*, p. 153.

17   D'Urban, op. cit., p. 216.

18   See Peter Edwards, *Albuera: Wellington's Fourth Peninsular Campaign*; Oman, *History*; Napier, *History of the Peninsular War*; Dempsey, *Albuera 1811*; M. Oliver and R. Partridge, *The Battle of Albuera, 1811: Field of Grief*; Fletcher, *Bloody Albuera*; Thompson, *The Fatal Hill*; Juan José Sanudo Bayon, *La Albuera, Gloriosos Campo de sufrimiento*.

19   While Zayas' 4th Division nominally exceeded 4,000 men, it would seem that his 2nd Brigade was not involved initially in the firefight.

20   Galbraith Lowry Cole (ed.), *The Correspondence of Colonel Wade, Colonel Napier, Major General Sir H. Hardinge and General the Hon. Sir Lowry G. Cole relating to the Battle of Albuera* (London: T. & W. Boone, 1841), p. 10. Hereafter, *Correspondence*.

21   It is worth noting that Harvey's Portuguese (11th and 23rd regiments) stood firm when attacked by La Tour-Maubourg's cavalry as they advanced under Cole. Whereas at Buçaco they fought the French infantry, here was further evidence of their ability to perform in battle, evidence of a well-trained force.

22   See Dempsey and Thompson, op. cit. In fact the manoeuvre undertaken by Cole involved not just moving the 4th Division forward on the British right to crush the French left, but a secondary movement whereby Abercrombie's brigade to the left of Hoghton's beleaguered force was used simultaneously to assault the French left. This latter movement was overseen by the energetic Hardinge. See Lowry Cole, *Correspondence*, p. 6. Colonels Rooke and Ward (at the time an ADC to Cole) supported the assertion that Cole was already contemplating the advance of the 4th Division before it was suggested by Hardinge.

23   H.A. Bruce (ed.), 'Letters to his Wife' in *Life of General Sir William Napier*, two volumes (London: John Murray, 1864), p. 312. Sir Herbert Taylor was private secretary to George III, George IV and William IV. In Wellington's government he was appointed Adjutant-General to the Forces. The reference to 'Murray' was probably Sir George Murray, who Wellington appointed Colonial Secretary in 1828.

24   Napier, op. cit., vol. III, p. 529 and ff. 548.

25   Wellington to Beresford, 23 April 1811 (WD 4, 763).

26 See *Strictures* and *Further Strictures* as well as *Report of the Operations of the Right Wing of the Allied Army under Field Marshal Sir Wm. Carr Beresford in the Alentejo and the Spanish Estremadura during the campaign of 1811, by Maj. General Sir Benjamin D'Urban*; published in Napier's *Peninsular War* and Beresford's *Strictures*.

27 Ibid. Report 'Preface', p. iii in which he describes the allegation as 'imaginary'.

28 D'Urban, *Further Strictures*, p. 111.

29 Beresford to Wellington, 15 May 1811 (WSD 7, 125).

30 D'Urban *Report*, ff. 21.

31 Beresford to Wellington, 17 May 1811 (WP1/330/88).

32 Oman calculated the Spanish force at Albuera at about 14,500 of which some 12,000 had arrived with Blake. Oman, *History*, p. 633. The Anglo-Portuguese force amounted to just over 20,000 including infantry, cavalry and artillery.

33 Beresford to Wellington, 15 May 1811 (WSD 7, 125–6).

34 Beresford to Wellington 12 May 1811 (WP1/330/86). Albuera was cavalry country and one of Beresford's difficulties in the battle was his huge inferiority of cavalry.

35 Beresford to Wellington, 20 May 1811 (WP1/330/28).

36 Ibid.

37 Wellington to Beresford, 14 May 1811 (WD 5, 12) and Wellington to Liverpool, 15 May 1811 (WD 5, 19).

38 Wellington to Beresford, 16 May 1811 (BL, Add MS 36,306) and Wellington to Charles Stuart, 16 May 1811 (WD 5, 24).

39 Wellington to Brent Spencer, 17 May 1811 (WD 5, 24).

40 Beresford to Wellington, 18 May 1811 (WD 5, 36).

41 Ibid. and see Wellington to Beresford, 23 April 1811 (WD 4, 763).

42 Napoleon post Jena, cited in Oliver and Partridge, *The Battle of Albuera*, p. 61.

43 D'Urban, *Report*, p. 30.

44 Contemporary accounts make it clear, however, that Stewart displayed personal bravery in leading his troops into battle. See Letter from Lieutenant George Crompton, 66th Regiment in *Journal of the Society for Army Historical Research*, 1922.

45 Colborne to Rev Duke Yonge, 18 May 1811, quoted in Dempsey, op. cit., p. 119. Dempsey in turn has found the letter in G.C.M. Smith's *Life of Seaton* (pp. 160–1). In addition Dempsey refers to a letter from George Crompton to his mother of the same date which is critical of Stewart.

46 This incident was the subject of a number of paintings and engravings including:
An aquatint drawn by Franz Joseph Manskirch and engraved by M. Dubourg; a print by T. Sutherland; a drawing in *The Book of Battles: or, Daring Deeds by Land and Sea* (London: Houlston and Wright, 1867).

47 Four squadrons of cavalry were involved, two British and two Spanish.

48 See Thompson, *The Spanish Report on the Battle of Albuera*, p. 45.

49 See D'Urban's *Report*, p. 31.

50 Napier, 'Justification' to volume III, p. 30.

51 The lance was about 9 feet (2.7 metres) long. However there was disagreement as to its effectiveness. While formidable in line, the length of the lance made it unwieldy in a melee. The 9th, 12th, 16th and 23rd regiments were equipped with lances resulting from an order of the Prince Regent dated 19 September 1816.

52 Major General Daniel Hoghton (1770–1811), an able and experienced soldier, fell at the head of his regiment at Albuera. He is buried in the British Cemetery at Elvas, established after the battle

by Marshal Beresford. He had served briefly with Beresford before the Peninsular War when he had transferred to the 88th Regiment and went with that regiment to India in 1800. Hoghton did not go to Egypt with Beresford and the 88th Regiment because he had secured a post on the staff of the Governor General, Richard Wellesley, recently created Marquess Wellesley. Lieutenant Colonel Sir William Myers was mortally wounded at Albuera when leading the Fusilier Brigade. He died at Valverde the following day and is remembered by a memorial raised at public expense in St Paul's cathedral.

53 *The United Service Magazine* (1831) quotes Baron Alten, Commander of the KGL, as saying that his orders were to quit the village with a view to taking up a position in the rear of it to cover the Valverde road.

54 At the time of the battle of Albuera Hartman (also Hartmann) was a Major in the King's German Artillery.

55 See *The United Service Magazine*, 1834, part 3, p. 92.

56 Napier, op. cit, vol. III, p. 539. Later Napier qualified his view; see 'A Letter to General Lord Viscount Beresford being An Answer to his Lordship's Assumed Refutation of Col. Napier's Justification of his Third Volume', op. cit., vol VI, p. lii. The rumour that Beresford had ordered a retreat was current in 1811 and Beresford denied it both then and later. See, for instance, Beresford to Sir George Hill, 12 March 1812 (PRONI, D/642/A/6/1-2).

57 Lieutenant William Tomkinson of the 16th Light Dragoons says Beresford ordered a retreat, but the 16th was not at Albuera so no great reliance should be placed on that comment.

58 A useful summary of all the troops present at the battle is contained in Oman, *History*, vol. IV, Appendix XV.

59 The point made in *Strictures* was that Stewart during his lifetime had never suggested Beresford had ordered a retreat.

60 The 16th Light Dragoons fought at Fuente de Oñoro. Tomkinson was a diarist as well as a soldier with the 16th Light Dragoons. In his diary he represented that Beresford determined to retreat but was talked out of it by D'Urban. However, D'Urban makes no such suggestion and Tomkinson was not an accurate witness. Indeed Tomkinson says that D'Urban did everything at the battle including begging Beresford to advance the Fusilier Brigade (part of the 4th Division); a suggestion not made by D'Urban. In fairness, however, Tomkinson concludes: 'It often occurs that a person not having the responsibility on his own shoulders can direct an affair with much more judgment than a principal, who feels everything at stake on his own decision.' William Tomkinson and James Tomkinson (ed.), *The Diary of a Cavalry Officer in the Peninsular War and Waterloo Campaign 1809–1815* (London: Swan Sonnenschein and Co., 1894). pp. 103–4.

61 All commentators note the substantial numerical advantage of the French cavalry at the Battle of Albuera. This advantage was enhanced by their being accustomed to fight under a unified command. Further, this superiority in cavalry made it dangerous to try and execute a pursuit of the French, even had the Allies not been exhausted. If Beresford had sought to organise a pursuit, it would have had to depend on Hamilton's fresh Portuguese brigade and a number of the Spanish brigades to spearhead it, and any repulse could have had serious consequences. Mindful of the situation, Beresford called back those pursuing the French. D'Urban, *Further Strictures*, p. 191.

62 D.G.F.D. de Pradt, *Mémoires Historiques sur la Révolution d'Espagne* (Paris: Chez Rosa, 1817), p. 243.

63 Georges Alexis Mocquery, later in 1811 made a General and a Baron of the Empire. Gazan to Soult (Duc de Dalmatie), 19 May 1811; enclosed with Beresford to Wellington, 21 May 1811 (WD 5, 40, and WD 5, Appendix II).

64 D'Urban, op. cit., p. 218.

65 Oman, *History*, vol. IV, pp. 395, 634–5.

66 Soult to Berthier, 21 May 1811 and Soult to Marmont 27 May 1811 (Marmont, *Mémoires du Maréchal Marmont, Duc de Raguse, de 1792 a 1841* (Paris: Perrotin, 1857), vol. 4, pp. 95–6).

67 There is some confusion regarding the number of such flags taken at Albuera, but it would seem at least one such trophy was brought afterwards to Cádiz and it hung for some time in the chapel of San Felipe Neri. See, Luis Sorando Muzás, 'Trophies of Albuera' (*The Napoleon Series*, March 2002). Available at: https://www.napoleon-series.org/military/battles/c_albueraflags.html (accessed 25 April 2018).

68 'House of Commons Debate, 7 June 1811' (*Hansard*, vol. 20, cc 519–32). The vote of thanks was proposed by the Chancellor of the Exchequer, Spencer Perceval, and seconded by Castlereagh. Perhaps unsurprisingly Beresford also received a letter of congratulations from General Charles François Dumouriez praising him for the victory at Albuera. Dumouriez had fought in the army of France under the Bourbons before commanding as a revolutionary general and subsequently defecting to the royalists, working for the British government as an adviser. Dumouriez to Beresford, 11 May 1811 (NAM 2008-03-26).

69 Beresford to Wellington, 21 May 1811 (WD 5, 40). Based on intercepted letters from General Gazan to Soult, Beresford was able to estimate the French losses as scarcely less than 9,000 men. Beresford to Wellington 21 May 1811 (WD 5, 40). In fact there would appear to have been more French wounded in the vicinity as Castaños refers to the French abandoning 200 wounded in the woods when they retreated towards Sevilla as they were unable to transport them. Castaños, 'Dispatch' 19 May 1811.

70 John Spencer Cooper, *Rough Notes of Seven Campaigns in Portugal, France, Spain and America, 1809–1815* (London: John Russell Smith, 1869), pp. 61–2. It is uncertain whether this was Napier's source (vol. III, p. 544). D'Urban in his *Journal* suggests the Spaniards were involved in moving the wounded and he also makes the point that English surgeons attended French wounded in Albuera; 19 May 1811, op. cit., vol. VI, p. 216.

71 Wellington to Peacocke, 20 May 1811 (WD 5, 25).

72 See Chapter 13.

73 Beresford to Wellington, 18 May 1811 (Hartley WP1/330/89).

74 Beresford to Wellington, 16 May 1811 (WD 5, 34–5).

75 Wellington to Beresford, 19 May 1811 (WD 5, 25).

76 Beresford to Wellington, 20 May 1811 (WSD 7, 133–4). See Napier, *History*, vol. III, p. 550.

77 D'Urban, *Journal*, p. 218.

78 Wellington, 31 December 1811 ('Memorandum of Operations in 1811', WD 5, 432–50).

79 'HC' (probably Henry Cadogan who commanded the 71st, Pack's old regiment) to Pack, 9 June 1811 observed: 'Albuera has knocked Fuentes de Onor [*sic*] out of all recollection, and I even think it will, if timeously announced in England obliterate the remembrance of Almeida' (Southampton University Archive MS 296).

80 D'Urban, op. cit., p, 229. The number of Portuguese killed at Albuera was put at only 102; injuries were some further 260. That there were not more killed and injured is due to Hamilton's Portuguese Brigade on the left flank not being engaged in any substantial way. Most of the Portuguese wounded came from the Portuguese brigade under Brigadier General William Harvey, part of the 4th Division.

81 Beresford to Blake, 23 May 1811 (TT, MNE CX 205, f. 598).

82 Wellington to Beresford, and Wellington to Stuart, 30 April 1811 (WD 4, 779–80).

83 Lapène, *Conquête de l'Andalousie*, p. 136.

84 Wellington to Hill, 27 May 1811 (WD 5, 52).

85 Beresford in his dispatch says the French were moving by 8 am and commenced their attack at 9 am. Beresford to Wellington, 18 May 1811 (WD 5, 36–9).

86 D'Urban, op. cit., pp. 216 and 230. See also 'A Prisoner of Albuera: Journal of Major William Brooke' in *Studies in the Napoleonic Wars* edited by Charles Oman (London: Methuen & Co., 1929), ff. 175. Brooke, who served with the 2/48th Regiment, was captured at the battle and led to the other (French) side of the river by a kindly dragoon as he was too weak to ford it. From there he watched the remainder of the battle and confirmed the French began to run about 2 pm. Over 500 men were reportedly captured at the same time as Brooke by the Polish Lancers, but half escaped at Usagre and Brooke himself escaped from Sevilla.

87 Beresford to Wellington, 18 May 1811 (WD 5, 36–9).

88 William Carr Beresford, *Refutation of Colonel Napier's Justification of His Third Volume* (London: John Murray, 1834), p. 193. Note: Castaños refers in his 'Dispatch' on the battle of 19 May 1811 (supra) that Blake was always at the head of his troops and during the battle suffered a minor injury to his arm due to a musket ball.

89 George Soane, *Life of the Duke of Wellington* (London: E. Churton 1839–40), vol. II, p. 36.

90 Beresford to Wellington, 18 May 1811 (WD 5, 36–9).

91 Beresford to Wellington, 17 May 1811 (WP1/330/88).

92 Wellington to Spencer, 19 May 1811 (WD 7, 573). His remark that 'the Spanish did not behave ill' is contrasted with his statement in the next sentence regarding the Portuguese who 'were but little engaged; those that were behaved well, and they have not suffered much'.

93 Wellington to E. Cooke, 23 May 1811 (WSD 7, 135).

94 D'Urban, op. cit., 16 May 1811, vol, V. p. 215.

95 D'Urban, *Report*, p. 30. This report is contained in the bound volume of Beresford's *Strictures*.

96 See, Thompson, *The Spanish Report on the Battle of Albuera*, prepared by António Burriel, Adjutant-General, Spanish Army, June 1811.

97 While praising the Spanish troops, Beresford observed 'had they had discipline, and in some instances better officers, they would have done everything that was wished'. Beresford to Wellington, 17 May 1811 (WP1/330/88).

98 Soult to Berthier, 21 May 1811 (quoted in WD 5, 770–1).

99 Soult sent the colours under the escort of a M. Lafitte with the assumption that he would be rewarded accordingly. Unfortunately for M. Lafitte, it appeared that he had previously fought for the Austrians and Napoleon was incensed, refusing to make him an ADC. Instead Lafitte was sent to the 9th Regiment of Light Horse. Napoleon to Berthier, 23 August 1811 quoted in *The Museum of Foreign Literature, Science and Art*, vol. 38, p. 258.

100 Proclamation of Duke of Dalmatia (Soult) 21 June 1811 (quoted in Cobbett's *Political Register* 1811, p. 147). Brooke, op. cit., ff. 175.

101 Barry Edward O'Meara, *Napoleon in Exile, or A Voice from St Helena*, two volumes (London: Jones and Co., 1822), vol. II, p. 124. Where Napoleon is reported as claiming to have censured Soult for failing to attack the British following the charge of the lancers.

102 This appointment must have been subsequent to the appointment of Wellington for he stresses that Beresford was more entitled than he in a letter to his brother Henry Wellesley, 1 June 1811 (WD V, 64–5). Perhaps it was due to Wellington's influence for Beresford was first offered a Marquisate of Castille, which Wellington observed was 'a title which can be purchased by any body'. On 20 July 1811 Wellington informed Liverpool that Beresford had been offered the position as Captain-General in the Spanish Army (WD 5, 174). There is a suggestion in Havard, *Wellington's Welsh General*, p. 161, that the

Cortes at Cádiz first voted Beresford the title of Marques de Albuera on 27 May 1811 but that this offer was withdrawn following adverse remarks about the conduct of Spanish troops at the battle and on 17 June he was instead made Captain-General.

103 Beresford to Lady Anne Beresford, 25 June 1809 (Beresford family papers). In April 1809 he had said to Waterford that he had not felt well since leaving London (in February); Beresford to 2nd Marquis of Waterford, 26 April 1809 (Beresford family papers).

104 Beresford to Wellington, 19 May 1811 (WP1/330/90).

105 Beresford to Charles Stewart, 25 May 1811 (PRONI, D3030/P/238/2). In November 1809 Beresford had offered Stewart command of the Portuguese cavalry, an offer which was repeated in 1810, but Stewart felt he was very near getting a brigade command in the British army, for which he expressed a preference. Charles Stewart to Beresford 21 May 1810 (PRONI, D3030/3319).

106 Beresford to Pack, 1 June 1811 (Southampton University Archive, MS 296).

107 HC to Denis Pack, 9 June 1811 (Southampton University Archive, MS 296. Papers of Sir Denis Pack). There is extensive correspondence between Cadogan and Pack in these papers. Cadogan commanded the 1st Battalion of the 71st Regiment from 1810 to 1812, having previously served as an ADC to Wellington. The 71st was brigaded in the 2nd Division in 1812. Cadogan was killed at the battle of Vitória in 1813.

108 Beresford, Ordens do Dia, show him at Calhariz (Lisbon) by 8 July, Sintra from 18 July–18 September, São José de Ribamar 27 September–15 October, and thereafter back at Calhariz until the end of the year.

109 D'Urban, op. cit., 1–30 November 1811, p. 233.

110 Wellington to Beresford, 13 December 1811 (BL, Add MS 36,036).

111 D'Urban, op. cit., 31 December 1811, p. 233.

112 Beresford to Torrens, 1 November 1811 (NYA/ZBA 21/10, f. 12).

113 Apart from fox hunting, officers engaged in shooting hares, rabbits, partridges, woodcock, snipe, plovers and swans. See Vandeleur, *With Wellington's Outposts*, 29 January 1811. On 24 December 1812 Sir George L'Estrange knocked down three snipe, two with one shot. George B. L'Estrange, *Recollections of Sir George B. L'Estrange* (London: Sampson Low, Marston, Low and Searle, 1894).

114 Hill and Hope were given independent responsibilities at different times. Hill had considerable success at Arroyo dos Molinos in 1811 and at the destruction of Almaraz in 1812; quite apart from commendable service when under Wellington. Hope was given independent command to enforce the siege of Bayonne in 1814. However, Wellington closely supervised them both. Further, in besieging Bayonne Hope was in no danger from a relieving army. There was none available and Wellington had Soult on the run eastwards.

115 Apart from three very detailed memoranda written on 23 April 1811, there are many letters and memoranda from Wellington to Beresford in the two months prior to the battle together with many relevant communications to third parties.

116 Wellington to Beresford, 16 March 1811 (WD 7, 351).

117 Beresford accumulated the cross and seven clasps for the battles of La Coruña, Buçaco, Albuera, Badajoz, Salamanca, Vitória, Pyrénées, Nivelle, Nive, Orthez and Toulouse. He was also present at the siege and capture of Ciudad Rodrigo, but only joined Wellington shortly before this event following the recovery of his health.

118 Wellington to Stuart, 11 September 1810 (WD 6, 401–4).

119 Wellington to Bathurst, 2 December 1812 (WSD 7, 484). Earl Bathurst was President of the Board of Trade 1807–12 and Secretary of State for the Colonies 1812–27, both cabinet posts.

120 *The Quarterly Review*, vol. 141 (1870), p. 475.

121   York to Bathurst, 28 December 1812, with Memorandum of 26 December 1812, (WSD 7, 516–17).

122   See Chapter 6.

123   Wellington to Bathurst, 26 January 1813 (WD 7, 22–3).

124   Wellington to Bathurst, 25 September 1813 (WSD 11, 143).

125   Oman, *History*, vol. IV, Appendix XV gives figures for the Allied army which differ from those of Napier. Oman states the combined allied infantry numbered approximately 31,000 (8,738 British, 9,131 Portuguese, 13,203 Spanish) with perhaps 3,800 cavalry (1,164 British, 849 Portuguese, 1,786 Spanish) whereas the French had about 20,000 infantry (Beresford says 20,000–22,000 in his report of 18 May 1811 and Napier says 19,000) and in excess of 4,000 cavalry. This suggests the French superiority in cavalry was not markedly so. Napier (op. cit., Book XII, ch. VI, p. 538) places Beresford with more than 2,000 cavalry. Napier (Chapters VI and VII) makes repeated references to the French superiority in cavalry numbers and the suitability of the terrain for cavalry both at the battle and during the subsequent French retreat. The Allies were outgunned with the French disposing of forty-eight guns as against thirty-eight for the Allies, and furthermore the French had a substantial number of 9-lb guns as against the Allies who for the most part relied on 6-lb guns.

126   D'Urban, op. cit., p. 184.

127   Beresford to Wellington, 20 May 1811 (WP1/330/28).

128   Beresford's early career had only seen him fighting as a subordinate officer with the exception of the capture of Buenos Aires, where he commanded a very small force. Since his arrival in the Peninsula in 1808 he had commanded a brigade in the retreat to La Coruña and a small force of some 9,000–10,000 men in the Porto campaign of 1809. Later that year he had led a force of over 18,000 into Spain, but it had not been involved in serious fighting. At Buçaco and in the Lines of Torres Vedras he had served under Wellington.

129   For instance, see Beresford's performance at Salamanca, Orthez and Toulouse.

130   Quoted in Dempsey, *Albuera 1811*, p. 246.

131   Philip Henry, 5th Earl Stanhope, *Notes of Conversations with the Duke of Wellington, 1831–1851* (New York: Longmans, Green and Co., 1888), 31 October 1836.

132   Beresford to Sir George Hill, 12 March 1812 (PRONI, D/642/A/6/1-2).

133   Napier was accused of inaccuracies, partiality and misrepresentation (see series of articles in the *Quarterly Review* – vols lvi, lvii and lxi – believed to be by Sir George Murray). He was censured by a number of others intimately involved in the Peninsular War including:

    i.   Viscount Strangford in his 'Observations on Some Passages in Lieutenant-Colonel Napier's History of the Peninsular War' (1828);

    ii.   Lieutenant Colonel Sorell's 'Notes on the Campaign, 1808–9', in Spain (1828);

    iii.   D.M. Perceval's Remarks on the Character ascribed by Col. Napier to the late Right Hon. Spencer Perceval (1835);

    iv.   H.B. Robinson in his *Memoirs of Lt. Gen. Sir Thomas Picton* suggested Napier failed to describe accurately Masséna's retreat in 1811 and in particular Picton's advance on Guarda;

    v.   General Giron alleged Napier's account was full of inaccuracies insofar as it referred to Spain and the Spaniards. See *United States Service Magazine*, vol. I, (1864), ff. 395.

    Napier obtained an advance of 1,000 guineas from the publisher John Murray in respect of volume I. Murray declined to publish further volumes on the basis that he had lost over £500 on this deal and Napier published the remainder himself.

134   Oman, *History*, vol. IV, pp. 374 and 398.

135   *The United Service Magazine* (1834), p. 93.

Chapter 12

1 Ordens do Dia 1811. He went to São José de Ribamar (between Belém and Cascais) to bathe in the sea during September–October. This may have been for his erysipelas.

2 In December he described a 'fever cold' as delaying his departure to join the army. Beresford to the 2nd Marquis of Waterford, 7 December 1811 (Beresford family papers).

3 Much correspondence regarding these matters is contained in AHM Div-14-55, 218 and 266. Other matters being pursued by Beresford during the autumn included the rebuilding of bridges on the Zezere (BL, Add MS 21,504). In November he advised Wellington of his decision to adopt similar regulations for staff officers to those prevailing in the British service. Inter alia badges for field officers had been introduced in the British army in 1810. See Beresford to Wellington, 16 November 1811 (BL, Add MS 21,504).

4 Charles Stuart, later Baron Stuart de Rothesay, was British Minister Plenipotentiary to Portugal 1810–14.

5 While this account does not seek to cover the exploits of the militia and ordenança in any detail, it is important not to forget the often heroic role played by each group. In certain areas they proved a real thorn in the side of the French. General Manuel Bacelar commanded five divisions of militia from his headquarters at Lamego (on the river Balsemão, a tributary of the Douro) including those under Colonel Trant (Porto to the Mondego), General Carlos Frederico Lecor (Castelo Branco) and General Silveira (guarding the border in Trás-os-Montes). Divisions or regiments of militia were moved to guard specific objectives, often well away from their home bases, such as late in 1811 when a number of Trant's and Wilson's (Brigadier General John Wilson) regiments were the garrison in Almeida.

6 Beresford, Ordem do Dia, 4 May 1811.

7 Two of the new regiments of caçadores were raised initially in Porto with the third recruited in Entre Douro e Minho.

8 Beresford to Wellington, 4 April 1811 (TT, MNE 067).

9 See de la Fuente, op. cit., fn. 561, which reports monthly recruiting running at less than 1,000 per month prior to July and over 3,000 for the remainder of 1811.

10 Beresford to Forjaz, 27 May 1811, and Forjaz to Councillor João Diogo de Barros Leitão e Carvalhosa, 29 May 1811 (TT-CX-056 and 057). Lieutenant Colonel Watling was sent to Mafra to assist General Blunt with training (TT, MNE 073).

11 AHM, 3-8, Caixa 4, 24 (Returns of the Army).

12 Forjaz to Beresford, 31 December 1811 (AHM, 1-14, Caixa 42).

13 Ordens do Dia, 3 June/12 July.

14 Stuart to Wellesley, 14 October 1811 (NA/FO 342/32). In early 1813 Beresford complained to Wellington of deserters escaping from prison and the lack of money which prevented the câmaras (local councils) from repairing the prisons. Beresford to Wellington, 1 February 1813 (WP1/366/43).

15 See de la Fuente, op. cit., ff. 225.

16 Beresford to Wellington, 5 November 1811 (BL, Add MS 21,504).

17 Wellington to Beresford, 10 November 1811 (BL, Add MS 21,504).

18 Beresford to Forjaz, 20 December 1811, 11 January 1812 and 5 April 1812; Forjaz to Beresford, 16 November and 30 December 1811 (AHM, 1-14 Caixa 26 and 42). For a good discussion of the difficulties regarding the cavalry, see de la Fuente, op. cit., pp. 217–21.

19 Beresford to Forjaz, 30 March 1812 (AHM, 1-14, Caixa 26).

20 The Portuguese infantry regiments with Wellington at the end of March 1811 were the 3rd, 7th, 8th, 9th, 11th, 12th, 15th, 19th, 21st and 23rd. Wellington to Beresford, 27 March 1811 (BL, Add MS 36,306).

21   Charles Stuart wrote to Richard Wellesley that although resolving the question of provisioning the Portuguese army was the reason Beresford returned to Lisbon in July, his illness kept him in Cintra, implying that he had a limited role in these events. Stuart to Richard Wellesley, 27 July 1811 (NA, FO 342/28).

22   De la Fuente, op. cit., p. 208.

23   Beresford to Lady Anne Beresford, 14 September 1811 (Beresford family papers).

24   Elizabeth Longford, *Wellington: The Years of the Sword* (London: Weidenfeld & Nicolson, 1969) refers to Wellington having two good packs of hounds sent out from England to Portugal in 1811. The huntsman was Tom Crane of the Coldstream Guards. Wellington usually kept eight hunters. Animals hunted included foxes, hares, wolf and wild cat. James Thornton, *Your Most Obedient Servant* (Exeter: Webb & Bower, 1985); introduction by Elizabeth Longford. Lieutenant George Woodberry also referred to General Stuart's [*sic*] pack of eighteen couples of hounds arriving in Lisbon on 18 February 1813: George Woodberry, *Journal du Lieutenant Woodberry: Campagnes de Portugal et d'Espagne, de France, de Belgique et de France, 1813–1815* (Paris: E. Plon, Nourrit et Cie, 1896).

25   Wellington to Beresford, 8 November 1811 (BL, Add MS 21,504).

26   Beresford to Wellington, 12 November 1811 (BL, Add MS 21,504).

27   Beresford to Lady Anne Beresford, 6 December 1811 (Beresford family papers).

28   Henry MacKinnon, *Journal*.

29   Although present at the latter stages of the siege, Beresford's battle honours did not include Ciudad Rodrigo. Wellington insisted that such honours were only awarded to those actively involved. The Ordens do Dia show Beresford at Gallegos on 16 January 1812.

30   John Theophilus Beresford (1792–1812) was the eldest son of Marcus Beresford and Lady Frances Leeson (daughter of the Earl of Milltown). This Marcus Beresford was the son of John Beresford 'The Commissioner' referred to in the Introduction. 'The Commissioner' was the brother of the 1st Marquis of Waterford and thus an uncle of Marshal William Carr Beresford.

31   Beresford had been appointed Colonel of the regiment on 9 February 1807 while still in South America; Lt. Col. H.F.N. Jourdain, *The Connaught Rangers* (London: Royal United Service Institution, 1924).

32   Grattan, *Adventures with the Connaught Rangers*, pp. 147–8.

33   Wellington named the four officers in command of the sap (each one appears to have been responsible for the volunteers from his regiment), including John Theophilus Beresford, noting 'they distinguished themselves not less in the storm of the place than they had in the performance of their laborious duty during the siege'. See Wellington to Liverpool, 20 January 1812 (WD 5, 474). That letter was of course written prior to the young Lieutenant's death.

34   Beresford, Marcus de la Poer, 'On a Lonely City Wall', *The New Ranger* (January 2016), pp. 12–21.

35   William Stavely was more fortunate. Writing to his mother he explained he was with MacKinnon when he and others were blown up, but Stavely was merely stunned and bruised though he lost his sword, hat and coat (Collection of Letters and Notes of William Stavely, NAM 1999-06-149). Not so lucky was Captain John Uniacke of the 95th Regiment who was severely wounded and died on 27 January. The Uniacke family from Waterford were related to the Beresfords through marriage.

36   Beresford to John Poo Beresford (later Sir John) NYA/ZBA 21/10.

37   Beresford to Lady Anne Beresford, 28 January 1811 (Beresford family papers).

38   Beresford to Lady Frances Beresford, 20 January 1812 (Beresford family papers).

39   Beresford to Lady Frances Beresford, 29 January 1812 (Beresford family papers).

40   Beresford to Lady Anne Beresford, 29 January 1812 (Beresford family papers).

41   Beresford to Lady Frances Beresford, 11 March 1812 (Beresford family papers).

42 Stuart to Marquis Wellesley, 1 and 2 February 1812 (NA, WO 1/401). Ricardo Nogueira, *Memória das causas mais notáveis que se trateram nas conferências do governo d'estes reinos desde o dia 9 de Agosto de 1810, em que entrei a server o logar de um dos governadores, ate 5 de Fevereiro de 1820* (Biblioteca Nacional, Lisbon 6848–6853, six volumes). Nogueira was a member of the Regency from 1810 until 1820. D'Urban, op. cit., p. 238, says Beresford was made President of the Council of War.

43 Stuart to Marquis Wellesley, 1 February 1812 (NA, FO 342).

44 Oman, *History*, vol. V, p. 228; Vichness, op. cit., pp. 452–3 suggests Beresford had little influence on the deliberations of the Regency at this time and that he took no identifiable role in the negotiations designed to address financial issues. In support of this suggestion he cites the lack of correspondence.

45 D'Urban, *Journal*, pp. 239 and 240 indicates Beresford left Lisbon on 2 March 1812.

46 D'Urban, *Journal*, p. 241; Fortescue, op. cit., vol. 8, p. 382. The Algarve Brigade consisted of elements of the 2nd and 14th Portuguese regiments of line which formed part of the 4th Division.

47 Michael Glover (ed.), *A Gentleman Volunteer: The Letters of George Hennell from the Peninsular War, 1812–1813* (London: Heinemann, 1979). Hennell to a friend, 5 April 1812. The 9th and 12th Portuguese regiments and the 5th Caçadores were with the Light Division at Badajoz.

48 Wellington to Liverpool, 7 April 1812 (WD 5, 578).

49 AHM 1-14, Caixa 24, quoted in Vichness, op. cit., p. 459.

50 The Portuguese brigades in Beresford's command were as follows:
Light Division: 9th and 21st Portuguese (two battalions each) and 12th Caçadores.
4th Division: 11th and 23rd Portuguese (two battalions each) and 7th Caçadores.
5th Division: 3rd and 15th Portuguese (two battalions each) and 8th Caçadores.

51 Beresford to Lady Anne Beresford, 7 July 1812 (Beresford family papers).

52 Bragge to father, 25 July 1812, in S.A.C. Cassels (ed.), *Peninsular Portrait 1811–1814: The Letters of Captain William Bragge Third (King's Own) Dragoons* (London: Oxford University Press, 1963).

53 General Zephyrino Brandão, 'Beresford Ferido na Batalha de Salamanca', *Revista Militar* 3 (1908), pp. 130–40. Dr David Barry from Roscommon, a surgeon attached to the 58th foot, operated on Beresford at Salamanca.

54 William Warre to his father, 24 July 1812 (Warre, *Letters*, p. 185).

55 Captain William Bragge in a letter of 28 July 1812 to his father reported that Marmont, Bonnet and Beresford were all dead, though in fact all three were seriously wounded. See Cassels, *Peninsular Portrait*. Wellington to Bathurst 24 July 1812 (WD 5, 755).

56 Wellington to Bathurst, 24 July 1812 (WD 5, 753–8 at 756).

57 Wellington to Bathurst, 24 July 1812 (second letter, WD 5, 758).

58 Wellington to Bathurst, 24 July 1812 (WD 5, 753–8 at 754).

59 Wellington to Beresford, 2 December 1812 (WD 6, 188).

60 Beresford to Lady Anne Beresford, 25 and 26 July 1812 (Beresford family papers).

61 Beresford to Wellington, 3 and 5 August 1812 (WP1/348/19 and 348/26).

62 Beresford to Wellington, 24 August 1812 (WP1/349/89).

63 Beresford to Lady Anne Beresford, 26 August 1812 (Beresford family papers).

64 D'Urban's report is enclosed with Beresford's letter to Wellington, 31 August 1812 (WP1/349/133). He refers to the 1st Regiment lacking cloaks and boots, the 11th Regiment having saddles of a very old description, 'very bad and heavy, cutting the horse backs every march'. Some of the men were allegedly too heavy for the horses, as well as being 'stupid'. The men of the 12th Regiment were reportedly 'totally unfit for dragoons and incapable of becoming so'. However, D'Urban praised the talents of individual Portuguese officers including Lieutenant Colonel João Luiz (1st), Lieutenant Colonel Domingo Bernardino (11th) as well as Viscount de Barbacena and Captain Figueiredo (12th).

65 Beresford to Wellington, 31 August 1812 (WP1/349/133).

66 Wellington to Beresford, 8 September 1812 (WP1/351/24).

67 Wellington to Beresford, 9 September 1812 (WP1/351/30).

68 William Warre to father, 29 August 1812 (Warre, *Letters*, p. 188).

69 Over land via Robliza (3 September), Fuente de Roble (4 September), Almeida (5 and 6 September), Santa Eufémia (between Pinhel and Trancoso, 7 September), A. de Barros (8 September), Lamego (9 September), Entre os Rios (10 September), Porto (11 September).

70 Beresford to Lady Anne Beresford, 11 September 1812 (Beresford family papers).

71 Beresford to 2nd Marquis Waterford, 19 September 1812 (Beresford family papers).

72 Beresford to 2nd Marquis of Waterford, 17 October 1812 (Beresford family papers).

73 Wellington to Beresford, 26 September and 5 October 1812 (WP1/351/73 and 106). See also WD 9, 465 and 466.

74 Wellington to Stuart, 24 April 1813 (WD 6, 445), and see also Stuart to Castlereagh, 21 November 1812 (NA, FO 342/39).

75 Beresford to Wellington, 1 August 1812 (WP1/348/6).

76 D'Urban, *Journal*, p. 301 refers to commissariat arrangements having failed during the retreat. Wellington's reprimand to his officers which caused so much dissension is dated 28 November 1812 (WD 6, 180–1).

77 Wellington to Beresford, 14 October 1812 (WP1/351/137).

78 See Mendo Castro Henriques, *Vitória e Pirenéus, 1813* (Lisbon: Tribuna da História, 2009), pp. 30–1. Henriques calculates that Portuguese losses on the retreat amounted to some 11 per cent of the men, whereas their British counterparts lost about 8 per cent. The 24th Regiment of line lost some 50 per cent of its men and its commander, Lieutenant Colonel Aires da Costa, and a number of other officers were condemned by the Council of War and deprived of their commissions.

79 Ordens do Dia, 7 January 1813. These were directed against captains, lieutenants and ensigns (alferes).

80 See de la Fuente, op. cit., pp. 213–15.

81 Stuart to Castlereagh, 3 April 1813 (NA, FO 342/41).

82 Wellington to Beresford, 22 September 1812 (WP1/351/67).

83 Wellington to Prince João, 12 April 1813 (WD 6, 417–20). It is unclear whether this letter was sent to Brazil or used to persuade the Regency to ameliorate matters.

84 Beresford was created Conde de Trancoso on 13 May 1811. Permission to use the title was granted by Prince George (later George IV) on 18 October 1811, the same date on which he gave authority to Wellington to accept the title of Conde de Vimeiro. Beresford had written to his half-sister Lady Anne Beresford on 14 September 1811 expressing doubt as to whether he would be allowed to accept the title (Beresford family papers).

85 David Barry and James McGrigor were two physicians created Knights of the Order.

86 On the same date as Beresford and Wellington were authorised to wear the Order, a similar permission was extended to Sir Robert Wilson and Colonel Nicholas Trant (*The Royal Military Chronicle*, 19 October 1811).

87 Wellington to Beresford, 22 September 1812 (WP1/351/67). 'If I should find that the Order of the Tower and the Sword is prostituted, I shall not wear it and will recommend to all British officers to follow my example and I will request you will inform M. de Forjaz of this determination or any other person who will convey it to the Prince Regent.'

88 Other recipients of the Order included Generals D'Urban, John Hamilton, George Murray and Lord Fitzroy Somerset.

89 Beresford to 2nd Marquis of Waterford, 14 December 1812 (Beresford family papers).

90 Wellington was in Cádiz from 24 December 1812 until 10 January 1813, during which time he agreed various reforms of the Spanish army with the Cortes. Included in these was agreement that appointments and the movement of Spanish troops would only be made with his approval, two topics that would later cause problems when the Cortes chose to follow its own course.

Chapter 13

1 Beresford held a series of dinners for Regency members in Lisbon. See BN 6849; Nogueira, *Memória*, 18 January 1813 quoted in Vichness, op. cit., p. 470.

2 AHM, 1-14, Cx 47; Circular Aos Generais das Provincias.

3 Forjaz to Beresford, 25 August 1813 (AHM, 1-14, Cx 47).

4 One problem which had to be faced was that soldiers (712 men) in the 4th and 10th Portuguese regiments had enlisted at the beginning of 1809 for a term of four years, which had now expired, and some of these men wished to return home. The solution to the problem as suggested by Wellington was that the law must be observed if they wished to leave the army, but that they would be liable to an immediate requirement to enlist again under the laws of the kingdom. He suggested therefore it would be better for them to continue to serve until given discharges at the end of the war. Beresford to Wellington, 13 February 1813 and Wellington to Beresford, 17 February 1813 (WP1/365/135 and 366/93).

5 Stuart to Castlereagh, 20 February 1813 (NA, FO 342/20). The procedure adopted for re-clothing the regiments was to take uniforms by water as far as possible and to then march the regiments to these landing depots where they were re-outfitted. Thus clothing was sent up the Tagus, to the Mondego and to Porto in early 1813.

6 Wellington to Beresford, 8 March 1813 (WP1/365/280).

7 See Chapter 6 above.

8 Wellington to Beresford, 2 December 1812 (WD 6, 188).

9 Wellington to Beresford, 10 December 1812 (WD 6, 205–6).

10 Wellington to Bathurst, 2 December 1812 (WSD 7, 484 and WD 9, 591).

11 Wellington to Beresford, 2 December 1812 (WD 6, 188–9).

12 Wellington to Bathurst, 2 December 1812 (WD 9, 591). Wellington urged Beresford not to resign, at least not before ascertaining whether a solution could be achieved. Wellington to Beresford, 6 February 1813 (WP1/365/104).

13 Wellington to Beresford, 2 December 1812 (WD 6, 188); Wellington to Bathurst, 26 January 1812 (WD 6, 248), in which Wellington cited the decision of the late Commander in Chief, Sir David Dundas (1809–11), referring to a letter from Dundas of 10 July 1809 in response to queries raised at that time by Wellington.

14 York to Bathurst, 28 December 1812, with Memorandum of 26 December 1812 (WSD 7, 516–17).

15 Beresford to Wellington, 2 and 3 February 1813 (WP1/366/46 and 51). Arbuthnot had told Beresford that his recall was generally spoken of in England.

16 Wellington to Beresford, 16 February 1813 (WP1/365/134).

17 Bathurst to Wellington, 27 January 1813 (NA, WO 6/51).

18 Oman, *History*, vol. VI, pp. 229–30.

19 Wellington to Beresford, 12 and 16 February 1812 (WD 6, 299 and 306).

20 Beresford to Wellington 12 February 1813 (WP1/366/90).

21 Beresford to Wellington, 22 January 1813 (WP1/364/90).

22 Wellington to Beresford, 16 January 1813 (WD 6, 245); Wellington to Beresford, 30 January 1813 (WP1/365/74).

23 Beresford to Wellington, 4 February 1813 (WP1/366/62).

24 New clothing and accoutrements were issued to the Portuguese regiments and contracts issued for the supply of meat and bread while on campaign. Vichness, op. cit., p. 471.

25 On 16 May, the second anniversary of the battle of Albuera, Wellington gave a dinner in Beresford's honour. D'Urban, op. cit., p. 306.

26 Wellington to Beresford, 24 April 1813 (WD 10, 322).

27 Oman suggests these figures; see *History*, vol. VI, Appendices VIII and IX. Giron was now commanding the Army of Galicia. Much to Wellington's annoyance the Cortes had removed Castaños as Captain-General of Galicia and replaced him with General Lacy.

28 Wellington to Bathurst, 22 June 1813 (WD 6, 539–43). The 3rd Division commanded by Picton included the Portuguese brigade commanded by Manley Power. The brigade was made up of 1st and 2nd battalions 9th Portuguese regiment of line, 1st and 2nd battalions 21st Portuguese regiment of line and 11th Caçadores. The 4th Division was commanded by Lowry Cole and included a Portuguese brigade under George Stubbs. This brigade was made up of 1st and 2nd battalions of the 11th Portuguese regiment of line, 1st and 2nd battalions of the 23rd Portuguese regiment of line and 7th Caçadores. Picton, who commanded the 3rd Division, eulogised 'the Portuguese brigade attached to the 3rd division was the admiration of the whole army'. Picton to Colonel Pleydell, 1 July 1813. Quoted in F.C. Beatson, *Wellington: The Crossing of the Gaves and the Battle of Orthez* (London: Heath Cranton Limited, 1925), p. 69.

29 Ibid. p. 542. Beresford and the Officers of the Portuguese army were specifically mentioned in the House of Commons vote of thanks for the battle (WSD 8, 67).

30 Wellington to Beresford, 22 August 1813 (WD 6, 703), and Wellington to Bathurst, 25 August 1813 (WSD 8, 205) enclosed the list of those entitled to a medal. However, the list is not attached to the letter as published.

31 Torrens to Wellington, 21 July 1813 and Palmerston to Wellington, 14 July 1813 (WSD 8, 73 and 95). It was the capture of Marshal Jourdan's baton by bugler Paddy Shannon of the 87th Regiment at Vitória that instigated a baton for Wellington in that he had sent Jourdan's baton to the Prince Regent (later George IV).

32 Wellington to Bathurst, 1 August 1812 (WD 6, 613).

33 Larpent, op. cit., 21 July 1813.

34 Beresford to Lady Anne Beresford, 20 September and 2 October 1813 (Beresford family papers).

35 Stuart to Wellington, 26 August 1813 (WSD 8, 210–11).

36 Bathurst to Wellington, 15 September 1813 (WSD 8, 253).

37 Torrens to Wellington, 21 September 1813 and Hope to Torrens, 17 September 1813 (WSD 8, 263–4).

38 Wellington to Bathurst, 18 October 1813 (WD 7, 70–2).

39 Stuart to Castlereagh, 23 and 30 October 1813 (NA, FO 342/45).

40 Wellington to Stuart, 8 November 1813 (WP1/381).

41 Lowry Cole alleges that Beresford sought this command from Wellington, and states that while at the battle of Nivelle Beresford had nominal command, in effect he received his orders from the Quartermaster General. Rather sourly, he implies that the objective was to get Beresford a peerage and that he had no objection as long as Beresford did not continue in command of the 4th Division. Cole was to be disappointed in his wish regarding command of the 4th Division and it is extremely unlikely Wellington would appoint anyone to a command in order to ensure them a peerage. Indeed, we have seen that several

months earlier Bathurst was suggesting Beresford as a candidate for a peerage (Lowry Cole and Gwynn, *Memoirs*).

Each of the divisions now under Beresford had a Portuguese brigade. The 3rd Division commanded by Picton included Major General Power's brigade being 9th and 21st Portuguese and 11th Caçadores. The 4th Division under Cole included a brigade under Colonel Stubbs made up of 11th and 23rd Portuguese and 7th Caçadores. The 7th division under Dalhousie included the brigade of Lecor made up of 7th and 19th Portuguese and 2nd Caçadores. Lecor in fact assumed command of the division when Dalhousie returned temporarily to England in November 1813, and in doing so became the only Portuguese commander of an allied division in Wellington's army. Silveira commanded the Portuguese Division in the Allied army in Hamilton's absence in 1813.

42 Beresford to Wellington, 27 October 1813 (WSD 8, 324–5), Note Bera is sometimes referred to as 'Vera' in English correspondence.

43 The isolated port of Santoña in north west Spain, forty-five kilometres from Santander, remained in French possession until May 1814 but represented no threat to the Allies and Wellington ignored it.

44 Bathurst to Wellington, 25 November 1813 (WSD 8, 400).

45 See letter of Lieutenant Colonel R.H.A. Frazer quoted in F.C. Beatson, *Wellington and the Invasion of France* (London: Edward Arnold & Co., 1931), p. 163.

46 Sir Richard D. Henegan, *Seven Years Campaigning in the Peninsula and the Netherlands, 1808–1815*, two volumes (London: Henry Colburn, 1846), vol. 2. See also *The Times*, 5 July 1813.

47 Before moving on the Nivelle, on 1 November Wellington issued an assurance to the French and Basque inhabitants that he had given orders to prevent pilfering and other outrages. He followed this up on 2 November with a stern order in similar terms to his own general officers. These proclamations are reproduced in Appendix B to Beatson, *Wellington and the Invasion of France*, vol. 2, p. 214. For details of the welcome see Hope to Wellington, 12 November 1813 (WSD 8, 364).

48 Most of Beresford's correspondence for this period is headed 'Ustaritz' though he was clearly moving around the area.

49 John Edgecombe Daniel, *Journal of an Officer in the Commissariat Department of the Army comprising a narrative of the campaigns under his Grace the Duke of Wellington in Portugal, Spain, France and the Netherlands in the years 1811, 1812, 1813, 1814, and 1815 and a short account of the Army of Occupation in France during the years 1816, 1817 & 1818* (London: Porter and King (printer), 1820).

50 Hope to Wellington, 11 December 1813 (WSD 8, 420–1). Hope highlighted the performance of Brigadier General Campbell's brigade.

51 Beresford to Lady Anne Beresford, 15 December 1813 (Beresford family papers).

52 Stewart to Hill, 14 December 1813 (WSD 8, 440).

53 Beresford to Lady Anne Beresford, 15 December 1813 (Beresford family papers).

54 Oman, *History*, vol. VII, pp. 286–7.

55 Stuart to Castlereagh, 18 March 1814 (NA, FO 342/46) and Forjaz to Beresford, 11 January 1814 (AHM 1-14 Cx 48).

56 Tradition is that a hunt was arranged involving both British and French officers in the weeks after the battle of Orthez, 27 February 1814. Major General Henry Fane was ordered to occupy Pau with his dragoons on 6 March 1814, so perhaps it was around this time the hunt took place. By the 1840s the Pau foxhounds were well established and it still exists today with its headquarters at Le Cercle Anglais in Pau.

57 On 15 April 1813, the Light Division had produced 'She stoops to Conquer' at Gallegos. The same Division also produced 'The Apprentice'. See Daniel, *Journal*.

58   Beresford to Lady Anne Beresford, 5 December 1813 (Beresford family papers).

59   Beresford to Lady Anne Beresford, 15 December 1813 (Beresford family papers).

60   Beresford to Lady Anne Beresford, 29 January 1814 (Beresford family papers).

Chapter 14

1   Beresford reciting 'the only reproaches we meet with' (in France). Beresford to Lady Anne Beresford, 26 February, 1814 (Beresford family papers).

2   Hubert Horace Lamb, *Climate History and the Modern World* (London: Methuen 1982).

3   Wellington to Bathurst, 21 November 1813 (WD 7 at 153). See also Daniel, *Journal*, p. 265.

4   Wellington to Bathurst, 14 December 1813 (WD 7, 194–7).

5   Wellington to Bathurst, 22 November 1813 (WD 7, 156–7).

6   L'Estrange, *Recollections*, p. 165. In Portugal and Spain he had shot and eaten snipe, woodcock, partridges, and even a bustard, p. 43.

7   Beresford to John Poo Beresford, 28 February 1814 (NYA/ZBA 21/10, f. 42), complains that two fowl cost 24 Francs in Ustaritz but only 2 Francs in Saint-Sever.

8   Wellington to Bathurst 13 February 1814 (WD 7, 319–20).

9   Wellington to Bathurst, 8 December 1813 (WD 7, 189).

10   Wellington was under pressure from the government to advance further in the winter of 1813/14, the government in turn having been urged by the Allies in northern Europe to get Wellington to do so. He responded with some asperity that he was farther into France than any of the allied powers and added: 'In military operations there are some things which cannot be done; one of these is to move troops in this country during or immediately after a violent fall of rain.' Wellington to Bathurst, 21 December 1813 (WD 7, 214).

11   Wellington to Bathurst, 8 December 1813 (WD 7, 189).

12   Indeed, Wellington claimed that if he had the money to put 40,000 Spaniards in the field he would have his outposts on the Garonne. Wellington to Bathurst, 21 December 1813 (WD 7, 213–16).

13   Ibid. at 216. The pay of some of the muleteers he observed was now twenty-six months in arrears.

14   Wellington to Bathurst, 8 January 1814 (WD 7, 246–8).

15   Wellington to Bathurst 15 December 1813 (second letter, WD 7, 204).

16   Wellington received £121,535 on 18 December and a further £99,987 was dispatched but had not reached him by 8 January 1814. Wellington to Bathurst, 8 January 1814 (WD 7, 246).

17   Wellington to Bathurst, 16 January 1814 (WD 7, 270).

18   Wellington to Beresford, 1 February 1814 (WD 7, 296).

19   Wellington to Colonel Bunbury, 4 February 1814 (WD 7, 302).

20   Wellington to Beresford, 7 February 1814 (WD 7, 305). This letter implies repayment of the monies previously 'borrowed' to help the Spaniards and the British cavalry earlier, as Wellington says it is in addition to the sum of $200,000.

21   Beresford to Forjaz, 2 January 1814 (AHM 1-14-33).

22   WSD 8, 581–2.

23   See Herbert, H. Kaplan, *Nathan Mayer Rothschild and the Creation of a Dynasty: The Critical Years 1806–1816* (Stanford, CA: Stanford University Press, 2006).

24   One example of this lack of supplies is noted by Larpent in his diary for 28 January 1814, where he refers to Wellington seeking to negotiate with Soult for the purchase of British soldiers' uniforms, a consignment of which had been captured en route to the Peninsula by a French privateer. See *Journal*, p. 373.

25 Wellington to Bathurst, 21 November 1813 (WD 7, 150–3). See also John Malcolm, 'Reminiscences of a Campaign in the Pyrenees and South of France', reproduced in *Constable's Miscellany of Original and Selected Publications in the Various Departments of Literature, Science and the Arts: Memorials of the Late War*, volume 1 ('Constable 1'), where he says that the Basques delighted to have British Officers in their houses as they are thus protected from the depravations of Spaniards and Portuguese.

26 Beresford to Lady Anne Beresford, 2 March 1814 (Lisbon: Gulbenkian Foundation, Beresford Papers, BC 919).

27 Wellington to Beresford, 28 January 1814 (WD 7, 289–90).

28 Wellington to Bathurst, 6 November 1813 (WD 7, 116).

29 Charles Stuart to Castlereagh, 1 January 1814 (Stuart de Rothesay correspondence; NA, FO 342/46). The Spaniards adopted the view that the only assistance they were bound to supply was buildings for hospitals.

30 Stuart to Castlereagh, 22 and 29 January 1814 (ibid. ff. 137 and 193). Major General Blunt and Colonel Brown were training recruits in depots at Mafra and Elvas, respectively.

31 Stuart to Castlereagh 18 March 1814 (Ibid. f. 691).

32 Wellington to Henry Wellesley, 14 January 1814 (WD 7, 262–3).

33 Soult was thus deprived of the infantry divisions of Boyer (9th) and Leval (7th) as well as Teilhard's cavalry division.

34 Correspondence de Napoleon Imperial Nat., t. 27, no. 21097.

35 The depradations of the French army were widely protested by local officials in what is now the Department of Pyrénées-Atlantiques. See Colonel Pierre Dupuy, *Soult et Wellington dans le Sud-Ouest* (Sauveterre-de-Béarn: Association Sauveterre Espace Culturel, 1996), pp. 16–17.

36 At that time the Adour was navigable from the sea to Saint-Sever, a distance of 128 kilometres. Soult sought to secure this section of the river with some twenty gunboats manned by sailors and marines from Rochefort. Sir Peter Hayman, *Soult: Napoleon's Maligned Marshal* (London: Arms and Armour, 1990), p. 203.

37 Beresford was also charged with interrupting river traffic on the Adour, by which the French continued to supply Bayonne. 'Movement of a part of the army', 10 February 1814 (WSD 8, 581).

38 Wellington to Beresford, 15 February 1814 (WD 7, 321).

39 Ibid. Wellington does not say whether he is referring to the Gave d'Oloron or the Gave de Pau, but in the event while there was some conflict on the Gave d'Oloron, the main engagement took place at Orthez after the Allies had crossed both rivers.

40 Beresford in fact sent a large reconnaissance over the Adour on 21 February but withdrew it that evening. During all this time he was making preparations to bridge the river.

41 Soult to Guerre (Clarke was Minister for War), 13 February 1814, quoted in Beatson, *Wellington: The Crossing of the Gaves*, p. 132.

42 On 24 February the army crossed the Gave d'Oloron at Viellenave (Lecor and Stewart), Montfort/Laàs (Clinton), Barraute/Andrein (Clinton). One of the objectives was to try to cut off the French in Sauveterre-de-Béarn from retreating to join the remainder of the army at Orthez; though this did not succeed. The retreating French blew up the bridge over the river at Sauveterre and it was on 25 February that Picton's troops entered the town. On the previous day the Allies had suffered a considerable reverse both upstream and downstream of Sauveterre when Keane's brigade (part of Picton's Division) and the 7th Hussars had been thrown back with substantial losses by the 119th Regiment of Line from the brigade of St Pol (Villatte's Division).

43 Villatte's Division had occupied Sauveterre (with that of Harispe on the heights behind it in or near Orion) and withdrew having blown up the bridge there, forcing the Allies to ford the Gave d'Oloron below the town.

44 Reportedly, Beresford heard of a miller who knew of this ford. He had the man brought to him by Major Hughes (as he then was) and he indicated the crossing which involved a small island in the middle of the river. The miller was put on horseback and led elements of Vivian's cavalry across first and the infantry followed, helped in part by the erection of a pontoon bridge. Note of Colonel Hughes; *United Service Journal* (1840), p. 446. This may have been James Hughes of the 18th Dragoons.

45 Beresford to John Poo Beresford, 28 February 1814 (NYA/ZBA 21/42).

46 Ibid. Beresford's force had moved so fast that when he wrote to his sister Anne that evening he said he had neither baggage nor a servant; but he commented on the friendly reception received from the people of the Béarn. Beresford to Lady Anne Beresford, 26 February 1814 (Beresford family papers).

47 George Murray also expressed the view that Soult would retreat in a letter to Hill, 26 February 1814 (see Edwin Sidney, *Life of Lord Hill*, quoted in Beatson, *Wellington: The Crossing of the Gaves*, p. 195). Wellington and his staff spent the night of 26 February based in Sauveterre-de-Béarn.

48 Beresford to Lady Anne Beresford, 26 February 1814 (Beresford family papers).

49 Memorandum by the Q.M.G. of the movements of the allied troops preparatory to and during the attack upon the enemy at Orthez (WD 7, 331–2).

50 Beresford to Wellington, 3 March 1814 (WSD 8, 611).

51 Foy said he was hit by a ball from one of Congreve's rockets. Hit in the shoulder, he lost all feeling in his left arm but still managed to ride to Sault-de-Navailles where he was treated by the Chief surgeon. He was sent to Toulouse to recuperate and managed to leave Toulouse before the battle after a further operation. Girod de l'Ain, *Vie Militaire*, p. 240.

52 Wellington to Bathurst, 1 March 1814 (WD 7, 336–42). Wellington entered Orthez about 4 pm riding Copenhagen, one of his favourite horses, which he also rode at Waterloo. He established his HQ at La Belle Hôtesse, previously occupied by Soult. Sir Robert Kennedy, Commissary-General was appointed Governor of the town and rigorous discipline was maintained. Wellington paid a further visit to Orthez when he passed through the town on 18 May on his way to Madrid.

53 See Beatson, *Wellington: The Crossing of the Gaves*, p. 253.

54 Beresford to Lady Anne Beresford, 2 March 1814 (Beresford family papers). Lowry Cole also testified to the bravery of the French at Orthez, writing to his Sister, Lady Grantham, on 3 March 1814: 'The enemy behaved much better than I have seen them do for a length of time, which was the less expected as we have been so much accustomed to drive them before us.' Lowry Cole and Gwynn, *Memoirs*.

55 Beresford to Lady Anne Beresford, 2 March 1814 (Beresford family papers).

56 Ibid.

57 *Parliamentary Debates*, vol. 27, 24 March 1814. Sir Frederick Flood was the MP who made the point concerning Ireland's production of Generals, while Whitsted Keene suggested the building of a house in Ireland for Wellington. No such house was built, but by the time of the debate £15,000 had already been raised for a testimonial to Wellington and that was later translated into the impressive Wellington Monument in Phoenix Park in Dublin.

58 Girod de l'Ain, *Vie Militaire*, p. 238.

59 Ibid. p. 239.

60 Guerre to Soult, 25 February 1814, quoted in Lieutenant-Colonel Jean-Baptiste Dumas, *Neuf Mois de Campagnes à la suite du Maréchal Soult* (Paris: Charles-Lavauzelle, 1907), p. 366.

61 Soult to Guerre, 26 February 1814. Ibid. p. 200.

62   Sub-Préfet d'Orthez writing on 18 February 1814: 'Our troops appear too penetrated with the superiority of the enemy, they have no doubt that his plan of invasion will succeed.' Quoted in Dumas, *Neuf Mois de Campagnes à la suite du Maréchal Soult*, p. 347.

63   The Duc d'Angoulême was the eldest son of the youngest brother (subsequently Charles X) of Louis XVI. He married Marie Thérèse, the eldest child of Louis XVI. On the abdication of his father in 1830 he would have succeeded to the throne had he not abdicated.

64   Wellington to Angoulême, 25 February 1814 (WD 7, 333).

65   Wellington to Angoulême, 3 March 1814 (WD 7, 343).

66   Wellington had received royalist agents from Bordeaux on 4 March indicating the city was prepared to renounce Napoleon; Alistair Nichols, *Wellington's Mongrel Regiment: A History of the Chasseurs Britanniques Regiment 1801–1814* (Staplehurst: Spellmount, 2005), p. 168.

67   Wellington to Beresford, 7 March 1814 (two letters, WD 7, 352–5).

68   Ibid. Second letter.

69   Wellington to Beresford, 12 March 1814 (WD 7, 366). Wellington particularly wanted to get Harvey back as it would appear there were problems with Lecor's Portuguese Division.

70   Beresford to Wellington, 10 March 1814 (WSD 8, 637).

71   Beresford to John Poo Beresford, 8 March 1814 (NYA/ZBA 21/10).

72   Jean-Baptiste Lynch, Mayor of Bordeaux (1749–1835). Not to be confused with his brother, Michel Lynch (1752–1840), Mayor of Pauillac. The Lynch family had emigrated from Galway following the defeat of James II and the Treaty of Limerick in 1691.

73   Letter from unidentified author, 14 March 1814 (NYA/ZBA 21/10).

74   Beresford to Wellington, 12 March 1814 (WD 7, 369). Impressively, Wellington was able to send on to Bathurst on 13 March Beresford's letter describing his entry into Bordeaux. At this stage Wellington was at Aire, some 160 kilometres from Bordeaux.

75   Beresford to Wellington, 13 March 1814 (WSD 8, 645). The commander at La Teste, the Chevalier de Mauleon, did in fact declare for the King on 16 March.

76   Stuart to Castlereagh, 31 March 1814 (Stuart de Rothesay correspondence, NA, FO 342/46, f. 717).

77   Wellington to Hope, 26 March 1814 (WD 7, 396–7). Wellington was at Saint-Lys.

78   On 26 March Beresford was encamped near La Salvetat-Saint-Gilles with the 4th and 6th divisions. This was only some thirteen kilometres from Toulouse. By 29 March he was at Colomiers, now a suburb of the city but then a village on its outskirts.

79   Beresford to John Poo Beresford, 25 March 1814 (NYA/ZBA 21/10).

80   QMG to Hill, 25 March 1814, and 'Arrangement for the movement of the army on 26 March 1814' (WD 7, 396).

81   Murray to Hill, 3 April 1814 (BL, Add MS 35,060).

82   The pontoon bridge consisted of seventeen boats; see Sir Joseph Thackwell, *The Military Memoirs of Lieutenant-General Sir Joseph Thackwell* (Uckfield: Naval and Military Press. Reprint of 1890 Original Edition, 2015).

83   A contemporary French account claims that a boat with hooks on its outside did in fact carry away part of the pontoon; 'C.D.', *Précis Historique de la Bataille Livrée le 10 Avril 1814, sous les murs de Toulouse* (Toulouse: Chez Benichet, 1815).

84   Anon, *Twelve years' military adventure in three quarters of the globe: The memoirs of an officer who served in the armies of His Majesty and of the East India Company, between the years 1802 and 1814, in which are contained the campaigns of the Duke of Wellington in India, and his last in Spain and the South of France,* two volumes (London: Henry Colburn, 1829).

85   Ibid.

86   Murray to Hill, 9 April 1814 (BL, Add MS 35,060).

87   The northern end of these heights is known as Mont Rave. The streets around the Calvinet Heights bear the names of the French generals there in 1814: Rue Soult, Clauzel, D'Erlon, Reille. There is also a Rue Dalmatie and a Rue 10 Avril.

88   Note that in contemporary accounts the river is sometimes referred to as the Ers.

89   A graphic first-hand account of the tough fighting on the Calvinet is given by Malcolm in 'Reminiscences', vol. 1. Malcolm was in fact captured by the French on the Heights and taken into Toulouse where he was operated on by a French surgeon and subsequently visited by an English surgeon who was a long-term resident of Toulouse. He refers also to the kindness of the French who fed him with soups and various fruits.

90   Malcolm, 'Reminiscences'.

91   Ibid.

92   Wellington put allied losses at Toulouse as 595 killed and 4,046 wounded with 18 missing (WD 7, 431).

93   This Portuguese brigade was part of the 6th Division. The brigade was made up of the 8th and 12th Portuguese regiments together with the 9th Caçadores. The 8th Regiment saw two officers killed at Toulouse (Lt Mascarnha and Ensign Benedits) and nearly all the wounded Portuguese officers in this battle came from the 8th and 12th regiments. In all ten Portuguese regiments of line and four regiments of caçadores were at Toulouse along with four regiments of cavalry.

94   Beresford to Wellington, 13 April 1814 (WD 7, 428–9).

95   Beresford to John Poo Beresford, 12 April 1814 (NYA/ZBA 21/10, f. 49).

96   Beresford to Wellington, 13 April 1814 (WSD 8, 739–41).

97   Q.M.G (Sir George Murray) to Beresford, 12 April 1814 (WD 7, 437).

98   Probably Labastide-Beauvoir about twenty-two kilometres from Toulouse.

99   Beresford to John Poo Beresford, 16 April (2 letters, NYA/ZBA 21/10, ff. 50 and 51).

100   The terms of the armistice noted that hostilities should cease at Bayonne, Saint-Jean-Pied-de-Port, Navarrenx, Blaye and the castle at Lourdes, all of which were still in French hands (WD 7, 458).

101   Bathurst to Wellington, 23 April 1814 (WSD 9, 29–30) confiding it was an unofficial communication.

102   See *Gentleman's Magazine*, 11 June 1814.

103   Beresford to John Poo Beresford, 2 September 1814 (NYA/ZBA 21/10, f. 55).

104   Beresford to John Poo Beresford, 18 September 1814 (NYA/ZBA 21/10, f. 56).

105   WSD 8, 373–4; 427–8; 545–6; 584–5 and 673–4. The figures would also suggest that the ratio of absentees to soldiers present was better in the Portuguese army than in its British counterpart.

106   João Centeno, 'Portuguese Army Actions 1808–1814' (*The Napoleon Series*, undated). Available at: https://www.napoleon-series.org/military/battles/portugal/c_portugal1.html and following (accessed 26 April 2018).

107   The British cavalry in some cases rode through France to the northern ports prior to embarkation. Those Portuguese with Dalhousie's 7th Division in Bordeaux travelled south to join their compatriots.

108   D'Urban as Quartermaster General accompanied the army. They reached Palencia (southwest of Burgos) on 10 July, Toro on 20 July and Braganza at the beginning of August. D'Urban, *Journal*, XXIV.

109   See 'The History of The Royal Irish Rifles' as quoted in Alice D. Berkeley, *New Lights on the Peninsular War: International Congress on the Iberian Peninsula, selected papers, 1780–1840* (Lisbon: The British Historical Society of Portugal, 1991), Appendix 4:

> They marched, in May, by slow stages, towards the coast, parting at Condom from their old comrades, the Portuguese of power's brigade (9th and 21st Line), who

had served beside them most faithfully and honourably from Busaco onward. The separation was bitterly felt on both sides. 'On the morning that we marched the Portuguese, ranged along the street, saluted us as we passed, and their hearty "vivas" and exclamations of regret evinced that they really felt moved.' Power's Brigade also included 11th Caçadores.

110   Beresford to John Poo Beresford, 16 April 1814 (NYA/ZBA 21/10, f. 51).
111   Wellington to Bathurst, 12 April 1814 (WD 7, 428).

Chapter 15

1   Personal correspondence is to be found in the NYA (ZBA series) and in the Beresford family papers. Individual letters will be referred to below.
2   John George was created Bishop of Cork and Ross in 1805 and in 1807 was appointed to the Bishopric of Raphoe. As Archbishop of Armagh and Primate of All Ireland he performed the marriage service of Richard Wellesley and Marianne Patterson in Dublin in 1825. Isabella Anne (sometimes Issy) married Sir John William Head Brydges in 1812. Elizabeth Louisa (sometimes Bess) married Major General Sir Denis Pack in 1816. William, Archbishop of Tuam, was created Lord Decies in 1812.
3   John Poo Beresford (1767–1844) was, like William Carr Beresford, a natural son of the 1st Marquis of Waterford, born prior to Waterford's marriage to Elizabeth Monck. He enjoyed a successful career in the Royal Navy ultimately rising to be an Admiral. He participated throughout the Revolutionary and Napoleonic wars with a number of different commands, being created a baronet in 1814. He married three times; first to Mary Anne Molloy, secondly to Harriet Peirse and thirdly to Amelia Peach, being succeeded by his son George from his first marriage.
4   Beresford to Waterford, 22 November 1808 (Beresford family papers).
5   Beresford to Angus McDonald (his agent in Pall Mall Court, London), 4 November 1808 (Beresford family papers) refers to sending home a favourite horse to be given to Lord Waterford. In 1809, Beresford was given a fine horse by the Junta of Catalonia which he arranged to send to Lord Waterford; Beresford to the 2nd Marquis of Waterford, 26 April 1809. He also sent him wines (notwithstanding Waterford suffered acutely from gout) and Merino sheep acquired in Spain; Maziere (Cork Merchant) to Beresford, 26 December 1810 confirming he has shipped wines onward to London and other articles have gone to Waterford (TT, MNE CX 207, f. 655). Henry's cousin, the politician John Claudius Beresford, complained of Henry's weakness as a correspondent, calling him 'indolent' (John Claudius Beresford to the 2nd Marquis of Waterford, Beresford family papers).
6   For instance, Waterford to John Poo Beresford, 5 June 1809 (NYA/ZBA 21/1).
7   Extensive correspondence of Lord John George Beresford is maintained in the Public Record Office of Northern Ireland (PRONI), D and T series.
8   Power of attorney, John Poo Beresford, 30 March 1798 (NYA/ZBA 21/1).
9   Beresford to Lady Anne Beresford, 3 March 1809, and Beresford to Waterford, same date (Beresford family papers).
10   Beresford to Lady Anne Beresford, 3 and 20 March 1809 (Beresford family papers). Rochefort is on the Charente estuary in south west France.
11   Beresford to Lady Anne Beresford, 20 February 1809, 14 September and 6 December 1811, 25 July, 26 and 27 August, and 20 September 1812 (Beresford family papers).
12   Beresford to Lady Anne Beresford, 6 December 1811 and 20 September 1813 (Beresford family papers).

13   Beresford to Lady Anne Beresford, 2 October 1813 and 29 January 1814 (Beresford family papers).

14   Beresford to Lady Anne Beresford, 2 October 1813 (Beresford family papers).

15   Beresford to Lady Anne Beresford, 15 December 1813 (Beresford family papers).

16   Waterford to John Poo Beresford, 5 and 25 June 1809; Beresford to John Poo Beresford, 9 June 1808, 9 May 1809 and 3 March 1811 (NYA/ZBA 21/10).

17   Wills of Captain John Poo Beresford dated 29 November 1808 and 6 August 1812, with codicil of 6 August 1812 (NYA/ZBA 21/1).

18   This correspondence is held by the NYA (ZBA series).

19   Beresford to John Poo Beresford, 23 January 1814 (NYA/ZBA 21/10).

20   Beresford to Lady Anne Beresford, 29 January and 13 February 1814 (Beresford family papers). In the latter letter he refers to getting rid of his 'unpleasant companions'. Beresford to John Poo Beresford, 6 February 1814 (NYA/ZBA 21/10).

21   Beresford to Lady Frances Beresford (nee Leeson) 10 August 1811 (Beresford family papers).

22   António was the son of a former Field Marshal of Portugal, João António Lemos de Lacerda Delgado.

23   William Lemos Willoughby was known as Guilherme Willoughby de Lemos in Portugal. While William Carr Beresford acknowledged him as his son, it did not prevent António Lemos, Visconte Juromenha, from registering him as *moço fidalgo* (young nobleman) in Rio de Janeiro when he was there in 1817. Though the Viscountess Juromenha was initially reluctant, William was brought over to England in 1827, attending first Charterhouse and subsequently Eton. He then joined the army, serving in the 23rd (Welsh Fusiliers) Regiment, rising to be a Captain before his retirement in 1845. In that year he married Louise Hermione. She died on 1 May 1846 giving birth to a girl. William died in England, 30 July 1861.

24   It is not clear whether William or Maria decided marriage was not the way forward.

25   BL, Add MS 30,099 ff. 197–8.

26   Lemos made at least two such trips in 1811 and in 1818.

27   Warre to James Warre (father), 31 December 1809 (*Letters from the Peninsula*, p. 59).

28   Ibid. 13 July and 10 October 1809, pp. 42 and 54. A query arose as to whether officers were in fact entitled to pay from both commissions which Beresford answered in the affirmative in a circular of 17 May 1810 (*The Dickson Manuscripts*, vol. II, pp. 221–2).

29   Warre to James Warre, 6 September 1809 and 7 September 1811 (*Letters from the Peninsula*, pp. 50 and 131).

30   Ibid. 31 December 1809, p. 61.

31   The performance of the Portuguese at the siege of Ciudad Rodrigo and Badajoz excited his particular admiration. Ibid. pp. 148 and 155.

32   Warre to Eleanor Warre (mother), 6 February 1810 (ibid. p. 69).

33   Warre to James Warre, 15 May 1810 (ibid. p. 80).

34   Beresford to John Poo Beresford, 29 October 1810 (NYA/ZBA 21/10, f. 5).

35   William Henry Sewell (c1786–1862). Joined the army in 1806 as an ensign in the 96th Foot. Promoted to Lieutenant in the 16th Light Dragoons in 1807 and Captain in 1812, rising to be Lieutenant General in 1854. He joined Beresford as an ADC in November 1808, remaining with him on the retreat to La Coruña in January 1809 (see Beresford to 2nd Marquis of Waterford, 22 November 1808; Beresford family papers). He then served as ADC to Beresford throughout the war, having returned to Portugal with him in March 1809. At the end of the war he remained in Portugal until 1816, commanding a cavalry regiment (*The Annual Register*, 1862, p. 396). Beresford did not seem to be greatly impressed with Angeja, saying a little later that while he was a favourite of the Prince he thought him a hypocrite or slothful (Beresford to John Poo Beresford, 18 September 1814; NYA/ZBA, 21/10, f. 56).

36 Beresford to John Poo Beresford, 29 October 1810 advising the latter he now had eight ADCs and about fourteen secretaries. This letter was written from his Headquarters in Casal Cochim in the Lines of Torres Vedras (NYA/ZBA 21/10, f. 5).

37 In 1812 Beresford became concerned based on a rumour that Arbuthnot had put it about Beresford intended to retreat at Albuera. Beresford could not believe the rumour (he wondered if the source was George Murray, Wellington's Quartermaster General) and it would seem that it was subsequently clarified to the effect that Arbuthnot had stated Beresford had ordered the retirement of two batteries of guns, having not noticed that the French were themselves retreating, until the move was pointed out by Arbuthnot. Brave, dedicated and efficient, Arbuthnot was a valuable member of staff. See Beresford to Torrens, 1 November 1811 and Beresford to John Poo Beresford, 12 March and 3 April 1812 (all in NYA/ZBA 21/10).

38 Thomas Bermingham Henry Daly Sewell was married to Harriet Beresford, a daughter of the Archbishop of Tuam. Arbuthnot came from Rockfleet in County Mayo.

39 When Pack died young in 1823, it was Beresford who secured a pension from the British government for Lady Pack. Beresford was godfather to Denis William Pack and on Beresford's death left his Irish estates to his godson on condition that he added the name Beresford to his own family name. This he did by Royal Licence in 1854.

40 Hardinge at the conclusion of the war was promoted to be Lieutenant Colonel of the 40th Foot and in July 1814 took command of the 1st Foot Guards. He later rose to be a Field Marshal and Governor of India. Ultimately he succeeded Wellington as Commander in Chief of the British army in 1852 and in that capacity was in charge at the time of the Crimean war.

41 D'Urban, *Journal* and extensive correspondence in both British and Portuguese archives (NAM, BL, NA, AHM, TT).

42 Thomas Hope had given Louisa on her wedding night the dowry of £3,000 received by Hope from the Archbishop.

43 At various times he resided at a house in Sintra. Of course he also had the use of houses in various towns where he established his Quartel General, such as Trancoso, Chamusca and Casal Cochim on the Lines of Torres Vedras.

44 Beresford to Waterford, 27 June 1809 (Beresford family papers).

45 Beresford to Sir John Poo Beresford, 9 May 1810 (NYA/ZBA 21/10, f. 3).

46 *The Times*, 21 July 1807.

47 See Chapter 2.

48 Remarkably Baird, having been removed from his position as Lieutenant-Governor of the Cape, and Popham, having been the subject of a Court Martial, and both in dispute as to prize money, were called upon to serve together in the British attack on Copenhagen in 1807.

49 Donnelly v. Sir Home Popham; 'Reports of Cases Argued and Determined in the Court of Common Pleas, Michaelmas Term 1807 to Easter Term 1809' per Mansfield. Ch. J. (vol. 1, pp. 3–4). There was an unfortunate knock-on effect in that Captain King, whom Popham had appointed Captain of the *Diadem*, on raising his own pennant as Commodore was adjudged not to be a captain and therefore not entitled to a captain's share of the prize money. See Cobbett's *Parliamentary Debates*, vol. 22, ff. 165.

50 There were a number of army agents who acted for British officers during the war, amongst the most substantial of which appears to have been Greenwood & Co. However, Angus MacDonald of 4 Pall Mall Court acted for a considerable clientele, including William Carr Beresford.

51 John Claudius Beresford (1766–1846) was a son of the Hon. John Beresford, the Revenue Commissioner, widely regarded as one of the most powerful men in Ireland. John was a brother of the 1st Marquis of

Waterford and John Claudius was therefore a cousin of William Carr Beresford. John Claudius held a number of income producing sinecures in Ireland (including Taster of Wines, 1798–1802) but was also a parliamentarian, holding seats at various times in Swords, Dublin City and Waterford County. He was elected a member of the Dublin Corporation in 1808 and remained one for many years, serving as Lord Mayor in 1814–15. He had reputedly acted with cruelty towards prisoners taken in the rebellion in Ireland of 1798 but vigorously opposed the Act of Union, whereby the Irish parliament ceased to exist and instead Ireland returned members to the parliament in London; going so far as to resign his position as Inspector General of Exports and Imports in order to show his principled opposition. A founder of the Grand Orange Lodge in Ireland, he was its first Grand Secretary. A complex political figure who, like Edmund Burke, hated clientelist politics believing MPs should act in the wider national interest. He did much to foster Irish industries.

52 Having sat for Swords and then Dublin, John Claudius was at this time a member for Waterford County.

53 Founded in 1793 and initially located in Beresford Place, the Beresford Bank later moved to Henry Street in Dublin. In 1799 the partners were listed as John Claudius Beresford, James Woodmason and James Farrell, but later both Farrell and Woodmason (1808) ceased to be partners, being replaced by Benjamin Ball, Mathew Plunkett and Philip Doyne. Following Beresford's withdrawal from the Bank it became Ball's Bank. See James William Gilbert, *The History of Banking in Ireland* (London: Longman, 1836).

54 John Claudius Beresford to the 2nd Marquis of Waterford, 5 June 1806 (Beresford family papers).

55 Beresford to 2nd Marquis of Waterford, 29 November 1808 (Beresford family papers).

56 Beresford to John Poo Beresford, 9 May 1810 (NYA/ZBA 21/10, f. 3). The Bishop referred to may have been Lord John George Beresford, the brother of the 2nd Marquis of Waterford, who was then Bishop of Raphoe and with whom the Marshal was on good terms.

57 House of Commons Debate, 7 June 1811 (*Hansard*, vol. 20, cc 519–32). Mathew on one occasion charged Wellington (when Chief Secretary for Ireland, as Arthur Wellesley) with corruption in respect of the Tipperary election.

58 The seats controlled by the Beresford interest included one member for each of Counties Londonderry and Waterford, one for the borough of Coleraine and one for the city of Londonderry. They would have also had influence elsewhere through marital and political alliances. The Beresfords were for the most part supporters of the Tory party, allied with Lord Castlereagh, the Wellesleys, Lord Liverpool and George Canning. Sir John Poo Beresford was MP for Coleraine from 1809–12 and 1814–23.

59 The Archbishop of Tuam (William de la Poer Beresford) sought the advice of the Chancellor of the Irish Exchequer on whether bankruptcy vacated the seat and further who might be the right person to succeed John Claudius. The Chancellor was clearly of the opinion that the Marshal was the appropriate person (Tuam to 2nd Marquis of Waterford, 27 March 1811, Beresford family papers). While the Chancellor is not named, it must have been John Foster, as William Wellesley Pole (later 3rd Earl of Mornington) was not appointed Chancellor until July 1811.

60 John Claudius' bankruptcy was declared in March 1811 (Archbishop of Tuam to Waterford, 27 March 1811, Beresford family papers). The mechanism by which he resigned his seat was to be appointed as Escheator of Munster, a sinecure abolished in 1838.

61 Archbishop of Tuam to 2nd Marquis of Waterford, 25 March 1811 (Beresford family papers).

62 *The House of Commons*, 691. John Claudius canvassed for the Marshal in his absence. John Claudius Beresford to the 2nd Marquis of Waterford, 26 June 1811 (Beresford family papers). Coincidentally, the writ for the by election in County Waterford was moved on 7 June, the same day as Prime Minister Perceval proposed the vote of thanks in parliament for Beresford's success at the Battle of Albuera. *Gentleman's Magazine & Historical Review*, vol. 195, p. 313.

Chapter 16

1 Andrew Pearson, *The Soldier Who Walked Away* (Edinburgh: Rollo, 1865), p. 9.

2 Throughout the war Dickson was assisted by various other artillery officers such as Major Victor von Arentschildt of the King's German Legion, and captains Francisco Cipriano Pinto and João da Cunha Preto. A good account is given by Nick Lipscombe, *Wellington's Guns: The Untold Story of Wellington and his Artillery in the Peninsula and at Waterloo* (Botley: Osprey Publishing, 2013).

3 Larpent, *Journal*, vol. II, p. 70.

4 Beresford was not involved at the combat on the Aire, but when he heard of the undignified retreat of the 2nd and 14th regiments and the flight of the commander of the brigade, Brigadier General Hipólito da Costa (part of the Portuguese Division with Hill, now commanded by Lecor), he had him sent back to Lisbon and dismissed from the service. The 2nd Regiment was in fact rallied by its Colonel, Jorge de Avilez, and remedied the situation on the day. De Avilez went on to be acting commander of the brigade at the battle of Toulouse. The combat on the Aire was one of the few occasions Beresford publicly expressed his concern regarding individual Portuguese officers, another one being the fall of Almeida.

5 Wellington to Liverpool, 30 September 1810 (WD 4, 304–9).

6 In July 1813 Picton said of the Portuguese: 'There was no difference between the British and Portuguese, they were equal in their exertions and deserving of an equal portion of the Laurel.' Picton to Lord Hastings, 26 July 1813, quoted in Glover, *A Gentleman Volunteer*, p. 10.

7 Girod de l'Ain, *Vie Militaire*, ff. 238.

8 Beresford to Lady Anne Beresford, 15 December 1813 (Beresford family papers).

9 Beresford to Wellington, 4 January 1811 (WSD 7, 38–40).

10 See Beresford to Wellington, 3 and 12 September 1809 (WSD 6, 345 and 3, 361) and Wellington to Beresford, 8 September 1809 (WD 3, 484–8).

11 Fortescue, *History of the British Army*, vol. 7, p. 420.

12 Beresford to Wellington, 2 October 1809 (WSD 6, 384–5).

13 August Ludolf Friedrich Schaumann, *On The Road With Wellington: The Diary of a War Commissary in the Peninsular Campaign* (London: W. Heinemann Ltd., 1924), p. 82.

14 Maxwell, *The Creevey Papers*, vol. II, pp. 126–7.

15 Warre to his sister, 2 September 1812, and Warre to mother, 6 February 1810 (Warre, op. cit., pp. 188 and 68–9).

16 Denis Pack had been with Beresford in South America. Robert Arbuthnot had been with him in South America and Madeira. The bond of those in arms worked both ways. Beresford had sought James McGrigor, who had been the surgeon to the 88th in Egypt, to head up the Portuguese army medical service, but the British government sent him to Walcheren in 1809 and he only came to the Peninsula subsequently, when he proved a very successful Surgeon-General to the British army.

17 Cooper, *Rough Notes*; Harris, op. cit., pp. 147–9; Pearson, *The Soldier Who Walked Away*, p. 9.

18 Wellington commented on the quality of Beresford's table when a newly-joined staff officer had to decline Wellington's own invitation to dine with him on the basis that he had already accepted an invitation from Hill: 'Go by all means. You will get a much better feed than here. As you are a stranger, I will give you some useful information. Cole gives the best dinners in the army, Hill the next best; mine are no great things; Beresford's and Picton's are very bad indeed.' Quoted in Antony Brett-James, *Life in Wellington's Army* (London: George Allen and Unwin, 1972), p. 125.

However, Lieutenant Woodberry was more complimentary of Beresford's table saying he offered excellent food and he did not spare the wine. Amongst the sixteen guests who attended with Woodberry on 24 February 1813, when Beresford held a dinner party at Cintra, were Admiral Sir George Martin,

Generals Hamilton and Brisbane and two Portuguese noblemen. See Woodberry, *Journal*, 24 February 1813.

19 Lady Anne Barnard, op. cit., p. 94.

20 Henegan, *Seven Years Campaigning*, vol. 2. The 48th Regiment served in the Peninsula from 1809–14.

21 Lady Anne Barnard, op. cit., p. 94.

22 *Gentleman's Magazine*, 11 June 1814.

23 Muir, *Wellington: The Path to Victory*, p. 585.

24 Michael Glover, *Wellington's Army in the Peninsula, 1808–1814* (Newton Abbot: David and Charles, 1977), p. 121.

25 Pulio do Luzo esforço a fina pedra

> O Illustre Beresford, Heróe preclaro;
> De sabia disciplina as Leis dictando,
> Valor no Campo manifesta raro (*Gazeta de Lisboa*, 23 June 1814).

26 Fortunato de São Boaventura Frade, *Noticias Biográficas do Marechal Beresford, escritas por F.F., M.C.D.T.* (Lisbon, 1812). Frade Fortunato (*c*1778–1844) was 'Monge Cisterciense de Alcobaça Doutor Theologo', hence M.C.D.T. He was Bishop of Evora 1832–44.

27 Noguiera, *Memória*. Quoted in Newitt and Robson, *Lord Beresford and British Intervention in Portugal*, p. 15.

Chapter 17

1   Beresford to John Poo Beresford, 18 September 1814 (NYA/ZBA 21/10, f. 55).

2   D'Urban, *Journal*, p. 335.

3   Ibid. p. 336.

4   Ibid. p. 328.

5   It is uncertain as to when the sword was presented to Beresford. The monies required were reportedly raised within one month of the agreement to subscribe. It had been intended to present it at a grand ceremony in 1817, but the sword was not completed in time and had to be handed over some time later. One newspaper report refers to the gold scabbard weighing 18 marcos and 7 oitavas (pre-metric weights used in Portugal – a marco was 0.229 kg; an oitava was 3.5 g). It was considered noteworthy enough to be exhibited at the Great Exhibition at Crystal Palace in 1851 and was the subject of an article in *Revista Universal Lisbonense*, vol. XI, no. 21 (1 January 1852), pp. 250–5.

6   Bathurst Papers, p. 324.

7   D'Urban, *Journal*, p. 335.

8   Beresford to Wellington, 14 April 1815 (WP1/473).

9   Wellington to Beresford, 24 March 1815 (PRONI, D3030/4464).

10 Beresford to Wellington, 14 April 1815 (WP1/473).

11 Beresford to Wellington, 7 May 1815 (WP1/473).

12 Beresford to Wellington, 4 May 1815 (WP1/459/22).

13 Beresford to Marquess of Abercorn, 2 June 1815 (PRONI, D623/A/244/1).

14 Beresford to Marquess of Abercorn, 10 August 1815 (PRONI, D623/A/244/5).

15 Beresford to Wellington, 12 May 1815 (WP1/473) refers to the opposition of various members of the Regency, in which Principal Sousa was most vocal while the Marquis of Borba and Forjaz were silent,

which Beresford deduced as meaning they were satisfied with the Principal's decision. Canning had noted difficulties between Beresford and Forjaz soon after his own arrival in Lisbon. Canning to Wellington, 16 January 1815 (WP1/448/36).

16 Beresford to Wellington, 8 July 1815 (WP1/473/56).

17 Bathurst to Wellington, 7 and 17 April 1815 (WP1/454 and 473).

18 D'Urban, *Journal*, p. 338.

19 Beresford to Wellington, 8 July 1815 (WP1/473/56).

20 George Canning had been appointed British Minister Plenipotentiary and Ambassador Extraordinary to Lisbon on 29 June 1814, with the intention of being in situ on the anticipated return of the royal family from Brazil, an indication of the importance attached to the post and to Portugal by the British government. On 29 October 1814, a squadron under Sir John Poo Beresford sailed for Brazil to escort Prince João and other members of the royal family to Lisbon. Lord Strangford's letter of 21 June 1814 to Castlereagh had, curiously enough, indicated that Prince João would be gratified if Sir John Poo Beresford was appointed to undertake the escort duty; see Robert Walsh (ed.), *Select Speeches of the Right Honourable George Canning; with a preliminary biographical sketch, and an appendix, of extracts from his writings and speeches* (Philadelphia: Key and Biddle, 1835), p. 236. On 10 April 1815, having learnt that João did not intend to return to Portugal at present, Canning tendered his resignation as Ambassador Extraordinary to Portugal (ibid. p. 244), a resignation which was accepted in the summer of that year following which Canning returned to Britain.

21 17 December 1815.

22 Lecor was appointed Governor and Captain-General of Montevideo. He advanced with 6,000 men along the Atlantic coastline protected by the Portuguese navy. On his right flank, Bernardo Silveira led a smaller force of some 3,000 with a reserve of 2,000 being held back under General Joaquim Curado. In late August 1816 the invasion began in earnest, with Lecor capturing Montevideo on 20 January 1817 after which he had to contend with guerilla warfare for several years. A curious footnote to this conquest occurred in 1824. After Brazilian independence in 1822, certain garrisons remained loyal to Portugal. One of these was Montevideo, which only surrendered in 1824 to General Lecor who was by then in Brazilian service.

23 Beresford to Wellington, 8 July 1815 (WP1/473).

24 Beresford to Elizabeth Pack (née Lady Elizabeth Beresford), 19 September 1816 (Beresford family papers).

25 Beresford to Denis Pack, 2 November 1816; Pack Beresford, *A Memoir of Major General Sir Denis Pack*, p. 110.

26 Palmerston to Lord Howard de Walden, 20 April 1839, in which he encloses a draft paper setting out the terms of the Treaty and describes events leading up to and subsequent to its ratification; House of Commons, *Parliamentary Papers*, vol. 49, no. 53.

27 Three army officers, all masons, appear to have come forward to denounce the conspiracy at various times. They were José Pinto de Morais Sarmento, João de Sá Pereira Soares and José Andrade Corvo. Sarmento may have been Beresford's primary informant.

28 The group to whom he brought the matter on 23 May 1817 are identified in the 'Apologia' which Beresford caused to be produced in 1822 by Joaquim Ferreira de Freitas. They were the Visconde de Santarém João Diogo de Barros, an old friend who had tried to dissuade Beresford from going to Rio in 1815 because he felt Beresford's presence was required to ensure stability in Portugal; Cipriano Ribeiro Freire, one-time member of the Regency; and the Auditor-General of the Army, José António d'Oliveira Leite de Barros. See Joaquim Ferreira de Freitas, *Memoria sobre A Conspiração de 1817, Vulgarmente*

Chamada A Conspiração de Gomes Freire (London: Ricardo and Artur Taylor, 1822), p. 121 (hereafter, '*Memoria*').

29   A number of those arrested were not prosecuted but were questioned and confined for a hundred days. These also were mostly soldiers but did include the Abbot of Carrazedo in Trás-os-Montes (ibid. p. 154).

30   Ten of those executed at the Campo de Santana (Campo Mártires da Pátria) were identified as Colonel Manuel Monteiro de Carvalho, Major José Campello de Miranda, Major José de Fonseca Neves, Alferes [ensign] retd António Cabral Calheiros de Lemos, Manuel Inácio de Figueiredo, Alferes [ensign] José Ribeiro Pinto, Maximiano dias Ribeiro, José Joaquim Pinto da Silva, Sargento de Brigada [RSM] Henrique José Garcia de Moraes and Captain Pedro Ricardo de Figueiro. General Gomes Freire de Andrade was accorded a private execution in the fort of São Julião da Barra outside Lisbon where his monument still exists today.

31   The remark attributed to Forjaz gave rise to a play of the same name by Luís de Sttau Monteiro published in 1961. It was full of symbolism and a barely concealed criticism of the Salazar regime.

32   De Freitas, *Memoria*, p. 52.

33   There was a story to the effect that a Colonel Haddock, also a mason, visited Gomes Freire de Andrade (Grand Master of the Order) offering him a chance to escape, but that the offer was declined; see Manuel Borges Grainha, *História da Franco-Maçonaria em Portugal: 1733–1912* (Lisboa: A Editora Limitada, 1912). This may have been Captain Robert Haddock of the 87th Regiment; who served in the 3rd and then 12th Caçadores (see Challis's 'Peninsular Roll Call'). Beresford refers to Colonel Haddock in a letter to General Campbell, 24 June 1817 (reproduced in de Freitas, *Memoria*, p. 46).

34   *The London Gazette*, 8 November 1817, 2270.

35   Beresford to Rear Admiral John Poo Beresford, May 1817 (North Yorkshire Archives, ZBA 21/10/75).

36   *New Monthly Magazine*, vol. 7 (1817), p. 551.

37   Beresford to D'Urban, 5 October 1817 (BL, Add MS 38,269).

38   D'Urban to Liverpool, 1 and 5 November and 21 December 1817 (BL, Add MS 38,269).

39   See for instance Beresford to Conde da Barca, 11 August 1817 (Arquivo Nacional de Rio de Janeiro, Cx 985 Maco 4) quoted in Malyn Newitt, 'Lord Beresford and the Governadores of Portugal' in Newitt and Robson (eds), *Lord Beresford and British Intervention in Portugal 1807–1820* (Lisbon: Imprensa das Ciências Sociais, 2004). The Conde de Barca was António de Araújo, who prior to the French invasions had shown definitely pro-French leanings as Secretary of State for Foreign Affairs and War, and who in 1807 had followed João to Rio, where he held various ministerial positions prior to his death in 1817. Here Beresford is writing after the defusing of the conspiracy and states:

> You must not think however that the difficulties of this kingdom are at an end, we should most extremely deceive ourselves if we so judged, its danger is most certainly postponed, but all depends upon the determination that you come to at the Rio, on the subject of His Majesty's return to Portugal and the fate of Monte Video [*sic*] ... I repeat to you, if you wish the Crown of Portugal to remain in the Royal Family of Braganca His Majesty must return here, and those who would make you think the contrary are the King's enemies.

40   BL, Add MS 38,574 letters Beresford/Liverpool.

41   Beresford to Wellington, 17 May 1819 (WP1/624).

42   NA, FO 63/223.

43   Beresford to Harriet Beresford, 17 June 1819 (Beresford family papers).

44 Beresford to Wellington, 24 July 1819 (WP1/628).

45 Beresford to Wellington, 28 January 1820 (WP1/637).

46 Beresford to Wellington, 26 February 1820 (WP1/639).

47 Wellington to Beresford, 12 February 1820 (WP1/640).

48 See Timothy E. Anna, 'The Buenos Aires Expedition and Spain's Secret Plan to Conquer Portugal, 1814–1820', *The Americas*, vol. 34, issue 3 (January 1978), pp. 356–80.

49 Beresford to Denis Pack, 11 March 1820 (Beresford family papers).

50 Beresford to Wellington, 14 February 1820 (WP1/639).

51 Wellington to Beresford, 28 March 1820 (WP1/ 642). Palmela feared a Gomes Freire-type conspiracy in Marshal Beresford's absence. The letter caught up with him in Rio and he read it to King João. See Beresford to Wellington, 30 July 1820 (WP1/649); Palmela to Wellington, 1 May 1820 (WP1/645).

52 Beresford to Lady Pack (his half-sister Elizabeth), 25 March 1820 (Beresford family papers).

53 The leader of the movement in Porto was a judge, Fernandes Tomás, who had earlier been a deputy commissary in the army. However, many mid-ranking army officers supported the coup including Brigadier General António Silveira and Colonel Bernardo Correia de Castro e Sepúlveda (18th Regiment).

54 Loring Hall, North Cray, near Bexley, where Castlereagh committed suicide in 1822.

55 After Ega had gone to France with Junot in 1808, the palace (otherwise known as the Palácio do pátio do Saldanha) was first used as a military hospital. It became Beresford's headquarters in 1814 and was given to him later by João. Following the revolution of 1820, Ega returned to Portugal, was rehabilitated, and recovered the palace, leading to a lengthy dispute resulting ultimately in Beresford receiving financial compensation for its loss.

Ж

MANUSCRIPT SOURCES

United Kingdom
British Library

Add MS 13,712; 21,504; 30,099; 30,106; 32,607; 35,059 and 35,060 (Rowland Hill papers); 35,704 (+Hardwicke Papers); 35,781 (Hardwicke Papers, Irish Application Book); 36,306; 40,722; 49,485.

RP 5296; 594. f. 24 (Portuguese Proclamations).

National Archives, Kew

ADM: 1–4200.

CO: 324–68.

FO: 63–58; 63–74; 63–75; 63–137; 63–188; 63–198; 72–60; 95–8; 342–11; 342–20; 342–26; 342–28; 342–32; 342–39; 341–2; 342–5; 342–6.

WO: 1–161; 1–162; 1–228; 1–229; 1–230; 1–231; 1–232; 1–233; 1–234; 1–235; 1–238; 1–239; 1–242; 1–243; 1–259; 1–260; 1–342; 1–354; 1–400; 1–401; 1–415; 1–416; 6–47; 6–51; 6–68; 17–209; 17–227; 25–744; 32–6866; 55–958; 78–5636; 78–5900; 164–517; 164–518; 164–519; 164–520.

National Army Museum

1995-09-87; 1999-06-149; 2003-08-3 (Journal of Charles Dudley Madden); 2008-03-26; 2007-03-83 (Livermore, Harold – Life of Beresford).

Report of the Operations of the Right Wing of the Allied Army under Field Marshal Sir William Carr Beresford in the Alentejo and the Spanish Extremadura during the Campaign of 1811 (microfilm).

2003-08-3 (Madden, Charles Dudley, Journal of Charles Dudley Madden, 4th Dragoons– certified copy).

Public Record Office of Northern Ireland (PRONI)

D3030.

North Yorkshire Archives (NYA)

ZBA Series (Papers of Sir John Poo Beresford): ZBA 20; ZBA 21.

University of Southampton Library

MS 61 Wellington Papers (WP).
WP1/166; WP1/167; WP1/177; WP1/178; WP1/179; WP1/259; WP1/260; WP1/262; WP1/263; WP1/264; WP1/265; WP1/268; WP1/269; WP1/327; WP1/330; WP1/348; WP1/349; WP1/351; WP1/364; WP1/365; WP1/366.
MS 296 (Pack Papers).

Ireland

National Library of Ireland

MS 21,740.

Private Collections

Beresford family papers from Curraghmore, Co. Waterford, and from the author's own collection.

Portugal

Arquivo Historico Militar (AHM)

4-72; 1-14 CX 11; 17; 18; 19; 20; 38; 39; 47; 162; 170; 186; 194; 268; 527.
Lv 1217; Lv 1219.

Torre do Tombo (TT)

Ministeiro do Reino, livro 324; 380.
MNE CX 204; 205; 206; 207; 885.

Arquivo Municipal de Mafra (AMM)

016; 022; 028; 029; 033; 034; 035; 038; 039; 041; 046; 048; 049; 055; 056; 062; 064; 065; 067; 068; 073; 078; 086 (note these are copies of letters in Torre de Tombo, MNE Series).

Gulbenkian Foundation, Lisbon

BC 919 (Beresford Papers).

Madeira

Day Books of Cossart Gordon & Co. for 1808.

United States of America

Rice University, Digital scholarship Archive: Coimbra 4-5-1809.
Rice University, Woodson Research Centre, Fondren Library.

BIBLIOGRAPHY

Books and Articles

'A Friend of the People', *Advantages of the Convention of Cintra, briefly stated in a candid review of that Transaction and of the circumstances under which it took place* (London, 1809).

Almazán, Bernardo, *Beresford, Gobernador de Buenos Aires* (Buenos Aires: Editorial Galerna, 1994).

Alorna, Marquês de, *Memórias Politicas: Apresentação de José Norton* (Lisbon: Tribuna da História, 2008).

Alves Caetano, António, *A Economia Portuguesa no Tempo do Napoleão* (Lisbon: Tribuna da História, 2008).

Amaral, Manuel, *Olivença 1801: Portugal em Guerra do Guadiana ao Paraguai* (Lisbon: Tribuna da História, 2004).

Amaral, Manuel (Apresentação), *A Luta Política em Portugal nos finais do Antigo Regime*, three volumes (Lisbon: Fábrica de Letras – Sociedade Gráfica, Lda., 2010).

Amaral, Manuel, 'The Portuguese Army and the Commencement of the Peninsular War', in Adelino de Matos Coelho (ed.), *O Exército Português e as Comemorações dos 200 Anos da Guerra Peninsular*, vol. I (Lisbon: Exército e Tribuna da História, 2008).

Anderson, Joseph, *Recollections of a Peninsular Veteran* (London: Edward Arnold, 1913).

Anglesey, Marquess of, *One-Leg: The Life and letters of Henry William Paget, First Marquess of Anglesey, K.G. 1768–1854* (New York: William Morrow & Co., 1961).

Anna, Timothy E., 'The Buenos Aires Expedition and Spain's Secret Plan to Conquer Portugal, 1814–1820', *The Americas*, vol. 34, issue 3 (January 1978), pp. 356–80.

Anon., *Mémoires relatifs à l'Expédition Anglaise de L'Inde et Égypte* (Paris: Imprimerie royale, 1826).

Anon., *Buenos Ayres: An authentic narrative of the proceedings of the Expedition against Buenos Ayres under the Command of Lieut. Gen Whitelocke, by an Irish Officer* (Dublin: W. Figgis, 1808).

Anon., *Narrative of the campaigns of the Loyal Lusitanian Legion under Brigadier General Sir Robert Wilson, with some Account of the Military Operations in Spain and Portugal during the years 1809, 1810 and 1811* (London: T. Egerton, 1812).

Anon., *A History of the campaigns of the British Forces in Spain and Portugal undertaken to relieve those countries from the French usurpation; comprehending memoirs of the operations of this interesting war, characteristic reports of the Spanish and Portuguese troops and illustrative anecdotes of distinguished military conduct of individuals, whatever their rank in the army* (London: T. Goddard, 1812).

Anon., *Twelve years military adventure in three quarters of the globe: the memoirs of an officer who serve in the armies of His Majesty and of the East India Company between the years 1802 and 1814 in which are contained the campaigns of the Duke of Wellington in India and his last in Spain and the South of France,* two volumes (London: Henry Colburn, 1829).

A.P.D.G., *Sketches of Portuguese life, manners, costume & character* (London: Geo. B. Whittaker, 1826).

Azeredo, Carlos de, *Invasão do Norte 1809* (Lisbon: Tribuna da História, 2004).

Baines, Edward, *History of the wars of the French Revolution, from the breaking out of the war in 1792 to the restoration of a general peace in 1815* (Philadelphia: M'Carty & Davis, 1819).

Balbi, Adrien, *Essai Statistique* (Lisbon: Imprensa Nacional Casa da Moeda, 2004).

Bamford, Andrew, *Sickness, Suffering and the Sword* (Norman, OK: University of Oklahoma Press, 2013).

Barnard, Lt. Col. Sir Andrew and Capt. M.C. Spurrier (ed.), *Letters of a Peninsular War Commanding Officer* (London, 1966).

Batcave, Louis, *La Bataille d'Orthez, 27 February 1814* (Monein, 2009).

Batchelor, Gordon, *The Beresfords of Bedgebury Park* (Goudhurst: Willam J.C. Musgrave, 1996).

Batty, Robert, *Campaign of the left wing of the Allied Army, in the Western Pyrenees and South of France in the years 1813–1814, under Field Marshal the Marquess of Wellington* (London: John Murray, 1823).

Beamish, N.L., *History of the King's German Legion* with plates, two volumes (London: Thomas and William Books, 1832).

Beatson, F.C., *Wellington and the Pyrenees Campaign*, two volumes (London: M. Goschen, 1914).

Beatson, F.C., *Wellington: The Crossing of the Gaves and the Battle of Orthez* (London: Heath Cranton Limited, 1925).

Beatson, F.C., *Wellington and the Invasion of France* (London: Edward Arnold & Co., 1931).

Belmas, J. (ed.), *Journaux des Siéges faits ou soutenus par les Français dans la Péninsule de 1807 a 1814,* four volumes (Paris: Chez Firmin Didot Fréres et Co., 1836–1837).

Beresford, Hugh de la Poer, *The Book of the Beresfords* (Chichester: Phillimore and Co. Ltd., 1977).

Beresford, Marcus de la Poer, 'On a Lonely City Wall', *The New Ranger* (January 2016).

Beresford, Marcus de la Poer, 'William Carr Beresford: The Capture of the Cape Colony and the Rio de la Plata Expedition of 1806', *The Irish Sword* XXIX, 117 (2012), pp. 241–62.

Beresford, Marshal Sir William ('Guilherme') Carr, *Ordens do Dia, 1809–1814* (Lisbon, 1809–23).

Beresford, Marshal Sir William Carr, *Instrucções para a formatura exercicio e movimentos dos Regimentos de Infanteria* (Lisbon: Impressão Regia, 1809).

Beresford, Marshal Sir William Carr, *Instrucções Provisórias para a Cavallaria* (Lisbon: Impressão Regia, 1810).

Beresford, Marshal Sir William Carr, *Sistema de Instrução e disciplina para os movimentos e deveres dos Caçadores* (Lisbon: Impressão Regia, 1810).

Beresford, Marshal Viscount William Carr, *Strictures on certain passages of Col. Napier's history of the Peninsular War which relate to the military opinions and conduct of General Lord Viscount Beresford* (London: Longman, Rees, Orme, Brown, Green and Co., 1831).

Beresford, William Carr, *Refutation of Colonel Napier's Justification of His Third Volume* (London: John Murray, 1834).

Bingham, Denis Arthur, *A selection from the letters and despatches of the First Napoleon* (London: Chapman and Hall, 1884).

Boletim do Arquivo Histórico Militar (various volumes).

Bonaparte, Joseph, *The Confidential Correspondence of Napoleon Bonaparte with his brother Joseph, Selected and Translated with explanatory notes from the Mémoire du Roi Joseph*, two volumes. (London: John Murray, 1855).

Bonaparte, Napoléon, *Correspondance générale de Napoléon Bonaparte*, vols 27 and 31.

Boothby, Charles, *Under England's Flag from 1804–1809: the memoirs, diary and correspondence of Charles Boothby, captain of Royal Engineers, compiled by the last survivors of his family, M.S.B and C.E.B* (London: Adam and Charles Black, 1900).

Borges, João Vieira, *A Artilharia na Guerra Peninsular* (Lisbon: Tribuna da História, 2009).

Boutflower, Charles, *Journal of an army surgeon during the Peninsular War* (Manchester: Refuge Printing Dept., 1912).

Bowen, Desmond and Jean Desmond, *Heroic Option* (Barnsley: Pen and Sword, 2005).

Bradford, Rev William, *Sketches of the country, character, and costume in Portugal and Spain, made during the campaign and on the route of the British Army 1808 and 1809* (London: John Booth, 1809).

Brandão, General Zephyrino, 'Beresford Ferido na Batalha de Salamanca', *Revista Militar*, 3 (1908), pp. 130–40.

Brett-James, Antony, *Wellington at War, 1794–1815* (London: Macmillan and Co. Ltd., 1961).

Brett-James, Antony, *Life in Wellington's Army* (London: George Allen and Unwin, 1972).

Bromley, Janet and David Bromley, *Wellington's Men Remembered: A Register of Memorials to Soldiers who fought in the Peninsular War and at Waterloo*, two volumes (Barnsley: Pen and Sword, 2015).

Brooke, William, 'A Prisoner of Albuera: Journal of Major William Brooke' in *Studies in the Napoleonic Wars* edited by Charles Oman (London: Methuen & Co., 1929).

Broughton, Samuel, *Letters from Portugal, Spain and France written during the campaigns of 1812, 1813 and 1814* (London: Longman, Hurst, Rees, Orme and Brown, 1815).

Bruce, H.A., *Napier and the Peninsula War* (Driffield reprint, 2010).

Bruce, James, *Travels to Discover the Source of the Nile, 1768–1773* (Edinburgh: G.G.J. and J. Robinson, 1790).

Bunbury, Sir Henry, *Narratives of some Passages in the Great War with France (1799–1810)* (London: P. Davies, 1927).

Burnham, Robert, *Charging Against Wellington: The French Cavalry in the Peninsular War, 1807–1814* (Barnsley: Frontline Books, 2011).

Burnham, Robert and Ron McGuigan, *The British Army against Napoleon: Facts, Lists and Trivia, 1805–1815* (Barnsley: Frontline Books, 2010).

Butler, Iris, *The Eldest Brother: The Marquess Wellesley, The Duke of Wellington's eldest brother* (London: Hodder & Stoughton, 1973).

Butler, Lewis, *Wellington's Operations in the Peninsula*, two volumes (London: T.F. Unwin, 1904).

Buttery, David, *Wellington Against Junot: The First Invasion of Portugal 1807–1808* (Barnsley: Pen and Sword, 2011).

Byron, George Gordon, *Childe Harold's Pilgrimage* (1812–18).

Caillaux de Almeida, Tereza, *Memória das 'Invasões Francesas' em Portugal (1807–1811)* (Lisbon: Ésquilo, 2010).

Cardoso, José Luis, 'The Transfer of the Court to Brazil, 200 years afterwards', *e-Journal of Portuguese History*, 7, 1 (2009).

Cassels, S.A.C. (ed.), *Peninsular Portrait 1811–1814: The Letters of Captain William Bragge Third (King's Own) Dragoons* (London: Oxford University Press, 1963).

Centeno, João, 'Portuguese Army Actions 1808–1814' (*The Napoleon Series*, undated). Available at: https://www.napoleon-series.org/military/battles/portugal/c_portugal1.html (and following. Accessed 26 April 2018).

Centeno João, 'Portuguese Artillery of the Napoleonic Wars' (*The Napoleon Series*, undated). Available at: https://www.napoleon-series.org/military/organization/portugal/c_portugalarty1.html (accessed 24 April 2018).

Cesar, Victor, 'A Evolução do Recrutamento em Portugal: Desde 1809 até 1901', *Revista Militar*, 2, 9 (Setembro 1909), pp. 577–92.

Cetre, Lieut. Col. F.O., 'Beresford and the Portuguese army, 1809–1814', in Alice D. Berkeley, *New Lights on the Peninsular War: International Congress on the Iberian Peninsula, selected papers, 1780–1840* (Lisbon: The British Historical Society of Portugal, 1991).

Cetre, Lieut. Col. F.O., *Beresford, Marshal of Portugal, His contribution to the success of the war in the Peninsula* (Lisbon: The British Historical Society of Portugal, 1999).

Challis, Lionel, S., 'Challis's "Peninsula Roll Call"' (*The Napoleon Series*, 2009). Available at: https://www.napoleon-series.org/research/biographies/GreatBritain/Challis/c_ChallisIntro.html (accessed 24 April 2018).

Chappell, Mike, *Wellington's Peninsula Regiments (1): The Irish* (Botley: Osprey Publishing, 2003).

Chartrand, René, *The Portuguese Army of the Napoleonic Wars* (Botley: Osprey Publishing, 2000).

Chartrand, René, 'Sir Robert Wilson and the Loyal Lusitanian Legion, 1808–1811', *Journal of the Society for Army Historical Research*, 79, 319 (Autumn 2001), pp. 197–208.

Clarke, – (ed.), *The Georgian Era: Memoirs of the Most Eminent Persons who have flourished in Great Britain. Volume 2: Military and Naval Commanders. Judges and Barristers. Physicians and Surgeons*, four volumes (London: Vizetelly, Branston and Co., 1832–34).

Clerc, Joseph Charles, *Campagne du Maréchal Soult dans les Pyrénées Occidentales en 1813–1814* (Paris: Librairie Militaire de L. Baudoin, 1894).

Clinton, Sir Henry, *A Few Remarks explanatory of the Motives which guided the operations of the British Army during the late short campaign in Spain* (London: T. Egerton, 1809).

Cobbett's *Political Register*.

Cole, John William, *Memoirs of British Generals distinguished during the Peninsular War*, two volumes (London: Richard Bentley, 1856).

Colleção das Ordens do Dia do Illustrissimo e Excellentissimo Senhor Guilherme Carr Beresford (Lisbon, 1809–14).

Collins, Bruce, *War and Empire: the expansion of Britain 1790–1830* (Harlow: Longman, 2010).

Colman, Oscar Tavani Perez, *Martínez de Fontes y la Fuga del General Beresford* (Buenos Aires: Editorial Dunken, 2005).

Cooper, John Spencer, *Rough Notes of Seven Campaigns in Portugal, France, Spain and America, 1809–1815* (London: John Russell Smith, 1869).

Correspondance de Napoleon I, publiée par ordre de l'Empereur Napoleon III. Volume 31 (Paris: H. Plon, J. Dumaine, 1858–70).

Corrigan, Gordon, *Wellington: A Military Life* (London: Continuum, 2001).

Corrigan, Gordon, *Waterloo: A New History of the Battle and its Armies* (London: Atlantic Books, 2014).

Costa, Ernestina, *English Invasion of the River Plate* (Buenos Aires: G. Kraft, Ltda, 1937).

Costello, Edward, *Adventures of a Soldier: Written by Himself. Being the Memoirs of Edward Costello, K.S.F* (London: Colburn and Co., 1852).

Creevey, Thomas and John Gore (ed.), *The Creevey Papers*, revised edition (London: B.T. Batsford, 1963).

Crumplin, Michael, *Men of Steel: Surgery in the Napoleonic Wars* (Shrewsbury: Quiller Press, 2007).

Crumplin, Michael, *Guthrie's War: A Surgeon of the Peninsula and Waterloo* (Barnsley: Pen and Sword, 2010).

Cruz, Miguel Dantas da, *A Neutralidade Portuguesa na Europa da Revolução (1792–1807)* (Lisbon: Tribuna da História, 2011).

Da Fonseca, João José Samouco, *História da Chamusca*, volume II (Chamusca: Câmara Municipal, 2002).

Dalrymple, Sir Hew, *Memoir of his Proceedings connected with the Affairs of Spain and the commencement of the Peninsular War* (London: T. and W. Boone, 1830).

Daniel, John Edgecombe, *Journal of an Officer in the Commissariat Department of the Army comprising a narrative of the campaigns under his Grace the Duke of Wellington in Portugal, Spain, France and the Netherlands in the years 1811, 1812, 1813, 1814, and 1815 and a short account of the Army of Occupation in France during the years 1816, 1817 & 1818* (London: Porter and King (printer), 1820).

Daniel, John Edgecombe, *Portugal to Waterloo with Wellington* (Driffield, 2010).

D'Arjuzon, Antoine, *Wellington* (Madrid: Torrelodones, 1998).

David, Saul, *All the King's Men: The British Soldier from the Restoration to Waterloo* (London: Viking, 2012).

Davies, Huw J., *Wellington's Wars: The Making of a Military Genius* (New Haven, CT: Yale University Press, 2012).

De Avillez, Pedro (ed.), *O Exército Português e as Comemorações dos 200 anos da Guerra Peninsular*, three volumes (Lisbon: Tribuna da História, 2011).

De la Fuente, Francisco A., *Dom Miguel Pereira Forjaz: His early career and Role in the Mobilization of the Portuguese Army and Defense of Portugal during the Peninsular War, 1807–1814*, translated by Amaral Manuel (Lisbon: Tribuna da Historia, 2011).

Delaforce, Patrick, *Wellington the Beau: The life and loves of the Duke of Wellington* (Barnsley: Pen and Sword, 2004).

Delderfield, R.F., *The March of the Twenty Six: The Story of Napoleon's Marshals* (London: Hodder & Stoughton, 1962).

Dempsey, Guy, *Albuera 1811: The Bloodiest Battle of the Peninsular War* (London: Frontline Books, 2008).

De Naylies, Joseph-Jacques, *Mémoires sur la guerre d'Espagne pendant les années 1808, 1809, 1810 et 1811* (Paris: Magimel, Anselin et Pochard, 1817).

Denon, Vivant, *Travels in Upper and Lower Egypt During the Campaign of General Bonaparte*, three volumes (London: T.N. Longman, 1803).

De Pradt, Dominique Georges Frederic, *Mémoires Historiques sur la Révolution d'Espagne* (Paris: Chez Rosa, 1817).

De Sousa Lobo, Francisco, *A Defesa de Lisboa: Linhas de Torres Vedras, Lisboa, Oriente e Sul do Tejo 1809–1814* (Lisbon: Tribuna da História, 2015).

Dictionary of National Biography (DNB).

D'Ivernois, Sir Francis, *Effets du Blocus continental sur le commerce: les finances, le crédit et la prospérité des Isles Britanniques* (London: J.B.G. Vogel, 1809).

Divall, Carole, *Wellington's Worst Scrape: The Burgos Campaign 1812* (Barnsley: Pen and Sword, 2012).

Divall, Carole, *Napoleonic Lives: Researching the British Soldiers of the Napoleonic Wars* (Barnsley: Pen and Sword, 2012).

Dodge, Theodore A., *Warfare in the age of Napoleon*, volume 6 (Driffield: Leonaur, 2011).

Dores Costa, Fernando, 'Army size, Military Recruitment and Financing During the Period of the Peninsula War – 1808–1811', *e-Journal of Portuguese History*, 6, 2 (Winter 2008). Available at: http://www.scielo.mec.pt/scielo.php?script=sci_arttext&pid=S1645-64322008000200003 (accessed 23 April 2018).

Drouet d'Erlon, Jean-Baptiste, *Le Maréchal Drouet d'Erlon: Notice sur la vie militaire* (Paris: Gustave Barba, 1844).

Duckers, Peter, *British Campaign Medals, 1815–1914* (Gosport: Shire Publications, 2000).

Dumas, Jean-Baptiste, *Neuf Mois de Campagnes à la suite du Maréchal Soult* (Paris: Charles-Lavauzelle, 1907).

Duplan, Carme, *Précis Historique de la Bataille Livrée le 10 Avril 1814, sous les murs de Toulouse* (Toulouse: Chez Benichet, 1815).

Dupuy, Colonel Pierre, *Soult et Wellington dans le Sud-Ouest* (Sauveterre de Béarn: Association Sauveterre Espace Culturel, 1996).

D'Urban, Benjamin, *Further Strictures on those parts of Col. Napier's History of the Peninsular War which relate to the military opinions and conduct of General Lord Viscount Beresford* (London: Longman, Rees, Orme, Brown, Green & Longman, 1832).

D'Urban, Sir Benjamin, *The Peninsular Journal 1808–1817* edited by I.J. Rousseau (London: Greenhill Books, 1990).

Ebke, Gabriele E. and Hans Ebke, *Journal der KGL-Artillerie 1804–1808: 4 Jahre in Portchester Castle in England* (Dusseldorf; Edition Winterwork, 2012).

Edgcumbe, Richard (ed.), *The Diary of Frances Lady Shelley 1787–1817* (London: C. Scribner & Sons, 1912).

Edinburgh Annual Register, various volumes.

Edwards, Peter, *Albuera: Wellington's Fourth Peninsular Campaign, 1811* (Marlborough: Crowood Press, 2008).

Edwards, Peter, *Salamanca 1812. Wellington's Year of Victories* (Barnsley: Praetorian, 2013).

English Naval Chronicle.

Ermitão, José Nogueira Rodrigues, 'A Desercão Militar no Periodo das Invasões Francesas/Guerra Peninsular'. Paper given to the *XX Colóquio de História Militar, 2011* (18 November 2011).

Escalettes, Jean-Paul, *Le 10 Avril 1814, La Dataille de Toulouse; Les Généraux, l'Armement, la Vie Quotidienne, Les Lieux* (Portet-sur-Garonne: Loubatières, 2003).

Esdaile, Charles, *The Peninsular War: A New History* (New York: Palgrave Macmillan, 2003).

Espirito Santo, Gabriel and Pedro de Brito, *A Logística do Exército Anglo-Luso na Guerra Peninsular: Uma Introdução (An Introduction to the Anglo-Portuguese army logistics in the Peninsular War)* (Lisbon: Tribuna da História, 2012).

Estrela, Paolo Jorge, *Ordens e Condecorações Portuguesas 1793–1824* (Lisbon: Tribuna da História, 2009).

European Magazine and London Review, vol. 59.

Fain, Baron Agathon Jean François, *Memoirs of the Invasion of France by the Allied Armies and of the Last Six Months of the Reign of Napoleon* (London: Henry Colburn, 1834).

Fergusson, William and James Fergusson (ed.), *Notes and recollections of a professional life* (London: Longman, Brown, Green and Longmans, 1846).

Fernyhough, Thomas, *Military Memoirs of Four Brothers, engaged in the service of their country, as well as the New World and Africa and on the Continent of Europe; by the survivor* (London: W. Sams, 1829).

Ferrão, António, *A 1ª Invasão Francesa: A Invasão de Junot vista através dos documentos da Intendência Geral da Policia, 1807–1808: estudo politico e social* (Coimbra, Imprensa da Universidade, 1923).

Fitchett, W.H., *Battles and Sieges of the Peninsular War* (Driffield: Leonaur, 2007).

Fletcher, Ian, *The Waters of Oblivion, The British Invasion of the Rio de la Plata 1806–1807* (Tunbridge Wells: Spellmount, 2006).

Fletcher, Ian, *Galloping at Everything: The British Cavalry in the Peninsular War and at Waterloo, 1808–1815* (Tunbridge Wells: Spellmount, 1999).

Fletcher, Ian, *Bloody Albuera: The 1811 Campaign in the Peninsula* (Marlborough: Crowood Press, 2001).

Fortescue, Hon Sir John W., *The County Lieutenancies and the Army 1803–1814* (London: Macmillan and Co., 1909).

Fortescue, Hon Sir John W., *History of the British Army*, thirteen volumes (London: Macmillan and Co., 1906–20).

Fortescue, Hon Sir John W., *Wellington* (London: Williams and Northgate, 1925).

Fortin, Jorge (ed.), *Invasiones Inglesas* (Buenos Aires: Colección Pablo Fortín, 1967).

Foy, General Maximilien Sebastien, *Histoire de la Guerre de la Péninsule sous Napoléon*, four volumes (Paris: Baudouin Fréres, 1827).

Frade, Fortunato de São Boaventura, *Noticias Biograficas do Marechal Beresford* (Lisbon, 1812).

Fraser, Edward, *The Soldiers Whom Wellington Led* (London: Methuen & Co. Ltd., 1913).

(de) Freitas, Joaquim Ferreira, *Memoria sobre A Conspiração de 1817, Vulgarmente Chamada A Conspiração de Gomes Freire* (London: Ricardo and Artur Taylor, 1822).

Fryman, Mildred L., 'Charles Stuart and the "common cause": The Anglo-Portuguese alliance, 1810–1814', (PhD thesis, Florida State University, 1974).

Gates, David, *The Spanish Ulcer: A History of the Peninsular War* (New York; W. W. Norton, 1986).

Gavin, William, 'Diary', published in *The Highland Light Infantry Chronicle 1920–1921*.

Geraldo, José Custódio Madaleno, 'José Maria Das Neves Costa e as Linhas de Torres Vedras' *Revista Militar* (February/March 2015). Available at: https://www.revistamilitar.pt/artigo/530 (accessed 24 April 2018).

Geschwind, H. and F. De Gélis, *La Bataille de Toulouse* (Toulouse: Imprimerie & Librairie Edouard Privat, 1914).

Gilbert, James William, *The History of Banking in Ireland* (London: Longman, 1836).

Gillespie, Alexander, *Gleanings and remarks collected during many months of residence in Buenos Ayres, and within the upper country* (Leeds: Printed by B. Dewhirst for the author, 1818).

Girod de l'Ain, Maurice, *Vie Militaire du Géneral Foy* (Paris: E. Plon, Nourrit et cie., 1900).

Glover, Gareth (ed.), *An Eloquent Soldier: The Peninsular War Journals of Lieutenant Charles Crowe of the Inniskillings, 1812–1814* (Barnsley: Frontline, 2011).

Glover, Gareth (ed.), *From Corunna to Waterloo: The Letters and Journals of Two Napoleonic Hussars, Major Edwin Griffith and Captain Frederick Philips* (Barnsley: Frontline, 2007).

Glover, Gareth (ed). *Wellington's Voice: The Candid Letters of Lieutenant Colonel John Fremantle, Coldstream Guards 1808–1837* (Barnsley: Frontline, 2012).

Glover, Gareth, *Waterloo: Myth and Reality* (Barnsley: Pen and Sword, 2014).

Glover, Michael, *Britannia Sickens: Sir Arthur Wellesley and the Convention of Cintra* (London: Leo Cooper Limited, 1970).

Glover, Michael, *Wellington's Army in the Peninsula, 1808–1814* (Newton Abbot: David and Charles, 1977).

Glover, Michael, *A Very Slippery Fellow: The Life of Sir Robert Wilson, 1777–1849* (Oxford: Oxford University Press, 1978).

Glover, Michael (ed.), *A Gentleman Volunteer: The Letters of George Hennell from the Peninsular War, 1812–1813* (London: Heinemann, 1979).

Gordon, Alexander, *The Journal of a cavalry officer in the Corunna Campaign 1808–1809* (London: J. Murray, 1913).

Gordon, Lieut. Col. J.W., *Military Transactions of the British Empire from the commencement of the year 1803 to the termination of 1807* (1808).

Grainger, J.D., 'The Royal Navy in the River Plate 1806–1807' *Navy Records Society*, vol. 135 (1996).

Grainha, Manuel Borges, *História da Franco-Maçonaria em Portugal: 1733–1912* (Lisboa: A Editora Limitada, 1912).

Grattan, William, *Adventures with the Connaught Rangers from 1809 to 1814* (London: H. Colburn, 1847).

Graves, Donald., *Dragon Rampant: The Royal Welch Fusiliers at War 1793–1815* (Barnsley: Frontline, 2010).

Gray, Anthony, *The French Invasions of Portugal 1807–1811: Rebellion, Reaction and Resistance* (MA thesis, University of York, 2011).

Gregory, Desmond, *The Beneficent Usurpers: A History of the British in Madeira* (Cranbury, NJ: Associated University Presses, 1988).

Grehan, John, *The Lines of Torres Vedras: The Cornerstone of Wellington's Strategy in the Peninsular War, 1809–1812* (Barnsley: Pen and Sword, 2000).

Griffith, Paddy (ed.), *A History of the Peninsular War, Modern Studies of the War in Spain and Portugal 1808–1814*, volume IX (London: Greenhill Books, 1999).

Guingret, Pierre, *Relation historique et militaire de la campagne de Portugal sous le Maréchal Masséna, Prince d'Essling* (Limoges: Chez Bargeas, 1817).

Guthrie, G.J., *Commentaries on the surgery of the war in Portugal, Spain, France and the Netherlands, from the Battle of Roliça, in 1808, to that of Waterloo, in 1815, showing the improvements made during and since that period in the great art and science of surgery on all the subjects to which they relate* (London: Henry Henshaw, 1853).

Gwilliam, John, *The Battle of Albuera, A poem: With An Epistle Dedicatory to Lord Wellington* (London: Gale and Curtis, 1811).

Hall, C.D. and J. Hill, 'Albuera and Vittoria: Letters from Lt. Col. J. Hill', *Journal of the Society for Army Historical Research*, 66, 268 (Winter 1988), pp. 193–8.

Hall, Christopher D., *British Strategy in the Napoleonic War 1803–1815* (Manchester: Manchester University Press, 1992).

Hall, John A., *A History of the Peninsular War. Volume VIII: The Biographical Dictionary of British Officers Killed and Wounded, 1808–1814* (London: Greenhill Books, 1998).

Halliday, Andrew, *Observations on the Present State of the Portuguese Army as Organised by Lieutenant-General Sir William Carr Beresford K.B.* (London: John Murray, 1811).

Hamilton, Anthony, *Hamilton's Campaigns with Moore and Wellington during the Peninsular War* (Staplehurst: Spellmount, 1998).

Hamilton, Thomas, *Annals of the Peninsular Campaigns* (London: T. Cadell, 1829).

Harvey, Robert, *The War of Wars: The Great European Conflict, 1793–1815* (London: Constable, 2006).

Hathaway, Eileen (ed.), *A Dorset Rifleman: The Recollections of Benjamin Harris* (Swanage, UK: Shinglepicker, 1995).

Havard, Robert, *Wellington's Welsh General: A Life of Sir Thomas Picton* (London: Aurum Press 1996).

Hayman, Sir Peter, *Soult: Napoleon's Maligned Marshal* (London: Arms and Armour, 1990).

Haythornthwaite, Philip J., *Die Hard! Dramatic Actions from the Napoleonic Wars* (London: Arms and Armour, 1996).

Haythornthwaite, Philip J., *British Napoleonic Infantry Tactics 1792–1815* (Botley: Osprey Publishing, 2008).

Haythornthwaite, Philip J., *The Napoleonic Source Book* (London: Arms and Armour, 1990).

Haythornthwaite, Philip J., *The Peninsular War: The Complete Companion to the Iberian Campaigns 1807–14* (London: Brasseys UK Ltd., 2004).

Hayward, Pat (ed.), *Surgeon Henry's Trifles: Events of a Military Life* (London: Chatto & Windus, 1970).

Heathcote, T.A., *Wellington's Peninsular War Generals and their Battles: A Biographical and Historical Dictionary* (Barnsley: Pen and Sword, 2010).

Henegan, Sir Richard D., *Seven Years Campaigning in the Peninsula and the Netherlands, 1808–1815*, two volumes (London: Henry Colburn, 1846).

Henriques, Mendo Castro, *Salamanca, 1812: Companheiros de Honra* (Lisbon: Prefácio, 2002).

Henriques, Mendo Castro, *Vitória e Pirenéus, 1813* (Lisbon: Tribuna da História, 2009).

Henry, Philip, 5th Earl Stanhope, *Notes of Conversations with the Duke of Wellington, 1831–1851* (New York: Longmans, Green and Co., 1888).

Herold, J. Christopher, *Bonaparte in Egypt* (Barnsley: Pen and Sword, 1963).

Hertslet, Lewis (ed.), *A Complete Collection of the Treaties and Conventions, and Reciprocal Regulations, at Present Subsisting between Great Britain and Foreign Powers*, vol. II (London: Butterworth, 1840).

Hill, Joanna, *Wellington's Right Hand: Rowland, Viscount Hill* (Stroud: Spellmount, 2011).

Hinde, Wendy, *George Canning* (London: Collins, 1973).

Hispanic American Historical Review, 1980 (Duke University Press).

Holmes, Richard., *Wellington: The Iron Duke* (London: Harper Collins, 2003).

Hook, Theodore, *The Life of General, The Right Honourable Sir David Baird*, two volumes (London: Richard Bentley, 1832).

Hope, James, *The Military Memoirs of an Infantry Officer, 1809–1816* (Edinburgh: Anderson & Bryce (printer), 1833).

Horward, Donald, *Napoleon and Iberia: The twin sieges of Ciudad Rodrigo and Almeida, 1810* (Tallahassee: University Presses of Florida, 1984).

Horward, Donald D., 'Wellington and the Defence of Portugal', *The International History Review*, 11, 1 (2010), pp. 39–54.

Hough, Henry, 'The Journal of Second Lieutenant Henry Hough, Royal Artillery, 1812–1813', *Journal of the Royal United Services Institution*, 61, 444 (1916), pp. 1–43.

House of Commons, *A copy of the Proceedings upon the Inquiry relative to the Armistice and Convention etc., made and concluded in Portugal, in August 1808, between the Commanders of the British and French armies, held at the Royal Hospital Chelsea, on Monday the 14th November 1808 and continued by adjournments until Tuesday the 27th December, 1808* (London, 1809).

House of Commons Debates, *Hansard*.

House of Commons, *Return of the names of the officers in the army who receive pensions* (London, 1818).

Hughes, Ben, *Conquer or Die! Wellington's Veterans and the Liberation of the New World* (Botley: Osprey Publishing, 2010).

Hughes, Ben, *The British Invasion of the River Plate, 1806–1807: How the Redcoats Were Humbled and a Nation Was Born* (Barnsley: Praetorian Press, 2013).

Hulot, Jacques-Louis, *Souvenirs Militaires du Baron Hulot (Jacques-Louis) général d'artillerie, 1773–1843* (Paris: *A la direction du spectateur militaire*, 1886).

Hunter, Arthur, *Wellington's Scapegoat: The Tragedy of Lieutenant Colonel Charles Bevan* (Barnsley: Leo Cooper, 2003).

Inglis, Henry David, *Constable's Miscellany of Original and Selected Publications in the various departments of Literature, Science and the Arts; Memorials of the last War*, vol. 1 (Edinburgh: Constable & Co., 1828).

Illustrated London News, 14 January 1854 (Obituary of Viscount Beresford).

Jackson, Caroline (ed.), *Diary of Captain James Maurice Primrose: 43rd Regiment of Foot* (Grahamstown: Rhodes University, 2016).

Jones, Sir John T., *Memoranda Relative to the Lines Thrown up to Cover Lisbon in 1810* (London, 1829).

Jones, Sir John T., *Journals of Sieges carried on by the army under the Duke of Wellington in Spain*, three volumes (London: John Weale, 1846).

Jourdain, Lieutenant Colonel H.F.N., *The Connaught Rangers* (London: Royal United Service Institution, 1924).

Journals of the House of Commons (1807–1814).

Journal of the Society for Army Historical Research (JSAHR), various volumes.

Journal of the Waterloo Association (various volumes).

Kaplan, Herbert H., *Nathan Mayer Rothschild and the Creation of a Dynasty: The Critical Years 1806–1816* (Stanford, CA: Stanford University Press, 2006).

Kelly, Catherine, 'War and the Militarization of British Army Medicine, 1793–1830', *Studies for the Social History of Medicine*, 5 (London: Routledge, 2011).

Knight, Roger, *Britain Against Napoleon: The Organization of Victory 1793–1815* (London: Penguin UK, 2013).

Knowles, Robert and J. MacCarthy, *The War in the Peninsula* and *Recollections of the Storming of the Castle of Badajos* (Stroud: The History Press, 2011).

Koch, Jean-Baptiste-Fréderic and António Ventura (ed.), *Memórias de Massena: Campanha de 1810 e 1811 em Portugal* (Lisbon: Livros Horizonte, 2007).

Lamb, Hubert, *Climate History and the Modern World* (London: Methuen, 1982).

Lapène, Édouard, *Conquête de l'Andalousie, Campagne de 1810 et 1811 dans le Midi de l'Espagne* (Paris: Chez Anselin, 1823).

Lapène, Édouard, *Mémoires d'un artilleur: Campagne de 1813 et 1814 sur l'Ebre, les Pyrénées et la Garonne; précédées de considérations sur la dernière guerre d'Espagne* (Paris: Chez Anselin, 1823).

Lapène, Édouard, *Événements Militaires devant Toulouse en 1814* (Paris: Chez Anselin, 1834).

Larpent, Francis S. and Larpent, Sir George (ed.) *The Private Journal of F.S. Larpent, Judge-Advocate General of the British Forces in the Peninsula attached to the headquarters of Lord Wellington during the Peninsular War from 1812 to its close*, two volumes (London: Richard Bentley, 1853).

Laurillard-Fallot, Salomon-Louis, *Souvenirs d'un médecin Hollandais sous les Aigles Françaises* (Paris: La Vouivre, t. X, 1998).

Law, Henry William and Irene Law, *The Book of the Beresford Hopes* (London: Heath Cranton, 1925).

Le Fers-Dupac, Pénélope, *Le Mousquetaire de Napoléon: L'autre vie du Maréchal Lannes, Duc de Montebello* (Portet-sur-Garonne: Empreinte Éditions, 2002).

Lenta, Margaret and Basil Le Cordeur (eds), *The Cape Diaries of Lady Anne Barnard 1799–1800* (Cape Town: Van Riebeeck Society, 1999).

Leslie, John (ed.), *The Dickson Manuscripts: Being Diaries, Letters, Maps, Account Books, With Various Papers of the late Major General Sir Alexander Dickson* (Woolwich: Royal Artillery Institution Printing House, 1908).

L'Estrange, Sir George B., *Recollections of Sir George B. L'Estrange* (London: Sampson Low, Marston, Low and Searle, 1894).

Lewin, Henry Ross, *The Life of a Soldier: a narrative of twenty-seven years' service in various parts of the world by a field officer*, three volumes (Dublin, 1824).

Liddell Hart, Basil Henry (ed.), *The Letters of Private Wheeler, 1809–1828* (London: Michael Joseph, 1951).

Light, Kenneth (ed.), *A Transferência da Capital e Corte para o Brasil* (Lisbon: Tribuna da História, 2007).

Lillie, John Scott, *A Narrative of the Campaigns of the Loyal Lusitanian Legion under Brigadier General Sir Robert Wilson* (London: T. Egerton, 1812).

Limpo Piriz, Luis Alfonso (ed.), *Badajoz y Elvas en 1811: Crónicas de Guerra, cartas de Francisco Xavier do Rego Aranha a Da María Luisa de Valleré* (Badajoz: Ayuntamiento, 2011).

(de) Liniers y Bremond, Santiago, *Oficio que el señor Don Santiago Liniers y Bremont, General en Xefe de las tropas victoriosas en la Reconquista de Buenos-Ayres, dirigió al Mayor General Inglés D. Guillermo Carr Beresford, después de verificada dicha Reconquista* (Buenos Aires: Impr. de los Niños Expósitos, 30 August 1806).

Lipscombe, Nick, *The Peninsular War Atlas* (Botley: Osprey Publishing, 2010).

Lipscombe, Nick, *Wellington's Guns: The Untold Story of Wellington and his Artillery in the Peninsula and at Waterloo* (Botley: Osprey Publishing, 2013).

Lipscombe, Nick, *Bayonne and Toulouse: Wellington Invades France* (Botley: Osprey Publishing, 2014).

Livermore, Harold, 'Beresford and the reform of the Portuguese army' in Paddy Griffith (ed.), *A History of the Peninsular War, vol. IX: Modern Studies of the War in Spain and Portugal, 1808–1814* (London: Greenhill, 1999).

Long, C.E., *The Albuera Medal* (London: British Library, 2011).

Longford, Elizabeth, *Wellington: The Years of the Sword* (London: Weidenfeld & Nicolson, 1969).

Lorblanchès, Jean-Claude, *Les soldats de Napoléon en Espagne et au Portugal, 1807–1814* (Paris: L'Harmattan, 2007).

Lowry Cole, Galbraith (ed.), *The Correspondence of Colonel Wade, Colonel Napier, Major General Sir H. Hardinge and General the Hon. Sir Lowry G. Cole relating to the Battle of Albuera* (London: T. & W. Boone, 1841).

Lowry Cole, Maud (ed.) and Stephen Gwynn, *Memoirs: Sir Lowry Cole* (Uckfield: The Naval & Military Press, 2011).

MacCarthy, Captain, *Recollections of the storming of the Castle of Badajos; by the Third Division under the Command of Lieut. Gen. Sir Thomas Picton, G.C.B.: A Personal Narrative by Captain MacCarthy, Late of the 50th Regiment* (London: Egerton's Military Library, 1836).

Macaulay, Rose, *They Went to Portugal* (London: Penguin, 1946).

Mackesy, Piers, *British Victory in Egypt, 1801: The End of Napoleon's Conquest* (Abingdon: Routledge, 1995).

Mackinnon, Henry, *A Journal of the Campaign in Portugal and Spain, Containing Remarks on the Inhabitants, Customs, Trade and Cultivation of those Countries from the year 1809 to 1812* (London: Longman, Hurst, and Co., 1812).

Malcolm, John, 'Reminiscences of a Campaign in the Pyrenees and South of France', reproduced in *Constable's Miscellany of Original and Selected Publications in the various Departments of Literature, Science and Arts: Memorials of the Late War*, vol. 1 (Edinburgh: Constable & Co., 1828).

Marcel, Capt. Nicolas, *Campagnes en Espagne et au Portugal, 1808–1814* (Paris: Tallandier, 2003).

Marindin A.H., *The Salamanca Campaign, 1812* (Uckfield: Naval and Military Press Ltd., 2005).

Marmont, *Mémoires du Maréchal Marmont, Duc de Raguse, de 1792 a 1841* (Paris: Perrotin, 1857).

Martelo, David, *Os Caçadores, Os Galos de combate do exército de Wellington* (Lisbon: Tribuna da Historia, 2007).

Martins, Ana Canas Delgado, *Governação e Arquivos: D. João VI no Brasil* (Lisbon: Instituto dos Arquivos Nacionais, 2007).

Martins, Francisco José Rocha, *Episodios da Guerra Peninsular: Os Três Invasões Francesas*, three volumes (Lisbon: Jornal do Cornércio, 1944).

Masséna, André and Général Koch (ed.) *Mémoires d'André Masséna, Duc de Rivoli, Prince d'Essling, Maréchal d'Empire*, seven volumes plus atlas (Paris; Jean de Bonnot, 1966).

Mauleverer, Bruce, *The Portuguese contribution to the Allied defeat of the French during the French Invasions of Portugal 1808–1811* (MA Dissertation, Buckingham University, 2011).

Maurice, Sir J.F., *The Diary of Sir John Moore*, two volumes (London: Edward Arnold, 1904).

Maxwell, Herbert (ed.), *The Creevey Papers: A Selection From the Correspondence & Diaries of the Late Thomas Creevey, M. P.* (London: John Murray, 1903).

Maxwell, William Hamilton, *Life of Field-Marshal His Grace The Duke of Wellington*, three volumes (London: A.H. Baily, 1834–41).

Maycock, F.W.O., *The Invasion of France, 1814* (London: G. Allen and Unwin, 1914).

McGregor, John James, *History of the French Revolution and the Wars resulting from that memorable event*, twelve volumes (London: G.B. Whittaker, 1828).

McGrigor, Sir James, *The Autobiography and Services of Sir James McGrigor, Late Director-General of the Army Medical Department* (London: Longman, Green, Longman and Roberts, 1861).

McGuffie, T.H. (ed.), *Peninsular Cavalry General 1811–1813: the Correspondence of Lieutenant-General Robert Ballard Long* (London: George G. Harrap & Co., 1951).

Mello, João C.C., *Lista dos Officiais do Exército em 1811 de Ordem de Sua Alteza Real o Principe Regente N.S.* (Lisbon: Impressão Régia, 1811).

Migliorini, Pierre and Jean Quatre Vieux, *Batailles de Napoléon dans le Sud-Ouest* (Anglet: Atlantica, 2002).

Millett, Major-General Allan F., 'Captain James H. Hausman and the Formation of the Korean Army, 1945–1950', *Armed Forces and Society*, 23, 4 (Summer 1997).

Mitre, Bartolomé, *Historia del Belgrano y de la Independencia Argentina*, sixth edition (Buenos Aires: Felix Lajouane, 1913).

Monick, S. (ed.), *The Iberian and Waterloo Campaigns: The Letters of Lt James Hope (92nd (Highland)Regiment) 1811–1815* (Uckfield: The Naval & Military Press, 2006).

Moore Smith, George Charles, *The Life of John Colborne, Field-Marshal Lord Seaton, compiled from his letters, records of his conversations, and other sources* (London: John Murray, 1903).

Moreira, Maria Cristina, 'Portuguese State Military Expenditure: British support of the Peninsular War efforts of the Erário Régio (Royal Treasury) from 1809 to 1811', in Stephen Conway and Rafael Torres Sánchez (eds), *The Spending of States, military expenditure during the long eighteenth century: patterns, organization, and consequences, 1650–1815* (Saarbrucken: VDM Verlag Dr. Müller GmbH & Co. KG, 2011).

Moura, Major-General Rui Fernando Baptista, 'Um erro repetido mil vezes torna-se "realidade": O "massacre" de Coimbra, 7 de Outubro 1810', *XX Colóquio de História Militar* (18 November 2011).

Muir, Rory, Robert Burnham, Howie Muir and Ron McGuigan, *Inside Wellington's Peninsular Army 1808–1814* (Barnsley: Pen and Sword, 2006).

Muir, Rory, *Britain and the Defeat of Napoleon, 1807–1815* (London: Yale University Press, 1996).

Muir, Rory, *At Wellington's Right Hand: The Letters of Lieutenant-Colonel Sir Alexander Gordon, 1808–1815* (Stroud: Sutton for Army Records Society, 2003).

Muir, Rory, *Wellington: The Path to Victory 1769–1814* (London: Yale University Press, 2013).

Munch-Petersen, Thomas, *Defying Napoleon: How Britain Bombarded Copenhagen and Seized the Danish fleet in 1807* (Stroud: Sutton Publishing Ltd, 2007).

Munster, Earl of, *An Account of the British Campaign in 1809 under Sir A. Wellesley in Portugal and Spain* (London: Henry Colburn and Richard Bentley, 1831).

Napier's Peninsular War, *Beresford's Strictures*. This is a compilation containing (i) Strictures (1831); (ii) Further Strictures (1832); (iii) D'Urban's Report (1831); (iv) Napier's Reply to various opponents (1832).

Napier, William F.P., *History of the War in the Peninsula and the South of France from the year 1807 to the year 1814* (London: Constable, 1828–40).

Napier, William F.P., *Colonel Napier's Justification of his third volume: forming a sequel to his reply to various opponents, and containing some new and curious facts relative to the battle of Albuera* (London: T. and W. Boone, 1833).

Neal, Larry, *The Rise of Financial Capitalism* (Cambridge: Cambridge University Press, 1993).

Neale, Adam, *Memorials of the late war: Journal of a soldier of the seventy-first regiment (Highland Light Infantry) from 1806 to 1815* (Edinburgh: Constable & Co., 1828).

Neale, Adam, *Letters from Portugal and Spain: Comprising an Account of the Operation of the Armies Under Their Excellencies Sir Arthur Wellesley and Sir John Moore from the Landing of the Troops in Mondego Bay to the Battle at Corunna* (London: Richard Phillips, 1809).

Newbolt, Sir Henry, *The Story of the Oxford and Buckinghamshire Light Infantry* (London: Country Life, 1915).

Newitt, Malyn (ed.), *War, Revolution and Society in the Rio de la Plata 1808–1810: Thomas Kinder's narrative of a journey to Madeira, Montevideo and Buenos Aires* (Oxford: Signal Books, 2010).

Newitt, Malyn and Martin Robson (eds), *Lord Beresford and British Intervention in Portugal 1807–1820* (Lisbon: Imprensa das Ciências Sociais, 2004).

Nichols, Alistair, *Wellington's Mongrel Regiment: A History of the Chasseurs Britanniques Regiment 1801–1814* (Staplehurst: Spellmount, 2005).

Nogueira, Ricardo, *Memória das causas mais notáveis que se trateram nas conferências do governo d'estes reinos desde o dia 9 de Agosto de 1810, em que entrei a server o logar de um dos governadores, ate 5 de Fevereiro de 1820* (Coimbra, 2012 reprint).

Norris, Daren Wayne, *Over the Hills and Far Away: The Life and Times of Thomas Norris 1778–1858* (Enstone: Writersworld, 2005).

O'Connell, M.J., *The Last Colonel of the Irish Brigade*, two volumes (London: Kegan, Paul, Trench, Trübner and Co., 1892).

Oliver, Michael and Richard Partridge, *The Battle of Albuera 1811: Glorious Field of Grief* (Barnsley: Pen and Sword, 2007).

Oman, Sir Charles, *A History of the Peninsular War*, seven volumes (Oxford: Clarendon, 1902–30).

Oman, Sir Charles, *Wellington's Army 1809–1814* (London: Edward Arnold, 1913).

Oman, Sir Charles, *Studies in the Napoleonic Wars* (London: Methuen & Co., Ltd., 1929).

O'Meara, Barry Edward, *Napoleon in Exile, or A Voice from St Helena*, two volumes (London: Jones and Co., 1822).

Ormsby, Reverend James Wilmot, *An Account of the Operations of the British Army: And of the State and Sentiments of the People of Portugal and Spain, During the Campaigns of the Years 1808 & 1809*, two volumes (London: James Carpenter, 1809).

Pack Beresford, Denis. R., *A Memoir of Major-General Sir Denis Pack, KCB* (Dublin, 1908).

Page, Julia (ed.), *Intelligence Officer in the Peninsula: The letters and diaries of the Hon. Edward Charles Cocks, 1786–1812* (Tunbridge Wells: Spellmount, 1986).

Panikkar, Margaret, *Daniel Hoghton, Hero of Albuera* (Preston, 1993).

Pearson, Andrew, *The Soldier Who Walked Away* (Edinburgh: Rollo, 1865).

Pelet, Jean Jacques, *The French campaign in Portugal 1810–1811*, edited and annotated by Donald D. Horward (Minnesota: University of Minnesota Press 1973).

Peltier, Jean-Gabriel, *La Campagne de Portugal en 1810 et 1811* (Paris: Chez A. Eymery-Le Normant, 1814).

Pereira, José Rodrigues, *Campanhas Navais 1793–1807: A Marinha Portuguesa na Época de Napoleão, 1807–1823, Volume I: A Armada e a Europa* (Lisbon: Tribuna da História, 2005).

Pereira, José Rodrigues, *Campanhas Navais 1807–1823: A Marinha Portuguesa na Época de Napoleão, Volume II: A Armada e o Brasil* (Lisbon: Tribuna da História, 2005).

Pinto, Alexandre Sousa, *A Cavalaria Na Guerra Peninsular* (Lisbon: Tribuna da História, 2008).

Pires, Nuno Lemos, 'Guerra Peninsular: Operações a partir de Trás-os-Montes', *Revista Científica Proelium*, 3 (2012), pp. 183–203.

Pires, Nuno, Lemos, 'El Ejército Portugués en las campañas de 1813–1814', *Revista de Historia Militar* (I extraordinario 1813), pp. 103–34.

Limpo Piriz, Luis Alfonso (ed.), *Badajoz y Elvas en 1811: Crónicas de Guerra, cartas de Francisco Xavier do Rego Aranha a Da María Luisa de Valleré* (Badajoz: Ayuntamiento, 2011).

Pistrucci, Benedetto, *The Waterloo Medal* (Waterloo200: Worcestershire Medal Service and Samlerhuset Group, 2014).

Pococke, Captain, 'Journal of Captain Pococke', *The Highland Light Infantry Chronicle* (Glasgow, 1899).

Popham, Home, *A full and correct report of the trial of Sir Home Popham, including the whole of the discussions which took place between that officer and Mr Jervis, Counsel for the Admiralty*

... and an appendix, in which are several important Documents ... and an interesting letter from Lord Grenville to Sir Home Popham (London: J. and J. Richardson, 1807).

Popham, Hugh, *A Damned Cunning Fellow: The Eventful Life of Rear-Admiral Sir Home Popham KCB, KCH, KM, FRS 1762–1820* (St Austell: Old Ferry Press, 1991).

Porter, Robert K., *Letters from Portugal and Spain Written During the March of the British Troops Under Sir John Moore* (London: Longman, Hurst, Rees and Orme, 1809).

Pyne, Peter, 'The Invasions of Buenos Aires, 1806–1807: The Irish Dimension', *Research Paper 20* (Liverpool: University of Liverpool, Institute of Latin American Studies, 1996).

Quarterly Review (various volumes).

Rait, Robert S., *The Life and Campaigns of Hugh, First Viscount Gough, Field Marshal*, two volumes (London, Archibald Constable & Co. Ltd., 1903).

Randolph, Reverend Herbert (ed.), *The Life of General Sir Robert Wilson*, vol. 1 (London: John Murray, 1862).

Ravina, Augustin Guimera and José María Blanco Núñez (eds), *Guerra Naval en la Revolución y el Imperio* (Madrid: Marcial Pons Ediciones De Historia, S.a., 2008).

Roberts, Carlos, *Las Invasiones Inglesas del Rio de la Plata (1806–1807) y la Influencia Inglesa en la Independencia y Organizacion de las Provincias del Rio de la Plata* (Buenos Aires: Talleres gráficos, S.a. Jacobo Peuser, ltda., 1938).

Roberts, Jenifer, *The Madness of Queen Maria* (Chippenham: Templeton Press, 2009).

Robinson, Heaton Bowstead, *Memoirs of Lieutenant-General Sir Thomas Picton, including his correspondence*, two volumes (London: Richard Bentley, 1835).

Robson, Martin, *Britain, Portugal and South America in the Napoleonic Wars: alliances and diplomacy in economic maritime conflict* (London: I.B. Tauris, 2011).

Rodrigues, Paulo Miguel, *A Política e as Questões Militares na Madeira. O Período das Guerras Napoleónicas* (Funchal: Centro de Estudos de História do Atlântico, 1999).

Ross-Lewin, Harry and John Wardell (ed.), *With 'the Thirty-Second' in the Peninsular and other Campaigns* (Dublin: Hodges, Figgis, 1904).

(de) Saint-Chamans, A.A.R., *Mémoires du Général Comte de Saint-Chamans, Ancien Aide-de-Camp du Maréchal Soult, 1802–1832* (Paris: Librairie Plon, 1896).

(de) Saint-Pierre, Louis and Antoinette de Saint-Pierre, *Mémoires du Maréchal Soult: Espagne et Portugal* (Paris: Hachette, 1955).

Sañudo Bayón, Juan José, *La Albuera 1811: Glorioso Campo de Sufrimiento!* (Madrid: Almena Ediciones, 2006).

Saraiva, José Hermano, *Portugal, A Companion History* (Manchester: Carcanet Press, 1997).

Sarmento, Alberto A., *Madeira: 1801–1802, 1807–1814 (notas e documentos sobre a ocupação Inglesa* (Funchal: As Freguesias da Madeira, 1932).

Schaumann, August Ludolf Friedrich, *On The Road With Wellington: The Diary of a War Commissary in the Peninsular Campaign* (London: W. Heinemann Ltd., 1924).

Sébastien, Jean-Yves, *La Bataille d'Orthez, 27 février 1814* (Pau: Périégète, 2013).

Severn, John, *Architects of Empire: The Duke of Wellington and his brothers* (Norman, OK: University of Oklahoma Press, 2007).

Shand, Alexander Innes, *Wellington's Lieutenants: The Campaigns and Battles of Eight British Generals in the Napoleonic Wars* (London: Smith, Elder & Company, 1902).

Sherer, Moyle, *Recollections of the Peninsula* (London: Longman, Hurst, Rees, Orme and Brown, 1823).

Sidney, Edwin, *Life of Lord Hill* (London: John Murray, 1845).

Simmons, George, *A British Rifle Man: The Journals and Correspondence of Major George Simmons, Rifle Brigade, during the Peninsular War and the Campaign of Waterloo* (London: A. & C. Black, 1899).

Sinclair, Joseph, *A Soldier of the Seventy-First: From de la Plata to the Battle of Waterloo* (Barnsley: Frontline, 2010).

Smith, Denis, *The Prisoners of Cabrera: Napoleon's Forgotten Soldiers 1809–1814* (Toronto: Macfarlane, Walter & Ross, 2001).

Smith, Harry George Wakelyn, *The Autobiography of Sir Harry Smith, 1787–1819: a classic story of love and war* (London: Constable, 1999).

Snow, Peter, *To War with Wellington: From the Peninsula to Waterloo* (St Ives: John Murray Publishers, 2010).

Soane, George, *Life of the Duke of Wellington*, two volumes (London: E. Churton 1839–40).

Sorell, Thomas Stephen, *Notes on the Campaign of 1808–1809 in the north of Spain, in reference to some passages in Lieut.-Col. Napier's History of the War in the Peninsula and in Sir Walter Scott's Life of Napoleon Bonaparte* (London; John Murray, 1828).

Soriano, Simão José da Luz, *História da Guerra Civil e do estabelecimento do governo parlamentar em Portugal comprehendendo a história diplomática, militar e política da este reino desde 1777 até 1834* (Lisbon: Imprensa Nacional, 1866–90).

Soult, Nicolas-Jean de Dieu and Napoléon Hector Soult, *Mémoires du maréchal-général Soult Duc de Dalmatie* (Paris: Librairie d'Amyot, 1854).

Sousa Pinto, Alexandre, José Carlos Antunes Calçada and Paulo Jorge Lopes da Silva, *A Cavalaria na Guerra Peninsular* (Lisbon: Tribuna da História, 2009).

Spencer, William, *Army Records: A Guide for Family Historians* (Kew, The National Archives, 2008).

Sprunglin, Colonel Emmanuel Frédéric, *Souvenirs des Campagnes d'Espagne et de Portugal* (Paris: Librairie Historique F. Teissedre, 1998).

Stanhope, James H. and Gareth Glover (ed.), *Eyewitness to the Peninsular War and the Battle of Waterloo: The Letters and Journals of Lieutenant Colonel the Honourable James Stanhope 1803–1825* (Barnsley: Pen and Sword, 2010).

Stewart, Major William and Robert Bremner (ed.), *The Journal of Major William Stewart: 30th (Cambridgeshire) Regiment of Foot, September 1810–May 1811: The Diary of a Traveller who Happened to be with Wellington's Army in Portugal* (Carcavelos: British Historical Society of Portugal, 2015).

Suchet, Marechal, *Mémoires du maréchal Suchet, duc d'Albufera, sur ses campagnes en Espagne, depuis 1808 jusqu'en 1814*, two volumes (Paris: Adolphe Bossange, 1828).

Supúlvede, Christovam Ayres de Magalhães, *Dicionário Bibliográfico de Guerra Peninsular*, four volumes (Coimbra, Imprensa da Universidade, 1924–30).

Thackwell, Sir Joseph, *The Military Memoirs of Lieutenant-General Sir Joseph Thackwell* (Uckfield: Naval and Military Press. Reprint of 1890 Original Edition, 2015).

The Gentleman's Magazine and Historical Review, various editions.

The Museum of Foreign Literature, Science and Art, volume 38.

The Philanthropic Society, *Subscription for the Relief of the Unfortunate Sufferers in Portugal, who have been plundered and treated by the French armies with the most unexampled Savage Barbarity* (London: The Philanthropic Society, 1811).

The Royal Military Calendar, various.

The Royal Military Chronicle, various.

The United Service Magazine, volume 83.

The Wellesley Papers, The life and correspondence of Richard Colley Wellesley, Marquess Wellesley, 1760–1842, two volumes, by the editor of 'The Windham Papers' (London: Herbert Jenkins, 1914).

Thiébault, Paul Charles Dieudonné, *Relation de l'expédition du Portugal: faite en 1807 et 1808* (Paris: Chez Magimel, 1817).

Thiébault, Paul Charles Dieudonné and Fernand Calmettes, *Mémoires du Général Thiébault* (Paris: Plon, 1893–5).

Thompson, Mark S., *The Fatal Hill: The Allied Campaign Under Beresford in Southern Spain in 1811* (Sunderland: Mark Thompson Publishing, 2002).

Thompson, Mark S., *Wellington's Engineers: Military Engineering in the Peninsular War 1808–1814* (Barnsley: Pen and Sword Books, 2015).

Thompson, Mark S., *The Spanish Report on the Battle of Albuera* (Sunderland: Mark Thompson Publishing, 2015).

Thompson, Mark S., *The Peninsular War Services of General Sir George Allen Madden* (Sunderland: Mark Thompson Publishing, 2014).

Thompson, Neville, *Earl Bathurst and the British Empire* (Barnsley: Leo Cooper, 1999).

Thornton, James, *Your Most Obedient Servant* (Exeter: Webb & Bower, 1985).

Tomkinson, William and James Tomkinson (ed.), *The Diary of a Cavalry Officer in the Peninsular War and Waterloo Campaign 1809–1815* (London: Swan Sonnenschein and Co., 1894).

(de) Toy, Brian, 'Admiral George Berkeley and Peninsular Victory, 1809–1812' in de Sousa, Maria Leonor Machado (ed.), *A Guerra Peninsular, Perspectivas Multidisciplinares* (Casal de Cambra: Caleidoscópio, 2008).

Tranié, Jean, and Juan-Carlos Carmigniani, *Napoléon et la Campagne d'Espagne 1807–1814* (Paris: Copernic, 1998).

Trant, Clarissa and C.G. Luard (ed.), *The Journal of Clarissa Trant 1800–1832* (London: John Lane, 1925).

Urban, Mark, *The Man Who Broke Napoleon's Codes: The story of George Scovell* (London: Faber and Faber, 2001).

Vandeleur, John, Andrew Bamford (ed.), *With Wellington's Outposts: The Peninsular and Waterloo Letters of John Vandeleur* (Barnsley: Frontline, 2015).

Walsh, Robert (ed.), *Select Speeches of the Right Honourable George Canning; with a preliminary biographical sketch, and an appendix, of extracts from his writings and speeches* (Philadelphia: Key and Biddle, 1835).

Ward, Stephen George Peregrine, *Wellington's Headquarters: A Study of the administrative problems in the Peninsula 1809–1814* (Oxford: Oxford University Press, 1957).

Warre, William, Warre, William A. and Warre, Edmond (ed.), *Letters from the Peninsula 1808–1812* (Staplehurst: Spellmount Publishers, 1999).

Wellesley, Jane, *Wellington: A Journey Through My Family* (London: Weidenfeld & Nicolson, 2008).

Wellington, Field Marshal the Duke of, *The Dispatches of Field Marshal the Duke of Wellington during his various campaigns in India, Denmark, Portugal, Spain, the Low Countries, and France*, compiled by John Gurwood, eight volumes and Index (London: Parker, Furnivall and Parker, 1844–7: WD).

Wellington, the Duke of, *The Despatches, Correspondence and Memoranda of Field Marshal the Duke of Wellington*, edited by his son, the Duke of Wellington (London: John Murray, 1857–80; WSD).

Wilcken, Patrick, *Empire Adrift: The Portuguese Court in Rio de Janeiro 1808–1821* (London: Bloomsbury, 2005).

Wilkin, Walter Harold, *The Life of Sir David Baird* (London: G. Allen, 1912).

Willis, R.C., 'Wellington and Beresford: Portugal and Brazil,' *Manchester Spanish & Portuguese Studies*, XVI (2007).

Wilson, Robert Thomas, *History of the British Expedition to Egypt* (London: C. Roworth, 1803).

Wilson, Sir Robert, *General Correspondence*, volume II: 1 February 1809–31 December 1812 (London, 1862).

Woodberry, George, *Journal du Lieutenant Woodberry: Campagnes de Portugal et d'Espagne, de France, de Belgique et de France, 1813–1815* (Paris: E. Plon, Nourrit et Cie, 1896).

Woolgar, C.M. (ed.), *Wellington Studies*, five volumes (Southampton: Hartley Institute, University of Southampton, 1996–2013).

Woolgar, C.M., *A summary catalogue of the Wellington papers* (Southampton: University of Southampton, 1984).

Wordsworth, William, *Concerning the Convention of Cintra, 1809 with Two letters of William Wordsworth written in 1811* (London: Humphrey Milford, 1915).

Vane, C.W. (Marquess of Londonderry), *Narrative of the Peninsular War from 1808 to 1813* (London; Henry Colburn, 1828).

Vane, Charles William (ed.), *Correspondence, Despatches and other Papers of Viscount Castlereagh, Second Marquess of Londonderry* (London: William Shoberl, 1851).

Ventura, António, *Guerra das Laranjas 1801* (Matosinhos: Quidnovi, 2008).

Ventura, António, *As Guerras Liberais, 1820–1834* (Matosinhos: Quidnovi, 2008).

Vicente, António Pedro, *Guerra Peninsular 1801–1814* (Matosinhos: Quidnovi, 2007).

Vichness, Samuel E., 'Marshall of Portugal: The Military Career of William Carr Beresford, 1785–1814' (Unpublished PhD thesis, Florida State University, 1976).

Vidal de la Blache, Paul Marie Joseph, *L'Evacuation de l'Espagne et l'invasion dans le Midi de la France (Juin 1813–Avril 1814)*, two volumes (Paris: Berger-Levrault, 1914).

Newspapers

England

Lancaster Gazette
London Gazette
Norfolk Chronicle
Northampton Mercury
The Morning Chronicle
The Times

France

Journal de Paris
Le Moniteur

Portugal

Gazeta de Lisboa (contains not just Ordens do Dia of Marshal Beresford but other declarations by Beresford and Forjaz, as well as reports from the front) 1809–14.

Online resources

The Napoleon Series (www.napoleon-series.org).

INDEX